Programming WCF Services

Other Microsoft .NET resources from O'Reilly

Related titles	COM and .NET Component Services Learning C# Learning WCF	Programming C# Programming .NET Components

---

.NET Books Resource Center *dotnet.oreilly.com* is a complete catalog of O'Reilly's books on .NET and related technologies, including sample chapters and code examples.

ONDotnet.com provides independent coverage of fundamental, interoperable, and emerging Microsoft .NET programming and web services technologies.

Conferences O'Reilly Media, Inc. brings diverse innovators together to nurture the ideas that spark revolutionary industries. We specialize in documenting the latest tools and systems, translating the innovator's knowledge into useful skills for those in the trenches. Visit *conferences.oreilly.com* for our upcoming events.

Safari Bookshelf (*safari.oreilly.com*) is the premier online reference library for programmers and IT professionals. Conduct searches across more than 1,000 books. Subscribers can zero in on answers to time-critical questions in a matter of seconds. Read the books on your Bookshelf from cover to cover or simply flip to the page you need. Try it today for free.

Programming WCF Services

Juval Löwy

O'REILLY®

Beijing · Cambridge · Farnham · Köln · Paris · Sebastopol · Taipei · Tokyo

Programming WCF Services
by Juval Löwy

Copyright © 2007 O'Reilly Media, Inc. All rights reserved.
Printed in the United States of America.

Published by O'Reilly Media, Inc., 1005 Gravenstein Highway North, Sebastopol, CA 95472.

O'Reilly books may be purchased for educational, business, or sales promotional use. Online editions
are also available for most titles (*safari.oreilly.com*). For more information, contact our
corporate/institutional sales department: (800) 998-9938 or *corporate@oreilly.com*.

Editor: John Osborn
Developmental Editor: Brian MacDonald
Production Editor: Laurel R.T. Ruma
Proofreader: Sada Preisch

Indexer: Ellen Troutman-Zaig
Cover Designer: Karen Montgomery
Interior Designer: David Futato
Illustrators: Robert Romano and Jessamyn Read

Printing History:

February 2007:   First Edition.

 This book uses RepKover™, a durable and flexible lay-flat binding.

ISBN 10: 0-596-52699-7
ISBN 13: 978-0-596-52699-3
[C]

To my daughters, Abigail and Eleanor

Table of Contents

Foreword

Juval Löwy, the author of this most excellent book, and I share a passion: designing and building distributed systems—or, as they are increasingly called today, connected systems. Both of us have walked a very similar path on the technology trail, even though we've always been working in different companies and on different projects and, for most of our careers, also on different continents.

In the early 1990s when both of us slowly got hooked on the idea of doing something on one computer that would cause something to happen on another computer, the world of distributed systems application platform technologies just began taking shape around us.

As workstations and server hardware became more affordable and increasingly commoditized, building large systems that weren't dependent on a single transaction hub in the middle became an economically attractive proposition. The same was true for wide-area data exchange options. It's difficult to believe these days, but my telephone company insisted back then that more than 1,200 bits per second would never be possible over phone lines. Today they run 6 MBps and more over the same copper. These were exciting times.

With the technology for affordable distributed computing coming together, two large distributed systems technology camps emerged in the early '90s: DCE, led by Digital Equipment Corporation (eventually gobbled up by Compaq, gobbled up by HP) and CORBA, driven by the OMG consortium, with a great dose of IBM backing. In 1996–1997, all of those great engineering efforts came to an effective stop. Here was the Internet and the world started to be obsessed with (a) HTML, (b) HTTP, (c) venture capital, and (d) IPOs.

It took the industry 10 years to recover from the bubble and its bursting. Not only economically, but also from a technology perspective. The good that came from that is that there are no longer two distributed system technology camps, but just one— or several dozen, depending on your perspective.

As of 2007, the industry is still in great disagreement about the "right way" to write code for distributed systems. Someone from Sun Microsystems or BEA will likely tell you that it's got to be Java; my colleagues here at Microsoft (and I) will most certainly tell you that we believe that C# or Visual Basic is the way to go. What neither Sun, nor BEA, nor IBM, nor we here at Microsoft are disagreeing about anymore is how to talk to each other on the wire. Given the DCE versus CORBA wars of the past, the fact that consensus was reached over the specification that is the foundation of this truce—SOAP 1.1—was quite a spectacular sensation.

More than six years have passed since SOAP 1.1 was submitted as a technical note to the W3C. Since then, a great number of SOAP-based specifications, ranging from fundamentals, such as addressing, and a broad range of security options up to enterprise protocols, such as atomic transaction coordination, have been developed and negotiated between many industry partners.

My team here at Microsoft, which still informally calls itself by its product's code name, "Indigo," has been at the heart of these development and negotiation efforts. Without IBM's, Microsoft's, and other partners' strong commitment to creating a common set of standards, even though we are all competing fiercely in the enterprise space, little of this open-standards framework would exist, much less would there be multiple implementations from so many vendors and such a variety of platforms.

Admittedly, it took a year or two longer than it probably should have. Agreement takes time and we would simply not have released our software, the Windows Communication Foundation, without making sure it would interoperate well with our industry partners and competitors. Design also takes time and we would not have released our software without knowing that we have a development experience that feels familiar to our customers who have invested time in learning and adopting our previous distributed systems technology wave, which included ASP.NET Services, the Web Services Enhancements (WSE), .NET Remoting, Messaging/MSMQ, and Enterprise Services/COM+.

The technology list I just cited has five technology names on it, and if you were counting the respective unmanaged code counterparts and underpinnings there would even be more. One of our most important design goals for the Windows Communication Foundation can be summed up in a simple phrase: one way to program. Whether you want to build a queuing application, a transactional N-Tier application, a mesh of P2P clients, an RSS feed server, or your own Enterprise Services Bus, you will no longer have to master a multitude of different technologies that each solve a part of the problem. The Windows Communication Foundation is what you learn and use. One way to program.

Programming WCF Services shows you in great detail what we here at Microsoft have built as a foundation for your applications and services, and the book conveys it with the accuracy, teaching skill, and dedication to architecture that Juval is justly renowned for around the globe.

We from the Connected Framework team at Microsoft are very satisfied with what we've built. We give you an infrastructure that unifies the distributed technology stack, is broadly interoperable, promotes service orientation, is straightforward to learn, and is very productive to build on. Juval Löwy is one of the most prominent distributed systems experts in the world today, and we are very proud that Juval is dedicated to the Windows Communication Foundation. We are quite confident that Juval will help you understand why we, Juval, and our early-adopter community are thrilled about the product and the new opportunities that it creates. Enjoy the book and have fun building your first WCF services.

—Clemens Vasters
Program Manager, Connected Framework Team
Microsoft Corporation

Preface

In August 2001 I first learned the details of an effort in Microsoft to rewrite COM+ using managed code. Nothing much happened after that. Then, in July 2002, during a C# 2.0 Strategic Design Review, the remoting program manager outlined in broad strokes plans to rework remoting into something that developers should actually use. At the same time, Microsoft was also working on incorporating the new security specs for web services into the ASMX stack and actively working with others on drafting a score of additional web services specs.

In July 2003 I was given access to a new transactional infrastructure that improved on the deficiencies in transactional .NET programming. As of yet, there was no cohesive programming model that unified these distinct technologies. Towards the end of 2003 I was privileged to be invited to join a small team of outside industry experts and participate in the strategic design review of a new development platform code-named Indigo. Some of the smartest and nicest people I know were part of that team. Over the next 2–3 years Indigo went through some three generations of programming models. The current declarative, endpoint-driven object model debuted in early 2005, was stabilized by August of that year, and was named the Windows Communication Foundation (WCF).

It is difficult to get a consistent answer from different people on what WCF is. To the web service developer, it is the ultimate interoperability solution, an implementation of a long list of industry standards. To the distributed application developer, it is the easiest way of making remote calls and even queued calls. To the system developer, it is the next generation of productivity-oriented features, such as transactions and hosting, that provide off-the-shelf plumbing for applications. To the application developer, it is a declarative programming model for structuring the application. And to the architect, it is how one can finally build service-oriented applications. WCF is in actuality all of those, simply because it was designed that way—to be the unified next generation of Microsoft's disparate technologies.

To me, WCF is simply the next development platform, which to a large extent subsumes raw .NET programming. WCF should be used by any .NET developer, regardless of the application type, size, or industry domain. WCF is a fundamental technology that provides an easy and clean way to generate services and applications in compliance with what I regard as sound design principles. WCF is engineered from the ground up to simplify application development and deployment, and to lower the overall cost of ownership. WCF services are used to build service-oriented applications, from standalone desktop applications to web-based applications and services to high-end Enterprise applications.

How This Book Is Organized

This book covers the topics and skills you need to design and develop service-oriented WCF-based applications. You will see how to take advantage of built-in features such as service hosting, instance management, concurrency management, transactions, disconnected queued calls, and security. While the book shows you how to use these features, it sets the focus on the "why" and the rationale behind particular design decisions. You'll not only learn WCF programming and the related system issues, but also relevant design options, tips, best practices, and pitfalls. I approached almost every topic and aspect from a software engineering standpoint because my objective is to make you not just a WCF expert, but also a better software engineer. Armed with such insights, you can engineer your application for maintainability, extensibility, reusability, and productivity.

The book avoids many implementation details of WCF and largely confines its coverage to the possibilities and the practical aspects of using WCF: how to apply the technology and how to choose among the available design and programming models. The book makes the most of what .NET 2.0 has to offer, and in some respects is an advanced C# book as well.

In addition, the book contains many useful utilities, tools, and helper classes I have written. My tools and helper classes or attributes aim at increasing your productivity and the quality of your WCF services. I literally developed a small framework that sits on top of WCF and compensates for some oversights in its design or simplifies and automates certain tasks. This book is as much about my tools, ideas, and techniques as it is about native WCF, and my framework also demonstrates how you can extend WCF.

During the past two years I have published a number of WCF articles in *MSDN Magazine*, and I presently write the WCF section of the Foundations column for the magazine as well. I used these articles to seed the chapters in this book, and I am grateful to the magazine for allowing me to do so. Even if you have read the articles, you should still read the corresponding chapters here. The chapters are much more comprehensive, offering additional angles, techniques, and samples, and often tie their subjects to other chapters.

Each chapter systematically addresses a single topic and discusses it in depth. However, each chapter does rely on the ones that precede it, so you should read the chapters in order.

Here is a brief summary of the chapters and appendixes in this book:

Chapter 1, *WCF Essentials*

Starts by explaining what WCF is, and then describes essential WCF concepts and building blocks, such as addresses, contracts, bindings, endpoints, hosting, and clients. The chapter ends with a discussion of the WCF architecture, which is really the linchpin of all that is enabled in the subsequent chapters. This chapter assumes you understand the basic motivation and benefit of service-orientation. If that is not the case, you should first read Appendix A. Even if you are already familiar with the basic concepts of WCF, I recommend you give this chapter at least, cursory reading, not only to ensure you have the solid foundation but also because some of the helper classes and terms introduced here will be used and extended throughout the book.

Chapter 2, *Service Contracts*

Is dedicated to designing and working with service contracts. You will first learn some useful techniques for service contract overloading and inheritance, and some advanced techniques. The chapter next discusses how to design and factor contracts that cater to reuse, maintainability, and extensibility. The chapter ends by showing you how to interact programmatically at runtime with the metadata of the exposed contracts.

Chapter 3, *Data Contracts*

Deals with how the client and the service can exchange data without ever actually sharing the data type itself or using the same development technology. You will see how to deal with some interesting real-life issues such as data versioning, and how to pass collections of items.

Chapter 4, *Instance Management*

Is dedicated to answering which service instance handles which client's request. WCF supports several service instance management, activation, and lifetime management techniques with drastic implications on scalability and performance. This chapter provides the rationale for each of the instance management modes, offers guidelines on when and how to best use them, and also addresses some related topics, such as throttling.

Chapter 5, *Operations*

Deals with the types of operations clients can invoke on a service and the related design guidelines, such as how to improve and extend the basic offering to support callback setup and teardown, manage callback ports and channels, and provide for type-safe duplex proxies.

Chapter 6, *Faults*

Is all about how services can report errors and exceptions back to their clients, since constructs such as exceptions and exception handling are technology-specific and should not transcend the service boundary. The chapter discusses the best practices of error handling, enabling you to decouple the client error handling from the service. The chapter also demonstrates how you can extend and improve on the basic error-handling mechanism.

Chapter 7, *Transactions*

Begins by providing the motivation for transactions in general, and then discusses the many aspects of transactional services: the transaction management architecture, transaction propagation configuration, the declarative transaction support offered by WCF, and how clients can create transactions. The chapter ends by discussing relevant design guidelines such as transactional service state management and instancing modes.

Chapter 8, *Concurrency Management*

Describes the powerful yet simple declarative way WCF offers for managing concurrency and synchronization, both for the client and the service. The chapter then presents more advanced aspects such as callbacks, reentrancy, thread affinity, and synchronization context and best practices and guidelines for avoiding deadlocks.

Chapter 9, *Queued Services*

Shows how clients can queue up calls to services, thus enabling asynchronous, disconnected work. The chapter starts by showing how to set up and configure queued services, and then focuses on aspects such as transactions, instance management, and failures and their impact on both the business model of the service and its implementation.

Chapter 10, *Security*

Demystifies service-oriented security by breaking down this multifaceted task into its basic elements, such as message transfer, authentication, and authorization. The chapter continues to demonstrate how to provide security for key scenarios such as intranet and Internet applications. Finally, you will see my framework for declarative WCF security, designed to automate security setup and to considerably simplify managing security.

Appendix A, *Introduction to Service-Orientation*

Is designed for readers who want to understand what service-orientation is all about. This appendix presents my take on service-orientation and what it means to put it in a concrete context. The appendix defines service-oriented applications (as opposed to mere architecture) and the services themselves, and examines the benefits of the methodology. The appendix then presents the principles of service-orientation and augments the abstract tenets with a few more practical points required by most applications.

Appendix B, *Publish-Subscribe Service*

Presents my framework for implementing a publish-subscribe event management solution. The framework lets you develop a publishing and a subscription service in literally one or two lines of code. While the publish-subscribe pattern could have just as well been part of Chapter 5, it is in a dedicated appendix because it utilizes aspects described in other chapters, such as transactions and queued calls.

Appendix C, *WCF Coding Standard*

Is basically a consolidated list of all the best practices and dos and don'ts mentioned throughout the book. The standard is all about the "how" and the "what," not the "why." The rationale behind the standard is found in the rest of the book. The standard also uses the helper classes discussed in this book.

Some Assumptions About the Reader

I assume you, the reader, are an experienced developer and that you are comfortable with object-oriented concepts such as encapsulation and inheritance. I will take advantage of your existing understanding of object and component technology and terminology, and port that knowledge to WCF. You should ideally have a fair understanding of .NET and know basic C# 2.0 (including use of generics and anonymous methods). Although the book uses C# for the most part, it is just as pertinent to Visual Basic 2005 developers.

What You Need to Use This Book

To use this book, you will need .NET 2.0, Visual Studio 2005, the released components of .NET 3.0, along with the .NET 3.0 development SDK and the .NET 3.0 extensions for Visual Studio 2005. Unless explicitly mentioned, the book applies to Windows XP, Windows Server 2003, and Windows Vista. You may also install additional Windows components, such as MSMQ and IIS.

Conventions Used in This Book

The following typographic conventions are used in this book:

Italic

Used for technical terms, online links, and filenames

`Constant width`

Used for code samples, statements, namespaces, classes, assemblies, interface directives, operators, attributes, and reserved words

`Constant width bold`

Used for code emphasis

This icon designates a note, which is an important aside to the nearby text.

 This icon designates a warning relating to the nearby text.

Whenever I wish to make a point in a code sample, I do so with the static `Assert` method of the `Debug` class:

```
int number = 1+2;
Debug.Assert(number == 3);
```

The `Assert` method accepts a Boolean statement, and throws an exception when the statement is `false`.

The book follows the recommended naming guidelines and coding style presented in Appendix E of my book *Programming .NET Components* (O'Reilly). Whenever it deviates from that standard it is likely the result of space or line length constraints. As for naming conventions, I use "Pascal casing" for public member methods and properties; this means the first letter of each word in the name is capitalized. For local variables and method parameters I use "camel casing," in which the first letter of the first word of the name is not capitalized. In the case of private members, I prefix such variables with `m_`:

```
public class SomeClass
{
   int m_Number;

   public int Number
   {get;set};
}
```

I use ellipses between curly braces to indicate the presence of code that is necessary but unspecified:

```
public class SomeClass
{...}
```

In the interest of clarity and space, code examples often do not contain all the using statements needed to specify all the namespaces the example requires; instead, such examples include only the new namespaces introduced in the preceding text.

Using Code Examples

This book is here to help you get your job done. In general, you may use the code in this book in your programs and documentation. You do not need to contact us for permission unless you're reproducing a significant portion of the code. For example, writing a program that uses several chunks of code from this book does not require permission. Selling or distributing a CD-ROM of examples from this book *does* require permission. Answering a question by citing this book and quoting example code does not require permission. Incorporating a significant amount of example code from this book into your product's documentation *does* require permission.

We appreciate, but do not require, attribution. An attribution usually includes the title, author, publisher, and ISBN. For example: "*Programming WCF Services* by Juval Löwy. Copyright 2007 O'Reilly Media, Inc., 978-0-596-52699-3."

If you feel your use of code examples falls outside fair use or the permission given above, feel free to contact us at *permissions@oreilly.com*.

How to Contact Us

Please address comments and questions concerning this book to the publisher:

O'Reilly Media, Inc.
1005 Gravenstein Highway North
Sebastopol, CA 95472
800-998-9938 (in the United States or Canada)
707-829-0515 (international/local)
707-829-0104 (fax)

There is a web page for this book, which lists errata, examples, or any additional information. You can access this page at:

http://www.oreilly.com/catalog/9780596526993

To comment or ask technical questions about this book, send email to:

bookquestions@oreilly.com

You can also contact the author at:

http://www.idesign.net

The author has posted a comprehensive code library on the IDesign web site with more than 120 downloads on WCF essentials, contract design, instance management, operations and calls, faults, transactions, concurrency, queuing, and security. The downloads articulate in a working fashion many of the code snippets in this book.

Safari® Enabled

 When you see a Safari® Enabled icon on the cover of your favorite technology book, that means the book is available online through the O'Reilly Network Safari Bookshelf.

Safari offers a solution that's better than e-books. It's a virtual library that lets you easily search thousands of top tech books, cut and paste code samples, download chapters, and find quick answers when you need the most accurate, current information. Try it for free at *http://safari.oreilly.com.*

Acknowledgments

I would not have been able to come to terms with WCF in its early days without the constant support and interaction with the WCF (then Indigo) program managers. I am especially grateful to my friend Steve Swartz, one of the WCF architects, not just for his knowledge and insight, but also for his patience with me, and those long IM sessions. Thanks go to Yasser Shohoud, Doug Purdy, and Shy Cohen for the fascinating strategic design reviews, and to Krish Srinivasan for his almost philosophical approach to engineering. Working with you guys has been the best part of learning WCF and a privilege on its own right. The following WCF program managers also shared their time and helped clarify WCF: Andy Milligan, Brian McNamara, Eugene Osovetsky, Kenny Wolf, Kirill Gavrylyuk, Max Feingold, Michael Marucheck, Mike Vernal, and Steve Millet. Thanks also to the group manager, Angela Mills.

Outside Microsoft, thanks to Norman Headlam and Pedro Felix for providing valuable feedback. I am grateful to Nicholas Paldino for his help. Nick's knowledge of the .NET framework is second to none, and his meticulous attention to details contributed greatly to the quality and cohesiveness of this book.

Finally, to my family: my wife, Dana, who keeps encouraging me to write down my ideas and techniques, while knowing too well that writing a book entails precious time away from the her and the girls; and to my parents, who imparted to me the love for engineering. I dedicate this book to my seven-year-old daughter, Abigail, and my four-year-old, Eleanor. You all mean the world to me.

CHAPTER 1

WCF Essentials

This chapter describes the essential concepts and building blocks of WCF and its architecture, enabling you to build simple services. You will learn the basic terms regarding addresses, bindings, contracts, and endpoints; see how to host a service, learn how to write a client; and understand some related topics, such as in-proc hosting and reliability. Even if you are already familiar with the basic concepts of WCF, I recommend you give this chapter at least a cursory reading, not only to ensure you have a solid foundation, but also because some of the helper classes and terms introduced here will be used and extended throughout the book.

What Is WCF?

Windows Communication Foundation (WCF) is an SDK for developing and deploying services on Windows. WCF provides a runtime environment for your services, enabling you to expose CLR types as services, and to consume other services as CLR types. Although in theory you could build services without WCF, in practice building services is significantly easier with WCF. WCF is Microsoft's implementation of a set of industry standards defining service interactions, type conversion, marshaling, and various protocols' management. Because of that, WCF provides interoperability between services. WCF provides developers with the essential off-the-shelf plumbing required by almost any application, and as such, it greatly increases productivity. The first release of WCF provides many useful facilities for developing services, such as hosting, service instance management, asynchronous calls, reliability, transaction management, disconnected queued calls, and security. WCF also has an elegant extensibility model that you can use to enrich the basic offering. In fact, WCF itself is written using this extensibility model. The rest of the chapters in this book are dedicated to those aspects and features. Most all of the WCF functionality is included in a single assembly called *System.ServiceModel.dll* in the System. ServiceModel namespace.

WCF is part of .NET 3.0 and requires .NET 2.0, so it can only run on operation systems that support it. Presently this list consists of Windows Vista (client and server), Windows XP SP2, and Windows Server 2003 SP1 or their later versions.

Services

A *service* is a unit of functionality exposed to the world. In that respect, it is the next evolutionary step in the long journey from functions to objects to components to services. *Service-orientation* (SO) is an abstract set of principles and best practices for building SO applications. If you are unfamiliar with the principles of service-orientation, Appendix A provides a concise overview and motivation for using service-orientation. The rest of this book assumes you are familiar with these principles. A *service-oriented application* (SOA) aggregates services into a single logical application similar to the way a component-oriented application aggregates components or an object-oriented application aggregates objects, as shown in Figure 1-1.

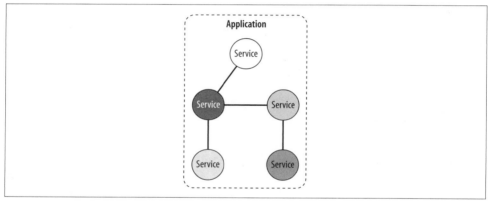

Figure 1-1. A service-oriented application

The services can be local or remote, developed by multiple parties using any technology, versioned independently, and even execute on different timelines. Inside a service, you will find concepts such as languages, technologies, platforms, versions, and frameworks, yet between services, only prescribed communication patterns are allowed.

The *client* of a service is merely the party consuming its functionality. The client can be literally anything—a Windows Forms class, an ASP.NET page, or another service.

Clients and services interact by sending and receiving messages. Messages may transfer directly from client to service or via an intermediary. With WCF, all messages are SOAP messages. Note that the messages are independent of transport protocols—unlike Web services, WCF services may communicate over a variety of transports, not just HTTP. WCF clients may interoperate with non-WCF services, and WCF services can interact with non-WCF clients. That said, typically if you develop both the client and the service, you could construct the application so that both ends require WCF to utilize WCF-specific advantages.

Because the making of the service is opaque from the outside, a WCF service typically exposes *metadata* describing the available functionality and possible ways of communicating with the service. The metadata is published in a predefined, technology-neutral way, such as using WSDL over HTTP-GET, or an industry standard for metadata exchange. A non-WCF client can import the metadata to its native environment as native types. Similarly, a WCF client can import the metadata of a non-WCF service and consume it as native CLR classes and interfaces.

Services' Execution Boundaries

With WCF, the client never interacts with the service directly, even when dealing with a local, in-memory service. Instead, the client always uses a proxy to forward the call to the service. The proxy exposes the same operations as the service, plus some proxy-management methods.

WCF allows the client to communicate with the service across all execution boundaries. On the same machine (see Figure 1-2), the client can consume services in the same app domain, across app domains in the same process, or across processes.

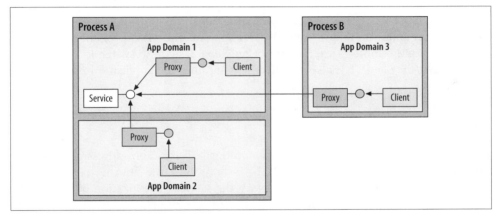

Figure 1-2. Same-machine communication using WCF

Across machine boundaries (Figure 1-3), the client can interact with services in its intranet or across the Internet.

WCF and location transparency

In the past, distributed computing technologies such as DCOM or .NET Remoting aspired to provide the same programming model to the client whether the object was local or remote. In the case of a local call, the client used a direct reference, and when

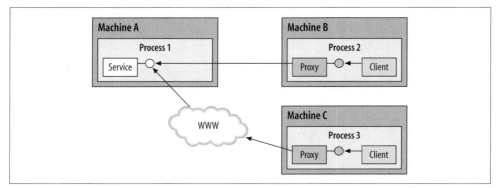

Figure 1-3. Cross-machine communication using WCF

dealing with a remote object, the client used a proxy. The problem with this approach of trying to take the local programming model and make it the remote programming model is that there is much more to a remote call than an object with a wire. Complex issues such as life cycle management, reliability, state management, scalability, and security raised their heads, making the remote programming model significantly more complex, all because it tried to be what it is not—a local object. WCF also strives to provide the client with the same programming model regardless of the location of the service. However, the WCF approach is the exact opposite: it takes the remote programming model of instantiating and using a proxy and uses it even in the most local case. Because all interactions are done via a proxy, requiring the same configuration and hosting, WCF maintains the same programming model for the local and remote cases; thus it not only enables you to switch locations without affecting the client, but also significantly simplifies the application programming model.

Addresses

In WCF, every service is associated with a unique address. The address provides two important elements: the location of the service and the transport protocol or *transport schema* used to communicate with the service. The location portion of the address indicates the name of the target machine, site, or network; a communication port, pipe, or queue; and an optional specific path or URI. A *URI* is a Universal Resource Identifier, and can be any unique string, such as the service name or a GUID.

WCF 1.0 supports the following transport schemas:

- HTTP
- TCP
- Peer network

- IPC (Inter-Process Communication over named pipes)
- MSMQ

Addresses always have the following format:

```
[base address]/[optional URI]
```

The base address is always in this format:

```
[transport]://[machine or domain][:optional port]
```

Here are a few sample addresses:

```
http://localhost:8001
http://localhost:8001/MyService
net.tcp://localhost:8002/MyService
net.pipe://localhost/MyPipe
net.msmq://localhost/private/MyService
net.msmq://localhost/MyService
```

The way to read an address such as

```
http://localhost:8001
```

is like this: "Using HTTP, go to the machine called localhost, where on port 8001 someone is waiting for my calls."

If there is also a URI such as:

```
http://localhost:8001/MyService
```

then the address would read as follows: "Using HTTP, go to the machine called localhost, where on port 8001 someone called MyService is waiting for my calls."

TCP Addresses

TCP addresses use net.tcp for the transport, and typically include a port number such as:

```
net.tcp://localhost:8002/MyService
```

When a port number is not specified, the TCP address defaults to port 808:

```
net.tcp://localhost/MyService
```

It is possible for two TCP addresses (from the same host, which will be discussed more later on in this chapter) to share a port:

```
net.tcp://localhost:8002/MyService
net.tcp://localhost:8002/MyOtherService
```

TCP-based addresses are used throughout this book.

 You can configure TCP-based addresses from different hosts to share a port.

HTTP Addresses

HTTP addresses use `http` for transport, and can also use `https` for secure transport. You typically use HTTP addresses with outward-facing Internet-based services, and can specify a port such as:

```
http://localhost:8001
```

When the port number is unspecified, it defaults to 80. Similar to TCP addresses, two HTTP addresses from the same host can share a port, even on the same machine.

HTTP-based addresses are also used throughout this book.

IPC Addresses

IPC addresses use `net.pipe` for transport, to indicate the use of the Windows named pipe mechanism. In WCF, services that use named pipes can only accept calls from the same machine. Consequently, you must specify either the explicit local machine name or `localhost` for the machine name, followed by a unique string for the pipe name:

```
net.pipe://localhost/MyPipe
```

You can only open a named pipe once per machine, and therefore it is not possible for two named pipe addresses to share a pipe name on the same machine.

IPC-based addresses are used throughout this book.

MSMQ Addresses

MSMQ addresses use `net.msmq` for transport, to indicate the use of the Microsoft Message Queue (MSMQ). You must specify the queue name. When you're dealing with private queues, you must specify the queue type, but that can be omitted for public queues:

```
net.msmq://localhost/private/MyService
net.msmq://localhost/MyService
```

Chapter 9 is dedicated to making queued calls.

Peer Network Address

Peer network addresses use `net.p2p` for transport, to indicate the use of the Windows peer network transport. You must specify the peer network name as well as a unique path and port. Using and configuring peer networks is beyond the scope of this book, and you will see very little mention of peer networks in subsequent chapters.

Contracts

In WCF, all services expose contracts. The *contract* is a platform-neutral and standard way of describing what the service does. WCF defines four types of contracts.

Service contracts

> Describe which operations the client can perform on the service. Service contracts are the subject of the next chapter, but are used extensively in every chapter in this book.

Data contracts

> Define which data types are passed to and from the service. WCF defines implicit contracts for built-in types such as int and string, but you can easily define explicit opt-in data contracts for custom types. Chapter 3 is dedicated to defining and using data contracts, and subsequent chapters make use of data contracts as required.

Fault contracts

> Define which errors are raised by the service, and how the service handles and propagates errors to its clients. Chapter 6 is dedicated to defining and using fault contracts.

Message contracts

> Allow the service to interact directly with messages. Message contracts can be typed or untyped, and are useful in interoperability cases and when there is an existing message format you have to comply with. As a WCF developer, you should use message contracts only rarely, so this book makes no use of message contracts.

The Service Contract

The ServiceContractAttribute is defined as:

```
[AttributeUsage(AttributeTargets.Interface|AttributeTargets.Class,
                Inherited = false)]
public sealed class ServiceContractAttribute : Attribute
{
   public string Name
   {get;set;}
   public string Namespace
   {get;set;}
   //More members
}
```

This attribute allows you to define a service contract. You can apply the attribute on an interface or a class, as shown in Example 1-1.

Example 1-1. Defining and implementing a service contract

```
[ServiceContract]
interface IMyContract
{
    [OperationContract]
    string MyMethod(string text);

    //Will not be part of the contract
    string MyOtherMethod(string text);
}
class MyService : IMyContract
{
    public string MyMethod(string text)
    {
        return "Hello " + text;
    }
    public string MyOtherMethod(string text)
    {
        return "Cannot call this method over WCF";
    }
}
```

The ServiceContract attribute maps a CLR interface (or inferred interface, as you will see later on) to a technology-neutral service contract. The ServiceContract attribute exposes a CLR interface (or a class) as a WCF contract, independently of that type's visibility. The type visibility has no bearing on WCF, because visibility is a CLR concept. Applying the ServiceContract attribute on an internal interface exposes that interface as a public service contract, ready to be consumed across the service boundary. Without the ServiceContract attribute, the interface is not visible to WCF clients, in line with the service-oriented tenet that service boundaries are explicit. To enforce that, all contracts must explicitly opt in: only interfaces (or classes) decorated with the ServiceContract attribute will be considered as WCF contracts. Other types will not.

In addition, none of the members of the type will ever be part of the contract when using the ServiceContract attribute. You must explicitly indicate to WCF which methods to expose as part of the WCF contract using the OperationContractAttribute, defined as:

```
[AttributeUsage(AttributeTargets.Method)]
public sealed class OperationContractAttribute : Attribute
{
    public string Name
    {get;set;}
    //More members
}
```

You can only apply the OperationContract attribute on methods, but not on properties, indexers, or events, which are CLR concepts. WCF only understands *operations*—logical functions—and the OperationContract attribute exposes a contract method as a logical operation to perform as part of the service contract. Other methods on the interface (or class) that do not have the OperationContract attribute will not be part of the contract. This enforces the explicit service boundary and maintains an explicit opt-in model for the operations themselves. In addition, a contract operation cannot use object references as parameters—only primitive types or data contracts are allowed.

Applying the ServiceContract attribute

WCF lets you apply the ServiceContract attribute on an interface or on a class. When you apply it on an interface, some class needs to implement the interface. In general, you use plain C# or VB to implement the interface, and nothing in the service class code pertains to it being a WCF service:

```
[ServiceContract]
interface IMyContract
{
    [OperationContract]
    string MyMethod( );
}
class MyService : IMyContract
{
    public string MyMethod( )
    {
        return "Hello WCF";
    }
}
```

You can use implicit or explicit interface implementation:

```
class MyService : IMyContract
{
    string IMyContract.MyMethod( )
    {
        return "Hello WCF";
    }
}
```

A single class can support multiple contracts by deriving and implementing multiple interfaces decorated with the ServiceContract attribute.

```
[ServiceContract]
interface IMyContract
{
    [OperationContract]
    string MyMethod( );
}
[ServiceContract]
interface IMyOtherContract
```

```
{
    [OperationContract]
    void MyOtherMethod( );
}

class MyService : IMyContract,IMyOtherContract
{
    public string MyMethod( )
    {...}
    public void MyOtherMethod( )
    {...}
}
```

There are, however, a few implementation constraints on the service implementation class. You should avoid parameterized constructors because only the default constructor will ever be used by WCF. Also, although the class can use internal properties, indexers, and static members, no WCF client will ever be able to access them.

WCF also lets you apply the ServiceContract attribute directly on the service class, without ever defining a separate contract first:

```
//Avoid
[ServiceContract]
class MyService
{
    [OperationContract]
    string MyMethod( )
    {
        return "Hello WCF";
    }
}
```

Under the covers, WCF will infer the contract definition. You can apply the OperationContract attribute on any method of the class, be it private or public.

 Avoid using the ServiceContract attribute directly on the service class. Always define a separate contract, so that you can use it in other contexts.

Names and namespaces

You can and should define a namespace for your contract. The contract namespace serves the same purpose in WCF as it does in .NET programming: to scope a type of contract and reduce the overall chance for a collision. You use the Namespace property of the ServiceContract attribute to provide a namespace:

```
[ServiceContract(Namespace = "MyNamespace")]
interface IMyContract
{...}
```

Unspecified, the contract namespace defaults to *http://tempuri.org*. For outward-facing services you would typically use your company's URL, and for intranet services you can use any meaningful unique name, such as MyApplication.

By default, the exposed name of the contract will be the name of the interface used. However, you could use an alias for a contract to expose a different name to the clients in the metadata using the Name property of the ServiceContract attribute:

```
[ServiceContract(Name = "IMyContract")]
interface IMyOtherContract
{...}
```

In similar manner, the name of the publicly exposed operation defaults to the method name, but you can use the Name property of the OperationContract attribute to alias it to a different publicly exposed name:

```
[ServiceContract]
interface IMyContract
{
    [OperationContract(Name = "SomeOperation")]
    void MyMethod(string text);
}
```

You will see a use for these properties in the next chapter.

Hosting

The WCF service class cannot exist in a void. Every WCF service must be hosted in a Windows process called the *host process*. A single host process can host multiple services, and the same service type can be hosted in multiple host processes. WCF makes no demand on whether or not the host process is also the client process. Obviously, having a separate process advocates fault and security isolation. It is also immaterial who provides the process or what kind of a process is involved. The host can be provided by IIS, by the Widows Activation Service (WAS) on Windows Vista, or by the developer as part of the application.

 A special case of hosting is in-process hosting, or *in-proc* for short, where the service resides in the same process as the client. The host for the in-proc case is, by definition, provided by the developer.

IIS Hosting

The main advantage of hosting a service in the Microsoft Internet Information Server (IIS) web server is that the host process is launched automatically upon the first client request, and you rely on IIS to manage the life cycle of the host process. The main disadvantage of IIS hosting is that you can only use HTTP. With IIS5, you are further restricted to having all services use the same port number.

Hosting in IIS is very similar to hosting a classic ASMX web service. You need to create a virtual directory under IIS and supply a *.svc* file. The *.svc* file functions similar to an *.asmx* file, and is used to identify the service code behind the file and class. Example 1-2 shows the syntax for the *.svc* file.

Example 1-2. A .svc file

```
<%@ ServiceHost
      Language  = "C#"
      Debug     = "true"
      CodeBehind = "~/App_Code/MyService.cs"
      Service   = "MyService"
%>
```

 You can even inject the service code inline in the *.svc* file, but that is not advisable, as is the case with ASMX web services.

When you use IIS hosting, the base address used for the service always has to be the same as the address of the *.svc* file.

Using Visual Studio 2005

You can use Visual Studio 2005 to generate a boilerplate IIS-hosted service. From the File menu, select New Website and then select WCF Service from the New Web Site dialog box. This causes Visual Studio 2005 to create a new web site, service code, and matching *.svc* file. You can also use the Add New Item dialog to add another service later on.

The Web.Config file

The web site config file (*Web.Config*) must list the types you want to expose as services. You need to use fully qualified type names, including the assembly name, if the service type comes from an unreferenced assembly:

```
<system.serviceModel>
   <services>
      <service name = "MyNamespace.MyService">
         ...
      </service>
   </services>
</system.serviceModel>
```

Self-Hosting

Self-hosting is the name for the technique used when the developer is responsible for providing and managing the life cycle of the host process. Self-hosting is used both in the case of wanting a process (or machine) boundary between the client and the service, and when using the service in-proc—that is, in the same process as the client. The process you need to provide can be any Windows process, such as a Windows Forms application, a Console application, or a Windows NT Service. Note that the process must be running before the client calls the service, which typically means you have to pre-launch it. This is not an issue for NT Services or in-proc. Providing a host can be done with only a few lines of code, and it does offer a few advantage over IIS hosting.

Similar to IIS hosting, the hosting application config file (*App.Config*) must list the types of the services you wish to host and expose to the world:

```
<system.serviceModel>
   <services>
      <service name = "MyNamespace.MyService">
         ...
      </service>
   </services>
</system.serviceModel>
```

In addition, the host process must explicitly register the service types at runtime and open the host for client calls, which is why the host process must be running before the client calls arrive. Creating the host is typically done in the Main( ) method using the class ServiceHost, defined in Example 1-3.

Example 1-3. The ServiceHost class

```
public interface ICommunicationObject
{
   void Open( );
   void Close( );
   //More members
}
public abstract class CommunicationObject : ICommunicationObject
{...}
public abstract class ServiceHostBase : CommunicationObject,IDisposable,...
{...}
public class ServiceHost : ServiceHostBase,...
{
   public ServiceHost(Type serviceType,params Uri[] baseAddresses);
   //More members
}
```

You need to provide the constructor of ServiceHost with the service type, and optionally with default base addresses. The set of base addresses can be an empty set. Even if you provide base addresses, the service can be configured to use different base addresses. Having a set of base addresses enables the service to accept calls on multiple addresses and protocols, and to use only a relative URI. Note that each ServiceHost instance is associated with a particular service type, and if the host process needs to host multiple types of services, you will need a matching number of

ServiceHost instances. By calling the Open( ) method on the host, you allow calls in, and by calling the Close( ) method, you gracefully exit the host instance, allowing calls in progress to complete, and yet refusing future client calls even if the host process is still running. Closing is typically done on host process shutdown. For example, to host this service in a Windows Forms application:

```
[ServiceContract]
interface IMyContract
{...}
class MyService : IMyContract
{...}
```

you would have the following hosting code:

```
public static void Main( )
{
    Uri baseAddress = new Uri("http://localhost:8000/");
    ServiceHost host = new ServiceHost(typeof(MyService),baseAddress);

    host.Open( );

    //Can do blocking calls:
    Application.Run(new MyForm( ));

    host.Close( );
}
```

Opening a host loads the WCF runtime and launches worker threads to monitor incoming requests. Since worker threads are involved, you can perform blocking operations after opening the host. Having explicit control over opening and closing the host provides for a nice feature not easily accomplished with IIS hosting: you can build a custom application control applet where the administrator explicitly opens and closes the host at will, without ever shutting down the host.

Using Visual Studio 2005

Visual Studio 2005 allows you to add a WCF service to any application project by selecting WCF Service from the Add New Item dialog box. The service added this way is, of course, in-proc toward the host process, but can be accessed by out-of-proc clients as well.

Self-hosting and base addresses

You can launch a service host without providing any base address by omitting the base addresses altogether:

```
public static void Main( )
{
    ServiceHost host = new ServiceHost(typeof(MyService));

    host.Open( );
```

```
   Application.Run(new MyForm());

   host.Close();
}
```

 Do not provide a null instead of an empty list, because that will throw
an exception:
```
ServiceHost host;
host = new ServiceHost(typeof(MyService),null);
```

You can also register multiple base addresses separated by a comma, as long as the
addresses do not use the same transport schema, as in the following snippet (note
the use of the params qualifier in Example 1-3):

```
Uri tcpBaseAddress  = new Uri("net.tcp://localhost:8001/");
Uri httpBaseAddress = new Uri("http://localhost:8002/");

ServiceHost host = new ServiceHost(typeof(MyService),
                        tcpBaseAddress,httpBaseAddress);
```

WCF lets you also list the base addresses in the host config file:

```
<system.serviceModel>
   <services>
      <service name = "MyNamespace.MyService">
         <host>
            <baseAddresses>
               <add baseAddress = "net.tcp://localhost:8001/"/>
               <add baseAddress = "http://localhost:8002/"/>
            </baseAddresses>
         </host>
         ...
      </service>
   </services>
</system.serviceModel>
```

When you create the host, it will use whichever base address it finds in the config
file, plus any base address you provide programmatically. Take extra care to ensure
the configured base addresses and the programmatic ones do not overlap in the
schema.

You can even register multiple hosts for the same type as long as the hosts use different base addresses:

```
Uri baseAddress1  = new Uri("net.tcp://localhost:8001/");
ServiceHost host1 = new ServiceHost(typeof(MyService),baseAddress1);
host1.Open();

Uri baseAddress2  = new Uri("net.tcp://localhost:8002/");
ServiceHost host2 = new ServiceHost(typeof(MyService),baseAddress2);
host2.Open();
```

However, with the exception of some threading issues discussed in Chapter 8, opening multiple hosts this way offers no real advantage. In addition, opening multiple hosts for the same type does not work with base addresses supplied in the config file and requires use of the ServiceHost constructor.

Advanced hosting features

The ICommunicationObject interface supported by ServiceHost offers some advanced features, listed in Example 1-4.

Example 1-4. The ICommunicationObject interface

```
public interface ICommunicationObject
{
   void Open( );
   void Close( );
   void Abort( );

   event EventHandler Closed;
   event EventHandler Closing;
   event EventHandler Faulted;
   event EventHandler Opened;
   event EventHandler Opening;

   IAsyncResult BeginClose(AsyncCallback callback,object state);
   IAsyncResult BeginOpen(AsyncCallback callback,object state);
   void EndClose(IAsyncResult result);
   void EndOpen(IAsyncResult result);

   CommunicationState State
   {get;}
   //More members
}
public enum CommunicationState
{
   Created,
   Opening,
   Opened,
   Closing,
   Closed,
   Faulted
}
```

If opening or closing the host is a lengthy operation, you can do so asynchronously with the BeginOpen( ) and BeginClose( ) methods. You can subscribe to hosting events such as state changes or faults, and you can use the State property to query for the host status. Finally, the ServiceHost class also implements the Abort( ) method. Abort( ) is an ungraceful exit—when called, it immediately aborts all service calls in progress and shuts down the host. Active clients will get an exception.

The ServiceHost<T> class

You can improve on the WCF-provided ServiceHost class by defining the ServiceHost<T> class, as shown in Example 1-5.

Example 1-5. The ServiceHost<T> class

```
public class ServiceHost<T> : ServiceHost
{
    public ServiceHost() : base(typeof(T))
    {}
    public ServiceHost(params string[] baseAddresses) :
                              base(typeof(T),Convert(baseAddresses))
    {}
    public ServiceHost(params Uri[] baseAddresses) :
                                 base(typeof(T),baseAddresses)
    {}
    static Uri[] Convert(string[] baseAddresses)
    {
        Converter<string,Uri> convert =  delegate(string address)
                                         {
                                             return new Uri(address);
                                         };
        return Array.ConvertAll(baseAddresses,convert);
    }
}
```

ServiceHost<T> provides simple constructors that do not require the service type as a construction parameter, and can operate on raw strings instead of the cumbersome Uri. I'll add quite a few extensions, features, and capabilities to ServiceHost<T> in the rest of the book.

WAS Hosting

The Windows Activation Service (WAS) is a system service available with Windows Vista. WAS is part of IIS7, but can be installed and configured separately. To use the WAS for hosting your WCF service, you need to supply a *.svc* file, just as with IIS. The main difference between IIS and WAS is that the WAS is not limited to HTTP and can be used with any of the available WCF transports, ports, and queues.

WAS offers many advantages over self-hosting, including application pooling, recycling, idle time management, identity management, and isolation, and is the host process of choice when available; that is, when you can target either a Vista Server machine for scalability or a Vista client machine used as a server machine for a handful of clients only.

Still, the self-hosted process offers singular advantages such as in-proc hosting, dealing with unknown customer environments, and easy programmatic access to the advanced hosting features described previously.

Bindings

There are multiple aspects of communication with any given service, and there are many possible communication patterns: messages can be synchronous request/reply or asynchronous fire-and-forget; messages can be bidirectional; messages can be delivered immediately or queued; and the queues can be durable or volatile. There are many possible transport protocols for the messages, such as HTTP (or HTTPS), TCP, P2P (peer network), IPC (named pipes), or MSMQ. There are a few possible message encoding options: you can chose plain text to enable interoperability, binary encoding to optimize performance, or MTOM (Message Transport Optimization Mechanism) for large payloads. There are a few options for securing messages: you can choose not to secure them at all, to provide transport-level security only, to provide message-level privacy and security, and of course there are numerous ways for authenticating and authorizing the clients. Message delivery might be unreliable or reliable end-to-end across intermediaries and dropped connections, and the messages might be processed in the order they were sent or in the order they were received. Your service might need to interoperate with other services or clients that are only aware of the basic web service protocol, or they may be capable of using the score of WS-* modern protocols such as WS-Security and WS-Atomic Transactions. Your service may need to interoperate with legacy clients over raw MSMQ messages, or you may want to restrict your service to interoperate only with another WCF service or client.

If you start counting all the possible communication and interaction options, the number of permutations is probably in the tens of thousands. Some of those choices may be mutually exclusive, and some may mandate other choices. Clearly, both the client and the service must be aligned on all these options in order to communicate properly. Managing this level of complexity adds no business value to most applications, and yet the productivity and quality implications of making the wrong decisions are severe.

To simplify these choices and make them more manageable, WCF groups together a set of such communication aspects in bindings. A *binding* is merely a consistent, canned set of choices regarding the transport protocol, message encoding, communication pattern, reliability, security, transaction propagation, and interoperability. Ideally, you would extract all these "plumbing" aspects out of your service code and allow the service to focus solely on the implementation of the business logic. Binding enables you to use the same service logic over drastically different plumbing.

You can use the WCF-provided bindings as is, you can tweak their properties, or you can write your own custom bindings from scratch. The service publishes its choice of binding in its metadata, enabling clients to query for the type and specific properties of the binding because the client must use the exact same binding values as the service. A single service can support multiple bindings on separate addresses.

The Standard Bindings

WCF defines nine standard bindings:

Basic binding
> Offered by the BasicHttpBinding class, this is designed to expose a WCF service as a legacy ASMX web service, so that old clients can work with new services. When used by the client, this binding enables new WCF clients to work with old ASMX services.

TCP binding
> Offered by the NetTcpBinding class, this uses TCP for cross-machine communication on the intranet. It supports a variety of features, including reliability, transactions, and security, and is optimized for WCF-to-WCF communication. As a result, it requires both the client and the service to use WCF.

Peer network binding
> Offered by the NetPeerTcpBinding class, this uses peer networking as a transport. The peer network-enabled client and services all subscribe to the same grid and broadcast messages to it. Peer networking is beyond the scope of this book since it requires an understanding of grid topology and mesh computing strategies.

IPC binding
> Offered by the NetNamedPipeBinding class, this uses named pipes as a transport for same-machine communication. It is the most secure binding since it cannot accept calls from outside the machine and it supports a variety of features similar to the TCP binding.

Web Service (WS) binding
> Offered by the WSHttpBinding class, this uses HTTP or HTTPS for transport, and is designed to offer a variety of features such as reliability, transactions, and security over the Internet.

Federated WS binding
> Offered by the WSFederationHttpBinding class, this is a specialization of the WS binding, offering support for federated security. Federated security is beyond the scope of this book.

Duplex WS binding
> Offered by the WSDualHttpBinding class, this is similar to the WS binding except it also supports bidirectional communication from the service to the client as discussed in Chapter 5.

MSMQ binding
> Offered by the NetMsmqBinding class, this uses MSMQ for transport and is designed to offer support for disconnected queued calls. Using this binding is the subject of Chapter 9.

MSMQ integration binding

Offered by the `MsmqIntegrationBinding` class, this converts WCF messages to and from MSMQ messages, and is designed to interoperate with legacy MSMQ clients. Using this binding is beyond the scope of this book.

Format and Encoding

Each of the standard bindings uses different transport and encoding, as listed in Table 1-1.

Table 1-1. Transport and encoding for standard bindings (default encoding is in bold)

Name	Transport	Encoding	Interoperable
BasicHttpBinding	HTTP/HTTPS	**Text**, MTOM	Yes
NetTcpBinding	TCP	Binary	No
NetPeerTcpBinding	P2P	Binary	No
NetNamedPipeBinding	IPC	Binary	No
WSHttpBinding	HTTP/HTTPS	**Text**, MTOM	Yes
WSFederationHttpBinding	HTTP/HTTPS	**Text**, MTOM	Yes
WSDualHttpBinding	HTTP	**Text**, MTOM	Yes
NetMsmqBinding	MSMQ	Binary	No
MsmqIntegrationBinding	MSMQ	Binary	Yes

Having a text-based encoding enables a WCF service (or client) to communicate over HTTP with any other service (or client) regardless of its technology. Binary encoding over TCP or IPC yields the best performance but at the expense of interoperability, by mandating WCF-to-WCF communication.

Choosing a Binding

Choosing a binding for your service should follow the decision-activity diagram shown in Figure 1-4.

The first question you should ask yourself is whether your service needs to interact with non-WCF clients. If the answer is yes, and if the client is a legacy MSMQ client, choose the `MsmqIntegrationBinding` that enables your service to interoperate over MSMQ with such a client. If you need to interoperate with a non-WCF client and that client expects basic web service protocol (ASMX web services), choose the `BasicHttpBinding`, which exposes your WCF service to the outside world as if it were an ASMX web service (that is, a WSI-basic profile). The downside is that you cannot take advantage of most of the modern WS-* protocols. However, if the non-WCF client can understand these standards, choose one of the WS bindings, such as `WSHttpBinding`, `WSFederationBinding`, or `WSDualHttpBinding`. If you can assume that

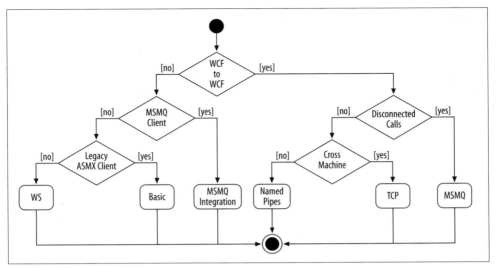

Figure 1-4. Choosing a binding

the client is a WCF client, yet it requires offline or disconnected interaction, choose the `NetMsmqBinding` that uses MSMQ for transporting the messages. If the client requires connected communication, but could be calling across machine boundaries, choose the `NetTcpBinding` that communicates over TCP. If the client is on the same machine as the service, choose the `NetNamedPipeBinding` that uses named pipes to maximize performance. You may fine-tune binding selections based on additional criteria such as the need for callbacks (`WSDualHttpBinding`) or federated security (`WSFederationBinding`).

 Most bindings work well even outside their target scenario. For example, you could use the TCP binding for same-machine or even in-proc communication, and you could use the basic binding for Intranet WCF-to-WCF communication. However, do try to choose a binding according to Figure 1-4.

Using a Binding

Each binding offers literally dozens of configurable properties. There are three modes of working with bindings. You can use the built-in bindings as is if they fit your requirements. You can tweak and configure some of their properties such as transaction propagation, reliability, and security. You can also write your own custom bindings. The most common scenario is using an existing binding almost as is, and merely configuring two or three of its aspects. Application developers will hardly ever need to write a custom binding, but framework developers may need to.

Endpoints

Every service is associated with an address that defines where the service is, a binding that defines how to communicate with the service, and a contract that defines what the service does. This triumvirate governing the service is easy to remember as the *ABC* of the service. WCF formalizes this relationship in the form of an endpoint. The *endpoint* is the fusion of the address, contract, and binding (see Figure 1-5).

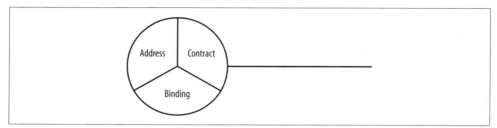

Figure 1-5. The endpoint

Every endpoint must have all three elements, and the host exposes the endpoint. Logically, the endpoint is the service's interface, and is analogous to a CLR or COM interface. Note in Figure 1-5 the use of the traditional "lollipop" to denote an endpoint.

 Conceptually, even in C# or VB, an interface is an endpoint: the address is the memory address of the type's virtual table, the binding is CLR JIT compiling, and the contract is the interface itself. Because in classic .NET programming you never deal with addresses or bindings, you take them for granted. In WCF the address and the binding are not ordained, and need to be configured.

Every service must expose at least one business endpoint and each endpoint has exactly one contract. All endpoints on a service have unique addresses, and a single service can expose multiple endpoints. These endpoints can use the same or different bindings and can expose the same or different contracts. There is absolutely no relationship between the various endpoints a service provides.

It is important to point out that nothing in the service code pertains to its endpoints and they are always external to the service code. You can configure endpoints either administratively using a config file or programmatically.

Administrative Endpoint Configuration

Configuring an endpoint administratively requires placing the endpoints in the hosting process' config file. For example, given this service definition:

```
namespace MyNamespace
{
```

```
        [ServiceContract]
        interface IMyContract
        {...}
        class MyService : IMyContract
        {...}
    }
```

Example 1-6 shows the required entries in the config file. Under each service type you list its endpoints.

Example 1-6. Administrative endpoint configuration

```
<system.serviceModel>
   <services>
      <service name = "MyNamespace.MyService">
         <endpoint
            address  = "http://localhost:8000/MyService/"
            binding  = "wsHttpBinding"
            contract = "MyNamespace.IMyContract"
         />
      </service>
   </services>
</system.serviceModel>
```

When you specify the service and the contract type, you need to use fully qualified type names. I will omit the namespace in the examples throughout the remainder of this book, but you should use a namespace when applicable. Note that if the endpoint provides a base address, then that address schema must be consistent with the binding, such as HTTP with WSHttpBinding. A mismatch causes an exception at the service load time.

Example 1-7 shows a config file defining a single service that exposes multiple endpoints. You can configure multiple endpoints with the same base address as long as the URI is different.

Example 1-7. Multiple endpoints on the same service

```
<service name = "MyService">
   <endpoint
      address  = "http://localhost:8000/MyService/"
      binding  = "wsHttpBinding"
      contract = "IMyContract"
   />
   <endpoint
      address  = "net.tcp://localhost:8001/MyService/"
      binding  = "netTcpBinding"
      contract = "IMyContract"
   />
   <endpoint
      address  = "net.tcp://localhost:8002/MyService/"
      binding  = "netTcpBinding"
      contract = "IMyOtherContract"
```

Example 1-7. Multiple endpoints on the same service (continued)

```
    />
</service>
```

Administrative configuration is the option of choice in the majority of cases because it provides the flexibility to change the service address, binding, and even exposed contracts without rebuilding and redeploying the service.

Using base addresses

In Example 1-7, each endpoint provided its own base address. When you provide an explicit base address, it overrides any base address the host may have provided.

You can also have multiple endpoints use the same base address, as long as the endpoint addresses differ in their URIs:

```
<service name = "MyService">
   <endpoint
       address  = "net.tcp://localhost:8001/MyService/"
       binding  = "netTcpBinding"
       contract = "IMyContract"
   />
   <endpoint
       address  = "net.tcp://localhost:8001/MyOtherService/"
       binding  = "netTcpBinding"
       contract = "IMyContract"
   />
</service>
```

Alternatively, if the host provides a base address with a matching transport schema, you can leave the address out, in which case the endpoint address will be the same as the base address of the matching transport:

```
<endpoint
   binding  = "wsHttpBinding"
   contract = "IMyContract"
/>
```

If the host does not provide a matching base address, loading the service host will fail with an exception.

When you configure the endpoint address you can add just the relative URI under the base address:

```
<endpoint
   address  = "SubAddress"
   binding  = "wsHttpBinding"
   contract = "IMyContract"
/>
```

The endpoint address in this case will be the matching base address plus the URI, and, again, the host must provide a matching base address.

Binding configuration

You can use the config file to customize the binding used by the endpoint. To that end, add the `bindingConfiguration` tag to the endpoint section, and name a customized section in the bindings section of the config file. Example 1-8 demonstrates using this technique to enable transaction propagation. What the `transactionFlow` tag does will be explained in Chapter 7.

Example 1-8. Service-side binding configuration

```
<system.serviceModel>
    <services>
        <service name = "MyService">
            <endpoint
                address  = "net.tcp://localhost:8000/MyService/"
                bindingConfiguration = "TransactionalTCP"
                binding  = "netTcpBinding"
                contract = "IMyContract"
            />
            <endpoint
                address  = "net.tcp://localhost:8001/MyService/"
                bindingConfiguration = "TransactionalTCP"
                binding  = "netTcpBinding"
                contract = "IMyOtherContract"
            />
        </service>
    </services>
    <bindings>
        <netTcpBinding>
            <binding name = "TransactionalTCP"
                transactionFlow = "true"
            />
        </netTcpBinding>
    </bindings>
</system.serviceModel>
```

As shown in Example 1-8, you can reuse the named binding configuration in multiple endpoints simply by referring to it.

Programmatic Endpoint Configuration

Programmatic endpoint configuration is equivalent to administrative configuration. Instead of resorting to a config file, you rely on programmatic calls to add endpoints to the ServiceHost instance. Again, these calls are always outside the scope of the service code. ServiceHost provides overloaded versions of the AddServiceEndpoint( ) method:

```
public class ServiceHost : ServiceHostBase
{
    public ServiceEndpoint AddServiceEndpoint(Type implementedContract,
                                              Binding binding,
```

```
                                            string address);
        //Additional members
    }
```

You can provide AddServiceEndpoint( ) methods with either relative or absolute addresses, just as with a config file. Example 1-9 demonstrates programmatic configuration of the same endpoints as in Example 1-7.

Example 1-9. Service-side programmatic endpoint configuration

```
ServiceHost host = new ServiceHost(typeof(MyService));

Binding wsBinding  = new WSHttpBinding( );
Binding tcpBinding = new NetTcpBinding( );

host.AddServiceEndpoint(typeof(IMyContract),wsBinding,
                        "http://localhost:8000/MyService");
host.AddServiceEndpoint(typeof(IMyContract),tcpBinding,
                        "net.tcp://localhost:8001/MyService");
host.AddServiceEndpoint(typeof(IMyOtherContract),tcpBinding,
                        "net.tcp://localhost:8002/MyService");

host.Open( );
```

When you add an endpoint programmatically, the address is given as a string, the contract as a Type, and the binding as one of the subclasses of the abstract class Binding, such as:

```
    public class NetTcpBinding : Binding,...
    {...}
```

To rely on the host base address, provide an empty string if you want to use the base address, or just the URI to use the base address plus the URI:

```
    Uri tcpBaseAddress = new Uri("net.tcp://localhost:8000/");

    ServiceHost host = new ServiceHost(typeof(MyService),tcpBaseAddress);

    Binding tcpBinding = new NetTcpBinding( );

    //Use base address as address
    host.AddServiceEndpoint(typeof(IMyContract),tcpBinding,"");
    //Add relative address
    host.AddServiceEndpoint(typeof(IMyContract),tcpBinding,"MyService");
    //Ignore base address
    host.AddServiceEndpoint(typeof(IMyContract),tcpBinding,
                                    "net.tcp://localhost:8001/MyService");
    host.Open( );
```

As with administrative configuration using a config file, the host must provide a matching base address; otherwise, an exception occurs. In fact, there is no difference between programmatic and administrative configuration. When you use a config file, all WCF does is parse the file and execute the appropriate programmatic calls in its place.

Binding configuration

You can programmatically set the properties of the binding used. For example, here is the code required to enable transaction propagation similar to Example 1-8:

```
ServiceHost host = new ServiceHost(typeof(MyService));

NetTcpBinding tcpBinding = new NetTcpBinding();

tcpBinding.TransactionFlow = true;

host.AddServiceEndpoint(typeof(IMyContract),tcpBinding,
                        "net.tcp://localhost:8000/MyService");
host.Open();
```

Note that when you're dealing with specific binding properties, you typically interact with a concrete binding subclass such as NetTcpBinding, and not its abstract base class Binding as in Example 1-9.

Metadata Exchange

A service has two options for publishing its metadata. You can provide the metadata over the HTTP-GET protocol, or you can use a dedicated endpoint, discussed later. WCF can provide the metadata over HTTP-GET automatically for your service; all you need is to enable it by adding an explicit service behavior. Behaviors are described in subsequent chapters. For now, all you need to know is that a behavior is a local aspect of the service, such as whether or not it wants to exchange its metadata over HTTP-GET. You can add this behavior administratively or programmatically. Example 1-10 shows a host application config file, where both hosted services reference a custom behavior section that enables the metadata exchange over HTTP-GET. The address the clients need to use for the HTTP-GET is the registered HTTP base address of the service. You can also specify in the behavior an external URL for this purpose.

Example 1-10. Enabling metadata exchange behavior using a config file

```
<system.serviceModel>
   <services>
      <service name = "MyService" behaviorConfiguration = "MEXGET">
         <host>
            <baseAddresses>
               <add baseAddress = "http://localhost:8000/"/>
            </baseAddresses>
         </host>
         ...
      </service>
      <service name = "MyOtherService" behaviorConfiguration = "MEXGET">
         <host>
            <baseAddresses>
               <add baseAddress = "http://localhost:8001/"/>
```

```
            </baseAddresses>
        </host>
        ...
    </service>
  </services>
  <behaviors>
    <serviceBehaviors>
      <behavior name = "MEXGET">
        <serviceMetadata httpGetEnabled = "true"/>
      </behavior>
    </serviceBehaviors>
  </behaviors>
</system.serviceModel>
```

Once you have enabled the metadata exchange over HTTP-GET, you can navigate to the HTTP base address (if present) using a browser. If all is well, you will get a confirmation page, such as the one shown in Figure 1-6, letting you know that you have successfully hosted a service. The confirmation page is unrelated to IIS hosting, and you can use a browser to navigate to the service address even when self-hosting.

Enabling Metadata Exchange Programmatically

To programmatically enable the metadata exchange over HTTP-GET, you first need to add the behavior to the collection of behaviors the host maintains for the service type. The ServiceHostBase class offers the Description property of the type ServiceDescription:

```
public abstract class ServiceHostBase : ...
{
   public ServiceDescription Description
   {get;}
   //More members
}
```

The service description, as its name implies, is the description of the service with all its aspects and behaviors. ServiceDescription contains a property called Behaviors of the type KeyedByTypeCollection<I> with IServiceBehavior as the generic parameter:

```
public class KeyedByTypeCollection<I> : KeyedCollection<Type,I>
{
   public T Find<T>( );
   public T Remove<T>( );
   //More members
}
public class ServiceDescription
{
   public KeyedByTypeCollection<IServiceBehavior> Behaviors
   {get;}
}
```

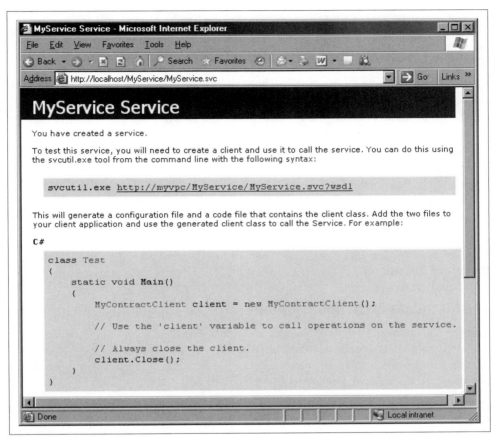

Figure 1-6. A service confirmation page

IServiceBehavior is the interface that all behavior classes and attributes implement. KeyedByTypeCollection<I> offers the generic method Find<T>( ), which returns the requested behavior if it is in the collection, and null otherwise. A given behavior type can only be found in the collection at most once. Example 1-11 shows how to enable the behavior programmatically.

Example 1-11. Enabling the metadata exchange behavior programmatically

```
ServiceHost host = new ServiceHost(typeof(MyService));

ServiceMetadataBehavior metadataBehavior;
metadataBehavior = host.Description.Behaviors.Find<ServiceMetadataBehavior>( );
if(metadataBehavior == null)
{
   metadataBehavior = new ServiceMetadataBehavior( );
   metadataBehavior.HttpGetEnabled = true;
   host.Description.Behaviors.Add(metadataBehavior);
```

Example 1-11. Enabling the metadata exchange behavior programmatically (continued)

```
}

host.Open( );
```

First the hosting code verifies that no MEX endpoint behavior was provided in the config file by calling the Find<T>( ) method of KeyedByTypeCollection<I> using ServiceMetadataBehavior as the type parameter. ServiceMetadataBehavior is defined in the System.ServiceModel.Description:

```
public class ServiceMetadataBehavior : IServiceBehavior
{
    public bool HttpGetEnabled
    {get;set;}
    //More members
}
```

If the returned behavior is null, the hosting code creates a new ServiceMetadataBehavior, sets HttpGetEnabled to true, and adds it to the behaviors in the service description.

The Metadata Exchange Endpoint

The service can also publish its metadata over a special endpoint called the *metadata exchange endpoint*, sometimes referred to as the *MEX endpoint*. Figure 1-7 shows a service with business and a metadata exchange endpoint. However, you typically do not show the metadata exchange endpoint in your design diagrams.

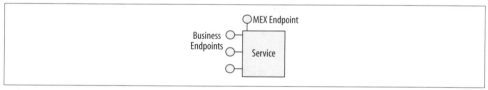

Figure 1-7. The metadata exchange endpoint

That endpoint supports an industry standard for exchanging metadata, represented in WCF by the IMetadataExchange interface:

```
[ServiceContract(...)]
public interface IMetadataExchange
{
    [OperationContract(...)]
    Message Get(Message request);
    //More members
}
```

The details of this interface are inconsequential. Like most of these industry standards, it is difficult to implement. Fortunately, WCF can have the service host automatically provide the implementation of IMetadataExchange and expose the metadata exchange endpoint. All you need to do is designate the address and the binding to use, as well as add the service metadata behavior. For the bindings, WCF provides dedicated binding transport elements for the HTTP, HTTPS, TCP, and IPC protocols. For the address, you can provide a full address or use any of the registered base addresses. There is no need to enable the HTTP-GET option, but there is no harm either. Example 1-12 shows a service that exposes three MEX endpoints, over HTTP, TCP, and IPC. For demonstration purposes, the TCP and IPC MEX endpoints use relative addresses and the HTTP one uses an absolute address.

Example 1-12. Adding MEX endpoints

```
<service name = "MyService" behaviorConfiguration = "MEX">
   <host>
      <baseAddresses>
         <add baseAddress = "net.tcp://localhost:8001/"/>
         <add baseAddress = "net.pipe://localhost/"/>
      </baseAddresses>
   </host>
   <endpoint
      address  = "MEX"
      binding  = "mexTcpBinding"
      contract = "IMetadataExchange"
   />
   <endpoint
      address  = "MEX"
      binding  = "mexNamedPipeBinding"
      contract = "IMetadataExchange"
   />
   <endpoint
      address  = "http://localhost:8000/MEX"
      binding  = "mexHttpBinding"
      contract = "IMetadataExchange"
   />
</service>
<behaviors>
   <serviceBehaviors>
      <behavior name = "MEX">
         <serviceMetadata/>
      </behavior>
   </serviceBehaviors>
</behaviors>
```

Adding MEX endpoints programmatically

Like any other endpoint, you can only add a metadata exchange endpoint programmatically before opening the host. WCF does not offer a dedicated binding type for the metadata exchange endpoint. Instead, you need to construct a custom binding that uses the matching transport binding element, and then provide that binding element as a construction parameter to an instance of a custom binding. Finally, call the AddServiceEndpoint( ) method of the host providing it with the address, the custom binding, and the IMetadataExchange contract type. Example 1-13 shows the code required to add a MEX endpoint over TCP. Note that before adding the endpoint you must verify the presence of the metadata behavior.

Example 1-13. Adding TCP MEX endpoint programmatically

```
BindingElement bindingElement = new TcpTransportBindingElement( );
CustomBinding binding = new CustomBinding(bindingElement);

Uri tcpBaseAddress = new Uri("net.tcp://localhost:9000/");
ServiceHost host = new ServiceHost(typeof(MyService),tcpBaseAddress);

ServiceMetadataBehavior metadataBehavior;
metadataBehavior = host.Description.Behaviors.Find<ServiceMetadataBehavior>( );
if(metadataBehavior == null)
{
   metadataBehavior = new ServiceMetadataBehavior( );
   host.Description.Behaviors.Add(metadataBehavior);
}
host.AddServiceEndpoint(typeof(IMetadataExchange),binding,"MEX");
host.Open( );
```

Streamlining with ServiceHost<T>

You can extend ServiceHost<T> to automate the code in Examples 1-11 and 1-13. ServiceHost<T> offers the EnableMetadataExchange Boolean property that you can call to both add the HTTP-GET metadata behavior and the MEX endpoints:

```
public class ServiceHost<T> : ServiceHost
{
   public bool EnableMetadataExchange
   {get;set;}
   public bool HasMexEndpoint
   {get;}
   public void AddAllMexEndPoints( );
   //More members
}
```

When set to true, EnableMetadataExchange adds the metadata exchange behavior, and if no MEX endpoint is available, EnableMetadataExchange adds a MEX endpoint for each registered base address scheme. Using ServiceHost<T>, Examples 1-11 and 1-13 are reduced to:

```
ServiceHost<MyService> host = new ServiceHost<MyService>( );
host.EnableMetadataExchange = true;
host.Open( );
```

ServiceHost<T> also offers the HasMexEndpoint Boolean property, which returns true if the service has any MEX endpoint (regardless of transport protocol), and the AddAllMexEndPoints( ) method, which adds a MEX endpoint for each registered base address of the scheme type of HTTP, TCP, or IPC. Example 1-14 shows the implementation of these methods.

Example 1-14. Implementing EnableMetadataExchange and its supporting methods

```
public class ServiceHost<T> : ServiceHost
{
   public bool EnableMetadataExchange
   {
      set
      {
         if(State == CommunicationState.Opened)
         {
            throw new InvalidOperationException("Host is already opened");
         }
         ServiceMetadataBehavior metadataBehavior;
         metadataBehavior = Description.Behaviors.Find<ServiceMetadataBehavior>();
         if(metadataBehavior == null)
         {
            metadataBehavior = new ServiceMetadataBehavior();
            metadataBehavior.HttpGetEnabled = value;
            Description.Behaviors.Add(metadataBehavior);
         }
         if(value == true)
         {
            if(HasMexEndpoint == false)
            {
               AddAllMexEndPoints();
            }
         }
      }
      get
      {
         ServiceMetadataBehavior metadataBehavior;
         metadataBehavior = Description.Behaviors.Find<ServiceMetadataBehavior>();
         if(metadataBehavior == null)
         {
            return false;
         }
         return metadataBehavior.HttpGetEnabled;
      }
   }
   public bool HasMexEndpoint
   {
      get
      {
         Predicate<ServiceEndpoint> mexEndPoint= delegate(ServiceEndpoint endpoint)
                                                 {
               return endpoint.Contract.ContractType == typeof(IMetadataExchange);
                                                 };
         return Collection.Exists(Description.Endpoints,mexEndPoint);
      }
   }
```

```
public void AddAllMexEndPoints( )
{
   Debug.Assert(HasMexEndpoint == false);

   foreach(Uri baseAddress in BaseAddresses)
   {
      BindingElement bindingElement = null;
      switch(baseAddress.Scheme)
      {
         case "net.tcp":
         {
            bindingElement = new TcpTransportBindingElement( );
            break;
         }
         case "net.pipe":
         {...}
         case "http":
         {...}
         case "https":
         {...}
      }
      if(bindingElement != null)
      {
         Binding binding = new CustomBinding(bindingElement);
         AddServiceEndpoint(typeof(IMetadataExchange),binding,"MEX");
      }
   }
}
}
```

EnableMetadataExchange verifies that the host has not been opened yet using the
State property of the CommunicationObject base class. EnableMetadataExchange does
not override the configured value from the config file and will only set the value if no
metadata behavior was found in the config file. When reading the value, the property checks if a value is configured. If no metadata behavior is configured at all,
EnableMetadataExchange returns false, and if a behavior is configured, it simply
returns its HttpGetEnabled value. The HasMexEndpoint property uses an anonymous
method* to initialize a predicate that checks if a given endpoint's contract is indeed
IMetadataExchange. The property then uses my static Collection class and calls the
Exists( ) method, providing the collection of endpoints available with the service
host. Exists( ) invokes the predicate on each item in the collection, and returns true
if any one of the items in the collection satisfies the predicate (that is, if the invocation of the anonymous method returned true), and false otherwise. The
AddAllMexEndPoints( ) method iterates over the BaseAddresses collection. For each

---

* If you are unfamiliar with anonymous methods, see my *MSDN Magazine* article "Create Elegant Code with
  Anonymous Methods, Iterators, and Partial Classes," May 2004.

base address found, it creates a matching MEX transport-binding element, creates a custom binding, and uses that, as in Example 1-13 to add the endpoint.

The Metadata Explorer

The metadata exchange endpoint provides metadata that describes not just contracts and operations, but also information about data contracts, security, transactions, reliability, and faults. To visualize the metadata of a running service I developed the Metadata Explorer tool, available along with the rest of the source code of this book. Figure 1-8 shows the Metadata Explorer reflecting the endpoints of Example 1-7. To use the Metadata Explorer, simply provide it with the HTTP-GET address or the metadata exchange endpoint of the running service to reflect the returned metadata.

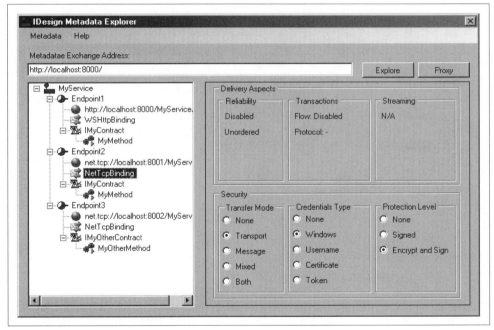

Figure 1-8. The Metadata Explorer

Client-Side Programming

To invoke operations on the service, the client first needs to import the service contract to the client's native representation. If the client uses WCF, the common way of invoking operations is to use a proxy. The proxy is a CLR class that exposes a single CLR interface representing the service contract. Note that if the service supports several contracts (over at least as many endpoints), the client needs a proxy per contract type. The proxy provides the same operations as service's contract, but also has additional methods for managing the proxy life cycle and the connection to the service. The proxy completely encapsulates every aspect of the service: its location, its implementation technology and runtime platform, and the communication transport.

Generating the Proxy

You can use Visual Studio 2005 to import the service metadata and generate a proxy. If the service is self-hosted, first launch the service and then select Add Service Reference... from the client project's context menu. If the service is hosted in IIS or the WAS, there is no need to pre-launch the service. Interestingly enough, if the service is self-hosted in another project in the same solution as the client project, you can launch the host in Visual Studio 2005 and still add the reference, because unlike most project settings, this option is not disabled during a debug session (see Figure 1-9).

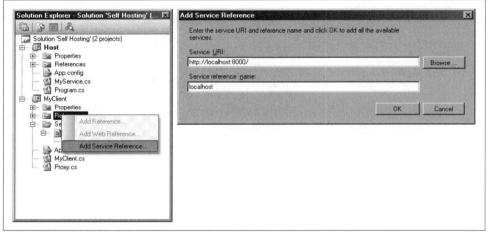

Figure 1-9. Generate a proxy using Visual Studio 2005

This brings up the Add Service Reference dialog box, where you need to supply the base address of the service (or a base address and a MEX URI) and the namespace to contain the proxy.

Instead of Visual Studio 2005, you can use the *SvcUtil.exe* command-line utility. You need to provide SvcUtil with the HTTP-GET address or the metadata exchange endpoint address and, optionally, with a proxy filename. The default proxy filename is *output.cs* but you can also use the /out switch to indicate a different name.

For example, if you're hosting the service MyService in IIS or the WAS, and have enabled metadata public sharing over HTTP-GET, simply run this command line:

```
SvcUtil http://localhost/MyService/MyService.svc /out:Proxy.cs
```

When you are hosting in IIS and selecting a port other than port 80 (such as port 81), you must provide that port number as part of the base address:

```
SvcUtil http://localhost:81/MyService/MyService.svc /out:Proxy.cs
```

With self-hosting, assuming the self-hosted service enabled metadata publishing over HTTP-GET, registers these base addresses and exposes the matching metadata exchange endpoints with a relative address of MEX:

```
http://localhost:8002/
net.tcp://localhost:8003
net.pipe://localhost/MyPipe
```

After launching the host, you can use the following commands to generate the proxy:

```
SvcUtil http://localhost:8002/MEX      /out:Proxy.cs
SvcUtil http://localhost:8002/         /out:Proxy.cs
SvcUtil net.tcp://localhost:8003/MEX   /out:Proxy.cs
SvcUtil net.pipe://localhost/MyPipe/MEX /out:Proxy.cs
```

 The main advantage of using SvcUtil over Visual Studio 2005 is the numerous options it offers through switches for controlling the generated proxies, as you will see later in this book.

For this service definition:

```
[ServiceContract(Namespace = "MyNamespace")]
interface IMyContract
{
    [OperationContract]
    void MyMethod();
}
class MyService : IMyContract
{
    public void MyMethod()
    {...}
}
```

SvcUtil generates the proxy shown in Example 1-15. You can safely remove the settings of Action and ReplyAction in most cases, since the default of using the method name is good enough.

Example 1-15. Client proxy file

```
[ServiceContract(Namespace = "MyNamespace")]
public interface IMyContract
{
    [OperationContract(Action = "MyNamespace/IMyContract/MyMethod",
                       ReplyAction = "MyNamespace/IMyContract/MyMethodResponse")]
    void MyMethod();
}

public partial class MyContractClient : ClientBase<IMyContract>,IMyContract
{
```

Example 1-15. Client proxy file (continued)

```
   public MyContractClient( )
   {}
   public MyContractClient(string endpointName) : base(endpointName)
   {}
   public MyContractClient(Binding binding,EndpointAddress remoteAddress) :
                                           base(binding,remoteAddress)
   {}
   /* Additional constructors */

   public void MyMethod( )
   {
      Channel.MyMethod( );
   }
}
```

The most glaring aspect of the proxy class is that it has no reference to the service-implementing class, only to the contract exposed by the service. You can use the proxy in conjunction with a client-side config file that provides the address and the binding, or you can use it without a config file. Note that each proxy instance points at exactly one endpoint. The endpoint to interact with is provided to the proxy at construction time. As I mentioned previously, if the service-side contract does not provide a namespace, it will implicitly use the *http://tempuri.org* namespace.

Administrative Client Configuration

The client needs to know where the service is located and use the same binding as the service, and, of course, import the service contract definition. In essence, this is exactly the same information captured in the service's endpoint. To reflect that, the client config file contains information about the target endpoints and even uses the same endpoint configuration schema as the host.

Example 1-16 shows the client configuration file required to interact with a service whose host is configured according to Example 1-6.

Example 1-16. Client config file

```
<system.serviceModel>
   <client>
      <endpoint name = "MyEndpoint"
         address  = "http://localhost:8000/MyService/"
         binding  = "wsHttpBinding"
         contract = "IMyContract"
      />
   </client>
</system.serviceModel>
```

The client config file may list as many endpoints as the services it deals with support, and the client may use any one of them. Example 1-17 shows the client config

---

file matching the host config file of Example 1-7. Note that each endpoint in the client config file has a unique name.

Example 1-17. Client config file with multiple target endpoints

```
<system.serviceModel>
   <client>
      <endpoint name = "FirstEndpoint"
         address  = "http://localhost:8000/MyService/"
         binding  = "wsHttpBinding"
         contract = "IMyContract"
      />
      <endpoint name = "SecondEndpoint"
         address  = "net.tcp://localhost:8001/MyService/"
         binding  = "netTcpBinding"
         contract = "IMyContract"
      />
      <endpoint name = "ThirdEndpoint"
         address  = "net.tcp://localhost:8002/MyService/"
         binding  = "netTcpBinding"
         contract = "IMyOtherContract"
      />
   </client>
</system.serviceModel>
```

Binding configuration

You can customize the client-side standard bindings to match the service binding in a manner identical to the service configuration, as shown in Example 1-18.

Example 1-18. Client-side binding configuration

```
<system.serviceModel>
   <client>
      <endpoint name = "MyEndpoint"
         address  = "net.tcp://localhost:8000/MyService/"
         bindingConfiguration = "TransactionalTCP"
         binding  = "netTcpBinding"
         contract = "IMyContract"
      />
   </client>
   <bindings>
      <netTcpBinding>
         <binding name = "TransactionalTCP"
            transactionFlow = "true"
         />
      </netTcpBinding>
   </bindings>
</system.serviceModel>
```

Generating the client config file

By default, SvcUtil also auto-generates a client-side config file called *output.config*. You can specify a config filename using the /config switch:

```
SvcUtil http://localhost:8002/MyService/  /out:Proxy.cs /config:App.Config
```

And you can suppress generating the config file using the /noconfig switch:

```
SvcUtil http://localhost:8002/MyService/  /out:Proxy.cs /noconfig
```

I recommend never letting SvcUtil generate the config file. The reason is that it generates fully articulated binding sections that often just state the default values, which tends to clutter the config file.

In-proc configuration

With in-proc hosting, the client config file is also the service host config file, and the same file contains both service and client entries, as shown in Example 1-19.

Example 1-19. In-proc hosting config file

```
<system.serviceModel>
   <services>
      <service name = "MyService">
         <endpoint
             address  = "net.pipe://localhost/MyPipe"
             binding  = "netNamedPipeBinding"
             contract = "IMyContract"
         />
      </service>
   </services>
   <client>
      <endpoint name = "MyEndpoint"
          address  = "net.pipe://localhost/MyPipe"
          binding  = "netNamedPipeBinding"
          contract = "IMyContract"
      />
   </client>
</system.serviceModel>
```

Note the use of the named pipe binding for in-proc hosting.

The SvcConfigEditor

WCF provides a config file editor called *SvcConfigEditor.exe* that can edit both host and client configuration files (see Figure 1-10). You can also launch the editor from within Visual Studio by right-clicking on the configuration file (both the client and the host files) and selecting Edit WCF Configuration.

I have mixed feelings about SvcConfigEditor. On the one hand, it edits the config files nicely and it saves developers the need to know the configuration schema. On

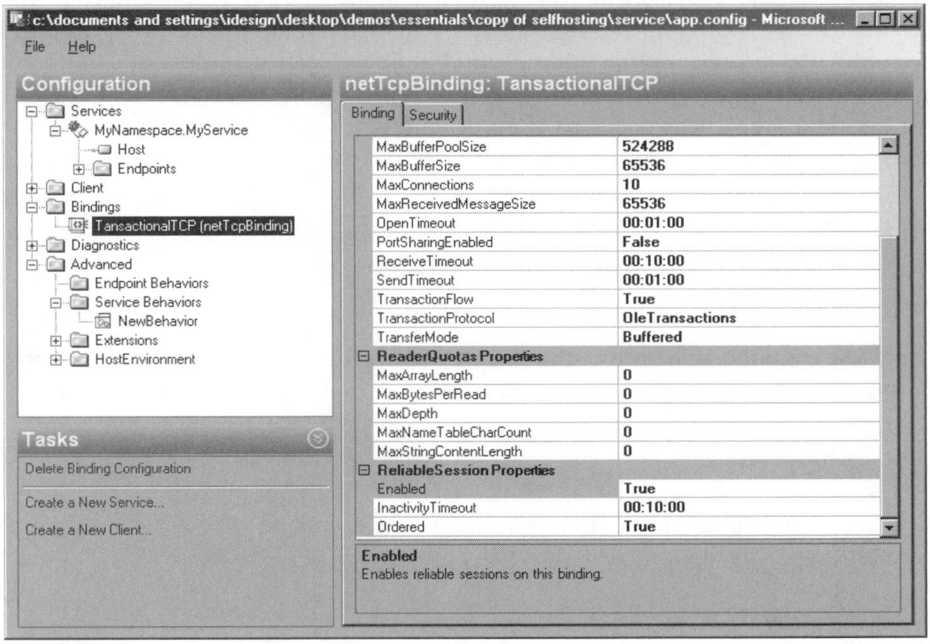

Figure 1-10. SvcConfigEditor is used to edit both host and client config files

the other hand, it does not save the need to thoroughly understand WCF configuration, and for the most part, the light editing done in a config file is faster by hand than editing using Visual Studio 2005.

Creating and Using the Proxy

The proxy class derives from the class ClientBase<T>, defined as:

```
public abstract class ClientBase<T> : ICommunicationObject,IDisposable
{
   protected ClientBase(string endpointName);
   protected ClientBase(Binding binding,EndpointAddress remoteAddress);
   public void Open( );
   public void Close( );
   protected T Channel
   {get;}
   //Additional members
}
```

ClientBase<T> accepts a single generic type parameter identifying the service contract that this proxy encapsulates. The Channel property of ClientBase<T> is of the type of that type parameter. The generated subclass of ClientBase<T> simply delegates to Channel the method call (see Example 1-15).

To use the proxy, the client first needs to instantiate a proxy object and to provide the constructor with endpoint information: either the endpoint section name from the config file, or the endpoint address and binding objects if you're not using a config file. The client can then use the proxy methods to call the service, and when the client is done, the client needs to close the proxy instance. For example, given the same definitions as in Examples 1-15 and 1-16, the client constructs the proxy, identifying the endpoint to use from the config file; invokes the method; and closes the proxy:

```
MyContractClient proxy = new MyContractClient("MyEndpoint");
proxy.MyMethod();
proxy.Close();
```

If only one endpoint is defined in the client config file for the type of contract the proxy is using, then the client can omit the endpoint name from the proxy's constructor:

```
MyContractClient proxy = new MyContractClient();
proxy.MyMethod();
proxy.Close();
```

However, if multiple endpoints are available for the same contract type then the proxy throws an exception.

Closing the proxy

It is a recommended best practice to always close the proxy when the client is done using it. You will see in Chapter 4 why the client needs to close the proxy in certain cases, because closing the proxy terminates the session with the service and closes the connection.

Alternatively, you can use the Dispose() method of the proxy to close it. The advantage of the Dispose() method is that you can use the using statement to call it even in the face of exceptions:

```
using(MyContractClient proxy = new MyContractClient())
{
    proxy.MyMethod();
}
```

If the client is declaring the contract directly instead of the concrete proxy class, the client can either query for the presence of IDisposable:

```
IMyContract proxy = new MyContractClient());
proxy.MyMethod();
IDisposable disposable = proxy as IDisposable;
if(disposable != null)
{
    disposable.Dispose();
}
```

or collapse the query inside the using statement:

```
IMyContract proxy = new MyContractClient();
```

```
using(proxy as IDisposable)
{
   proxy.MyMethod( );
}
```

Call timeout

Each call made by a WCF client must complete within a configurable timeout. If for whatever reason the call duration exceeds the timeout, the call is aborted and the client gets a TimeoutException. The exact value of the timeout is a property of the binding, where the default timeout is one minute. To provide a different timeout, set the SendTimeout property of the abstract Binding base class:

```
public abstract class Binding : ...
{
   public TimeSpan SendTimeout
   {get;set;}
   //More members
}
```

For example, when using the WSHttpBinding:

```
<client>
   <endpoint
      ...
      binding = "wsHttpBinding"
      bindingConfiguration = "LongTimeout"
      ...
   />
</client>
<bindings>
   <wsHttpBinding>
      <binding name = "LongTimeout" sendTimeout = "00:05:00"/>
   </wsHttpBinding>
</bindings>
```

Programmatic Client Configuration

Instead of relying on a config file, the client can programmatically construct address and binding objects matching the service endpoint and provide them to the proxy constructor. There is no need to provide the contract, since that was provided in the form of the generic type parameter of the proxy. To represent the address, the client needs to instantiate an EndpointAddress class, defined as:

```
public class EndpointAddress
{
   public EndpointAddress(string uri);
   //More members
}
```

Example 1-20 demonstrates this technique, showing the code equivalent to Example 1-16 targeting the service in Example 1-9.

Example 1-20. Programmatic client configuration

```
Binding wsBinding = new WSHttpBinding( );
EndpointAddress endpointAddress = new
                    EndpointAddress("http://localhost:8000/MyService/");

MyContractClient proxy = new MyContractClient(wsBinding,endpointAddress);

proxy.MyMethod( );
proxy.Close( );
```

Similar to using a binding section in a config file, the client can programmatically configure the binding properties:

```
WSHttpBinding wsBinding = new WSHttpBinding( );
wsBinding.SendTimeout = TimeSpan.FromMinutes(5);
wsBinding.TransactionFlow = true;

EndpointAddress endpointAddress = new
                    EndpointAddress("http://localhost:8000/MyService/");

MyContractClient proxy = new MyContractClient(wsBinding,endpointAddress);
proxy.MyMethod( );
proxy.Close( );
```

Again, note the use of the concrete subclass of `Binding` in order to access binding-specific properties such as the transaction flow.

Programmatic Versus Administrative Configuration

The two techniques shown so far for configuring both the client and service complement each other. Administrative configuration gives you the option to change major aspects of the service and the client post-deployment, without even the need to rebuild or redeploy. The major downside of administrative configuration is that it is not type-safe, and configuration errors will only be discovered at runtime.

Programmatic configuration is useful when the configuration decision is either completely dynamic—when it is taken at runtime based on the current input or conditions—or when the decision is static and never changes, in which case you might as well hardcode it. For example, if you are interested in hosting in-proc calls only, you might as well hardcode the use of the `NetNamedPipeBinding` and its configuration. However, by and large, most clients and services do resort to using a config file.

WCF Architecture

So far in this chapter, I've covered all that is required to set up and consume simple WCF services. However, as described in the rest of the book, WCF offers immensely valuable support for reliability, transactions, concurrency management, security, and instance activation, all of which rely on the WCF interception-based architecture.

Having the client interact with a proxy means that WCF is always present between the service and the client, intercepting the call and performing pre- and post-call processing. The interception starts when the proxy serializes the call stack frame to a message and sends the message down a chain of channels. The *channel* is merely an interceptor, whose purpose is to perform a specific task. Each client-side channel does pre-call processing of the message. The exact structure and composition of the chain depends mostly on the binding. For example, one of the channels may be responsible for encoding the message (binary, text, or MTOM), another for passing security call context, another for propagating the client transaction, another for managing the reliable session, another for encrypting the message body (if so configured), and so on. The last channel on the client side is the transport channel, which sends the message over the configured transport to the host.

On the host side, the message goes through a chain of channels as well, which perform host-side pre-call processing of the message. The first channel on the host side is the transport channel, which receives the message from the transport. Subsequent channels perform various tasks, such as decryption of the message body, decoding of the message, joining the propagated transaction, setting the security principal, managing the session, and activating the service instance. The last channel on the host side passes the message to the dispatcher. The dispatcher converts the message to a stack frame and calls the service instance. This sequence is depicted in Figure 1-11.

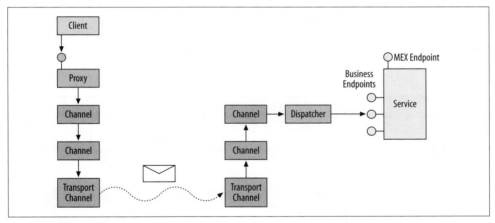

Figure 1-11. The WCF architecture

The service has no way of knowing it was not called by a local client. In fact, it *was* called by a local client—the dispatcher. The interception both on the client and the service side ensures that the client and the service get the runtime environment they require to operate properly. The service instance executes the call and returns control to the dispatcher, which then converts the returned values and error information (if any) to a return message. The process is now reversed: the dispatcher passes the message through the host-side channels to perform post-call processing, such as managing the transaction, deactivating the instance, encoding the reply, encrypting it, and so on. The returned message goes to the transport channel, which sends it to the client-side channels for client-side post-call processing, which consists of tasks such as decryption, decoding, committing or aborting the transaction, and so on. The last channel passes the message to the proxy. The proxy converts the returned message to a stack frame and returns control to the client.

Most noteworthy is that almost all the points in the architecture provide hooks for extensibility—you can provide custom channels for proprietary interaction, custom behaviors for instance management, custom security behavior, and so on. In fact, the standard facilities that WCF offers are all implemented using the same extensibility model. You will see many examples and uses for extensibility throughout this book.

Host Architecture

It is also interesting to explore how the transition is made from a technology-neutral, service-oriented interaction to CLR interfaces and classes. The bridging is done via the host. Each .NET host process can have many app domains. Each app domain can have zero or more service host instances. However, each service host instance is dedicated to a particular service type. When you create a host instance, you are in effect registering that service host instance with all the endpoints for that type on the host machine that correspond to its base addresses. Each service host instance has zero or more contexts. The *context* is the innermost execution scope of the service instance. A context is associated with at most one service instance, meaning it could also be empty, without any service instance. This architecture is shown in Figure 1-12.

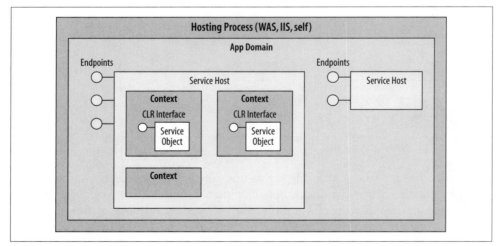

Figure 1-12. The WCF host architecture

The WCF context is conceptually similar to the Enterprise Services context or the .NET context-bound object context.

It is the combined work of the service host and the context that exposes a native CLR type as a service. After the message is passed through the channels, the host maps that message to a new or existing context (and the object instance inside) and lets it process the call.

Working with Channels

You can use channels directly to invoke operations on the service without ever resorting to using a proxy class. The ChannelFactory<T> class (and its supporting types), shown in Example 1-21, enables you to create a proxy on the fly.

Example 1-21. TheChannelFactory<T> class

```
public class ContractDescription
{
   public Type ContractType
   {get;set;}
   //More members
}

public class ServiceEndpoint
{
   public ServiceEndpoint(ContractDescription contract,Binding binding,
                                                 EndpointAddress address);
   public EndpointAddress Address
   {get;set;}
   public Binding Binding
   {get;set;}
   public ContractDescription Contract
   {get;}
   //More members
}

public abstract class ChannelFactory : ...
{
   public ServiceEndpoint Endpoint
   {get;}
   //More members
}
public class ChannelFactory<T> : ChannelFactory,...
{
   public ChannelFactory(ServiceEndpoint endpoint);
   public ChannelFactory(string configurationName);
   public ChannelFactory(Binding binding,EndpointAddress endpointAddress);
   public static T CreateChannel(Binding binding,EndpointAddress endpointAddress);
   public T CreateChannel();
```

Example 1-21. TheChannelFactory<T> class (continued)

```
   //More Members
}
```

You need to provide the constructor of ChannelFactory<T> with the endpoint—either the endpoint name from the client config file, or the binding and address objects, or a ServiceEndpoint object. Next, use the CreateChannel( ) method to obtain a reference to the proxy and use its methods. Finally, close the proxy by either casting it to IDisposable and calling the Dispose( ) method or to ICommunicationObject and calling the Close( ) method:

```
ChannelFactory<IMyContract> factory = new ChannelFactory<IMyContract>( );

IMyContract proxy1 = factory.CreateChannel( );
using(proxy1 as IDisposable)
{
    proxy1.MyMethod( );
}

IMyContract proxy2 = factory.CreateChannel( );
proxy2.MyMethod( );
ICommunicationObject channel = proxy2 as ICommunicationObject;
Debug.Assert(channel != null);
channel.Close( );
```

You can also use the shorthand static CreateChannel( ) method to create a proxy given a binding and an address, without directly constructing an instance of ChannelFactory<T>:

```
Binding binding = new NetTcpBinding( );
EndpointAddress address = new EndpointAddress("net.tcp://localhost:8000");

IMyContract proxy = ChannelFactory<IMyContract>.CreateChannel(binding,address);
using(proxy as IDisposable)
{
    proxy1.MyMethod( );
}
```

The InProcFactory Class

To demonstrate the power of ChannelFactory<T>, consider my static helper class InProcFactory, defined as:

```
public static class InProcFactory
{
    public static I CreateInstance<S,I>( ) where I : class
                                           where S : I;
    public static void CloseProxy<I>(I instance) where I : class;
    //More members
}
```

InProcFactory is designed to streamline and automate in-proc hosting. The CreateInstance( ) method takes two generic type parameters: the type of the service

S and the type of the supported contract I. CreateInstance( ) constrains S to derive from I. Using InProcFactory is straightforward:

```
IMyContract proxy = InProcFactory.CreateInstance<MyService,IMyContract>( );

proxy.MyMethod( );

InProcFactory.CloseProxy(proxy);
```

It literally takes a service class and hoists it up as a WCF service. It is as close as you can get in WCF to the old Win32 call of LoadLibrary( ).

Implementing InProcFactory<T>

All in-proc calls should use named pipes, and should also flow all transactions. You can use programmatic configuration to automate the configurations of both the client and the service, and use ChannelFactory<T> to avoid the need for a proxy. Example 1-22 shows the implementation of InProcFactory with some of the code removed for brevity.

Example 1-22. The InProcFactory class

```
public static class InProcFactory
{
   struct HostRecord
   {
      public HostRecord(ServiceHost host,string address)
      {
         Host = host;
         Address = address;
      }
      public readonly ServiceHost Host;
      public readonly string Address;
   }
   static readonly Uri BaseAddress = new Uri("net.pipe://localhost/");
   static readonly Binding NamedPipeBinding;
   static Dictionary<Type,HostRecord> m_Hosts = new Dictionary<Type,HostRecord>( );

   static InProcFactory( )
   {
      NetNamedPipeBinding binding = new NetNamedPipeBinding( );
      binding.TransactionFlow = true;
      NamedPipeBinding = binding;
      AppDomain.CurrentDomain.ProcessExit += delegate
                                {
                          foreach(KeyValuePair<Type,HostRecord> pair in m_Hosts)
                                {
                                   pair.Value.Host.Close( );
                                }
                                };
   }
   public static I CreateInstance<S,I>( ) where I : class
                                 where S : I
```

Example 1-22. The InProcFactory class (continued)

```
   {
      HostRecord hostRecord = GetHostRecord<S,I>();
      return ChannelFactory<I>.CreateChannel(NamedPipeBinding,
                                   new EndpointAddress(hostRecord.Address));
   }
   static HostRecord GetHostRecord<S,I>() where I : class
                                          where S : I
   {
      HostRecord hostRecord;
      if(m_Hosts.ContainsKey(typeof(S)))
      {
         hostRecord = m_Hosts[typeof(S)];
      }
      else
      {
         ServiceHost host = new ServiceHost(typeof(S), BaseAddress);
         string address = BaseAddress.ToString() + Guid.NewGuid().ToString();
         hostRecord = new HostRecord(host,address);
         m_Hosts.Add(typeof(S),hostRecord);
         host.AddServiceEndpoint(typeof(I),NamedPipeBinding,address);
         host.Open();
      }
      return hostRecord;
   }
   public static void CloseProxy<I>(I instance) where I : class
   {
      ICommunicationObject proxy = instance as ICommunicationObject;
      Debug.Assert(proxy != null);
      proxy.Close();
   }
}
```

The main challenge facing InProcFactory is that CreateInstance() can be called to instantiate services of every type. For every service type, there should be a single matching host (an instance of ServiceHost). Allocating a host instance for each call is not a good idea. The problem is what should CreateInstance() do when it is asked to instantiate a second object of the same type:

```
IMyContract proxy1 = InProcFactory.CreateInstance<MyService,IMyContract>();
IMyContract proxy2 = InProcFactory.CreateInstance<MyService,IMyContract>();
```

The solution is to internally manage a dictionary that maps service types to a particular host instance. When CreateInstance() is called to create an instance of a particular type, it looks in the dictionary, using a helper method called GetHostRecord(), which creates the host only if the dictionary does not already contain the service type. If it needs to create a host, GetHostRecord() programmatically adds to that host an endpoint, using a new GUID as a unique pipe name. CreateInstance() then grabs the address of the endpoint from the host record and uses ChannelFactory<T> to create the proxy. In its static constructor, which is called upon the first use of the class, InProcFactory subscribes to the process exit event, using an anonymous method to close all hosts when the process shuts down. Finally, to help the clients close the proxy, InProcFactory provides the CloseProxy( ) method, which queries the proxy to ICommunicationObject and closes it.

Reliability

WCF and other service-oriented technologies make a distinction between transport reliability and message reliability. *Transport reliability* (such as the one offered by TCP) offers point-to-point guaranteed delivery at the network packet level, as well as guarantees the order of the packets. Transport reliability is not resilient to dropping network connections and a variety of other communication problems.

Message reliability, as the name implies, deals with reliability at the message level independent of how many packets are required to deliver the message. Message reliability provides for end-to-end guaranteed delivery and order of messages, regardless of how many intermediaries are involved, and how many network hops are required to deliver the message from the client to the service. Message reliability is based on an industry standard for reliable message-based communication that maintains a session at the transport level. It offers retries in case of transport failures such as dropping a wireless connection; it automatically deals with congestion, message buffering, and flow control; and it can adjust the number of messages accordingly. Message reliability also deals with managing the connection itself via connection verification and cleanup when no longer needed.

Binding and Reliability

In WCF, reliability is controlled and configured in the binding. A particular binding can support or not support reliable messaging, and if supported, it can be enabled or disabled. Which binding supports which reliability value is driven by the target scenario for that particular binding. Table 1-2 summarizes the relationship between binding, reliability, and ordered delivery and their respective default values.

Table 1-2. Reliability and binding

Name	Supports reliability	Default reliability	Supports ordered	Default ordered
BasicHttpBinding	No	N/A	No	N/A
NetTcpBinding	Yes	Off	Yes	On
NetPeerTcpBinding	No	N/A	No	N/A
NetNamedPipeBinding	No	N/A (On)	Yes	N/A (On)
WSHttpBinding	Yes	Off	Yes	On
WSFederationHttpBinding	Yes	Off	Yes	On
WSDualHttpBinding	Yes	On	Yes	On

Table 1-2. Reliability and binding (continued)

Name	Supports reliability	Default reliability	Supports ordered	Default ordered
NetMsmqBinding	No	N/A	No	N/A
MsmqIntegrationBinding	No	N/A	No	N/A

Reliability is not supported by the `BasicHttpBinding`, `NetPeerTcpBinding`, and the two MSMQ bindings, `NetMsmqBinding` and `MsmqIntegrationBinding`. The reason is that the `BasicHttpBinding` is oriented toward the legacy ASMX web services world, which does not have reliability. `NetPeerTcpBinding` is designed for broadcast scenarios. The MSMQ bindings are for disconnected calls, where no transport session is possible anyway.

Reliability is always enabled on `WSDualHttpBinding` to keep the callback channel to the client alive even over HTTP.

Reliability is disabled by default but can be enabled on the `NetTcpBinding` and the various WS bindings. Finally, the `NetNamedPipeBinding` is considered inherently reliable because it always has exactly one hop from the client to the service.

Ordered Messages

Message reliability also provides ordered delivery assurance, allowing messages to be executed in the order they were sent, not in the order in which they were delivered. In addition, it guarantees that messages are delivered exactly once.

WCF lets you enable reliability but not ordered delivery, in which case messages are delivered in the order in which they were received. The default for all bindings that support reliability is that when reliability is enabled, ordered delivery is enabled as well.

Configuring Reliability

You can configure reliability (and ordered delivery) both programmatically and administratively. When you enable reliability, you must do so on both the client and the service host sides, otherwise the client will not be able communicate with the service. You can only configure reliability for the bindings that support it. Example 1-23 shows the service-side config file that uses a binding configuration section to enable reliability when using the TCP binding.

Example 1-23. Enabling reliability with the TCP binding

```
<system.serviceModel>
   <services>
      <service name = "MyService">
         <endpoint
            address  = "net.tcp://localhost:8000/MyService"
```

Example 1-23. Enabling reliability with the TCP binding (continued)

```
           binding  = "netTcpBinding"
           bindingConfiguration = "ReliableTCP"
           contract = "IMyContract"
        />
      </service>
   </services>
   <bindings>
      <netTcpBinding>
         <binding name = "ReliableTCP">
            <reliableSession enabled = "true"/>
         </binding>
      </netTcpBinding>
   </bindings>
</system.serviceModel>
```

When it comes to programmatic configuration, the TCP and the WS bindings offer slightly different properties for configuring reliability. For example, the `NetTcpBinding` binding accepts a Boolean construction parameter for enabling reliability:

```
public class NetTcpBinding : Binding,...
{
   public NetTcpBinding(...,bool reliableSessionEnabled);
   //More members
}
```

You can only enable reliability at construction time, so when you set reliability programmatically, you need to construct the binding as reliable:

```
Binding reliableTcpBinding = new NetTcpBinding(...,true);
```

`NetTcpBinding` also offers the read-only `ReliableSession` class, letting you retrieve the reliability status:

```
public class ReliableSession
{
   public TimeSpan InactivityTimeout
   {get;set;}
   public bool Ordered
   {get;set;}
   //More members
}
public class OptionalReliableSession : ReliableSession
{
   public bool Enabled
   {get;set;}
   //More members
}
public class NetTcpBinding : Binding,...
{
   public OptionalReliableSession ReliableSession
   {get;}
   //More members
}
```

Requiring Ordered Delivery

In theory, the service code and the contract definition should be independent of the binding used and of its properties. The service should not care about the binding, and nothing in service code pertains to the binding used. The service should be able to work with any aspect of the configured binding. In practice, the service implementation or the contract itself may depend on ordered delivery of the messages. To enable the contract or service developer to constrain the allowed bindings, WCF defines the DeliveryRequirementsAttribute:

```
[AttributeUsage(AttributeTargets.Class|AttributeTargets.Interface
                AllowMultiple = true)]
public sealed class DeliveryRequirementsAttribute : Attribute,...
{
   public Type TargetContract
   {get;set;}
   public bool RequireOrderedDelivery
   {get;set;}

   //More members
}
```

The DeliveryRequirements attribute can be applied at the service level, affecting all endpoints of the service, or only at the endpoints that expose a particular contract. When applied at the service level, it means that requiring ordered delivery is an implementation decision. The attribute can also be used at the contract level, affecting all services that support that contract. When applied at the contract level, it means that requiring ordered delivery is a design decision. Enforcing the constraint is done at the service load time. If an endpoint has a binding that does not support reliability, or supports reliability and has reliability disabled, or has reliability enabled yet ordered delivery is disabled, loading the service will fail with InvalidOperationException.

 The named pipe binding satisfies the ordered delivery constraint.

For example, to demand that all endpoints of the service, regardless of contracts, have ordered delivery enabled, apply the attribute directly on the service class:

```
[DeliveryRequirements(RequireOrderedDelivery = true)]
class MyService : IMyContract,IMyOtherContract
{...}
```

By setting the TargetContract property, you can demand that only endpoints of the service that support that contract be constrained to have reliable ordered delivery:

```
[DeliveryRequirements(TargetContract = typeof(IMyContract),
                      RequireOrderedDelivery = true)]
class MyService : IMyContract,IMyOtherContract
{...}
```

By applying the DeliveryRequirements attribute on the contract interface, you place the constraint on all services that support it:

```
[DeliveryRequirements(RequireOrderedDelivery = true)]
[ServiceContract]
interface IMyContract
{...}

class MyService : IMyContract
{...}

class MyOtherService : IMyContract
{...}
```

The default of the RequireOrderedDelivery is false, so merely applying the attribute has no effect. For example, these statements are equivalent:

```
[ServiceContract]
interface IMyContract
{...}

[DeliveryRequirements]
[ServiceContract]
interface IMyContract
{...}

[DeliveryRequirements(RequireOrderedDelivery = false)]
[ServiceContract]
interface IMyContract
{...}
```

CHAPTER 2

Service Contracts

The ServiceContract attribute presented in the previous chapter exposes an interface (or a class) as a service-oriented contract, allowing you to program in languages like C#, using constructs like interfaces, while exposing the constructs as WCF contracts and services. This chapter starts by discussing how to better bridge the gap between the two programming models by enabling operation overloading and contract inheritance. Next you will see a few simple yet powerful service contract design and factoring guidelines and techniques. The chapter ends by showing how to interact programmatically at run runtime with the metadata of the exposed contracts.

Operation Overloading

Programming languages such as C++ and C# support method overloading: defining two methods with the same name but with different parameters. For example, this is a valid C# interface definition:

```
interface ICalculator
{
    int Add(int arg1,int arg2);
    double Add(double arg1,double arg2);
}
```

However, operation overloading is invalid in the world of WSDL-based operations. Consequently, while the following contract definition compiles, it will throw an InvalidOperationException at the service host load time:

```
//Invalid contract definition:
[ServiceContract]
interface ICalculator
{
    [OperationContract]
    int Add(int arg1,int arg2);

    [OperationContract]
    double Add(double arg1,double arg2);
}
```

However, you can manually enable operation overloading. The trick is using the `Name` property of the `OperationContract` attribute to alias the operation:

```
[AttributeUsage(AttributeTargets.Method)]
public sealed class OperationContractAttribute : Attribute
{
   public string Name
   {get;set;}
   //More members
}
```

You need to alias the operation both on the service and on the client side. On the service side, provide a unique name for the overloaded operations, as shown in Example 2-1.

Example 2-1. Service-side operation overloading

```
[ServiceContract]
interface ICalculator
{
   [OperationContract(Name = "AddInt")]
   int Add(int arg1,int arg2);

   [OperationContract(Name = "AddDouble")]
   double Add(double arg1,double arg2);
}
```

When the client imports the contract and generates the proxy, the imported operations will have the aliased names:

```
[ServiceContract]
public interface ICalculator
{
   [OperationContract]
   int AddInt(int arg1,int arg2);

   [OperationContract]
   double AddDouble(double arg1,double arg2);
}
public partial class CalculatorClient : ClientBase<ICalculator>,ICalculator
{
   public int AddInt(int arg1,int arg2)
   {
      return Channel.AddInt(arg1,arg2);
   }
   public double AddDouble(double arg1,double arg2)
   {
      return Channel.AddDouble(arg1,arg2);
   }
   //Rest of the proxy
}
```

The client can use the generated proxy and contract as is, but you can also rework those to provide overloading on the client side. Rename the methods on the imported contract and the proxy to the overloaded name, and make sure the proxy class makes calls on the internal proxy using the overloaded methods, such as:

```
public int Add(int arg1,int arg2)
{
   return Channel.Add(arg1,arg2);
}
```

Finally, use the Name property on the imported contract on the client side to alias and overload the methods, matching the imported operation names, as shown in Example 2-2.

Example 2-2. Client-side operation overloading

```
[ServiceContract]
public interface ICalculator
{
   [OperationContract(Name = "AddInt")]
   int Add(int arg1,int arg2);

   [OperationContract(Name = "AddDouble")]
   double Add(double arg1,double arg2);
}

public partial class CalculatorClient : ClientBase<ICalculator>,ICalculator
{
   public int Add(int arg1,int arg2)
   {
      return Channel.Add(arg1,arg2);
   }
   public double Add(double arg,double arg2)
   {
      return Channel.Add(arg1,arg2);
   }
   //Rest of the proxy
}
```

Now the client can benefit from the readable and smooth programming model offered by overloaded operations:

```
CalculatorClient proxy = new CalculatorClient();

int result1 = proxy.Add(1,2);
double result2 = proxy.Add(1.0,2.0);

proxy.Close();
```

Contract Inheritance

Service contract interfaces can derive from each other, enabling you to define a hierarchy of contracts. However, the ServiceContract attribute is not inheritable:

```
[AttributeUsage(Inherited = false,...)]
public sealed class ServiceContractAttribute : Attribute
{...}
```

Consequently, every level in the interface hierarchy must explicitly have the ServiceContract attribute, as shown in Example 2-3.

Example 2-3. Service-side contract hierarchy

```
[ServiceContract]
interface ISimpleCalculator
{
   [OperationContract]
   int Add(int arg1,int arg2);
}
[ServiceContract]
interface IScientificCalculator : ISimpleCalculator
{
   [OperationContract]
   int Multiply(int arg1,int arg2);
}
```

When it comes to implementing a contract hierarchy, a single service class can implement the entire hierarchy, just as with classic C# programming:

```
class MyCalculator : IScientificCalculator
{
   public int Add(int arg1,int arg2)
   {
      return arg1 + arg2;
   }
   public int Multiply(int arg1,int arg2)
   {
      return arg1 * arg2;
   }
}
```

The host can expose a single endpoint for the bottom most interface in the hierarchy:

```
<service name = "MyCalculator">
   <endpoint
      address  = "http://localhost:8001/MyCalculator/"
      binding  = "basicHttpBinding"
      contract = "IScientificCalculator"
   />
</service>
```

Client-Side Contract Hierarchy

When the client imports the metadata of a service endpoint whose contract is part of an interface hierarchy, the resulting contract on the client side does not maintain the original hierarchy. Instead it will include a flattened hierarchy in the form of a single contract named after the endpoint's contract. The single contract will have a union of all the operations from all the interfaces leading down to it in the hierarchy, including itself. However, the imported interface definition will maintain, in the `Action` and `ResponseAction` properties of the `OperationContract` attribute, the name of the original contract that defined each operation:

```
[AttributeUsage(AttributeTargets.Method)]
public sealed class OperationContractAttribute : Attribute
{
   public string Action
   {get;set;}
   public string ReplyAction
   {get;set;}
   //More members
}
```

Finally, a single proxy class will implement all methods in the imported contract. Given the definitions of Example 2-3, Example 2-4 shows the imported contract and the generated proxy class.

Example 2-4. Client-side flattened hierarchy

```
[ServiceContract]
public interface IScientificCalculator
{
   [OperationContract(Action = ".../ISimpleCalculator/Add",
                      ReplyAction = ".../ISimpleCalculator/AddResponse")]
   int Add(int arg1,int arg2);

   [OperationContract(Action = ".../IScientificCalculator/Multiply",
                      ReplyAction = ".../IScientificCalculator/MultiplyResponse")]
   int Multiply(int arg1,int arg2);
}

public partial class ScientificCalculatorClient :
           ClientBase<IScientificCalculator>, IScientificCalculator
{
   public int Add(int arg1,int arg2)
   {...}
   public int Multiply(int arg1,int arg2)
   {...}
   //Rest of the proxy
}
```

Restoring the hierarchy on the client

The client can manually rework the proxy and the imported contract definitions to restore the contract hierarchy as shown in Example 2-5.

Example 2-5. Client-side contract hierarchy

```
[ServiceContract]
public interface ISimpleCalculator
{
   [OperationContract]
   int Add(int arg1,int arg2);
}
public partial class SimpleCalculatorClient : ClientBase<ISimpleCalculator>,
                                              ISimpleCalculator
{
   public int Add(int arg1,int arg2)
   {
      return Channel.Add(arg1,arg2);
   }
   //Rest of the proxy
}

[ServiceContract]
public interface IScientificCalculator : ISimpleCalculator
{
   [OperationContract]
   int Multiply(int arg1,int arg2);
}
public partial class ScientificCalculatorClient :
                         ClientBase<IScientificCalculator>,IScientificCalculator
{
   public int Add(int arg1,int arg2)
   {
      return Channel.Add(arg1,arg2);
   }
   public int Multiply(int arg1,int arg2)
   {
      return Channel.Multiply(arg1,arg2);
   }
   //Rest of the proxy
}
```

Using the value of the Action property in the various operations, the client can factor out the definitions of the comprising contracts in the service contract hierarchy and provide interface and proxy definitions, for example. ISimpleCalculator and SimpleCalculatorClient in Example 2-5. There is no need to set the Action and ResponseAction properties, and you can safely remove them all. Next, manually add the interface to the inheritance chain as required:

```
[ServiceContract]
public interface IScientificCalculator : ISimpleCalculator
{...}
```

Even though the service may have exposed just a single endpoint for the bottom-most interface in the hierarchy, the client can view it as different endpoints with the same address, where each endpoint corresponds to a different level in the contract hierarchy:

```
<client>
   <endpoint name = "SimpleEndpoint"
      address  = "http://localhost:8001/MyCalculator/"
      binding  = "basicHttpBinding"
      contract = "ISimpleCalculator"
   />
   <endpoint name = "ScientificEndpoint"
      address  = "http://localhost:8001/MyCalculator/"
      binding  = "basicHttpBinding"
      contract = "IScientificCalculator"
   />
</client>
```

The client can now write the following code, taking full advantage of the contract hierarchy:

```
SimpleCalculatorClient proxy1 = new SimpleCalculatorClient();
proxy1.Add(1,2);
proxy1.Close();

ScientificCalculatorClient proxy2 = new ScientificCalculatorClient();
proxy2.Add(3,4);
proxy2.Multiply(5,6);
proxy2.Close();
```

The advantage of the proxy refactoring in Example 2-5 is that each level in the contract is kept separately and decoupled from the levels underneath it. Anyone on the client side that expects a reference to ISimpleCalculator can now be given a reference to IScientificCalculator:

```
void UseCalculator(ISimpleCalculator calculator)
{...}

ISimpleCalculator proxy1 = new SimpleCalculatorClient();
ISimpleCalculator proxy2 = new ScientificCalculatorClient();
IScientificCalculator  proxy3 = new ScientificCalculatorClient();
SimpleCalculatorClient  proxy4 = new SimpleCalculatorClient();
ScientificCalculatorClient proxy5 = new ScientificCalculatorClient();

UseCalculator(proxy1);
UseCalculator(proxy2);
UseCalculator(proxy3);
UseCalculator(proxy4);
UseCalculator(proxy5);
```

However, there is no Is-A relationship between the proxies. Even though the IScientificCalculator interface derives from ISimpleCalculator, a ScientificCalculatorClient is not a SimpleCalculatorClient. In addition, you have to repeat the implementation of the base contract in the proxy for the subcontract. You can rectify that by using a technique I call *proxy chaining*, shown in Example 2-6.

Example 2-6. Proxy chaining

```
public partial class SimpleCalculatorClient : ClientBase<IScientificCalculator>,
                                              ISimpleCalculator
{
   public int Add(int arg1,int arg2)
   {
      return Channel.Add(arg1,arg2);
   }
   //Rest of the proxy
}

public partial class ScientificCalculatorClient : SimpleCalculatorClient,
                                                  IScientificCalculator
{
   public int Multiply(int arg1,int arg2)
   {
      return Channel.Multiply(arg1,arg2);
   }
   //Rest of the proxy
}
```

Only the proxy that implements the top most base contract derives directly from ClientBase<T>, providing it as a type parameter with the bottom most subinterface. All the other proxies derive from the proxy immediately above them and the respective contract.

Proxy chaining gives you an Is-A relationship between the proxies as well as code reuse. Anyone on the client side that expects a reference to SimpleCalculatorClient can be given now a reference to ScientificCalculatorClient:

```
void UseCalculator(SimpleCalculatorClient calculator)
{...}

SimpleCalculatorClient proxy1 = new SimpleCalculatorClient();
SimpleCalculatorClient proxy2 = new ScientificCalculatorClient();
ScientificCalculatorClient proxy3 = new ScientificCalculatorClient();

UseCalculator(proxy1);
UseCalculator(proxy2);
UseCalculator(proxy3);
```

Service Contracts Factoring and Design

Syntax aside, how do you go about designing service contracts? How do you know which operations to allocate to which service contract? How many operations should each contract have? Answering these questions has little to do with WCF and a lot to do with abstract service-oriented analysis and design. An in-depth discussion of how to decompose a system into services and how to discover contract methods is beyond the scope of this book. Nonetheless, this section offers a few pieces of advice to guide you in your service contracts design effort.

Contract Factoring

A service contract is a grouping of logically related operations. What constitutes "logically related" is usually domain-specific. You can think of service contracts as different facets of some entity. Once you have identified (after requirements analysis) all the operations the entity supports, you need to allocate them to contracts. This is called *service contract factoring*. When you factor a service contract, always think in terms of reusable elements. In a service-oriented application, the basic unit of reuse is the service contract. Would this particular contract factoring yield contracts that other entities in the system can reuse? What facets of the entity can logically be factored out and used by other entities?

As a concrete yet simple example, suppose you wish to model a dog service. The requirements are that the dog should be able to bark and fetch, that the dog should have a veterinary clinic registration number, and that you could vaccinate it. You can define the IDog service contract and have different kinds of services, such as the PoodleService and the GermanShepherdService implement the IDog contract:

```
[ServiceContract]
interface IDog
{
   [OperationContract]
   void Fetch();

   [OperationContract]
   void Bark();

   [OperationContract]
   long GetVetClinicNumber();

   [OperationContract]
   void Vaccinate();
}
class PoodleService : IDog
{...}
class GermanShepherdService : IDog
{...}
```

However, such a composition of the IDog service contract is not well factored. Even though all the operations are things a dog should support, Fetch() and Bark() are more logically related to each other than to GetVetClinicNumber() and Vaccinate(). Fetch() and Bark() involve one facet of the dog, as a living, active canine entity, while GetVetClinicNumber() and Vaccinate() involve a different facet, one that relates it as a record of a pet in a veterinary clinic. A better approach is to factor out

the GetVetClinicNumber( ) and Vaccinate( ) operations to a separate contract called
IPet:

```
[ServiceContract]
interface IPet
{
   [OperationContract]
   long GetVetClinicNumber( );

   [OperationContract]
   void Vaccinate( );
}

[ServiceContract]
interface IDog
{
   [OperationContract]
   void Fetch( );

   [OperationContract]
   void Bark( );
}
```

Because the pet facet is independent of the canine facet, other entities (such as cats)
can reuse the IPet service contract and support it:

```
[ServiceContract]
interface ICat
{
   [OperationContract]
   void Purr( );

   [OperationContract]
   void CatchMouse( );
}

class PoodleService : IDog,IPet
{...}

class SiameseService : ICat,IPet
{...}
```

This factoring, in turn, allows you to decouple the clinic-management aspect of the
application from the actual service (be it dogs or cats). Factoring operations into separate interfaces is usually done when there is a weak logical relation between the
operations. However, identical operations are sometimes found in several unrelated
contracts, and these operations are logically related to their respective contracts. For
example, both cats and dogs need to shed fur and feed their offspring. Logically,
shedding is just a dog operation as is barking, and is also just a cat operation as is
purring.

In such cases, you can factor the service contracts into a hierarchy of contracts
instead of separate contracts:

```
[ServiceContract]
interface IMammal
{
    [OperationContract]
    void ShedFur();

    [OperationContract]
    void Lactate();
}
[ServiceContract]
interface IDog : IMammal
{...}

[ServiceContract]
interface ICat : IMammal
{...}
```

Factoring Metrics

As you can see, proper contract-factoring results in more specialized, loosely coupled, fine-tuned, and reusable contracts, and subsequently, those benefits apply to the system as well. In general, contract factoring results in contracts with fewer operations.

When you design a service-based system, however, you need to balance out two countering forces (see Figure 2-1). One is the cost of implementing the service contracts and the other is the cost of putting them together or integrating them into a cohesive application.

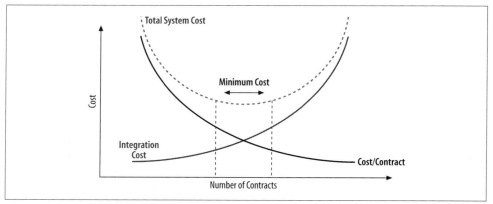

Figure 2-1. Balancing the number of services and their size

If you have too many granular service contracts, it will be easy to implement each contract, but the overall cost of integrating all those service contracts will be prohibitive. On the other hand, if you have only a few complex, large service contracts, the cost of implementing those contracts will be a prohibitive factor, even though the cost of integrating them might be low.

The relationship between cost and size of a service contract to implementation is not linear, because complexity is not linear to size—something twice as big is four or six times as complex. Similarly, the relationship between integration cost and the number of service contracts to integrate is not linear, because the number of possible connections is not linear to the number of participating services.

In any given system, the total effort involved in designing and maintaining the services that implement the contracts is the sum of those two factors (cost of implementation and the cost of integration). As you can see from Figure 2-1, there is an area of minimum cost or effort in relation to the size and number of the service contracts. A well-designed system has not too many but not too few services, and those services are not too big but not too small.

Because these contracts-factoring issues are independent of the service technology used, I can extrapolate from my own and others' experiences of factoring and architecting large-scale applications and share a few rules of thumb and metrics I have collected about service contracts factoring.

Service contracts with just one operation are possible, but you should avoid them. A service contract is a facet of an entity, and that facet must be pretty dull if you can express it with just one operation. Examine that single operation: is it using too many parameters? Is it too coarse, and therefore, should it be factored into several operations? Should you factor this operation into an already existing service contract?

The optimal number of service contracts members (in my opinion and experience) is between three and five. If you design a service contract with more operations—say, six to nine—you are still doing relatively well. However, try to look at the operations to determine whether any can be collapsed into each other, since it's quite possible to overfactor operations. If you have a service contract with 12 or more operations, you should definitely find ways to factor the operations into either separate service contracts or a hierarchy of contracts. Your coding standard should set some upper limit never to be exceeded, regardless of the circumstances (say, 20).

Another rule involves the use of property-like operations such as:

```
[OperationContract]
long GetVetClinicNumber( );
```

You should avoid such operations. Service contracts allow clients to invoke abstract operations, without caring about actual implementation details. Property-like operations are known as *just-enough-encapsulation*. You can encapsulate the business logic of setting and reading that variable's value on the service side, but ideally, you shouldn't bother clients with properties at all. Clients should invoke operations and let the service worry about how to manage its state. The interaction should be in terms of DoSomething( ) like Vaccinate( ). How the service goes about doing that and whether or not a vet clinic number was involved should be of no concern to the client.

A word of caution about factoring metrics: rules of thumb and generic metrics are only tools to help you gauge and evaluate your particular design. There is no substitute for domain expertise and experience. Always be practical, apply judgment, and question what you do in light of these guidelines.

Contract Queries

Sometimes the client needs to programmatically verify whether a particular endpoint (identified by its address) supports a particular contract. For example, imagine an application where the end user specifies or configures the application during setup (or even at runtime) to consume and interact with a service. If the service does not support the required contracts, the application should alert the user that an invalid address was specified, and ask for an alternative or a correct address. For example, the Credentials Manager application used in Chapter 10 has just such a feature: the user needs to provide it with the address of the security credentials service that manages accounts membership and roles. Credentials Manager only allows the user to select a valid address, after verifying the address supports the required service contracts.

Programmatic Metadata Processing

In order to support such functionality, the application needs to retrieve the metadata of the service endpoints and see if at least one of the endpoints supports the requested contract. As explained in Chapter 1, the metadata is available in special metadata exchange endpoints that the service might support or over the HTTP-GET protocol. When you use HTTP-GET, the address of the metadata exchange is the HTTP-GET address (usually just the base address of the service suffixed by ?wsdl). To ease the task of parsing the returned metadata, WCF offers a few helper classes, available in the `System.ServiceModel.Description` namespaces, as shown in Example 2-7.

Example 2-7. Metadata processing supporting types

```
public enum MetadataExchangeClientMode
{
   MetadataExchange,
   HttpGet
}
class MetadataSet : ...
{...}
public class ServiceEndpointCollection : Collection<ServiceEndpoint>
{...}

public class MetadataExchangeClient
{
   public MetadataExchangeClient();
```

Example 2-7. Metadata processing supporting types (continued)

```
   public MetadataExchangeClient(Binding mexBinding);
   public MetadataSet GetMetadata(Uri address,MetadataExchangeClientMode mode);
   //More members
}
public abstract class MetadataImporter
{
   public abstract ServiceEndpointCollection ImportAllEndpoints();
   //More members
}
public class WsdlImporter : MetadataImporter
{
   public WsdlImporter(MetadataSet metadata);
   //More members
}
public class ServiceEndpoint
{
   public EndpointAddress Address
   {get;set;}
   public Binding Binding
   {get;set;}
   public ContractDescription Contract
   {get;}
   //More members
}
public class ContractDescription
{
   public string Name
   {get;set;}
   public string Namespace
   {get;set;}
   //More members
}
```

MetadataExchangeClient can use the binding associated with metadata exchange in the application config file. You can also provide the constructor MetadataExchangeClient with an already initialized binding instance that has some custom values, such as a capacity for larger messages if the metadata returned exceeds the default received message size. The GetMetadata() method of MetadataExchangeClient accepts an endpoint address instance, wrapping the meta-data exchange address as well as an enum specifying the access method, and returns the metadata in an instance of MetadataSet. You should not work with that type directly. Instead, instantiate a subclass of MetadataImporter such as WsdlImporter and provide the raw metadata as a construction parameter, and then call the ImportAllEndpoints() method to obtain a collection of all endpoints found in the metadata. The endpoints are represented by the ServiceEndpoint class.

ServiceEndpoint provides the Contract property of the type ContractDescription. ContractDescription provides the name and namespace of the contract.

Using HTTP-GET, to find out if a specified base address supports a particular contract, follow the steps just described yielding the collection of endpoints. For each endpoint in the collection, compare the `Name` and `Namespace` properties in the `ContractDescription` with the requested contract, as shown in Example 2-8.

Example 2-8. Querying an address for a contract

```
bool contractSupported = false;

string mexAddress = "...?WSDL";

MetadataExchangeClient MEXClient = new MetadataExchangeClient(new Uri(mexAddress),
                                        MetadataExchangeClientMode.HttpGet);
MetadataSet metadata =  MEXClient.GetMetadata( );
MetadataImporter importer = new WsdlImporter(metadata);
ServiceEndpointCollection endpoints = importer.ImportAllEndpoints( );

foreach(ServiceEndpoint endpoint in endpoints)
{
   if(endpoint.Contract.Namespace == "MyNamespace" &&
      endpoint.Contract.Name == "IMyContract")
   {
      contractSupported = true;
      break;
   }
}
```

 The Metadata Explorer tool presented in Chapter 1 follows steps similar to Example 2-8 to retrieve the service endpoints. When given an HTTP-based address, the tool tries both HTTP-GET and an HTTP-based metadata exchange endpoint. The Metadata Explorer can also retrieve the metadata using a TCP- or IPC-based metadata exchange endpoint. The bulk of the implementation of the tool was in processing the metadata and rendering it because the difficult task of retrieving and parsing the metadata is done by the WCF-provided classes.

The MetadataHelper Class

I encapsulated and generalized the steps on Example 2-8 in my general-purpose static utility class called `MetadataHelper` in the `QueryContract( )` method:

```
public static class MetadataHelper
{
   public static bool QueryContract(string mexAddress,Type contractType);
   public static bool QueryContract(string mexAddress,string contractNamespace,
                                        string contractName);

   //More members
}
```

You can provide `MetadataHelper` with either the `Type` of the contract you wish to query for or with the name and namespace of the contract:

```
string address = "...";
bool contractSupported = MetadataHelper.QueryContract(address,typeof(IMyContract));
```

For a metadata exchange address, you can provide MetadataHelper with an HTTP-GET address, or a metadata exchange endpoint address over HTTP, HTTPS, TCP, or IPC. Example 2-9 shows the implementation of MetadataHelper.QueryContract( ), with some of the error handling code removed.

Example 2-9. Implementing MetadataHelper.QueryContract()

```
public static class MetadataHelper
{
  const int MessageMultiplier = 5;

  static ServiceEndpointCollection QueryMexEndpoint(string mexAddress,
                                                    BindingElement bindingElement)
  {
    CustomBinding binding = new CustomBinding(bindingElement);

    MetadataExchangeClient MEXClient = new MetadataExchangeClient(binding);
    MetadataSet metadata = MEXClient.GetMetadata
                                        (new EndpointAddress(mexAddress));
    MetadataImporter importer = new WsdlImporter(metadata);
    return importer.ImportAllEndpoints();
  }

  public static ServiceEndpoint[] GetEndpoints(string mexAddress)
  {
    /* Some error handling */
    Uri address = new Uri(mexAddress);
    ServiceEndpointCollection endpoints = null;

    if(address.Scheme == "net.tcp")
    {
      TcpTransportBindingElement tcpBindingElement =
                                      new TcpTransportBindingElement();
      tcpBindingElement.MaxReceivedMessageSize *= MessageMultiplier;
      endpoints = QueryMexEndpoint(mexAddress,tcpBindingElement);
    }
    if(address.Scheme == "net.pipe")
    {...}
    if(address.Scheme == "http")  //Checks for HTTP-GET as well
    {...}
    if(address.Scheme == "https") //Checks for HTTPS-GET as well
    {...}
    return Collection.ToArray(endpoints);

  }
  public static bool QueryContract(string mexAddress,Type contractType)
  {
    if(contractType.IsInterface == false)
    {
      Debug.Assert(false,contractType + " is not an interface");
      return false;
    }
```

Example 2-9. Implementing MetadataHelper.QueryContract() (continued)

```
      object[] attributes = contractType.GetCustomAttributes(
                                  typeof(ServiceContractAttribute),false);
      if(attributes.Length == 0)
      {
         Debug.Assert(false,"Interface " + contractType +
                      " does not have the ServiceContractAttribute");
         return false;
      }
      ServiceContractAttribute attribute = attributes[0] as
                                           ServiceContractAttribute;
      if(attribute.Name == null)
      {
         attribute.Name = contractType.ToString( );
      }
      if(attribute.Namespace == null)
      {
         attribute.Namespace = "http://tempuri.org/";
      }
      return QueryContract(mexAddress,attribute.Namespace,attribute.Name);
   }
   public static bool QueryContract(string mexAddress,string contractNamespace,
                                            string contractName)
   {
      if(String.IsNullOrEmpty(contractNamespace))
      {
         Debug.Assert(false,"Empty namespace");
         return false;
      }
      if(String.IsNullOrEmpty(contractName))
      {
         Debug.Assert(false,"Empty name");
         return false;
      }
      try
      {
         ServiceEndpoint[] endpoints = GetEndpoints(mexAddress);
         foreach(ServiceEndpoint endpoint in endpoints)
         {
            if(endpoint.Contract.Namespace == contractNamespace &&
               endpoint.Contract.Name == contractName)
            {
               return true;
            }
         }
      }

      catch
      {}
      return false;
   }
}
```

In Example 2-9, the GetEndpoints() method parses out the schema of the metadata exchange address. According to the transport schema found (such as TCP), GetEndpoints() constructs a binding element to use so that it could set its MaxReceivedMessageSize property:

```
public abstract class TransportBindingElement : BindingElement
{
    public virtual long MaxReceivedMessageSize
    {get;set;}
}
public abstract class ConnectionOrientedTransportBindingElement :
                                        TransportBindingElement,...
{...}
public class TcpTransportBindingElement : ConnectionOrientedTransportBindingElement
{...}
```

MaxReceivedMessageSize defaults to 64K. While it is adequate for simple services, services that have many endpoints that use complex types will generate larger messages that will fail the call to MetadataExchangeClient.GetMetadata(). My experimentations indicate that 5 is an adequate fudge factor for most cases. GetEndpoints() then uses the QueryMexEndpoint() private method to actually retrieve the metadata. QueryMexEndpoint() accepts the metadata exchange endpoint address and the binding element to use. It uses the binding element to construct a custom binding and provide it to an instance of MetadataExchangeClient, which retrieves the metadata and returns the endpoint collection. Instead of returning a ServiceEndpointCollection, GetEndpoints() uses my Collection helper class to return an array of endpoints.

The QueryContract() method that accepts a Type first verifies that the type is an interface and that it is decorated with the ServiceContract attribute. Because the ServiceContract attribute can be used to alias both the name and namespace of the requested type of contract, QueryContract() uses those for looking up the contract. If no aliasing is used, QueryContract() uses the name of the type and the default *http://tempuri.org* for the namespace, and calls the QueryContract() that operates on the name and namespace. That version of QueryContract()—calls GetEndpoints() to obtain the array of endpoints and then it iterates over the array and returns true if it finds at least one endpoint that supports the contract. Any errors make QueryContract() return false.

Example 2-10 shows additional metadata querying methods offered by MetadataHelper.

Example 2-10. The MetadataHelper class

```
public static class MetadataHelper
{
    public static ServiceEndpoint[] GetEndpoints(string mexAddress);
    public static string[] GetAddresses(Type bindingType,string mexAddress,
                                                    Type contractType);
    public static string[] GetAddresses(string mexAddress,Type contractType);
```

Example 2-10. The MetadataHelper class (continued)

```
   public static string[] GetAddresses(Type bindingType,string mexAddress,
                                        string contractNamespace,string contractName)
                                                         where B : Binding;
   public static string[] GetAddresses(string mexAddress,string contractNamespace,
                                                          string contractName);
   public static string[] GetContracts(Type bindingType,string mexAddress);
   public static string[] GetContracts(string mexAddress);
   public static string[] GetOperations(string mexAddress,Type contractType);
   public static string[] GetOperations(string mexAddress,
                                        string contractNamespace,
                                        string contractName);
   public static bool QueryContract(string mexAddress,Type contractType);
   public static bool QueryContract(string mexAddress,
                                    string contractNamespace,string contractName);

   //More members
}
```

These powerful and useful features are often required during setup or in administration applications and tools, and yet the implementation of them is all based on processing the array of endpoints returned from the GetEndpoints( ) method.

The GetAddresses( ) methods return all the endpoint addresses that support a particular contract or only the addresses of the endpoints that also use a particular binding.

Similarly, GetContracts( ) returns all the contracts supported across all endpoints or the contracts supported across all endpoints that use a particular binding. Finally, GetOperations( ) returns all the operations on a particular contract.

 Chapter 10 uses the the MetadataHelper class in the Credentials Manager application, and Appendix B uses it for administering persistent subscribers.

CHAPTER 3

Data Contracts

In the abstract, all that WCF provides for is the ability to host and expose native CLR types (interfaces and classes) as services, and the ability to consume services as native CLR interfaces and classes. WCF service operations accept and return CLR types such as integers and strings, and the WCF clients pass in and process returned CLR types. However, such CLR types are specific to .NET, of course. One of the core tenets of service-orientation is that services do not betray their implementation technology across the service boundary. As a result, any client, regardless of its own technology, can interact with the service. This obviously means that WCF cannot allow you to expose the CLR data types across the service boundary. What you need is a way of converting CLR types to and from a standard neutral representation. That representation is a simple XML-based schema or an *infoset*. In addition, the service needs a formal way for declaring how such conversion is to take place. This formal way is called a *data contract*, and it is the subject of this chapter. This first part of the chapter shows how data contracts enable type marshaling and conversions and how the infrastructure deals with class hierarchies and data contract versioning. The second part shows how to use various .NET types such as enumerations, delegates, data tables, and collections as data contracts.

Serialization

The data contract is part of the contractual operations the service supports, just like the service contract is part of that contract. The data contract is published in the service metadata, which allows clients to convert the neutral, technology-agnostic representation to the client's native representation. Because objects and local references are CLR concepts, you cannot pass to and from a WCF service operation your CLR objects and references. Allowing you to do so would not just violate the core service-oriented principle discussed previously, but would also be impractical, since the object is comprised of both the state and the code manipulating it. There is no way of sending the code or the logic as part of a C# or Visual Basic method invocation, let alone marshaling it to another platform and technology. In fact, when passing an object (or a value type) as an operation parameter, all you really need to send is the state of that object, and you let the receiving side convert it back to its own native representation. Such an approach for passing state around is called *marshaling by value*. The easiest way to perform marshaling by value is to rely on the built-in support most platforms (.NET included) offer for serialization. The approach is simple enough, as shown in Figure 3-1.

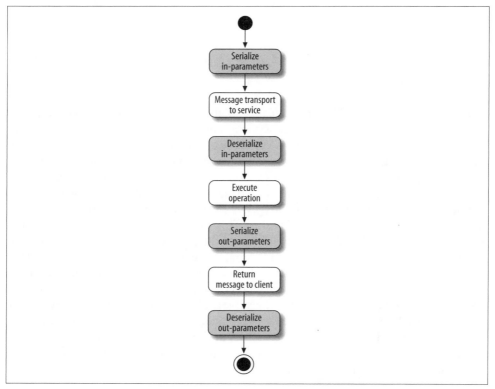

Figure 3-1. Serialization and deserialization during an operation call

On the client side, WCF will serialize the in-parameters from the CLR native representation to an XML infoset and bundle them in the outgoing message to the client. Once the message is received on the service side, WCF will deserialize it and convert the neutral XML infoset to the corresponding CLR representation before dispatching the call to the service. The service will then process the native CLR parameters. Once the service finishes executing the operation, WCF will serialize the out-parameters and the returned values into a neutral XML infoset, package them in the returned message, and post the returned message to the client. Finally, on the client, WCF will deserialize the returned values into native CLR types and return them to the client.

.NET Serialization

WCF could make use of the ready-made support .NET offers for serialization. .NET automatically serializes and deserializes the objects using reflection. .NET captures the value of every field of an object and serializes it to memory, a file, or a network connection. For deserializing, .NET creates a new object of the matching type; reads its persisted field values; and sets the value of its fields, using reflection. Because reflection can access private fields, including base-class fields, .NET takes a complete snapshot of the state of an object during serialization and perfectly reconstructs that state during deserialization. .NET serializes the object state into a stream. A *stream* is a logical sequence of bytes, independent of a particular medium such as a file, memory, a communication port, or other resource.

The Serializable attribute

By default, user-defined types (classes and structs) are not serializable. The reason is that .NET has no way of knowing whether a reflection-based dump of the object state to a stream makes sense. Perhaps the object members have some transient value or state (such as an open database connection or communication port). If .NET simply serialized the state of such an object, then after constructing a new object by deserializing it from the stream, you would end up with a defective object. Consequently, serialization has to be performed by consent of the class' developer.

To indicate to .NET that instances of your class are serializable, you add the SerializableAttribute to your class or struct definition:

```
[AttributeUsage(AttributeTargets.Delegate|
                AttributeTargets.Enum   |
                AttributeTargets.Struct |
                AttributeTargets.Class,
                Inherited=false)]
public sealed class SerializableAttribute : Attribute
{}
```

For example:

```
[Serializable]
public class MyClass
{...}
```

When a class is serializable, .NET insists that all its member variables be serializable as well, and if it discovers a nonserializable member, it throws an exception. However, what if the class or a struct has a member that cannot be serialized? That type will not have the Serializable attribute and will preclude the containing type from being serialized. Commonly, that nonserializable member is a reference type requiring some special initialization. The solution to this problem requires marking such a member as nonserializable and taking a custom step to initialize it during deserialization.

To allow a serializable type to contain a nonserializable type as a member variable, you need to mark the member with the NonSerialized field attribute; for example:

```
public class MyOtherClass
{..}

[Serializable]
public class MyClass
{
   [NonSerialized]
   MyOtherClass m_OtherClass;
   /* Methods and properties */
}
```

When NET serializes a member variable, it first reflects it to see whether it has the NonSerialized attribute. If so, .NET ignores that variable and simply skips over it.

This allows you to preclude from serialization even normally serializable types such as the string:

```
[Serializable]
public class MyClass
{
   [NonSerialized]
   string m_Name;
}
```

The .NET formatters

.NET offers two formatters used for serializing and deserializing types. The BinaryFormatter serializes into a compact binary format, enabling fast serialization and deserialization because no parsing is required. The SoapFormatter uses a .NET-specific SOAP XML format, and it introduces composition overhead during serialization and parsing overhead during deserialization.

Both formatters support the IFormatter interface, defined as:

```
public interface IFormatter
{
   object Deserialize(Stream serializationStream);
   void Serialize(Stream serializationStream,object graph);
   // More members
}

public sealed class BinaryFormatter : IFormatter,...
{...}
public sealed class SoapFormatter : IFormatter,...
{...}
```

Regardless of the format used, in addition to the state of the object, both formatters persist the type's assembly and versioning information to the stream, so that they can deserialize it back to the correct type. This renders them inadequate for service-oriented interaction because it requires the other party to have the type assembly, and of course be using .NET in the first place. The use of the Stream is also an imposition because it requires the client and the service to somehow share the stream.

The WCF Formatters

Due to the deficiencies of the classic .NET formatters, WCF has to provide its own service-oriented formatter. The WCF formatter DataContractSerializer is capable of sharing just the data contract, not the underlying type information. DataContractSerializer is defined in the System.Runtime.Serialization namespace and is partially listed in Example 3-1.

Example 3-1. The DataContractSerializer

```
public abstract class XmlObjectSerializer
{
   public virtual object ReadObject(Stream stream);
   public virtual object ReadObject(XmlReader reader);
   public virtual void WriteObject(XmlWriter writer,object graph);
   public void WriteObject(Stream stream,object graph);
   //More members
}
public sealed class DataContractSerializer : XmlObjectSerializer
{
   public DataContractSerializer(Type type);
   //More members
}
```

DataContractSerializer only captures the state of the object according to the serialization or data contract schema. Note also that DataContractSerializer does not support IFormatter.

WCF automatically uses DataContractSerializer under the covers, and developers never need to interact with it directly. However, you can use DataContractSerializer to serialize types to and from a .NET stream, similar to using the legacy formatters. Unlike the binary or SOAP formatters, you need to supply the constructor of DataContractSerializer with the type to operate on, because no type information will be present in the stream:

```
MyClass obj1 = new MyClass();
DataContractSerializer formatter = new DataContractSerializer(typeof(MyClass));

using(Stream stream = new MemoryStream())
{
   formatter.WriteObject(stream,obj1);
   stream.Seek(0,SeekOrigin.Begin);
   MyClass obj2 = (MyClass)formatter.ReadObject(stream);
}
```

While you can use DataContractSerializer with .NET streams, you can also use it in conjunction with XML readers and writers, when the only form of input is the raw XML itself, as opposed to some media like a file or memory.

Note the use of the amorphous object in the definition of DataContractSerializer in Example 3-1. This means that there will be no compile-time type safety because the constructor can accept one type, the WriteObject( ) method can accept a second type, and the ReadObject( ) can cast to yet a third type.

To compensate for that, you can define your own generic wrapper around DataContractSerializer, as shown in Example 3-2.

Example 3-2. The generic DataContractSerializer<T>

```
public class DataContractSerializer<T> : XmlObjectSerializer
{
    DataContractSerializer m_DataContractSerializer;

    public DataContractSerializer( )
    {
        m_DataContractSerializer = new DataContractSerializer(typeof(T));
    }
    public new T ReadObject(Stream stream)
    {
        return (T)m_DataContractSerializer.ReadObject(stream);
    }
    public new T ReadObject(XmlReader reader)
    {
        return (T)m_DataContractSerializer.ReadObject(reader);
    }
    public void WriteObject(Stream stream,T graph)
    {
        m_DataContractSerializer.WriteObject(stream,graph);
    }
    public void WriteObject(XmlWriter writer,T graph)
    {
        m_DataContractSerializer.WriteObject(writer,graph);
    }
    //More members
}
```

The generic class DataContractSerializer<T> is much safer to use than the object-based DataContractSerializer:

```
MyClass obj1 = new MyClass( );
DataContractSerializer<MyClass> formatter = new
                                DataContractSerializer<MyClass>( );
using(Stream stream = new MemoryStream( ))
{
    formatter.WriteObject(stream,obj1);
    stream.Seek(0,SeekOrigin.Begin);
    MyClass obj2 = formatter.ReadObject(stream);
}
```

WCF also offers the `NetDataContractSerializer` formatter, which is polymorphic with IFormatter:

```
public sealed class NetDataContractSerializer : IFormatter,...
{...}
```

As its name implies, similar to the legacy .NET formatters, the `NetDataContractSerializer` formatter captures the type information in addition to the state of the object, and is used just like the legacy formatters:

```
MyClass obj1 = new MyClass();
IFormatter formatter = new NetDataContractSerializer();

using(Stream stream = new MemoryStream())
{
   formatter.Serialize(stream,obj1);
   stream.Seek(0,SeekOrigin.Begin);
   MyClass obj2 = (MyClass)formatter.Deserialize(stream);
}
```

`NetDataContractSerializer` is designed to complement `DataContractSerializer`. You can serialize a type using `NetDataContractSerializer` and deserialize using `DataContractSerializer`:

```
MyClass obj1 = new MyClass();
Stream stream = new MemoryStream();

IFormatter formatter1 = new NetDataContractSerializer();
formatter1.Serialize(stream,obj1);

stream.Seek(0,SeekOrigin.Begin);

DataContractSerializer formatter2 = new DataContractSerializer(typeof(MyClass));
MyClass obj2 = (MyClass)formatter2.ReadObject(stream);
stream.Close();
```

This ability opens the way for versioning tolerance and for migrating legacy code that shares type information into a more service-oriented approach where only the data schema is maintained.

Data Contract via Serialization

When a service operation accepts or returns any type or parameter, WCF uses `DataContractSerializer` to serialize and deserialize that parameter. This means that you can pass any serializable type as a parameter or returned value from a contract operation, as long as the other party has the definition of the data schema or the data contract. All the .NET built-in primitive types are serializable. For example, here are the definitions of the int and the string:

```
[Serializable]
public struct Int32 : ...
{...}
```

```
[Serializable]
public sealed class String : ...
{...}
```

This is the only reason why any of the service contracts shown in the previous chapters actually worked. WCF offers an *implicit data contract* for the primitive types because there is an industry standard for the schema of those types.

To be able to use a custom type as an operation parameter, two things need to happen: first, the type must be serializable, and second, both client and service need to have a local definition of that type that results in the same data schema.

For example, consider the IContactManager service contract used to manage a contacts list:

```
[Serializable]
struct Contact
{
    public string FirstName;
    public string LastName;
}

[ServiceContract]
interface IContactManager
{
    [OperationContract]
    void AddContact(Contact contact);

    [OperationContract]
    Contact[] GetContacts();
}
```

If the client uses an equivalent definition of the Contact structure, it will be able to pass a contact to the service. An equivalent definition might be anything that results in the same data schema for serialization. For example, the client might use this definition as well:

```
[Serializable]
struct Contact
{
    public string FirstName;
    public string LastName;

    [NonSerialized]
    public string Address;
}
```

Data Contract Attributes

While the Serializable attribute is workable, it is inadequate for service-oriented interaction between clients and services. It denotes all members in the type as serializable and therefore part of the data schema for that type. It is much better to have an opt-in approach, where only members the contract developer wants to explicitly include in the data contract are included. The `Serializable` attribute forces the data type to be serializable in order to be used as a parameter in a contract operation, and does not offer clean separation between the serviceness aspect of the type (ability to use it as a WCF operation parameter) and the ability to serialize it. The attribute offers no support for aliasing type name or members, or for mapping a new type to a predefined data contract. The attribute operates directly on member fields, and completely bypasses any logical properties used to access those fields. It would be better to allow those properties to add their values when accessing the fields. Finally, there is no direct support for versioning because any versioning information is supposedly captured by the formatters. Consequently, it is difficult to deal with versioning over time.

Yet again, the solution is to come up with new WCF service-oriented opt-in attributes. The first of these attributes is the `DataContractAttribute` defined in the `System.Runtime.Serialization` namespace:

```
[AttributeUsage(AttributeTargets.Enum   |
                AttributeTargets.Struct|
                AttributeTargets.Class,
                Inherited = false)]
public sealed class DataContractAttribute : Attribute
{
   public string Name
   {get;set;}
   public string Namespace
   {get;set;}
}
```

Applying the `DataContract` attribute on a class or struct does not cause WCF to serialize any of its members:

```
[DataContract]
struct Contact
{
   //Will not be part of the data contract
   public string FirstName;
   public string LastName;
}
```

All the `DataContract` attribute does is merely opt-in the type, indicating that the type is willing to be marshaled by value. To serialize any of its members, you must apply the `DataMemberAttribute` defined as:

```
[AttributeUsage(AttributeTargets.Field|AttributeTargets.Property,
                Inherited = false)]
public sealed class DataMemberAttribute : Attribute
{
   public bool IsRequired
   {get;set;}
   public string Name
   {get;set;}
```

```
   public int Order
   {get;set;}
}
```

You can apply the DataMember attribute on the fields directly:

```
[DataContract]
struct Contact
{
   [DataMember]
   public string FirstName;

   [DataMember]
   public string LastName;
}
```

Or you can apply it on properties:

```
[DataContract]
struct Contact
{
   string m_FirstName;
   string m_LastName;

   [DataMember]
   public string FirstName
   {
      get
      {...}
      set
      {...}
   }

   [DataMember]
   public string LastName
   {
      get
      {...}
      set
      {...}
   }
}
```

Similar to service contracts, the visibility of the data members or the data contract itself is of no consequence to WCF. You can include internal types with private data members in the data contract:

```
[DataContract]
struct Contact
{
   [DataMember]
   string m_FirstName;

   [DataMember]
   string m_LastName;
}
```

Most of the text in this chapter applies the `DataMember` attribute directly on public data members, for brevity's sake. In real code you should of course use properties instead of public members.

 Data contracts are case-sensitive, both at the type and member level.

Importing a Data Contract

When a data contract is used in a contract operation, it is published in the service metadata. When the client imports the definition of the data contract, the client will end up with an equivalent definition, but not an identical one. The imported definition will maintain the original type designation of a class or a structure. In addition, unlike a service contract, by default the important definition will maintain the original type namespace.

For example, given this service-side definition:

```
namespace MyNamespace
{
   [DataContract]
   struct Contact
   {...}

   [ServiceContract]
   interface IContactManager
   {
      [OperationContract]
      void AddContact(Contact contact);

      [OperationContract]
      Contact[] GetContacts();
   }
}
```

The imported definition will be:

```
namespace MyNamespace
{
   [DataContract]
   struct Contact
   {...}
}
[ServiceContract]
interface IContactManager
{
   [OperationContract]
   void AddContact(Contact contact);

   [OperationContract]
   Contact[] GetContacts();
}
```

To override this and provide an alternative namespace for the data contract, you can assign a value to the Namespace property of the DataContract attribute. For example, given this service-side definition:

```
namespace MyNamespace
{
    [DataContract(Namespace = "MyOtherNamespace")]
    struct Contact
    {...}
}
```

The imported definition will be:

```
namespace MyOtherNamespace
{
    [DataContract]
    struct Contact
    {...}
}
```

The imported definition will always have properties decorated with the DataMember attribute, even if the original type on the service side did not define any properties. If the original service-side definition applied the DataMember attribute on fields directly, then the imported type definition will have properties accessing fields whose names will be the name of the data member suffixed with Field. For example, for this service-side definition:

```
[DataContract]
struct Contact
{
    [DataMember]
    public string FirstName;

    [DataMember]
    public string LastName;
}
```

the imported client-side definition will be:

```
[DataContract]
public partial struct Contact
{
    string FirstNameField;
    string LastNameField;

    [DataMember]
    public string FirstName
    {
        get
        {
            return FirstNameField;
        }
        set
        {
```

```
                    FirstNameField = value;
            }
        }

        [DataMember]
        public string LastName
        {
            get
            {
                return LastNameField;
            }
            set
            {
                LastNameField = value;
            }
        }
    }
```

The client can of course manually rework any imported definition to be just like a service-side definition.

 Even if the DataMember attribute on the service side is applied on a private field or property:
```
        [DataContract]
        struct Contact
        {
            [DataMember]
            string FirstName
            {get;set;}

            [DataMember]
            string LastName;
        }
```
the imported definition will have a public property instead.

If the DataMember attribute is applied on a property as part of the service-side data contract, the imported definition will have an identical set of properties. The client-side properties will wrap a field named after the property suffixed by Field. For example, given this service-side data contract:
```
[DataContract]
public partial struct Contact
{
    string m_FirstName;
    string m_LastName;

    [DataMember]
    public string FirstName
    {
        get
        {
            return m_FirstName;
```

```
      }
      set
      {
         m_FirstName = value;
      }
   }

   [DataMember]
   public string LastName
   {
      get
      {
         return m_LastName;
      }
      set
      {
         m_LastName = value;
      }
   }
}
```

the imported definition will be:

```
[DataContract]
public partial struct Contact
{
   string FirstNameField;
   string LastNameField;

   [DataMember]
   public string FirstName
   {
      get
      {
         return FirstNameField;
      }
      set
      {
         FirstNameField = value;
      }
   }

   [DataMember]
   public string LastName
   {
      get
      {
         return LastNameField;
      }
      set
      {
         LastNameField = value;
      }
   }
}
```

When the DataMember attribute is applied on a property (either on the service or the client side), that property must have get and set accessors. Without them, you will get an InvalidDataContractException at call time. The reason is that when the property itself is the data member, WCF uses the property during serialization and deserialization, letting you apply any custom logic in the property.

 Do not apply the DataMember attribute both on a property and on its underlying field—this will result in a duplication of the members on the importing side.

It is important to realize that the way described so far for utilizing the DataMember attribute applies both for the service and the client side. When the client uses the DataMember attribute (and its related attributes described elsewhere in this chapter), it affects the data contract it is using to serialize and send parameters to the service, or deserialize and use the returned values from the service. It is quite possible for the two parties to use equivalent yet not identical data contracts, and, as you will see later on, even to use nonequivalent data contracts. The client controls and configures its data contracts independently of the service.

Data Contract and the Serializable Attribute

The service can still use a type that is only marked with the Serializable attribute:

```
[Serializable]
struct Contact
{
    string m_FirstName;
    public string LastName;
}
```

When importing the metadata of such a type, the imported definition will use the DataContract attribute. In addition, since the Serializable attribute affects fields only, it would be as if every serializable member, public or private, is a data member, resulting in a set of wrapping properties named exactly like the original fields:

```
[DataContract]
public partial struct Contact
{
    string LastNameField;
    string m_FirstNameField;

    [DataMember(...)]
    public string LastName
    {
        ... //Accesses LastNameField
    }
    [DataMember(...)]
    public string m_FirstName
    {
```

```
    ... //Accesses m_FirstNameField
    }
}
```

In much the same way, the client can use the `Serializable` attribute on its data contract and have the *wire representation*—that is, the way it is marshaled—be the same as just described.

 A type marked only with the `DataContract` attribute cannot be serialized using the legacy formatters. If you want to serialize the type, you can apply both the `DataContract` attribute and the `Serializable` attribute. The wire representation of such a type is as if only the `DataContract` attribute was applied, and you still need to use the `DataMember` attribute on the members.

Data Contract and XML Serialization

.NET offers yet another serialization mechanism—raw XML serialization, using a dedicated set of attributes. When you're dealing with a data type that requires explicit control over the XML serialization, you can use the `XmlSerializerFormatAttribute` on individual operations in the contract definition to instruct WCF to use XML serialization at runtime. If all operations on the contract require this form of serialization, you can use the `/serializer:XmlSerializer` switch of SvcUtil to instruct it to automatically apply the `XmlSerializerFormat` attribute on all operations in all imported contracts. Use caution with that switch, because it will affect all data contracts, including those that do not require explicit control over the XML serialization.

Composite Data Contracts

When you define a data contract, you can apply the `DataMember` attribute on members that are themselves data contracts, as shown in Example 3-3.

Example 3-3. A composite data contract

```
[DataContract]
struct Address
{
    [DataMember]
    public string Street;

    [DataMember]
    public string City;

    [DataMember]
    public string State;

    [DataMember]
```

Example 3-3. A composite data contract (continued)

```
    public string Zip;
}
[DataContract]
struct Contact
{
    [DataMember]
    public string FirstName;

    [DataMember]
    public string LastName;

    [DataMember]
    public Address Address;
}
```

Being able to aggregate other data contracts this way illustrates the fact that data contracts are actually recursive in nature. When you serialize a composite data contract, the DataContractSerializer will chase all references in the object graph and capture their state as well. When you publish a composite data contract, all its comprising data contracts will be published as well. For example, using the same definitions as Example 3-3, the metadata for this service contract:

```
    [ServiceContract]
    interface IContactManager
    {
        [OperationContract]
        void AddContact(Contact contact);

        [OperationContract]
        Contact[] GetContacts();
    }
```

will include the definition of the Address structure as well.

Data Contract Events

.NET 2.0 introduced support for serialization events for serializable types, and WCF provides the same support for data contracts. WCF calls designated methods on your data contract when serialization and deserialization take place. Four serialization and deserialization events are defined. The *serializing event* is raised just before serialization takes place, and the *serialized event* is raised just after serialization. Similarly, the *deserializing event* is raised just before deserialization, and the *deserialized event* is raised after deserialization. You designate methods as serialization event handlers using method attributes, as shown in Example 3-4.

Example 3-4. Applying the serialization event attributes

```
[DataContract]
class MyDataContract
{
    [OnSerializing]
    void OnSerializing(StreamingContext context)
    {...}

    [OnSerialized]
    void OnSerialized(StreamingContext context)
    {...}

    [OnDeserializing]
    void OnDeserializing(StreamingContext context)
    {...}

    [OnDeserialized]
    void OnDeserialized(StreamingContext context)
    {...}
    //Data members
}
```

Each serialization event-handling method must have the following signature:

```
void <Method Name>(StreamingContext context);
```

This is required because internally WCF still uses delegates to subscribe and invoke the event-handling methods. If the attributes are applied on methods with incompatible signatures, WCF will throw an exception.

StreamingContext is a structure informing the type of why it is being serialized, but it can be ignored for WCF data contracts. The event attributes are defined in the System.Runtime.Serialization namespace.

As the attribute names imply, the OnSerializing attribute designates a method handling the serializing event, and the OnSerialized attribute designates a method handling the serialized event. Similarly, the OnDeserializing attribute designates a method handling the deserializing event, and the OnDeserialized attribute designates the method handling the deserialized event. Figure 3-2 is an activity diagram depicting the order in which events are raised during serialization.

WCF first raises the serializing event, thus invoking the corresponding event handler. Next, WCF serializes the object, and finally the serialized event is raised and its event handler is invoked.

Figure 3-3 is an activity diagram depicting the order in which deserialization events are raised.

Note that in order to call the deserializing event-handling method, WCF has to first construct an object—however, it does so without ever calling your data contract class default constructor.

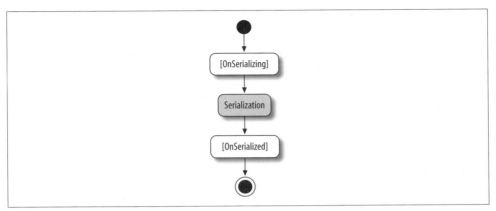

Figure 3-2. Events during serialization

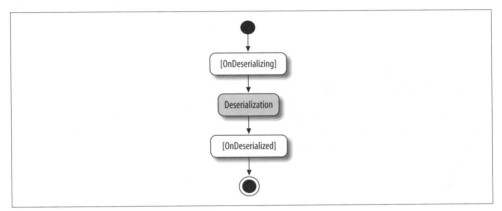

Figure 3-3. Events during deserialization

 WCF does not allow you to apply the same serialization event attribute on multiple methods of the data contract type. This is somewhat regretful because it precludes support for partial types, where each part deals with its own serialization events.

Using the deserializing event

Since no constructor calls are ever made during deserialization, the deserializing event-handling method is logically your deserialization constructor. It is intended for performing some custom pre-deserialization steps—typically, initialization of class members not marked as data members. Any value settings done on members marked as data members will be in vain, because WCF will set those members again during deserialization, using values from the message. Other steps you can take in the deserializing event-handling method are setting specific environment variables (such as thread local storage), performing diagnostics, or signaling some global synchronization events.

Using the deserialized event

The deserialized event lets your data contract initialize or reclaim nondata members, while using already deserialized values. Example 3-5 demonstrates this point: it uses the event to initialize a database connection. Without the event, the data contract will not be able to function properly.

Example 3-5. Initializing nonserializable resources using the deserialized event

```
[DataContract]
class MyDataContract
{
   IDbConnection m_Connection;

   [OnDeserialized]
   void OnDeserialized(StreamingContext context)
   {
      m_Connection = new SqlConnection(...);
   }
   /* Data members */
}
```

Data Contract Hierarchy

Your data contract class may be the subclass of another data contract class. WCF requires that every level in the class hierarchy explicitly opt in for a given data contract, because the DataContract attribute is not inheritable:

```
[DataContract]
class Contact
{
   [DataMember]
   public string FirstName;

   [DataMember]
   public string LastName;
}
[DataContract]
class Customer : Contact
{
   [DataMember]
   public int OrderNumber;
}
```

Failing to designate every level in the class hierarchy as serializable or as a data contract will result in an InvalidDataContractException at the service load time. WCF lets you mix the Serializable and DataContract attribute in the class hierarchy:

```
[Serializable]
class Contact
{...}
```

```
[DataContract]
class Customer : Contact
{..}
```

But typically the Serializable attribute will be at the root of the class hierarchy, if at all, because new classes should use the DataContract attribute. When you export a data contract hierarchy, the metadata maintains the hierarchy, and all levels of the class hierarchy are exported when making use of the subclass in a service contract:

```
[ServiceContract]
interface IContactManager
{
   [OperationContract]
   void AddCustomer(Customer customer);//Contact is exported as well
   ...
}
```

Known Types

While languages such as C# let you substitute a subclass for a base class, this is not the case with WCF operations. By default, you cannot use a subclass of a data contract class instead of its base class. Consider this service contract:

```
[ServiceContract]
interface IContactManager
{
   //Cannot accept Customer object here:
   [OperationContract]
   void AddContact(Contact contact);

   //Cannot return Customer objects here:
   [OperationContract]
   Contact[] GetContacts();
}
```

Suppose the client defined the Customer class as well:

```
[DataContract]
class Customer : Contact
{
   [DataMember]
   public int OrderNumber;
}
```

While the following code compiles successfully, it fails at runtime:

```
Contact contact = new Customer();
contact.FirstName = "Juval";
contact.LastName = "Lowy";

ContactManagerClient proxy = new ContactManagerClient();
//Service call will fail:
proxy.AddContact(contact);
proxy.Close();
```

The reason is that when you pass in a Customer instead of a Contact as in the previous example, the service does not know how to deserialize the Contact object it received—it does not know about the Customer object.

Much the same way, when a Customer is returned instead of a Contact, the client does not know how to deserialize it, because all it knows about are contacts, not customers:

```
////////////////////////// Service Side ///////////////////////////////
[DataContract]
class Customer : Contact
{
    [DataMember]
    public int OrderNumber;
}
class CustomerManager : IContactManager
{
    List<Customer> m_Customers = new List<Customer>();

    public Contact[] GetContacts()
    {
        return m_Customers.ToArray();
    }
    //Rest of the implementation
}
////////////////////////// Client Side ///////////////////////////////
ContactManagerClient proxy = new ContactManagerClient();
//Call will fail:
Contact[] contacts = proxy.GetContacts();
proxy.Close();
```

The solution is to explicitly tell WCF about the Customer class using the KnownTypeAttribute, defined as:

```
[AttributeUsage(AttributeTargets.Struct|AttributeTargets.Class,
                AllowMultiple = true)]
public sealed class KnownTypeAttribute : Attribute
{
    public KnownTypeAttribute(Type type);
    //More members
}
```

The KnownType attribute allows you to designate acceptable subclasses for the data contract:

```
[DataContract]
[KnownType(typeof(Customer))]
class Contact
{...}

[DataContract]
class Customer : Contact
{...}
```

On the host side, the KnownType attribute affects all contracts and operations using the base class, across all services and endpoints, allowing it to accept subclasses instead of base classes. In addition, it includes the subclass in the metadata, so that the client will have its own definition of the subclass, and can pass the subclass instead of the base class. If the client also applies the KnownType attribute on its copy of the base class, then it can receive the known subclass back from the service.

Service Known Types

The downside of using the KnownType attribute is that it may be too broad in scope. WCF also provides the ServiceKnownTypeAttribute, defined as:

```
[AttributeUsage(AttributeTargets.Interface|
                AttributeTargets.Method   |
                AttributeTargets.Class,
                AllowMultiple = true)]
public sealed class ServiceKnownTypeAttribute : Attribute
{
   public ServiceKnownTypeAttribute(Type type);
   //More members
}
```

Instead of using the KnownType attribute on the base data contract, when the ServiceKnownType attribute is applied on a specific operation on the service side, then only that operation (across all supporting services) can accept the known subclass:

```
[DataContract]
class Contact
{...}

[DataContract]
class Customer : Contact
{...}

[ServiceContract]
interface IContactManager
{
   [OperationContract]
   [ServiceKnownType(typeof(Customer))]
   void AddContact(Contact contact);

   [OperationContract]
   Contact[] GetContacts();
}
```

Other operations cannot accept the subclass.

When the ServiceKnownType attribute is applied at the contract level, all the operations on that contract can accept the known subclass across all implementing services:

```
[ServiceContract]
[ServiceKnownType(typeof(Customer))]
interface IContactManager
```

```
{
    [OperationContract]
    void AddContact(Contact contact);

    [OperationContract]
    Contact[] GetContacts( );
}
```

 Do not apply the ServiceKnownType attribute on the service class itself. Although it compiles, it is only available when you don't define the service contract as an interface, something I strongly discourage in any case. If you apply the ServiceKnownType attribute on the service class while there is a separate contract definition, it will have no effect.

Whether you apply the ServiceKnownType attribute at the operation or the contract level, the exported metadata and the generated proxy have no trace of it, and will include the KnownType attribute on the base class only. For example, given this service-side definition:

```
[ServiceContract]
[ServiceKnownType(typeof(Customer))]
interface IContactManager
{...}
```

The imported definition will be:

```
[DataContract]
[KnownType(typeof(Customer))]
class Contact
{...}
[DataContract]
class Customer : Contact
{...}
[ServiceContract]
interface IContactManager
{...}
```

You can manually rework the client-side proxy class to reflect correctly the service-side semantic by removing the KnownType attribute from the base class and applying the ServiceKnownType attribute to the appropriate level in the contract.

Multiple Known Types

You can apply both the KnownType and the ServiceKnownType attributes multiple times to inform WCF about as many known types as required:

```
[DataContract]
class Contact
{...}

[DataContract]
class Customer : Contact
{...}
```

```
[DataContract]
class Person : Contact
{...}

[ServiceContract]
[ServiceKnownType(typeof(Customer))]
[ServiceKnownType(typeof(Person))]
interface IContactManager
{...}
```

Note that you must explicitly add all levels in the data contract class hierarchy. Adding a subclass does not add its base class(es):

```
[DataContract]
class Contact
{...}

[DataContract]
class Customer : Contact
{...}

[DataContract]
class Person : Customer
{...}

[ServiceContract]
[ServiceKnownType(typeof(Customer))]
[ServiceKnownType(typeof(Person))]
interface IContactManager
{...}
```

Configuring Known Types

The main downside of the known types attributes is that they require the service or the client to know in advance about all possible subclasses the other party may want to use. Adding a new subclass necessitates changing the code, recompiling, and redeploying. To alleviate this, WCF lets you configure the known types in the service's or client's config file, as shown in Example 3-6. You need to provide not just the type name but also the full name of their containing assemblies.

Example 3-6. Known types in config file

```
<system.runtime.serialization>
   <dataContractSerializer>
      <declaredTypes>
         <add type = "Contact,Host,Version=1.0.0.0,Culture=neutral,
                                                   PublicKeyToken=null">
            <knownType type = "Customer,MyClassLibrary,Version=1.0.0.0,
                                        Culture=neutral,PublicKeyToken=null"/>
         </add>
      </declaredTypes>
   </dataContractSerializer>
</system.runtime.serialization>
```

Interestingly enough, using a config file to declare a known type is the only way to add a known type if that known type is internal to another assembly.

Object and Interfaces

The base type of a data contract class or a struct can be an interface:

```
interface IContact
{
   string FirstName
   {get;set;}
   string LastName
   {get;set;}
}
[DataContract]
class Contact : IContact
{...}
```

You can use such a base interface in your service contract or as data members in data contracts, as long as you use the ServiceKnownType attribute to designate the actual data type:

```
[ServiceContract]
[ServiceKnownType(typeof(Contact))]
interface IContactManager
{
   [OperationContract]
   void AddContact(IContact contact);

   [OperationContract]
   IContact[] GetContacts();
}
```

You cannot apply the KnownType attribute on the base interface because the interface itself will not be included in the exported metadata. Instead, the exported service contract will be object-based, and will include the data contract subclass or struct without the derivation:

```
//Imported definitions:
[DataContract]
class Contact
{...}

[ServiceContract]
public interface IContactManager
{
   [OperationContract]
   [ServiceKnownType(typeof(Contact))]
   [ServiceKnownType(typeof(object[]))]
   void AddContact(object contact);

   [OperationContract]
   [ServiceKnownType(typeof(Contact))]
```

```
    [ServiceKnownType(typeof(object[]))]
    object[] GetContacts( );
}
```

The imported definition will have the ServiceKnownType attribute always applied at the operation level, even if it was originally defined at the scope of the contract. In addition, every operation will include a union of all the ServiceKnownType attributes required by all the operations. You can manually rework the imported definition to have only the required ServiceKnownType attributes:

```
[DataContract]
class Contact
{...}

[ServiceContract]
public interface IContactManager
{
    [OperationContract]
    [ServiceKnownType(typeof(Contact))]
    void AddContact(object contact);

    [OperationContract]
    [ServiceKnownType(typeof(Contact))]
    object[] GetContacts( );
}
```

If you have the definition of the base interface on the client side, you can use that instead of object, for an added degree of type safety, as long as you add a derivation from the interface to the data contract:

```
[DataContract]
class Contact : IContact
{...}

[ServiceContract]
public interface IContactManager
{
    [OperationContract]
    [ServiceKnownType(typeof(Contact))]
    void AddContact(IContact contact);

    [OperationContract]
    [ServiceKnownType(typeof(Contact))]
    IContact[] GetContacts( );
}
```

However, you cannot replace the object in the imported contract with the concrete data contract type, because it is no longer compatible:

```
//Invalid client-side contract
[ServiceContract]
public interface IContactManager
{
```

```
    [OperationContract]
    void AddContact(Contact contact);

    [OperationContract]
    Contact[] GetContacts();
}
```

Data Contract Equivalence

Two data contracts are considered equivalent if they have the same wire representation. This can be the case when defining the same type (but not necessarily the same version of the type), or if the two data contracts refer to two different types with the same names for the contract and the members. Equivalent data contracts are interchangeable: WCF will let any service that was defined with one data contract operate on an equivalent data contract.

The most common way of defining an equivalent data contract is to use the Name property of the DataContract or DataMember attribute to map one data contract to another. In the case of the DataContract attribute, the Name property defaults to the type's name, so these two definitions are identical:

```
[DataContract]
struct Contact
{...}

[DataContract(Name = "Contact")]
struct Contact
{...}
```

In fact, the full name of the data contract always includes its namespace as well, but as you have seen, you can assign a different namespace. In the case of the DataMember attribute, the Name defaults to member name, so these two definitions are identical:

```
[DataMember]
public string FirstName;

[DataMember(Name = "FirstName")]
public string FirstName;
```

By assigning different names to the contract and the members you can generate an equivalent data contract from a different type.

For example, these two data contracts are equivalent:

```
[DataContract]
struct Contact
{
    [DataMember]
    public string FirstName;

    [DataMember]
    public string LastName;
}
```

```
[DataContract(Name = "Contact")]
struct Person
{
   [DataMember(Name = "FirstName")]
   public string Name;

   [DataMember(Name = "LastName")]
   public string Surname;
}
```

In addition to having identical names, the types of the data members have to match.

 A class and a structure that support the same data contract are inter-changeable.

Serialization Order

Equivalent data contracts must serialize and deserialize their members in the same order. The default serialization order inside a type is simply alphabetical, and across class hierarchy the order is top-down. In case of a mismatch in the serialization order, the members will be initialized to their default values. For example, when serializing a Customer instance, defined as:

```
[DataContract]
class Contact
{
   [DataMember]
   public string FirstName;

   [DataMember]
   public string LastName;
}
[DataContract]
class Customer : Contact
{
   [DataMember]
   public int CustomerNumber;
}
```

the members will be serialized in the following order: FirstName, LastName, CustomerNumber.

The problem now is that combining data contract hierarchy with aliasing contracts and members might break the serialization order. For example, the following data contract is now not equivalent to the Customer data contract:

```
[DataContract(Name = "Customer")]
public class Person
{
   [DataMember(Name = "FirstName")]
   public string Name;
```

```
    [DataMember(Name = "LastName")]
    public string Surname;

    [DataMember]
    public int CustomerNumber;
}
```

because the serialization order is CustomerNumber, FirstName, LastName. To resolve this conflict, you need to provide WCF with the order of serialization by setting the Order property of the DataMember attribute. The Order property defaults to −1, meaning the default WCF ordering, but you can assign to it values indicating the required order:

```
[DataContract(Name = "Customer")]
public class Person
{
    [DataMember(Name = "FirstName",Order = 1)]
    public string Name;

    [DataMember(Name = "LastName",Order = 2)]
    public string Surname;

    [DataMember,Order = 3)]
    public int CustomerNumber;
}
```

If another member has the same value for its Order property, WCF will order them alphabetically. You can take advantage of this by assigning the same number to all members coming from the same level in the original class hierarchy, or better yet, assign them simply their level in that hierarchy:

```
[DataContract(Name = "Customer")]
public class Person
{
    [DataMember(Name = "FirstName",Order = 1)]
    public string Name;

    [DataMember(Name = "LastName",Order = 1)]
    public string Surname;

    [DataMember,Order = 2)]
    public int CustomerNumber;
}
```

Versioning

Services should be decoupled as much as possible from their clients, especially when it comes to versioning and technologies. Any version of the client should be able to consume any version of the service, and should do so without resorting to version numbers, such as those in assemblies, because those are .NET-specific. When a service and a client share a data contract, an important objective is allowing the service and client to evolve their versions of the data contract separately. To allow such decoupling, WCF needs to enable both backward and forward compatibility, without even sharing types or version information. There are three main versioning scenarios:

- New members
- Missing members
- Round tripping, where a new version is passed to and from an old version, requiring both backward and forward compatibility

By default, data contracts are version tolerant and will silently ignore incompatibilities.

New Members

The most common change done with data contracts is adding new members on one side and sending the new contract to an old client or service. The new members will simply be ignored by `DataContractSerializer` when deserializing the type. As a result, both the service and the client can accept data with new members that were not part of original contract. For example, the service may be built against this data contract:

```
[DataContract]
struct Contact
{
   [DataMember]
   public string FirstName;

   [DataMember]
   public string LastName;
}
```

and yet the client may send it this data contract instead:

```
[DataContract]
struct Contact
{
   [DataMember]
   public string FirstName;

   [DataMember]
   public string LastName;

   [DataMember]
   public string Address;
}
```

Note that adding new members and having them ignored this way breaks the data contract schema compatibility, because a service (or a client) that is compatible with one schema is all of a sudden compatible with a new schema.

Missing Members

By default, WCF lets either party remove members from the data contract. You can serialize it without the missing members and send it to another party that expects the missing members. Although normally you are unlikely to intentionally remove members, the more common scenario is when a client is written against an old definition of the data contract, which interacts with a service written against a newer definition of that contract that expects new members. When DataContractSerializer on the receiving side does not find in the message the information required to deserialize those members, it will silently deserialize them to their default value; that is, null for a reference type and a zero whitewash for value types. It would be as if the sending party never initialized those members. This default policy enables the service to accept data with missing members, or return data with missing members to the client. Example 3-7 demonstrates this point.

Example 3-7. Missing members are initialized to their default value

```
/////////////////////////// Service Side ///////////////////////////////
[DataContract]
struct Contact
{
   [DataMember]
   public string FirstName;

   [DataMember]
   public string LastName;

   [DataMember]
   public string Address;
}

[ServiceContract]
interface IContactManager
{
   [OperationContract]
   void AddContact(Contact contact);
   ...
}

class ContactManager : IContactManager
{
   public void AddContact(Contact contact)
   {
      Trace.WriteLine("First name = " + contact.FirstName);
      Trace.WriteLine("Last name = " + contact.LastName);
      Trace.WriteLine("Address = " + (contact.Address ?? "Missing"));
      ...
   }
   ...
}
```

Example 3-7. Missing members are initialized to their default value (continued)

```
/////////////////////////// Client Side ////////////////////////////////
[DataContract]
struct Contact
{
   [DataMember]
   public string FirstName;

   [DataMember]
   public string LastName;
}

Contact contact = new Contact();
contact.FirstName = "Juval";
contact.LastName = "Lowy";

ContactManagerClient proxy = new ContactManagerClient();
proxy.AddContact(contact);

proxy.Close();
```

The output of Example 3-7 will be:

```
First name = Juval
Last name = Lowy
Address = Missing
```

because the service received `null` for the `Address` data member and coalesced the trace to `Missing`.

Using the OnDeserializing event

You can use the `OnDeserializing` event to initialize potentially missing data members based on some local heuristic. If the message contains the values, it will override your settings in the `OnDeserializing` event; if not, you will have some non-default value:

```
[DataContract]
struct Contact
{
   [DataMember]
   public string FirstName;

   [DataMember]
   public string LastName;

   [DataMember]
   public string Address;

   [OnDeserializing]
   void OnDeserializing(StreamingContext context)
   {
      Address = "Some default address";
   }
}
```

in which case the output of Example 3-7 will be:

```
First name = Juval
Last name = Lowy
Address = Some default address
```

Required members

Unlike ignoring new members, which for the most part is benign, the default handling of missing members may very likely cause the receiving side to fail further down the call chain, because the missing members may be essential for correct operation. This may have disastrous results. You can instruct WCF to avoid invoking the operation and to fail the call if a data member is missing by setting the `IsRequired` property of the `DataMember` attribute to `true`:

```
[DataContract]
struct Contact
{
   [DataMember]
   public string FirstName;

   [DataMember]
   public string LastName;

   [DataMember(IsRequired = true)]
   public string Address;
}
```

The default value of `IsRequired` is `false`; that is, to ignore the missing member. When `DataContractSerializer` on the receiving side does not find the information required to deserialize a member marked as required in the message, it will abort the call, resulting in a `NetDispatcherFaultException` on the sending side. If the data contract on the service side in Example 3-7 were to mark the `Address` member as required, the call would not have reached the service. The fact that a particular member is required is published in the service metadata and when it is imported to the client, the generated proxy file definition will include the correct setting for it.

Both the client and the service can mark some or all of the data members on their data contracts as required, completely independently of each other. The more members that are marked as required, the safer the interaction is with a service or a client, but at the expense of flexibility and versioning tolerance.

When a data contract that has a required new member is sent to a receiving party that is not even aware of that member, such a call is actually valid and will be allowed to go through. In other words, even if `IsRequired` is set to `true` on a new member by Version 2 (V2) of a data contract, you can send V2 to a party expecting Version 1 (V1) that does not even have the member in the contract. The new member will simply be ignored. `IsRequired` only has an effect when the member is missed by V2-aware parties. Assuming that V1 does not know about a new member added by V2, Table 3-1 lists the possible permutations of allowed or disallowed interactions as a product of the versions involved and the value of the IsRequired property.

Table 3-1. Versioning tolerance with required members

IsRequired	V1 to V2	V2 to V1
False	Yes	Yes
True	No	Yes

An interesting situation relying on required members is serializable types. Since serializable types have no tolerance toward missing members by default, when they are exported the resulting data contract will have all data members as required. For example, this Contact definition:

```
[Serializable]
struct Contact
{
    public string FirstName;
    public string LastName;
}
```

will have the metadata representation of:

```
[DataContract]
struct Contact
{
    [DataMember(IsRequired = true)]
    public string FirstName
    {get;set;}

    [DataMember(IsRequired = true)]
    public string LastName
    {get;set;}
}
```

In order to have the same versioning tolerance regarding missing members as with the DataContract attribute, apply the OptionalField attribute on the member. For example, this Contact definition:

```
[Serializable]
struct Contact
{
    public string FirstName;

    [OptionalField]
    public string LastName;
}
```

will have the metadata representation of:

```
[DataContract]
struct Contact
{
```

```
    [DataMember(IsRequired = true)]
    public string FirstName
    {get;set;}

    [DataMember]
    public string LastName
    {get;set;}
}
```

Versioning Round-Trip

The versioning tolerance techniques discussed so far for ignoring new members and defaulting missing ones are suboptimal. They enable a point-to-point client-to-service call but have no support for a wider-scope pass-through scenario. Consider the two interactions shown in Figure 3-4.

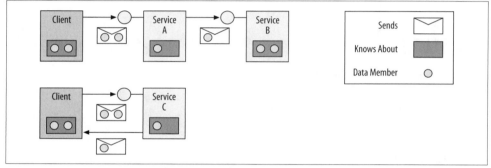

Figure 3-4. Versioning round-trip may degrade overall interaction

In the first interaction, a client that is built against a new data contract with new members is passing that data contract to Service A, which does not know about the new members. Service A then passes the data to Service B, which is aware of the new data contract. However, the data passed from Service A to Service B does not contain the new members—they were silently dropped during deserialization from the client because they were not part of the data contract for Service A. A similar situation occurs when a client that is aware of the new data contract with new members passes the data to Service C, which is aware only of the old contract that does not have the new members. If Service C returns the data to the client, the data will not have the new members.

This situation of new-old-new interaction is called *versioning round-trip*. WCF supports handling of versioning round-tripping. A service (or client) that knows about the old contract can just pass though the state of the new members without dropping them. The problem is how to serialize and deserialize the unknown members without their schema, and where to store them in between calls. The solution is to have the data contract type implement the IExtensibleDataObject interface defined as:

```
public interface IExtensibleDataObject
{
   ExtensionDataObject ExtensionData
   {get;set;}
}
```

IExtensibleDataObject defines a single property of the type ExtensionDataObject. The exact definition of ExtensionDataObject is irrelevant since developers never have to interact with it directly. ExtensionDataObject has an internal linked list of object references and type information, and that is where the unknown data members are stored. If the data contract type supports IExtensibleDataObject, then when unrecognized new members are available in the message, they are deserialized and stored in that list. When the service (or client) calls out, passing the old data contract type, which now includes the unknown data members inside ExtensionDataObject, the unknown members are serialized out into the message. If the receiving side knows about the new data contract, it will get a valid new data contract without any missing members. Example 3-8 demonstrates implementing and relying on IExtensibleDataObject. As you can see, the implementation is straightforward—just add an ExtensionDataObject property that accesses a matching member variable.

Example 3-8. Implementing IExtensibleDataObject

```
[DataContract]
class Contact : IExtensibleDataObject
{
   ExtensionDataObject m_ExtensionData;

   public ExtensionDataObject ExtensionData
   {
      get
      {
         return m_ExtensionData;
      }
      set
      {
         m_ExtensionData = value;
      }
   }

   [DataMember]
   public string FirstName;

   [DataMember]
   public string LastName;
}
```

Schema compatibility

While implementing IExtensibleDataObject enables round-tripping, it has the downside of enabling a service that is compatible with one data contract schema to interact successfully with another service that expects another data contract schema. In some esoteric cases, the service may decide to disallow round-tripping, and enforce its own version of the data contract on downstream services. The service can instruct WCF to override the handling of unknown members by IExtensibleDataObject and ignore them even if the data contract supports IExtensibleDataObject. To that end, you need to use the ServiceBehavior attribute. The next chapter will discuss behaviors and this attribute at length. For the purposes of this discussion, the ServiceBehavior attribute offers the Boolean property IgnoreExtensionDataObject, defined as:

```
[AttributeUsage(AttributeTargets.Class)]
public sealed class ServiceBehaviorAttribute : Attribute,...
{
    public bool IgnoreExtensionDataObject
    {get;set;}
    //More members
}
```

The default value of IgnoreExtensionDataObject is false. By setting it to true, all unknown data members across all data contracts used by the service will always be ignored:

```
[ServiceBehavior(IgnoreExtensionDataObject = true)]
class ContactManager : IContactManager
{...}
```

When you import a data contract using SvcUtil or Visual Studio, the generated data contract type always supports IExtensibleDataObject, even if the original data contract did not. I believe that the best practice is to always have your data contracts implement IExtensibleDataObject and to avoid setting IgnoreExtensionDataObject to true. IExtensibleDataObject decouples the service from its downstream services, allowing them to evolve separately.

 There is no need for implementing IExtensibleDataObject when dealing with known types because the subclass is always deserialized without a loss.

Enumerations

Enumerations are always serializable by definition. When you define a new enum, there is no need to apply the DataContract attribute on it, and you can freely use it in a data contract, as shown in Example 3-9. All the values in the enum will implicitly be included in the data contract.

Example 3-9. Using an enum in a data contract

```
enum ContactType
{
    Customer,
    Vendor,
    Partner
```

Example 3-9. Using an enum in a data contract (continued)

```
}

[DataContract]
struct Contact
{
   [DataMember]
   public ContactType ContactType;

   [DataMember]
   public string FirstName;

   [DataMember]
   public string LastName;
}
```

If you want to exclude certain enum values from the data contract, you need to first decorate the enum with the DataContract attribute. Then, explicitly apply the EnumMemberAttribute to all enum values you want to include in the enum data contract. The EnumMember attribute is defined as:

```
[AttributeUsage(AttributeTargets.Field,Inherited = false)]
public sealed class EnumMemberAttribute : Attribute
{
   public string Value
   {get;set;}
}
```

Any enum value not decorated with the EnumMember attribute will not be part of the data contract for that enum. For example, this enum:

```
[DataContract]
enum ContactType
{
   [EnumMember]
   Customer,

   [EnumMember]
   Vendor,

   //Will not be part of data contract
   Partner
}
```

will result in this wire representation:

```
enum ContactType
{
   Customer,
   Vendor
}
```

The other use for the EnumMember attribute is to alias certain enum values to an already existing enum data contract using the Value property. For example, this enum:

```
[DataContract]
enum ContactType
{
    [EnumMember(Value = "MyCustomer")]
    Customer,

    [EnumMember]
    Vendor,

    [EnumMember]
    Partner
}
```

will result with this wire representation:

```
enum ContactType
{
    MyCustomer,
    Vendor,
    Partner
}
```

The affect the EnumMember attribute has is local to the party using it. When publishing the metadata (or when defining it on the client side) the resulting data contract has no trace of it, and only the final product is used.

Delegates and Data Contracts

All delegate definitions are compiled into serializable classes, and so in theory your data contract types could contain delegates as member variables:

```
[DataContract]
class MyDataContract
{
    [DataMember]
    public EventHandler MyEvent;
}
```

or even as events (note the use of the field qualifier):

```
[DataContract]
class MyDataContract
{
    [field:DataMember]
    public event EventHandler MyEvent;
}
```

In practice, the imported data contract contains an invalid delegate definition when it refers to a custom delegate. While you could manually fix that definition, the bigger problem is that when you serialize an object that has a delegate member variable, the internal invocation list of the delegates is serialized too. In most cases, this is not the desired effect with services and clients, because the exact structure of the list is local to the client or the service, and should not be shared across the service boundary. In addition, there are no guaranties that the target objects in the internal list are serializable or are valid data contracts. Consequently, sometimes the serialization will work, and sometimes it will fail.

The simplest way to avoid this pitfall is not to apply the `DataMember` attribute on delegates. If the data contract is a serializable type, you need to explicitly exclude the delegate from the data contract:

```
[Serializable]
public class MyClass
{
   [NonSerialized]
   EventHandler m_MyEvent;
}
```

Data Sets and Tables

One of the most common types of data contracts exchanged between clients and services is data that originates in or is destined to a database. In .NET, the native way of interacting with databases is via ADO.NET's data set and data table types. Applications can use the raw `DataSet` and `DataTable` types, or use the data access management tools in Visual Studio to generate type-safe derivatives.

The raw `DataSet` and `DataTable` types are serializable, marked with the `Serializable` attribute:

```
[Serializable]
public class DataSet : ...
{...}

[Serializable]
public class DataTable : ...
{...}
```

This means that you can define valid service contracts that accept or return data tables or data sets:

```
[DataContract]
struct Contact
{...}

[ServiceContract]
interface IContactManager
{
   [OperationContract]
   void AddContact(Contact contact);

   [OperationContract]
```

```
    void AddContacts(DataTable contacts);

    [OperationContract]
    DataTable GetContacts( );
}
```

When importing the definition of this service contract above, the generated proxy file will contain the definition of the DataTable data contract—only the schema of DataTable, without any of the code. You can freely remove this definition from the file and reference ADO.NET instead.

You can also use the type-safe subclasses of DataSet and DataTable in your contract. For example, suppose you have a table in a database called ContactsDataTable, containing your contacts, with columns such as FirstName and LastName. You can use Visual Studio to generate a type-safe data set called MyDataSet, which has a nested class called ContactsDataTable, as well as a type-safe row and type-safe data adapter, as shown in Example 3-10.

Example 3-10. Type-safe data set and data table

```
[Serializable]
public partial class MyDataSet : DataSet
{
    public ContactsDataTable Contacts
    {get;}

    [Serializable]
    public partial class ContactsDataTable : DataTable,IEnumerable
    {
        public void AddContactsRow(ContactsRow row);
        public ContactsRow AddContactsRow(string FirstName,string LastName);
        //More members
    }

    public partial class ContactsRow : DataRow
    {
        public string FirstName
        {get;set;}

        public string LastName
        {get;set;}
        //More members
    }
    //More members
}
public partial class ContactsTableAdapter : Component
{
    public virtual MyDataSet.ContactsDataTable GetData( );
    //More members
}
```

You can use the type-safe data table in your service contract:

```
[DataContract]
struct Contact
{...}

[ServiceContract]
interface IContactManager
{
   [OperationContract]
   void AddContact(Contact contact);

   [OperationContract]
   void AddContacts(MyDataSet.ContactsDataTable contacts);

   [OperationContract]
   MyDataSet.ContactsDataTable GetContacts();
}
```

> The data row itself is not serializable, so you cannot use it (or its type-safe subclass) in operations:
> ```
> //Invalid definition
> [OperationContract]
> void AddContact(MyDataSet.ContactsRow contact);
> ```

The type-safe data table will be part of the published metadata of the service. When importing it to the client, SvcUtil and Visual Studio are smart enough to regenerate the type-safe data table, and the proxy file will include not just the data contract but the code itself. If the client already has a local definition of the type-safe table, you can remove the definition from the proxy file.

Arrays Instead of Tables

ADO.NET and the Visual Studio tools make it trivial for both a WCF client and service to use DataSet and DataTable and their type-safe derivatives. However, these data access types are specific to .NET. While they are serializable, their resulting data contract schema is so complex that trying to interact with it on other platforms is impractical. There are additional drawbacks for using a table or a data set in a service contract: you may be exposing your internal data structure to the world. Also, future changes to the database schema may affect your clients. While inside an application it may be permissible to pass the data table, sending the data table across an application or public service boundary is rarely a good idea. It is better in general to expose operations on the data as opposed to the data itself.

If you do need to pass around the data itself, it is best to do so using a neutral data structure such as an array. To streamline the task of converting a data table to an array, you can use my DataTableHelper class, defined as:

```
public static class DataTableHelper
{
```

```
    public static T[] ToArray<R,T>(DataTable table,Converter<R,T> converter)
                                                        where R : DataRow;
    }
```

All DataTableHelper requires is a converter from a data row in the table to the data contract. DataTableHelper also adds some compile-time and runtime type-safety verification. Example 3-11 demonstrates using DataTableHelper.

Example 3-11. Using DataTableHelper

```
[DataContract]
struct Contact
{
    [DataMember]
    public string FirstName;

    [DataMember]
    public string LastName;
}
[ServiceContract]
interface IContactManager
{
    [OperationContract]
    Contact[] GetContacts();
    ...
}
class ContactManager : IContactManager
{
    public Contact[] GetContacts()
    {
        ContactsTableAdapter adapter = new ContactsTableAdapter();
        MyDataSet.ContactsDataTable contactsTable = adapter.GetData();

        Converter<MyDataSet.ContactsRow,Contact> converter;
        Converter = delegate(MyDataSet.ContactsRow row)
                    {
                        Contact contact = new Contact();
                        contact.FirstName = row.FirstName;
                        contact.LastName  = row.LastName;
                        return contact;
                    };

        return DataTableHelper.ToArray(contactsTable,converter);
    }
    //Rest of the implementation
}
```

In Example 3-11, the GetContacts() method uses the type-safe table adapter ContactsTableAdapter (listed in Example 3-10) to get the records from the database in the form of the type-safe table MyDataSet.ContactsDataTable. GetContacts(), then defines an anonymous method that converts an instance of the type-safe data row MyDataSet.ContactsRow to a Contact instance. GetContacts() then calls DataTableHelper.ToArray(), providing it with the table and the converter.

Example 3-12 shows the implementation of `DataTableHelper.ToArray()`.

Example 3-12. The DataTableHelper class

```
public static class DataTableHelper
{
    public static T[] ToArray<R,T>(DataTable table,Converter<R,T> converter)
                                                        where R : DataRow
    {
        if(table.Rows.Count == 0)
        {
            return new T[]{};
        }
        //Verify [DataContract] or [Serializable] on T
        Debug.Assert(IsDataContract(typeof(T)) || typeof(T).IsSerializable);

        //Verify table contains correct rows
        Debug.Assert(MatchingTableRow<R>(table));

        return Collection.UnsafeToArray(table.Rows,converter);
    }
    static bool IsDataContract(Type type)
    {
        object[] attributes =
                    type.GetCustomAttributes(typeof(DataContractAttribute),false);
        return attributes.Length == 1;
    }
    static bool MatchingTableRow<R>(DataTable table)
    {
        if(table.Rows.Count == 0)
        {
            return true;
        }
        return table.Rows[0] is R;
    }
}
```

In essence, all `DataTableHelper.ToArray()` does is use the `myCollection` helper class to invoke the converter on every row in the table, converting every row to a single `Contact` and returning the resulted array. `DataTableHelper` adds some type safety. At compile time, it places constraints on the type parameter R to be a data row. At runtime, the `ToArray()` method returns an empty array if the table is empty. It verifies that the type parameter T is decorated either with the `DataContract` attribute or the `Serializable` attribute. Verifying the `DataContract` attribute is done via the helper method `IsDataContract()`, which uses reflection to look up the attribute. Verifying the `Serializable` attribute is done by checking whether the `IsSerializable` bit is set on the type. The last verification done by `ToArray()` is to ensure that the provided table has the rows specified with the type parameter R. This is done via the `MatchingTableRow()` helper method, which gets the first row and verifies its type.

Generics

You cannot define WCF contracts that rely on generic type parameters. Generics are specific to .NET, and using them would violate the service-oriented nature of WCF. However, you can use bounded generic types in your data contracts, as long as you specify the type parameters in the service contract and as long as the specified type parameters have valid data contracts, as shown in Example 3-13.

Example 3-13. Using bounded generic types

```
[DataContract]
class MyClass<T>
{
   [DataMember]
   public T m_MyMember;
}

[ServiceContract]
interface IMyContract
{
   [OperationContract]
   void MyMethod(MyClass<int> obj);
}
```

When you import the metadata of a data contract such as the one in Example 3-13, the imported types have all type parameters replaced with specific types, and the data contract itself is renamed to:

```
<Original name>Of<Type parameter names><hash>
```

Using the same definitions as in Example 3-13, the imported data contract and service contract will look like this:

```
[DataContract]
class MyClassOfint
{
   int MyMemberField;

   [DataMember]
   public int  MyMember
   {
      get
      {
         return MyMemberField;
      }
      set
      {
         MyMemberField = value;
      }
   }
}

[ServiceContract]
interface IMyContract
```

```
{
    [OperationContract]
    void MyMethod(MyClassOfint obj);
}
```

If instead of the int the service contract were to use a custom type such as SomeClass:

```
[DataContract]
class SomeClass
{...}

[DataContract]
class MyClass<T>
{...}

[OperationContract]
void MyMethod(MyClass<SomeClass> obj);
```

then the exported data contract may look like this:

```
[DataContract]
class SomeClass
{...}

[DataContract]
class MyClassOfSomeClassMTRdqN6P
{...}

[OperationContract(...)]
void MyMethod(MyClassOfSomeClassMTRdqN6P obj);
```

Where MTRdqN6P is some quasi-unique hash of the generic type parameter and the containing namespace. Different data contracts and namespaces will generate different hashes. The hash is in place to reduce the overall potential for a conflict with another data contract that might use another type parameter with the same name. No hash is created for the implicit data contracts of the primitives when they are used as generic type parameters.

In most cases the hash is a cumbersome overprecaution. You can specify a different name for the exported data contract by simply assigning it to the Name property of the data contract. For example, given this service-side data contract:

```
[DataContract]
class SomeClass
{...}

[DataContract(Name = "MyClass")]
class MyClass<T>
{...}

[OperationContract]
void MyMethod(MyClass<SomeClass> obj);
```

the exported data contract will be:

```
[DataContract]
class SomeClass
{...}

[DataContract]
class MyClass
{...}

[OperationContract]
void MyMethod(MyClass obj);
```

If you would still like to combine the name of the generic type parameter with that of the data contract, use the {<number>} directive, where the number is the ordinal number of the type parameter. For example, given this service-side definition:

```
[DataContract]
class SomeClass
{...}

[DataContract(Name = "MyClassOf{0}{1}")]
class MyClass<T,U>
{...}

[OperationContract]
void MyMethod(MyClass<SomeClass,int> obj);
```

the exported definition will be:

```
[DataContract]
class SomeClass
{...}

[DataContract]
class MyClassOfSomeClassint
{...}

[OperationContract(...)]
void MyMethod(MyClassOfSomeClassint obj);
```

The number of type parameters specified is not verified at compile time. Any mismatch will yield a runtime exception.

Finally, you can append # after the number to generate the unique hash. For example, given this data contract definition:

```
[DataContract]
class SomeClass
{...}

[DataContract(Name = "MyClassOf{0}{#}")]
class MyClass<T>
{...}
```

```
[OperationContract]
void MyMethod(MyClass<SomeClass> obj);
```

the exported definition will be:

```
[DataContract]
class SomeClass
{...}

[DataContract]
class MyClassOfSomeClassMTRdqN6P
{...}

[OperationContract]
void MyMethod(MyClassOfSomeClassMTRdqN6P obj);
```

Collections

In .NET, a collection is any type that supports the IEnumerable or IEnumerable<T>
interfaces. All of the built-in collections in .NET, such as the array, the list, and the
stack support these interfaces. A data contract can include a collection as a data
member, or a service contract can define operations that interact with a collection
directly. Because .NET collections are .NET-specific, WCF cannot expose them in
the service metadata, yet because they are so useful, WCF offers dedicated marshaling rules for collections.

Whenever you're defining a service operation that uses any of the following collection interfaces: IEnumerable<T>, IList<T>, and ICollection<T>, the wire representation always uses an array. For example, this service contract definition and
implementation:

```
[ServiceContract]
interface IContactManager
{
   [OperationContract]
   IEnumerable<Contact> GetContacts();
   ...
}
class ContactManager : IContactManager
{
   List<Contact> m_Contacts = new List<Contact>();

   public IEnumerable<Contact> GetContacts()
   {
      return m_Contacts;
   }
   ...
}
```

will be exported as:

```
[ServiceContract]
interface IContactManager
```

```
    {
        [OperationContract]
        Contact[] GetContacts();
    }
```

Concrete Collections

If the collection in the contract is a concrete collection (not an interface), and is a
serializable collection—that is, it is marked with the `Serializable` attribute but not
with the `DataContract` attribute—WCF can normalize the collection automatically to
an array of the collection's type, provided the collection contains an `Add()` method
with either one of these signatures:

```
public void Add(object obj); //Collection uses IEnumerable
public void Add(T item);     //Collection uses IEnumerable<T>
```

For example, consider this contract definition:

```
[ServiceContract]
interface IContactManager
{
    [OperationContract]
    void AddContact(Contact contact);

    [OperationContract]
    List<Contact> GetContacts();
}
```

The list class is defined as:

```
public interface ICollection<T> : IEnumerable<T>
{...}
public interface IList<T> : ICollection<T>
{...}
[Serializable]
public class List<T> : IList<T>
{
    public void Add(T item);
    //More members
}
```

Because it is a valid collection and it has an `Add()` method, the resulting wire representation of the contract will be:

```
[ServiceContract]
interface IContactManager
{
    [OperationContract]
    void AddContact(Contact contact);

    [OperationContract]
    Contact[] GetContacts();
}
```

That is, the List<Contacts> is marshaled as a Contact[]. The service may still return a List<Contacts>, and yet the client will interact with an array, as shown in Example 3-14.

Example 3-14. Marshaling a list as an array

```
//////////////////////////// Service Side ////////////////////////////
[ServiceContract]
interface IContactManager
{
   [OperationContract]
   void AddContact(Contact contact);

   [OperationContract]
   List<Contact> GetContacts();
}
//Service implementation
class ContactManager : IContactManager
{
   List<Contact> m_Contacts = new List<Contact>();

   public void AddContact(Contact contact)
   {
      m_Contacts.Add(contact);
   }

   public List<Contact> GetContacts()
   {
      return m_Contacts;
   }
}
//////////////////////////// Client Side ////////////////////////////
[ServiceContract]
interface IContactManager
{
   [OperationContract]
   void AddContact(Contact contact);

   [OperationContract]
   Contact[] GetContacts();
}
public partial class ContactManagerClient : ClientBase<IContactManager>,
                                                         IContactManager
{
   public Contact[] GetContacts()
   {
      return Channel.GetContacts();
   }
}
//Client code
ContactManagerClient proxy = new ContactManagerClient();
Contact[] contacts = proxy.GetContacts();
proxy.Close();
```

Note that while the collection must have the Add( ) method for it to be marshaled as an array, the collection need not implement the Add( ) method at all.

Custom Collections

The ability to automatically marshal a collection as an array is not limited to the built-in collections. Any custom collection can abide by the same prerequisites and be marshaled as an array, as shown in Example 3-15. In the example, the collection MyCollection<string> is marshaled as a string[ ].

Example 3-15. Marshaling a custom collection as an array

```
///////////////////////// Service Side /////////////////////////////
[Serializable]
public class MyCollection<T> : IEnumerable<T>
{
   public void Add(T item)
   {}

   IEnumerator<T>  IEnumerable<T>.GetEnumerator( )
   {...}
   //Rest of the implementation
}
[ServiceContract]
interface IMyContract
{
   [OperationContract]
   MyCollection<string> GetCollection( );
}


///////////////////////// Client Side /////////////////////////////
[ServiceContract]
interface IMyContract
{
   [OperationContract]
   string[] GetCollection( );
}
```

Collection Data Contract

The mechanism shown so far for marshaling a concrete collection is suboptimal. First, it requires the collection to be serializable, and does not work with the service-oriented DataContract attribute. While one party is dealing with a collection, the other is dealing with an array. The two are not semantically equivalent—the collection is likely to offer some advantages, or it would not have been used in the first place. There is no compile-time or run-time verification of the presence of the Add( ) method or the IEnumerable and IEnumerable<T> interfaces, resulting in an unworkable data contract if they are missing. The solution is yet another dedicated attribute called CollectionDataContractAttribute, defined as:

```
[AttributeUsage(AttributeTargets.Struct|AttributeTargets.Class,Inherited = false)]
public sealed class CollectionDataContractAttribute : Attribute
{
   public string Name
   {get;set;}
   public string Namespace
   {get;set;}
   //More members
}
```

CollectionDataContract attribute is analogous to the DataContract attribute, and it does not make the collection serializable. When applied on a collection, the CollectionDataContract attribute exposes the collection to the client as a generic linked list. While the linked list may have nothing to do with the original collection, it does offer a more collection-like interface than an array.

For example, given this collection definition:

```
[CollectionDataContract(Name = "MyCollectionOf{0}")]
public class MyCollection<T> : IEnumerable<T>
{
   public void Add(T item)
   {}

   IEnumerator<T>  IEnumerable<T>.GetEnumerator()
   {...}
   //Rest of the implementation
}
```

and this service-side contract definition:

```
[ServiceContract]
interface IContactManager
{
   [OperationContract]
   void AddContact(Contact contact);

   [OperationContract]
   MyCollection<Contact> GetContacts();
}
```

the definitions the client ends up with after importing the metadata will be:

```
[CollectionDataContract]
public class MyCollectionOfContact : List<Contact>
{}

[ServiceContract]
interface IContactManager
{
   [OperationContract]
   void AddContact(Contact contact);

   [OperationContract]
   MyCollectionOfContact GetContacts();
}
```

In addition, the CollectionDataContract attribute verifies at the service load time the presence of the Add( ) method as well as IEnumerable or IEnumerable<T>. Failing to have these on the collection will result in an InvalidDataContractException.

Note that you cannot apply both the DataContract attribute and CollectionDataContract attribute on the collection, and again this is verified at the service load time.

Referencing the Collection

WCF can even let you preserve the same collection on the client side as on the service side. The SvcUtil utility offers the /collectionType switch (or /ct for short), allowing you to reference a particular collection assembly on the client side and have it be used in the contract definition. You need to specify the location of the collection assembly, and the assembly must of course be available to the client.

For example, the service could define the following contract that makes use of the Stack<T> collection:

```
[ServiceContract]
interface IContactManager
{
   [OperationContract]
   void AddContact(Contact contact);

   [OperationContract]
   Stack<Contact> GetContacts( );
}
```

The client points SvcUtil at the service metadata exchange address (such as *http:// localhost:8000*), uses the /r switch to reference the *System.dll* assembly containing the Stack<t> class, and the /ct switch to indicate it wants to preserve the original collection:

```
SvcUtil http://localhost:8000/
        /r:C:\WINDOWS\Microsoft.NET\Framework\v2.0.50727\System.dll
        /ct:System.Collections.Generic.Stack`1
```

The resulting client-side contract definition will be using Stack<t>:

```
[ServiceContract]
interface IContactManager
{
   [OperationContract]
   void AddContact(Contact contact);

   [OperationContract]
   Stack<Contact> GetContacts( );
}
```

Obviously, the use of /rct switch is not very service-oriented. It requires intimate knowledge beforehand of the collection used, and it works only in WCF-to-WCF interactions.

Client-Side Collection

Interacting with collections so far was discussed in the context of the service defining and using a collection, while letting the client interact with either an array or a list. As it turns out, it can actually work the other way around: the service can be defined in terms of an array, and the client can use a compatible collection.

For example, consider this service contract definition:

```
[ServiceContract]
interface IMyContract
{
   [OperationContract]
   void ProcessArray(string[] array);
}
```

By default, the imported service and proxy definitions will be identical. However, the client can manually rework the contract and the proxy to use any collection interface:

```
//Reworked definition:
[ServiceContract]
interface IMyContract
{
   [OperationContract]
   void ProcessArray(IList<string> list);
}
```

and supply at call time a collection with the Add( ) method (serializable or with the CollectionDataContract attribute):

```
IList<string> list = new List<string>();
MyContractClient proxy = new MyContractClient( );
proxy.ProcessArray(list);
proxy.Close( );
```

C# Iterators

The iterators[*] feature of C# 2.0 lets you rely on the compiler to generate the implementation of a custom iterator on a collection. However, that implementation is done on a nested class that is not marked with the Serializable attribute. Consequently, you cannot return that collection directly from a service method:

```
[ServiceContract]
interface IContactManager
```

---

[*] If you are unfamiliar with C# 2.0 iterators, see my *MSDN Magazine* article "Create Elegant Code with Anonymous Methods, Iterators, and Partial Classes," May 2004.

```
{
   [OperationContract]
   IEnumerable<Contact> GetContacts();
   ...
}
class ContactManager : IContactManager
{
   List<Contact> m_Contacts = new List<Contact>();

   //Invalid implementation
   public IEnumerable<Contact> GetContacts()
   {
      foreach(Contact contact in m_Contacts)
      {
         yield return contact;
      }
   }
   ...
}
```

> In the next release of C# (along with the rest of .NET 3.5) the compiler will add the Serializable attribute to the nested class generated by the yield return statement, thus enabling returning an iterator directly from a service method.

Dictionaries

Dictionaries are a special type of a collection that maps one data contract type to another. As such, they do not fit well either as an array or as a list. Not surprisingly, dictionaries get their own representation in WCF.

If the dictionary is a serializable collection that supports the IDictionary interface, then it will be exposed as a Dictionary<object,object>. For example, this service contract definition:

```
[Serializable]
public class MyDictionary : IDictionary
{...}

[ServiceContract]
interface IContactManager
{
   ...
   [OperationContract]
   MyDictionary GetContacts();
}
```

will be exposed as this definition:

```
[ServiceContract]
interface IContactManager
{
   ...
```

```
    [OperationContract]
    Dictionary<object,object> GetContacts( );
}
```

This, by the way, includes using the HashTable collection.

If the serializable collection supports the IDictionary<K,T> interface, such as:

```
[Serializable]
public class MyDictionary<K,T> : IDictionary<K,T>
{...}

[ServiceContract]
interface IContactManager
{
    ...
    [OperationContract]
    MyDictionary<int,Contact> GetContacts( );
}
```

then its wire representation will be as a Dictionary<K,T>:

```
[ServiceContract]
interface IContactManager
{
    ...
    [OperationContract]
    Dictionary<int,Contact> GetContacts( );
}
```

This includes making direct use of the Dictionary<K,T> in the original definition.

If instead of a mere serializable collection the dictionary is decorated with the CollectionDataContract, it will be marshaled as a subclass of the respective representation. For example, this service contract definition:

```
[CollectionDataContract]
public class MyDictionary : IDictionary
{...}

[ServiceContract]
interface IContactManager
{
    ...
    [OperationContract]
    MyDictionary GetContacts( );
}
```

will have this wire representation:

```
[CollectionDataContract]
public class MyDictionary : Dictionary<object,object>
{}

[ServiceContract]
```

```
interface IContactManager
{
    ...
    [OperationContract]
    MyDictionary GetContacts( );
}
```

while this generic collection:

```
[CollectionDataContract]
public class MyDictionary<K,T> : IDictionary<K,T>
{...}

[ServiceContract]
interface IContactManager
{
    ...
    [OperationContract]
    MyDictionary<int,Contact> GetContacts( );
}
```

will be published in the metadata as:

```
[CollectionDataContract]
public class MyDictionary : Dictionary<int,Contact>
{}

[ServiceContract]
interface IContactManager
{
    ...
    [OperationContract]
    MyDictionary GetContacts( );
}
```

CHAPTER 4

Instance Management

Instance management is the name for a set of techniques used by WCF to bind client requests to service instances, governing which service instance handles which client request. You need instance management because applications differ too much in their needs for scalability, performance, throughput, transactions, and queued calls. When it comes to those needs, there simply isn't a one-size-fits-all solution. However, there are a few canonical instance management techniques that are applicable across the range of applications, thus enabling a wide variety of scenarios and programming models. These techniques are the subject of this chapter, and understanding them is essential to developing scalable and consistent service-oriented applications. WCF supports three types of instance activation: *per-call services* allocate (and destroy) a new service instance per client request. *Sessionful services* allocate a service instance per client connection. Finally, with a *singleton service*, all clients share the same service instance across all connections and activations. This chapter provides the rationale for each of the instance management modes; offers guidelines on when and how to best use them; and also addresses some related topics such as behaviors, contexts, demarcating operations, instance deactivation, and throttling.[*]

Behaviors

By and large, the service instance mode is strictly a service-side implementation detail that should not manifest itself on the client side in any way. To support that and a few other local service-side aspects, WCF defines the notion of behaviors. A *behavior* is a local attribute of a service that does not affect its communication patterns. Clients should be unaware of behaviors, and behaviors do not manifest themselves in the service's binding or published metadata. WCF defines two types of service-side

---

[*] This chapter contains excerpts from my article "WCF Essentials: Discover Mighty Instance Management Techniques for Developing WCF Apps," *MSDN Magazine*, June 2006.

behaviors governed by two corresponding attributes: the `ServiceBehaviorAttribute` is used to configure *service behaviors*; that is, behaviors that affect all endpoints (all contracts and operations) of the service. The `ServiceBehavior` attribute is applied directly on the service implementation class. In the context of this chapter, the `ServiceBehavior` attribute is used to configure the service instance mode. As shown in Example 4-1, the attribute defines the `InstanceContextMode` property of the enum type `InstanceContextMode`. The value of the `InstanceContextMode` enum controls which instance mode is used for the service.

Example 4-1. The ServiceBehaviorAttribute used to configure instance context mode

```
public enum InstanceContextMode
{
   PerCall,
   PerSession,
   Single
}
[AttributeUsage(AttributeTargets.Class)]
public sealed class ServiceBehaviorAttribute : Attribute,...
{
   public InstanceContextMode InstanceContextMode
   {get;set;}
   //More members
}
```

The `OperationBehaviorAttribute` is used to configure *operation behaviors*, that is, a behaviors that affect a particular operation's implementation only. The `OperationBehavior` attribute can be applied only on a method that implements a contract operation, never on the operation definition in the contract itself. You will see the use of the `OperationBehavior` later on in this chapter and in subsequent chapters as well.

Per-Call Services

When the service type is configured for *per-call activation*, a service instance (the CLR object) exists only while a client call is in progress. Every client request (that is, a method call on the WCF contract) gets a new dedicated service instance. The following list details how per call activation works; its steps are illustrated in Figure 4-1.

1. The client calls the proxy and the proxy forwards the call to the service.
2. WCF creates a service instance and calls the method on it.
3. When the method call returns, if the object implements `IDisposable`, WCF calls `IDisposable.Dispose( )` on it.
4. The client calls the proxy and the proxy forwards the call to the service.
5. WCF creates an object and calls the method on it.

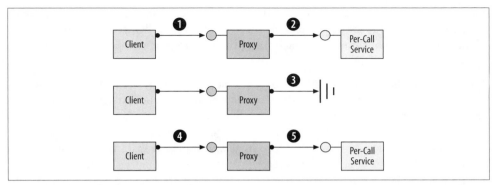

Figure 4-1. Per-call instantiation mode

Disposing of the service instance is an interesting point. As I just mentioned, if the service supports the IDisposable interface, WCF will automatically call the Dispose( ) method, allowing the service to perform any required cleanup. Note that Dispose( ) is called on the same thread that dispatched the original method call, and that Dispose( ) has an operation context (presented later on). Once Dispose( ) is called, WCF disconnects the instance from the rest of the WCF infrastructure, making it a candidate for garbage collection.

Benefits of Per-Call Services

In the classic client-server programming model, using languages such as C++ or C#. every client gets its own dedicated server object. The fundamental problem with this approach is that it doesn't scale well. The server object may hold expensive or scarce resources such as database connections, communication ports, or files. Imagine an application that has to serve many clients. Typically, these clients create the objects they need when the client application starts and dispose of them when the client application shuts down. What impedes scalability with the client-server model is that the client applications can hold onto objects for long periods of time, while actually using the objects for only a fraction of that time. If you allocate an object for each client, you will tie up such crucial or limited resources for long periods and will eventually run out of resources.

A better activation model is to allocate an object for a client only while a call is in progress from the client to the service. That way, you have to create and maintain in memory only as many objects as there are concurrent calls, not as many objects as there are outstanding clients. In a typical Enterprise system only 1 percent of all clients make concurrent calls (a high-load Enterprise system has 3 percent of concurrent calls). If your system can concurrently sustain only 100 expensive service instances, this means it can typically serve as many as 10,000 outstanding clients. This is exactly what the per-call instance activation mode offers, because in between calls the client holds a reference on a proxy that doesn't have an actual object at the end of the wire. The obvious benefit of that is the fact that you can now dispose of the expensive resources the service instance occupies long before the client disposes of the proxy. By that same token, acquiring the resources is postponed until they are actually needed by a client.

Keep in mind that creating and destroying a service instance repeatedly on the service side without tearing down the connection to the client (with its client-side proxy) is a lot cheaper than creating an instance and a connection. The second benefit is that forcing the service instance to reallocate or connect to its resources on every call caters very well to transactional resources and transactional programming as discussed in Chapter 7, because it eases the task of enforcing consistency with the instance state. The third benefit of per-call services is that they can be used in conjunction with queued disconnected calls as described in Chapter 9, because they allow easy mapping of service instances to discrete queued messages.

Configuring Per-Call Services

To configure a service type as a per-call service, you apply the ServiceBehavior attribute with the InstanceContextMode property set to InstanceContextMode.PerCall:

```
[ServiceContract]
interface IMyContract
{...}

[ServiceBehavior(InstanceContextMode = InstanceContextMode.PerCall)]
class MyService : IMyContract
{...}
```

Example 4-2 lists a simple per-call service and its client. As you can see from the program output, for each client method call a new service instance is constructed.

Example 4-2. Per-call service and client

```
///////////////////////// Service code /////////////////////
[ServiceContract]
interface IMyContract
{
   [OperationContract]
   void MyMethod( );
}
[ServiceBehavior(InstanceContextMode = InstanceContextMode.PerCall)]
class MyService : IMyContract,IDisposable
{
   int m_Counter = 0;

   MyService( )
   {
      Trace.WriteLine("MyService.MyService( )");
   }
   public void MyMethod( )
   {
```

Example 4-2. Per-call service and client (continued)

```
        m_Counter++;
        Trace.WriteLine("Counter = " + m_Counter);
    }
    public void Dispose( )
    {
        Trace.WriteLine("MyService.Dispose( )");
    }
}
/////////////////////////// Client code ///////////////////////
MyContractClient proxy = new MyContractClient( );

proxy.MyMethod( );
proxy.MyMethod( );

proxy.Close( );

//Possible Output
MyService.MyService( )
Counter = 1
MyService.Dispose( )
MyService.MyService( )
Counter = 1
MyService.Dispose( )
```

Designing Per-Call Services

Although in theory you can use per-call instance activation mode on any service type, in practice you need to design the service and its contracts to support the per-call activation mode from the ground up. The main problem is that the client doesn't know it's getting a new instance each time. Per-call services must be *state-aware*; that is, they must proactively manage their state, giving the client the illusion of a continuous session. A state-aware service isn't the same as a stateless service. In fact, if the per-call service were truly stateless, there would be no need for per-call activation in the first place. It is precisely because it has state, and an expensive state at that, that you need the per-call mode. An instance of a per-call service is created just before every method call and is destroyed immediately after each call. Therefore, at the beginning of each call, the object should initialize its state from values saved in some storage, and at the end of the call it should return its state to the storage. Such storage is typically either a database or the filesystem, but it can be a volatile storage like static variables.

Not all of the object's state can be saved as is, however. For example, if the state contains a database connection, the object must reacquire the connection at construction or at the beginning of every call (or at the constructor) and dispose of the connection at the end of the call or in its implementation of IDisposable.Dispose( ). Using per-call instance mode has one important implication for operation design: every operation must include a parameter to identify the service instance whose state needs to be retrieved. The instance uses that parameter to get its state from the storage and not the state of another instance of the same type. Examples for such parameters are the account number for bank account service, the order number for services processing orders, and so on. Example 4-3 shows a template for implementing a per-call service.

Example 4-3. Implementing a per-call service

```
[DataContract]
class Param
{...}

[ServiceContract]
interface IMyContract
{
   [OperationContract]
   void MyMethod(Param stateIdentifier);
}
[ServiceBehavior(InstanceContextMode = InstanceContextMode.PerCall)]
class MyPerCallService : IMyContract,IDisposable
{
   public void MyMethod(Param stateIdentifier)
   {
      GetState(stateIdentifier);
      DoWork();
      SaveState(stateIdentifier);
   }
   void GetState(Param stateIdentifier)
   {...}
   void DoWork()
   {...}
   void SaveState(Param stateIdentifier)
   {...}
   public void Dispose()
   {...}
}
```

The class implements the MyMethod( ) operation, which accepts a parameter of type Param (a pseudotype invented for this example) that identifies the instance:

```
   public void MyMethod(Param stateIdentifier);
```

The instance then uses the identifier to retrieve its state and to save the state back at the end of the method call. Any piece of state that is common to all clients can be allocated at the constructor and disposed of in Dispose( ).

Also, the per-call activation mode works best when the amount of work to be done in each method call is finite, and there are no more activities to complete in the background once a method returns. For this reason, you should not spin off background threads or dispatch asynchronous calls back into the instance, because the object will be discarded once the method returns. Because the per-call service retrieves its state from some storage in every method call, per-call services work very well in conjunction with a load-balancing machine, as long as the state repository is some global resource accessible to all machines. The load balancer can redirect calls to different machines at will, knowing that each per-call service can execute the call after retrieving its state.

Per-call and performance

Per-call services clearly offer a trade-off in performance (the overhead of reconstructing the instance state on each method call) with scalability (holding on to the state and the resources it ties in). There are no hard-and-fast rules as to when and to what extent you should trade some performance for a lot of scalability. You may need to profile your system and ultimately design some services to use per-call activation and some not to use it.

Cleanup operations

Whether or not the service type supports IDisposable is of no relevance to the client and is an implementation detail. In fact, the client has of course no way of calling the Dispose( ) method anyway. When you design a contract for a per-call service, avoid defining operations that are dedicated for state or resource cleanup, like this:

```
//Avoid
[ServiceContract]
interface IMyContract
{
   void DoSomething( );
   void Cleanup( );
}
[ServiceBehavior(InstanceContextMode = InstanceContextMode.PerCall)]
class MyPerCallService : IMyContract,IDisposable
{
   public void DoSomething( )
   {...}
   public void Cleanup( )
   {...}
   public void Dispose( )
   {
      Cleanup( );
   }
}
```

The folly of such as design is obvious: if the client does call the cleanup method, it has the detrimental effect of creating an object just so the client can call Cleanup( ) on it, followed by a call to IDisposable.Dispose( ) (if present) by WCF for doing the cleanup again.

Choosing Per-Call Services

While the programming model of per-call services looks somewhat alien to client/server developers, per-call services are actually the preferred instance management mode for WCF services. The first argument in favor of per-call services is that they simply scale better. When designing a service, my golden rule for scalability is 10X. That is, every service should be designed to handle a load at least an order of magnitude greater that what its requirements call for. The reason for this is that in every other engineering discipline, engineers never design a system to handle its exact nominal specified load. You would not want to enter a building whose beams support exactly the load they were required to handle, ride in an elevator whose cable can handle exactly six passengers as stated on the elevator, and so on. Software systems are no different—why design a system for the specific current load while every other person in the company is working to increase business and the implied load? You should design software system to last years and sustain current and future loads. As a result, when using the 10X golden rule, you very quickly end up needing the scalability of the per-call service. The second argument in favor of per-call services is transactions. As you will see in Chapter 7, transactions are absolutely essential in any system, and per-call services lend themselves very well for the transactional programming model, regardless of the system load.

Per-Session Services

WCF can maintain a session between a client and a particular service instance. When the client creates a new proxy to a service configured as a *sessionful service*, the client gets a new dedicated service instance that is independent of all other instances of the same service. That instance will remain in service usually until the client no longer needs it. This activation mode is very much like the classic client-server model. This mode is also sometimes referred to as *private sessions*. Each private session uniquely binds a proxy and its set of client- and service-side channels to a particular service instance (actually to its context, as discussed later on).

Because the service instance remains in memory throughout the session, it can maintain state in memory, and the programming model is very much like that of the classic client/server. Consequently, it also suffers from the same scalability and transaction issues as the classic client/server model. A service configured for private sessions cannot typically support more than a few dozen (or perhaps up to a hundred or two) outstanding clients due to the cost associated with each such dedicated service instance.

 The client session is per service endpoint per proxy. If the client creates another proxy to the same or a different endpoint, that second proxy will be associated with a new instance and session.

Configuring Private Sessions

Supporting a session has three elements to it—behavior, binding, and contract. The behavior part is required so that WCF will keep the service instance alive throughout the session and to direct the client messages to it. This local behavior facet is achieved by setting the `InstanceContextMode` property of the `ServiceBehavior` attribute to `InstanceContextMode.PerSession`:

```
[ServiceBehavior(InstanceContextMode = InstanceContextMode.PerSession)]
class MyService : IMyContract
{...}
```

Since `InstanceContextMode.PerSession` is the default value of the `InstanceContextMode` property, these definitions are equivalent:

```
class MyService : IMyContract
{...}

[ServiceBehavior]
class MyService : IMyContract
{...}

[ServiceBehavior(InstanceContextMode = InstanceContextMode.PerSession)]
class MyService : IMyContract
{...}
```

The session typically terminates when the client closes the proxy. This causes the proxy to notify the service that the session has ended. If the service supports `IDisposable`, then the `Dispose()` method will be called asynchronously to the client. However, `Disposed()` will be called on a worker thread without an operation context.

In order to correlate all messages from a particular client to a particular instance, WCF needs to be able to identify the client. One way of doing that is to rely on a *transport-level session*; that is, a continuous connection at the transport level, such as the one maintained by the TCP and IPC protocols. As a result, when using the `NetTcpBinding` or the `NetNamedPipeBinding`, WCF associates that connection with the client. The situation is more complex when it comes to the connectionless nature of the HTTP protocol. Conceptually, each message over HTTP reaches the services on a new connection. Consequently, you cannot maintain a transport-level session over the `BasicHttpBinding`. The WS binding, on the other hand, is capable of emulating a transport-level session by including a logical session ID in the message headers that uniquely identifies the client. In fact, the `WSHttpBinding` will emulate a transport session whenever security or reliable messaging is enabled.

The contractual element is required across the service boundary because the client-side WCF runtime needs to know it should use a session. The `ServiceContract` attribute offers the property `SessionMode` of the enum type `SessionMode`:

```
public enum SessionMode
{
```

```
    Allowed,
    Required,
    NotAllowed
}
[AttributeUsage(AttributeTargets.Interface|AttributeTargets.Class,
                Inherited=false)]
public sealed class ServiceContractAttribute : Attribute
{
    public SessionMode SessionMode
    {get;set;}
    //More members
}
```

SessionMode defaults to SessionMode.Allowed. The configured SessionMode value is included in the service metadata and is reflected correctly when the client imports the contract metadata.

SessionMode.Allowed

SessionMode.Allowed is the default value of the property, so these definitions are equivalent:

```
[ServiceContract]
interface IMyContract
{...}

[ServiceContract(SessionMode = SessionMode.Allowed)]
interface IMyContract
{...}
```

All bindings support configuring the contract on the endpoint with SessionMode. Allowed. The SessionMode property does not refer to the instancing mode, but rather to the presence of a transport-level session (or its emulation in the case of the WS bindings). As its name implies, when the SessionMode property is configured with SessionMode.Allowed, it merely allows transport sessions, but does not enforce it. The exact resulting behavior is a product of the service configuration and the binding used. If the service is configured for per-call, it still behaves as per-call service, as is the case in Example 4-2. When the service is configured for a per-session service, it will behave as a per-session service only if the binding used maintains a transport-level session. For example, the BasicHttpBinding can never have a transport-level session due to the connectionless nature of the HTTP protocol. The WSHttpBinding without security and without reliable messaging will also not maintain a transport-level session. In both of these cases, even though the service is configured with InstanceContextMode.PerSession and the contract with SessionMode.Allowed, the service will behave as a per-call service, and the calls to Dispose() are asynchronous; that is, the client is not blocked after the call while WCF disposes of the instance.

However, if you use the WSHttpBinding with security (its default configuration) or with reliable messaging, or the NetTcpBinding, or the NetNamedPipeBinding, then the service will behave as a per-session service. For example, assuming use of the NetTcpBinding, this service behaves as sessionful:

```
[ServiceContract]
interface IMyContract
{...}

class MyService : IMyContract
{...}
```

Note that the previous code snippet simply takes the default of both the SessionMode and the InstanceContextMode properties.

SessionMode.Required

The SessionMode.Required value mandates the use of a transport-level session, but not necessarily an application-level session. You cannot have a contract configured with SessionMode.Required with a service's endpoint whose binding does not maintain a transport-level session, and this constraint is verified at the service load time. However, you can still configure the service to be a per-call service, and the service instance will be created and destroyed on each client call. Only if the service is configured as a sessionful service will the service instance persist throughout the client's session:

```
[ServiceContract(SessionMode = SessionMode.Required)]
interface IMyContract
{...}

class MyService : IMyContract
{...}
```

 When designing a sessionful contract, I recommend explicitly using SessionMode.Required and not relying on the default of SessionMode.Allowed. The rest of the code samples in this book actively apply SessionMode.Required when sessionful interaction is by design.

Example 4-4 lists the same service and client as in Example 4-2, except the contract and service are configured to require a private session. As you can see from the output, the client got a dedicated instance.

Example 4-4. Per-session service and client

```
//////////////////////////// Service code ////////////////////////////
[ServiceContract(SessionMode = SessionMode.Required)]
interface IMyContract
{
    [OperationContract]
    void MyMethod( );
}
class MyService : IMyContract,IDisposable
{
    int m_Counter = 0;
```

Example 4-4. Per-session service and client (continued)

```
   MyService( )
   {
      Trace.WriteLine("MyService.MyService( )");
   }
   public void MyMethod( )
   {
      m_Counter++;
      Trace.WriteLine("Counter = " + m_Counter);
   }
   public void Dispose( )
   {
      Trace.WriteLine("MyService.Dispose( )");
   }
}
////////////////////////// Client code //////////////////////
MyContractClient proxy = new MyContractClient( );

proxy.MyMethod( );
proxy.MyMethod( );

proxy.Close( );

//Output
MyService.MyService( )
Counter = 1
Counter = 2
MyService.Dispose( )
```

SessionMode.NotAllowed

SessionMode.NotAllowed disallows the use of a transport-level session, which precludes an application-level session. Regardless of the service configuration, it always behaves as a per-call service. If the service implements IDisposable, then Dispose( ) will be called asynchronously toward the client; that is, control will return to the client, and in the background (on the incoming call thread) WCF will call Dispose( ). Since both the TCP and IPC protocols maintain a session at the transport level, you cannot configure a service endpoint to expose a contract marked with SessionMode. NotAllowed that uses the NetTcpBinding or the NetNamedPipeBinding, and this is verified at the service load time. However, the use of the WSHttpBinding with an emulated transport session is still allowed. In the interest of readability, I recommend that when selecting SessionMode.NotAllowed, always configure the service as per-call also:

```
   [ServiceContract(SessionMode = SessionMode.NotAllowed)]
   interface IMyContract
   {...}

   [ServiceBehavior(InstanceContextMode = InstanceContextMode.PerCall)]
   class MyService : IMyContract
   {...}
```

Since the BasicHttpBinding cannot have a transport-level session, endpoints that use it behave as if the contract is always configured with SessionMode.NotAllowed, always yielding an asynchronous Dispose( ).

Binding, contract, and service behavior

Table 4-1 summarizes the resulting instance mode as a product of the binding being used, the session mode in the contract, and the configured instance context mode in the service behavior. The table does not list invalid configurations, such as SessionMode.Required with BasicHttpBinding.

Table 4-1. Instance mode as a product of the binding, contract configuration, and service behavior

Binding	Session mode	Context mode	Async Dispose()	Instance mode
Basic	Allowed/ NotAllowed	PerCall/ PerSession	Yes	PerCall
TCP, IPC	Allowed/Required	PerCall	No	PerCall
TCP, IPC	Allowed/Required	PerSession	Yes	PerSession
WS (no security, no reliability)	NotAllowed/ Allowed	PerCall/ PerSession	Yes	PerCall
WS (with security or reliability)	Allowed/Required	PerSession	Yes	PerSession
WS (with security or reliability)	NotAllowed	PerCall/ PerSession	Yes	PerCall

Consistent configuration

I strongly recommend that if one contract the service implements is a sessionful contract, then all contracts should be sessionful, and that you should avoid mixing percall and sessionful contracts on the same per-session service type, even though it is allowed by WCF:

```
[ServiceContract(SessionMode = SessionMode.Required)]
interface IMyContract
{...}

[ServiceContract(SessionMode = SessionMode.NotAllowed)]
interface IMyOtherContract
{...}

//Avoid
class MyService : IMyContract,IMyOtherContract
{...}
```

The reason is obvious: per-call services need to proactively manage their state, while per-session services do not. While the two contracts will be exposed on two different endpoints and can be consumed independently by two different clients, it introduces cumbersome implementation for the underlying service class.

Sessions and Reliability

This session between the client and the service instance is only as reliable as the underlying transport session. Consequently, a service that implements a sessionful contract should have all the endpoints that expose that contract use bindings that support reliable transport session. Make sure to always use a binding that supports reliability and that you explicitly enable it at both the client and the service either programmatically or administratively, as shown in Example 4-5.

Example 4-5. Enabling reliability for per-session services

```
<!--Host configuration:-->
<system.serviceModel>
   <services>
      <service name = "MyPerSessionService">
         <endpoint
            address  = "net.tcp://localhost:8000/MyPerSessionService"
            binding  = "netTcpBinding"
            bindingConfiguration = "TCPSession"
            contract = "IMyContract"
         />
      </service>
   </services>
   <bindings>
      <netTcpBinding>
         <binding name = "TCPSession">
            <reliableSession enabled = "true"/>
         </binding>
      </netTcpBinding>
   </bindings>
</system.serviceModel>

<!--Client configuration:-->
<system.serviceModel>
   <client>
      <endpoint
         address  = "net.tcp://localhost:8000/MyPerSessionService/"
         binding  = "netTcpBinding"
         bindingConfiguration = "TCPSession"
         contract = "IMyContract"
      />
   </client>
   <bindings>
      <netTcpBinding>
         <binding name = "TCPSession">
            <reliableSession enabled = "true"/>
         </binding>
      </netTcpBinding>
   </bindings>
</system.serviceModel>
```

The one exception to this rule is the named pipes binding. This binding has no need for the reliable messaging protocol (all calls will be on the same machine anyway), and it is considered an inherently reliable transport. Just as a reliable transport session is optional, so is ordered delivery of messages, and WCF will provide for a session even when ordered delivery is disabled. Obviously, by the very nature of an application session, a client that interacts with a sessionful service expects that all messages are delivered in the order they are sent. Luckily, ordered delivery is enabled by default when reliable transport session is enabled, so no additional setting is required.

Session ID

Every session has a unique ID that both the client and the service can obtain. The session ID is in the form of a GUID, and it can be used for logging and diagnostics. The service can access the session ID via the operation call context. Every service operation has an *operation call context*—a set of properties that are used in addition to the session ID for callbacks, transaction management, security, host access, and access to the object representing the execution context itself. The class OperationContext provides access to all those, and the service obtains a reference to the operation context of the current method via the Current static method of the OperationContext class:

```
public sealed class OperationContext : ...
{
    public static OperationContext Current
    {get; set;}
    public string SessionId
    {get;}
}
```

To access the session ID, the service needs to read the value of the SessionId property, which returns a GUID in the form of a string:

```
string sessionID = OperationContext.Current.SessionId;
Trace.WriteLine(sessionID);
//Traces:
//urn:uuid:c8141f66-51a6-4c66-9e03-927d5ca97153
```

If a per-call service without a transport session (such as with the BasicHttpBinding or with SessionMode.NotAllowed) accesses the SessionId property, it will return null, since there is no session and therefore no ID.

> In the IDisposable.Dispose( ) method, the service has no operation context and subsequently cannot access the session ID.

The client can access the session ID via the proxy. As introduced in Chapter 1, the class ClientBase<T> is the base class of the proxy generated by either Visual Studio 2005 or SvcUtil. ClientBase<T> provides the read-only property InnerChannel of the type IClientChannel. IClientChannel derives from the interface IContextChannel, which provides the SessionId property that returns the session ID in the form of a string:

```
public interface IContextChannel : ...
{
   string SessionId
   {get;}
   //More members
}
public interface IClientChannel : IContextChannel,...
{...}
public abstract class ClientBase<T> : ...
{
   public IClientChannel InnerChannel
   {get;}
   //More members
}
```

Given the definitions of Example 4-4, obtaining the session ID by the client might look like this:

```
MyContractClient proxy = new MyContractClient();
proxy.MyMethod();

string sessionID = proxy.InnerChannel.SessionId;
Trace.WriteLine(sessionID);
//Traces:
//urn:uuid:c8141f66-51a6-4c66-9e03-927d5ca97153
```

However, to what degree the client-side session ID matches that of the service, and when the client is allowed to even access the SessionId property is a product of the binding used and its configuration. What correlates the client-side and service-side session ID is the reliable session at the transport level. If the TCP binding is used, when a reliable session is enabled (as it should be) the client can only obtain a valid session ID after issuing the first method call to the service to establish the session (or after explicitly opening the proxy). If it is accessed before the first call, the SessionId property will be set to null. The session ID obtained by the client will match that of the service. If the TCP binding is used but reliable sessions are disabled, the client can access the session ID before making the first call, but the ID obtained will be different from that obtained by the service. With any one of the WS bindings, with reliable messaging, the session ID will be null until after the first call (or after opening the proxy), but after that the client and the service will always have the same session ID. Without reliable messaging, you must first use the proxy (or just open it) before accessing the session ID or risk an InvalidOperationException. After opening the proxy, the client and the service will have a correlated session ID. With the named-pipe binding, the client can access the SessionId property before making the first call, but the client will always get a session ID different from that of the service. When using the named-pipe binding, it is therefore better to ignore the session ID altogether.

Session Termination

Typically, the session will end once the client closes the proxy. However, in case the client terminates ungracefully or in case of a communication problem, each session also has an idle-time timeout that defaults to 10 minutes. The session will automatically terminate after 10 minutes of inactivity from the client, even if the client still intends to use the session. Once the session is terminated due to the idle-timeout, if the client tries to use its proxy, the client will get a `CommunicationObjectFaultedException`. Both the client and the service can configure a different timeout by setting a different value in the binding. The bindings that support a reliable transport-level session provide the `ReliableSession` property of the type `ReliableSession` or `OptionalReliableSession`. The `ReliableSession` class offers the `TimeSpan` `InactivityTimeout` property that you can use to configure a new idle-time timeout:

```
public class ReliableSession
{
    public TimeSpan InactivityTimeout
    {get;set;}
    //More members
}
public class OptionalReliableSession : ReliableSession
{
    public bool Enabled
    {get;set;}
    //More members
}
public class NetTcpBinding : Binding,...
{
    public OptionalReliableSession ReliableSession
    {get;}
    //More members
}
public abstract class WSHttpBindingBase : ...
{
    public OptionalReliableSession ReliableSession
    {get;}
    //More members
}
public class WSHttpBinding : WSHttpBindingBase,...
{...}
public class WSDualHttpBinding : Binding,...
{
    public ReliableSession ReliableSession
    {get;}
    //More members
}
```

For example, here is the code required to programmatically configure an idle time-out of 25 minutes for the TCP binding:

```
NetTcpBinding tcpSessionBinding = new NetTcpBinding( );
tcpSessionBinding.ReliableSession.Enabled = true;
tcpSessionBinding.ReliableSession.InactivityTimeout = TimeSpan.FromMinutes(25);
```

Here is the equivalent configuration setting using a config file:

```
<netTcpBinding>
    <binding name = "TCPSession">
        <reliableSession enabled = "true" inactivityTimeout = "00:25:00"/>
    </binding>
</netTcpBinding>
```

If both the client and the service configure a timeout, then the shorter timeout prevails.

 There is another esoteric service-side configuration for session termination. The ServiceBehavior attribute offers an advanced option for managing the session shutdown via the AutomaticSessionShutdown property. This property is intended for optimizing certain callback scenarios, and can be safely ignored in most cases. In a nutshell, AutomaticSessionShutdown defaults to true so that when the client closes the proxy, the session is terminated. Setting it to false causes the session to continue until the service explicitly closes its sending channel. When set to false, the client of a duplex session (discussed in Chapter 5) must manually close the output session on the duplex client channel, otherwise the client will hang waiting for the session to terminate.

Singleton Service

The singleton service is the ultimate sharable service. When a service is configured as a *singleton*, all clients independently get connected to the same single well-known instance, regardless of which endpoint of the service they connect to. The singleton service lives forever and is only disposed of once the host shuts down. The singleton is created exactly once, when the host is created.

Using a singleton does not require the clients to maintain a session with the singleton instance, or to use a binding that supports a transport-level session. If the contract the client consumes has a session, then during the call the singleton will have the same session ID as the client (binding permitting), but closing the client proxy will only terminate the session, not the singleton instance. In addition, the session will never expire. If the singleton service supports contracts without a session, those contracts will not be per-call: they too will be connected to the same instance. By its very nature, the singleton is shared, and each client should simply create its own proxies to it.

You configure a singleton service by setting the `InstanceContextMode` property to `InstanceContextMode.Single`:

```
[ServiceBehavior(InstanceContextMode = InstanceContextMode.Single)]
class MySingleton : ...
{...}
```

Example 4-6 demonstrates a singleton service with two contracts, one that requires a session and one that does not. As you can see from the client call, the calls on the two endpoints were routed to the same instance, and closing the proxies did not terminate the singleton.

Example 4-6. A singleton service and client

```
///////////////////////// Service code /////////////////////////
[ServiceContract(SessionMode = SessionMode.Required)]
interface IMyContract
{
   [OperationContract]
   void MyMethod( );
}
[ServiceContract(SessionMode = SessionMode.NotAllowed)]
interface IMyOtherContract
{
   [OperationContract]
   void MyOtherMethod( );
}
[ServiceBehavior(InstanceContextMode=InstanceContextMode.Single)]
class MySingleton : IMyContract,IMyOtherContract,IDisposable
{
   int m_Counter = 0;

   public MySingleton( )
   {
      Trace.WriteLine("MySingleton.MySingleton( )");
   }
   public void MyMethod( )
   {
      m_Counter++;
      Trace.WriteLine("Counter = " + m_Counter);
   }
   public void MyOtherMethod( )
   {
      m_Counter++;
      Trace.WriteLine("Counter = " + m_Counter);
   }
   public void Dispose( )
   {
      Trace.WriteLine("Singleton.Dispose( )");
   }
}
///////////////////////// Client code /////////////////////////
MyContractClient proxy1 = new MyContractClient( );
```

Example 4-6. A singleton service and client (continued)

```
proxy1.MyMethod( );
proxy1.Close( );

MyOtherContractClient proxy2 = new MyOtherContractClient( );
proxy2.MyOtherMethod( );
proxy2.Close( );

//Output
MySingleton.MySingleton( )
Counter = 1
Counter = 2
```

Initializing a Singleton

Sometimes you may not want to create and initialize the singleton using just the default constructor. Perhaps initializing that state requires some custom steps or specific knowledge not available to the clients or that the clients should not be bothered with. To support such scenarios, WCF allows you to directly create the singleton instance beforehand using normal CLR instantiation, initialize it, and then open the host with that instance in mind as the singleton service. The ServiceHost class offers a dedicated constructor that accepts an object:

```
public class ServiceHost : ServiceHostBase,...
{
    public ServiceHost(object singletonInstance,
                       params Uri[] baseAddresses);
    public virtual object SingletonInstance
    {get;}
    //More members
}
```

Note that the object must be configured as a singleton. For example, consider the code in Example 4-7. The class MySingleton will be first initialized and then hosted as a singleton.

Example 4-7. Initializing and hosting a singleton

```
//Service code
[ServiceContract]
interface IMyContract
{
    [OperationContract]
    void MyMethod( );
}
[ServiceBehavior(InstanceContextMode = InstanceContextMode.Single)]
class MySingleton : IMyContract
{
    int m_Counter = 0;

    public int Counter
```

Example 4-7. Initializing and hosting a singleton (continued)

```
   {
      get
      {
         return m_Counter;
      }
      set
      {
         m_Counter = value;
      }
   }
   public void MyMethod( )
   {
      m_Counter++;
      Trace.WriteLine("Counter = " + Counter);
   }
}
//Host code
MySingleton singleton = new MySingleton( );
singleton.Counter = 42;

ServiceHost host = new ServiceHost(singleton);
host.Open( );
//Do some blocking calls then
host.Close( );

//Client code
MyContractClient proxy = new MyContractClient( );
proxy.MyMethod( );
proxy.Close( );

//Outoput:
Counter = 43
```

If you do initialize and host a singleton this way, you may also want to be able to access it directly on the host side. WCF enables downstream objects to reach back into the singleton directly using the SingletonInstance property of ServiceHost. Any party on the call chain leading down from an operation call on the singleton can always access the host via the operation context's read-only Host property:

```
public sealed class OperationContext : ...
{
   public ServiceHostBase Host
   {get;}
   //More members
}
```

Once you have the singleton reference, you can interact with it directly:

```
ServiceHost host = OperationContext.Current.Host as ServiceHost;
Debug.Assert(host != null);
MySingleton singleton = host.SingletonInstance as MySingleton;
Debug.Assert(singleton != null);
singleton.Counter = 388;
```

If no singleton instance was provided to the host, SingletonInstance returns null.

Streamlining with ServiceHost<T>

The ServiceHost<T> class presented in Chapter 1 can be extended to offer type-safe singleton initialization and access:

```
public class ServiceHost<T> : ServiceHost
{
    public ServiceHost(T singleton,params Uri[] baseAddresses)
                                    : base(singleton,baseAddresses)
    {}
    public virtual T Singleton
    {
        get
        {
            if(SingletonInstance == null)
            {
                return default(T);
            }
            return (T)SingletonInstance;
        }
    }
    //More members
}
```

The type parameter provides type-safe binding for the object used for construction:

```
MySingleton singleton = new MySingleton();
singleton.Counter = 42;

ServiceHost<MySingleton> host = new ServiceHost<MySingleton>(singleton);
host.Open();
```

and the object returned from the Singleton property.

```
ServiceHost<MySingleton> host = OperationContext.Current.Host
                                    as ServiceHost<MySingleton>;
Debug.Assert(host != null);
host.Singleton.Counter = 388;
```

 In a similar manner, InProcFactory<T> presented in Chapter 1 is also extended to initialize a singleton instance.

Choosing a Singleton

The singleton service is the sworn enemy of scalability. The reason is the singleton state synchronization. Having a singleton implies the singleton has some valuable state that you wish to share across multiple clients. The problem is that when multiple clients connect to the singleton, they may all do so concurrently, and the incoming client calls will be on multiple worker threads. The singleton must synchronize access to its state to avoid state corruption. This in turn means that only one client at a time can access the singleton. This may degrade throughput, responsiveness, and availability to the point that the singleton is unusable in a decent-size system. For example, if an operation on a singleton takes one-tenth of a second, then the singleton can only service 10 clients a second. If there are more (say 20 or 100), the system's performance will be inadequate.

In general, use a singleton object if it maps well to a natural singleton in the application domain. A *natural singleton* is a resource that is by its very nature single and unique. Examples for natural singletons are a global logbook that all services should log their activities to, a single communication port, or a single mechanical motor. Avoid using a singleton if there is even the slightest chance that the business logic will allow more than one such service in the future, such as adding another motor or a second communication port. The reason is clear: if your clients all depend on implicitly being connected to the well-known instance, and more than one service instance is available, the clients would suddenly need to have a way to bind to the correct instance. This can have severe implications on the application's programming model. Because of these limitations, I recommend that you avoid singletons in the general case and find ways to share the state of the singleton instead of the singleton instance itself. That said, there are cases when using a singleton is acceptable as mentioned above.

Demarcating Operations

Sometimes, a sessionful contract has an implied order to operation invocations. Some operations cannot be called first, while other operations must be called last. For example, consider this contract used to manage customer orders:

```
[ServiceContract(SessionMode = SessionMode.Required)]
interface IOrderManager
{
   [OperationContract]
   void SetCustomerId(int customerId);

   [OperationContract]
   void AddItem(int itemId);

   [OperationContract]
   decimal GetTotal();

   [OperationContract]
   bool ProcessOrders();
}
```

The contract has the following constraints: the client must provide the customer ID as the first operation in the session, or else no other operations can take place; items may be added, and the total calculated, in any order, and as often as the client wishes; processing the order terminates the session, and therefore must come last.

WCF allows contract designers to designate contract operations as operations that can or cannot start or terminate the session using the IsInitiating and IsTerminating properties of the OperationContract attribute:

```
[AttributeUsage(AttributeTargets.Method)]
public sealed class OperationContractAttribute : Attribute
{
   public bool IsInitiating
   {get;set;}
   public bool IsTerminating
   {get;set;}
   //More members
}
```

Using these properties may demarcate the boundary of the session; hence I call this technique *demarcating operations*. During the service load time (or the proxy use time on the client side), if these properties are set to their nondefault values, WCF verifies that the demarcating operations are part of a contract that mandates sessions (SessionMode is set to SessionMode.Required), and will throw an InvalidOperationException otherwise. Both a sessionful service and a singleton can implement a contract that uses demarcating operations to manage their client sessions.

The default values of these properties are IsInitiating set to true and IsTerminating set to false. Consequently these two definitions are equivalent:

```
[ServiceContract(SessionMode = SessionMode.Required)]
interface IMyContract
{
   [OperationContract]
   void MyMethod( );
}
[ServiceContract(SessionMode = SessionMode.Required)]
interface IMyContract
{
   [OperationContract(IsInitiating = true,IsTerminating = false)]
   void MyMethod( );
}
```

As you can see, you can set both properties on the same method. In addition, operations do not demarcate the session boundary by default—operations can be called first, last, or in between any other operation in the session. Using nondefault values enables you to dictate that a method is not called first, or that it is called last, or both:

```
[ServiceContract(SessionMode = SessionMode.Required)]
interface IMyContract
{
   [OperationContract]
   void StartSession( );
```

```
    [OperationContract(IsInitiating = false)]
    void CannotStart();

    [OperationContract(IsTerminating = true)]
    void EndSession();

    [OperationContract(IsInitiating = false,IsTerminating = true)]
    void CannotStartCanEndSession();
}
```

Going back to the order management contract, you can use demarcating operations to enforce the interaction constraints:

```
[ServiceContract(SessionMode = SessionMode.Required)]
interface IOrderManager
{
    [OperationContract]
    void SetCustomerId(int customerId);

    [OperationContract(IsInitiating = false)]
    void AddItem(int itemId);

    [OperationContract(IsInitiating = false)]
    decimal GetTotal();

    [OperationContract(IsInitiating = false,IsTerminating = true)]
    bool ProcessOrders();
}
//Client code
OrderManagerClient proxy = new OrderManagerClient();

proxy.SetCustomerId(123);
proxy.AddItem(4);
proxy.AddItem(5);
proxy.AddItem(6);
proxy.ProcessOrders();

proxy.Close();
```

When IsInitiating is set to true (its default) it means the operation will start a new session if it is the first method called by the client, but that it will be part of the on-going session if another operation is called first. When IsInitiating is set to false, it means that the operation can never be called as the first operation by client in a new session, and that the method can only be part of an ongoing session.

When IsTerminating is set to false (its default), it means the session continues after the operation returns. When IsTerminating is set to true, it means the session terminates once the method returns, and WCF disposes of the service instance asynchronously. The client will not be able to issue additional calls on the proxy. Note that the client should still close the proxy.

When you generate a proxy to a service that uses demarcating operations, the imported contract definition contains the property settings. In addition, WCF enforces the demarcation separately on the client and on the service side, so that you could actually employ them separately.

Instance Deactivation

The sessionful service instance management technique as described so far connects a client (or clients) to a service instance. Yet, the real picture is more complex. Recall from Chapter 1 that each service instance is hosted in a context, as shown in Figure 4-2.

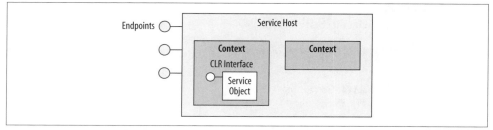

Figure 4-2. Contexts and instances

What sessions actually do is correlate the client messages not to the instance but to the context that hosts it. When the session starts, the host creates a new context. When the session ends, the context is terminated. By default, the lifetime of the context is the same as that of the instance it hosts. However, for optimization purposes, WCF provides the service designer with the option of separating the two lifetimes and deactivating the instance separately from its context. In fact, WCF also allows the situation of a context that has no instance at all, as shown in Figure 4-2. I call this instance management technique *context deactivation*. The common way of controlling context deactivation is via the `ReleaseInstanceMode` property of the `OperationBehavior` attribute:

```
public enum ReleaseInstanceMode
{
   None,
   BeforeCall,
   AfterCall,
   BeforeAndAfterCall,
}
[AttributeUsage(AttributeTargets.Method)]
public sealed class OperationBehaviorAttribute : Attribute,...
{
   public ReleaseInstanceMode ReleaseInstanceMode
   {get;set;}
   //More members
}
```

ReleaseInstanceMode is of the enum type ReleaseInstanceMode. The various values of ReleaseInstanceMode control when to release the instance in relation to the method call: before, after, before and after, or not at all. When releasing the instance, if the service supports IDisposable, then the Dispose( ) method is called and Dispose( ) has an operation context.

You typically apply instance deactivation only on some service methods, but not all of them, or with different values on different methods:

```
[ServiceContract(SessionMode = SessionMode.Required)]
interface IMyContract
{
   [OperationContract]
   void MyMethod( );

   [OperationContract]
   void MyOtherMethod( );
}
class MyService : IMyContract,IDisposable
{
   [OperationBehavior(ReleaseInstanceMode = ReleaseInstanceMode.AfterCall)]
   public void MyMethod( )
   {...}
   public void MyOtherMethod( )
   {...}
   public void Dispose( )
   {...}
}
```

The reason you typically apply it sporadically is that if you were to apply it uniformly you would have ended up with a per-call-like service, so you might as well have configured the service as per-call. If relying on instance deactivation assumes a certain call order, you can try and enforce that order using demarcating operations.

Configuring with ReleaseInstanceMode.None

The default value for the ReleaseInstanceMode property is ReleaseInstanceMode.None, so these two definitions are equivalent:

```
[OperationBehavior(ReleaseInstanceMode = ReleaseInstanceMode.None)]
public void MyMethod( )
{...}

public void MyMethod( )
{...}
```

ReleaseInstanceMode.None means that the instance lifetime is not affected by the call, as shown in Figure 4-3.

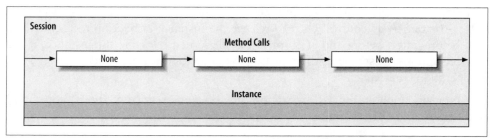

Figure 4-3. Instance lifetime with methods configured with ReleaseInstanceMode.None

Configuring with ReleaseInstanceMode.BeforeCall

When a method is configured with `ReleaseInstanceMode.BeforeCall`, if there is already an instance in the session, before forwarding the call, WCF will deactivate it, create a new instance in its place, and let that new instance service the call, as shown in Figure 4-4.

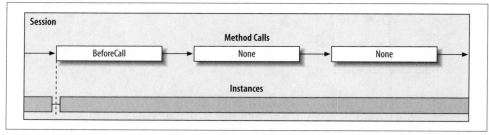

Figure 4-4. Instance lifetime with methods configured with ReleaseInstanceMode.BeforeCall

WCF deactivates the instance and calls `Dispose( )` before the call is done on the incoming call thread, while the client blocks. This makes sure that the deactivation is indeed done before the call and not concurrently to it. `ReleaseInstanceMode.BeforeCall` is designed to optimize methods such as `Open( )` that acquire some valuable resources and yet wish to release the previously allocated resources. Instead of acquiring the resource when the session starts, you wait until the call to the `Open( )` method, and then both release the previously allocated resources and allocate new ones. After `Open( )` is called, you are ready to start calling other methods on the instance that are typically configured with `ReleaseInstanceMode.None`.

Configuring with ReleaseInstanceMode.AfterCall

When a method is configured with `ReleaseInstanceMode.AfterCall`, WCF deactivates the instance after the call, as shown in Figure 4-5.

This is designed to optimize methods such as `Close( )` that clean up valuable resources the instance holds, without waiting for the session to terminate.

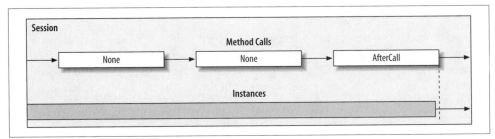

Figure 4-5. Instance lifetime with methods configured with ReleaseInstanceMode.AfterCall

ReleaseInstanceMode.AfterCall is typically applied on methods called after methods configured with ReleaseInstanceMode.None.

Configuring with ReleaseInstanceMode.BeforeAndAfterCall

When a method is configured with ReleaseInstanceMode.BeforeAndAfterCall, as its name implies, it has the combined effect of ReleaseInstanceMode.BeforeCall and ReleaseInstanceMode.AfterCall. If the context has an instance before the call is made, then just before the call, WCF deactivates that instance, creates a new instance to service the call, and deactivates the new instance after the call, as shown in Figure 4-6.

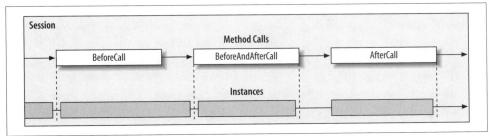

Figure 4-6. Instance lifetime with methods configured with ReleaseInstanceMode. BeforeAndAfterCall

ReleaseInstanceMode.BeforeAndAfterCall may look superfluous at first glance, but it actually complements the other values. It is designed to be applied on methods called after methods marked with ReleaseInstanceMode.BeforeCall or None, or before methods marked with ReleaseInstanceMode.AfterCall or None. Consider a situation where the sessionful service wants to benefit from state-aware behavior (like a per-call service), while holding onto resources only when needed to optimize resource allocation and security lookup. If ReleaseInstanceMode.BeforeCall was the only available option, then there would be a period of time after the call where the resources would still be allocated to the object but not in use. A similar situation occurs if ReleaseInstanceMode.AfterCall were the only available option, because there would be a period of time before the call where the resource would be wasted.

Explicit Deactivation

Instead of making a design-time decision on which methods to use to deactivate the instance, you can make a runtime decision to deactivate the instance after the method returns. You do that by calling the ReleaseServiceInstance( ) method on the instance context. You obtain the instance context via the InstanceContext property of the operation context:

```
public sealed class InstanceContext : CommunicationObject,...
{
   public void ReleaseServiceInstance( );
   //More members
}
public sealed class OperationContext : ...
{
   public InstanceContext InstanceContext
   {get;}
   //More members
}
```

Example 4-8 demonstrates this technique.

Example 4-8. Using ReleaseServiceInstance( )

```
[ServiceContract(SessionMode = SessionMode.Required)]
interface IMyContract
{
   [OperationContract]
   void MyMethod( );
}
class MyService : IMyContract,IDisposable
{
   public void MyMethod( )
   {
      //Do some work then
      OperationContext.Current.InstanceContext.ReleaseServiceInstance( );
   }
   public void Dispose( )
   {...}
}
```

Calling ReleaseServiceInstance( ) has a similar effect to using ReleaseInstanceMode. AfterCall. When used in a method decorated with ReleaseInstanceMode.BeforeCall it has a similar effect to using ReleaseInstanceMode.BeforeAndAfterCall.

 Instance deactivation affects a singleton as well, although combining the two makes little sense—by its very definition, it is permissible and even desirable to never deactivate the singleton.

Using Instance Deactivation

Instance deactivation is an optimization technique, and like all such optimization techniques, you should avoid it in the general case. Consider using instance deactivation only after failing to meet both your performance and scalability goals and when careful examination and profiling has proven beyond a doubt that using instance deactivation will improve the situation. If scalability and throughput are your concern, you should take advantage of the simplicity of the per-call instancing mode, and avoid instance deactivation.

Throttling

While it is not a direct instance management technique, *throttling* enables you to restrain client connections and the load they place on your service. Throttling enables you to avoid maxing out your service and the underlying resources it allocates and uses. When throttling is engaged, if the settings you configure are exceeded, WCF will automatically place the pending callers in a queue and serve them out of the queue in order. If the client's call timeout expires while pending in the queue, the client will get a TimeoutException. Throttling is done per service type; that is, it affects all instances of the service and all its endpoints. This is done by associating the throttle with every channel dispatcher the service uses.

WCF allows you to control some or all of the following service consumption parameters:

- Maximum number of concurrent sessions—the overall number of outstanding clients that have a session at the transport level with the service. In plain terms, this number means the maximum overall number of outstanding clients using TCP, IPC, or any of the WS bindings with sessions. When using the basic binding or any of the WS bindings without a transport session, this number has no effect because of the connectionless nature of a basic HTTP connection. The default value is 10.

- Maximum number of concurrent calls—the total number of calls currently in progress across all service instances. This number should be kept usually at 1 to 3 percent of the maximum number of concurrent sessions. The default value is set to 16.

- Maximum number of concurrent instances—this number actually stands for the total number of contexts concurrently alive. The default value is unlimited. How instances map to contexts is a product of the instance context management mode as well as context and instance deactivation. With a per-session service, the maximum number of instances is both the total number of concurrently active instances and the total number of concurrent sessions. When instance deactivation is employed, there could be far fewer instances than contexts, and yet clients will be blocked if the number of contexts has reached the maximum number of concurrent instances. With a per-call service, the number of instances is actually the same as the number of concurrent calls. Consequently, the maximum number of instances with a per-call service is the lesser of the maximum concurrent instances and the maximum concurrent calls. The value of maximum concurrent instances is ignored with a singleton service since it can only have a single instance anyway.

 Throttling is a hosting and deployment aspect. When you design a service, make no assumptions about throttling configuration—always assume your service will bear the full brunt of the client's load. This is why although it is fairly easy to write a throttling behavior attribute, WCF does not offer one.

Configuring Throttling

Throttling is typically configured by administrators in the config file. This enables you to throttle the same service code differently over time or across deployment sites. The host can also programmatically configure throttling based on some runtime decisions.

Administrative throttling

Example 4-9 shows how to configure throttling in the host config file. Using the behaviorConfiguration tag, you add to your service a custom behavior that sets throttled values.

Example 4-9. Administrative throttling

```
<system.serviceModel>
   <services>
      <service name = "MyService" behaviorConfiguration = "ThrottledBehavior">
         ...
      </service>
   </services>
   <behaviors>
      <serviceBehaviors>
         <behavior name = "ThrottledBehavior">
            <serviceThrottling
               maxConcurrentCalls     = "12"
               maxConcurrentSessions  = "34"
               maxConcurrentInstances = "56"
            />
         </behavior>
      </serviceBehaviors>
   </behaviors>
</system.serviceModel>
```

Programmatic throttling

The host process can programmatically throttle the service based on some runtime parameters. You can only do so before the host is opened. Although the host can override the throttling behavior found in the config file by removing it and adding its own, you typically should provide a programmatic throttling behavior only when there is no throttling behavior in the config file.

The `ServiceHostBase` class offers the `Description` property of the type `ServiceDescription`:

```
public abstract class ServiceHostBase : ...
{
   public ServiceDescription Description
   {get;}
   //More members
}
```

The service description, as its name implies, is the description of the service with all its aspects and behaviors. `ServiceDescription` contains a property called `Behaviors` of the type `KeyedByTypeCollection<I>`, with `IServiceBehavior` as the generic parameter.

Example 4-10 shows how to set the throttled behavior programmatically.

Example 4-10. Programmatic throttling

```
ServiceHost host = new ServiceHost(typeof(MyService));

ServiceThrottlingBehavior throttle;
throttle = host.Description.Behaviors.Find<ServiceThrottlingBehavior>();
if(throttle == null)
{
   throttle = new ServiceThrottlingBehavior();
   throttle.MaxConcurrentCalls     = 12;
   throttle.MaxConcurrentSessions  = 34;
   throttle.MaxConcurrentInstances = 56;
   host.Description.Behaviors.Add(throttle);
}

host.Open();
```

First the hosting code verifies that no service throttling behavior was provided in the config file. This is done by calling the `Find<T>()` method of `KeyedByTypeCollection<I>` using `ServiceThrottlingBehavior` as the type parameter.

`ServiceThrottlingBehavior` is defined in the `System.ServiceModel.Design` namespace:

```
public class ServiceThrottlingBehavior : IServiceBehavior
{
   public int MaxConcurrentCalls
   {get;set;}
   public int MaxConcurrentSessions
   {get;set;}
   public int MaxConcurrentInstances
```

```
      {get;set;}
      //More members
   }
```

If the returned throttle is null, the hosting code creates a new ServiceThrottlingBehavior, sets its values, and adds it to the behaviors in the service description.

Streamlining with ServiceHost<T>

You can extend ServiceHost<T> to automate the code in Example 4-10, as shown in Example 4-11.

Example 4-11. Extending ServiceHost<T> to handle throttling

```
public class ServiceHost<T> : ServiceHost
{
   public void SetThrottle(int maxCalls,int maxSessions,int maxInstances)
   {
      ServiceThrottlingBehavior throttle = new ServiceThrottlingBehavior( );
      throttle.MaxConcurrentCalls = maxCalls;
      throttle.MaxConcurrentSessions = maxSessions;
      throttle.MaxConcurrentInstances = maxInstances;
      SetThrottle(throttle);
   }
   public void SetThrottle(ServiceThrottlingBehavior serviceThrottle)
   {
      SetThrottle(serviceThrottle,false);
   }
   public void SetThrottle(ServiceThrottlingBehavior serviceThrottle,
                           bool overrideConfig)
   {
      if(State == CommunicationState.Opened)
      {
         throw new InvalidOperationException("Host is already opened");
      }
      ServiceThrottlingBehavior throttle =
                           Description.Behaviors.Find<ServiceThrottlingBehavior>( );
      if(throttle != null && overrideConfig == false)
      {
         return;
      }
      if(throttle != null) //overrideConfig == true, remove the configured one
      {
         Description.Behaviors.Remove(throttle);
      }
      if(throttle == null)
      {
         Description.Behaviors.Add(serviceThrottle);
      }
   }
   public ServiceThrottlingBehavior ThrottleBehavior
   {
      get
      {
```

Example 4-11. Extending ServiceHost<T> to handle throttling (continued)

```
         return Description.Behaviors.Find<ServiceThrottlingBehavior>( );
      }
   }
   //More members
}
```

ServiceHost<T> offers the SetThrottle( ) method, which accepts the throttle to use, as well as a Boolean flag indicating whether or not to override the configured values, if present. The default value (using an overloaded version of SetThrottle( )) is false. SetThrottle( ) verifies that the host has not been opened yet using the State property of the CommunicationObject base class. If it is required to override the configured throttle, SetThrottle( ) removes it from the description. The rest of Example 4-11 is similar to Example 4-10. Here is how you can use ServiceHost<T> to set a throttle programmatically:

```
ServiceHost<MyService> host = new ServiceHost<MyService>( );
host.SetThrottle(12,34,56);
host.Open( );
```

In a similar manner, InProcFactory<T> presented in Chapter 1 is also extended to streamline throttling.

Reading throttled values

The throttled values can be read at runtime by service developers for diagnostic and analytical purposes. At runtime, the service instance can access its throttled properties from its dispatcher. First, obtain a reference to the host from the operation context. The host base class ServiceHostBase offers the read-only ChannelDispatchers property:

```
public abstract class ServiceHostBase : CommunicationObject,...
{
   public ChannelDispatcherCollection ChannelDispatchers
   {get;}
   //More members
}
```

ChannelDispatchers is a strongly typed collection of ChannelDispatcherBase objects:

```
public class ChannelDispatcherCollection :
                               SynchronizedCollection<ChannelDispatcherBase>
{...}
```

Each item in the collection is of the type ChannelDispatcher. ChannelDispatcher offers the property ServiceThrottle:

```
public class ChannelDispatcher : ChannelDispatcherBase
{
   public ServiceThrottle ServiceThrottle
   {get;set;}
   //More members
```

```
    }
    public sealed class ServiceThrottle
    {
        public int MaxConcurrentCalls
        {get;set;}
        public int MaxConcurrentSessions
        {get;set;}
        public int MaxConcurrentInstances
        {get;set;}
    }
```

ServiceThrottle contains the configured throttled values:

```
    class MyService : ...
    {
        public void MyMethod( ) //Contract operation
        {
            ChannelDispatcher dispatcher = OperationContext.Current.
                                  Host.ChannelDispatchers[0] as ChannelDispatcher;

            ServiceThrottle serviceThrottle = dispatcher.ServiceThrottle;

            Trace.WriteLine("Max Calls = " + serviceThrottle.MaxConcurrentCalls);
            Trace.WriteLine("Max Sessions = " + serviceThrottle.MaxConcurrentSessions);
            Trace.WriteLine("Max Instances = " + serviceThrottle.MaxConcurrentInstances);
        }
    }
```

Note that the service can only read the throttled values and has no way of affecting them. If the service tries to set throttled values, it will get an InvalidOperationException.

Again, you can streamline the throttle lookup via ServiceHost<T>. First, add a ServiceThrottle property:

```
    public class ServiceHost<T> : ServiceHost
    {
        public ServiceThrottle Throttle
        {
            get
            {
                if(State == CommunicationState.Created)
                {
                    throw new InvalidOperationException("Host is not opened");
                }

                ChannelDispatcher dispatcher = OperationContext.Current.
                                    Host.ChannelDispatchers[0] as ChannelDispatcher;
                return dispatcher.ServiceThrottle;
            }
        }
        //More members
    }
```

Then, use `ServiceHost<T>` to host the service and use the `ServiceThrottle` property to access the configured throttle:

```
//Hosting code
ServiceHost<MyService> host = new ServiceHost<MyService>();
host.Open();

class MyService : ...
{
   public void MyMethod()//Contract operation
   {
      ServiceHost<MyService> host = OperationContext.Current.
                                           Host as ServiceHost<MyService>;

      ServiceThrottle serviceThrottle = host.Throttle;
      ...
   }
}
```

> You can only access the `Throttle` property of `ServiceHost<T>` after the host is opened. This is because the dispatcher collection is initialized only after opening the host.

Throttled Connections in the Binding

When you use the TCP and named-pipe bindings, you can also configure the maximum connection number for a particular endpoint in the binding itself. Both the `NetTcpBinding` and the `NetNamedPipeBinding` offer the `MaxConnections` property:

```
public class NetTcpBinding : Binding,...
{
   public int MaxConnections
   {get;set;}
}
public class NetNamedPipeBinding : Binding,...
{
   public int MaxConnections
   {get;set;}
}
```

On the host side, you can set that property either programmatically or by using a config file:

```
<bindings>
   <netTcpBinding>
      <binding name = "TCPThrottle" maxConnections = "25"/>
   </netTcpBinding>
</bindings>
```

`MaxConnections` defaults to 10. When both a binding-level throttle and a service-behavior throttle sets the max connection value, WCF chooses the lesser of the two.

CHAPTER 5
Operations

The classic object- or component-oriented programming models offered only a single way for clients to call a method: the client would issue a call, block while the call was in progress, and continue executing once the method returned. Any other calling model had to be handcrafted, often incurring productivity and quality penalties. While WCF supports this classic invocation model, it also provides built-in support for additional operation types: one-way calls for fire-and-forget operations, duplex callbacks for allowing the service to call back to the client, and streaming to allow the client or the service to handle large payloads. In general, the type of operation used is part of the service contract and is an intrinsic part of the service design. The operation type even has some constraints on the allowed bindings. Consequently, clients and services should be designed from the ground up with the operation type in mind, and you will not be able to easily switch between the various operation types. This chapter is dedicated to the various ways of invoking WCF operations and the related design guidelines. Two other ways of invoking operations—asynchronously or queued—are addressed in subsequent chapters.*

Request-Reply Operations

All the samples in the previous chapters included contracts whose operations are of the type known as *request-reply*. As the name implies, the client issues a request in the form of a message, and blocks until it get the reply message. If the service does not respond within a default timeout of one minute, the client will get a `TimeoutException`. Request-reply is the default operation mode. Programming against request-reply operations is simple enough and resembles programming using the classic client/server model. The returned response message containing the results or returned values is converted to normal method returned values. In addition, the

---

* This chapter contains excerpts from my article "WCF Essentials: What You Need to Know About One-Way Calls, Callbacks, and Events," *MSDN Magazine*, October 2006.

proxy will throw an exception on the client side if there are any communication or service-side exceptions. With the exception of the `NetPeerTcpBinding` and `NetMsmqBinding`, all bindings support request-reply operations.

One-Way Operations

There are cases when an operation has no returned values, and the client does not care about the success or failure of the invocation. To support this sort of fire-and-forget invocation, WCF offers *one-way* operations. Once the client issues the call, WCF generates a request message, but no correlated reply message will ever return to the client. As a result, one-way operations cannot return values, and any exception thrown on the service side will not make its way to the client. Ideally, once the client calls a one-way method, it should be blocked only for the briefest moment it takes to dispatch the call. However, in reality, one-way calls do not equate asynchronous calls. When one-way calls reach the service, they may not be dispatched all at once, and may be queued up on the service side to be dispatched one at a time, all according to the service's configured concurrency mode behavior. (Chapter 8 will discuss concurrency management and one-way calls in depth.) How many messages (be it one-way operations or request-reply ones) the service is willing to queue up is a product of the configured channel and reliability mode. If the number of queued messages has exceeded the queue's capacity then the client will block, even when issuing a one-way call. However, once the call is queued (which is usually the case), the client is unblocked and can continue executing, while the service processes the operation in the background. All the WCF bindings support one-way operations.

Configuring One-Way Operations

The `OperationContract` attribute offers the Boolean `IsOneWay` property:

```
[AttributeUsage(AttributeTargets.Method)]
public sealed class OperationContractAttribute : Attribute
{
   public bool IsOneWay
   {get;set;}
   //More members
}
```

`IsOneWay` defaults to `false`, which means a request-reply operation (hence the WCF default). However, setting `IsOneWay` to `true` configures the method as a one-way operation:

```
[ServiceContract]
interface IMyContract
{
   [OperationContract(IsOneWay = true)]
   void MyMethod( );
}
```

There is nothing special or different the client has to do when invoking a one-way operation. The value of the IsOneWay property is reflected in the service metadata. Note that both the service contract definition and the definition imported by the client must have the same value for IsOneWay.

Because there is no reply associated with a one-way operation, there is no point in having any returned values or results. For example, here is an invalid definition of a one-way operation that returns a value:

```
//Invalid contract
[ServiceContract]
interface IMyContract
{
   [OperationContract(IsOneWay = true)]
   int MyMethod( );
}
```

In fact, WCF enforces this by verifying the method signature when loading up the host, and throwing an InvalidOperationException in the case of a mismatch.

One-Way Operations and Reliability

The fact that the client does not care about the result of the invocation does not mean that the client does not care whether the invocation took place at all. In general, you should turn on reliability for your services, even for one-way calls. This will ensure delivery of the requests to the service. However, with one-way calls, the client may or may not care about the invocation order of the one-way operations. This is one of the main reasons why WCF allows you to separate enabling reliable delivery from enabling ordered delivery and execution. Obviously, both the client and the service have to agree beforehand on these details, otherwise the binding configuration will not match.

One-Way Operations and Sessionful Services

WCF will let you design a sessionful contract with one-way operations:

```
[ServiceContract(SessionMode = SessionMode.Required)]
interface IMyContract
{
   [OperationContract(IsOneWay = true)]
   void MyMethod( )
}
```

If the client issues a one-way call, and then closes the proxy while the method executes, the client is blocked until the operation completes.

However, I believe that in general, one-way operations in a sessionful contract indicate bad design. The reason is that having a session usually implies that the service manages state on behalf of the client. Any exception that happens will be likely to fault that state, and yet, the client may be unaware of it. In addition, typically the client (or the service) will choose a sessionful interaction because the contract used requires some lock-step execution advancing through some state machine. One-way calls do not fit this model very well. Consequently, I recommend that one-way operations should be applied on per-call or singleton services only.

If you employ one-way operations on a sessionful contract, strive to have only the last operation terminating the session as a one-way operation (make sure it complies with one-way rules, such as a void return type). You can use demarcating operations to enforce that:

```
[ServiceContract(SessionMode = SessionMode.Required)]
interface IOrderManager
{
   [OperationContract]
   void SetCustomerId(int customerId);

   [OperationContract(IsInitiating = false)]
   void AddItem(int itemId);

   [OperationContract(IsInitiating = false)]
   decimal GetTotal();

   [OperationContract(IsOneWay = true,IsInitiating = false,
                                     IsTerminating = true)]
   void ProcessOrders();
}
```

One-Way Operations and Exceptions

It is wrong to perceive a one-way operation as a one-way street or a "black hole" that nothing can come out of. First, when dispatching a one-way operation, any error in trying to dispatch the call because of communication problems (such as a wrong address or the host being unavailable) will throw an exception on the client side trying to invoke the operation. Second, depending on the service instance mode and the binding used, the client may be affected by service-side exceptions. The following discussion assumes that the service does not throw a FaultException or a derived exception, as discussed in Chapter 6.

Per-call services and one-way exceptions

In the case of a per-call service, when there is no transport session (such as when using the BasicHttpBinding or the WSHttpBinding without reliable messaging and security), if an exception takes place when invoking a one-way operation, the client is unaffected and can continue to issue calls on the same proxy instance:

```
[ServiceContract]
interface IMyContract
{
   [OperationContract(IsOneWay = true)]
   void MethodWithError();
```

```
    [OperationContract]
    void MethodWithoutError( );
}

class MyService : IMyContract
{
    public void MethodWithError( )
    {
        throw new Exception( );
    }
    public void MethodWithoutError( )
    {}
}
//Client side when using basic binding:
MyContractClient proxy = new MyContractClient( );
proxy.MethodWithError( );
proxy.MethodWithoutError( );
proxy.Close( );
```

However, when using the WSHttpBinding with security or the NetTcpBinding without reliable messaging or the NetNamedPipeBinding, a service-side exception, including those thrown by one-way operations, will fault the channel, and the client will not be able to issue any new calls using the same proxy instance:

```
[ServiceContract]
interface IMyContract
{
    [OperationContract(IsOneWay = true)]
    void MethodWithError( );

    [OperationContract]
    void MethodWithoutError( );
}

class MyService : IMyContract
{
    public void MethodWithError( )
    {
        throw new Exception( );
    }
    public void MethodWithoutError( )
    {}
}
//Client side when using TCP or IPC binding:
MyContractClient proxy = new MyContractClient( );
proxy.MethodWithError( );
try
{
    proxy.MethodWithoutError( ); //Will throw because channel is at fault
    proxy.Close( );
}
catch
{}
```

The client will not even be able to safely close the proxy.

When using the WSHttpBinding or the NetTcpBinding with reliable messaging, the exception will not fault the channel and the client can continue to issue more calls.

I find these inconsistencies to be disturbing to say the least, first because the choice of a binding should not affect the client code, but also because it is a violation of the semantic of one-way operations, enabling the caller to discover that something went wrong on the service during a one-way invocation.

 A sessionless singleton in this respect behaves similarly to the per-call service.

Sessionful services and one-way exceptions

The situation is even more complex when it comes to sessionful services throwing an exception in a one-way method. With NetTcpBinding and the NetNamedPipeBinding, the exception terminates the session; WCF disposes of the service instance and faults the channel. Subsequent operation calls using the same proxy yield CommunicationException (or CommunicationObjectFaultedException, when reliability is enabled on the TCP and WS bindings) because there is no longer a session or a service instance. If Close( ) is the only method called on the proxy after the exception, Close( ) throws CommunicationException (or CommunicationObjectFaultedException). If the client closes the proxy before the error takes place, Close( ) is blocked until the error takes place, then Close( ) throws the exception. This intricate behavior is yet another reason to avoid one-way calls on a sessionful service.

In the case of WS bindings with a transport session, the exception faults the channel, and the client cannot issue new calls on the proxy. Closing the proxy immediately after the call that threw the exception behaves similar to the other bindings.

 A sessionful singleton in this respect behaves similarly to the per-session service.

Callback Operations

WCF supports allowing the service to call back to its clients. During a callback, in many respects the tables are turned: the service is the client and the client becomes the service (see Figure 5-1).

The client also has to facilitate hosting the callback object. Callback operations can be used in a variety of scenarios and applications, but they are especially useful when it comes to events, or notifying the clients that some event has happened on the service side. Not all bindings support callback operations. Only bidirectional-capable

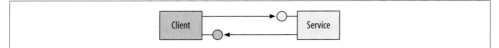

Figure 5-1. A callback allows the service to call back to the client

bindings can be used for callbacks. For example, because of its connectionless nature, HTTP cannot be used for callbacks, and therefore you cannot use callbacks over `BasicHttpBinding` or `WSHttpBinding`. WCF offers callback support for `NetTcpBinding` and `NetNamedPipeBinding`, because by their very nature, the TCP and the IPC protocols support duplex communication. To support callbacks over HTTP, WCF offers the `WSDualHttpBinding`, which actually sets up two HTTP channels: one for the calls from the client to the service and one for the calls from the service to the client.

Callback Contract

Callback operations are part of the service contract, and it is up to the service contract to define its own callback contract. A service contract can have at most one callback contract. Once defined, the clients are required to support the callback and provide the callback endpoint to the service in every call. To define a callback contract, the `ServiceContract` attribute offers the `CallbackContract` property of the type `Type`:

```
[AttributeUsage(AttributeTargets.Interface|AttributeTargets.Class)]
public sealed class ServiceContractAttribute : Attribute
{
   public Type CallbackContract
   {get;set;}
   //More members
}
```

When you define a service contract with a callback contract, you need to provide the `ServiceContract` attribute with the type of the callback contract and the definition of the callback contract, as shown in Example 5-1.

Example 5-1. Defining and configuring a callback contract

```
interface ISomeCallbackContract
{
   [OperationContract]
   void OnCallback();
}

[ServiceContract(CallbackContract = typeof(ISomeCallbackContract))]
interface IMyContract
{
   [OperationContract]
   void DoSomething();
}
```

Note that the callback contract need not be marked with a `ServiceContract` attribute—the `ServiceContract` attribute is implied because it is defined as a callback contract, and will be included in the service metadata. Of course, you still need to mark all the callback interface methods with the `OperationContract` attribute.

Once the client imports the metadata of the callback contract, the imported callback interface will not have the same name as in the original service-side definition. Instead, it will be have the name of the service contract interface suffixed with the word `Callback`. For example, if the client imports the definitions of Example 5-1, the client would get these definitions instead:

```
interface IMyContractCallback
{
   [OperationContract]
   void OnCallback();
}
[ServiceContract(CallbackContract = typeof(IMyContractCallback))]
interface IMyContract
{
   [OperationContract]
   void DoSomething();
}
```

> For simplicity's sake, I recommend even on the service side to name the callback contract as the service contract interface suffixed by Callback.

Client Callback Setup

It is up to the client to host the callback object and expose a callback endpoint. Recall from Chapter 1 that the innermost execution scope of the service instance is the instance context. The `InstanceContext` class provides a constructor that takes the service instance to the host:

```
public sealed class InstanceContext : CommunicationObject,...
{
   public InstanceContext(object implementation);
   public object GetServiceInstance();
   //More members
}
```

All the client needs to do to host a callback object is to instantiate the callback object and construct a context around it:

```
class MyCallback : IMyContractCallback
{
   public void OnCallback()
   {...}
}
IMyContractCallback callback = new MyCallback();
InstanceContext context = new InstanceContext(callback);
```

It is also worth mentioning that although the callback methods are on the client side, they are WCF operations in every respect, and therefore have an operation call context, accessible via OperationContext.Current.

Duplex proxy

Whenever you're interacting with a service endpoint whose contract defines a callback contract, the client must use a proxy that will set up the bidirectional communication and pass the callback endpoint reference to the service. To that end, the proxy the client uses must derive from the specialized proxy class DuplexClientBase<T> shown in Example 5-2.

Example 5-2. The DuplexClientBase<T> class

```
public interface IDuplexContextChannel : IContextChannel
{
   InstanceContext CallbackInstance
   {get;set;}
   //More members
}
public abstract class DuplexClientBase<T> : ClientBase<T> where T : class
{
   protected DuplexClientBase(InstanceContext callbackContext);
   protected DuplexClientBase(InstanceContext callbackContext,
                              string endpointName);
   protected DuplexClientBase(InstanceContext callbackContext,
                              Binding binding,
                              EndpointAddress remoteAddress);
   protected DuplexClientBase(object callbackInstance);
   protected DuplexClientBase(object callbackInstance,
                              string endpointConfigurationName);
   protected DuplexClientBase(object callbackInstance,Binding binding,
                              EndpointAddress remoteAddress);

   public IDuplexContextChannel InnerDuplexChannel
   {get;}
   //More members
}
```

The client needs to provide the constructor of DuplexClientBase<T> with the instance context hosting the callback object (as well as the service endpoint information as with a regular proxy). The proxy will construct an endpoint around the callback context, while inferring the details of the callback endpoint from the service endpoint configuration: the callback endpoint contract is the one defined by the service contract callback type. The callback endpoint will use the same binding (and transport) as the outgoing call. For the address, WCF will use the client's machine name and even select a port when using HTTP. Simply passing the instance context to the duplex proxy and using the proxy to call the service will expose that client-side callback endpoint. To streamline the process, DuplexClientBase<T> also offers constructors that accept the callback object directly and wrap it internally with a context. If for any reason the client needs to access that context, the `DuplexClientBase<T>` also offers the `InnerDuplexChannel` property of the type `IduplexContextChannel`, which offers the context via the `CallbackInstance` property.

When using SvcUtil or Visual Studio 2005 to generate a proxy class targeting a service with a callback contract, the tools will generate a class that derives from `DuplexClientBase<T>` as shown in Example 5-3.

Example 5-3. Tool-generated duplex proxy

```
partial class MyContractClient : DuplexClientBase<IMyContract>,IMyContract
{
    public MyContractClient(InstanceContext callbackContext) : base(callbackContext)
    {}

    public MyContractClient(InstanceContext callbackContext,string endpointName) :
                                          base(callbackContext,endpointName)
    {}
    public MyContractClient(InstanceContext callbackContext,Binding binding,
                                    EndpointAddress remoteAddress) :
                             base(callbackContext,binding,remoteAddress)
    {}
    //More constructors

    public void DoSomething( )
    {
        Channel.DoSomething( );
    }
}
```

Using that derived proxy class, the client can construct a callback instance, host it in a context, create a proxy, and call the service, thus passing the callback endpoint reference:

```
class MyCallback : IMyContractCallback
{
    public void OnCallback( )
    {...}
}
IMyContractCallback callback = new MyCallback( );
InstanceContext context = new InstanceContext(callback);

MyContractClient proxy = new MyContractClient(context);
proxy.DoSomething( );
```

Note that as long as the client is expecting callbacks, the client cannot close the proxy. Doing so will close the callback endpoint and cause an error on the service side when the service tries to call back.

It is often the case that the client itself implements the callback contract, in which case the client will typically use a member variable for the proxy and close it when the client is disposed, as shown in Example 5-4.

Example 5-4. Client implementing the callback contract

```
class MyClient : IMyContractCallback,IDisposable
{
   MyContractClient m_Proxy;

   public void CallService()
   {
      InstanceContext context = new InstanceContext(this);
      m_Proxy = new MyContractClient(context);
      m_Proxy.DoSomething();
   }
   public void OnCallback()
   {...}

   public void Dispose()
   {
      m_Proxy.Close();
   }
}
```

Interestingly enough, the generated proxy does not take advantage of the stream-lined constructors of DuplexClientBase<T> that accept the callback object directly, but you can rework the proxy manually to add that support, as shown in Example 5-5.

Example 5-5. Using a reworked object-based proxy

```
partial class MyContractClient : DuplexClientBase<IMyContract>,IMyContract
{
   public MyContractClient(object callbackInstance) : base(callbackInstance)
   {}
   //More constructors
   public void DoSomething()
   {
      Channel.DoSomething();
   }
}
class MyClient : IMyContractCallback,IDisposable
{
   MyContractClient m_Proxy;

   public void CallService()
   {
      m_Proxy = new MyContractClient(this);
      m_Proxy.DoSomething();
   }
   public void OnCallback()
   {...}
   public void Dispose()
   {
      m_Proxy.Close();
   }
}
```

Service-Side Callback Invocation

The client-side callback endpoint reference is passed along with every call the client makes to the service, and is part of the incoming message. The OperationContext class provides the service with easy access to the callback reference via the generic method GetCallbackChannel<T>( ):

```
public sealed class OperationContext : ...
{
    public T GetCallbackChannel<T>( );
    //More members
}
```

Exactly what the service does with the callback reference and when it decides to use it is completely at the discretion of the service. The service can extract the callback reference from the operation context and store it for later use, or it can use it during the service operation to call back to the client. Example 5-6 demonstrates the first option.

Example 5-6. Storing the callback references for later use

```
[ServiceBehavior(InstanceContextMode = InstanceContextMode.PerCall)]
class MyService : IMyContract
{
    static List<ISomeCallbackContract> m_Callbacks =
                                        new List<ISomeCallbackContract>( );
    public void DoSomething( )
    {
        ISomeCallbackContract callback = OperationContext.Current.
                                GetCallbackChannel<ISomeCallbackContract>( );

        if(m_Callbacks.Contains(callback) == false)
        {
            m_Callbacks.Add(callback);
        }
    }
    public static void CallClients( )
    {
      Action<ISomeCallbackContract> invoke = delegate(ISomeCallbackContract callback)
                                 {
                                     callback.OnCallback( );
                                 };
        m_Callbacks.ForEach(invoke);
    }
}
```

Using the same definitions as Example 5-1, the service uses a static, generic linked list to store references to interfaces of the type ISomeCallbackContract. Because the service is not aware of which client is calling it and whether or not the client has called it already, in every call the service checks to see whether the list already contains the callback reference. If the list does not contain the reference, the service adds the callback to the list. The service class also offers the static method `CallClients( )`. Any party on the host side can simply use that to call back to the clients:

```
MyService.CallClients( );
```

Invoked this way, the invoking party is using some host-side thread for the callback invocation. That thread is unrelated to any thread executing an incoming service call.

 Example 5-6 (and similar examples in this chapter) does not synchronize access to the callbacks list. Obviously, real application code will need to do that. Concurrency management (and, in particular, synchronizing access to shared resources) is discussed in Chapter 8.

Callback reentrancy

The service may also want to invoke the callback reference passed in or a saved copy of it during the execution of a contract operation. However, such invocations are disallowed by default. The reason is the default service concurrency management. By default, the service class is configured for single-threaded access: the service instance is associated with a lock, and only one thread at a time can own the lock and access the service instance. Calling out to the client during an operation call requires blocking the service thread and invoking the callback. The problem is that processing the reply message from the client once the callback returns requires ownership of the same lock, and so a deadlock would occur. Note that the service may still invoke callbacks to other clients or call other services. It is the callback to the calling client that will cause the deadlock.

To avoid a deadlock, if the single-threaded service instance tries to call back to its client, WCF will throw an `InvalidOperationException`. There are three possible solutions. The first is to configure the service for multithreaded access, which would not associate it with a lock and would therefore allow the callback, but would also increase the burden on the service developer because of the need to provide synchronization for the service. The second solution is to configure the service for reentrancy. When configured for reentrancy, the service instance is still associated with a lock and only a single-threaded access is allowed. However, if the service is calling back to its client, WCF will silently release the lock first. Chapter 8 is dedicated to the synchronization modes and their implications on the programming model. For now, if your service needs to call back to its clients, configure its concurrency behavior to either multithreaded or reentrant using the `ConcurrencyMode` property of the `ServiceBehavior` attribute:

```
public enum ConcurrencyMode
{
    Single, //Default
    Reentrant,
    Multiple
}
```

```
[AttributeUsage(AttributeTargets.Class)]
public sealed class ServiceBehaviorAttribute : ...
{
    public ConcurrencyMode ConcurrencyMode
    {get;set;}
    //More members
}
```

Example 5-7 demonstrates a service configured for reentrancy. During the operation execution, the service reaches to the operation context, grabs the callback reference and invokes it. Control will only return to the service once the callback returns, and the service's own thread will need to reacquire the lock.

Example 5-7. Configure for reentrancy to allow callbacks

```
[ServiceContract(CallbackContract = typeof(IMyContractCallback))]
interface IMyContract
{
    [OperationContract]
    void DoSomething();
}
interface IMyContractCallback
{
    [OperationContract]
    void OnCallback();
}
[ServiceBehavior(ConcurrencyMode = ConcurrencyMode.Reentrant)]
class MyService : IMyContract
{
    public void DoSomething()
    {
        IMyContractCallback callback = OperationContext.Current.
                            GetCallbackChannel<IMyContractCallback>();

        callback.OnCallback();
    }
}
```

The third solution that allows the service to safely call back to the client is to have the callback contract operations configured as one-way operations. Doing so will enable the service to call back even when concurrency is set to single-threaded, because there will not be any reply message to contend for the lock. Example 5-8 demonstrates this configuration. Note that the service defaults to single-threaded concurrency mode.

Example 5-8. One-way callbacks are allowed by default

```
[ServiceContract(CallbackContract = typeof(IMyContractCallback))]
interface IMyContract
{
    [OperationContract]
    void DoSomething();
}
```

Example 5-8. One-way callbacks are allowed by default (continued)

```
interface IMyContractCallback
{
   [OperationContract(IsOneWay = true)]
   void OnCallback();
}
class MyService : IMyContract
{
   public void DoSomething()
   {
      IMyContractCallback callback = OperationContext.Current.
                                 GetCallbackChannel<IMyContractCallback>();

      callback.OnCallback();
   }
}
```

Callback Connection Management

The callback mechanism supplies nothing like a higher-level protocol for managing the connection between the service and the callback endpoint. It is up to the developer to come up with some application-level protocol or a consistent pattern for managing the life cycle of the connection. As mentioned previously, the service can only call back to the client if the client-side channel is still open, typically done by not closing the proxy. Keeping the proxy open will also prevent the callback object from being garbage-collected. If the service maintains a reference on a callback endpoint and the client-side proxy is closed or the client application itself is gone, when the service invokes the callback, it will get an ObjectDisposedException from the service channel. It is therefore preferable for the client to inform the service when it no longer wishes to receive callbacks or when the client application is shutting down. To that end, you can add an explicit Disconnect() method to the service contract. Since every method call carries with it the callback reference, in the Disconnect() method the service can remove the callback reference from its internal store.

In addition, for symmetry's sake, I recommend also adding an explicit Connect() method. Having a Connect() method will enable the client to connect or disconnect multiple times, as well as provide a clearly delineated point in time as to when to expect a callback (only after a call to Connect()). Example 5-9 demonstrates this technique. In both the Connect() and Disconnect() methods, the service needs to obtain the callback reference. In Connect(), the service verifies that the callback list does not already contain the callback reference before adding it to the list (this makes multiple calls to Connect() benign). In Disconnect() the service verifies that the list contains the callback reference and it throws an exception otherwise.

Example 5-9. Explicit callback connection management

```
[ServiceContract(CallbackContract = typeof(IMyContractCallback))]
interface IMyContract
```

Example 5-9. Explicit callback connection management (continued)

```
{
   [OperationContract]
   void DoSomething( );

   [OperationContract]
   void Connect( );

   [OperationContract]
   void Disconnect( );
}
interface IMyContractCallback
{
   [OperationContract]
   void OnCallback( );
}
[ServiceBehavior(InstanceContextMode = InstanceContextMode.PerCall)]
class MyService : IMyContract
{
   static List<IMyContractCallback> m_Callbacks = new List<IMyContractCallback>( );
   public void Connect( )
   {
      IMyContractCallback callback = OperationContext.Current.
                                  GetCallbackChannel<IMyContractCallback>( );
      if(m_Callbacks.Contains(callback) == false)
      {
         m_Callbacks.Add(callback);
      }
   }
   public void Disconnect( )
   {
      IMyContractCallback callback = OperationContext.Current.
                                  GetCallbackChannel<IMyContractCallback>( );
      if(m_Callbacks.Contains(callback) == true)
      {
         m_Callbacks.Remove(callback);
      }
      else
      {
         throw new InvalidOperationException("Cannot find callback");
      }
   }
   public static void CallClients( )
   {
    Action<IMyContractCallback> invoke = delegate(IMyContractCallback callback)
                                       {
                                          callback.OnCallback( );
                                       };
      m_Callbacks.ForEach(invoke);
   }
   public void DoSomething( )
   {...}
}
```

Connection management and instance mode

A per-call service can use the callback reference during the operation call itself or store it in some kind of a global repository such as a static variable, as you have seen in examples so far. The reason is clear: any instance state the service may use to store the reference will be gone when the operation returns. As such, using a Disconnect( )-like method is especially required by a per-call service. A similar need exists with a singleton service. The singleton lifetime has no end, and as such it will accumulate an open number of callback references, and as time goes by most of them will become stale as the callback clients are no longer there. Having a Disconnect( ) method will keep the singleton connected only to the relevant alive clients.

Interestingly enough, a per-session service may get by without a Disconnect( ) method at all, as long as it maintains the callback reference in some instance member variable. The reason is that the service instance will automatically be disposed of when the session ends (when the client closes the proxy or times out), and there is no danger in keeping the reference throughout the session—it is guaranteed to always be valid. However, if the sessionful service stores its callback reference in some global repository for the use of other host-side parties or across sessions, adding a Disconnect( ) method is required in order to remove the callback reference explicitly, because the callback reference is not available during the call to Dispose( ).

Finally, you may want to add the Connect( ) and Disconnect( ) pair on a sessionful service simply as a feature, because it enables the client to decide when to start or stop receiving callbacks during the session.

Duplex Proxy and Type Safety

The WCF-provided DuplexClientBase<T> is not strongly typed to the callback interface used. The compiler will let you pass in any object, even an invalid callback interface. The compiler will even let you use for T a service contract type that has no callback contract defined at all. At runtime, you can successfully instantiate the proxy. The incompatibility will be discovered only when you try to use the proxy, yielding an InvalidOperationException. Much the same way, InstanceContext is object-based and is not verified at compile time to actually have a valid callback contract instance. When passed as a constructor parameter to the duplex proxy, there is no compile-time check to correlate the InstanceContext with the callback instance the duplex proxy expects, and the error will be discovered when you try to use the proxy. You can use generics to compensate to some degree for these oversights and discover the error at runtime, as soon as you instantiate the proxy.

First, define the type-safe generic InstanceContext<T> class, shown in Example 5-10.

Example 5-10. The InstanceContext<T> class

```
public class InstanceContext<T>
{
   InstanceContext m_InstanceContext;

   public InstanceContext(T implementation)
   {
      m_InstanceContext = new InstanceContext(implementation);
   }
   public InstanceContext Context
   {
      get
      {
         return m_InstanceContext;
      }
   }
   public T ServiceInstance
   {
      get
      {
         return (T)m_InstanceContext.GetServiceInstance();
      }
   }
}
```

By using generics, you also provide type-safe access to the hosted callback object and capture the desired callback type.

Next, define a new type-safe, generic subclass of DuplexClientBase<T>, as shown in Example 5-11.

Example 5-11. TheDuplexClientBase<T,C>class

```
//T is the service contract and C is the callback contract
public abstract class DuplexClientBase<T,C> : DuplexClientBase<T> where T : class
{
   protected DuplexClientBase(InstanceContext<C> context) : base(context.Context)
   {}
   protected DuplexClientBase(InstanceContext<C> context,string endpointName) :
                                          base(context.Context,endpointName)

   {}
   protected DuplexClientBase(InstanceContext<C> context,Binding binding,
                        EndpointAddress remoteAddress) :
                                    base(context.Context,binding,remoteAddress)

   {}
   protected DuplexClientBase(C callback) : base(callback)
   {}
   protected DuplexClientBase(C callback,string endpointName) :
                                          base(callback,endpointName)

   {}
   protected DuplexClientBase(C callback,Binding binding,
                        EndpointAddress remoteAddress) :
                                    base(callback,binding,remoteAddress)
```

Example 5-11. TheDuplexClientBase<T,C>class (continued)

```
{}

/* More constructors */

static DuplexClientBase( )
{
   VerifyCallback( );
}
internal static void VerifyCallback( )
{
   Type contractType = typeof(T);
   Type callbackType = typeof(C);

   object[] attributes = contractType.GetCustomAttributes(
                             typeof(ServiceContractAttribute),false);
   if(attributes.Length != 1)
   {
      throw new InvalidOperationException("Type of " + contractType +
                          " is not a service contract");
   }
   ServiceContractAttribute serviceContractAttribute;
   serviceContractAttribute = attributes[0] as ServiceContractAttribute;
   if(callbackType != serviceContractAttribute.CallbackContract)
   {
      throw new InvalidOperationException("Type of " + callbackType +
               " is not configured as callback contract for " + contractType);
   }
}
}
}
```

The DuplexClientBase<T,C> class uses two type parameters: T is used for the service contract type parameter and C is used for the callback contract type parameter. The constructors of DuplexClientBase<T,C> can accept either a raw C instance or an instance of InstanceContext<C> wrapping a C instance. These enable the compiler to ensure that only compatible contexts are used. However, C# 2.0 does not support a way to constrain a declarative relationship between T and C. The workaround is to perform a single runtime check before any use of DuplexClientBase<T,C>, and abort the use of the wrong type immediately, before any damage could take place. The trick is to place the runtime verification in the C# static constructor. The static constructor of DuplexClientBase<T,C> calls the static helper method VerifyCallback( ). What VerifyCallback( ) does is to use reflection to first verify that T is decorated with the ServiceContract attribute. Then, it verifies that it has a type set for the callback contract that is the type parameter C. By throwing an exception in the static constructor, you will discover the error as soon as possible at runtime.

Performing the callback contract verification in the static constructor is a technique applicable to any constraint that you cannot enforce at compile time, yet you have some programmatic way of determining and enforcing it at runtime.

Next, you need to rework the machine-generated proxy class on the client side to derive from the type-safe DuplexClientBase<T,C> class:

```
partial class MyContractClient : DuplexClientBase<IMyContract,IMyContractCallback>,
                                  IMyContract
{
   public MyContractClient(InstanceContext<IMyContractCallback> context)
                                                          : base(context)
   {}
   public MyContractClient(IMyContractCallback callback) : base(callback)
   {}

   /* Rest of the constructors */

   public void DoSomething()
   {
      Channel.DoSomething();
   }
}
```

You can either provide the reworked proxy with a type-safe instance context or with the callback instance directly:

```
//Client code
class MyClient : IMyContractCallback
{...}

IMyContractCallback callback = new MyClient();
MyContractClient proxy1 = new MyContractClient(callback);

InstanceContext<IMyContractCallback> context = new
                       InstanceContext<IMyContractCallback>(callback);
MyContractClient proxy2 = new MyContractClient(context);
```

Either way, the compiler will verify that the type parameters provided to the proxy match the context type parameter or the callback instance, and the static constructor will verify the relationship between the service contract and the callback instance upon instantiation.

Duplex Factory

Similar to the ChannelFactory<T> class, WCF also offers DuplexChannelFactory<T>, which can be used for setting up duplex proxies programmatically:

```
public class DuplexChannelFactory<T> : ChannelFactory<T>
{
   public DuplexChannelFactory(object callback);
   public DuplexChannelFactory(object callback,string endpointName);
   public DuplexChannelFactory(InstanceContext context,string endpointName);

   public T CreateChannel(InstanceContext context);
   public static T CreateChannel(object callback,string endpointName);
   public static T CreateChannel(InstanceContext context,string endpointName);
```

```
        public static T CreateChannel(object callback,Binding binding,
                                    EndpointAddress endpointAddress);
        public static T CreateChannel(InstanceContext context,Binding binding,
                                    EndpointAddress endpointAddress);
        //More members
    }
```

DuplexChannelFactory<T> is used just like its base class, ChannelFactory<T>, except its
constructors expect either a callback instance or a callback context. Note again the
use of object for the callback instance and the lack of type safety. Similar to fixing up
the   DuplexClientBase<T>   class,   Example 5-12   shows   the   reworked
DuplexChannelFactory<T,C> class, which provides both compile-time and runtime
type safety.

Example 5-12. The DuplexChannelFactory<T,C> class

```
public class DuplexChannelFactory<T,C> : DuplexChannelFactory<T> where T : class
{
    static DuplexChannelFactory( )
    {
        DuplexClientBase<T,C>.VerifyCallback( );
    }

    public static T CreateChannel(C callback,string endpointName)
    {
        return DuplexChannelFactory<T>.CreateChannel(callback,endpointName);
    }
    public static T CreateChannel(InstanceContext<C> context,string endpointName)
    {
        return DuplexChannelFactory<T>.CreateChannel(context.Context,endpointName);
    }
    public static T CreateChannel(C callback,Binding binding,
                                EndpointAddress endpointAddress)
    {
        return DuplexChannelFactory<T>.CreateChannel(callback,binding,
                                                    endpointAddress);
    }
    public static T CreateChannel(InstanceContext<C> context,Binding binding,
                                EndpointAddress endpointAddress)
    {
        return DuplexChannelFactory<T>.CreateChannel(context,binding,
                                                    endpointAddress);
    }
    public DuplexChannelFactory(C callback) : base(callback)
    {}
    public DuplexChannelFactory(C callback,string endpointName):
                                        base(callback,endpointName)
    {}
    public DuplexChannelFactory(InstanceContext<C> context,string endpointName) :
                                        base(context.Context,endpointName)
    {}
    //More constructors
}
```

As an example for utilizing the duplex channel factory, consider Example 5-13, which adds callback ability to the InProcFactory static helper class presented in Chapter 1.

Example 5-13. Adding duplex support to InProcFactory

```
public static class InProcFactory
{
   public static I CreateInstance<S,I,C>(C callback) where I : class
                                         where S : class,I
   {
      InstanceContext<C> context = new InstanceContext<C>(callback);
      return CreateInstance<S,I,C>(context);
   }
   public static I CreateInstance<S,I,C>(InstanceContext<C> context)
                                         where I : class
                                         where S : class,I
   {
      HostRecord hostRecord = GetHostRecord<S,I>();
      return  DuplexChannelFactory<I,C>.CreateChannel(
              context,NamedPipeBinding,new EndpointAddress(hostRecord.Address));
   }
   //More members
}
//Sample client
IMyContractCallback callback = new MyClient();

IMyContract proxy = InProcFactory.CreateInstance
                          <MyService,IMyContract,IMyContractCallback>(callback);
proxy.DoSomething();
InProcFactory.CloseProxy(proxy);
```

Callback Contract Hierarchy

There is an interesting constraint on the design of callback contracts. A service contract can only designate a callback contract if that contract is a subinterface of all callback contracts defined by the contract's own base contracts. For example, here is an invalid definition of callback contracts:

```
interface ICallbackContract1
{...}

interface ICallbackContract2
{...}

[ServiceContract(CallbackContract = typeof(ICallbackContract1))]
interface IMyBaseContract
{...}

//Invalid
[ServiceContract(CallbackContract = typeof(ICallbackContract2))]
interface IMySubContract : IMyBaseContract
{...}
```

IMySubContract cannot designate ICallbackContract2 as a callback contract because ICallbackContract2 is not a subinterface of ICallbackContract1, while IMyBaseContract (the base of IMySubContract) defines ICallbackContract1 as its own callback contract. The reason for the constraint is obvious: if a client passes an endpoint reference to a service implementation of IMySubContract, that callback reference must satisfy the callback type expected by IMyBaseContract. WCF verifies the callback contract hierarchy at the service load time and throws an InvalidOperationException in the case of a violation.

The straightforward way to satisfy the constraint is to reflect the service contract hierarchy in the callback contract hierarchy:

```
interface ICallbackContract1
{...}

interface ICallbackContract2 : ICallbackContract1
{...}

[ServiceContract(CallbackContract = typeof(ICallbackContract1))]
interface IMyBaseContract
{...}

[ServiceContract(CallbackContract = typeof(ICallbackContract2))]
interface IMySubContract : IMyBaseContract
{...}
```

However, you can also use multiple interface inheritance by a single callback contract and avoid mimicking the service contract hierarchy:

```
interface ICallbackContract1
{...}
interface ICallbackContract2
{...}
interface ICallbackContract3 : ICallbackContract2,ICallbackContract1
{...}

[ServiceContract(CallbackContract = typeof(ICallbackContract1))]
interface IMyBaseContract1
{...}
[ServiceContract(CallbackContract = typeof(ICallbackContract2))]
interface IMyBaseContract2
{...}
[ServiceContract(CallbackContract = typeof(ICallbackContract3))]
interface IMySubContract : IMyBaseContract1,IMyBaseContract2
{...}
```

Note, also, that a service can implement its own callback contract:

```
[ServiceContract(CallbackContract = typeof(IMyContractCallback))]
interface IMyContract
{...}
[ServiceContract]
interface IMyContractCallback
{...}
```

```
class MyService : IMyContract,IMyContractCallback
{...}
```

The service can even store a reference to itself in some callback store (if it wished to be called back as if it were a client).

Callback, Ports, and Channels

When you use either the NetTcpBinding or the NetNamedPipeBinding, the callbacks enter the client on the outgoing channel maintained by the binding to the service. There is no need to open a new port or a pipe for the callbacks. When you use the WSDualHttpBinding, WCF maintains a separate HTTP channel dedicated for the callbacks, because HTTP itself is a unidirectional protocol. For that callback channel, WCF selects port 80 by default and passes the service a callback address that uses HTTP, the client machine name, and port 80.

While using port 80 makes sense for Internet-based services, it is of little value to intranet-based services. In addition, if the client machine happens to also have IIS running, port 80 will be reserved already, and the client will not be able to host the callback endpoint. While the likelihood of an intranet application being forced to use WSDualHttpBinding is somewhat low, it is quite common for developers who develop Internet-based applications to have IIS installed on their machines and have the callback port therefore conflict with IIS during testing and debugging.

Assigning a callback address

Fortunately, the WSDualHttpBinding binding offers the ClientBaseAddress property, where you can configure on the client a different callback URI:

```
public class WSDualHttpBinding : Binding,...
{
   public Uri ClientBaseAddress
   {get;set;}
   //More members
}
```

For example, here is how to configure a base address in the client's config file:

```
<system.serviceModel>
   <client>
      <endpoint
         address  = "http://localhost:8008/MyService"
         binding  = "wsDualHttpBinding"
         bindingConfiguration = "ClienCallback"
         contract = "IMyContract"
      />
   </client>
   <bindings>
      <wsDualHttpBinding>
         <binding name = "ClientCallback"
```

```
        clientBaseAddress = "http://localhost:8009/"
      />
    </wsDualHttpBinding>
  </bindings>
</system.serviceModel>
```

However, since the callback port need not be known to the service in advance, in actuality any available port will do. It is therefore better to set the client base address programmatically to any available port. You can automate this using the WsDualProxyHelper static helper class shown in Example 5-14.

Example 5-14. The WsDualProxyHelper class

```
public static class WsDualProxyHelper
{
   public static void SetClientBaseAddress<T>(DuplexClientBase<T> proxy,int port)
                                                                where T : class
   {
      WSDualHttpBinding binding = proxy.Endpoint.Binding as WSDualHttpBinding;
      Debug.Assert(binding != null);
      binding.ClientBaseAddress = new Uri("http://localhost:"+ port + "/");
   }
   public static void SetClientBaseAddress<T>(DuplexClientBase<T> proxy)
                                                                where T : class
   {
      lock(typeof(WsDualProxyHelper))
      {
         int portNumber = FindPort();
         SetClientBaseAddress(proxy,portNumber);
         proxy.Open();
      }
   }
   internal static int FindPort()
   {
      IPEndPoint endPoint = new IPEndPoint(IPAddress.Any,0);
      using(Socket socket = new Socket(AddressFamily.InterNetwork,
                                  SocketType.Stream,
                                  ProtocolType.Tcp))
      {
         socket.Bind(endPoint);
         IPEndPoint local = (IPEndPoint)socket.LocalEndPoint;
         return local.Port;
      }
   }
}
```

WsDualProxyHelper offers two overloaded versions of the SetClientBaseAddress( ) method. The first simply takes a proxy instance and port number. It verifies the proxy is using the WSDualHttpBinding binding, and then it sets the client base address using the provided port. The second version of SetClientBaseAddress( ) automatically selects an available port and calls the first one with the available port. To avoid a race condition with other concurrent invocations of SetClientBaseAddress( ) in the same app domain, it locks on the type itself during the sequence of looking up the available port and setting the base address, and then it opens the proxy to lock in the port. Note that a race condition is still possible with other processes or app domains on the same machine.

Using `WsDualProxyHelper` is straightforward:

```
//Sample client code:
class MyClient : IMyContractCallback
{...}

IMyContractCallback callback = new MyClient( );
InstanceContext context = new InstanceContext(callback);

MyContractClient proxy = new MyContractClient(context);

WsDualProxyHelper.SetClientBaseAddress(proxy);
```

Another advantage of programmatically setting the callback address (as opposed to hardcoding it in the config file) is that it supports launching a few clients on the same machine during testing.

Assigning callback address declaratively

You can even automate the process further and assign the callback port declaratively using a custom attribute. `CallbackBaseAddressBehaviorAttribute` is a contract behavior attribute affecting only the callback endpoints that use `WSDualHttpBinding`. `CallbackBaseAddressBehaviorAttribute` offers a single integer property called `CallbackPort`:

```
[AttributeUsage(AttributeTargets.Class)]
public class CallbackBaseAddressBehaviorAttribute : Attribute,IEndpointBehavior
{
   public int CallbackPort
   {get;set;}
}
```

`CallbackPort` defaults to 80. Unset, applying the `CallbackBaseAddressBehavior` attribute will result in the default behavior for `WSDualHttpBinding`, so these two definitions are equivalent:

```
class MyClient : IMyContractCallback
{...}

[CallbackBaseAddressBehavior]
class MyClient : IMyContractCallback
{...}
```

You can explicitly specify a callback port:

```
[CallbackBaseAddressBehavior(CallbackPort = 8009)]
class MyClient : IMyContractCallback
{...}
```

However, if you set `CallbackPort` to 0, `CallbackBaseAddressBehavior` will automatically select any available port for the callback:

```
[CallbackBaseAddressBehavior(CallbackPort = 0)]
class MyClient : IMyContractCallback
{...}
```

Example 5-15 lists the code of `CallbackBaseAddressBehaviorAttribute`.

Example 5-15. The CallbackBaseAddressBehaviorAttribute

```
[AttributeUsage(AttributeTargets.Class)]
public class CallbackBaseAddressBehaviorAttribute : Attribute,IEndpointBehavior
{
   int m_CallbackPort = 80;

   public int CallbackPort //Accesses m_CallbackPort
   {get;set;}
   void IEndpointBehavior.AddBindingParameters(ServiceEndpoint endpoint,
                              BindingParameterCollection bindingParameters)
   {
      if(CallbackPort == 80)
      {
         return;
      }
      lock(typeof(WsDualProxyHelper))
      {
         if(CallbackPort == 0)
         {
            CallbackPort = WsDualProxyHelper.FindPort();
         }
         WSDualHttpBinding binding = endpoint.Binding as WSDualHttpBinding;
         if(binding != null)
         {
            binding.ClientBaseAddress = new Uri(
                              "http://localhost:" + CallbackPort + "/");
         }
      }
   }
   //Do-nothing methods of IEndpointBehavior
}
```

`CallbackBaseAddressBehaviorAttribute` is an endpoint behavior attribute allowing you to intercept (either on the client or service side) the configuration of the endpoint. The attribute supports the `IContractBehavior` interface:

```
public interface IEndpointBehavior
{
   void AddBindingParameters(ServiceEndpoint endpoint,
                     BindingParameterCollection bindingParameters);
   //More members
}
```

WCF calls the `AddBindingParameters()` method on the client side just before using the proxy to the service for the first time, allowing the attribute to configure the binding used for the callback. `AddBindingParameters()` checks the value of `CallbackPort`. If it is 80, it does nothing. If it is 0, `AddBindingParameters()` finds an available port and assigns it to `CallbackPort`. Then, `AddBindingParameters()` looks up the binding used to call the service. If the call is `WSDualHttpBinding`, `AddBindingParameters()` sets the client base address using the callback port.

 With `CallbackBaseAddressBehaviorAttribute`, a race condition is possible with another callback object grabbing the same port, even in the same app domain.

Events

The basic WCF callback mechanism does not indicate anything about the nature of the interaction between the client and the service. They could be equal peers in a commutative interaction, each calling and receiving calls from the other.

However, the canonical use for duplex callbacks is with events. *Events* allow the client or clients to be notified about something that occurred on the service side. The event may result from a direct client call, or it may be the result of something the service monitors. The service firing the event is called the *publisher*, and the client receiving the event is called the *subscriber*. Events are a required feature in almost any type of application, as shown in Figure 5-2.

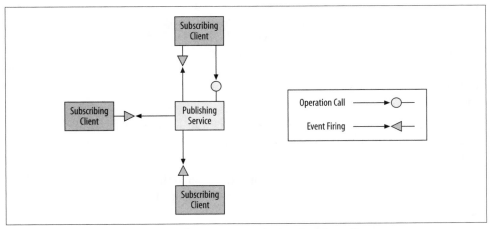

Figure 5-2. A publishing service can fire events at multiple subscribing clients

While events in WCF are noting more than callback operations, by their very nature events usually imply a looser relationship between the publisher and the subscriber, compared with the relationship between a client and a service. When dealing with events, the service typically publishes the same event to multiple subscribing clients. The publisher often does not care about the order of the invocation of the subscribers. The publishing service usually does not care about errors the subscribers might have while processing the events. All the publisher knows is that it should deliver the event to the subscribers. If they have a problem with the event, there is nothing the service can do about it anyway. In addition, the service does not care about returned results from the subscribers. Consequently, event-handling operations should have a void return type, should not have any outgoing parameters, and should be marked as one-way. I also recommend factoring the events to a separate callback contract, and not mixing events with regular callbacks on the same contract:

```
interface IMyEvents
{
    [OperationContract(IsOneWay = true)]
    void OnEvent1( );

    [OperationContract(IsOneWay = true)]
    void OnEvent2(int number);

    [OperationContract(IsOneWay = true)]
    void OnEvent3(int number,string text);
}
```

On the subscriber side, even when using one-way callback operations, the implementation of the event handling methods should be of short duration. The reason is that if there is a large volume of events to publish, the publisher may get blocked if a subscriber has maxed out its ability to queue up callbacks because it was still processing the previous events. Blocking the publisher may prevent the event from reaching other subscribers in a timely manner. The publisher may add dedicated operations to its contract, allowing clients to explicitly subscribe to or unsubscribe from the events. If the publisher supports multiple event types, it may want to allow the subscribers to choose exactly which event they want to subscribe to or unsubscribe from.

How the service internally goes about managing the subscribers list and their preferences is completely a service-side implementation detail that should not affect the clients.

The publisher can even use .NET delegates to manage the list of subscribers and the publishing act itself. Example 5-16 demonstrates this technique as well as the other design considerations discussed so far.

Example 5-16. Events management using delegates

```
enum EventType
{
    Event1 = 1,
    Event2 = 2,
```

Example 5-16. Events management using delegates (continued)

```
   Event3 = 4,
   AllEvents = Event1|Event2|Event3
}
[ServiceContract(CallbackContract = typeof(IMyEvents))]
interface IMyContract
{
   [OperationContract]
   void DoSomething( );

   [OperationContract]
   void Subscribe(EventType mask);

   [OperationContract]
   void Unsubscribe(EventType mask);
}
[ServiceBehavior(InstanceContextMode = InstanceContextMode.PerCall)]
class MyPublisher : IMyContract
{
   static GenericEventHandler m_Event1            = delegate{};
   static GenericEventHandler<int> m_Event2       = delegate{};
   static GenericEventHandler<int,string> m_Event3 = delegate{};

   public void Subscribe(EventType mask)
   {
      IMyEvents subscriber =  OperationContext.Current.
                                          GetCallbackChannel<IMyEvents>( );

      if((mask & EventType.Event1) == EventType.Event1)
      {
         m_Event1 += subscriber.OnEvent1;
      }
      if((mask & EventType.Event2) == EventType.Event2)
      {
         m_Event2 += subscriber.OnEvent2;
      }
      if((mask & EventType.Event3) == EventType.Event3)
      {
         m_Event3 += subscriber.OnEvent3;
      }
   }
   public void Unsubscribe(EventType mask)
   {
      //Similar to Subscribe( ) but uses -=
   }
   public static void FireEvent(EventType eventType)
   {
      switch(eventType)
      {
         case EventType.Event1:
         {
            m_Event1( );
            return;
```

Example 5-16. Events management using delegates (continued)

```
      }
      case EventType.Event2:
      {
         m_Event2(42);
         return;
      }
      case EventType.Event3:
      {
         m_Event3(42,"Hello");
         return;
      }
      default:
      {
         throw new InvalidOperationException("Unknown event type");
      }
   }
}
public void DoSomething()
{...}
}
```

The service contract IMyContract defines the Subscribe() and Unsubscribe() methods. These methods take an enum of the type EventType, whose individual fields are set to integer powers of 2. This enables the subscribing client to combine the values into a mask indicating the types of event it wants to subscribe to or unsubscribe from. For example, to subscribe to Event1 and Event3 but not Event2, the subscriber would call like this:

```
class MySubscriber : IMyEvents
{
   void OnEvent1()
   {...}
   void OnEvent2(int number)
   {...}
   void OnEvent2(int number,string text)
   {...}
}
IMyEvents subscriber = new MySubscriber();
InstanceContext context = new InstanceContext(subscriber);
MyContractClient proxy = new MyContractClient(context);
proxy.Subscribe(EventType.Event1|EventType.Event3);
```

Internally, MyPublisher maintains three static delegates; each corresponds to an event type. The delegates are all of the generic delegate type GenericDelegate:

```
public delegate void GenericEventHandler();
public delegate void GenericEventHandler<T>(T t);
public delegate void GenericEventHandler<T,U>(T t,U u);
public delegate void GenericEventHandler<T,U,V>(T t,U u,V v);
public delegate void GenericEventHandler<T,U,V,W>(T t,U u,V v,W w);
public delegate void GenericEventHandler<T,U,V,W,X>(T t,U u,V v,W w,X x);
public delegate void GenericEventHandler<T,U,V,W,X,Y>(T t,U u,V v,W w,X x,Y y);
```

GenericDelegate allows you to literally express any event-handling signature.

> For more information about delegates and GenericDelegate, see Chapter 6 in my book *Programming .NET Components* (O'Reilly).

Both the Subscribe( ) and Unsubscribe( ) methods check the supplied EventType value, and add or remove the subscriber's callback to the corresponding delegate. To fire an event, MyPublisher offers the static FireEvent( ) method. FireEvent( ) accepts which event to fire and invokes the corresponding delegate.

Again, the fact that the MyPublisher service uses delegates is purely an implementation detail simplifying the events lookup. The service could have used a linked list, although with more complex code.

> Appendix B presents a framework for supporting a better design approach for events called publish-subscriber.

Streaming

By default, when the client and the service exchange messages, these messages are buffered on the receiving end and delivered once the entire message is received. This is true whether it is the client sending a message to the service or the service returning a message to the client. When the client calls the service, the service is invoked when the message is received in its entirety. The client is unblocked when the returned message with the results of the invocation is received in its entirety. For sufficiently small message sizes, this exchange pattern provides for a simple programming model because the latency caused by receiving the message is usually negligible compared with the message processing itself. However, when it comes to much larger messages, such as ones involving multimedia content, large files, or batches of data, blocking every time until the message is received may be impractical. To handle such cases, WCF enables the receiving side (be it the client or the service) to start processing the data in the message while the message is still being received by the channel. Such processing is called *streaming transfer mode*. With large payloads, streaming provides improved throughput and responsiveness because neither the receiving nor sending side is blocked when sending or receiving the message.

I/O Streams

For message streaming, WCF requires the use of the .NET Stream class. In fact, the contract operations used for streaming look just like conventional I/O methods. The Stream class is the base class of all the I/O streams in .NET (such as the FileStream, NetworkStream, and MemoryStream classes) allowing you to stream content from any of these I/O sources. All you need to do is to return or receive a Stream as an operation parameter, as shown in Example 5-17.

Example 5-17. Streaming operations

```
[ServiceContract]
interface IMyContract
{
   [OperationContract]
   Stream StreamReply1( );

   [OperationContract]
   void StreamReply2(out Stream stream);

   [OperationContract]
   void StreamRequest(Stream stream);

   [OperationContract(IsOneWay = true)]
   void OneWayStream(Stream stream);
}
```

Note that you can only define as an operation parameter the abstract class Stream or a specific serializable subclass such as MemoryStream. Subclasses such as FileStream are not serializable and you will have to use the base Stream.

WCF lets services stream the reply, the request, or both the request and the reply, using one-way streaming.

To stream the reply, either return the Stream from the operation:

```
[OperationContract]
Stream GetStream1( );
```

or provide the stream as an out parameter:

```
[OperationContract]
void GetStream2(out Stream stream);
```

To stream the request, provide a Stream as a method parameter:

```
[OperationContract]
void SetStream1(Stream stream);
```

Finally, you can even stream the request for a one-way operation:

```
//One-way streaming
[OperationContract(IsOneWay = true)]
void SetStream2(Stream stream);
```

Streaming and Binding

Only the BasicHttpBinding, NetTcpBinding, and NetNamedPipeBinding support streaming. With all these bindings streaming is disabled by default, and the binding will buffer the message in its entirety, even when a Stream is used. You have to enable streaming by setting the `TransferMode` Boolean property according to the desired streaming mode; for example, when using `BasicHttpBinding`:

```
public enum TransferMode
{
    Buffered, //Default
    Streamed,
    StreamedRequest,
    StreamedResponse
}
public class BasicHttpBinding : Binding,...
{
    public TransferMode TransferMode
    {get;set;}
    //More members
}
```

`TransferMode.Streamed` supports all streaming modes, and is the only transfer mode that can support all the operations in Example 5-17. However, if the contract contains only a specific type of streaming such as streamed reply:

```
[ServiceContract]
interface IMyContract
{
    //Stream reply
    [OperationContract]
    Stream GetStream1( );

    [OperationContract]
    int MyMethod( );
}
```

you can have a buffered request and streamed reply by selecting `TransferMode.StreamedResponse`.

You will need to configure the binding on the client or service side (or both) per the required stream mode:

```
<configuration>
    <system.serviceModel>
        <client>
            <endpoint
                binding = "basicHttpBinding"
                bindingConfiguration = "StreamedHTTP"
                ...
            />
        </client>
        <bindings>
            <basicHttpBinding>
                <binding name = "StreamedHTTP" transferMode = "Streamed">
                </binding>
            </basicHttpBinding>
        </bindings>
    </system.serviceModel>
</configuration>
```

Streaming and Transport

It is important to realize that WCF streaming is merely a programming model nicety. The underlying transport itself (such as HTTP) is not streamed, and the default maximum message size is set to 64 KB. This may be a problem with the sort of data you are likely to use streaming with, because streamed messages tend to be very large (hence the motivation for streaming in the first place). You may find the need to increase the max message size on the receiving side to accommodate the large message by setting the MaxReceivedMessageSize property to the expected maximum message size:

```
public class BasicHttpBinding : Binding,...
{
   public long MaxReceivedMessageSize
   {get;set;}
   //More memebrs
}
```

Typically you would place that piece of configuration in the config file and avoid doing it programmatically, as message size tends to be deployment-specific:

```
<bindings>
   <basicHttpBinding>
      <binding name = "StreamedHTTP" transferMode = "Streamed"
            maxReceivedMessageSize = "120000">
      </binding>
   </basicHttpBinding>
</bindings>
```

Stream Management

When the client passes a request stream to the service, the service may read from the stream long after the client is gone. The client has no way of knowing when the service is done using the stream. Consequently the client should not close the stream—WCF will automatically close the client-side stream once the service is done using the stream.

A similar problem exists when the client interacts with a response stream. The stream was produced on the service side, and yet the service does not know when the client is done using the stream, nor can WCF help, because it has no idea what the client is doing with the stream. The client is always responsible for closing reply streams.

 When you use streaming, you cannot use message-level transfer security. You will see more on security in Chapter 10. When streaming with the TCP binding, you also cannot enable reliable messaging.

There a few additional implications on streamed messages: first you need to synchronize access to the streamed content; for example, by opening the file stream in a read-only mode to allow other parties to access the file, or opening the stream in an exclusive mode to prevent others from accessing it if so required. In addition, you cannot use streaming with a sessionful service—the session implies a lock-step execution and has a well-defined demarcation, unlike streaming, which may be continuous for a long period of time.

CHAPTER 6

Faults

Any service operation can at any moment encounter an unexpected error. The question is how (if at all) that error should be reported back to the client. Concepts such as exceptions and exception handling are technology-specific and should not transcend the service boundary. In addition, typically error handling is a local implementation detail that should not affect the client, partly because the client may not care about the details of the errors (other than the fact that something went wrong), but mostly because in a well-designed application, the service is encapsulated so that the client does not have anything meaningful to do about the error anyway. A well-designed service should be autonomous as much as possible, and should not depend on its client to handle and recover the error. Anything beyond a blank error notification should in fact be part of the contractual interaction between the client and the service. This chapter describes just how the service and the client should handle these declared faults, and how you can extend and improve on the basic mechanism.

Errors and Exceptions

In raw .NET programming, any unhandled exception immediately terminates the process it took place in. That is not the WCF behavior, however. If a service call on behalf of one client causes an exception, it must not be allowed to take down the hosting process. Other clients accessing the service, or other services hosted by the same process, should not be affected. As a result, when an unhandled exception leaves the service scope, the dispatcher silently catches and handles it by serializing it in the returned message to the client. When the returned message reaches the proxy, the proxy throws an exception on the client side.

The client can actually encounter three types of errors when trying to invoke the service. The first type of error is communication errors such as network availability, wrong address, host process not running, and so on. Communication exceptions are manifested on the client side by the CommunicationException.

The second type of error the client might encounter is related to the state of the proxy and the channels, such as trying to access an already closed proxy, resulting in an `ObjectDisposedException`, or a mismatch in the contract and the binding security protection level.

The third type of error is the one that originated in the service call, either by the service throwing an exception or as a result of the service calling another object or resource and having that internal call throw an exception. These errors are the subject of this chapter.

In the interest of encapsulation and decoupling, by default all exceptions thrown on the service side always reach the client as `FaultException`:

```
public class FaultException : CommunicationException
{...}
```

By having all service exceptions indistinguishable from each other, WCF decouples the client from the service. The less the client knows about what happened on the service side, the more decoupled the interaction will be.

Exceptions and Instance Management

While WCF does not take down the host process when the service instance encounters an exception, the error may affect the service instance and the ability of the client to continue using the proxy (or actually the channel) to the service. The exact effect the exception has on the client and the service instance depends on the instance mode.

Per-call service and exceptions

If the call encounters an exception, after the exception the service instance is disposed and the proxy throws a `FaultException` on the client's side. By default, all service-thrown exceptions (with the exception of `FaultException`-derived classes) fault the channel so that even if the client catches that exception, it cannot issue subsequent calls because those yield a `CommunicationObjectFaultedException`. The client can only close the proxy.

Sessionful service and exceptions

When you use any of the WCF sessionful bindings, by default all exceptions (with the exception of `FaultException`-derived classes) terminate the session. WCF disposes of the instance and the client gets a `FaultException`. Even if the client catches that exception, it cannot continue using the proxy because subsequent calls yield a `CommunicationObjectFaultedException`. The only thing the client can safely do is to close the proxy, because once the service instance participating in the session encounters an error, the session should no longer be used.

Singleton service and exceptions

When you call a singleton service and encounter an exception, the singleton instance is not terminated and continues running. By default, all exceptions (with the exception of FaultException-derived classes) fault the channel and the client cannot issue subsequent calls other than closing the proxy. If the client had a session with the singleton, that session is terminated.

Faults

The fundamental problem with exceptions is that they are technology-specific and as such should not be shared across the service boundary. For seamless interoperability, you need a way to map technology-specific exceptions to some neutral error information. This representation is called *soap faults*. Soap faults are based on an industry standard that is independent of any technology-specific exceptions such as CLR, Java, or C++ exceptions. To throw a soap fault (or just a fault for short) the service cannot throw a raw CLR exception. Instead, the service should throw an instance of the FaultException<T> class, defined in Example 6-1.

Example 6-1. The FaultException<T> class

```
[Serializable] //More attributes
public class FaultException : CommunicationException
{
   public FaultException( );
   public FaultException(string reason);
   public FaultException(FaultReason reason);
   public virtual MessageFault CreateMessageFault( );
   //More members
}

[Serializable]
public class FaultException<T> : FaultException
{
   public FaultException(T detail);
   public FaultException(T detail,string reason);
   public FaultException(T detail,FaultReason reason);
   //More members
}
```

FaultException<T> is a specialization of FaultException, so any client that programs against FaultException will be able to handle FaultException<T> as well.

The type parameter T for FaultException<T> conveys the error details. The detailing type can be any type, not necessarily an Exception-derived class. The only constraint is that the type must be serializable or a data contract.

Example 6-2 demonstrates a simple calculator service that throws a FaultException<DivideByZeroException> in its implementation of the Divide( ) operation when asked to divide by zero.

Example 6-2. Throwing a FaultException<T>

```
[ServiceContract]
interface ICalculator
{
   [OperationContract]
   double Divide(double number1,double number2);
   //More methods
}

class Calculator : ICalculator
{
   public double Divide(double number1,double number2)
   {
      if(number2 == 0)
      {
         DivideByZeroException exception = new DivideByZeroException( );
         throw new FaultException<DivideByZeroException>(exception);
      }
      return number1 / number2;
   }
   //Rest of the implementation
}
```

Instead of FaultException<DivideByZeroException> the service could have also thrown a non-Exception-derived class:

```
throw new FaultException<double>( );
```

However, I find that using an Exception-derived detailing type is more aligned with the conventional .NET programming practices, and results in more readable code. In addition, it allows for exception promotion, discussed later on.

The reason parameter passed to the constructor of FaultException<T> is used as the exception message. You can pass a mere string for the reason:

```
DivideByZeroException exception = new DivideByZeroException( );
throw new FaultException<DivideByZeroException>(exception,"number2 is 0");
```

or you can pass a FaultReason, which is useful when localization is required.

Fault Contracts

By default, any exception thrown by the service reaches the client as a FaultException. The reason is that anything beyond communication errors that the service wishes to share with the client must be part of the service contractual behavior. To that end, WCF provides *fault contracts*—a way for the service to list the type of errors it can throw. The idea is that these types of errors should be the same as the type parameters used with FaultException<T>, and by listing them in a fault contract, a WCF client will be able to distinguish between contracted faults and other errors.

The service defines its fault contracts using the FaultContractAttribute:

```
[AttributeUsage(AttributeTargets.Method,AllowMultiple = true,Inherited = false)]
public sealed class FaultContractAttribute : Attribute
{
   public FaultContractAttribute(Type detailType);
   //More members
}
```

You apply the FaultContract attribute directly on a contract operation, specifying the error detailing type, as shown in Example 6-3.

Example 6-3. Defining a fault contract

```
[ServiceContract]
interface ICalculator
{
   [OperationContract]
   double Add(double number1,double number2);

   [OperationContract]
   [FaultContract(typeof(DivideByZeroException))]
   double Divide(double number1,double number2);
   //More methods
}
```

The effect of the FaultContract attribute is limited to the method it decorates. Only that method can throw that fault and have it propagated to the client. In addition, if the operation throws an exception that is not in the contract, it will reach the client as a plain FaultException. To propagate the exception, the service must throw exactly the same detailing type listed in the fault contract. For example, to satisfy this fault contract definition:

```
[FaultContract(typeof(DivideByZeroException))]
```

The service must throw FaultException<DivideByZeroException>. The service cannot even throw a subclass of the fault contract's detailing type and have it satisfy the contract:

```
[ServiceContract]
interface IMyContract
{
   [OperationContract]
   [FaultContract(typeof(Exception))]
   void MyMethod( );
}

class MyService : IMyContract
{
   public void MyMethod( )
   {
      //Will not satisfy contract
      throw new FaultException<DivideByZeroException>(new DivideByZeroException( ));
   }
}
```

The `FaultContract` attribute is configured to allow multiple usages so that you can list multiple fault contracts in a single operation:

```
[ServiceContract]
interface ICalculator
{
   [OperationContract]
   [FaultContract(typeof(InvalidOperationException))]
   [FaultContract(typeof(string))]
   double Add(double number1,double number2);

   [OperationContract]
   [FaultContract(typeof(DivideByZeroException))]
   double Divide(double number1,double number2);
   //More methods
}
```

This enables the service to throw any of the exceptions in the contracts and have them propagate to the client.

 You cannot provide a fault contract on a one-way operation, because in theory nothing should be returned from a one-way operation:

```
//Invalid definition
[ServiceContract]
interface IMyContract
{
   [OperationContract(IsOneWay = true)]
   [FaultContract(...)]
   void MyMethod( );
}
```

Trying to do so will result with an `InvalidOperationException` at the service load time.

Fault Handling

The fault contracts are published along with the rest of the service metadata. When a WCF client imports that metadata, the contract definitions contain the fault contracts as well as the fault detailing type definition, including the relevant data contract. This last point is important if the detailing type is some custom exception type with various dedicated fields.

The client can expect to catch and handle the imported fault types. For example, when you write a client against the contract shown in Example 6-3, the client can catch `FaultException<DivideByZeroException>`:

```
CalculatorClient proxy = new CalculatorClient( );
try
{
   proxy.Divide(2,0);
   proxy.Close( );
}
```

```
catch(FaultException<DivideByZeroException> exception)
{...}

catch(CommunicationException exception)
{...}
```

Note that the client can still encounter communication exceptions.

The client can choose to treat all noncommunication service-side exceptions uniformly by simply handling only the FaultException base exception:

```
CalculatorClient proxy = new CalculatorClient();
try
{
    proxy.Divide(2,0);
    proxy.Close();
}

catch(FaultException exception)
{...}

catch(CommunicationException exception)
{...}
```

 A somewhat esoteric case is when the client's developer manually changes the definition of the imported contract by removing the fault contract on the client side. In that case, when the service throws an exception listed in the service-side fault contract, the exception will manifest itself on the client as FaultException, not as the contracted fault.

When the service throws an exception listed in the service-side fault contract, the exception will not fault the communication channel. The client can catch that exception and continue using the proxy, or safely close the proxy.

Unknown Faults

The FaultException<T> class is derived from the class FaultException. The service (or any downstream object it uses) can throw an instance of FaultException directly:

```
throw new FaultException("Some Reason");
```

FaultException is a special type of an exception I call an *unknown fault*. An unknown fault is propagated to the client as a FaultException. The unknown fault will not fault the communication channel, so the client can keep using the proxy as if the exception was part of the fault contract.

 Note that any FaultException<T> thrown by the service always reaches the client as a FaultException<T> or as FaultException. If no fault contract is in place (or if T is not in the contract) then both FaultException and FaultException<T> thrown by the service reach the client as FaultException.

The Message property of the exception object on the client side will be set to the reason construction parameter of FaultException. The main use of FaultException is by downstream objects that are unaware of the fault contracts being used by their calling services. To avoid coupling such downstream objects to the top-level service, they can throw FaultException if they do not wish to fault the channel or if they wish to allow the client to handle the exception separately from any other communication error.

Fault Debugging

For a service already deployed, it is preferable to decouple that service from its clients, declare in the service fault contracts only the absolute bare minimum, and provide as little information as possible about the original error. However, during testing and debugging, it is very useful to include all exceptions in the information sent back to the client. This enables you to use a test client and a debugger to analyze the source of the error, instead of dealing with the all-encompassing yet opaque FaultException. For that purpose, use the ExceptionDetail class defined as:

```
[DataContract]
public class ExceptionDetail
{
    public ExceptionDetail(Exception exception);

    [DataMember]
    public string HelpLink
    {get;private set;}

    [DataMember]
    public ExceptionDetail InnerException
    {get;private set;}

    [DataMember]
    public string Message
    {get;private set;}

    [DataMember]
    public string StackTrace
    {get;private set;}

    [DataMember]
    public string Type
    {get;private set;}
}
```

You need to create an instance of ExceptionDetail and initialize it with the exception you want to propagate to the client. Next, instead of throwing the indented exception, throw a FaultException<ExceptionDetail> with the instance of ExceptionDetail as a construction parameter, and also provide the original exception's message as the fault reason. This sequence is shown in Example 6-4.

Example 6-4. Including the service exception in the fault message

```
[ServiceContract]
interface IMyContract
{
   [OperationContract]
   void MethodWithError( );
}
class MyService : IMyContract
{
   public void MethodWithError( )
   {
      InvalidOperationException exception =
                              new InvalidOperationException("Some error");
      ExceptionDetail detail = new ExceptionDetail(exception);
      throw new FaultException<ExceptionDetail>(detail,exception.Message);
   }
}
```

Doing so will enable the client to discover the original exception type and message. The client-side fault object will have the Detail.Type property that contains the name of the original service exception, and the Message property will contain the original exception message. Example 6-5 shows the client code processing the exception thrown in Example 6-4.

Example 6-5. Processing the included exception

```
MyContractClient proxy = new MyContractClient(endpointName);
try
{
   proxy.MethodWithError( );
}
catch(FaultException<ExceptionDetail> exception)
{
   Debug.Assert(exception.Detail.Type ==
                typeof(InvalidOperationException).ToString( ));
   Debug.Assert(exception.Message == "Some error");
}
```

Declarative exceptions inclusion

The ServiceBehavior attribute offers the Boolean property IncludeExceptionDetailInFaults, defined as:

```
[AttributeUsage(AttributeTargets.Class)]
public sealed class ServiceBehaviorAttribute : Attribute, ...
{
   public bool IncludeExceptionDetailInFaults
   {get;set;}
   //More members
}
```

IncludeExceptionDetailInFaults defaults to false. Setting it to true as in this snippet:

```
[ServiceBehavior(IncludeExceptionDetailInFaults = true)]
class MyService : IMyContract
{...}
```

has the same effect as in Example 6-4, only automated: all noncontractual faults and exceptions thrown by the service or any of its downstream objects are propagated to the client and included in the returned fault message for the client program to process them, as in Example 6-5:

```
[ServiceBehavior(IncludeExceptionDetailInFaults = true)]
class MyService : IMyContract
{
    public void MethodWithError()
    {
        throw new InvalidOperationException("Some error");
    }
}
```

Any fault thrown by the service (or its downstream objects) that is listed in the fault contract is unaffected, and is propagated as is to the client.

While including all exceptions is beneficial for debugging, great care should be taken to avoid shipping and deploying the service with IncludeExceptionDetailInFaults set to true. To automate this and avoid the potential pitfall, you can use conditional compilation as shown in Example 6-6.

Example 6-6. SettingIncludeExceptionDetailInFaults to true in debug only

```
public static class DebugHelper
{
    public const bool IncludeExceptionDetailInFaults =
#if DEBUG
        true;
#else
        false;
#endif
}

[ServiceBehavior(IncludeExceptionDetailInFaults =
                 DebugHelper.IncludeExceptionDetailInFaults)]
class MyService : IMyContract
{...}
```

 When IncludeExceptionDetailInFaults is true, the exception will actually fault the channel, so the client cannot issue subsequent calls.

Host and exceptions diagnostics

Obviously, including all exceptions in the fault message contributes greatly in debugging, but it also has a use when trying to analyze a problem in an already-deployed service. Fortunately, you can set IncludeExceptionDetailInFaults to true by the host, both programmatically and administratively in the host config file. When you set it programmatically, before opening the host, you need to find the service behavior in the service description and set the IncludeExceptionDetailInFaults property:

```
ServiceHost host = new ServiceHost(typeof(MyService));

ServiceBehaviorAttribute debuggingBehavior =
                    host.Description.Behaviors.Find<ServiceBehaviorAttribute>();

debuggingBehavior.IncludeExceptionDetailInFaults = true;

host.Open();
```

You can streamline this procedure by encapsulating it in ServiceHost<T>, as shown in Example 6-7.

Example 6-7. ServiceHost<T> and returning unknown exceptions

```
public class ServiceHost<T> : ServiceHost
{
   public bool IncludeExceptionDetailInFaults
   {
      set
      {
         if(State == CommunicationState.Opened)
         {
            throw new InvalidOperationException("Host is already opened");
         }
         ServiceBehaviorAttribute debuggingBehavior =
                       Description.Behaviors.Find<ServiceBehaviorAttribute>();
         debuggingBehavior.IncludeExceptionDetailInFaults = value;
      }
      get
      {
         ServiceBehaviorAttribute debuggingBehavior =
                       Description.Behaviors.Find<ServiceBehaviorAttribute>();
         return debuggingBehavior.IncludeExceptionDetailInFaults;
      }
   }
}
```

Using ServiceHost<T> is trivial and readable:

```
ServiceHost<MyService> host = new ServiceHost<MyService>();
host.IncludeExceptionDetailInFaults = true;
host.Open();
```

To apply this behavior administratively, add a custom behavior section in the host config file and reference it in the service definition, as shown in Example 6-8.

Example 6-8. Administratively including exceptions in the fault message

```
<system.serviceModel>
   <services>
      <service name = "MyService" behaviorConfiguration = "Debugging">
         ...
      </service>
   </services>
   <behaviors>
      <serviceBehaviors>
         <behavior name = "Debugging">
            <serviceDebug includeExceptionDetailInFaults = "true"/>
         </behavior>
      </serviceBehaviors>
   </behaviors>
</system.serviceModel>
```

The advantage of administrative configuration in this case is the ability to toggle the behavior in production post-deployment without affecting the service code.

Faults and Callbacks

Callbacks to the client can of course fail due to communication exceptions or because the callback itself threw an exception. Similar to service contract operations, callback contract operations can too define fault contracts, as shown in Example 6-9.

Example 6-9. Callback contract with fault contract

```
[ServiceContract(CallbackContract = typeof(IMyContractCallback))]
interface IMyContract
{
   [OperationContract]
   void DoSomething();
}
interface IMyContractCallback
{
   [OperationContract]
   [FaultContract(typeof(InvalidOperationException))]
   void OnCallBack();
}
```

Callbacks in WCF are usually configured as one-way calls, and as such cannot define their own fault contracts.

However, unlike normal service invocation, what is propagated to the service and how the error manifests itself is also the product of the following:

- When the callback is being invoked; meaning, whether the callback is being invoked during a service call to its calling client, or whether it is invoked out-of-band by some other party on the host side.
- The binding used.
- The type of the exception thrown.

If the callback is invoked out-of-band—that is, by some party besides the service during a service operation—then the callback behaves like a normal WCF operation invocation. Example 6-10 demonstrates out-of-band invocation of the callback contract defined in Example 6-9.

Example 6-10. Fault handling in out-of-band invocation

```
[ServiceBehavior(InstanceContextMode = InstanceContextMode.PerCall)]
class MyService : IMyContract
{
   static List<IMyContractCallback> m_Callbacks =
                                    new List<IMyContractCallback>();
   public void DoSomething()
   {
      IMyContractCallback callback =
             OperationContext.Current.GetCallbackChannel<IMyContractCallback>();

      if(m_Callbacks.Contains(callback) == false)
      {
         m_Callbacks.Add(callback);
      }
   }
   public static void CallClients()
   {
   Action<IMyContractCallback> invoke = delegate(IMyContractCallback callback)
                                        {
                                           try
                                           {
                                              callback.OnCallback();
                                           }
                        catch(FaultException<InvalidOperationException> exception)
                                           {...}
                                           catch(FaultException exception)
                                           {...}
                                           catch(CommunicationException exception)
                                           {...}
                                        };
      m_Callbacks.ForEach(invoke);
   }
}
```

As you can see, it is valid to expect to handle the callback fault contract because faults are propagated to the host side according to it. If the client callback throws an exception listed in the callback fault contract, or if the callback threw a FaultException, it will not fault the callback channel and you can catch the exception and continue using the callback channel. However, as with service calls, after an exception that is not part of the fault contract, avoid using the callback channel.

If the callback is invoked by the service during a service operation and the exception is listed in the fault contract or if the client callback threw a FaultException, the callback fault behaves just as with the out-of-band invocation:

```
[ServiceBehavior(ConcurrencyMode = ConcurrencyMode.Reentrant)]
class MyService : IMyContract
{
    public void DoSomething()
    {
        IMyContractCallback callback =
                OperationContext.Current.GetCallbackChannel<IMyContractCallback>();
        try
        {
            callback.OnCallBack();
        }
        catch(FaultException<int> exception)
        {...}
    }
}
```

Note that the service must be configured for reentrancy to avoid a deadlock, as explained in Chapter 5. Because the callback operation defines a fault contract, it is guaranteed not to be a one-way method, hence the need for reentrancy.

Both the out-of-band and the service callbacks as described so far provide for the expected intuitive behavior.

The scenario gets considerably more complex when the service invokes the callback and the callback operation throws an exception not listed in the fault contract (or not a FaultException).

If the service uses either the TCP or the IPC binding, then when the callback throws an exception not in the contract, the client that called the service in the first place immediately receives a CommunicationException, even if the service catches the exception. The service then gets a FaultException. The service can catch and handle the exception, but the exception faults the channel, so that the service cannot reuse it:

```
[ServiceBehavior(ConcurrencyMode = ConcurrencyMode.Reentrant)]
class MyService : IMyContract
{
    public void DoSomething()
    {
        IMyContractCallback callback =
                OperationContext.Current.GetCallbackChannel<IMyContractCallback>();
        try
```

```
    {
        callback.OnCallBack();
    }
    catch(FaultException exception)
    {...}
    }
}
```

If the service uses the dual WS binding, when the callback throws an exception not in the contract, the client that called the service in the first place immediately receives a CommunicationException, even if the service catches the exception. Meanwhile, the service is blocked and will eventually be unblocked with a timeout exception:

```
[ServiceBehavior(ConcurrencyMode = ConcurrencyMode.Reentrant)]
class MyService : IMyContract
{
    public void DoSomething()
    {
        IMyContractCallback callback =
                OperationContext.Current.GetCallbackChannel<IMyContractCallback>();
        try
        {
            callback.OnCallBack();
        }
        catch(TimeoutException exception)
        {...}
    }
}
```

The service cannot reuse the callback channel.

 The large degree of discrepancy in callback behaviors just described is a design deficiency of WCF; that is, it is by design and not a defect. That said, it may be partially addressed in future releases.

Callbacks debugging

While the callback can use the same technique shown in Example 6-4 to manually include the exception in the fault message, the CallbackBehavior attribute provides the Boolean property IncludeExceptionDetailInFaults, used to include all nonfault contract exceptions (besides FaultException) in the message:

```
[AttributeUsage(AttributeTargets.Class)]
public sealed class CallbackBehaviorAttribute : Attribute,...
{
    public bool IncludeExceptionDetailInFaults
    {get;set;}
    //More members
}
```

Similar to the service, including the exceptions is instrumental in debugging:

```
[CallbackBehavior(IncludeExceptionDetailInFaults = true)]
class MyClient : IMyContractCallback
```

```
{
   public void OnCallBack( )
   {
      ...
      throw new InvalidOperationException( );
   }
}
```

You can also configure this behavior administratively in the client config file:

```
<client>
   <endpoint ... behaviorConfiguration = "Debug"
   ...
   />
</client>
<behaviors>
   <endpointBehaviors>
      <behavior name = "Debug">
         <callbackDebug includeExceptionDetailInFaults = "true"/>
      </behavior>
   </endpointBehaviors>
</behaviors>
```

Note the use of the endpointBehaviors tag to affect the client's callback endpoint.

Error-Handling Extensions

WCF enables developers to customize the default exception reporting and propagation, and even provide for a hook for custom logging. This extensibility is applied per channel dispatcher, although you are more than likely to simply utilize it across all dispatchers.

To install your own error-handling extension, you need to provide the dispatchers with an implementation of the IErrorHandler interface defined as:

```
public interface IErrorHandler
{
   bool HandleError(Exception error);
   void ProvideFault(Exception error,MessageVersion version,ref Message fault);
}
```

Any party can provide this implementation, but typically it will be provided either by the service itself or by the host. In fact, you can have multiple error-handling extensions chained together. You will see later in this section just how to install the extensions.

Providing a Fault

The ProvideFault( ) method of the extension object is called immediately after any exception is thrown by the service or any object on the call chain down from a service operation. WCF calls ProvideFault( ) before returning control to the client and before terminating the session (if present) and before disposing of the service instance (if required). Because ProvideFault( ) is called on the incoming call thread while the client it still blocked waiting for the operation to complete, you should avoid lengthy execution inside ProvideFault( ).

Using ProvideFault( )

ProvideFault( ) is called regardless of the type of exception thrown, be it a regular CLR exception, a fault, or a fault in the fault contract. The error parameter is a reference to the exception just thrown. If ProvideFault( ) does nothing, the client will get an exception according to the fault contract (if any) and the exception type being thrown, as discussed previously in this chapter:

```
class MyErrorHandler : IErrorHandler
{
   public bool HandleError(Exception error)
   {...}

   public void ProvideFault(Exception error,MessageVersion version,
                                                 ref Message fault)
   {
      //Nothing here - exception will go up as usual
   }
}
```

However, ProvideFault( ) can examine the error parameter and either return it to the client as is, or ProvideFault( ) can provide an alternative fault. This alternative behavior will affect even exceptions that are in the fault contract. To provide an alternative fault, you need to use the CreateMessageFault( ) method of FaultException to create an alternative fault message. If you are providing a new fault contract message, you must create a new detailing object, and you cannot reuse the original error reference. You then provide the created fault message to the static CreateMessage( ) method of the Message class:

```
public abstract class Message
{
   public static Message CreateMessage(MessageVersion version,
                                 MessageFault fault,string action);
   //More members
}
```

Note that you need to provide CreateMessage( ) with the action of the fault message used. This intricate sequence is demonstrated in Example 6-11.

Example 6-11. Creating an alternative fault

```
class MyErrorHandler : IErrorHandler
{
   public bool HandleError(Exception error)
   {...}
   public void ProvideFault(Exception error,MessageVersion version,
                                     ref Message fault)
```

Example 6-11. Creating an alternative fault (continued)

```
    {
        FaultException<int> faultException = new FaultException<int>(3);
        MessageFault messageFault = faultException.CreateMessageFault();
        fault = Message.CreateMessage(version,messageFault,faultException.Action);
    }
}
```

In Example 6-11, the ProvideFault() method provides FaultException<int> with a value of 3 as the fault thrown by the service, irrespective of the actual exception that was thrown.

The implementation of ProvideFault() can also set the fault parameter to null:

```
    class MyErrorHandler : IErrorHandler
    {
        public bool HandleError(Exception error)
        {...}
        public void ProvideFault(Exception error,MessageVersion version,
                                                        ref Message fault)
        {
            fault = null;//Suppress any faults in contract
        }
    }
```

Doing so will result with all exceptions propagated to the client as a FaultException, even if the exceptions were according to the fault contract. Setting fault to null is an effective way of suppressing any fault contract that may be in place.

Exception promotion

One possible use for ProvideFault() is a technique I call *exception promotion*. The service may use downstream objects. The objects could be called by a variety of services. In the interest of decoupling, these objects may very well be unaware of the particular fault contracts of the service calling them. In case of errors, the objects simply throw regular CLR exceptions. What the service could do is use an error-handling extension to examine the exception thrown. If that exception is of the type T, where FaultException<T> is part of the operation fault contract, the service could promote that exception to a full-fledged FaultException<T>. For example, given this service contract:

```
    interface IMyContract
    {
        [OperationContract]
        [FaultContract(typeof(InvalidOperationException))]
        void MyMethod();
    }
```

if the downstream object throws an InvalidOperationException, ProvideFault() will promote it to FaultException<InvalidOperationException>, as shown in Example 6-12.

Example 6-12. Exception promotion

```
class MyErrorHandler : IErrorHandler
{
   public bool HandleError(Exception error)
   {...}
   public void ProvideFault(Exception error,MessageVersion version,
                                                       ref Message fault)
   {
      if(error is InvalidOperationException)
      {
         FaultException<InvalidOperationException> faultException =
                              new FaultException<InvalidOperationException>(
                              new InvalidOperationException(error.Message));
         MessageFault messageFault = faultException.CreateMessageFault();
         fault = Message.CreateMessage(version,messageFault,faultException.Action);
      }
   }
}
```

The problem with Example 6-12 is that the code is coupled to a specific fault contract, and it requires a lot of tedious work across all services to implement it, not to mention that any change to the fault contract will necessitate a change to the error extension.

Fortunately, you can automate exception promotion using my `ErrorHandlerHelper` static class:

```
public static class ErrorHandlerHelper
{
   public static void PromoteException(Type serviceType,
                                       Exception error,
                                       MessageVersion version,
                                       ref Message fault);
   //More members
}
```

The `ErrorHandlerHelper.PromoteException()` requires the service type as a parameter. It will then use reflection to examine all the interfaces and operations on that service type, looking for fault contracts for the particular operation. It gets the faulted operation by parsing the error object. `PromoteException()` will promote a CLR exception to a contracted fault if the exception type matches any one of the detailing types defined in the fault contracts for that operation.

Using `ErrorHandlerHelper`, Example 6-12 can be reduced to one or two lines of code:

```
class MyErrorHandler : IErrorHandler
{
   public bool HandleError(Exception error)
   {...}
   public void ProvideFault(Exception error,MessageVersion version,
                                                       ref Message fault)
   {
```

```
        Type serviceType = ...;
        ErrorHandlerHelper.PromoteException(serviceType,error,version,ref fault);
    }
}
```

The implementation of PromoteException( ) has little to do with WCF and as such is not listed in this chapter. Instead you can examine it as part of the source code available with this book. The implementation makes use of some advanced C# programming techniques such as generics and reflection, string parsing, anonymous methods, and late binding.

Handling a Fault

The HandleError( ) method of IErrorHandler is defined as:

```
bool HandleError(Exception error);
```

HandleError( ) is called by WCF after control returns to the client. HandleError( ) is strictly for service-side use, and nothing it does affects the client in any way. HandleError( ) is called on a separate worker thread, not the thread that was used to process the service request (and the call to ProvideFault( )). Having a separate thread used in the background enables you to perform lengthy processing, such as logging to a database without impeding the client.

Because you could have multiple error-handling extensions installed in a list, WCF also enables you to control whether extensions down the list should be used. If HandleError( ) returns false, then WCF will continue to call HandleError( ) on the rest of the installed extensions. If HandleError( ) returns true, WCF stops invoking the error-handling extensions. Obviously, most extensions should return false.

The error parameter of HandleError( ) is the original exception thrown. The classic use for HandleError( ) is logging and tracing, as shown in Example 6-13.

Example 6-13. Logging the error log to a logbook service

```
class MyErrorHandler : IErrorHandler
{
   public bool HandleError(Exception error)
   {
      try
      {
         LogbookServiceClient proxy = new LogbookServiceClient( );
         proxy.Log(...);
         proxy.Close( );
      }
      catch
      {}
      finally
      {
         return false;
      }
   }
```

Example 6-13. Logging the error log to a logbook service (continued)

```
   }
   public void ProvideFault(Exception error,MessageVersion version,
                                              ref Message fault)
   {...}
}
```

The Logbook service

The source code available with this book contains a standalone service called LogbookService, dedicated to error logging. LogbookService logs the errors into a SQL Server database. The service contract also provides operations for retrieving the entries in the logbook and clearing the logbook. The source code also contains a simple logbook viewer and management tool. In addition to error logging, LogbookService allows you to log entries explicitly into the logbook independently of exceptions. The architecture of this framework is depicted in Figure 6-1.

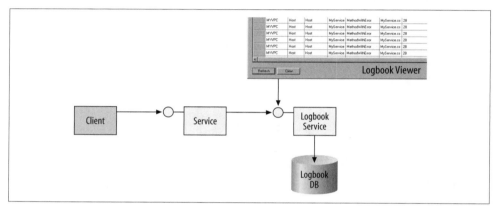

Figure 6-1. The LogbookService and viewer

You can automate error logging to LogbookService using the LogError( ) method of my ErrorHandlerHelper static class:

```
public static class ErrorHandlerHelper
{
   public static void LogError(Exception error);
   //More members
}
```

The error parameter is simply the exception you wish to log. LogError( ) encapsulates the call to LogbookService. For example, instead of Example 6-13, you can simply write a single line:

```
class MyErrorHandler : IErrorHandler
{
   public bool HandleError(Exception error)
   {
```

```
        ErrorHandlerHelper.LogError(error);
        return false;
    }
    public void ProvideFault(Exception error,MessageVersion version,
                                                    ref Message fault)
    {...}
}
```

In addition to the raw exception information, `LogError( )` performs extensive parsing of the exception and other environment variables for a comprehensive record of the error and its related information.

Specifically, `LogError( )` captures the following information:

- Where the exception occurred (machine name and host process name)
- The code where the exception took place (the assembly name, the filename, and the line number)
- The type where the exception took place and the member being accessed
- The date and time of the exception
- The exception name and message

Implementing `LogError( )` has little to do with WCF and therefore is not shown in this chapter. The code, however, makes extensive use of interesting .NET programming techniques such as string and exception parsing, along with obtaining the environment information. The error information is passed in a dedicated data contract to `LogbookService`.

Installing Error-Handling Extensions

Every channel dispatcher in WCF offers a collection of error extensions:

```
public class ChannelDispatcher : ChannelDispatcherBase
{
    public Collection<IErrorHandler> ErrorHandlers
    {get;}
    //More members
}
```

Installing your own custom implementation of `IErrorHandler` requires merely adding it to the desired dispatcher (usually all of them).

You must add the error extensions before the first call arrives to the service and yet after the collection of dispatchers is constructed by the host. This narrow window of opportunity exists after the host is initialized but not yet opened. To act in that window, the best solution is to treat error extensions as custom service behaviors, because the behaviors are given the opportunity to interact with the dispatchers at just the right time. As mentioned in Chapter 4, all service behaviors implement the `IServiceBehavior` interface defined as:

```
public interface IServiceBehavior
{
```

```
        void AddBindingParameters(ServiceDescription description,
                                  ServiceHostBase host,
                                  Collection<ServiceEndpoint> endpoints,
                                  BindingParameterCollection parameters);

        void ApplyDispatchBehavior(ServiceDescription description,
                                   ServiceHostBase host);

        void Validate(ServiceDescription description,ServiceHostBase host);
    }
```

The ApplyDispatchBehavior( ) method is your cue to add the error extension to the dispatchers. You can safely ignore all other methods of IServiceBehavior and provide an empty implementation.

In ApplyDispatchBehavior( ) you need to access the collection of dispatchers available in the ChannelDispatchers property of ServiceHostBase:

```
public class ChannelDispatcherCollection :
                                SynchronizedCollection<ChannelDispatcherBase>
{}
public abstract class ServiceHostBase : ...
{
    public ChannelDispatcherCollection ChannelDispatchers
    {get;}
    //More members
}
```

Each item in ChannelDispatchers is of the type ChannelDispatcher. You can add the implementation of IErrorHandler to all dispatchers or just add it to specific dispatchers associated with a particular binding. Example 6-14 demonstrates adding an implementation of IErrorHandler to all dispatchers of a service.

Example 6-14. Adding an error extension object

```
class MyErrorHandler : IErrorHandler
{...}

class MyService : IMyContract,IServiceBehavior
{
    public void ApplyDispatchBehavior(ServiceDescription description,
                                      ServiceHostBase host)
    {
        IErrorHandler handler = new MyErrorHandler( );
        foreach(ChannelDispatcher dispatcher in host.ChannelDispatchers)
        {
            dispatcher.ErrorHandlers.Add(handler);
        }
    }
    public void Validate(...)
    {}
    public void AddBindingParameters(...)
    {}
}
```

In Example 6-14, the service itself implements ISeviceBehavior. In ApplyDispatchBehavior( ), the service obtains the dispatchers collection and adds an instance of the MyErrorHandler class to each dispatcher. Instead of relying on an external class to implement IErrorHandler, the service class itself can support IErrorHandler directly, as shown in Example 6-15.

Example 6-15. Supporting IErrorHandler by the service class

```
class MyService : IMyContract,IServiceBehavior,IErrorHandler
{
   public void ApplyDispatchBehavior(ServiceDescription description,
                                     ServiceHostBase host)
   {
      foreach(ChannelDispatcher dispatcher in host.ChannelDispatchers)
      {
         dispatcher.ErrorHandlers.Add(this);
      }
   }
   public bool HandleError(Exception error)
   {...}

   public void ProvideFault(Exception error,MessageVersion version,
                                            ref Message fault)
   {...}
   //More members
}
```

Error-Handling attribute

The problem both with Examples 6-14 and 6-15 is that they pollute the service class code with WCF plumbing. Instead of having the service focus on the business logic, it also has to wire up error extensions. Fortunately, you can provide the same plumbing declaratively using my ErrorHandlerBehaviorAttribute, defined as:

```
public class ErrorHandlerBehaviorAttribute : Attribute,IErrorHandler,
                                             IServiceBehavior
{
   protected Type ServiceType
   {get;set;}
}
```

Applying the ErrorHandlerBehavior attribute is straightforward:

```
[ErrorHandlerBehavior]
class MyService : IMyContract
{...}
```

The attribute installs itself as the error-handling extension. Its implementation uses ErrorHandlerHelper to both automatically promote exceptions to fault contracts if required, and to automatically log the exception to LogbookService. Example 6-16 lists the code for the ErrorHandlerBehavior attribute.

Example 6-16. The ErrorHandlerBehavior attribute

```
[AttributeUsage(AttributeTargets.Class)]
public class ErrorHandlerBehaviorAttribute : Attribute,IServiceBehavior,
                                             IErrorHandler
{
   protected Type ServiceType
   {get;set;}

   void IServiceBehavior.ApplyDispatchBehavior(ServiceDescription description,
                                               ServiceHostBase host)
   {
      ServiceType = description.ServiceType;
      foreach(ChannelDispatcher dispatcher in host.ChannelDispatchers)
      {
         dispatcher.ErrorHandlers.Add(this);
      }
   }
   bool IErrorHandler.HandleError(Exception error)
   {
      ErrorHandlerHelper.LogError(error);
      return false;
   }
   void IErrorHandler.ProvideFault(Exception error,MessageVersion version,
                                                   ref Message fault)
   {
      ErrorHandlerHelper.PromoteException(ServiceType,error,version,ref fault);
   }
   void IServiceBehavior.Validate(...)
   {}
   void IServiceBehavior.AddBindingParameters(...)
   {}
}
```

Note in Example 6-16 that `ApplyDispatchBehavior( )` saves the service type in a protected property. The reason is that the call to `ErrorHandlerHelper.PromoteException( )` in `ProvideFault( )` requires the service type.

Host and Error Extensions

While the `ErrorHandlerBehavior` attribute greatly simplifies the act of installing an error extension, it does require the service developer to apply the attribute. It would be nice if the host could add error extensions independently of whether or not the service provides one. However, due to the narrow timing window of installing the extension, having the host add such an extension requires multiple steps. First, you need to provide an error-handling extension type that supports both `IServiceBehavior` and `IErrorHandler`. The implementation of `IServiceBehavior` will add the error extension to the dispatchers as shown previously. Next, derive a custom host class from

ServiceHost and override the OnOpening( ) method defined by the CommunicationObject base class:

```
public abstract class CommunicationObject : ICommunicationObject
{
   protected virtual void OnOpening( );
   //More memebrs
}
public abstract class ServiceHostBase : CommunicationObject ,...
{...}
public class ServiceHost : ServiceHostBase,...
{...}
```

In OnOpening( ) you need to add the custom error-handling type to the collection of service behaviors in the service description. That behaviors collection was described in Chapters 1 and 4:

```
public class Collection<T> : IList<T>,...
{
   public void Add(T item);
   //More members
}
public abstract class KeyedCollection<K,T> : Collection<T>
{...}
public class KeyedByTypeCollection<I> : KeyedCollection<Type,I>
{...}
public class ServiceDescription
{
   public KeyedByTypeCollection<IServiceBehavior> Behaviors
   {get;}
}
public abstract class ServiceHostBase : ...
{
   public ServiceDescription Description
   {get;}
   //More members
}
```

This sequence of steps is already encapsulated and automated in ServiceHost<T>:

```
public class ServiceHost<T> : ServiceHost
{
   public void AddErrorHandler(IErrorHandler errorHandler);
   public void AddErrorHandler( );
   //More members
}
```

ServiceHost<T> offers two overloaded versions of the AddErrorHandler( ) method. The one that takes an IErrorHandler object will internally associate it with a behavior so that you could provide it with any class that supports just IErrorHandler, not IServiceBehavior:

```
class MyService : IMyContract
{...}
```

```
class MyErrorHandler : IErrorHandler
{...}

SerivceHost<MyService> host = new SerivceHost<MyService>();
host.AddErrorHandler(new MyErrorHandler());
host.Open();
```

The AddErrorHandler() method that takes no parameters will install an error-handling extension that uses ErrorHandlerHelper, just as if the service class was decorated with the ErrorHandlerBehavior attribute:

```
class MyService : IMyContract
{...}

SerivceHost<MyService> host = new SerivceHost<MyService>();
host.AddErrorHandler();
host.Open();
```

Actually, for this last example, ServiceHost<T> does use internally an instance of the ErrorHandlerBehaviorAttribute.

Example 6-17 shows the implementation of the AddErrorHandler() method.

Example 6-17. Implementing AddErrorHandler()

```
public class ServiceHost<T> : ServiceHost
{
   class ErrorHandlerBehavior : IServiceBehavior,IErrorHandler
   {
      IErrorHandler m_ErrorHandler;

      public ErrorHandlerBehavior(IErrorHandler errorHandler)
      {
         m_ErrorHandler = errorHandler;
      }
      void IServiceBehavior.ApplyDispatchBehavior(ServiceDescription description,
                                                  ServiceHostBase host)
      {
         foreach(ChannelDispatcher dispatcher in host.ChannelDispatchers)
         {
            dispatcher.ErrorHandlers.Add(this);
         }
      }
      bool IErrorHandler.HandleError(Exception error)
      {
         return m_ErrorHandler.HandleError(error);
      }
      void IErrorHandler.ProvideFault(Exception error,MessageVersion version,
                                                       ref Message fault)
      {
         m_ErrorHandler.ProvideFault(error,version,ref fault);
      }
      //Rest of the implementation
   }
```

Example 6-17. Implementing AddErrorHandler() (continued)

```
   List<IServiceBehavior> m_ErrorHandlers = new List<IServiceBehavior>();

   public void AddErrorHandler(IErrorHandler errorHandler)
   {
      if(State == CommunicationState.Opened)
      {
         throw new InvalidOperationException("Host is already opened");
      }
      IServiceBehavior errorHandler = new ErrorHandlerBehavior(errorHandler);
      m_ErrorHandlers.Add(errorHandlerBehavior);
   }
   public void AddErrorHandler()
   {
      if(State == CommunicationState.Opened)
      {
         throw new InvalidOperationException("Host is already opened");
      }
      IServiceBehavior errorHandler = new ErrorHandlerBehaviorAttribute();
      m_ErrorHandlers.Add(errorHandlerBehavior);
   }
   protected override void OnOpening()
   {
      foreach(IServiceBehavior behavior in m_ErrorHandlers)
      {
         Description.Behaviors.Add(behavior);
      }
      base.OnOpening();
   }
   //Rest of the implementation
}
```

To avoid forcing the provided IErrorHandler reference to also support
IServiceBehavior, ServiceHost<T> defines a private nested class called
ErrorHandlerBehavior. ErrorHandlerBehavior implements both IErrorHandler and
IServiceBehavior. To construct ErrorHandlerBehavior, you need to provide it with an
implementation of IErrorHandler. That implementation is saved for later use. The
implementation of IServiceBehavior adds the instance itself to the error-handler collection of all dispatchers. The implementation of IErrorHandler simply delegates to
the saved construction parameter. ServiceHost<T> defines a list of IServiceBehavior
references in the m_ErrorHandlers member variable. The AddErrorHandler() method
that accepts an IErrorHandler reference uses it to construct an instance of
ErrorHandlerBehavior and then adds it to m_ErrorHandlers. The AddErrorHandler()
method that takes no parameter uses an instance of the
ErrorHandlerBehaviorAttribute, because the attribute is merely a class that supports
both IErrorHandler and IServiceBehavior. The attribute instance is also added to
m_ErrorHandlers. Finally, the OnOpening() method iterates over m_ErrorHandlers,
adding each behavior to the behavior collection.

Callbacks and Error Extensions

The client-side callback object can also provide an implementation of IErrorHandler for error handling. Compared with the service-error extensions, the main difference is that to install the callback extension, you need to use the IEndpointBehavior interface defined as:

```
public interface IEndpointBehavior
{
    void AddBindingParameters(ServiceEndpoint serviceEndpoint,
                              BindingParameterCollection bindingParameters);
    void ApplyClientBehavior(ServiceEndpoint serviceEndpoint,
                             ClientRuntime behavior);
    void ApplyDispatchBehavior(ServiceEndpoint serviceEndpoint,
                               EndpointDispatcher endpointDispatcher);
    void Validate(ServiceEndpoint serviceEndpoint);
}
```

IEndpointBehavior is the interface supported by all callback behaviors. The only relevant method for the purpose of installing an error extension is the ApplyClientBehavior() method, which lets you associate the error extension with the single dispatcher of the callback. The behavior parameter is of the type ClientRuntime, which offers the CallbackDispatchRuntime property of the type DispatchRuntime. The DispatchRuntime class offers the ChannelDispatcher with its collection of error handlers:

```
public sealed class ClientRuntime
{
    public DispatchRuntime CallbackDispatchRuntime
    {get;}
    //More members
}
public sealed class DispatchRuntime
{
    public ChannelDispatcher ChannelDispatcher
    {get;}
    //More members
}
```

As with a service-side error-handling extension, you need to add to that collection your custom error-handling implementation of IErrorHandler.

The callback object itself can implement IEndpointBehavior, as shown in Example 6-18.

Example 6-18. Implementing IEndpointBehavior

```
class MyErrorHandler : IErrorHandler
{...}

class MyClient : IMyContractCallback,IEndpointBehavior
{
    public void OnCallBack()
```

Example 6-18. Implementing IEndpointBehavior (continued)

```
{...}

void IEndpointBehavior.ApplyClientBehavior(ServiceEndpoint serviceEndpoint,
                                           ClientRuntime behavior)
{
   IErrorHandler handler = new MyErrorHandler( );

   behavior.CallbackDispatchRuntime.ChannelDispatcher.
                                             ErrorHandlers.Add(handler);
}

void IEndpointBehavior.AddBindingParameters(...)
{}
void IEndpointBehavior.ApplyDispatchBehavior(...)
{}
void IEndpointBehavior.Validate(...)
{}
}
```

Instead of using an external class for implementing `IErrorHandler`, the callback class itself can implement `IErrorHandler` directly:

```
class MyClient : IMyContractCallback,IEndpointBehavior,IErrorHandler
{
   public void OnCallBack( )
   {...}

   void IEndpointBehavior.ApplyClientBehavior(ServiceEndpoint serviceEndpoint,
                                              ClientRuntime behavior)
   {
      behavior.CallbackDispatchRuntime.ChannelDispatcher.ErrorHandlers.Add(this);
   }
   public bool HandleError(Exception error)
   {...}
   public void ProvideFault(Exception error,MessageVersion version,
                                                    ref Message fault)
   {...}
}
```

Callback error-handling attribute

To automate code such as in Example 6-18, `CallbackErrorHandlerBehaviorAttribute` is defined as:

```
public class CallbackErrorHandlerBehaviorAttribute : ErrorHandlerBehaviorAttribute,
                                                     IEndpointBehavior
{
   public CallbackErrorHandlerBehaviorAttribute(Type clientType);
}
```

The `CallbackErrorHandlerBehavior` attribute derives from the service-side `ErrorHandlerBehavior` attribute, and adds explicit implementation of `IEndpointBehavior`. The attribute uses `ErrorHandlerHelper` to promote and log the exception.

In addition, the attribute requires as a construction parameter the type of the callback it is applied on:

```
[CallbackErrorHandlerBehavior(typeof(MyClient))]
class MyClient : IMyContractCallback
{
   public void OnCallBack()
   {...}
}
```

The type is required because there is no other way to get a hold of the callback type, which is required by `ErrorHandlerHelper.PromoteException()`.

The implementation of `CallbackErrorHandlerBehaviorAttribute` is shown in Example 6-19.

Example 6-19. Implementing CallbackErrorHandlerBehavior attribute

```
public class CallbackErrorHandlerBehaviorAttribute : ErrorHandlerBehaviorAttribute,
                                                     IEndpointBehavior
{
   public CallbackErrorHandlerBehaviorAttribute(Type clientType)
   {
      ServiceType = clientType;
   }
   void IEndpointBehavior.ApplyClientBehavior(ServiceEndpoint serviceEndpoint,
                                              ClientRuntime behavior)
   {
      behavior.CallbackDispatchRuntime.ChannelDispatcher.ErrorHandlers.Add(this);
   }
   void IEndpointBehavior.AddBindingParameters(...)
   {}
   void IEndpointBehavior.ApplyDispatchBehavior(...)
   {}
   void IEndpointBehavior.Validate(...)
   {}
}
```

Note in Example 6-19 how the provided callback client type is stored in the `ServiceType` protected property, defined as protected in Example 6-16.

CHAPTER 7

Transactions

Transactions are the key to building robust, high-quality service-oriented applications. WCF provides simple, declarative transaction support for service developers, enabling you to configure parameters such as enlistment and voting, all outside the scope of your service. In addition, WCF allows client applications to create transactions and to propagate transactions across service boundaries. This chapter starts by introducing the problem space transactions address and the basic transactions terminology, and then discusses the support for transactions and transaction management offered by WCF. The rest of the chapter is dedicated to transactional programming models, both by services and clients, and how transactions relate to other aspects of WCF, such as instance management and callbacks.

The Recovery Challenge

Proper error handling and recovery is the Achilles' heel of many applications. Once an application fails to perform a particular operation, you should recover from it and restore the system—that is, the collection of interacting services and clients—to a consistent state, usually the state the system was at before the operation that caused the error took place. Typically, any operation that can fail consists of multiple, potentially concurrent, smaller steps. Some of those steps can fail while the others succeed. The problem with recovery is the sheer number of partial success and partial failure permutations that you have to code against. For example, an operation comprising 10 smaller, concurrent steps has some three million recovery scenarios, because for the recovery logic, the order in which the operations fails matters as well, and the factorial of 10 is roughly three million.

Trying to handcraft recovery code in a decent-size application is often a futile attempt, resulting in fragile code that is very susceptible to any change in the application execution or the business use case, incurring both productivity and performance penalties. The productivity penalty results from simply putting in all the effort for handcrafting the recovery logic. The performance penalty is inherited with such an approach because you need to execute huge amounts of code after every operation to verify all is well. In reality, developers tend to deal only with the easy recovery cases; that is, the cases that they are both aware of and know how to deal with. More insidious error scenarios, such as intermediate network failures or disk crashes, go unaddressed. In addition, because recovery is all about restoring the system to a consistent state (typically the state before the operations), the real problem is the operations that succeeded, rather than those that failed. The reason is that the failed operations failed to affect the system. The challenge here is the need to undo successful steps, such as deleting a row from a table, or a node from a linked list, or a call to a remote service. The scenarios involved could be very complex, and your manual recovery logic is almost bound to miss a few successful suboperations.

The more complex the recovery logic becomes, the more error-prone the recovery logic itself becomes. If you have an error in the recovery, how would you recover the recovery? How do developers go about designing, testing, and debugging complex recovery logic? How do they simulate the endless number of errors and failures possible? Not only that, but what if before the operation failed, as it was progressing along executing operations successfully, some other party accessed your applications and acted upon the state of the system—the state that you are going to roll back during the recovery? That other party is now acting on inconsistent information and, by definition, is in error too. Moreover, your operation may be just a step in some other, much wider operation that spans multiple services from multiple vendors on multiple machines. How would you recover the system as a whole in such a case? Even if you have a miraculous way of recovering your service, how would that recovery logic plug into the cross-service recovery?

Transactions

The best (or perhaps only) way of maintaining system consistency and dealing properly with the error recovery challenge is to use transactions. A *transaction* is a set of potentially complex operations in which the failure of any single operation causes the entire set to fail, as one atomic operation. As illustrated in Figure 7-1, while the transaction is in progress, the system is allowed to be in a temporary inconsistent state, but once the transaction is complete, you are guaranteed to be in a consistent state, either a new consistent state (B) or the original consistent state the system was at before the transaction started (A).

If the transaction executed successfully, and managed to transfer the system from the consistent state A to the consistent state B, it is called a *committed transaction*. If the transaction encountered any error during its execution and rolled back all the intermediate steps that have already succeeded, it is called an *aborted transaction*. If the transaction failed to either commit or abort, it is called an *in-doubt transaction*. In-doubt transactions usually require administrator or user assistance to resolve and are beyond the scope of this book.

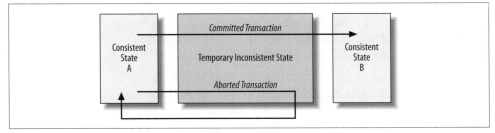

Figure 7-1. A Transaction transfers the system between consistent states

Transactional Resources

Transactional programming requires working with a resource such as a database or a message queue that is capable of participating in a transaction, and being able to commit or roll back the changes made during the transaction. Such resources have been around in one form or another for decades. Traditionally, you had to inform a resource that you would like to perform transactional work against it. This is called *enlisting* the resource in the transaction. Some resources may support *auto-enlistment*, that is, they can detect they are being accessed by a transaction and automatically enlist in it. Once enlisted, you then perform work against the resource, and if no error occurs, the resource is asked to commit the changes made to its state. If you encounter any error, the resource is ask to roll back the changes. During a transaction it is vital that you do not access any nontransactional resource (such as the filesystem on Windows XP), because changes made to those resources will not roll back if the transaction is aborted.

Transaction Properties

When you make use of transactions in your service-oriented applications, you must abide by four core properties, known as ACID: atomic, consistent, isolated, and durable. When you design transactional services, you must adhere to the ACID requirements—they are not optional. As you will see throughout this chapter, WCF enforces them rigorously.

The Atomic property

*Atomic** means that when a transaction completes, all the changes it made to the resource state must be made as if they were all one atomic, indivisible operation. The changes made to the resource are made as if everything else in the universe stops, the changes are made, and then everything resumes. It must not be possible for a party

---

* The word "atom" comes from the Greek word "atomos," meaning *indivisible*. The ancient Greeks thought that if you start dividing matter, and continue dividing it, eventually you get to indivisible pieces, which they called "atomos," The ancient Greeks were of course wrong, as atoms can be divided to subatomic particles such as electrons, protons, and neutrons. Transactions, however, are truly atomic.

outside the transaction to observe the resources involved with only some of the changes but not all of them. A transaction should not leave things to do in the background once it is done, as those operations violate atomicity. Every operation resulting from the transaction must be included in the transaction itself.

Because transactions are atomic, a client application becomes a lot easier to develop. The client does not have to manage partial failure of its requests, or have complex recovery logic. The client knows that the transaction either succeeded or failed as a whole. In the case of failure, the client can choose to issue a new request (start a new transaction), or something else, such as alerting the user. The important thing is that the client does not have to recover the system.

The Consistent property

Consistent means the transaction must leave the system in a consistent state. Note that consistency is different from atomicity. Even if all the changes are committed as one atomic operation, the transaction is required to guarantee that all those changes are consistent—that they "make sense." Usually it is up to the developer to ensure that the semantics of the operations are consistent. All the transaction is required to do is to transfer the system from one consistent state to another.

The Isolated property

Isolated means no other entity (transactional or not) is able to see the intermediate state of the resources during the transaction, because it may be inconsistent. In fact, even if it is consistent, the transaction could still abort, and the changes could be rolled back. Isolation is crucial to overall system consistency. Suppose transaction A allows transaction B access to its intermediate state. Transaction A aborts, and transaction B decides to commit. The problem is that transaction B based its execution on system state that was rolled back, and therefore transaction B is left unknowingly inconsistent. Managing isolation is not trivial. The resources participating in a transaction must lock the data accessed by the transaction from all other parties, and must unlock access to that data when the transaction commits or aborts.

The Durable property

Traditionally, transactional support by a resource implies not just a transaction-aware resource, but also a *durable* one. This is because at any moment, the application could crash, and the memory it was using could be erased. If the changes to the system's state were in-memory changes, they would be lost, and the system would be in an inconsistent state. However, durability is really a range of options. How resilient to such catastrophes the resource should be is an open question that depends on the nature and sensitivity of the data, your budget, available time and available system administration staff, and so on. If durability is a range that actually means various degrees of persistence, then you could also consider the far end of the spectrum—volatile, in-memory resources. The advantage of volatile resources is that they offer better performance than durable resources, and, more importantly, they allow you to approximate much better conventional programming models, while using transaction support for error recovery. You will see later on in this chapter how and when your services can benefit from volatile resource managers (VRMs).

Transaction Management

WCF services can work directly against a transactional resource and manage the transaction explicitly using programming models such as that offered by ADO.NET. Using this model, you are responsible for explicitly starting and managing the transaction, as shown in Example 7-1.

Example 7-1. Explicit transaction management

```
[ServiceContract]
interface IMyContract
{
   [OperationContract]
   void MyMethod( );
}

class MyService : IMyContract
{
   public void MyMethod( )
   {
      //Avoid this programming model:

      string connectionString = "...";
      IDbConnection connection = new SqlConnection(connectionString);
      connection.Open( );
      IDbCommand command = new SqlCommand( );
      command.Connection = connection;
      IDbTransaction transaction = connection.BeginTransaction( );//Enlisting
      command.Transaction = transaction;
      try
      {
         /* Interact with database here, then commit the transaction */
         transaction.Commit( );
      }
      catch
      {
         transaction.Rollback( ); //Abort transaction
      }
      finally
      {
         connection.Close( );
         command.Dispose( );
         transaction.Dispose( );
      }
   }
}
```

You obtain an object representing the underlying database transaction by calling BeginTransaction( ) on the connection object. BeginTransaction( ) returns an implementation of the interface IDbTransaction used to manage the transaction. When the database is enlisted, it does not really execute any of the requests made. Instead it merely logs the requests against the transaction. If all updates or other changes made to the database are consistent and no error took place, you simply call Commit( ) on the transaction object. This will instruct the database to commit the changes as one atomic operation. If any exception occurred, it skips over the call to Commit( ), and the catch statement aborts the transaction by calling Rollback( ). Aborting the transaction instructs the database to discard all the changes logged so far.

The transaction management challenge

While the explicit programming model is straightforward, requiring nothing of the service performing the transaction, it is most suitable for a client calling a single service interacting with a single database (or a single transactional resource), where the service starts and manages the transaction, as shown in Figure 7-2.

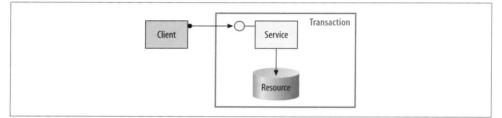

Figure 7-2. Single service/single resource transaction

This is due to the transaction coordination problem. Consider, for example, a service-oriented application where the client interacts with multiple services that in turn interact with each other and with multiple resources, as shown in Figure 7-3.

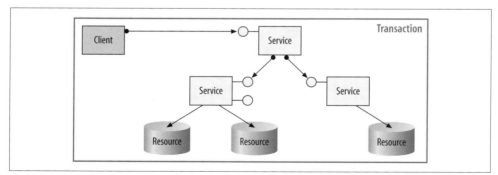

Figure 7-3. Distributed transactional service-oriented application

The question now is, which one of the participating services is responsible for beginning the transaction and enlisting each resource? If all of them will do that, you will end up with multiple transactions. Putting the enlistment logic in the service code will create a great deal of coupling between the services and the resources. Furthermore, which one of the services is responsible for committing or rolling back the transactions? How would one service know what the rest of the services feel about the transaction? How would the service managing the transaction inform other services about the transaction's outcome? Trying to pass the transaction object or some identifier as an operation parameter is not service-oriented, because the clients and the services could all be using any implementation platform and technology. The services could of course be deployed in different processes or even across different machines or sites, and issues such as network failures or machine crashes introduce additional complexity for managing the transaction, because one service can crash, while others can continue processing the transaction. One possible solution is to couple the clients and the services by adding logic for the transaction coordination, but such an approach is very fragile and would not withstand even minor changes to the business flow or the number of participating services. In addition, the services in Figure 7-3 could have been developed by different vendors, which would preclude any such coordination. Even if you find a way of solving the coordination problem at the service level, when multiple resources are involved, you have multiple independent points of failure, because each of the resources could fail independently of the services.

Distributed transactions

The predicament just described is called a *distributed transaction*. A distributed transaction contains two or more independent services (often in different execution contexts), or even just a single service with two or more transactional resources. It is impractical to try to explicitly manage the potential error cases of a distributed transaction. For a distributed transaction, you need to rely on the two-phase commit protocol, and a dedicated transaction manager. A *transaction manager* is a third party that will manage the transaction for you, because the last thing you want is to place the transaction management logic in your service code.

The two-phase commit protocol

To overcome the complexity of a distributed transaction, the transaction manager uses a transaction management protocol called the *two-phase commit* protocol to decide on the outcome of the transaction as well as to commit or roll back the changes to the system state. The two-phase commit protocol is what enforces atomicity and consistency in a distributed system. The protocol enables WCF to support transactions that involve multiple clients, services, and resources. You will see later in this chapter just how transactions start and how they flow across service boundaries. For now, the important thing to note is that while a transaction is in progress, the transaction manager stays largely out of the way. New services may join the transaction, and every resource accessed is enlisted with that transaction. The services execute business logic, and the resources record the changes made under the scope of the transaction. During the transaction, all the services (and the clients participating in the transaction) must *vote* if they want to commit the changes they performed or if they want to abort the transaction for whatever reason.

When the transaction ends (and you will see when transactions end later on), the transaction manager checks the combined vote of the participating services. If any service or client voted to abort, the transaction is doomed. All the participating resources are instructed to discard the changes made during the transaction. If all the services in the transaction voted to commit, the two-phase commit protocol starts. In the first phase, the transaction manager asks all the resources that took part in the transaction if they have any reservations in committing the changes recorded during the transaction. That is, if they were asked to commit, would they? Note that the transaction manager is not instructing the resources to commit the changes. It is merely asking for their vote on the matter. At the end of the first phase, the transaction manager has the combined vote of the resources. The second phase of the protocol is acting upon that combined vote. If all the resources voted to commit the transaction in the first phase, then the transaction manager instructs all of them to commit the changes. If even one of the resources said in phase one that it could not commit the changes, then in phase two the transaction manager instructs all the resources to roll back the changes made, thus aborting the transaction and restoring the system to its pre-transaction state.

It is important to emphasize that a resource vote that it would commit if asked to is special: it is an unbreakable promise. If a resource votes to commit a transaction, it means that it cannot fail if subsequently, in the second phase, it is instructed to commit. The resource should verify before voting to commit that all the changes are consistent and legitimate. A resource can never go back on its vote. This is the basis for enabling distributed transactions. The various resource vendors have gone to great lengths to implement this behavior exactly.

WCF Resource Managers

A *WCF Resource Manager* (RM) is any resource that supports both automatic enlistment and the two-phase commit protocol managed by one of WCF's transaction managers. The resource must detect that it is being accessed by a transaction and automatically enlist in it exactly once. The RM can be either a durable resource or a volatile resource, such as a transactional integer, string, or collection. While the RM must support the two-phase commit protocol, the RM can optionally implement an optimized protocol used when it is the only RM in the transaction. The optimized protocol is called the single-phase commit protocol, when the RM is the one informing the transaction manager in one step about the success or failure of an attempt to commit.

Transaction Propagation

WCF can propagate transactions across the service boundary. This enables a service to participate in the client's transaction, and for the client to include operations on multiple services in the same transaction. The client itself may or may not be a WCF service. Both the binding and the operation contract configuration control the decision whether or not the client transaction is propagated to the service. I call a *transaction-aware binding* any binding that is capable of propagating the client's transaction to the service if configured to do so. Not all bindings are transaction-aware; only the TCP-, IPC- and WS-related bindings are transaction-aware (those would be the `NetTcpBinding`, the `NetNamedPipeBinding`, the `WSHttpBinding`, the `WSDualHttpBinding` and the `WSFederationHttpBinding`, respectively).

Transaction Flow and Binding

By default, transaction-aware bindings do not propagate transactions. The reason is that like most everything else in WCF, it is an opt-in setting. The service host or administrator has to explicitly give its consent to accepting incoming transactions, potentially from across the organization or the business boundaries. To propagate a transaction, you must explicitly enable it at the binding on both the service host and the client sides. All transaction-aware bindings offer the Boolean property `TransactionFlow`, such as:

```
public class NetTcpBinding : Binding,...
{
   public bool TransactionFlow
   {get;set;}
   //More members
}
```

`TransactionFlow` defaults to `false`.

To enable propagation, simply set this property to true, either programmatically or in the host config file; for example, in the case of the TCP binding:

```
NetTcpBinding tcpBinding = new NetTcpBinding( );
tcpBinding.TransactionFlow = true;
```

or when using a config file:

```
<bindings>
   <netTcpBinding>
      <binding name = "TransactionalTCP"
         transactionFlow = "true"
      />
   </netTcpBinding>
</bindings>
```

Note that the value of the TransactionFlow property is not published in the service metadata. If you use Visual Studio 2005 or SvcUtil to generate the client config file, you will still need to manually enable or disable transaction flow as required.

Transactions and Reliability

Strictly speaking, transactions do not require reliable messaging. The reason is that when reliability is disabled, if the WCF messages are dropped or the client or service becomes disconnected, the transaction will abort. Because the client is guaranteed complete success or complete failure of the transactional operation, transactions are reliable in their own way. However, enabling reliability will decrease the likelihood of aborted transactions because it will make the communication reliable, and so the transaction will be unlikely to abort due to communication problems. I therefore recommend as a best practice when enabling transactions with NetTcpBinding and WSHttpBinding to also enable reliability:

```
<netTcpBinding>
    <binding name = "TransactionalTCP"
                            transactionFlow = "true">
       <reliableSession enabled = "true"/>
    </binding>
</netTcpBinding>
```

There is no need to enable reliability for the NetNamedPipeBinding and WSDualHttpBinding because, as discussed in Chapter 1, these two bindings are always reliable.

Transaction Flow and Operation Contract

Using a transaction-aware binding and even enabling transaction flow does not mean that the service wants to use the client's transaction in every operation, or that the client has a transaction to propagate in the first place. Such service-level decisions should be part of the contractual agreement between the client and the service. To that end, WCF provides the TransactionFlowAttribute method attribute that controls if and when the client's transaction flows into the service:

```
public enum TransactionFlowOption
{
    Allowed,
    NotAllowed,
    Mandatory
}

[AttributeUsage(AttributeTargets.Method)]
public sealed class TransactionFlowAttribute : Attribute,IOperationBehavior
{
    public TransactionFlowAttribute(TransactionFlowOption flowOption);
}
```

Note that the TransactionFlow attribute is a method-level attribute because WCF insists that the decision on transaction flow be made on a per-operation level, not at the service level.

```
[ServiceContract]
interface IMyContract
{
    [OperationContract]
    [TransactionFlow(TransactionFlowOption.Allowed)]
    void MyMethod(...);
}
```

This is deliberate, to enable the granularity of having some methods that use the client's transaction and some that do not.

The value of the TransactionFlow attribute is included in the published metadata of the service, and so when you import a contract definition, the imported definition will contain the configured value. WCF will also let you apply the TransactionFlow attribute directly on the service class implementing the operation:

```
[ServiceContract]
interface IMyContract
{
    [OperationContract]
    void MyMethod(...);
}
class MyService : IMyContract
{
    [TransactionFlow(TransactionFlowOption.Allowed)]
    public void MyMethod(...)
    {...}
}
```

But such use is discouraged because it splits the definition of the logical service contract that will be published.

TransactionFlowOption.NotAllowed

When the operation is configured to disallow transaction flow, the client cannot propagate its transaction to the service. Even if transaction flow is enabled at the binding and the client has a transaction, it will be silently ignored and not propagate to the service. As a result, the service will never use the client's transaction, and the service and the client can select any binding with any configuration. TransactionFlowOption.NotAllowed is the default value of the TransactionFlowOption attribute, so these two definitions are equivalent:

```
[ServiceContract]
interface IMyContract
{
    [OperationContract]
    void MyMethod(...);
}
```

```
[ServiceContract]
interface IMyContract
{
    [OperationContract]
    [TransactionFlow(TransactionFlowOption.NotAllowed)]
    void MyMethod(...);
}
```

TransactionFlowOption.Allowed

When the operation is configured to allow transaction flow by providing `TransactionFlowOption.Allowed` to the `TransactionFlowOption` attribute, if the client has a transaction, the service will allow the client's transaction to flow across the service boundary. However, the service may or may not use the client's transaction even though it was propagated. When you choose `TransactionFlowOption.Allowed`, the service can be configured to use any binding, be it transaction-aware or not, but the client and the service must be compatible in their binding configuration. In the context of transaction flow, compatible means that when the service operation allows transaction flow but the binding disallows it, the client should also disallow it in the binding on its side. Trying to flow the client transaction will cause an error because the transaction information in the message will not be understood by the service. However, when the service-side binding configuration is set to allow transaction flow, the client may or may not want to enable propagation on its side, and so may elect to set `TransactionFlow` to `false` in the binding even if the service has it set to `true`.

TransactionFlowOption.Mandatory

When the operation is configured for `TransactionFlowOption.Mandatory`, the service and client must use a transaction-aware binding with transaction flow enabled. WCF verifies this requirement at the service load time and throws an `InvalidOperationException` if the service has at least one incompatible endpoint. `TransactionFlowOption.Mandatory` means the client must have a transaction to propagate to the service. Trying to call a service operation without a transaction throws a `FaultException` on the client side stating that the service requires a transaction. With mandatory flow, the client's transaction always propagates to the service. Yet again, the service may or may not use the client's transaction.

One-Way Calls

Propagating the client transaction to the service requires, by its very nature, allowing the service to abort the client transaction if so desired. This implies that you cannot flow the client transaction to a service over a one-way operation, because that call does not have a reply message. WCF validates this at the service load time, and will throw an exception when a one-way operation is configured for anything but `TransactionFlowOption.NotAllowed`.

```
//Invalid definition:
[ServiceContract]
interface IMyContract
{
   [OperationContract(IsOneWay = true)]
   [TransactionFlow(TransactionFlowOption.Allowed)]
   void MyMethod(...);
}
```

Transaction Protocols and Managers

Depending on the execution scope of the participating parties in the transaction, WCF will use a different transaction management protocol. The word *protocol* may be misleading here, because in the abstract the protocol being used is the two-phase commit protocol. The differences between the transaction management protocols have to do with the type of remote calls and communication protocol used and the kind of boundaries it can cross.

Lightweight protocol

This protocol is used to manage transactions in a local context only, inside the same app domain. It cannot propagate the transaction across the app domain boundary (let alone the process or machine boundary), nor can it flow the transaction across any service boundary (that is, from a client to a service). The lightweight protocol is used only inside a service or outside services. The Lightweight protocol yields the best performance compared with the other protocols.

OleTx protocol

This protocol is used to propagate transactions across app domain, process, and machine boundaries, and to manage the two-phase commit protocol. The protocol uses RPC calls, and the exact binary format of the calls is Windows-specific. As a result of the use of both the RPC and the Windows-specific format, it cannot go across firewalls or interoperate with non-Windows parties. This is usually not a problem because the primary use for the OleTx protocol is for managing transactions in an intranet, in a homogenous Windows environment, and when a single transaction manager is involved.

WS-Atomic Transaction (WSAT) protocol

This protocol is similar to the OleTx protocol in that it too can propagate the transaction across app domain, process, and machine boundaries, and manage the two-phase commit protocol. However, unlike the OleTx protocol, the WSAT protocol is based on an industry standard and, when used over HTTP with text encoding, can go across firewalls. Although you can use the WSAT protocol in an intranet, its primary use is for transaction management across the Internet, where multiple transaction managers are involved.

Protocols and Bindings

No binding supports the lightweight protocol, because the protocol cannot propagate the transaction across the service boundary anyway. However, the various transaction-aware bindings differ in their support for the two other transaction-management protocols. The TCP and IPC bindings can be configured to work with both OleTx and WSAT protocols or with just one of them. Both bindings default to the OleTx protocol and will switch to the WSAT protocol if required. In addition, these two intranet bindings let you configure the protocol either in a config file or programmatically like any other binding property.

WCF provides the `TransactionProtocol` abstract class defined as:

```
public abstract class TransactionProtocol
{
   public static TransactionProtocol Default
   {get;}
   public static TransactionProtocol OleTransactions
   {get;}
   public static TransactionProtocol WSAtomicTransactionOctober2004
   {get;}
}
```

Both the `NetTcpBinding` and the `NetNamedPipeBinding` offer the `TransactionProtocol` property of the matching type, for example:

```
public class NetTcpBinding : Binding,...
{
   TransactionProtocol TransactionProtocol
   {get;set;}
   //More members
}
```

To set the protocol programmatically, first construct the specific binding type, then set the property using one of the static methods:

```
NetTcpBinding tcpBinding = new NetTcpBinding();
//Protocol only matters with propagation
tcpBinding.TransactionFlow = true;
tcpBinding.TransactionProtocol = TransactionProtocol.WSAtomicTransactionOctober2004;
```

Note that the transaction protocol configuration is only meaningful when transaction propagation is enabled as well.

To configure the protocol in a config file, define a binding section as usual:

```
<bindings>
   <netTcpBinding>
      <binding name = "TransactionalTCP"
         transactionFlow = "true"
         transactionProtocol = "WSAtomicTransactionOctober2004"
      />
   </netTcpBinding>
</bindings>
```

When you configure a protocol for the TCP or IPC binding, the service and the client must use the same protocol.

Since the TCP and IPC bindings can only be used in an intranet, there is really no practical value for configuring them for the WSAT protocol, and this ability is available largely for completeness' sake.

The WS bindings (`WSHttpBinding`, `WSDualHttpBinding`, and `WSFederationHttpBinding`) are designed for use across the Internet, when multiple transaction managers are involved using the WSAT protocol. However, in an Internet scenario when only a single transaction manager is involved, these bindings will default for the OleTx protocol. There is no need or ability to configure a particular protocol.

Transaction Managers

Recall from the discussion at the beginning of this chapter that the last thing you should do is manage the transaction yourself. The best solution is to have a third party called the transaction manager manage the two-phase commit protocol for your clients and services. WCF can work with not one but three different transaction managers in a provider model, shown in Figure 7-4.

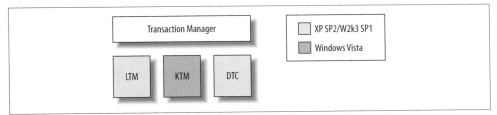

Figure 7-4. WCF transaction managers

The three transaction managers are the *Lightweight Transaction Manager* (LTM), the *Kernel Transaction Manager* (KTM), and the *Distributed Transaction Coordinator* (DTC). As a function of the platform used, what the application does, the services it calls, and the resources it consumes, WCF will assign the appropriate transaction manager. By automatically assigning the transaction manager, WCF decouples the transaction management from service code and from the transaction protocol used. Developers need never bother themselves with the transaction managers, and the following discussion is only intended to alleviate some common concerns regarding performance and efficiency.

The LTM

The LTM can only manage a local transaction; that is, a transaction inside a single app domain. The LTM uses the lightweight transaction protocol to manage the two-phase commit protocol. It can only manage a transaction that involves at most a single durable resource manager. The LTM can also manage as many volatile resource managers as present. If only a single resource manager is present, and that resource supports single-phase commit, then the LTM will use that optimized protocol. Most importantly, the LTM can only manage a transaction inside a single service, and only when that service does not flow the transaction to other services. The LTM is the most performant transaction manager.

The KTM

The KTM can be used to manage transactional kernel resource managers (KRM) on Windows Vista, specifically the transactional filesystem (TXF) and the transactional registry (TXR). The KTM uses the lightweight transaction protocol over both direct memory and kernel calls. The KTM can manage the transaction as long as it involves at most a single durable KRM, but the transaction can have as many volatile resource managers as desired. Similar to the LTM, the transaction can involve at most one service, as long as that service does not propagate the transaction to other services.

The DTC

The DTC is capable of managing a transaction across any execution boundary, from the most local (such as the same app domain) across all boundaries, such as process, machine, or site boundaries. The DTC can use either the OleTx or the WSAT protocols. The DTC is the transaction manager used when transactions flow across the service boundary. The DTC can easily manage a transaction that involves any number of services and resource managers as desired.

The DTC is a system service available by default on every machine running WCF. The DTC is tightly integrated with WCF. The DTC is the one that creates new transactions, propagates transactions across machines, collects the votes of the resource managers, and instructs the resource managers to roll back or commit. For example, consider the service-oriented application shown in Figure 7-5, where a nontransactional client calls to a service on Machine A. The service on Machine A is configured to use a transaction. That service becomes the *root* of the transaction, and it will get the opportunity not just to start the transaction but also to indicate when the transaction is done.

 Every transaction in WCF has at most one root service, because a non-service client can also be the root of the transaction. In any case, the root not only starts the transaction but also ends it.

When a service that is part of a transaction on Machine A tries to access another service or a resource on Machine B, it actually has a proxy to the remote service or resource. That proxy propagates the transaction ID to Machine B. The interception on Machine B contacts the local DTC on Machine B, passing it the transaction ID, informing it to start managing that transaction on Machine B. Because the transaction ID gets propagated to Machine B, resource managers on Machine B can now auto-enlist with it. Similarly, the transaction ID is propagated to Machine C.

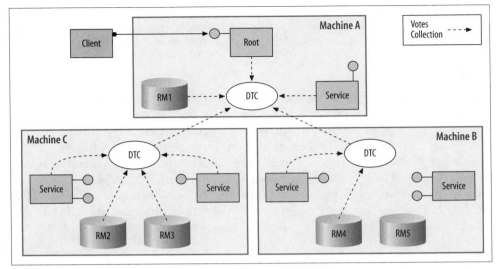

Figure 7-5. DTC managed transaction

When the transaction is done, if the combined services' vote was to try to commit the transaction, then it is time to start the two-phase commit protocol. The DTC on the root machine collects the resource managers' votes on the root machine and contacts the DTC on every machine that took part in the transaction, instructing them to conduct the first phase on their machines. The DTCs on the remote machines collect the resource managers' votes on their machines and forward the results back to the DTC on the root machine. After the DTC on the root machine receives the results from all the remote DTCs, it has the combined resource managers vote. If all of them vote to commit, then the DTC on the root machine again contacts all the DTCs on the remote machines, instructing them to conduct phase two on their respective machines and to commit the transaction. If even one resource manager voted to abort the transaction, however, then the DTC on the root machine informs all the DTCs on the remote machines to conduct phase two on their respective machines and to abort the transaction. Note that only the DTC on the root machine has the combined vote of phase one, and only it can instruct the final abort or commit.

Transaction Manager Promotion

WCF dynamically assigns the appropriate transaction manager for the transaction. If one transaction manager is inadequate, WCF will *promote* the transaction; that is, ask the next-level-up transaction manager to handle the transaction. A single transaction can be promoted multiple times. Once promoted, the transaction stays elevated and cannot be demoted. The previous transaction manager used to manage the transaction is relegated to a pass-through mode. Because of the dynamic promotion, developers are precluded from interacting with the transaction managers directly, because that would bypass promotion. Promotion is yet another reason why you should not write code such as Example 7-1, because it precludes any chance of promotion.

LTM promotion

Every transaction in WCF always starts out as a transaction managed by the LTM. As long as the transaction interacts with a single durable resource and as long as there is no attempt to flow the transaction to a WCF service, the LTM can manage the transaction and yield the best throughput and performance. However, if the transaction tries to enlist a second durable resource or the transaction is propagated to a service, WCF will promote the transaction from the LTM to the DTC. Another type of promotion takes place if the first durable resource accessed is a KTM resource, in which case WCF will promote the transaction from the LTM to the KTM.

KTM promotion

The KTM can manage a transaction as long as it interacts with a single KRM and as long as the transaction is local. The KTM can manage as many volatile resource managers as required. The KTM transaction is promoted to the DTC when the transaction flows to another service or when any second durable resource (kernel or regular) is enlisted.

Resources and promotion

At the time of this writing, the only resources that can participate in an LTM transaction are volatile resource managers and the various flavors of SQL Server 2005. Legacy resource managers such as SQL Server 2000, Oracle, DB2, and MSMQ can only participate in a DTC transaction. Consequently, when a legacy resource is accessed by an LTM transaction, even if it is the single resource in the transaction, the transaction is automatically promoted to the DTC. The relationship between resources and transaction managers is summarized in Table 7-1.

Table 7-1. Resources and transaction managers

Resource	LTM	KTM	DTC
Volatile	Yes	Yes	Yes
SQL Server 2005	Yes	No	Yes
Kernel	No	Yes	Yes
Any other RM	No	No	Yes

The Transaction Class

The Transaction class from the System.Transactions namespace, introduced in .NET 2.0, represents the transaction all WCF transaction managers work with:

```
[Serializable]
public class Transaction : IDisposable,ISerializable
{
   public static Transaction Current
   {get;set;}

   public void Rollback(); //Abort the transaction
   public void Dispose();

   //More members
}
```

Developers rarely need to interact with the Transaction class directly. The main use of the Transaction class is to manually abort the transaction by calling the Rollback() method. Additional features of the Transaction class include enlisting resource managers, setting the isolation level, subscribing to transaction events, cloning the transaction for concurrent threads, and obtaining transaction status and information.

The Ambient Transaction

.NET 2.0 defines a concept called an ambient transaction. The *ambient transaction* is the transaction in which your code executes. To obtain a reference to the ambient transaction, call the static Current property of Transaction:

```
Transaction ambientTransaction = Transaction.Current;
```

If there is no ambient transaction, Current will return null. Every piece of code, be it client or service, can always reach out for its ambient transaction. The ambient transaction object is stored in the thread local storage (TLS). As a result, when the thread winds its way across multiple objects and methods on the same call chain, all objects and methods can access their ambient transactions.

In the context of WCF, the ambient transaction is paramount. When present, any WCF resource manager will automatically enlist in the ambient transaction. When a client calls a WCF service, if the client has an ambient transaction, and the binding and the contract are configured to allow transaction flow, the ambient transaction will propagate to the service.

 The client cannot propagate an already aborted transaction to the service. Doing so will yield an exception.

Local Versus Distributed Transaction

The Transaction class is used both for local and distributed transactions. Each transaction has two identifiers used to identify the local and the distributed transaction. You obtain the transaction identifiers by accessing the TransactionInformation property of the Transaction class:

```
[Serializable]
public class Transaction : IDisposable,ISerializable
{
    public TransactionInformation TransactionInformation
    {get;}
    //More members
}
```

The TransactionInformation property is of the type TransactionInformation defined as:

```
public class TransactionInformation
{
    public Guid DistributedIdentifier
    {get;}
    public string LocalIdentifier
    {get;}
    //More members
}
```

TransactionInformation offers access to the two identifiers. The main use of these identifiers is for logging, tracing, and analysis. In this chapter, I will use the identifiers as a convenient way to demonstrate transaction flow in code as a result of configuration.

Local transaction identifier

The *local transaction identifier* (local ID) contains both an identifier for the LTM in the current app domain as well as an ordinal number enumerating the transaction. You access the local ID via the LocalIdentifier property of TransactionInformation. The local ID is always available with the ambient transaction, and as such is never null. As long as there is an ambient transaction, it will have a valid local ID. The value of the local ID has two parts to it: a constant GUID that is unique for each app domain representing the assigned LTM for that app domain, and an incremented integer enumerating the transactions managed so far by that LTM.

For example, if a service traces three consecutive transactions, starting with the first call, it would get something like:

```
8947aec9-1fac-42bb-8de7-60df836e00d6:1
8947aec9-1fac-42bb-8de7-60df836e00d6:2
8947aec9-1fac-42bb-8de7-60df836e00d6:3
```

The GUID is constant per app domain. If the service is hosted in the same app domain as the client, they will have the same GUID. If the client makes a cross-app domain call, the client will have its own unique GUID identifying its own local LTM.

Distributed transaction identifier

The *distributed transaction identifier* (distributed ID) is generated automatically whenever an LTM or KTM managed transaction is promoted to a DTC managed transaction (such as when the ambient transaction flows to another service). You access the distributed ID via the `DistributedIdentifier` property of `TransactionInformation`. The distributed ID is unique per transaction, and no two transactions will ever have the same distributed ID. Most importantly, the distributed ID will be uniform across the service boundaries and across the entire call chain from the topmost client through every service and object down the call chain. As such, it is useful in logging and tracing. Note that the value of the distributed ID may be `Guid.Empty` when the transaction has not been promoted yet. The distributed ID is usually `Guid.Empty` on the client side when the client is the root of the transaction and the client did not call a service yet, and on the service side it will be empty if the service does not use the client's transaction and instead starts its own local transaction.

Transactional Service Programming

For services, WCF offers a simple and elegant declarative programming model. This model is unavailable for nonservice code called by service or for nonservice WCF clients, however.

Ambient Transaction Setting

By default, the service class and all its operations have no ambient transaction. This is the case even when the client transaction is propagated to the service. Consider the following service:

```
[ServiceContract]
interface IMyContract
{
   [OperationContract]
   [TransactionFlow(TransactionFlowOption.Mandatory)]
   void MyMethod(...);
}
class MyService : IMyContract
{
   public void MyMethod(...)
   {
      Transaction transaction = Transaction.Current;
      Debug.Assert(transaction == null);
   }
}
```

The ambient transaction of the service will be null, even though the mandatory transaction flow guarantees the client's transaction propagation. In order to have an ambient transaction, for each contract method, the service must indicate that it wants WCF to scope the body of the method with a transaction. For that purpose, WCF provides the TransactionScopeRequired property of OperationBehaviorAttribute:

```
[AttributeUsage(AttributeTargets.Method)]
public sealed class OperationBehaviorAttribute : Attribute,...
{
   public bool TransactionScopeRequired
   {get;set;}
   //More members
}
```

The default value of TransactionScopeRequired is false, which is why by default the service has no ambient transaction. Setting TransactionScopeRequired to true provides the operation with an ambient transaction:

```
class MyService : IMyContract
{
   [OperationBehavior(TransactionScopeRequired = true)]
   public void MyMethod( )
   {
      Transaction transaction = Transaction.Current;
      Debug.Assert(transaction != null);
   }
}
```

If the client transaction is propagated to the service, WCF will set the client transaction as the operation's ambient transaction. If not, WCF creates a new transaction for that operation and set the new transaction as the ambient transaction.

 The service class constructor does not have a transaction: it can never participate in the client transaction, and you cannot ask WCF to scope it with a transaction. Unless you manually create a new ambient transaction (as shown later on), do not perform transactional work in the service constructor.

Figure 7-6 demonstrates which transaction a WCF service uses as a product of the binding configuration, the contract operation, and the local operation behavior attribute.

In the figure, a nontransactional client calls Service 1. The operation contract is configured with TransactionFlowOption.Allowed. Even though transaction flow is enabled in the binding, since the client has no transaction, no transaction is propagated. The operation behavior on Service 1 is configured to require a transaction scope. As a result, WCF creates a new transaction for Service 1, Transaction A in Figure 7-6. Service 1 then calls three other services, each configured differently. The binding used for Service 2 has transaction flow enabled, and the operation contract mandates the flow of the client transaction. Since the operation behavior is configured

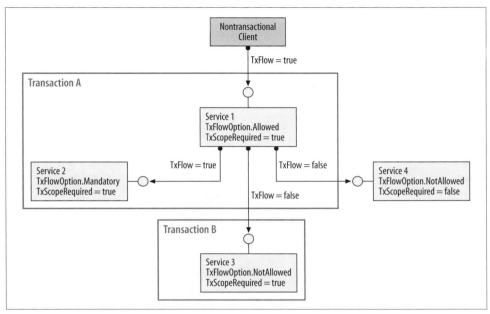

Figure 7-6. Transaction propagation as product of contract, binding, and operation behavior

to require transaction scope, WCF sets Transaction A as the ambient transaction for Service 2. The call to Service 3 has the binding and the operation contract disallow transaction flow. However, since Service 3 has its operation behavior require a transaction scope, WCF creates a new transaction for Service 3 (Transaction B) and sets it as the ambient transaction for Service 3. Similar to Service 3, the call to Service 4 has the binding and the operation contract disallow transaction flow. Since Service 4 does not require a transaction scope, it has no ambient transaction.

Transaction Propagation Modes

Which transaction the service uses is the product of the flow property of the binding (two values), the flow option in the operation contract (three values), and the value of the transaction scope property in the operation behavior (two values). There are therefore 12 possible configuration settings. Out of these 12, 4 are inconsistent and are precluded by WCF (such as flow disabled in the binding, yet mandatory flow in the operation contract) or are just plain impractical. Table 7-2 lists the remaining eight permutations.*

---

* I first presented my designation of transaction propagation modes in *MSDN Magazine*, May 2007.

Table 7-2. Transaction modes as product of binding, contract, and behavior

Binding transaction flow	TransactionFlowOption	TransactionScopeRequired	Transaction mode
False	Allowed	False	None
False	Allowed	True	Service
False	**NotAllowed**	**False**	**None**
False	**NotAllowed**	**True**	**Service**
True	Allowed	False	None
True	**Allowed**	**True**	**Client/Service**
True	Mandatory	False	None
True	**Mandatory**	**True**	**Client**

Those eight permutations actually result with only four transaction propagation modes. I call these four modes Client/Service, Client, Service, and None. Table 7-2 also shows in bold font the recommended way to configure each mode. Each of these modes has its place in designing your application, and understanding how to select the correct mode greatly simplifies thinking about and configuring transaction support.

Client/Service transaction

The Client/Service mode, as its name implies, ensures the service uses the client transaction if possible, or a service-side transaction when the client does not have a transaction. To configure this mode:

1. Select a transactional binding and enable flow by setting `TransactionFlow` to true.
2. Set the transaction flow option in the operation contract to `TransactionFlowOption.Allowed`.
3. Set the `TransactionScopeRequired` property of the operation behavior to true.

The Client/Service mode is the most decoupled configuration, because the service minimizes its assumptions about what the client is doing. The service will join the client transaction if the client has a transaction to flow. Joining the client transaction is always good for overall system consistency. Imagine the service has a transaction separate from that of the client. It opens the way for one of these two transactions to commit while the other one aborts, and leave the system in an inconsistent state. When the service joins the client transaction, all the work done by the client and the service (and potentially other services the client calls) will be committed or aborted as one atomic operation. If the client does not have a transaction, the service still requires the protection of the transaction, and so this mode provides a contingent transaction to the service, by making it the root of a new transaction. Example 7-2 shows a service configured for the Client/Service transaction mode.

Example 7-2. Configuring for the Client/Service transaction mode

```
[ServiceContract]
interface IMyContract
{
   [OperationContract]
   [TransactionFlow(TransactionFlowOption.Allowed)]
   void MyMethod(...);
}

class MyService : IMyContract
{
   [OperationBehavior(TransactionScopeRequired = true)]
   public void MyMethod(...)
   {
      Transaction transaction = Transaction.Current;
      Debug.Assert(transaction != null);
   }
}
```

Note in Example 7-2 that the service can assert it always has a transaction. The service cannot assume or assert whether or not it is the client's transaction or a locally created one. The Client/Service mode is applicable when the service can be used standalone or as part of a bigger transaction. When you select this mode, you should be mindful of potential deadlocks—if the resulting transaction is a service-side transaction, it may deadlock with other transactions trying to access the same resources, because the resources would isolate access per transaction, and the service-side transaction will be a new transaction. When you use the Client/Service mode, the service may or may not be the root of the transaction, and the service must not behave differently when it is the root or when it is joining the client's transaction.

Requiring transaction flow

The Client/Service mode requires the use of a transaction-aware binding with transaction flow enabled, and yet this is not enforced by WCF at the service load time. To tighten this loose screw, you can use my BindingRequirementAttribute:

```
[AttributeUsage(AttributeTargets.Class)]
public class BindingRequirementAttribute : Attribute,IServiceBehavior
{
   public bool TransactionFlowEnabled //Default is false
   {get;set;}
   //More members
}
```

You apply the attribute directly on the service class. The default of TransactionFlowEnabled is false. However, when you set it to true, per endpoint, if the contract of the endpoint has at least one operation with the TransactionFlow attribute set to TransactionFlowOption.Allowed, the BindingRequirement attribute will enforce that the endpoint uses a transaction-aware binding with the TransactionFlow property set to true:

```
[ServiceContract]
interface IMyContract
{
   [OperationContract]
   [TransactionFlow(TransactionFlowOption.Allowed)]
   void MyMethod(...);
}

[BindingRequirement(TransactionFlowEnabled = true)]
class MyService : IMyContract
{...}
```

Enforcing the binding requirement is done by throwing an InvalidOperationException when launching the host. Example 7-3 shows the somewhat simplified implementation of the BindingRequirementAttribute.

Example 7-3. The BindingRequirementAttribute

```
[AttributeUsage(AttributeTargets.Class)]
public class BindingRequirementAttribute : Attribute,IServiceBehavior
{
   public bool TransactionFlowEnabled
   {get;set;}

   void IServiceBehavior.Validate(ServiceDescription description,
                                  ServiceHostBase host)
   {
      if(TransactionFlowEnabled == false)
      {
         return;
      }
      foreach(ServiceEndpoint endpoint in description.Endpoints)
      {
         Exception exception = new InvalidOperationException(...);

         foreach(OperationDescription operation in endpoint.Contract.Operations)
         {
            foreach(IOperationBehavior behavior in operation.Behaviors)
            {
               if(behavior is TransactionFlowAttribute)
               {
                  TransactionFlowAttribute  attribute =
                                            behavior as TransactionFlowAttribute;
                  if(attribute.Transactions == TransactionFlowOption.Allowed)
                  {
                     if(endpoint.Binding is NetTcpBinding)
                     {
                        NetTcpBinding tcpBinding =
                                            endpoint.Binding as NetTcpBinding;
                        if(tcpBinding.TransactionFlow == false)
                        {
```

Example 7-3. The BindingRequirementAttribute (continued)

```
                        throw exception;
                    }
                    break;
                }
                ... //Similar checks for the rest of the transaction-aware
                    //bindings

                throw new InvalidOperationException(...);
            }
        }
      }
    }
   }
  }
  void IServiceBehavior.AddBindingParameters(...)
  {}
  void IServiceBehavior.ApplyDispatchBehavior(...)
  {}
}
```

The BindingRequirementAttribute class is a service behavior, and so it supports the
IServiceBehavior interface introduced in Chapter 6. The Validate( ) method of
IServiceBehavior is called during the host launch-time, enabling you to abort the service load sequence. The first thing Validate( ) does is to check whether the
TransactionFlowEnabled property is set to false. If so, Validate( ) does nothing and
returns. If TransactionFlowEnabled is true, Validate( ) iterates over the collection of
service endpoints available in the service description. For each endpoint, it obtains
the collection of operations. For each operation, it accesses its collection of operation behaviors. All operation behaviors implement the IOperationBehavior interface,
including the TransactionFlowAttribute. If the behavior is TransactionFlowAttribute,
Validate( ) checks if the attribute is configured for TransactionFlowOption.Allowed. If
so, Validate( ) checks the binding. For each transaction-aware binding, it verifies that
the binding has the TransactionFlow property set to true, and if not, it will throw an
InvalidOperationException. Validate( ) also throws an InvalidOperationException if a
nontransactional binding is used for that endpoint.

> The technique shown in Example 7-3 for implementing
> BindingRequirementAttribute is a general-purpose technique you can
> use to enforce any binding requirement. For example,
> BindingRequirementAttribute has another property called WCFOnly that
> enforces the use of WCF-to-WCF bindings only and the
> ReliabilityRequired property that insists on using a reliable binding
> with reliability enabled:
>
> ```
> [AttributeUsage(AttributeTargets.Class)]
> public class BindingRequirementAttribute :
>                          Attribute,IServiceBehavior
> {
>    public bool ReliabilityRequired
> ```

```
      {get;set;}
      public bool TransactionFlowEnabled
      {get;set;}
       public bool WCFOnly
      {get;set;}
   }
```

Client transaction

The Client mode ensures the service only uses the client's transaction. To configure this mode:

1. Select a transactional binding and enable flow by setting `TransactionFlow` to true.

2. Set the transaction flow option in the operation contract to `TransactionFlowOption.Mandatory`.

3. Set the `TransactionScopeRequired` property of the operation behavior to true.

You select the Client transaction mode when the service must use its client's transactions and can never be used standalone, by design. The main motivation for this is to avoid deadlocks and maximize overall system consistency. By having the service share the client's transaction, you reduce the potential for a deadlock because all resources accessed will enlist in the same transaction so there will not be another transaction that competes for access to the same resources and underlying locks. By having a single transaction you maximize consistency, because that transaction will commit or abort as one atomic operation. Example 7-4 shows a service configured for the Client transaction mode.

Example 7-4. Configuring for the Client transaction mode

```
[ServiceContract]
interface IMyContract
{
   [OperationContract]
   [TransactionFlow(TransactionFlowOption.Mandatory)]
   void MyMethod(...);
}
class MyService : IMyContract
{
   [OperationBehavior(TransactionScopeRequired = true)]
   public void MyMethod(...)
   {
      Transaction transaction = Transaction.Current;
      Debug.Assert(transaction.TransactionInformation.
               DistributedIdentifier != Guid.Empty);
   }
}
```

Note in Example 7-4 that the method asserts the fact that the ambient transaction is a distributed one, meaning it originated with the client.

Service transaction

The Service mode ensures that the service always has a transaction, separate from any transaction its clients may or may not have. The service will always be the root of a new transaction. To configure this mode:

1. You can select any binding. If you select a transaction-aware binding, leave its default value of the `TransactionFlow` property or explicitly set it to `false`.
2. Do not apply the `TransactionFlow` attribute or set it with transaction flow set to `TransactionFlowOption.NotAllowed`.
3. Set the `TransactionScopeRequired` property of the operation behavior to `true`.

You select the Service transaction mode when the service needs to perform transactional work outside the scope of the client's transaction. For example, when you want to perform some logging or audit operations, or when you want to publish events to subscribers regardless of whether your client transaction commits or aborts. For example, consider a logbook service that performs error logging into a database. When an error occurs on the client side, the client would use the logbook service to log it or some other entries. In case of an error, after logging, the error on the client side aborts the client's transaction. If the service were to use the client transaction, once the client transaction aborts, the logged error would be discarded from the database, and you would have no trace of it, defeating the purpose of the logging in the first place. By configuring the service to have its own transaction, logging the error would be committed even when the client transaction aborts. The downside is of course the potential for jeopardizing the system consistency, because the service transaction could abort while the client's commits.

The heuristic you need to make when selecting this mode is that the service transaction is much more likely to succeed and commit than the client's transaction. In the example of the logging service, this is often the case, because once deterministic logging is in place, it will usually work, as opposed to business transactions that may fail due to a variety of reasons. In general, you should be extremely careful when using the Service transaction mode, and verify that the two transactions (the client's transaction and the service's transaction) do not jeopardize consistency if one aborts and the other commits. Logging and auditing services are the classic candidates for this mode.

Example 7-5 shows a service configured for the Service transaction mode.

Example 7-5. Configuring for the Service transaction mode

```
[ServiceContract]
interface IMyContract
{
   [OperationContract]
   void MyMethod(...);
}
class MyService : IMyContract
```

Example 7-5. Configuring for the Service transaction mode (continued)

```
{
   [OperationBehavior(TransactionScopeRequired = true)]
   public void MyMethod(...)
   {
      Transaction transaction = Transaction.Current;
      Debug.Assert(transaction.TransactionInformation.
                   DistributedIdentifier == Guid.Empty);
   }
}
```

Note in Example 7-5: the service can assert that it actually has a local transaction.

None transaction

The None transaction mode means the service never has a transaction. To configure this mode:

1. You can select any binding. If you select a transaction-aware binding, leave its default value of the TransactionFlow property or explicitly set it to false.

2. Do not apply the TransactionFlow attribute or set it with transaction flow set to TransactionFlowOption.NotAllowed.

3. No need to set the TransactionScopeRequired property of the operation behavior, and if you do, set it to false.

The None transaction mode is useful when the operations performed by the service are nice to have but not essential, and should not abort the client's transaction if the operations fail. For example, a service that prints a receipt for a money transfer should not be able to abort the client transaction if the printer is out of paper. Another example where the None mode is useful is when you want to provide some custom behavior, and you need to perform your own programmatic transaction support or manually enlist resources, such as calling legacy code as in Example 7-1. Obviously, there is danger in the None mode because it can jeopardize the system consistency: if the calling client has a transaction and it calls a service configured as None then the client aborted its transaction, and changes made to the system state by the service will not roll back. Another pitfall of this mode is when a service configured for None calls another service configured for a Client transaction. Such a call will fail because the calling service has no transaction to propagate.

Example 7-6 shows a service configured for the None mode.

Example 7-6. Configuring for the None transaction mode

```
[ServiceContract]
interface IMyContract
{
   [OperationContract]
   void MyMethod();
}
```

Example 7-6. Configuring for the None transaction mode (continued)

```
class MyService : IMyContract
{
   public void MyMethod( )
   {
      Transaction transaction = Transaction.Current;
      Debug.Assert(transaction == null);
   }
}
```

Note that the service in Example 7-6 can assert it has no ambient transaction.

The None mode allows you to have a nontransactional service called by a transactional client. As stated previously, configuring for the None mode is mostly for nice-to-have operations. The problem with that is that any exception thrown by the None service will abort the calling client's transaction, something that should be avoided with a nice-to-have operations. The solution is to have the client catch all exceptions from the None service to avoid contaminating the client's transaction; for example, calling the service from Example 7-6:

```
MyContractClient proxy = new MyContractClient( );
try
{
   proxy.MyMethod( );
   proxy.Close( );
}
catch
{}
```

> You need to encase the call to the None service in a catch statement even when configuring the operations of the None service as one-way operations, because one-way operations could still throw delivery exceptions.

Choosing a service transaction mode

Out of the four modes, the Service and None modes are somewhat esoteric. They are useful in the context of the particular scenarios mentioned, but other than that they harbor the danger of jeopardizing the system consistency. You should use the Client/Service or Client transaction modes, and choose the mode based on the ability of the service to be used standalone as a function of potential deadlocks and consistency. Avoid the Service and None modes.

Voting and Completion

Although WCF is responsible for every aspect of the transaction propagation and overall management of the two-phase commit protocol across the resource managers, it does not know whether the transaction should commit or abort. WCF simply has no way of knowing whether the changes made to the system state are consistent; that is, if they make sense. Every participating service must vote on the outcome of the transaction and voice an opinion about whether the transaction should commit or abort. In addition, WCF does not know when to start the two-phase commit protocol; that is, when the transaction ends and when all the services are done with their work. That too is something the services (actually, just the root service) need to indicate to WCF. WCF offers two programming models for services to vote on the outcome of the transaction: a declarative model and an explicit model. As you will see, voting is strongly related to completing and ending the transaction.

Declarative voting

WCF can automatically vote on behalf of the service to commit or abort the transaction. Automatic voting is controlled via the Boolean TransactionAutoComplete property of the OperationBehavior attribute:

```
[AttributeUsage(AttributeTargets.Method)]
public sealed class OperationBehaviorAttribute : Attribute,...
{
   public bool TransactionAutoComplete
   {get;set;}
   //More members
}
```

The TransactionAutoComplete property defaults to true, so these two definitions are equivalent:

```
[OperationBehavior(TransactionScopeRequired = true,TransactionAutoComplete = true)]
public void MyMethod(...)
{...}

[OperationBehavior (TransactionScopeRequired = true)]
public void MyMethod(...)
{...}
```

When set to true, if there were no unhandled exceptions in the operation, WCF will automatically vote to commit the transaction. If there was an unhandled exception, WCF will vote to abort the transaction. Note that even though WCF has to catch the exception in order to abort the transaction, it rethrows it, allowing it to go up the call chain. To rely on automatic voting, the service method must have TransactionScopeRequired set to true because automatic voting only works when it was WCF who set the ambient transaction for the service.

It is very important when TransactionScopeRequired is set to true to avoid catching and handling exceptions and explicitly voiding to abort:

```
//Avoid
[OperationBehavior(TransactionScopeRequired = true)]
public void MyMethod(...)
{
   try
   {
      ...
```

```
    }
    catch
    {
        Transaction.Current.Rollback( );
    }
}
```

The reason is that your service could be part of a much larger transaction that spans multiple services, machines, and sites. All other parties of this transaction are working hard, consuming system resources; yet it is all in vain because your service voted to abort, and nobody knows about it. By allowing the exception to go up the call chain, it will abort all objects in its path, eventually reaching the root service or client and terminating the transaction. By not handling the exception, you improve throughput and performance. If you want to catch the exception for some local handling such as logging, make sure to rethrow it:

```
[OperationBehavior(TransactionScopeRequired = true)]
public void MyMethod(...)
{
    try
    {
        ...
    }
    catch
    {
        /* Some local handling here */
        throw;
    }
}
```

Explicit voting

Explicit voting is required when TransactionAutoComplete is set to false. You can only set TransactionAutoComplete to false when TransactionScopeRequired is set to true.

When declarative voting is disabled, WCF will vote to abort all transactions by default, regardless of exceptions or lack thereof. You must explicitly vote using the SetTransactionComplete( ) method of the operation context:

```
public sealed class OperationContext : ...
{
    public void SetTransactionComplete( );
    //More members
}
```

Make sure you do not perform any work, especially transactional work, after the call to SetTransactionComplete( ). Calling SetTransactionComplete( ) should be the last line of code in the operation just before returning:

```
[OperationBehavior(TransactionScopeRequired = true,
                   TransactionAutoComplete = false)]
```

```
public void MyMethod(...)
{
    /* Do transactional work here, then: */
    OperationContext.Current.SetTransactionComplete( );
}
```

If you try to perform any transactional work (including accessing Transaction.
Current) after the call to SetTransactionComplete( ), WCF will throw
InvalidOperationException and abort the transaction.

By not performing any work after SetTransactionComplete( ), any exception before
the call to SetTransactionComplete( ) would skip over it and have WCF default to
aborting the transaction. As a result, there is no need to catch the exception, unless
you want to do some local handling. As with declarative voting, if you do catch the
exception, make sure to rethrow it so that it will expedite aborting the transaction:

```
[OperationBehavior(TransactionScopeRequired = true,
                   TransactionAutoComplete = false)]
public void MyMethod(...)
{
    try
    {
        /* Do transactional work here, then: */
        OperationContext.Current.SetTransactionComplete( );
    }
    catch
    {
        /* Do some error handling then */
        throw;
    }
}
```

Explicit voting is designed for the case when the vote depends on other information
obtained throughout the transaction besides exceptions and errors. However, for the
vast majority of applications and services, you should prefer the simplicity of declarative voting.

 Setting TransactionAutoComplete to false should not be done lightly,
and in fact it is only allowed for a per-session service, because it has
drastic effects on the affinity of the service instance to a transaction. In
order to obtain information for the vote throughout the transaction, it
must be the same transaction and the same instance. You will see later
on why, when, and how you can set TransactionAutoComplete to
false.

Terminating a transaction

When the transaction ends is a product of who starts it. Consider a client that either
does not have a transaction or just does not propagate its transaction to the service,
and that client calls a service operation configured with TransactionScopeRequired set
to true. That service operation becomes the root of the transaction. The root service

---

can call other services and propagate the transaction to them. The transaction will end once the root operation completes the transaction. The root operation can complete the transaction either declaratively by setting `TransactionAutoComplete` to true, or explicitly by setting it to `false` and calling `SetTransactionComplete( )`. This is partly why both `TransactionAutoComplete` and `SetTransactionComplete( )` are named the way they are—they do more than mere voting; they complete and terminate the transaction for a root service. Note that any of the downstream services called by the root operation can only vote on the transaction, not complete it. Only the root both votes and completes the transaction.

When a nonservice client starts the transaction, the transaction ends when the client disposes of the transaction object. You will see more on that in the section on explicit transaction programming.

Transaction Isolation

In general, the more isolated the transactions, the more consistent their results are. The highest degree of isolation is called *serializable,* meaning the results obtained from a set of concurrent transactions are identical to the results obtained by running each transaction serially. To achieve serialization, all the resources a transaction touches are locked from any other transaction. If other transactions try to access those resources, they are blocked and cannot continue executing until the original transaction commits or aborts. Isolation level is defined using the `IsolationLevel` enumeration defined in the `System.Transactions` namespace:

```
public enum IsolationLevel
{
    Unspecified,
    ReadUncommitted,
    ReadCommitted,
    RepeatableRead,
    Serializable,
    Chaos,    //No isolation whatsoever
    Snapshot //Special form of ReadCommitted supported by SQL 2005
}
```

The difference between the four isolation levels (`ReadUncommitted`, `ReadCommitted`, `RepeatableRead`, and `Serializable`) is in the way the different levels use read and write locks. A lock can be held only when the transaction accesses the data in the resource manager, or it can be held until the transaction is committed or aborted. The former is better for throughput; the latter for consistency. The two kinds of locks and the two kinds of operations (read/write) give four basic isolation levels. In addition, not all resource managers support all levels of isolation, and they may elect to take part in the transaction at a higher level than the one configured. Every isolation level besides serializable is susceptible to some sort of inconsistency resulting from other transactions accessing the same information.

Selecting an isolation level other than serializable is commonly used for read-intensive systems, and it requires a solid understanding of transaction processing theory and the semantics of the transaction itself, the concurrency issues involved, and the consequences for system consistency. The reason isolation configuration is available is that a high degree of isolation comes at the expense of overall system throughput, because the resource managers involved have to hold on to both read and write locks for as long as a transaction is in progress, and all other transactions are blocked. However, there are some situations where you may be willing to trade system consistency for throughput by lowering the isolation level. Imagine, for example, a banking system. One of the requirements is to retrieve the total amount of money in all customer accounts combined. Although it is possible to execute that transaction with the serializable isolation level, if the bank has hundreds of thousands of accounts, it may take quite a while to complete. The transaction may possibly time out and abort, because some accounts are likely being accessed by other transactions at the same time. But the number of accounts may be a blessing in disguise. On average, statistically speaking, if the transaction is allowed to run at a lower transaction level, it may get the wrong balance on some accounts, but those incorrect balances would tend to cancel each other out. The actual resulting error may be acceptable for the bank's need.

In WCF, the isolation is a service behavior, so that all methods on the service use the same configured isolation. Isolation is configured via the `TransactionIsolationLevel` property of the `ServiceBehavior` attribute:

```
[AttributeUsage(AttributeTargets.Class)]
public sealed class ServiceBehaviorAttribute : Attribute,...
{
    public IsolationLevel TransactionIsolationLevel
    {get;set;}
    //More members
}
```

There is no way to configure isolation level in the host configuration file. You can only set the `TransactionIsolationLevel` property if the service has at least one operation configured with `TransactionScopeRequired` set to true.

Isolation and transaction flow

The default value of `TransactionIsolationLevel` is `IsolationLevel.Unspecified`, so these two statements are equivalent:

```
class MyService : IMyContract
{...}

[ServiceBehavior(TransactionIsolationLevel = IsolationLevel.Unspecified)]
class MyService : IMyContract
{...}
```

When the service joins the client transaction and the service is configured for IsolationLevel.Unspecified, the service will use the client's isolation level.

However, if the service specifies an isolation level other than IsolationLevel. Unspecified, the client must match that level, and a mismatch will throw a FaultException on the client's side.

When the service is the root of the transaction and the service is configured for IsolationLevel.Unspecified, WCF will set the isolation level to IsolationLevel. Serializable. If the root service provides a level other than IsolationLevel. Unspecified, WCF will use that specified level.

Transaction Timeout

Due to the use of isolation, the introduction of the isolation locks raises the possibility of a deadlock when one transaction tries to access a resource manager owned by another. If the transaction takes a long time to complete, it may be indicative of a transactional deadlock. To address that, the transaction will automatically abort if executed for more than a predetermined timeout (60 seconds by default). Once aborted, any attempt to flow that transaction to a service will result in an exception. Even if no exceptions take place, the transaction will eventually abort. All that the participating clients and services do is complete the transaction. The transaction time-out is configurable both programmatically and administratively.

The timeout is a service behavior property, and all operations across all endpoints of the service use the same timeout. You configure the timeout by setting the TransactionTimeout time-span string property of ServiceBehaviorAttribute:

```
[AttributeUsage(AttributeTargets.Class)]
public sealed class ServiceBehaviorAttribute : Attribute,...
{
    public string TransactionTimeout
    {get;set;}
    //More members
}
```

For example, use the following to configure a 30-second timeout:

```
[ServiceBehavior(TransactionTimeout = "00:00:30")]
class MyService : ...
{...}
```

You can also configure the transaction timeout in the host config file by creating a custom behavior section and referencing it at the service section:

```
<services>
    <service name = "MyService" behaviorConfiguration = "ShortTransactionBehavior">
        ...
    </service>
</services>
<behaviors>
```

```
    <serviceBehaviors>
        <behavior name = "ShortTransactionBehavior"
            transactionTimeout = "00:00:30"
        />
    </serviceBehaviors>
</behaviors>
```

The maximum allowed transaction timeout is 10 minutes. The value of 10 minutes is used even when larger values are specified. If you want to override the default maximum timeout of 10 minutes, and specify, say, 30 minutes, add the following to *machine.config*:

```
<configuration>
    <system.transactions>
        <machineSettings maxTimeout = "00:30:00"/>
    </system.transactions>
</configuration>
```

 Setting any value in *machine.config* will affect all applications on the machine.

Configuring such a long timeout is useful mostly for debugging, when you want to try to isolate a problem in your business logic by stepping through your code, and you do not want the transaction you're debugging to time out while you figure out the problem. Be extremely careful with long timeouts in all other cases, because it means there are no safeguards against transaction deadlocks.

You typically set the timeout to a value less than the default in two cases. The first is during development, when you want to test the way your application handles aborted transactions. By setting the timeout to a small value (such as one millisecond), you cause your transaction to fail and can thus observe your error-handling code.

The second case in which you set the transaction timeout to be less than the default timeout is when you have reason to believe that a service is involved in more than its fair share of resource contention, resulting in deadlocks. In that case, you want to abort the transaction as soon as possible and not wait for the default timeout to expire.

Transaction flow and timeout

When a transaction flows into a service that is configured with a shorter timeout than the incoming transaction, the transaction adopts the service's timeout, and the service gets to enforce the shorter timeout. This is designed to support resolving deadlocks in problematic services as just discussed. When a transaction flows into a service that is configured with a longer timeout than the incoming transaction, the service configuration has no effect.

Explicit Transaction Programming

The transactional programming model described so far can only be used declaratively by transactional services. Nonservice clients, nontransactional services, or just plain .NET objects called downstream by a service cannot take advantage of it. For all these cases, WCF relies on the transactional infrastructure available with .NET 2.0 in the System.Transactions namespace. In addition, you may rely on System.Transactions even in transactional services when exploiting some advanced features such as transaction events, cloning, asynchronous commit, and manual transactions. I described the System.Transactions capabilities in my MSDN whitepaper "Introducing System.Transactions in the .NET Framework 2.0" (published April 2005; updated December 2005). The flowing sections contain excerpts from that article describing how to use the core aspects of System.Transactions in the context of WCF. Please refer to the whitepaper for detailed discussions of the rest of the features.

The TransactionScope Class

The most common way of using transactions explicitly is via the TransactionScope class:

```
public class TransactionScope : IDisposable
{
   public TransactionScope( );
   //Additional constructors

   public void Complete( );
   public void Dispose( );
}
```

As the name implies, the TransactionScope class is used to scope a code section with a transaction, as demonstrated in Example 7-7.

Example 7-7. Using TransactionScope

```
using(TransactionScope scope = new TransactionScope( ))
{
   /* Perform transactional work here */

   //No errors - commit transaction
   scope.Complete( );
}
```

The scope constructor can create a new LTM transaction and make it the ambient transaction by setting Transaction.Current, or can join an existing ambient transaction. TransactionScope is a disposable object—if the scope creates a new transaction, the transaction will end once the Dispose( ) method is called (the end of the using statement in Example 7-7). The Dispose( ) method also restores the original ambient transaction (null in the case of Example 7-7).

Finally, if the `TransactionScope` object is not used inside a `using` statement, it would become garbage once the transaction timeout is expired and the transaction is aborted.

TransactionScope voting

The `TransactionScope` object has no way of knowing whether the transaction should commit or abort. To address this, every `TransactionScope` object has a consistency bit, which is by default is set to `false`. You can set the consistency bit to `true` by calling the `Complete()` method. Note that you can only call `Complete()` once. Subsequent calls to `Complete()` will raise an `InvalidOperationException`. This is deliberate, to encourage developers to have no transactional code after the call to `Complete()`.

If the transaction ends (due to calling `Dispose()` or garbage collection) and the consistency bit is set to `false`, the transaction will abort. For example, the following scope object will abort its transaction, because the consistency bit is never changed from its default value:

```
using(TransactionScope scope = new TransactionScope())
{}
```

By having the call to `Complete()` as the last action in the scope, you have an automated way for voting to abort in case of an error. The reason is that any exception thrown inside the scope will skip over the call to `Complete()`; the `finally` statement in the `using` statement will dispose of the `TransactionScope` object; and the transaction will abort. On the other hand, if you do call `Complete()` and the transaction ends with the consistency bit set to `true` as in Example 7-7, the transaction will try to commit. Note that after calling `Complete()`, you cannot access the ambient transaction, and trying to do so will result in an `InvalidOperationException`. You can access the ambient transaction (via `Transaction.Current`) again once the scope object is disposed of.

The fact that the code in the scope called `Complete()` does not guarantee committing the transaction. Even if you call `Complete()` and the scope is disposed of, all that will do is try to commit the transaction. The ultimate success or failure of that attempt is the product of the two-phase commit protocol, which may involve multiple resources and services your code is unaware of. As a result, `Dispose()` will throw `TransactionAbortedException` if it fails to commit the transaction. You can catch and handle that exception, perhaps by alerting the user, as shown in Example 7-8.

Example 7-8. TransactionScope and error handling

```
try
{
   using(TransactionScope scope = new TransactionScope())
   {
      /* Perform transactional work here */
      //No errors - commit transaction
```

Example 7-8. TransactionScope and error handling (continued)

```
      scope.Complete( );
   }
}
catch(TransactionAbortedException e)
{
   Trace.Writeline(e.Message);
}
catch //Any other exception took place
{
   Trace.Writeline("Cannot complete transaction");
   throw;
}
```

Transaction Flow Management

Transaction scopes can nest both directly and indirectly. In Example 7-9, scope2 simply nests inside scope1.

Example 7-9. Direct scope nesting

```
using(TransactionScope scope1 = new TransactionScope( ))
{
   using(TransactionScope scope2 = new TransactionScope( ))
   {
      scope2.Complete( );
   }
   scope1.Complete( );
}
```

The scope can also nest indirectly when calling a method that uses TransactionScope from within a method that uses its own scope, as is the case with the RootMethod( ) in Example 7-10.

Example 7-10. Indirect scope nesting

```
void RootMethod( )
{
   using(TransactionScope scope = new TransactionScope( ))
   {
      /* Perform transactional work here */
      SomeMethod( );
      scope.Complete( );
   }
}
void SomeMethod( )
{
   using(TransactionScope scope = new TransactionScope( ))
   {
      /* Perform transactional work here */
      scope.Complete( );
   }
}
```

A transaction scope can also nest in a service method, as in Example 7-11. The service method may or may not be transactional.

Example 7-11. Scope nesting inside a service method

```
class MyService : IMyContract
{
   [OperationBehavior(TransactionScopeRequired = true)]
   public void MyMethod(...)
   {
      using(TransactionScope scope = new TransactionScope())
      {
         scope.Complete();
      }
   }
}
```

If the scope creates a new transaction for its use, it is called the *root scope*. Whether or not a scope becomes a root scope depends on the scope configuration and the presence of an ambient transaction. Once a root scope is established, there is an implicit relationship between it and all its nested scopes or downstream services called.

The TransactionScope class provides several overloaded constructors that accept an enum of the type TransactionScopeOption:

```
public enum TransactionScopeOption
{
   Required,
   RequiresNew,
   Suppress
}
public class TransactionScope : IDisposable
{
   public TransactionScope(TransactionScopeOption scopeOption);
   public TransactionScope(TransactionScopeOption scopeOption,
                           TransactionOptions transactionOptions);
   public TransactionScope(TransactionScopeOption scopeOption,
                           TimeSpan scopeTimeout);
   //Additional constructors and memebrs
}
```

The value of TransactionScopeOption lets you control whether the scope takes part in a transaction and, if so, whether it will join the ambient transaction or will be the root scope of a new transaction.

For example, here is how you specify the value of the TransactionScopeOption in the scope's constructor:

```
using(TransactionScope scope
                       = new TransactionScope(TransactionScopeOption.Required))
   {...}
```

The default value for the scope option is TransactionScopeOption.Required, meaning this is the value used when you call one of the constructors that does not accept a TransactionScopeOption parameter, so these two definitions are equivalent:

```
using(TransactionScope scope = new TransactionScope())
{...}
using(TransactionScope scope
                        = new TransactionScope(TransactionScopeOption.Required))
{...}
```

The TransactionScope object determines which transaction to belong to when it is constructed. Once determined, the scope will always belong to that transaction. TransactionScope bases its decision on two factors: whether an ambient transaction is present, and the value of the TransactionScopeOption parameter.

A TransactionScope object has three options:

- Join the ambient transaction
- Be a new scope root; that is, start a new transaction and have that transaction be the new ambient transaction inside its own scope
- Not take part in a transaction at all

If the scope is configured with TransactionScopeOption.Required, and an ambient transaction is present, the scope will join that transaction. If, on the other hand, there is no ambient transaction, then the scope will create a new transaction and become the root scope.

If the scope is configured with TransactionScopeOption.RequiresNew, then it will always be a root scope. It will start a new transaction, and its transaction will be the new ambient transaction inside the scope.

If the scope is configured with TransactionScopeOption.Suppress it will never be part of a transaction, regardless of whether an ambient transaction is present. A scope configured with TransactionScopeOption.Suppress will always have null as its ambient transaction.

Voting inside a nested scope

It is important to realize that although a nested scope can join the ambient transaction of its parent scope, the two scope objects will have two distinct consistency bits. Calling Complete() in the nested scope has no effect on the parent scope:

```
using(TransactionScope scope1 = new TransactionScope())
{
    using(TransactionScope scope2 = new TransactionScope())
    {
        scope2.Complete();
    }
    //scope1's consistency bit is still false
}
```

Only if all the scopes, from the root scope down to the last nested scope, vote to commit the transaction will the transaction commit. In addition, only the root scope dictates the life span of the transaction. When a TransactionScope object joins an ambient transaction, disposing of that scope does not end the transaction. The transaction ends only when the root scope is disposed, or when the service method that started the transaction returns.

TransactionScopeOption.Required

TransactionScopeOption.Required is not just the most common value used; it is also the most decoupled value. If your scope has an ambient transaction, it will join the ambient transaction to improve consistency. However, if it cannot, the scope will at least provide the code with a new ambient transaction. When TransactionScopeOption.Required is used, the code inside the TransactionScope must not behave differently when it is the root or when it is just joining the ambient transaction. It should operate identically in both cases. On the service side, the most common use for TransactionScopeOption.Required is by nonservice downstream classes called by the service, as shown in Example 7-12.

Example 7-12. Using TransactionScopeOption.Required in a downstream class

```
class MyService : IMyContract
{
   [OperationBehavior(TransactionScopeRequired = true)]
   public void MyMethod(...)
   {
      MyClass obj = new MyClass();
      obj.SomeMethod();
   }
}
class MyClass
{
   public void SomeMethod()
   {
      using(TransactionScope scope = new TransactionScope())
      {
         //Do some work then
         scope.Complete();
      }
   }
}
```

While the service itself can use TransactionScopeOption.Required directly, such practice adds no value:

```
   class MyService : IMyContract
   {
      [OperationBehavior(TransactionScopeRequired = true)]
      public void MyMethod(...)
```

```
    {
        //One transaction only
        using(TransactionScope scope = new TransactionScope())
        {
            //Do some work then
            scope.Complete();
        }
    }
}
```

The reason is obvious: the service can simply ask WCF to scope the operation with a transaction scope by setting TransactionScopeRequired to true (this is also the origin of that property's name). Note that even though the service may use declarative voting, any downstream (or directly nested) scope must still explicitly call Complete() in order for the transaction to commit.

The same is true when the service method uses explicit voting:

```
[OperationBehavior(TransactionScopeRequired = true,
                   TransactionAutoComplete = false)]
public void MyMethod(...)
{
    using(TransactionScope scope = new TransactionScope())
    {
        //Do some work then
        scope.Complete();
    }
    /* Do transactional work here, then: */
    OperationContext.Current.SetTransactionComplete();
}
```

In short, voting to abort in a scope with TransactionScopeRequired nested in a service call will abort the service transaction regardless of exceptions or the use of declarative voting (via TransactionAutoComplete) or explicit voting by the service (via SetTransactionComplete()).

TransactionScopeOption.RequiresNew

Configuring the scope with TransactionScopeOption.RequiresNew is useful when you want to perform transactional work outside the scope of the ambient transaction; for example, when you want to perform some logging or audit operations, or when you want to publish events to subscribers, regardless of whether your ambient transaction commits or aborts:

```
class MyService : IMyContract
{
    [OperationBehavior(TransactionScopeRequired = true)]
    public void MyMethod(...)
    {
        //Two distinct transactions
        using(TransactionScope scope =
                        new TransactionScope(TransactionScopeOption.RequiresNew))
        {
```

```
            //Do some work then
            scope.Complete();
        }
    }
}
```

Note that you must complete the scope in order for the new transaction to commit. You may also want to consider encasing a scope that uses TransactionScopeOption.RequiresNew in a try and catch statement to isolate it from the service's ambient transaction.

You should be extremely careful when using TransactionScopeOption.RequiresNew and verify that the two transactions (the ambient transaction and the one created for your scope) do not jeopardize consistency if one aborts and the other commits.

TransactionScopeOption.Suppress

TransactionScopeOption.Suppress is useful for both the client and the service when the operations performed by the code section are nice to have and should not abort the ambient transaction if the operations fail. TransactionScopeOption.Suppress allows you to have a nontransactional code section inside a transactional scope or service operation, as shown in Example 7-13.

Example 7-13. Using TransactionScopeOption.Suppress

```
[OperationBehavior(TransactionScopeRequired = true)]
public void MyMethod(...)
{
   try
   {
      //Start of nontransactional section
      using(TransactionScope scope = new
                           TransactionScope(TransactionScopeOption.Suppress))
      {
          //Do nontransactional work here
      }//Restores ambient transaction here
   }
   catch
   {}
}
```

Note in Example 7-13 that there is no need to call Complete() on the suppressed scope. Another example where TransactionScopeOption.Suppress is useful is when you want to provide some custom behavior and you need to perform your own programmatic transaction support or manually enlist resources.

That said, you should be careful when mixing transactional scopes or service methods with nontransactional scopes, as that can jeopardize isolation and consistency, because changes made to the system state inside the suppressed scope will not roll back along with the containing ambient transaction. In addition, the nontransactional scope may have errors, but those errors should not affect the ambient transaction outcome. This is why in Example 7-13 the suppressed scope is encased in a try and catch statement that also suppresses any exception coming out of it.

 Do not call a service configured for Client transactions (basically with mandatory transaction flow) inside a suppressed scope, because that call is guaranteed to fail.

TransactionScope timeout

If the code inside the transactional scope takes a long time to complete, it may be indicative of a transactional deadlock. To address that, the transaction will automatically abort if executed for more than a predetermined timeout (60 seconds by default). You can configure the default timeout in the application config file. For example, to configure a default timeout of 30 seconds, add this to the config file:

```
<system.transactions>
   <defaultSettings timeout = "00:00:30"/>
</system.transactions>
```

Placing the new default in the application config file affects all scopes used by all clients and services in that application. You can also configure a timeout for a specific transaction scope. A few of the overloaded constructors of TransactionScope accept a value of type TimeSpan, used to control the timeout of the transaction, for example:

```
public TransactionScope(TransactionScopeOption scopeOption,
                        TimeSpan scopeTimeout);
```

To specify a timeout different from the default of 60 seconds, simply pass in the desired value:

```
TimeSpan timeout = TimeSpan.FromSeconds(30);
using(TransactionScope scope
                = new TransactionScope(TransactionScopeOption.Required,timeout))
{...}
```

When a TransactionScope joins the ambient transaction, yet specifies a shorter timeout than the one the ambient transaction is set to, it has the effect of enforcing the new, shorter timeout on the ambient transaction, and the transaction must end within the nested time specified, or it is automatically aborted. If the scope's timeout is greater than that of the ambient transaction, it has no effect.

TransactionScope isolation level

If the scope is a root scope, by default the transaction will execute with the isolation level set to serializable. Some of the overloaded constructors of TransactionScope accept a structure of the type TransactionOptions, defined as:

```
public struct TransactionOptions
{
    public IsolationLevel IsolationLevel
```

```
        {get;set;}
        public TimeSpan Timeout
        {get;set;}
        //Other members
    }
```

Although you can use the `TransactionOptions` `Timeout` property to specify a timeout, the main use for `TransactionOptions` is for specifying isolation level. You could assign into `TransactionOptions` `IsolationLevel` property a value of the enum type `IsolationLevel` presented earlier:

```
    TransactionOptions options = new TransactionOptions();
    options.IsolationLevel = IsolationLevel.ReadCommitted;
    options.Timeout = TransactionManager.DefaultTimeout;

    using(TransactionScope scope
                    = new TransactionScope(TransactionScopeOption.Required,options))
    {...}
```

When a scope joins an ambient transaction, it must be configured to use exactly the same isolation level as the ambient transaction, otherwise an `ArgumentException` is thrown.

Nonservice Clients

Although services can take advantage of `TransactionScope`, by far its primary use is by nonservice clients. Using a transaction scope is practically the only way a nonservice client can group multiple service calls into single transaction, as shown in Figure 7-7.

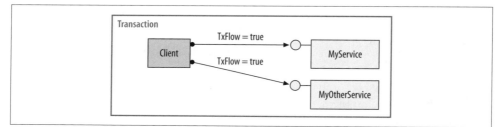

Figure 7-7. A nonservice client using a single transaction to call multiple services

Having the option to create a root transaction scope enables the client to flow its transaction to services and to manage and commit the transaction based on the aggregated result of the services, as shown in Example 7-14.

Example 7-14. Using TransactionScope to call services in a single transaction

```
//////////////////////////// Service Side ////////////////////////////
[ServiceContract]
interface IMyContract
{
```

```
    [OperationContract]
    [TransactionFlow(TransactionFlowOption.Allowed)]
    void MyMethod(...);
}
[ServiceContract]
interface IMyOtherContract
{
    [OperationContract]
    [TransactionFlow(TransactionFlowOption.Mandatory)]
    void MyOtherMethod(...);
}
class MyService : IMyContract
{
    [OperationBehavior(TransactionScopeRequired = true)]
    public void MyMethod(...)
    {...}
}
class MyOtherService : IMyOtherContract
{
    [OperationBehavior(TransactionScopeRequired = true)]
    public void MyOtherMethod(...)
    {...}
}
///////////////////////// Client Side /////////////////////////
using(TransactionScope scope = new TransactionScope())
{
    MyContractClient proxy1 = new MyContractClient();
    proxy1.MyMethod(...);
    proxy1.Close();

    MyOtherContractClient proxy2 = new MyOtherContractClient();
    proxy2.MyOtherMethod(...);
    proxy2.Close();

    scope.Complete();
}

//Can combine in single using block:
using(MyContractClient proxy3 = new MyContractClient())
using(MyOtherContractClient proxy4 = new MyOtherContractClient())
using(TransactionScope scope = new TransactionScope())
{
    proxy3.MyMethod(...);
    proxy4.MyOtherMethod(...);
    scope.Complete();
}
```

Service State Management

The sole propose of transactional programming is to address the recovery challenge by always leaving the system in a consistent state. The state of the system consists of all the resources that were involved in the transaction plus the in-memory clients and service instances. Besides the advantage of a WCF resource manager such as auto-enlistment and participation in the two-phase commit protocol, the basic and obvious advantage of using a resource manager is that any change made to its state during a transaction will automatically roll back if the transaction aborts. This, however, is not true when it comes to the in-memory instance members and static members of the participating services. Consequently, the system would not be in a consistent state after the transaction. The problem is compounded by the fact that the transaction the service participates in may span multiple services, machines, and sites. Even if the service instance encounters no errors and votes to commit transaction, the transaction may eventually be aborted by other parties across the service boundary. If the service were to simply store its state in memory, how would it know about the outcome of the transaction so that it would somehow manually roll back the changes it made to its state?

The solution for the service instance state management problem is to develop the service as a state-aware service and proactively manage its state. As explained in Chapter 4, a state-aware service is not the same as a stateless service. If the service were truly stateless, there would not be any problem with instance state rollback. As long as a transaction is in progress, the service instance is allowed to maintain state in memory. Between transactions, the service should store its state in a resource manager. That state resource manager may not be related to any other business-logic-specific resource accessed during the transaction, or it may be one and the same. At the beginning of the transaction, the service should retrieve its state from the resource and by doing so enlist the resource in the transaction. At the end of the transaction, the service should save its state back to the resource manager. The elegant thing about this technique is that it provides for state auto-recovery. Any changes made to the instance state would commit or roll back as part of the transaction. If the transaction commits, the next time the service gets its state it will have the new state. If the transaction aborts, then it will have its pre-transaction state. Either way, the service will have a consistent state ready to be accessed by a new transaction. To force the service instance to indeed purge all its in-memory state this way, by default once the transaction completes, WCF destroys the service instance, ensuring no leftovers in memory that might jeopardize consistency.

Transaction Boundary

There are two remaining problems with writing transactional state-aware services. The first is how would the service know when transactions start and end so that it could get and save its state? The service may be part of a much larger transaction that spans multiple services and machines. At any moment between service calls the transaction might end. Who would call the service, letting it know to save its state? The second problem is isolation—different clients might call the service concurrently on different transactions. How would the service isolate the change made to its state by one transaction from the other? The service cannot allow cross-transactional calls because doing so would jeopardize isolation. If the other transaction were to access its state and operate based on its values, that transaction would be contaminated with foul state once the original transaction aborted and the changes rolled back.

The solution to both problems is for the service to equate method boundaries with transaction boundaries. At the beginning of every method, the service should read its state, and at the end of each method, the service should save its state to the resource manager. By doing so, when the transaction ends between method calls, the service is assured its state will persist or roll back with it. Because the service equates method boundaries with transaction boundaries, the service instance must therefore also vote on the transaction's outcome at the end of every method. From the service perspective, the transaction completes once the method returns. This is really why the TransactionAutoComplete property is called that instead of something like TransactionAutoVote. The service states that, as far as it is concerned, the transaction is complete. If the service is also the root of the transaction, completing it will indeed terminate the transaction.

In addition, reading and storing the state in the resource manager in each method call addresses the isolation challenge because the service simply lets the resource manager isolate access to the state between concurrent transactions.

State Identifier

Because there could be many instances of the same service type accessing the same resource manager, every operation must contain some parameters that allow the service instance to find its state in the resource manager and bind against it. The best approach is to have each operation contain some key as a parameter identifying the state. I call that parameter the *state identifier*. The client must provide the state identifier. Typical state identifiers are account numbers, order numbers, and so on. For example, the client creates a new transactional order-processing object, and on every method call, the client must provide the order number as a parameter, in addition to other parameters.

Example 7-15 shows a template for implementing a transactional per-call service.

Example 7-15. Implementing a transactional service

```
[DataContract]
class Param
{...}

[ServiceContract]
interface IMyContract
{
   [OperationContract]
   [TransactionFlow(...)]
   void MyMethod();
```

Example 7-15. Implementing a transactional service (continued)

```
}
[ServiceBehavior(InstanceContextMode = InstanceContextMode.PerCall)]
class MyService : IMyContract,IDisposable
{
   [OperationBehavior(TransactionScopeRequired = true)]
   public void MyMethod(Param stateIdentifier)
   {
      GetState(stateIdentifier);
      DoWork();
      SaveState(stateIdentifier);
   }
   void GetState(Param stateIdentifier)
   {...}
   void DoWork()
   {...}
   void SaveState(Param stateIdentifier)
   {...}
   public void Dispose()
   {...}
}
```

The MyMethod( ) signature contains a state identifier parameter of the type Param (a pseudotype invented for this example) used to get the state from a resource manager with the GetState( ) helper method. The service instance then performs its work using the DoWork( ) helper method. The service instance then saves its state back to the resource manager using the SaveState( ) method, specifying its identifier.

 With a per-call service, the resource managers used to store the service state can also be volatile resource managers accessed as static member variables.

Note that not all of the service instance state can be saved by value to the resource manager. If the state contains references to other objects, GetState( ) should create those objects, and SaveState( ) (or Dispose( )) should dispose of them.

Instance Management and Transactions

Because the service instance goes through the trouble of retrieving its state and saving it on every method call, why wait till the end of the transaction to destroy the object? A per-call service would therefore be the most natural programming model for a transactional WCF service. In addition, the behavioral requirements for a state-aware transactional object and the requirements of a per-call object are the same—both retrieve and save their state at the method boundaries (compare Example 4-3 with Example 7-15). In spite of the fact that the per-call instancing mode is the most congenial for transactions, WCF does support a per-session and even a singleton service, albeit with a considerably more complex programming model.

Per-Call Transactional Service

A far as a per-call service call is concerned, transactional programming is almost incidental. Every call on the service gets a new instance, and that call may or may not be in the same transaction as the previous call (see Figure 7-8).

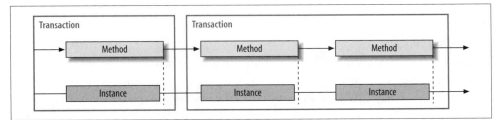

Figure 7-8. Per-call service and transactions

Regardless of transactions, in every call the service gets and saves its state from a resource manager, so the methods are always guaranteed to operate on consistent state from the previous transaction or on the temporary yet well-isolated state of the current transaction in progress. A per-call service must vote and complete its transaction in every method call. In fact, a per-call service must always use auto-completion (have TransactionAutoComplete set to true—its default).

From the client perspective, the same service proxy can participate in multiple transactions or in the same transactions. For example, in the following code snippet, every call will be in a different transaction:

```
MyContractClient proxy = new MyContractClient();

using(TransactionScope scope = new TransactionScope())
{
   proxy.MyMethod(...);
   scope.Complete();
}
using(TransactionScope scope = new TransactionScope())
{
   proxy.MyMethod(...);
   scope.Complete();
}

proxy.Close();
```

Or, the client can use the same proxy multiple times in the same transaction, and even close the proxy independently of any transactions:

```
MyContractClient proxy = new MyContractClient();
using(TransactionScope scope = new TransactionScope())
{
   proxy.MyMethod(...);
   proxy.MyMethod(...);
```

```
        scope.Complete( );
    }
    proxy.Close( );
```

 The call to Dispose( ) on a per-call service has no ambient transaction.

Transaction life cycle

When the per-call service is the root of a transaction (that is, when it is configured for Client/Service and there is no client transaction, or when it is configured for Service transaction) the transaction ends once the service instance is deactivated. As soon as the method returns, WCF completes and ends the transaction, even before Dispose( ) is called. When the client is the root of the transaction (or whenever the client's transaction flows to the service and the service joins it) the transaction ends when the client's transaction ends.

Per-Session Transactional Service

The default transaction configuration of WCF will turn any service, regardless of its instancing mode, into a per-call service. This behavior is geared toward consistency in the service state management, requiring the service to be state-aware. However, having a state-aware service negates the very need for a per-session service in the first place. WCF does allow you to maintain the session semantic with a transactional service. A per-session transactional service instance can be accessed by multiple transactions, or the instance can establish an affinity to a particular transaction, in which case, until it completes, only that transaction is allowed to access it. However, as you will see, this support harbors a disproportional cost in programming model complexity.

Releasing service instance

The life cycle of any non-per-call transactional service is controlled by the ReleaseServiceInstanceOnTransactionComplete Boolean property of the ServiceBehavior attribute:

```
[AttributeUsage(AttributeTargets.Class)]
public sealed class ServiceBehaviorAttribute : Attribute,...
{
    public bool ReleaseServiceInstanceOnTransactionComplete
    {get;set;}
    //More members
}
```

When ReleaseServiceInstanceOnTransactionComplete is set to true (the default value), it disposes of the service instance once the instance completes the transaction. Note

---

that the release takes place once the instance completes the transaction, not necessarily when the transaction really completes (which could be much later). When ReleaseServiceInstanceOnTransactionComplete is true, the instance has two ways of completing the transaction and being released: at the method boundary if the method has TransactionAutoComplete set to true, or when any method that has TransactionAutoComplete set to false calls SetTransactionComplete( ).

ReleaseServiceInstanceOnTransactionComplete has two interesting interactions with other service and operation behavior properties. First, it cannot be set (to either true or false) unless at least one operation on the service has TransactionScopeRequired set to true. This is validated at the service load time by the set accessor of the ReleaseServiceInstanceOnTransactionComplete property.

For example, this is a valid configuration:

```
[ServiceBehavior(ReleaseServiceInstanceOnTransactionComplete = true)]
class MyService : IMyContract
{
   [OperationBehavior(TransactionScopeRequired = true)]
   public void MyMethod( )
   {...}

   [OperationBehavior(...)]
   public void MyOtherMethod( )
   {...}
}
```

What this constraint means is that even though the default of ReleaseServiceInstanceOnTransactionComplete is true, the following two definitions are not semantically equivalent, because the second one will throw an exception at the service load time:

```
class MyService : IMyContract
{
   public void MyMethod( )
   {...}
}

//Invalid definition
[ServiceBehavior(ReleaseServiceInstanceOnTransactionComplete = true)]
class MyService : IMyContract
{
   public void MyMethod( )
   {...}
}
```

The second constraint involved in using ReleaseServiceInstanceOnTransactionComplete relates to concurrent multithreaded access to the service instance.

Concurrency management is the subject of the next chapter. For now, the ConcurrencyMode property of the ServiceBehavior attribute controls concurrent access to the service instance:

```
public enum ConcurrencyMode
{
    Single,
    Reentrant,
    Multiple
}

[AttributeUsage(AttributeTargets.Class)]
public sealed class ServiceBehaviorAttribute : ...
{
    public ConcurrencyMode ConcurrencyMode
    {get;set;}
    //More members
}
```

The default value of ConcurrencyMode is ConcurrencyMode.Single.

WCF will verify at the service load time that if at least one operation on the service has   TransactionScopeRequired   set   to   true   when ReleaseServiceInstanceOnTransactionComplete is true (by default or explicitly), the service concurrency mode must be ConcurrencyMode.Single.

For example, given this contract:

```
[ServiceContract]
interface IMyContract
{
    [OperationContract]
    [TransactionFlow(...)]
    void MyMethod( );

    [OperationContract]
    [TransactionFlow(...)]
    void MyOtherMethod( );
}
```

the following two definitions are equivalent and valid:

```
class MyService : IMyContract
{
    [OperationBehavior(TransactionScopeRequired = true)]
    public void MyMethod( )
    {...}

    public void MyOtherMethod( )
    {...}
}

[ServiceBehavior(ConcurrencyMode = ConcurrencyMode.Single,
                 ReleaseServiceInstanceOnTransactionComplete = true)]
```

```
class MyService : IMyContract
{
   [OperationBehavior(TransactionScopeRequired = true)]
   public void MyMethod( )
   {...}

   public void MyOtherMethod( )
   {...}
}
```

The following definition is also valid since no method requires a transaction scope even though ReleaseServiceInstanceOnTransactionComplete is true:

```
[ServiceBehavior(ConcurrencyMode = ConcurrencyMode.Multiple)]
class MyService : IMyContract
{
   public void MyMethod( )
   {...}

   public void MyOtherMethod( )
   {...}
}
```

In contrast, the following definition is invalid, because at least once method requires a transaction scope, ReleaseServiceInstanceOnTransactionComplete is true, and yet the concurrency mode is not ConcurrencyMode.Single.

```
//Invalid configuration:
[ServiceBehavior(ConcurrencyMode = ConcurrencyMode.Multiple)]
class MyService : IMyContract
{
   [OperationBehavior(TransactionScopeRequired = true)]
   public void MyMethod( )
   {...}

   public void MyOtherMethod( )
   {...}
}
```

The concurrency constraint applies to all instancing modes.

The ReleaseServiceInstanceOnTransactionComplete property can enable a transactional session interaction between the client and the service. By default it will have its value of true, which means that once the service instance completes the transaction (either declaratively or explicitly), the return of the method will deactivate the service instance as if it were a per-call service.

For example, the service in Example 7-16 behaves just like a per-call service.

Example 7-16. Per-session yet per-call transactional service

```
[ServiceContract(SessionMode = SessionMode.Required)]
interface IMyContract
{
   [OperationContract]
   [TransactionFlow(...)]
   void MyMethod();
}
class MyService : IMyContract
{
   [OperationBehavior(TransactionScopeRequired = true)]
   public void MyMethod()
   {...}
}
```

Every time the client calls MyMethod( ), the client will get a new service instance. The new client call may come in on a new transaction as well, and the service instance has no affinity to any transaction. The relationship between the service instances and the transactions is just as in Figure 7-8.

Disabling releasing the service instance

Obviously, a configuration such as Example 7-16 adds no value. To behave per-session, the service can set ReleaseServiceInstanceOnTransactionComplete to false, as in Example 7-17.

Example 7-17. Per-session transactional service

```
[ServiceContract(SessionMode = SessionMode.Required)]
interface IMyContract
{
   [OperationContract]
   [TransactionFlow(...)]
   void MyMethod();
}
[ServiceBehavior(ReleaseServiceInstanceOnTransactionComplete = false)]
class MyService : IMyContract
{
   [OperationBehavior(TransactionScopeRequired = true)]
   public void MyMethod()
   {...}
}
```

When ReleaseServiceInstanceOnTransactionComplete is false, the instance will not be disposed of once transactions complete, as shown in Figure 7-9.

For example, the interaction of Figure 7-9 may be the result of the following client code, where all calls went to the same service instance:

```
MyContractClient proxy = new MyContractClient();
using(TransactionScope scope = new TransactionScope())
```

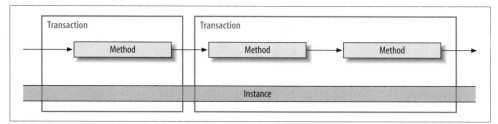

Figure 7-9. Sessionful transactional instance and transactions

```
{
   proxy.MyMethod( );
   scope.Complete( );
}

using(TransactionScope scope = new TransactionScope( ))
{
   proxy.MyMethod( );
   proxy.MyMethod( );
   scope.Complete( );
}
proxy.Close( );
```

State-aware per-session service

When `ReleaseServiceInstanceOnTransactionComplete` is `false`, WCF will stay out of the way, and will let the developer of the service worry about managing the state of the service instance in the face of transactions. Obviously, you have to somehow monitor transactions and roll back any changes made to the state of the instance if the transaction aborts. The per-session service still must equate method boundaries with transaction boundaries because every method may be in a different transaction. There are two possible programming models. The first is to be state-aware, but use the session ID as a state identifier. At the beginning of every method the service would get its state from a resource manager using the session ID as a key, and at the end of every method the service instance would save the state back to the resource manager, as shown in Example 7-18.

Example 7-18. State-aware, transactional per-session service

```
[ServiceBehavior(ReleaseServiceInstanceOnTransactionComplete = false)]
class MyService : IMyContract,IDisposable
{
   readonly string m_StateIdentifier;

   public MyService( )
   {
      InitializeState( );
      m_StateIdentifier = OperationContext.Current.SessionId;
      SaveState( );
   }
```

Example 7-18. State-aware, transactional per-session service (continued)

```
[OperationBehavior(TransactionScopeRequired = true)]
public void MyMethod( )
{
   GetState( );
   DoWork( );
   SaveState( );
}
public void Dispose( )
{
   RemoveState( );
}

//Helper methods

void InitializeState( )
{...}
void GetState( )
{
   //Use m_StateIdentifier to get state
   ...
}
void DoWork( )
{...}
void SaveState( )
{
   //Use m_StateIdentifier to save state
   ...
}
void RemoveState( )
{
   // Use m_StateIdentifier to remove the state from the RM
   ...
}
}
```

In Example 7-18, the constructor first initializes the state of the object, and then saves the state to a resource manager, so that any method can retrieve it. Note that the per-session object maintains the illusion of a stateful, sessionful interaction with its client. The client does not need to pass an explicit state identifier. The service must be disciplined, and retrieve and save the state in every operation call. When the session ends, the service purges its state from the resource manager in the Dispose( ) method.

Stateful per-session service

The second and more modern programming model is to use volatile resource managers for the service members (see the sidebar "Volatile Resource Managers"), as shown in Example 7-19.

Volatile Resource Managers

In the article "Volatile Resource Managers in .NET Bring Transactions to the Common Type" (*MSDN Magazine*, May 2005) I presented my technique for implementing a general-purpose volatile resource manager called `Transactional<T>`:

```
public class Transactional<T> : ...
{
   public Transactional(T value);
   public Transactional();
   public T Value
   {get;set;}
   /* Conversion operators to and from T */
}
```

By specifying any serializable type parameter such as an `int` or a `string` to `Transactional<T>`, you turn that type into a full-blown volatile resource manager that auto-enlists in the ambient transaction, participates in the two-phase commit protocol, and isolates the current changes from all other transactions using my original transaction-based lock.

For example, in the following code snippet the scope is not completed. As a result the transaction aborts and the values of `number` and `city` revert to their pre-transaction state:

```
Transactional<int> number = new Transactional<int>(3);
Transactional<string> city
                  = new Transactional<string>("New York");

using(TransactionScope scope = new TransactionScope())
{
   city.Value = "London";
   number.Value = 4;
   number.Value++;
   Debug.Assert(number.Value == 5);
   Debug.Assert(number == 5);
}
Debug.Assert(number == 3);
Debug.Assert(city == "New York");
```

In addition to `Transactional<T>` I also provided a transactional array called `TransactionalArray<T>` and well as a transactional version for all of the collections in `System.Collections.Generic`, such as `TransactionalDictionary<K,T>` and `TransactionalList<T>`. The implementation of my volatile resource managers has nothing to do with WCF, and therefore I chose not to include it in this book. The implementation, however, makes intense use of the more advanced features of C# 2.0, `System.Transactions`, and .NET system programming, and it may be of interest for its own merit.

Example 7-19. Using volatile resource managers to achieve stateful per-session transactional service

```
[ServiceBehavior(ReleaseServiceInstanceOnTransactionComplete = false)]
class MyService : IMyContract
{
   Transactional<string> m_Text =
                          new Transactional<string>("Some initial value");

   TransactionalArray<int> m_Numbers = new TransactionalArray<int>(3);

   [OperationBehavior(TransactionScopeRequired = true)]
   public void MyMethod( )
   {
      m_Text.Value = "This value will roll back if the transaction aborts";

      //These will roll back if the transaction aborts
      m_Numbers[0] = 11;
      m_Numbers[1] = 22;
      m_Numbers[2] = 33;
   }
}
```

Example 7-19 uses my Transactional<T> and TransactionalArray<T> volatile resource managers, which are available with the source code of this book. Using generics, Transactional<T> can take any serializable type and provide transactional access to it. So, the per-session service can safely set ReleaseServiceInstanceOnTransactionComplete to false and yet freely access its members. The use of the volatile resource managers enables a stateful programming model, and the service instance simply accesses its state as if no transactions were involved. The volatile resource managers auto-enlist in the transaction and isolate that transaction from all other transactions. Any changes made to the state will commit or roll back with the transaction.

Transaction life cycle

When the per-session service is the root of the transaction, the transaction ends once the service completes the transaction, which is when the method returns. When the client is the root of transaction (or when a transaction flows to the service) the transaction ends when the client's transaction ends. If the per-session service provides an IDisposable implementation, the Dispose( ) method will not have any transaction regardless of the root.

Concurrent transactions

Because a per-session service can engage the same service instance in multiple client calls, it could also sustain multiple concurrent transactions. Given the service definition of Example 7-17, Example 7-20 shows some client code that launches concurrent transactions on the same instance. scope2 will use a new transaction separate from that of scope1, and yet access the same service instance in the same session.

Example 7-20. Launching concurrent transactions

```
using(TransactionScope scope1 = new TransactionScope())
{
    MyContractClient proxy = new MyContractClient();
    proxy.MyMethod();

    using(TransactionScope scope2
                    = new TransactionScope(TransactionScopeOption.RequiresNew))
    {
        proxy.MyMethod();
        scope2.Complete();
    }
    proxy.MyMethod();

    proxy.Close();
    scope1.Complete();
}
```

The resulting transactions of Example 7-20 are depicted in Figure 7-10.

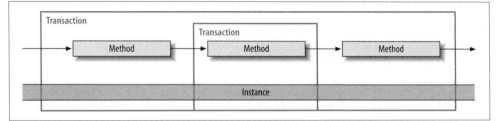

Figure 7-10. Concurrent transactions

 Code such as in Example 7-20 will almost certainly result in a transactional deadlock over the underlying resources the service accesses. The first transaction will obtain the resource lock. The second transaction will wait to own that lock while the first transaction waits for the second to complete.

Completing on session end

WCF offers yet another programming model for transactional per-session services, which is completely independent of ReleaseServiceInstanceOnTransactionComplete. This model is available for the case when the lifeline of the session is only a part of the transaction lifeline, meaning the entire session fits into a single transaction. The idea is that the service should not complete the transaction inside the session, because that is what causes WCF to release the service instance. To avoid completing the transaction, a per-session service can set TransactionAutoComplete to false, as shown in Example 7-21.

Example 7-21. Setting TransactionAutoComplete to false

```
[ServiceContract(SessionMode = SessionMode.Required)]
interface IMyContract
{
   [OperationContract]
   [TransactionFlow(...)]
   void MyMethod1( );

   [OperationContract]
   [TransactionFlow(...)]
   void MyMethod2( );

   [OperationContract]
   [TransactionFlow(...)]
   void MyMethod3( );
}
class MyService : IMyContract
{
   [OperationBehavior(TransactionScopeRequired = true,
                      TransactionAutoComplete = false)]
   public void MyMethod1( )
   {...}

   [OperationBehavior(TransactionScopeRequired = true,
                      TransactionAutoComplete = false)]
   public void MyMethod2( )
   {...}

   [OperationBehavior(TransactionScopeRequired = true,
                      TransactionAutoComplete = false)]
   public void MyMethod3( )
   {...}
}
```

Note that only a per-session service can set TransactionAutoComplete to false, and that is verified at the service load time. The problem with Example 7-21 is that the transaction the service participates in will always abort because the service does not vote to commit it. If the lifetime of the session is completely included in a single transaction, the service should vote once the session ends. For that purpose the ServiceBehavior attribute provides the Boolean property TransactionAutoCompleteOnSessionClose, defined as:

```
[AttributeUsage(AttributeTargets.Class)]
public sealed class ServiceBehaviorAttribute : Attribute,...
{
   public bool TransactionAutoCompleteOnSessionClose
   {get;set;}
   //More members
}
```

The default of TransactionAutoCompleteOnSessionClose is false. However, when set to true, it will auto-complete all uncompleted methods in the session. If no exceptions occurred during the session, when TransactionAutoCompleteOnSessionClose is true the service will vote to commit. For example, here is how to retrofit Example 7-21; Figure 7-11 shows the resulting instance and its session:

```
[ServiceBehavior(TransactionAutoCompleteOnSessionClose = true)]
class MyService : IMyContract
{...}
```

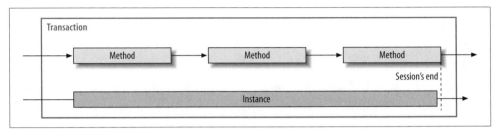

Figure 7-11. Setting TransactionAutoCompleteOnSessionClose to true

During the session, the instance can maintain and access its state in member variables, and there is no need for state awareness or volatile resource managers.

 When joining the client's transaction and relying on auto-completion on session close, the service must avoid lengthy processing in Dispose() or, in practical terms, avoid implementing IDisposable altogether. The reason is the following race condition. Recall from Chapter 4, that Dispose() is called asynchronously at the end of the session. Auto-completion at session end takes place once the instance is disposed. If the client has control before the instance is disposed, the transaction will abort because the service did not complete it yet.

Note that using TransactionAutoCompleteOnSessionClose is risky because it is always subjected to the transaction timeout. Sessions are by their very nature long-living entities, while well-designed transactions are short-lived. This programming model is available for the case when the vote decision requires information obtained by future calls throughout the session.

Because having TransactionAutoCompleteOnSessionClose set to true equates the session's end with the transaction's end, it is required that when the client's transaction is used, that the client terminates the session within that transaction:

```
using(TransactionScope scope = new TransactionScope())
{
   MyContractClient proxy = new MyContractClient();
   proxy.MyMethod();
   proxy.MyMethod();
   proxy.Close();

   scope.Complete();
}
```

Failing to do so will abort the transaction. A side effect of this is that the client cannot easily stack the using statements of the transaction scope and the proxy because that may cause the proxy to be disposed after the transaction:

```
//This always aborts:
using(MyContractClient proxy = new MyContractClient())
using(TransactionScope scope = new TransactionScope())
{
    proxy.MyMethod();
    proxy.MyMethod();

    scope.Complete();
}
```

In addition, because the proxy is basically good for only one-time use, there is little point in storing the proxy in member variables.

Transactional affinity

Setting `TransactionAutoComplete` to `false` has a unique effect that nothing else in WCF provides: it creates an affinity between the service instance and the transaction, so that only that single transaction can ever access the service instance. The affinity is established once the first transaction accesses the service instance, and once established it is fixed for the life of the instance (until the session ends). Transactional affinity is only available for per-session services because only a per-session service can set `TransactionAutoComplete` to `false`. Affinity is crucial because the service is not state-aware—it uses normal members, and it must isolate access to them from any other transaction, in case the transaction it has an affinity to aborts. Affinity thus offers a crude form of transaction-based locking. With transaction affinity, code such as Example 7-20 is guaranteed to deadlock (and eventually abort due to timing out) because the second transaction is blocked (independently of any resources the service accesses) waiting for the first transaction to finish, while the first transaction is blocked waiting for the second.

Hybrid state management

WCF also supports a hybrid mode of the two programming models shown so far, combining both a state-aware and a stateful transactional per-session service. The hybrid mode is designed to allow the service instance to maintain in-memory state until it can complete the transaction and then recycle state using `ReleaseServiceInstanceOnTransactionComplete`. Consider the service in Example 7-22 that implements the contract from Example 7-21.

Example 7-22. Hybrid per-session service

```
[ServiceBehavior(TransactionAutoCompleteOnSessionClose = true)]
class MyService : IMyContract
{
    [OperationBehavior(TransactionScopeRequired = true,
                       TransactionAutoComplete = false)]
```

Example 7-22. Hybrid per-session service (continued)

```
    public void MyMethod1( )
    {...}
    [OperationBehavior(TransactionScopeRequired = true,
                       TransactionAutoComplete = false)]
    public void MyMethod2( )
    {...}
    [OperationBehavior(TransactionScopeRequired = true)]
    public void MyMethod3( )
    {...}
}
```

The service uses the default of TransactionAutoCompleteOnSessionClose (false) and yet it has two methods (MyMethod1( ) and MyMethod2( )) that do not complete the transaction and have TransactionAutoComplete set to false, which creates an affinity to a particular transaction. The affinity isolates access to its members from any other transaction, in case the transaction it has an affinity to aborts. The problem now is that the service will always abort that transaction because it does not complete it. To compensate for that, the service offers MyMethod3( ), which does complete the transaction. Because the service uses the default of ReleaseServiceInstanceOnTransactionComplete (true), after calling MyMethod3( ), the transaction is completed and the instance is disposed of, as shown in Figure 7-12. Note that MyMethod3( ) could have instead used explicit voting via SetTransactionComplete( ). The important thing is that it completes the transaction.

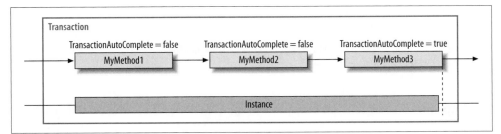

Figure 7-12. Hybrid state management

The hybrid mode is inherently a brittle proposition. First, the service instance must complete the transaction before it times out. Since there is no telling when the client will call the completing method, you risk timing out before that. In addition, the service also prolongs holding on to any locks on resource managers it may access for the duration of the session. The longer the locks are held, the higher the likelihood of other transactions timing out or deadlocking with this service's transaction. Finally, the service is at the mercy of the client because the client must call the completing method to end the session. You can and should use demarcating operations to try to force this on the client:

```
    [ServiceContract(SessionMode = SessionMode.Required)]
    interface IMyContract
```

```
{
    [OperationContract]
    [TransactionFlow(...)]
    void MyMethod1();

    [OperationContract(IsInitiating = false)]
    [TransactionFlow(...)]
    void MyMethod2();

    [OperationContract(IsInitiating = false,IsTerminating = true)]
    [TransactionFlow(...)]
    void MyMethod3();
}
```

Choosing per-session transactional service

Transactional sessions are available for situations when the transaction execution and subsequent voting decision requires information obtained throughout the session. Consider, for example, the following contract used for order processing:

```
[ServiceContract(SessionMode = SessionMode.Required)]
interface IOrderManager
{
    [OperationContract]
    [TransactionFlow(...)]
    void SetCustomerId(int customerId);

    [OperationContract(IsInitiating = false)]
    [TransactionFlow(...)]
    void AddItem(int itemId);

    [OperationContract(IsInitiating = false,IsTerminating = true)]
    [TransactionFlow(...)]
    bool ProcessOrders();
}
```

The implementing service can only process the order once it has the customer ID and all its ordered items. However, relying on transactional sessions usually indicates poor design because of its inferior throughput and scalability implications. The service must maintain locks longer and risk deadlocks. I consider a transactional session a design aberration at best and an anathema at worst. The disproportional complexity of a transactional session resulting from the state management, transactional affinity, and transaction completion outweigh the perceived benefit of a session. It is usually better to factor the contract so that it does not rely on a session:

```
[ServiceContract]
interface IOrderManager
{
    [OperationContract]
    [TransactionFlow(...)]
    bool ProcessOrders(int customerId,int[] itemIds);
}
```

I prefer the simplicity of the per-call service and avoid transactional sessions.

Transactional Singleton

By default, a transactional singleton behaves like a per-call service. The reason is that by default ReleaseServiceInstanceOnTransactionComplete is true, and so after the singleton auto-completes a transaction, WCF disposes of the singleton, in the interest of state management and consistency. This in turn implies that the singleton must be state-aware, and proactively manage its state in every method call, in and out of a resource manager. The big difference compared to a per-call service is that WCF will enforce the semantic of the single instance, so at any point in time there is at most a single instance running. WCF uses concurrency management and instance deactivation to enforce this rule. Recall that when ReleaseServiceInstanceOnTransactionComplete is true, the concurrency mode must be ConcurrencyMode.Single to disallow concurrent calls. WCF keeps the singleton context and merely deactivates the instance hosted in the context, as discussed in Chapter 4. What this means is that even though the singleton needs be state-aware, it does not need an explicit state identifier to be provided by the client in every call. The singleton can use any type-level constant to identify its state in the state resource manager, as shown in Example 7-23.

Example 7-23. State-aware singleton

```
[ServiceBehavior(InstanceContextMode = InstanceContextMode.Single)]
class MySingleton : IMyContract
{
   readonly static string m_StateIdentifier = typeof(MySingleton).GUID.ToString( );

   [OperationBehavior(TransactionScopeRequired = true)]
   public void MyMethod( )
   {
      GetState( );
      DoWork( );
      SaveState( );
   }

   //Helper methods
   void GetState( )
   {
      //Use m_StateIdentifier to get state
   }
   void DoWork( )
   {}
   public void SaveState( )
   {
      //Use m_StateIdentifier to save state
   }
   public void RemoveState( )
   {
```

Example 7-23. State-aware singleton (continued)

```
        //Use m_StateIdentifier to remove the state from the resource manager
    }
}
//Hosting code
MySingleton singleton  = new MySingleton();
singleton.SaveState();//Create the initial state in the resource manager

ServiceHost host = new ServiceHost(singleton);
host.Open();

/* Some blocking calls */

host.Close();
singleton.RemoveState();
```

In the example, the singleton uses the unique GUID associated with every type as a
state identifier. At the beginning of every method the singleton reads its state, and at
the end of each method its saves the state back to the resource manager. However,
the first call on the first instance ever must also be able to bind to the state, so you
must prime the resource manager with the state before the first call ever arrives. To
that end, before launching the host, you need to create the singleton, save its state to
the resource manager, and then provide the singleton instance to host to ServiceHost
as explained in Chapter 4. After the host shuts down, make sure to remove the singleton state from the resource manager, as shown in Example 7-23. Note that you
cannot create the initial state in the singleton constructor, because the constructor
will be called for each operation on the singleton and override the previous state
saved. While a state-aware singleton is certainly possible (as demonstrated in
Example 7-23), the overall complexity involved makes it a technique to avoid. It is
better to use a stateful transactional singleton as presented next.

Stateful singleton

By setting ReleaseServiceInstanceOnTransactionComplete to false, you regain the
singleton semantic. The singleton will be created just once when the host is launched
and the same single instance will be shared across all clients and transactions. The
problem is of course how to manage the state of the singleton. The singleton has to
have state; otherwise there is no point in making it a singleton in the first place. The
solution as before with the stateful per-session service is to use volatile resource managers as member variables, as shown in Example 7-24.

Example 7-24. Achieving stateful singleton transactional service

```
///////////////////// Service Side ////////////////////////////////////////
[ServiceBehavior(InstanceContextMode = InstanceContextMode.Single,
                 ReleaseServiceInstanceOnTransactionComplete = false)]
class MySingleton : IMyContract
{
```

```
    Transactional<int> m_Counter = new Transactional<int>( );

    [OperationBehavior(TransactionScopeRequired = true)]
    public void MyMethod( )
    {
       m_Counter.Value++;
       Trace.WriteLine("Counter: " + m_Counter.Value);
    }
}
/////////////////// Client Side ///////////////////////////////////////
using(TransactionScope scope1 = new TransactionScope( ))
{
    MyContractClient proxy = new MyContractClient( );
    proxy.MyMethod( );
    proxy.Close( );
    scope1.Complete( );
}
using(TransactionScope scope2 = new TransactionScope( ))
{
    MyContractClient proxy = new MyContractClient( );
    proxy.MyMethod( );
    proxy.Close( );
}
using(TransactionScope scope3 = new TransactionScope( ))
{
    MyContractClient proxy = new MyContractClient( );
    proxy.MyMethod( );
    proxy.Close( );
    scope3.Complete( );
}
/////////////////// Output ///////////////////////////////////////
Counter: 1
Counter: 2
Counter: 2
```

In Example 7-24, a client creates three transactional scopes, each with its own new proxy to the singleton. In each call, the singleton increments a counter it maintains as a Transactional<int> volatile resource manager. scope1 completes the transaction and commits the new value of the counter (1). In scope2, the client calls the singleton and temporarily increments the counter to 2. However, scope2 does not complete its transaction. The volatile resource manager rejects the increment and reverts to its previous value of 1. The call in scope3 then increments the counter again from 1 to 2, as shown in the trace output.

Note that when setting ReleaseServiceInstanceOnTransactionComplete, the singleton must have at least one method with TransactionScopeRequired set to true.

In addition, the singleton must have TransactionAutoComplete set to true on every method, which of course precludes any transactional affinity, and allows concurrent transactions. All calls and all transactions are routed to the same instance. For example, the following client code will result in the transaction diagram shown in Figure 7-13 using (MyContractClient proxy = new MyContractClient( )).

```
using(TransactionScope scope = new TransactionScope( ))
{
   proxy.MyMethod( );
   scope.Complete( );
}

using(MyContractClient proxy = new MyContractClient( ))
using(TransactionScope scope = new TransactionScope( ))
{
   proxy.MyMethod( );
   proxy.MyMethod( );
   scope.Complete( );
}
```

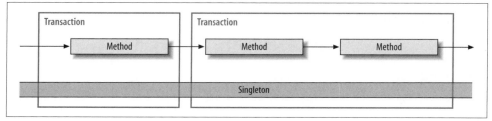

Figure 7-13. Stateful transactional singleton

Instancing Modes and Transactions

As you can see from the discussion so far, the moment you configure your transactional service for anything besides per-call instancing mode, you incur a disproportional increase in the complexity of the programming model. While WCF is powerful and extensible enough to support the widest range of configuration permutations, I recommend that you stick with the per-call service. A transactional singleton using a volatile resource manager is agreeable, as long as you can tolerate the singleton in the first place. To summarize the topic of instance management modes and transactions, Table 7-3 lists the configurations discussed so far. Note that Table 7-3 only lists the possible configurations and their resulting effects. Other combinations may be technically allowed but are nonsensical, or are plainly disallowed by WCF.

Table 7-3. Instancing mode, configurations and transactions

Configured instance mode	Auto-complete	Release on complete	Complete on session end	Resulting instance mode	State management	Transaction affinity
Per call	True	True/false	True/false	Per call	State-aware	Call
Session	False	True/false	True	Session	Stateful	Instance

Table 7-3. Instancing mode, configurations and transactions (continued)

Configured instance mode	Auto-complete	Release on complete	Complete on session end	Resulting instance mode	State management	Transaction affinity
Session	True	False	True/false	Session	Stateful (State-aware, VRM)	Call
Session	True	True	True/false	Per call	State-aware	Call
Session	Hybrid	True	True/false	Hybrid	Hybrid	Instance
Singleton	True	True	True/false	Per call	State-aware	Call
Singleton	True	False	True/false	Singleton	Stateful (State-aware, VRM)	Call

Callbacks

Callback contracts, just like service contracts, can propagate the service transaction to the callback client. You apply the TransactionFlow attribute, as with a service contract, for example:

```
interface IMyContractCallback
{
   [OperationContract]
   [TransactionFlow(TransactionFlowOption.Allowed)]
   void OnCallback();
}
[ServiceContract(CallbackContract = typeof(IMyContractCallback))]
interface IMyContract
{...}
```

The callback method implementation can use the OperationBehavior attribute just like a service operation and specify requiring a transaction scope and auto-completion:

```
class MyClient : IMyContractCallback
{
   [OperationBehavior(TransactionScopeRequired = true)]
   public void OnCallback()
   {
      Transaction transaction = Transaction.Current;
      Debug.Assert(transaction != null);
   }
}
```

Callback Transaction Modes

The callback client can have four modes of configuration: Service, Service/Callback, Callback, and None, analogous to the service transaction modes, except the service now plays the client role and the callback plays the service role in the previous service-side modes. For example, to configure the callback for Service transaction mode (that is, always using the service transaction), follow these steps:

1. Use a transaction-aware duplex binding with transaction flow enabled.

2. Set transaction flow to mandatory on the callback operation.

3. Configure the callback operation to require a transaction scope.

Example 7-25 shows a callback client configured for Service transaction.

Example 7-25. Configuring the callback for Service transaction

```
interface IMyContractCallback
{
   [OperationContract]
   [TransactionFlow(TransactionFlowOption.Mandatory)]
   void OnCallback();
}

class MyClient : IMyContractCallback
{
   [OperationBehavior(TransactionScopeRequired = true)]
   public void OnCallback()
   {
      Transaction transaction = Transaction.Current;
      Debug.Assert(transaction.TransactionInformation.
               DistributedIdentifier != Guid.Empty);
   }
}
```

When the callback operation is configured for mandatory transaction flow, WCF will enforce the use of a transaction-ware binding with transaction flow enabled.

When configuring for Service/Callback transaction propagation mode, WCF does not enforce the use of a transaction aware binding or that transaction flow is enabled. You can use my BindingRequirement attribute to verify this:

```
interface IMyContractCallback
{
   [OperationContract]
   [TransactionFlow(TransactionFlowOption.Allowed)]
   void OnCallback();
}
[BindingRequirement(TransactionFlowEnabled = true)]
class MyClient : IMyContractCallback
{
   [OperationBehavior(TransactionScopeRequired = true)]
   public void OnCallback()
   {...}
}
```

I extended the BindingRequirement attribute to verify callback binding by implementing the IEndpointBehavior interface:

```
public interface IEndpointBehavior
{
```

```
        void AddBindingParameters(ServiceEndpoint endpoint,
                               BindingParameterCollection bindingParameters);
        void ApplyClientBehavior(ServiceEndpoint serviceEndpoint,
                               ClientRuntime behavior);
        void ApplyDispatchBehavior(ServiceEndpoint endpoint,
                               EndpointDispatcher endpointDispatcher);
        void Validate(ServiceEndpoint serviceEndpoint);
    }
```

As explained in Chapter 6, the `IEndpointBehavior` interface lets you configure the client-side endpoint used for the callback by the service. In the case of the `BindingRequirement` attribute, it uses the `IEndpointBehavior.Validate( )` method, and the implementation is almost identical to that of Example 7-3.

Isolation and timeouts

Similar to a service, the `CallbackBehavior` attribute enables a callback type to control its transaction's timeout and isolation level:

```
[AttributeUsage(AttributeTargets.Class)]
public sealed class CallbackBehaviorAttribute: Attribute,IEndpointBehavior
{
    public IsolationLevel TransactionIsolationLevel
    {get;set;}
    public string TransactionTimeout
    {get;set;}
    //More members
}
```

These properties accept the same values as in the service case, and choosing a particular value follows the same reasoning.

Callback Voting

By default, WCF will use automatic voting for the callback operation, just as with a service operation. Any exception in the callback will vote to abort the transaction, and without an error WCF will vote to commit the transaction, as is the case in Example 7-25. However, unlike a service instance, the callback instance life cycle is managed by the client, and it has no instancing mode. Any callback instance can be configured for explicit voting by setting `TransactionAutoComplete` to `false`, and then voting explicitly using `SetTransactionComplete( )`:

```
class MyClient : IMyContractCallback
{
    [OperationBehavior(TransactionScopeRequired = true,
                      TransactionAutoComplete = false)]
    public void OnCallback( )
    {
        /* Do some transactional work then */

        OperationContext.Current.SetTransactionComplete( );
    }
}
```

As with a per-session service, explicit voting is for the case when the vote depends on other things besides exceptions. Do not perform any work, especially transactional work after the call to SetTransactionComplete(). Calling SetTransactionComplete() should be the last line of code in the callback operation just before returning. If you try to perform any transactional work (including accessing Transaction.Current) after the call to SetTransactionComplete(), WCF will throw an InvalidOperationException and abort the transaction.

Using Transactional Callbacks

While WCF provides the infrastructure for propagating the service transaction to the callback, in reality callbacks and service transactions do not mix well. First, callbacks are usually one-way operations, and as such cannot propagate transactions. Second, to be able to invoke the callback, the service cannot be configured with ConcurrencyMode.Single; otherwise, WCF will abort the call to avoid the deadlock. Typically services are configured for Client/Service or Client transaction propagation modes. Ideally, the service should be able to propagate its original calling client's transaction to the callbacks it invokes. Yet, for the service to use the client's transaction, TransactionScopeRequired must be set to true. Since ReleaseServiceInstanceOnTransactionComplete is true by default, it requires ConcurrencyMode.Single, thus precluding the callback.

Out-of-band transactional callbacks

There are two ways of making transactional callbacks. The first is out-of-band callbacks by nonservice parties on the host side using callback references stored by the service. Such parties can easily propagate their transactions (usually in a TransactionScope) to the callback because there is no risk of a deadlock, as shown in Example 7-26.

Example 7-26. Out-of-band callbacks

```
[ServiceBehavior(InstanceContextMode = InstanceContextMode.PerCall)]
class MyService : IMyContract
{
   static List<IMyContractCallback> m_Callbacks = new List<IMyContractCallback>();

   public void MyMethod()
   {
      IMyContractCallback callback = OperationContext.Current.
                               GetCallbackChannel<IMyContractCallback>();

      if(m_Callbacks.Contains(callback) == false)
      {
         m_Callbacks.Add(callback);
      }
   }
   public static void CallClients()
   {
```

Example 7-26. Out-of-band callbacks (continued)

```
      Action<IMyContractCallback> invoke = delegate(IMyContractCallback callback)
                                           {
                                              using(TransactionScope scope
                                                          = new TransactionScope())
                                              {
                                                 callback.OnCallback();
                                                 scope.Complete();
                                              }
                                           };
      m_Callbacks.ForEach(invoke);
   }
}
//Out-of-band callbacks:
MyService.CallClients();
```

Service transactional callback

The second option is to carefully configure the transactional service so that it is able
to call back to its calling client. To that end, configure the service with
ConcurrencyMode.Reentrant, set ReleaseServiceInstanceOnTransactionComplete to
false, and make sure at least one operation has TransactionScopeRequired set to
true, as shown in Example 7-27.

Example 7-27. Configuring for transactional callbacks

```
[ServiceContract(CallbackContract = typeof(IMyContractCallback))]
interface IMyContract
{
   [OperationContract]
   [TransactionFlow(TransactionFlowOption.Allowed)]
   void MyMethod(...);
}
interface IMyContractCallback
{
   [OperationContract]
   [TransactionFlow(TransactionFlowOption.Allowed)]
   void OnCallback();
}
[ServiceBehavior(InstanceContextMode = InstanceContextMode.PerCall,
               ConcurrencyMode = ConcurrencyMode.Reentrant,
               ReleaseServiceInstanceOnTransactionComplete = false)]
class MyService : IMyContract
{
   [OperationBehavior(TransactionScopeRequired = true)]
   public void MyMethod(...)
   {
      Trace.WriteLine("Service ID:    " +
               Transaction.Current.TransactionInformation.DistributedIdentifier);

      IMyContractCallback callback =
               OperationContext.Current.GetCallbackChannel<IMyContractCallback>();
      callback.OnCallback();
```

Example 7-27. Configuring for transactional callbacks (continued)

```
    }
}
```

The rationale behind this constraint is explained in the next chapter.

Given the definitions of Example 7-27 and transaction flow enabled in the binding, the following client code:

```
class MyClient : IMyContractCallback
{
    [OperationBehavior(TransactionScopeRequired = true)]
    public void OnCallback()
    {
        Trace.WriteLine("OnCallback ID: " +
                Transaction.Current.TransactionInformation.DistributedIdentifier);
    }
}
MyClient client = new MyClient();
InstanceContext context = new InstanceContext(client);
MyContractClient proxy = new MyContractClient(context);

using(TransactionScope scope = new TransactionScope())
{
    proxy.MyMethod();

    Trace.WriteLine("Client ID:     " +
            Transaction.Current.TransactionInformation.DistributedIdentifier);
    scope.Complete();
}
proxy.Close();
```

yields output similar to this:

```
Service ID:     23627e82-507a-45d5-933c-05e5e5a1ae78
OnCallback ID: 23627e82-507a-45d5-933c-05e5e5a1ae78
Client ID:      23627e82-507a-45d5-933c-05e5e5a1ae78
```

indicating that the client transaction was propagated to the service and into the callback.

Obviously, setting ReleaseServiceInstanceOnTransactionComplete to false means WCF will not recycle the instance once the transaction completes. The best remedy for that is to prefer per-call services for transactional callbacks (as in Example 7-27) because they will be destroyed after the method returns anyway, and their state-aware programming model is independent of ReleaseServiceInstanceOnTransactionComplete.

If you are using a per-session service, you need to follow the guidelines mentioned previously on how to manage the state of a per-session service when ReleaseServiceInstanceOnTransactionComplete is false; namely, state-aware programming or utilizing volatile resource managers.

CHAPTER 8

Concurrency Management

Incoming client calls are dispatched to the service on threads from the thread pool. Since multiple clients can make multiple concurrent calls, the service itself can sustain those calls on multiple threads. If those calls are dispatched to the same instance, you must provide thread-safe access to the service's in-memory state or risk state corruption and errors. The same is true for the client's in-memory state during callbacks, since callbacks too are dispatched on threads from the thread pool. In addition to synchronizing access to the instance state when applicable, all services need to synchronize access to resources shared between instances, such as static variables or user-interface controls. Another dimension altogether for concurrency management is ensuring that, if required, the service (or the resources it accesses) executes on particular threads.

WCF offers two modes for synchronization. Automatic synchronization instructs WCF to synchronize access to the service instance. Automatic synchronization is easy and simple to use, but it is only available for service and callback classes. Manual synchronization puts the full burden of synchronization on the developer, and requires application-specific integration. The developer needs to employ the .NET synchronization locks, and it is by far an expert discipline. The advantages of manual synchronization are that it is available for service and nonservice classes alike and it allows developers to optimize throughput and scalability. This chapter starts by describing the basic concurrency modes available and then presents more advanced aspects such as resourcing safety and synchronization, thread affinity and custom synchronization context, callbacks, and asynchronous calls. Throughout, the chapter shares best practices and concurrency management design guidelines.

Instance Management and Concurrency

Service-instance thread safety is closely related to the service-instancing mode. A per-call service instance is thread-safe by definition because each call gets its own dedicated instance. That instance will only be accessible by its assigned worker thread and therefore will have no need for synchronization because no other threads will be accessing it. However, a per-call service is typically state-aware. The state store can also be in-memory resources such as static variables. The state store can be subject to multithreaded access because the service can sustain concurrent calls. Consequently, you must synchronize access to the state store.

A per-session service does require concurrency management and synchronization. The reason is that the client may use the same proxy and yet dispatch calls on multiple client-side threads to the service. A singleton service is even more susceptible to concurrent access, and must have synchronized access. The singleton has some in-memory state that all clients implicitly share. On top of the possibility for dispatching calls on multiple threads as with a per-session service, a singleton may simply have multiple clients in different execution contexts, each using its own thread to call the service. All these calls will enter the singleton on different threads from the thread pool, hence the need for synchronization.

Service Concurrency Mode

Concurrent access to the service instance is governed by the `ConcurrencyMode` property of the `ServiceBehavior` attribute:

```
public enum ConcurrencyMode
{
    Single,
    Reentrant,
    Multiple
}

[AttributeUsage(AttributeTargets.Class)]
public sealed class ServiceBehaviorAttribute : ...
{
    public ConcurrencyMode ConcurrencyMode
    {get;set;}
    //More members
}
```

The value of the `ConcurrencyMode` enum controls if and when concurrent calls are allowed on the service instance.

ConcurrencyMode.Single

When the service is set with `ConcurrencyMode.Single`, WCF will provide automatic synchronization to the service instance and disallow concurrent calls by associating the service instance with a synchronization lock. Every call coming into the service must first try to acquire the lock. If the lock is unowned, the caller will lock the lock and be allowed in. Once the operation returns, WCF will unlock the lock and thus allow another caller in. The important thing is that only one caller at a time is ever allowed. If there are multiple concurrent callers while the lock is locked, the callers are all placed in a queue, and are served out of the queue in order. If the call times out while blocked, WCF will remove the caller from the queue and the client will get a TimeoutException. ConcurrencyMode.Single is the WCF default setting, so these definitions are equivalent:

```
[ServiceBehavior(InstanceContextMode = InstanceContextMode.PerCall)]
class MyService : IMyContract
{...}

[ServiceBehavior(InstanceContextMode = InstanceContextMode.PerCall,
                 ConcurrencyMode = ConcurrencyMode.Single)]
class MyService : IMyContract
{...}
```

Because the default concurrency mode is synchronized access, the susceptible instancing modes of per-session and singleton are also synchronized by default:

```
[ServiceContract(SessionMode = SessionMode.Required)]
interface IMyContract
{...}

//These stateful services are thread-safe

class MyService1 : IMyContract
{...}

[ServiceBehavior(InstanceContextMode = InstanceContextMode.PerSession)]
class MyService2 : IMyContract
{...}

[ServiceBehavior(InstanceContextMode = InstanceContextMode.Single)]
class MySingleton : IMyContract
{...}
```

 In the case of a sessionful or singleton service, keep the duration of the operation execution short and avoid blocking clients for long. Because the service instance is synchronized, if the operation takes a while to complete, you risk timing out pending callers.

Synchronized access and transactions

As explained in Chapter 7, WCF will verify at the service load time that if at least one operation on the service has TransactionScopeRequired set to true and ReleaseServiceInstanceOnTransactionComplete is true, the service concurrency mode must be ConcurrencyMode.Single. This is done deliberately to ensure that the service instance can be recycled at the end of the transaction without having another thread accessing the disposed instance.

ConcurrencyMode.Multiple

When the service is set with ConcurrencyMode.Mutiple, WCF will stay out of the way and will not synchronize access in any way to the service instance. ConcurrencyMode. Mutiple simply means that the service instance is not associated with any synchronization lock, so concurrent calls are allowed on the service instance. Put differently, when a service instance is configured with ConcurrencyMode.Mutiple, WCF will not queue up the client messages and dispatch them to the service instance as soon as they arrive.

 A large number of concurrent client calls will not result in a matching number of concurrently executing calls on the service. The maximum number of concurrent calls dispatched to the service is the product of the configured maximum concurrent calls' throttled value. As mentioned in Chapter 4, the default max concurrent calls value is 16.

Obviously, this is of great concern to sessionful and singleton services, but also sometimes to a per-call service, as you will see later on. Such services must manually synchronize access to their state. The common way of doing that is to use .NET locks such as Monitor or a WaitHandle-derived class. Manual synchronization is not for the faint of heart and is covered in great depth in Chapter 8 of my book *Programming .NET Components* (O'Reilly). Manual synchronization does enable the service developer to optimize the throughput of client calls on the service instance, because you can lock the service instance just when and where synchronization is required, thus allowing other clients calls on the same service instance in between the synchronized sections. Such a manually synchronized service is shown in Example 8-1.

Example 8-1. Manual synchronization using fragmented locking

```
[ServiceContract(SessionMode = SessionMode.Required)]
interface IMyContract
{
   void MyMethod( );
}
[ServiceBehavior(ConcurrencyMode = ConcurrencyMode.Multiple)]
class MyService : IMyContract
{
   int[] m_Numbers;
   List<string> m_Names;

   public void MyMethod( )
   {
      lock(m_Numbers)
      {
       ...
      }

      /* Don't access members here */
```

Example 8-1. Manual synchronization using fragmented locking (continued)

```
        lock(m_Names)
        {
          ...
        }
    }
}
```

The service in Example 8-1 is configured for concurrent access. Since the critical sections of the operations that require synchronization are any member variable access, the service uses a Monitor (encapsulated in the lock statement) to lock the object before accessing it. Local variables require no synchronization because they are visible only to the thread that created them on its own call stack. The problem with the technique shown in Example 8-1 is that it is deadlock- and error-prone. It only provides for thread-safe access if every other operation on the service is as disciplined to always lock the members before accessing them. But even if all operations lock all members, you may still risk deadlocks—if one operation on Thread A locks member M1 trying to access member M2 while another operation executing concurrently on Thread B locks member M2 while trying to access member M1, you will end up with a deadlock.

 WCF resolves service calls deadlock by eventually timing out the call and throwing a TimeoutException. Avoid using a long timeout as it decreases WCF's ability to resolve deadlocks in a timely manner.

I therefore recommend avoiding fragmented locking. It is better to lock the entire service instance instead:

```
    public void MyMethod()
    {
        lock(this)
        {
          ...
        }

        /* Don't access members here */

        lock(this)
        {
          ...
        }
    }
```

The problem with this approach is that it is still fragmented and thus error-prone—if at some point in the future someone adds a method call in the unsynchronized code section that does access the members, it will not be a synchronized access. It is better still to lock the entire body of the method:

```
public void MyMethod()
{
    lock(this)
    {
        ...
    }
}
```

You can even instruct .NET to automate injecting the call to lock the instance using the MethodImpl attribute with the MethodImplOptions.Synchronized flag:

```
[ServiceBehavior(ConcurrencyMode = ConcurrencyMode.Multiple)]
class MyService : IMyContract
{
    int[] m_Numbers;
    List<string> m_Names;

    [MethodImpl(MethodImplOptions.Synchronized)]
    public void MyMethod()
    {
        ...
    }
}
```

You will need to repeat the assignment of the MethodImpl attribute on all the service operations implementations.

The problem now is that while the code is thread-safe, you gain little from the use of ConcurrencyMode.Multiple because the net effect will be similar to using ConcurrencyMode.Single in terms of synchronization, yet you have increased the overall code complexity and reliance on developers' discipline. There are cases where just such a configuration is required, however—in particular when callbacks are involved, as you will see later on.

Unsynchronized access and transactions

When the service is configured for ConcurrencyMode.Multiple, if at least one operation has TransactionScopeRequired set to true, then ReleaseServiceInstanceOnTransactionComplete must be set to false. For example, this is a valid definition because no method has TransactionScopeRequired set to true even though ReleaseServiceInstanceOnTransactionComplete defaults to true:

```
[ServiceBehavior(ConcurrencyMode = ConcurrencyMode.Multiple)]
class MyService : IMyContract
{
    public void MyMethod()
    {...}
    public void MyOtherMethod()
    {...}
}
```

The following, on the other hand, is an invalid definition because at least one method has TransactionScopeRequired set to true:

```
//Invalid configuration:
[ServiceBehavior(ConcurrencyMode = ConcurrencyMode.Multiple)]
class MyService : IMyContract
{
   [OperationBehavior(TransactionScopeRequired = true)]
   public void MyMethod( )
   {...}
   public void MyOtherMethod( )
   {...}
}
```

A transactional unsynchronized service must set ReleaseServiceInstanceOnTransactionComplete explicitly to false:

```
[ServiceBehavior(ConcurrencyMode = ConcurrencyMode.Multiple,
                 ReleaseServiceInstanceOnTransactionComplete = false)]
class MyService : IMyContract
{
   [OperationBehavior(TransactionScopeRequired = true)]
   public void MyMethod( )
   {...}
   public void MyOtherMethod( )
   {...}
}
```

The rationale behind this constraint is that only a sessionful or a singleton service could possibly benefit from unsynchronized access, so in the case of transactional access, WCF wants to enforce the semantic of the configured instancing mode. In addition, this will avoid having a caller accessing the instance, completing the transaction and releasing the instance all while the instance is still being used by another caller.

ConcurrencyMode.Reentrant

The ConcurrencyMode.Reentrant value is a refinement of ConcurrencyMode.Single. Similar to ConcurrencyMode.Single, ConcurrencyMode.Reentrant associates the service instance with a synchronization lock, so concurrent calls on the same instance are never allowed. However, if the reentrant service calls out to another service or a callback, and that call chain (or *causality*) somehow winds its way back to the service instance as shown in Figure 8-1, then that call is allowed to reenter the service instance.

ConcurrencyMode.Reentrant implementation is very simple—when the reentrant service calls out over WCF, WCF silently releases the synchronization lock associated with the instance. ConcurrencyMode.Reentrant is designed to avoid the potential deadlock of reentrancy. If the service were to maintain the lock while calling out, then if the causality tried to enter the same instance, a deadlock would occur.

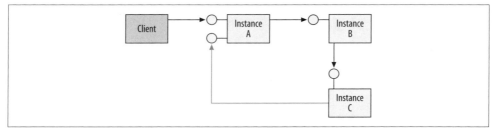

Figure 8-1. Call reentrancy

Reentrancy support is instrumental in a number of scenarios:

- A singleton service calling out risks a deadlock if any of the downstream services it calls try to call back into the singleton.
- In the same app domain, if the client stores a proxy reference in some globally available static variable, then some of the downstream services called by the referenced service use the proxy reference to call back to the original service.
- Callbacks on non-one-way operations must be allowed to reenter the calling service.
- If the callout the service performs is of long duration, even without reentrancy, you may want to optimize throughput by allowing other clients to use the same service instance.

 A service configured with ConcurrencyMode.Multiple is by definition also reentrant, because no lock is held during the callout. However, unlike a reentrant service, which is inherently thread-safe, a service with ConcurrencyMode.Multiple must provide for its own synchronization, such as by locking the instance during every call, as explained previously. It is up to the developer of such a service to decide if it wants to release the lock of the instance before calling out to avoid reentrancy deadlock.

Designing for reentrancy

It is very important to realize the liability associated with reentrancy. First, when the reentrant service calls out, it must leave the service state in a workable consistent state, because others could be allowed into the service instance while the service calls out. A consistent thread-safe state means that the reentrant service has no more interactions with its own members or any other local object or static variable, and that when the callout returns, the reentrant service could simply return control to its client. For example, suppose the reentrant service modified the state of some linked list, and leaves it in an inconsistent state (such as missing a head node) because it needs the value of the new head from another service. The reentrant service then calls to the other service, but now it leaves other clients vulnerable, because if they call into the reentrant service and access the linked list, they will encounter an error.

Much the same way, when the reentrant service returns from its callout, it must refresh all local method state. For example, if the service has a local variable that contains a copy of the state of a member variable, that local variable may have the wrong value now because during the callout another party could have entered the reentrant service and modified the member variable.

Reentrancy and transactions

A reentrant service faces exactly the same design constraints regarding transactions as a service configured with ConcurrencyMode.Multiple; namely, if at least one operation has TransactionScopeRequired set to true, then ReleaseServiceInstanceOnTransactionComplete must be set to false.

Callbacks and reentrancy

Callbacks are the main reason reentrancy is available. As explained in Chapter 5, if a WCF service wants to invoke a duplex callback to its calling client, the service requires reentrancy (or no synchronization at all via ConcurrencyMode.Multiple). The reason is that processing the reply message from the client once the callback returns requires ownership of the instance lock, and so a deadlock would occur if a service with ConcurrencyMode.Single were allowed to call back to its clients. To allow callbacks, the service must be configured with either ConcurrencyMode.Multiple or preferably ConcurrencyMode.Reentrant. This is required even of a per-call service, which otherwise has no need for anything but ConcurrencyMode.Single. Note that the service may still invoke callbacks to other clients or call other services. It is the callback to the calling client that is disallowed.

If a service configured with ConcurrencyMode.Single tries to invoke a duplex callback, WCF will throw an InvalidOperationException. Example 8-2 demonstrates a service configured for reentrancy. During the operation execution, the service calls back to its client. Control will only return to the service once the callback returns, and the service's own thread will need to reacquire the lock.

Example 8-2. Configure for reentrancy to allow callbacks

```
[ServiceContract(CallbackContract = typeof(IMyContractCallback))]
interface IMyContract
{
   [OperationContract]
   void DoSomething( );
}
interface IMyContractCallback
{
   [OperationContract]
   void OnCallback( );
}
[ServiceBehavior(ConcurrencyMode = ConcurrencyMode.Reentrant)]
class MyService : IMyContract
{
```

Example 8-2. Configure for reentrancy to allow callbacks (continued)

```
public void DoSomething( )
{
    IMyContractCallback callback = OperationContext.Current.
                            GetCallbackChannel<IMyContractCallback>( );
    callback.OnCallback( );
}
}
```

As also mentioned in Chapter 5, the only case where a service configured with `ConcurrencyMode.Single` can call back to its clients is when the callback contract operation is configured as one-way because there will not be any reply message to contend for the lock.

Instances and Concurrent Access

Using the same proxy, a single client can issue multiple concurrent calls to the service. The client could use multiple threads to invoke calls on the service, or the client could issue one-way calls in rapid succession. In both of these cases, concurrent processing of the calls from the same client is a product of the service's configured instancing mode, the service's concurrency mode, and the configured delivery; that is, the binding type and the session mode.

Per-Call Services

In the case of a per-call service, if there is no transport-level session; that is, if the call is made over the `BasicHttpBinding`, or over any of the WS bindings when the contract is configured for `SessionMode.NotAllowed`, or for `SessionMode.Allowed` yet without security and reliable messaging, concurrent processing of calls is allowed. Calls are dispatched as they arrive, each to a new instance, and execute concurrently. This is the case regardless of the service concurrency mode. I consider this to be the correct behavior.

If the per-call service has a transport-level session—that is, the binding is either TCP or IPC, or a WS binding when the contract has its `SessionMode` set to either `SessionMode.Allowed` with security or reliable messaging, or `SessionMode.Required`—concurrent processing of calls is a product of the service concurrency mode. If the service is configured with `ConcurrencyMode.Single`, then concurrent processing of the pending calls is not allowed. While this is a direct result of the channel architecture, I consider this to be a flawed design, since the lock should be associated with an instance, not a type. If the service is configured with `ConcurrencyMode.Multiple`, concurrent processing is allowed. Calls are dispatched as they arrive, each to a new instance, and execute concurrently. When the service is configured with `ConcurrencyMode.Reentrant`, if the service does not call out, it behaves similarly to `ConcurrencyMode.Single`. If the service does call out, the next call is allowed in, and the returning call has to negotiate the lock like all other pending calls.

Sessionful and Singleton Services

In the case of a sessionful or a singleton service, the configured concurrency mode alone governs the concurrent execution of pending calls. If the service is configured with ConcurrencyMode.Single, then calls will be placed to the service instance one at a time. Pending calls will be placed in a queue. You should avoid lengthy processing of calls because it may risk call timeouts.

If the service instance is configured with ConcurrencyMode.Mutiple then concurrent processing of calls is allowed. Calls will be executed by the service instance as fast as they come off the channel (up to the throttle limit). As is always the case with a stateful unsynchronized service instance, you must of course synchronize access to the service instance or risk state corruption.

If the service instance is configured with ConcurrencyMode.Reentrant, it behaves just as with the ConcurrencyMode.Single. However, if the service does call out, the next call (be it one-way or not) is allowed to execute. You must follow the guidelines discussed previously regarding programming in a reentrant environment.

 For a per-session service configured with ConcurrencyMode.Mutiple to experience concurrent calls, the client must use multiple worker threads to access the same proxy instance. However, if the client threads rely on the auto-open feature of the proxy (that is, just invoking a method and having that call open the proxy if the proxy is not opened yet) and call the proxy concurrently, then the calls will actually be serialized until the proxy is opened, and be concurrent after that. If you want to dispatch concurrent calls regardless of the state of the proxy, the client needs to explicitly open the proxy (by calling the Open( ) method) before issuing any calls on the worker threads.

Resources and Services

Synchronizing access to the service instance using ConcurrencyMode.Single or an explicit synchronization lock only manages concurrent access to the service instance state itself. It does not provide safe access to the underlying resources the service may be using. These resources must also be thread-safe. For example, consider the application shown in Figure 8-2.

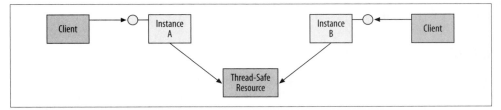

Figure 8-2. Applications must synchronize access to resources

Even though the service instances are thread-safe, the two instances try to concurrently access the same resource (such as a static variable, a helper static class, or a file), and therefore the resource itself must have synchronized access. This is true regardless of the service instancing mode. Even a per-call service could run into the situation shown in Figure 8-2.

Deadlocked Access

The naive solution to providing thread-safe access to resources is providing each resource with its own lock, potentially encapsulating that lock in the resource itself, and asking the resource to lock the lock when accessed and unlock it when the service is done with the resource. The problem with this approach is that it is deadlock-prone. Consider the situation of Figure 8-3.

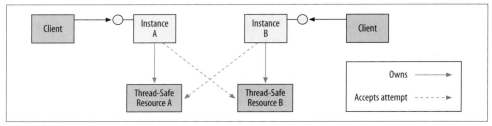

Figure 8-3. Deadlock over resources access

If the figure, Instance A of the service accesses the thread-safe Resource A. Resource A has its own synchronization lock and Instance A acquires that lock. In the same way, Instance B accesses Resource B and acquires its lock. A deadlock occurs when Instance A tries to access Resource B while Instance B tries to access Resource A, since each instance will be waiting for the other to release its lock.

The concurrency and instancing modes of the service are almost irrelevant to avoiding this deadlock. The only case that avoids it is if the service is configured both with InstanceContextMode.Single and ConcurrencyMode.Single, because a synchronized singleton by definition can only have one client at a time and there is no other instance to deadlock with over access to resources. All other combinations are still susceptible to this kind of deadlock. For example, a per-session synchronized service may have two separate thread-safe instances associated with two different clients, yet the two instances deadlock when accessing the resources.

Deadlocked Avoidance

There are a few possible ways to avoid the deadlock. If all instances of the service meticulously access all resources in the same order, such as always trying to acquire the lock of Resource A first, and then the lock of Resource B, then there would be no deadlock. The problem with the approach is that it is difficult to enforce over the life of the service, and over time, during code maintenance, someone may deviate from this strict guideline (even inadvertently by calling methods on helper classes) and trigger the deadlock.

Another solution is to have all resources use the same shared lock. In order to minimize the chances for a deadlock, you also want to minimize the number of locks in the system and have the service itself also use the same lock. To that end, you can configure the service itself with ConcurrencyMode.Multiple (even with a per-call service) to avoid using the WCF-provided lock. The first service instance to acquire the shared lock will lock out all other instances and own all underlying resources. A simple technique for using such a shared lock is locking on the service type, as shown in Example 8-3.

Example 8-3. Using the service type as a shared lock

```
[ServiceBehavior(InstanceContextMode = InstanceContextMode.PerCall,
                 ConcurrencyMode = ConcurrencyMode.Multiple)]
class MyService : IMyContract
{
   public void MyMethod()
   {
      lock(typeof(MyService))
      {
         ...
         MyResource.DoWork();
         ...
      }
   }
}
static class MyResource
{
   public static void DoWork()
   {
      lock(typeof(MyService))
      {
         ...
      }
   }
}
```

The resources themselves must also lock on the service type (or some other shared type agreed upon in advance). There are two problems with this approach of using a shared lock. First, it introduces coupling between the resources and the service, because the resource developer has to know about the type of the service or the type used for synchronization. While you could minimize that by providing the type as a resource construction parameter, it will likely not be applicable with third-party provided resources. The second problem is that while your service instance is executing, all other instances (and their respective clients) are blocked. In the interest of throughput and responsiveness, you should avoid lengthy operations when using a shared lock.

Services should never share resources. Regardless of concurrency management, resources are local implementation details and therefore should not be shared across services. Most importantly, sharing resources across the service boundary is also deadlock-prone. Such shared resources have no easy way to share locks across technologies and organizations, and the services need to somehow coordinate the locking order. This would imply a high degree of coupling between the services and would violate the best practices and tenets of service-orientation.

Resource Synchronization Context

Incoming service calls execute on worker threads. These threads are managed by WCF and are unrelated to any service or resource threads. This means that by default the service cannot rely on any kind of *thread affinity*, which is always being accessed by the same thread. Much the same way, the service cannot rely by default on executing on some host-side custom threads created by the host or service developers. The problem with this situation is that some resources may rely on thread affinity, for example user-interfaces resources updated by the service must execute and be accessed only by the user-interface (UI) thread. Another example is a resource (or a service) that makes use of the thread local storage (TLS) to store out-of-band information shared globally by all parties on the same thread. Using the TLS mandates use of the same thread. In addition, for scalability and throughput purposes, some resources or frameworks may require being access by their own pool of threads.

Whenever an affinity to a particular thread or threads is expected, the service cannot simply execute the call on the incoming WCF worker thread. Instead, the service must marshal the call to the correct thread(s) required by the resource it accesses.

.NET 2.0 Synchronization Contexts

.NET 2.0 introduced the concept of a *synchronization context*. The idea is that any party can provide an execution context and have other parties marshal the calls to that context. The synchronization context can be a single thread or any number of designated threads, although typically it will be just a single, yet particular, thread. All the synchronization context does is assure that the call executes on the correct thread or threads. Note that the word *context* is overloaded. Synchronization contexts have absolutely nothing to do with the service instance context or the operation context described so far in this book.

While conceptually, synchronization contexts are a simple enough design pattern to use, implementing a synchronization context is a complex programming task that is not intended for developers to normally attempt.

The SynchronizationContext class

The class `SynchronizationContext` from the `System.Threading` namespace represents a synchronization context:

```
public delegate void SendOrPostCallback(object state);

public class SynchronizationContext
{
   public virtual void Post(SendOrPostCallback callback,object state);
   public virtual void Send(SendOrPostCallback callback,object state);
   public static void SetSynchronizationContext(SynchronizationContext context);
   public static SynchronizationContext Current
   {get;}
   //More members
}
```

Every thread in .NET 2.0 may have a synchronization context associated with it. You can obtain a thread's synchronization context by accessing the static `Current` property of `SynchronizationContext`. If the thread does not have a synchronization context, then `Current` will return `null`. You can also pass the reference to the synchronization context between threads, so that one thread can marshal a call to another thread.

To represent the call to invoke in the synchronization context, you wrap a method with a delegate of the type `SendOrPostCallback`. Note that the signature of the delegate uses an amorphous `object`. If you want to pass multiple parameters, pack those in a structure and pass the structure as an `object`.

 Synchronization contexts use an amorphous `object`. Exercise caution when using synchronization contexts due to the lack of compile-time type safety.

Working with the synchronization context

There are two ways of marshaling a call to the synchronization context: synchronously and asynchronously, by sending or posting a work item respectively. The `Send()` method will block the caller until the call has completed on the other synchronization context, while `Post()` would merely dispatch it to the synchronization context and then return control to its caller.

For example, to synchronously marshal a call to a particular synchronization context, first you somehow obtain a reference to that synchronization context, and then use the `Send()` method:

```
//Obtain synchronization context
SynchronizationContext context = ...

SendOrPostCallback doWork = delegate(object arg)
```

```
                              {
                                  //The code here guaranteed to
                                  //execute on correct thread(s)
                              };
      context.Send(doWork,"Some argument");
```

Example 8-4 shows a less abstract example.

Example 8-4. Calling a resource on the correct synchronization context

```
class MyResource
{
   public int DoWork()
   {...}
   public SynchronizationContext MySynchronizationContext
   {get;}
}
class MyService : IMyContract
{
   MyResource GetResource()
   {...}

   public void MyMethod()
   {
      MyResource resource = GetResource();
      SynchronizationContext context = resource.MySynchronizationContext;

      int result = 0;
      SendOrPostCallback doWork = delegate
                                  {
                                     result = resource.DoWork();
                                  };
      context.Send(doWork,null);
   }
}
```

In the example, the service MyService needs to interact with the resource MyResource and have it perform some work by executing the DoWork() method and returning a result. However, MyResource requires that all calls to it execute on its particular synchronization context. MyResource makes that execution context available via the MySynchronizationContext property. The service operation MyMethod() executes on a WCF worker thread. MyMethod() first obtains the resource and its synchronization context. MyMethod() then defines an anonymous method that wraps the call to DoWork(), and assigns that anonymous method to the doWork delegate of the type SendOrPostCallback. Finally MyMethod() calls Send() and passes null for the argument, since the DoWork() method on the resource requires no parameters. Note the technique used in Example 8-4 to retrieve a returned value from the invocation. Since Send() returns void, the anonymous method assigns the returned value of DoWork() into an outer variable. Without anonymous methods, this task would have required the complicated use of a synchronized member variable.

The problem with Example 8-4 is the excessive degree of coupling between the service and the resource. The service needs to know the resource is sensitive to its synchronization context, obtain the context, and manage the execution. It is much better to encapsulate the need in the resource itself, as shown in Example 8-5.

Example 8-5. Encapsulating the synchronization context

```
class MyResource
{
   public int DoWork()
   {
      int result = 0;
      SendOrPostCallback doWork = delegate
                                  {
                                     result = DoWorkInternal();
                                  };
      MySynchronizationContext.Send(doWork,null);
      return result;
   }
   SynchronizationContext MySynchronizationContext
   {get;}
   int DoWorkInternal()
   {...}
}
[ServiceBehavior(InstanceContextMode = InstanceContextMode.PerCall)]
class MyService :  IMyContract
{
   MyResource GetResource()
   (...}
   public void MyMethod()
   {
      MyResource resource = GetResource();
      int result = resource.DoWork();
   }
}
```

Compare Example 8-5 to Example 8-4. All the service in Example 8-5 has to do is access the resource. It is up to the service internally to marshal the call to its synchronization context.

UI Synchronization Context

The canonical case for utilizing synchronization contexts is with Windows user interface frameworks such as Windows Forms or the Windows Presentation Foundation (WPF). For simplicity's sake, the rest of the discussion in this chapter will refer only to Windows Forms, although it equally applies to WPF. A Windows UI application relies on the underlying Windows messages and a message-processing loop (the *message pump*) to process them. The message loop must have thread affinity because messages to a window are delivered only to the thread that created it. In general, you must always marshal to the UI thread any attempt to access a Windows control or a form, or risk errors and failures. This becomes an issue if your services need to update some user interface, as a result of client calls or some other event. Fortunately, Windows Forms support the synchronization context pattern. The thread that pumps messages has a synchronization context. That synchronization context is the `WindowsFormsSynchronizationContext` class:

```
public sealed class WindowsFormsSynchronizationContext : SynchronizationContext,...
{...}
```

Whenever you call the `Application.Run()` method of Windows Forms to bring up the main window of your application, it not only starts processing windows messages, it also installs `WindowsFormsSynchronizationContext` as the current thread's synchronization context.

What `WindowsFormsSynchronizationContext` does is convert the call to `Send()` or `Post()` to a custom Windows message and post that Windows message to the UI thread's message queue. Every Windows Forms UI class that derives from `Control` has a special method that handles this custom message by invoking the supplied `SendOrPostCallback` delegate. At some point the custom Windows message is processed by the UI thread and the delegate is invoked.

Because the window or control can also be called already in the correct synchronization context, to avoid a deadlock when calling `Send()`, the implementation of the Windows Forms synchronization context verifies that marshaling the call is indeed required. If marshaling is not required, it uses direct invocation on the calling thread.

UI access and updates

When a service needs to update some user interface, it must have some proprietary mechanisms to find the window to update in the first place. Once the service has the correct window, it must somehow get hold of that window's synchronization context and marshal the call to it. Such a possible interaction is shown in Example 8-6.

Example 8-6. Using the form synchronization context

```
partial class MyForm : Form
{
   Label m_CounterLabel;
   SynchronizationContext m_SynchronizationContext;

   public MyForm()
   {
      InitializeComponent();
      m_SynchronizationContext = SynchronizationContext.Current;
      Debug.Assert(m_SynchronizationContext != null);
   }
   public SynchronizationContext MySynchronizationContext
   {
      get
      {
```

Example 8-6. Using the form synchronization context (continued)

```
            return m_SynchronizationContext;
         }
      }
      public int Counter
      {
         get
         {
            return Convert.ToInt32(m_CounterLabel.Text);
         }
         set
         {
            m_CounterLabel.Text = value.ToString( );
         }
      }
}
[ServiceContract]
interface IFormManager
{
   [OperationContract]
   void IncrementLabel( );
}
[ServiceBehavior(InstanceContextMode = InstanceContextMode.PerCall)]
class MyService : IFormManager
{
   public void IncrementLabel( )
   {
      MyForm form = Application.OpenForms[0] as MyForm;
      Debug.Assert(form != null);

      SendOrPostCallback callback = delegate
                                    {
                                        form.Counter++;
                                    };
      form.MySynchronizationContext.Send(callback,null);
   }
}
static class Program
{
   static void Main( )
   {
      ServiceHost host = new ServiceHost(typeof(MyService));
      host.Open( );

      Application.Run(new MyForm( ));

      host.Close( );
   }
}
```

Example 8-6 shows the form MyForm that provides the property MySynchronizationContext, allowing its clients to obtain its synchronization context.

MyForm initializes MySynchronizationContext in its constructor by obtaining the synchronization context of the current thread. The thread has a synchronization context because the Main() method called Application.Run(), which triggered the message pump. MyForm also offers the Counter property that updates the value of a counting Windows Forms label. Counter must be accessed by the thread that owns the form. The service MyService implements the IncrementLabel() operation. In that operation, the service obtains a reference to the form via the static OpenForms collection of the Application class:

```
public class FormCollection : ReadOnlyCollectionBase
{
    public virtual Form this[int index]
    {get;}
    public virtual Form this[string name]
    {get;}
}

public sealed class Application
{
    public static FormCollection OpenForms
    {get;}
    //Rest of the members
}
```

Once IncrementLabel() has the form to update, it accesses the synchronization context via the MySynchronizationContext, and calls the Send() method. Send() is provided with an anonymous method that updates Counter. Example 8-6 is a concrete example of the programming model shown in Example 8-4. Much the same way, the technique of Example 8-6 suffers from the same deficiency; namely, tight coupling between the service and the form. If the service needs to update multiple controls, that also results in a cumbersome programming model. Any change to the user interface layout, the controls on the forms, and the required behavior is likely to cause major changes to the service code.

Safe controls

It is better to encapsulate the interaction with the Windows Forms synchronization context in safe controls or safe methods on the form to decouple them from the service and to simplify the overall programming model. Example 8-7 lists the code for SafeLabel, a Label-derived class that provides a thread-safe access to its Text property. Because SafeLabel derives from Label, you still have all the design-time visual experience and integration with Visual Studio, yet you surgically affect just the property that requires the safe access.

Example 8-7. Encapsulating the synchronization context

```
public class SafeLabel : Label
{
    SynchronizationContext m_SynchronizationContext =
                                  SynchronizationContext.Current;
```

Example 8-7. Encapsulating the synchronization context (continued)

```
override public string Text
{
   set
   {
      SendOrPostCallback setText = delegate(object text)
                                   {
                                       base.Text = text as string;
                                   };
      m_SynchronizationContext.Send(setText,value);
   }
   get
   {
      string text = String.Empty;
      SendOrPostCallback getText = delegate
                                   {
                                       text = base.Text;
                                   };
      m_SynchronizationContext.Send(getText,null);
      return text;
   }
}
}
```

Upon construction, SafeLabel caches its synchronization context. SafeLabel overrides its base class Text property, and uses an anonymous method in the get and set accessors to send the call to the correct UI thread. Note in the get accessor the use of an outer variable to return a value from Send( ) as discussed previously. Using SafeLabel, the code in Example 8-6 is reduced to the code shown in Example 8-8.

Example 8-8. Using a safe control

```
class MyForm : Form
{
   Label m_CounterLabel;

   public MyForm( )
   {
      InitializeComponent( );
   }
   void InitializeComponent( )
   {
      ...
      m_CounterLabel = new SafeLabel( );
      ...
   }
   public int Counter
   {
      get
      {
         return Convert.ToInt32(m_CounterLabel.Text);
      }
      set
```

Example 8-8. Using a safe control (continued)

```
      {
         m_CounterLabel.Text = value.ToString( );
      }
   }
}
[ServiceBehavior(InstanceContextMode = InstanceContextMode.PerCall)]
class MyService : IFormManager
{
   public void IncrementLabel( )
   {
      MyForm form = Application.OpenForms[0] as MyForm;
      Debug.Assert(form != null);

      form.Counter++;
   }
}
```

Note in Example 8-8 that the service simply accesses the form directly:

```
      form.Counter++;
```

and that the form is written as a normal form. Example 8-8 is a concrete example of the programming model shown in Example 8-5.

 The source code accompanying this book contains, in the assembly *ServiceModelEx.dll,* the code not only for SafeLabel but also for other commonly used controls, such as SafeButton, SafeListBox, SafeProgressBar, SafeStatusBar, and SafeTextBox.

Service Synchronization Context

The programming techniques showed so far put the onus of accessing the resource on the correct thread squarely on the service or resource developer. It would be preferable if the service had a way of associating itself with a particular synchronization context, and then have WCF detect that context and automatically marshal the call from the worker thread to the service synchronization context. WCF lets you do just that. You can instruct WCF to maintain affinity between all service instances from a participle host and a specific synchronization context. The ServiceBehavior attribute offers the UseSynchronizationContext Boolean property, defined as:

```
      [AttributeUsage(AttributeTargets.Class)]
      public sealed class ServiceBehaviorAttribute : ...
      {
         public bool UseSynchronizationContext
         {get;set;}
         //More members
      }
```

Affinity between the service type, its host, and a synchronization context is locked in when the host is opened. If the thread opening the host has a synchronization context and UseSynchronizationContext is true, WCF will establish an affinity between that synchronization context and all instances of the service hosted by that host. WCF will automatically marshal all incoming calls to the service's synchronization context. All the thread-specific information stored in the TLS, such as the client's transaction or the security information (discussed in Chapter 10) will be marshaled correctly to the synchronization context.

If UseSynchronizationContext is false, regardless of any synchronization context the opening thread might have, the service will have no affinity to any synchronization context. Much the same way, even if UseSynchronizationContext is true, if the opening thread has no synchronization context, then the service will not have one.

The default value of UseSynchronizationContext is true, so these definitions are equivalent:

```
[ServiceContract]
interface IMyContract
{...}

class MyService : IMyContract
{...}

[ServiceBehavior(UseSynchronizationContext = true)]
class MyService : IMyContract
{...}
```

Hosting on the UI Thread

The classic use for UseSynchronizationContext is to enable the service to update user interface controls and windows directly, without resorting to techniques such as Examples 8-6 and 8-7. WCF greatly simplifies UI updates by providing an affinity between all service instances from a particular host and specific UI thread. To that end, host the service on the UI thread that also creates the windows or controls that the service needs to interact with. Since the Windows Forms synchronization context is established during the message pump initialization of Application.Run(), which is a blocking operation (that brings up the window or form), opening the host before or after Application.Run() is pointless—before Application.Run(), there is still no synchronization context, and after it the application is usually shutting down. The simple solution is to have the window or form that the service needs to interact with be the one that opens the host before loading the form, as shown in Example 8-9.

Example 8-9. Hosting the service by the form

```
[ServiceBehavior(InstanceContextMode = InstanceContextMode.PerCall)]
class MyService : IMyContract
{...}

partial class HostForm : Form
{
   ServiceHost m_Host;

   public HostForm( )
   {
      InitializeComponent( );

      m_Host = new ServiceHost(typeof(MyService));

      m_Host.Open( );
   }
   void OnFormClosed(object sender,EventArgs e)
   {
      m_Host.Close( );
   }
}
static class Program
{
   static void Main( )
   {
      Application.Run(new HostForm( ));
   }
}
```

The service in Example 8-9 defaults to using whichever synchronization context its host encounters. The form HostForm stores the service host in a member variable so that the form can close the service when the form is closed. The constructor of HostForm already has a synchronization context so when it opens the host, affinity to that synchronization context is established.

Accessing the form

Even though the service in Example 8-9 is hosted by the form, the service instances must have some proprietary application-specific mechanism to reach into the form. If the service instance needs to update multiple forms, you can use the Application. OpenForms collections (as in Example 8-6) to find the correct form. Once the service has the form, it can freely access it directly, as opposed to Example 8-6, which required marshaling:

```
[ServiceBehavior(InstanceContextMode = InstanceContextMode.PerCall)]
class MyService : IFormManager
{
   public void IncrementLabel( )
   {
      HostForm form = Application.OpenForms[0] as HostForm;
```

```
            Debug.Assert(form != null);
            form.Counter++;
      }
   }
```

You could also store references to the forms to use in static variables. The problem with such global variables is that if multiple UI threads are used to pump messages to difference instances of the same form type, you cannot use a single static variable for each form type—you need a static variable for each thread used, which complicates things significantly.

Instead, the form (or forms) can store a reference to itself in the TLS, and have the service instance access that store and obtain the reference. The problem with the TLS is that it is a cumbersome non-type-safe programming model. An improvement on this approach is to use thread-relative static variables. By default, static variables are visible to all threads in an app domain. With thread-relative static variables, each thread in the app domain gets its own copy of the static variable. You use the ThreadStaticAttribute to mark a static variable as thread-relative. Thread-relative static variables are always thread-safe because they can be accessed only by a single thread and because each thread gets its own copy of the static variable. Thread-relative static variables are stored in the TLS, yet they provide a type-safe simplified programming model over the TLS. Example 8-10 demonstrates this technique.

Example 8-10. Storing form reference in a thread-relative static variable

```
partial class HostForm : Form
{
   Label m_CounterLabel;
   ServiceHost m_Host;

   [ThreadStatic]
   static HostForm m_CurrentForm;

   public static HostForm CurrentForm
   {
      get
      {
         return m_CurrentForm;
      }
      set
      {
         m_CurrentForm = value;
      }
   }
   public int Counter
   {
      get
      {
         return Convert.ToInt32(m_CounterLabel.Text);
      }
      set
```

```
        {
            m_CounterLabel.Text = value.ToString( );
        }
    }
    public HostForm( )
    {
        InitializeComponent( );

        CurrentForm = this;

        m_Host = new ServiceHost(typeof(MyService));
        m_Host.Open( );
    }
    void OnFormClosed(object sender,EventArgs e)
    {
        m_Host.Close( );
    }
}
[ServiceContract]
interface IFormManager
{
    [OperationContract]
    void IncrementLabel( );
}
[ServiceBehavior(InstanceContextMode = InstanceContextMode.PerCall)]
class MyService : IFormManager
{
    public void IncrementLabel( )
    {
        HostForm form = HostForm.CurrentForm;
        form.Counter++;
    }
}
static class Program
{
    static void Main( )
    {
        Application.Run(new HostForm( ));
    }
}
```

The form HostForm stores a reference to itself in a thread-relative static variable called m_CurrentForm. The service accesses the static property CurrentForm and obtains a reference to the instance of HostForm on that UI thread.

Multiple UI threads

Your service host process can actually have multiple UI threads, each pumping messages to its own set of windows. Such a setup is usually required with UI-intensive applications that want to avoid having multiple windows sharing a single UI thread and hosting the services, because while the UI thread is processing a service call (or a

---

complicated UI update), not all of the windows will be responsive. Since the service synchronization context is established per host, if you have multiple UI threads you need to open a service host instance for the same service type on each UI thread. Each service host will therefore have a different synchronization context for its service instances. As mentioned in Chapter 1, in order to have multiple hosts for the same service type, you must provide each host with a different base address. The easiest way of doing that is to provide the form constructor with the base address to use as a construction parameter. I also recommend in such a case to use base address relative addresses for the service endpoints. The clients still invoke calls on the various service endpoints, yet each endpoint now corresponds to a different host according to the base address schema and the binding used. Example 8-11 demonstrates this configuration.

Example 8-11. Hosting on multiple UI threads

```
partial class HostForm : Form
{
   public HostForm(string baseAddress)
   {
      InitializeComponent();

      CurrentForm = this;

      m_Host = new ServiceHost(typeof(MyService),new Uri(baseAddress));
      m_Host.Open();
   }
   //Rest same as Example 8-10
}
static class Program
{
   static void Main()
   {
      ParameterizedThreadStart threadMethod = delegate(object baseAddress)
                                    {
                                       string address = baseAddress as string;
                                       Application.Run(new HostForm(address));
                                    };

      Thread thread1 = new Thread(threadMethod);
      thread1.Start("http://localhost:8001/");

      Thread thread2 = new Thread(threadMethod);
      thread2.Start("http://localhost:8002/");
   }
}
/* MyService same as Example 8-10 */

///////////////////////////// Host Config File  /////////////////////////////
<services>
   <service name = "MyNamespace.MyService">
      <endpoint
         address  = "MyService"
```

Example 8-11. Hosting on multiple UI threads (continued)

```
            binding = "basicHttpBinding"
            contract = "IFormManager"
        />
    </service>
</services>
/////////////////////////////// Client Config File ///////////////////////////////
<client>
    <endpoint name = "Form A"
        address  = "http://localhost:8001/MyService/"
        binding  = "basicHttpBinding"
        contract = "IFormManager"
    />
    <endpoint name = "Form B"
        Address  = "http://localhost:8002/MyService/"
        binding  = "basicHttpBinding"
        contract = "IFormManager"
    />
</client>
```

In Example 8-11, the Main( ) method launches two UI threads, each with its own instance of HostForm. Each form instance accepts as a construction parameter a base address that it in turn provides for its own host instance. Once the host is opened, it establishes an affinity to that UI thread's synchronization context. Calls from the client to the corresponding base address are now routed to the respective UI thread. Note that the service exposes an endpoint over HTTP using BasicHttpBinding. If the service were to expose a second endpoint over the TCP binding you would have to provide the host with a TCP base address as well.

Form As a Service

The main motivation for hosting a WCF service on the UI thread is if the service needs to update the UI or the form. The problem is always how does the service reach out and obtain a reference to the form? While the techniques and ideas shown in the examples so far certainly work, it would be simpler yet if the form were the service and would host itself. For this to work, the form (or any window) must be a singleton service. The reason is that singleton is the only instancing mode that enables you to provide WCF with a live instance to host. In addition, you would not want a form that only exists during a client call (which is usually very brief) nor would you want a form that only a single client can establish a session with and update. When a form is also a service, having that form as a singleton is the best instancing mode all around. Example 8-12 lists just such a service.

Example 8-12. Form as a singleton service

```
[ServiceContract]
interface IFormManager
{
    [OperationContract]
```

Example 8-12. Form as a singleton service (continued)

```
    void IncrementLabel( );
}
[ServiceBehavior(InstanceContextMode = InstanceContextMode.Single)]
partial class MyForm : Form,IFormManager
{
    Label m_CounterLabel;
    ServiceHost m_Host;

    public MyForm( )
    {
        InitializeComponent( );
        m_Host = new ServiceHost(this);
        m_Host.Open( );
    }
    void OnFormClosed(object sender,EventArgs args)
    {
        m_Host.Close( );
    }
    public void IncrementLabel( )
    {
        Counter++;
    }
    public int Counter
    {
        get
        {
            return Convert.ToInt32(m_CounterLabel.Text);
        }
        set
        {
            m_CounterLabel.Text = value.ToString( );
        }
    }
}
```

MyForm implements the IFormManager contract and is configured as a WCF singleton
service. MyForm has a ServiceHost as a member variable, same as before. When MyForm
constructs the host, it uses the host constructor that accepts an object reference as
shown in Chapter 4. MyForm passes itself as the object. MyForm opens the host when
the form is created and closes the host when the form is closed. Updating the form's
controls as a result of client calls is done by accessing them directly, because the
form, of course, runs on its own synchronization context.

The FormHost<F> class

You can streamline and automate the code in Example 8-12 using my FormHost<F>
class, defined as:

```
[ServiceBehavior(InstanceContextMode = InstanceContextMode.Single)]
public abstract class FormHost<F> : Form where F : Form
{
```

```
        public FormHost(params string[] baseAddresses);

        protected ServiceHost<F> Host
        {get;set;}
    }
```

Using FormHost<F>, Example 8-12 is reduced to:

```
    partial class MyForm : FormHost<MyForm>,IFormManager
    {
        Label m_CounterLabel;

        public MyForm()
        {
            InitializeComponent();
        }
        public void IncrementLabel()
        {
            Counter++;
        }
        public int Counter
        {
            get
            {
                return Convert.ToInt32(m_CounterLabel.Text);
            }
            set
            {
                m_CounterLabel.Text = value.ToString();
            }
        }
    }
```

> The Windows Forms designer is incapable of rendering a form that has an abstract base class, let alone one that uses generics. You will have to change the base class to Form for visual editing, then revert back to FormHost<F> for debugging. Hopefully, these annoying deficiencies will be addressed in the future.

Example 8-13 shows the implementation of FormHost<F>.

Example 8-13. Implementing FormHost<F>

```
[ServiceBehavior(InstanceContextMode = InstanceContextMode.Single)]
public abstract class FormHost<F> : Form where F : Form
{
    ServiceHost<F> m_Host;

    protected ServiceHost<F> Host
    {
        get
        {
            return m_Host;
```

Example 8-13. Implementing FormHost<F> (continued)

```
      }
      set
      {
         m_Host = value;
      }
   }
   public FormHost(params string[] baseAddresses)
   {
      m_Host = new ServiceHost<F>(this as F,baseAddresses);

      Load += delegate
              {
                 if(Host.State == CommunicationState.Created)
                 {
                    Host.Open( );
                 }
              };
      FormClosed += delegate
                 {
                    if(Host.State == CommunicationState.Opened)
                    {
                       Host.Close( );
                    }
                 };
   }
}
```

FormHost<F> is an abstract class configured as a singleton service. FormHost<F> is a generic class and it takes a single type parameter F. F is constrained to be a Windows Forms Form class. FormHost<F> uses my ServiceHost<T> as a member variable, specifying F for the type parameter for the host. FormHost<F> offers access to the host to the derived forms, mostly for advanced configuration, so the Host property is marked as protected. The constructor of FormHost<F> creates the host, but does not open it. The reason is that the subform may want to perform some host initialization such as configuring a throttle. This initialization can only be done before opening the host. The subclass should place that initialization in its own constructor:

```
public MyForm( )
{
   InitializeComponent( );
   Host.SetThrottle(10,20,1);
}
```

To allow for this, the constructor uses an anonymous method to subscribe to the form's Load event, where it first verifies it was not opened yet by the subform, and then opens the host. In a similar manner, the constructor subscribes to the form's FormClosed event, where it closes the host.

UI Thread and Concurrency Management

Whenever you use hosting on the UI thread (or in any other case of a single-thread affinity synchronization context) deadlocks are possible. For example, the following setup is guaranteed to result with a deadlock: A Windows Forms application is hosting a service with `UseSynchronizationContext` set to `true` and UI thread affinity is established. The Windows Forms application then calls the service in-proc over one of its endpoints. The call to the service blocks the UI thread, while WCF posts a message to the UI thread to invoke the service. That message is never processed due to the blocking UI thread, hence the deadlock.

Another possible case for a deadlock occurs when a Windows Forms application is hosting a service with `UseSynchronizationContext` set to `true` and UI thread affinity is established. The service receives a call from a remote client. That call is marshaled to the UI thread and is eventually executed on that thread. If the service is allowed to call out to another service, that may result in a deadlock if the callout causality tries somehow to update the UI or call back to the service's endpoint, since all service instances associated with any endpoint (regardless of the service instancing mode) share the same UI thread. Similarly, you risk a deadlock if the service is configured for reentrancy and it calls back to its client. You risk a deadlock if the callback causality tries to update the UI or enter the service, since that reentrance must be marshaled to the blocked UI thread.

UI responsiveness

Every client call to a service hosted on the UI thread is converted to a Windows message and is eventually executed on the UI thread, the same thread that is responsible for updating the UI, and for continuing to respond to the user input as well as updating the UI and the user about the state of the application. While the UI thread is processing the service call, it does not process UI messages. Consequently, you should avoid lengthy execution in the service operation because that can severely degrade the UI responsiveness. You can somewhat alleviate this by pumping Windows messages in the service operation by explicitly calling the static method `Application.DoEvents()` to process all the queued-up Windows messages, or by using a method such as `MessageBox.Show()` that pumps some but not all of the queued messages. The downside of trying to refresh the UI this way is that it may dispatch client calls to the service instance that are queued and may cause unwanted reentrancy or a deadlock.

To make things even worse, as a product of the service concurrency mode (discussed next) even if the service calls are of short duration, what if a number of them are dispatched to the service all at once by clients? Those calls will all be queued back-to-back in the Windows message queue, and processing them in order might take time, all the while not updating the UI. Whenever hosting on a UI thread, carefully examine the calls' duration and their frequency to see if the resulting degradation in UI responsiveness is acceptable. What is acceptable may be application-specific, but as a rule of thumb, most users will not mind a UI latency of less than half a second, will notice a delay of more than three quarters of a second, and will be annoyed if the delay is more than a second. If that is the case, consider hosting parts of the UI (and the associated services) on multiple UI threads, as explained previously. By having multiple UI threads, you maximize responsiveness because while one thread is busy servicing a client call, the rest can still update their windows and controls. If using multiple UI threads is impossible in the application, and processing service calls introduces unacceptable UI responsiveness, examine what the service operations do and what is causing the latency. Typically, the latency would be caused not by the UI updates but rather by performing lengthy operations such as calling other services or computational-intensive operations such as image processing. Because the service is hosted on the UI thread, WCF performs all that work on the UI thread, not just the critical part that interacts with the UI directly. If that is indeed your situation, disallow the affinity to the UI thread altogether by setting UseSynchronizationContext to false:

```
[ServiceBehavior(InstanceContextMode = InstanceContextMode.PerCall,
                 UseSynchronizationContext = false)]
class MyService : IMyContract
{
   public void MyMethod()
   {
      Debug.Assert(Application.MessageLoop == false);
      //Rest of the implementation
   }
}
```

(You can even assert that the thread executing the service call does not have a message loop.) Perform the lengthy operations on the incoming worker thread, and use safe controls (such as SafeLabel) to marshal the calls to the UI thread just when required as opposed to all the time. The downside of this approach is that it is an expert programming model: the service cannot be the window or form itself (by relying on the simplicity of FormHost<F>) so you need a way of binding to the form, and the service developer has to work together with the UI developers to ensure they use the safe controls or provide access to the form's synchronization context.

UI thread and concurrency modes

A service with a UI thread affinity is inherently thread-safe because only the UI thread can ever call its instances. Since only a single thread (and the same thread at that) can ever access an instance, that instance is by definition thread-safe. As a result, configuring the service with ConcurrencyMode.Single adds no safety because the service is single-threaded anyway. When you configure with ConcurrencyMode.Single, concurrent client calls are first queued up by the instance lock and are dispatched to the service's message loop one at a time, in order. These client calls are therefore given the opportunity of being interleaved with other UI Windows messages, and so ConcurrencyMode.Single yields the best responsiveness, because the UI thread will alternate between processing client calls and user interactions. When configured with `ConcurrencyMode.Multiple`, client calls are dispatched to the service message loop as soon as they arrive off the channel, and are invoked in order. The problem is that it allows the possibility of a batch of client calls either back-to-back or in proximity to each other in the Windows message queue, and when the UI thread processes that batch, the UI will be unresponsive. Consequently, `ConcurrencyMode.Multiple` is the worst for UI responsiveness. When configured with `ConcurrencyMode.Reentrant`, the service is not reentrant at all, and deadlocks are still possible, as explained at the beginning of this section. Clearly, the best practice with UI thread affinity is to configure the service with `ConcurrencyMode.Single`. Avoid `ConcurrencyMode.Multiple` due to its detrimental effect on responsiveness and `ConcurrencyMode.Reentrant` due to its unfulfilled safety.

Custom Service Synchronization Context

While synchronization context is a general-purpose pattern, out of the box, .NET 2.0 and WCF only implement a single occurrence of it: the Windows Forms synchronization context. Developing a custom service synchronization context has two aspects. The first is implementing a custom synchronization context, and the second is installing it or even applying it declaratively on the service. The first aspect of implementing a custom synchronization context has nothing to do with WCF and is therefore not discussed in this book. Instead in this section I will use my ready-made `AffinitySynchronizer` class, defined as:

```
public class AffinitySynchronizer : SynchronizationContext,IDisposable
{
   public AffinitySynchronizer();
   public AffinitySynchronizer(string threadName);
   public void Dispose();
}
```

`AffinitySynchronizer` executes all calls marshaled to it on the same private worker thread. When attached to the thread that opens a host, all instances of the service, regardless of instance mode, concurrency mode, endpoints, and contracts, will execute on the same worker thread. The implementation of `AffinitySynchronizer` is available along with the source code of this book. In a nutshell, `AffinitySynchronizer` creates a worker thread and maintains a synchronized queue of work items. You can even provide `AffinitySynchronizer` with a thread name as a constructor parameter for debugging and logging purposes. Unassigned, the worker thread name will default to "AffinitySynchronizer Worker Thread." Each work item in the queue contains a delegate of the type `SendOrPostCallback`. When the `Post()` or `Send()` methods are called, `AffinitySynchronizer` wraps a work item around the delegate and posts it to the queue. The worker thread monitors the queue. As long as long there are work items in the queue, the worker thread de-queues the first item in the queue and invokes the delegate. To terminate the worker threads, dispose of the

AffinitySynchronizer instance. In a similar manner, you can develop a custom synchronization context that marshals all incoming calls to a private, small pool of threads, where only those threads are allowed to execute the calls.

The second aspect of implementing a custom synchronization context—that is, installing it—serves as a great example for WCF extensibility and as a checklist of points to consider regarding the how and when of installing such extensions.

Thread-Affinity Services

With a WCF service, AffinitySynchronizer is useful when it is the service that creates and then interacts with resources that require thread affinity, such as the TLS. A service that uses AffinitySynchronizer is always thread-safe, since only the internal worker thread of a particular AffinitySynchronizer can ever call it. When the service is configured with ConcurrencyMode.Single, the service gains no additional thread safety because the service instance is single-threaded anyway. You do get double queuing of concurrent calls: all concurrent calls to the service are first queued in the lock's queue, and then are dispatched to the worker thread one at a time. With ConcurrencyMode.Multiple, calls are dispatched to the worker thread's queue as fast as they arrive and are then queued up, later to be invoked in order and never concurrently. Note that if you use a custom synchronization context that marshals its calls to a pool of threads instead of a single thread, ConcurrencyMode.Multiple will yield the best throughput. Finally, with ConcurrencyMode.Reentrant, the service is of course not reentrant, because the incoming reentering call will be queued up and a deadlock would occur. The recommended mode with AffinitySynchronizer is ConcurrencyMode.Single.

Installing a Service Synchronization Context

Example 8-14 demonstrates installing AffinitySynchronizer before opening the host so that all instances of the service run on the same thread.

Example 8-14. Installing AffinitySynchronizer

```
SynchronizationContext synchronizationContext = new AffinitySynchronizer();
SynchronizationContext.SetSynchronizationContext(synchronizationContext);

using(synchronizationContext as IDisposable)
{
   ServiceHost host = new ServiceHost(typeof(MyService));
   host.Open();
   /* Some blocking operations */
   host.Close();
}
```

To attach a synchronization context to the current thread, call the static SetSynchronizationContext() method of SynchronizationContext. Once the host is opened, it will use the provided synchronization context. Note in Example 8-14 that after closing the host, the example disposes of AffinitySynchronizer to shut down the worker thread used.

You can streamline the code in Example 8-14 by encapsulating the installation of AffinitySynchronizer in a custom host, as with my ServiceHost<T>:

```
public class ServiceHost<T> : ServiceHost
{
   public void SetThreadAffinity(string threadName);
   public void SetThreadAffinity();
   //More members
}
```

Using SetThreadAffinity() to attach AffinitySynchronizer is straightforward:

```
ServiceHost<MyService> host = new ServiceHost<MyService>();
host.SetThreadAffinity();

host.Open();

/* Some blocking operations */

host.Close();
```

Example 8-15 lists the implementation of the SetThreadAffinity() methods.

Example 8-15. Adding thread affinity support to ServiceHost<T>

```
public class ServiceHost<T> : ServiceHost
{
   AffinitySynchronizer m_AffinitySynchronizer;

   public void SetThreadAffinity(string threadName)
   {
      if(State == CommunicationState.Opened)
      {
         throw new InvalidOperationException("Host is already opened");
      }
      m_AffinitySynchronizer = new AffinitySynchronizer(threadName);
      SynchronizationContext.SetSynchronizationContext(m_AffinitySynchronizer);
   }
   public void SetThreadAffinity()
   {
      SetThreadAffinity("Executing all endpoints of " + typeof(T));
   }
   protected override void OnClosing()
   {
      using(m_AffinitySynchronizer)
      {}
      base.OnClosing();
   }
   //More members
}
```

ServiceHost<T> maintains a member variable of the type AffinitySynchronizer and offers two versions of SetThreadAffinity( ). The parameterized one takes the thread name to provide for AffinitySynchronizer's worker thread, and the parameterless SetThreadAffinity( ) calls the other SetThreadAffinity( ) method specifying a thread name inferred from the hosted service type, such as "Executing all endpoints of MyService." SetThreadAffinity( ) first checks that the host is not opened yet, because you can only attach a synchronization context before the host is opened. If the host is not opened, SetThreadAffinity( ) constructs a new AffinitySynchronizer, providing it with the thread name to use and attaches it to the current thread. Finally, ServiceHost<T> overrides its base class OnClosing( ) method in order to call dispose on the AffinitySynchronizer member to shut down its worker thread. Since the AffinitySynchronizer member could be null if no one called SetThreadAffinity( ), OnClosing( ) uses the using statement that internally checks for null assignment before calling Dispose( ).

The ThreadAffinityBehavior attribute

The previous section showed how to install AffinitySynchronizer by the host, regardless of the service configuration. However, if by design the service is required to always execute on the same thread, it is better not to be at the mercy of the host and the thread that happens to open it. Use my ThreadAffinityBehaviorAttribute defined as:

```
[AttributeUsage(AttributeTargets.Class)]
public class ThreadAffinityBehaviorAttribute : Attribute,
                                     IContractBehavior,IServiceBehavior
{
   public ThreadAffinityBehaviorAttribute(Type serviceType);
   public ThreadAffinityBehaviorAttribute(Type serviceType,string threadName);
   public string ThreadName
   {get;set;}
}
```

As the name of the attribute implies, ThreadAffinityBehavior provides a local behavior enforcing the fact that all service instances always run on the same thread. The ThreadAffinityBehavior attribute uses my AffinitySynchronizer class internally. When applying the attribute, you need to provide the type of the service and optionally a thread name:

```
[ServiceBehavior(InstanceContextMode = InstanceContextMode.PerCall)]
[ThreadAffinityBehavior(typeof(MyService))]
class MyService : IMyContract
{...}
```

The thread name defaults to "Executing all endpoints of <service type>."

The ThreadAffinityBehavior attribute is a custom contract behavior because it implements the interface IContractBehavior, introduced in Chapter 5. IContractBehavior offers the ApplyDispatchBehavior() method, allowing you to affect an individual endpoint dispatcher's runtime and set its synchronization context:

```
public interface IContractBehavior
{
   void ApplyDispatchBehavior(ContractDescription description,
                              ServiceEndpoint endpoint,
                              DispatchRuntime dispatch);
   //More members
}
```

Each endpoint has its own dispatcher, and each dispatcher has its own synchronization context, so the attribute is instantiated and ApplyDispatchBehavior() is called per endpoint. Example 8-16 shows most of the implementation of the ThreadAffinityBehavior attribute.

Example 8-16. Implementing ThreadAffinityBehaviorAttribute

```
[AttributeUsage(AttributeTargets.Class)]
public class ThreadAffinityBehaviorAttribute : Attribute,
                                               IContractBehavior,
                                               IServiceBehavior
{
   string m_ThreadName;
   Type m_ServiceType;

   public string ThreadName //Accesses m_ThreadName
   {get;set;}

   public ThreadAffinityBehaviorAttribute(Type serviceType) :
                                          this(serviceType,null)
   {}
   public ThreadAffinityBehaviorAttribute(Type serviceType,string threadName)
   {
      m_ThreadName = threadName;
      m_ServiceType = serviceType;
   }
   void IContractBehavior.ApplyDispatchBehavior(ContractDescription description,
                              ServiceEndpoint endpoint,
                              DispatchRuntime dispatch)
   {
      m_ThreadName = m_ThreadName ?? "Executing endpoints of " + m_ServiceType;
      ThreadAffinityHelper.ApplyDispatchBehavior(m_ServiceType,m_ThreadName,
                                                 dispatch);
   }
   void IContractBehavior.Validate(...)
   {}
   void IContractBehavior.AddBindingParameters(...)
   {}
   void IContractBehavior.ApplyClientBehavior(...)
   {}

   void IServiceBehavior.Validate(ServiceDescription description,
                        ServiceHostBase serviceHostBase)
```

Example 8-16. Implementing ThreadAffinityBehaviorAttribute (continued)

```
   {
      serviceHostBase.Closed += delegate
                                {
                                   ThreadAffinityHelper.CloseThread(m_ServiceType);
                                };
   }
   void IServiceBehavior.AddBindingParameters(...)
   {}
   void IServiceBehavior.ApplyDispatchBehavior(...)
   {}
}
```

The constructors of the `ThreadAffinityBehavior` attribute save the provided service type and thread name.

 The `ApplyDispatchBehavior()` method in Example 8-16 uses the ?? null-coalescing operator (introduced in C# 2.0) to assign a thread name if it needs to. The expression:

```
m_ThreadName = m_ThreadName ?? "Executing endpoints
                                of " + m_ServiceType;
```

is shorthand for:

```
if(m_ThreadName == null)
{
   m_ThreadName = "Executing endpoints of " +
                                m_ServiceType;
}
```

The `ThreadAffinityBehavior` attribute serves as a top-level coordinator, delegating the actual implementation of `ApplyDispatchBehavior()` to the helper static class `ThreadAffinityHelper`:

```
public static class ThreadAffinityHelper
{
   internal static void ApplyDispatchBehavior(Type type,string threadName,
                                DispatchRuntime dispatch)
   public static void CloseThread(Type type);
}
```

The class `ThreadAffinityHelper` also offers the static method `CloseThread()` that shuts down the worker thread associated with the service type synchronization context. `ThreadAffinityBehavior` is also a service behavior. It implements `IServiceBehavior` so that in its implementation of `Validate()` it can obtain a reference to the service host and subscribe to the `Closed` event using an anonymous method. That anonymous method shuts down the worker thread by calling `ThreadAffinityHelper.CloseThread()` and providing the service type. Example 8-17 shows the implementation of the `ThreadAffinityHelper` class.

Example 8-17. Implementing ThreadAffinityHelper

```
public static class ThreadAffinityHelper
{
   static Dictionary<Type,AffinitySynchronizer> m_Contexts =
                         new Dictionary<Type,AffinitySynchronizer>();

   [MethodImpl(MethodImplOptions.Synchronized)]
   internal static void ApplyDispatchBehavior(Type type,string threadName,
                                        DispatchRuntime dispatch)
   {
      Debug.Assert(dispatch.SynchronizationContext == null);

      if(m_Contexts.ContainsKey(type) == false)
      {
         m_Contexts[type] = new AffinitySynchronizer(threadName);
      }
      dispatch.SynchronizationContext = m_Contexts[type];
   }

   [MethodImpl(MethodImplOptions.Synchronized)]
   public static void CloseThread(Type type)
   {
      if(m_Contexts.ContainsKey(type))
      {
         m_Contexts[type].Dispose();
         m_Contexts.Remove(type);
      }
   }
}
```

The DispatchRuntime class provides the SynchronizationContext property ThreadAffinityHelper, used to assign a synchronization context for the dispatcher:

```
public sealed class DispatchRuntime
{
   public SynchronizationContext SynchronizationContext
   {get;set;}
   //More members
}
```

Before making the assignment, ThreadAffinityHelper verifies that the dispatcher has no other synchronization context, since that would indicate some unresolved conflict. The task of ThreadAffinityHelper is to associate all dispatchers of all endpoints of the provided service type with the same instance of a synchronization context. To handle this single-association scenario, ThreadAffinityHelper uses a static dictionary internally that maps a type to its synchronization context. ThreadAffinityHelper, in ApplyDispatchBehavior(), checks if the dictionary already contains a synchronization context for the type at hand. If no matching entry is found, ThreadAffinityHelper creates a new synchronization context (with the thread name) and adds it to the dictionary. It then looks up in the dictionary the synchronization context for the type and assigns it to the dispatcher. The CloseThread() method uses the provided type as a key to look up in the dictionary the associated synchronization context and then dispose of it, thus shutting down the thread. All access to the static dictionary is synchronized declaratively using the `MethodImpl` attribute with the `MethodImplOptions.Synchronized` flag.

Callbacks and Client Safety

There are quite a few cases when a client might receive concurrent callbacks. If the client provided a callback reference to multiple services, those services could call back concurrently to the client. But even with a single callback reference, the service might launch multiple threads and use all of them to call on that single reference. Duplex callbacks enter the client on worker threads and might corrupt the client state if done concurrently without synchronization. The client must synchronize access to its own in-memory state, but also to any resources the callback thread might access. Similar to a service, a callback client can use either manual or declarative synchronization. The `CallbackBehavior` attribute introduced in Chapter 6 offers the `ConcurrencyMode` and the `UseSynchronizationContext` properties:

```
[AttributeUsage(AttributeTargets.Class)]
public sealed class CallbackBehaviorAttribute : Attribute,...
{
   public ConcurrencyMode ConcurrencyMode
   {get;set;}
   public bool UseSynchronizationContext
   {get;set;}
}
```

Both of these properties default to the same values as with the `ServiceBehavior` attribute and behave in a similar manner. For example, the default of the `ConcurrencyMode` property is `ConcurrencyMode.Single`, so these two definitions are equivalent:

```
class MyClient : IMyContractCallback
{...}

[CallbackBehavior(ConcurrencyMode = ConcurrencyMode.Single)]
class MyClient : IMyContractCallback
{...}
```

Callbacks with ConcurrencyMode.Single

When the callback is configured with `ConcurrencyMode.Single` (the default), only one callback is allowed at a time to enter the callback object. The big difference, compared with a service, is that callback objects often have an existence independent of WCF. While the service instance is owned by WCF and only worker threads dispatched by WCF ever access the service instance, a callback object may also interact with local client-side threads. These client threads are unaware of the

synchronization lock associated with the callback object when using
ConcurrencyMode.Single. All that ConcurrencyMode.Single does for a callback object is
serialize the access by WCF threads. You must therefore manually synchronize
access to the callback state and any other resource accessed by the callback method,
as shown in Example 8-18.

Example 8-18. Manually synchronizing the callback with ConcurrencyMode.Single

```
interface IMyContractCallback
{
   [OperationContract]
   void OnCallback( );
}
class MyClient : IMyContractCallback,IDisposable
{
   MyContractClient m_Proxy;

   public void CallService( )
   {
      InstanceContext callbackContext = new InstanceContext(this);
      m_Proxy = new MyContractClient(callbackContext);
      m_Proxy.DoSomething( );
   }
   //This method invoked by one callback at a time, plus client threads
   public void OnCallback( )
   {
      //Access state and resources, synchronize manually
      lock(this)
      {...}
   }
   public void Dispose( )
   {
      m_Proxy.Close( );
   }
}
```

Callbacks with ConcurrencyMode.Multiple

When configuring the callback with ConcurrencyMode.Multiple, WCF will allow concurrent calls on the callback instance. This means you need to synchronize access in
the callback operations because they could be invoked concurrently both by WCF
worker threads and by client-side threads, as shown in Example 8-19.

Example 8-19. Manually synchronizing callback with ConcurrencyMode.Multiple

```
[CallbackBehavior(ConcurrencyMode = ConcurrencyMode.Multiple)]
class MyClient : IMyContractCallback,IDisposable
{
   MyContractClient m_Proxy;

   public void CallService( )
```

```
   {
      InstanceContext callbackContext = new InstanceContext(this);
      m_Proxy = new MyContractClient(callbackContext);
      m_Proxy.DoSomething( );
   }
   //This method can be invoked concurrently by callbacks,
   //plus client threads
   public void OnCallback( )
   {
      //Access state and resources, synchronize manually
      lock(this)
      {...}
   }
   public void Dispose( )
   {
      m_Proxy.Close( );
   }
}
```

Callbacks with ConcurrencyMode.Reentrant

Since the callback object can also perform outgoing calls over WCF, those calls may eventually try to reenter the callback object. To avoid a deadlock when using ConcurrencyMode.Single, you can configure the callback with ConcurrencyMode. Reentrant as needed:

```
[CallbackBehavior(ConcurrencyMode = ConcurrencyMode.Reentrant)]
class MyClient : IMyContractCallback
{...}
```

Configuring the callback for reentrancy also enables other services to call the callback when the callback object itself is engaged in WCF callouts.

Callbacks and Synchronization Context

Similar to a service invocation, the callback may need to access resources that rely on some kind of thread(s) affinity. In addition, the callback instance itself may require thread affinity for its own use of the TLS or for interacting with a UI thread. While the callback can use techniques such as those in Examples 8-4 and 8-5 to marshal the interaction to the resource synchronization context, you can also have WCF associate the callback with a particular synchronization context by setting the UseSynchronizationContext property to true. However, unlike the service, the client does not use any host to expose the endpoint. If the UseSynchronizationContext property is true, the synchronization context to use is locked in when the proxy is opened, or, more commonly, when the client makes the first call to the service using the proxy, if Open( ) is not explicitly called. If the calling client thread has a synchronization context, this will be the synchronization context used by WCF for all callbacks to the client's endpoint associated with that proxy. Note that only the first call (or the call to Open( )) made on the proxy is given the opportunity to determine the synchronization context. Subsequent calls have no say in the matter. If the calling client thread has no synchronization context, even if UseSynchronizationContext is true, no synchronization context will be used for the callbacks.

Callbacks and UI Synchronization Context

If the callback object is running in a Windows Forms synchronization context, or if it needs to update some UI, you must marshal the callbacks or the updates to the UI thread. You can use techniques such as those in Examples 8-6 or 8-8. However, the more common use for UI updates over callbacks is to have the form itself implement the callback contract and update the UI as in Example 8-20.

Example 8-20. Relying on the UI synchronization context for callbacks

```
partial class MyForm : Form,IMyContractCallback
{
   MyContractClient m_Proxy;

   public MyForm( )
   {
      InitializeComponent( );
      InstanceContext callbackContext = new InstanceContext(this);
      m_Proxy = new MyContractClient(callbackContext);
   }
   //Called as a result of a UI event
   public void OnCallService(object sender,EventArgs args)
   {
      m_Proxy.DoSomething( );//Affinity established here
   }
   //This method always runs on the UI thread
   public void OnCallback( )
   {
      //No need for synchronization and marshaling
      Text = "Some Callback";
   }
   public void OnClose(object sender,EventArgs args)
   {
      m_Proxy.Close( );
   }
}
```

In Example 8-20 the proxy is first used in the CallService( ) method, which is called by the UI thread as a result of some UI event. Calling the proxy on the UI synchronization context establishes the affinity to it, so the callback can directly access and update the UI without marshaling any calls. In addition, since only one thread (and the same thread at that) will ever execute in the synchronization context, the callback is guaranteed to be synchronized.

You can also explicitly establish the affinity to the UI synchronization context by opening the proxy in the form's constructor without invoking an operation. This is especially useful if you want to dispatch calls to the service on worker threads (or perhaps even asynchronously as discussed at the end of this chapter), and yet have the callbacks enter on the UI synchronization context, as shown in Example 8-21.

Example 8-21. Explicitly opening a proxy to establish synchronization context

```
partial class MyForm : Form,IMyContractCallback
{
   MyContractClient m_Proxy;

   public MyForm( )
   {
      InitializeComponent( );
      InstanceContext callbackContext = new InstanceContext(this);
      m_Proxy = new MyContractClient(callbackContext);

      //Establish affinity to UI synchronization context here:
      m_Proxy.Open( );
   }
   //Called as a result of a UI event
   public void CallService(object sender,EventArgs args )
   {
      ThreadStart invoke = delegate
                           {
                              m_Proxy.DoSomething( );
                           };
      Thread thread = new Thread(invoke);
      thread.Start( );
   }
   //This method always runs on the UI thread
   public void OnCallback( )
   {
      //No need for synchronization and marshaling
      Text = "Some Callback";
   }
   public void OnClose(object sender,EventArgs args)
   {
      m_Proxy.Close( );
   }
}
```

UI thread callbacks and responsiveness

When callbacks are processed on the UI thread, the UI itself is not responsive. Even if you perform relatively short callbacks, if the callback is configured with ConcurrencyMode.Multiple, there could be multiple callbacks back-to-back in the UI message queue, and processing them all at once will degrade responsiveness. You should avoid lengthy callback processing on the UI thread and opt for configuring the callback with ConcurrencyMode.Single so that the callback object lock will queue up the multiple callbacks, and by dispatching them one at a time to the callback object you enable interleaving them among the UI messages.

UI thread callbacks and concurrency management

Configuring the callback for affinity to the UI thread may trigger a deadlock. Consider the following setup: A Windows Forms client establishes affinity between a callback object (or even itself) and the UI synchronization context. The client then calls a service passing the callback reference. The service is configured for reentrancy and it calls the client. A deadlock occurs now because the callback to the client needs to execute on the UI thread, and that thread is blocked waiting for the service call to return. Configuring the callback as a one-way operation will not resolve the problem here because the one-way call still needs to be marshaled first to the UI thread. The only way to resolve the deadlock in this case is to turn off using the UI synchronization context by the callback, and to manually and asynchronously marshal the update to the form using its synchronization context. Example 8-22 demonstrates using this technique.

Example 8-22. Avoiding callback deadlock on the UI thread

```
//////////////////////// Client Side //////////////////////
[CallbackBehavior(UseSynchronizationContext = false)]
partial class MyForm : Form,IMyContractCallback
{
   SynchronizationContext m_Context;
   MyContractClient m_Proxy;

   public MyForm( )
   {
      InitializeComponent( );
      m_Context = SynchronizationContext.Current;
      InstanceContext callbackContext = new InstanceContext(this);
      m_Proxy = new MyContractClient(callbackContext);
   }

   public void CallService(object sender,EventArgs args)
   {
      m_Proxy.DoSomething( );
   }
   //Callback runs on worker threads
   public void OnCallback( )
   {
      SendOrPostCallback setText = delegate
                                   {
                                      Text = "Manually marshaling to UI thread";
                                   };
      m_Context.Post(setText,null);
   }
   public void OnClose(object sender,EventArgs args)
   {
```

Example 8-22. Avoiding callback deadlock on the UI thread (continued)

```
      m_Proxy.Close( );
   }
}
/////////////////////////// Service Side ///////////////////////
[ServiceContract(CallbackContract = typeof(IMyContractCallback))]
interface IMyContract
{
   [OperationContract]
   void DoSomething( );
}
interface IMyContractCallback
{
   [OperationContract]
   void OnCallback( );
}
[ServiceBehavior(ConcurrencyMode = ConcurrencyMode.Reentrant)]
class MyService : IMyContract
{
   public void DoSomething( )
   {
      IMyContractCallback callback = OperationContext.Current.
                                GetCallbackChannel<IMyContractCallback>( );
      callback.OnCallback( );
   }
}
```

As shown in Example 8-22, you must use the Post( ) method of the synchronization context. Under no circumstances should you use the Send( ) method—even though the callback is executing on the worker thread, the UI thread is still blocked on the outbound call. Calling Send( ) would trigger the deadlock you are trying to avoid because Send( ) will block until the UI thread can process the request. Much the same way, the callback in Example 8-22 cannot use any of the safe controls (such as SafeLabel) because those too use the Send( ) method.

Callback Custom Synchronization Context

Similar to a service custom synchronization context, you can install a custom synchronization context for the use of the callback. All that is required is that the thread that opens the proxy (or calls it for the first time) has the custom synchronization context attached to it. Example 8-23 shows how to attach my AffinitySynchronizer class to the callback object by attaching it before using the proxy.

Example 8-23. Setting custom synchronization context for the callback

```
interface IMyContractCallback
{
   [OperationContract]
   void OnCallback( );
}
```

Example 8-23. Setting custom synchronization context for the callback (continued)

```
class MyClient : IMyContractCallback
{
    //This method always invoked by the same thread
    public void OnCallback()
    {....}
}

MyClient client = new MyClient();
InstanceContext callbackContext = new InstanceContext(client);
MyContractClient proxy = new MyContractClient(callbackContext);

SynchronizationContext synchronizationContext = new AffinitySynchronizer();
SynchronizationContext.SetSynchronizationContext(synchronizationContext);

using(synchronizationContext as IDisposable)
{
    proxy.DoSomething();
    /* Some blocking operations till after the callback*/
    proxy.Close();
}
```

The CallbackThreadAffinityBehaviorAttribute

Much the same way as the service, you can also assign a custom synchronization context for a callback endpoint using an attribute. For example, here is my CallbackThreadAffinityBehaviorAttribute:

```
[AttributeUsage(AttributeTargets.Class)]
public class CallbackThreadAffinityBehaviorAttribute : Attribute,IEndpointBehavior
{
    public CallbackThreadAffinityBehaviorAttribute(Type callbackType);
    public CallbackThreadAffinityBehaviorAttribute(Type callbackType,
                                                   string threadName);
    public string ThreadName
    {get;set;}
}
```

The CallbackThreadAffinityBehavior attribute makes all callbacks across all callback contracts the client supports execute on the same thread. Since the attribute needs to affect the callback endpoints, it implements the IEndpointBehavior interface presented in Chapter 6. You apply the attribute directly on the callback type, as shown in Example 8-24.

Example 8-24. Applying the CallbackThreadAffinityBehavior attribute

```
[CallbackThreadAffinityBehavior(typeof(MyClient))]
class MyClient : IMyContractCallback,IDisposable
{
    MyContractClient m_Proxy;

    public void CallService()
```

```
   {
      InstanceContext callbackContext = new InstanceContext(this);
      m_Proxy = new MyContractClient(callbackContext);
      m_Proxy.DoSomething( );
   }
   //This method invoked by same callback thread, plus client threads
   public void OnCallback( )
   {
      //Access state and resources, synchronize manually
   }
   public void Dispose( )
   {
      m_Proxy.Close( );
   }
}
```

The attribute requires as a construction parameter the type of the callback it is deco-
rating. Note that although the callback is always invoked by WCF on the same
thread, you still may need to synchronize access to it if other client-side threads
access the method as well.

Using the `CallbackThreadAffinityBehavior` attribute as in Example 8-24,
Example 8-23 is reduced to:

```
   MyClient client = new MyClient( );
   InstanceContext callbackContext = new InstanceContext(client);
   MyContractClient proxy = new MyContractClient(callbackContext);

   proxy.DoSomething( );
   /* Some blocking operations till after the callback*/
   proxy.Close( );
```

Example 8-25 shows the implementation of the `CallbackThreadAffinityBehavior`
attribute.

Example 8-25. Implementing CallbackThreadAffinityBehaviorAttribute

```
[AttributeUsage(AttributeTargets.Class)]
public class CallbackThreadAffinityBehaviorAttribute : Attribute,IEndpointBehavior
{
   string m_ThreadName;
   Type m_CallbackType;

   public string ThreadName //Accesses m_ThreadName
   {get;set;}

   public CallbackThreadAffinityBehaviorAttribute(Type callbackType)
                                                 : this(callbackType,null)
   {}
   public CallbackThreadAffinityBehaviorAttribute(Type callbackType,
                                       string threadName)
```

```
   {
      m_ThreadName = threadName;
      m_CallbackType = callbackType;
      AppDomain.CurrentDomain.ProcessExit += delegate
                                  {
                           ThreadAffinityHelper.CloseThread(m_CallbackType);
                                  };
   }
   void IEndpointBehavior.ApplyClientBehavior(ServiceEndpoint serviceEndpoint,
                              ClientRuntime clientRuntime)
   {
      m_ThreadName = m_ThreadName ?? "Executing callbacks of " + m_CallbackType;

      ThreadAffinityHelper.ApplyDispatchBehavior(m_CallbackType,m_ThreadName,
                                 clientRuntime.CallbackDispatchRuntime);

   }
   void IEndpointBehavior.AddBindingParameters(...)
   {}
   void IEndpointBehavior.ApplyDispatchBehavior(...)
   {}
   void IEndpointBehavior.Validate(...)
   {}
}
```

The constructor of CallbackThreadAffinityBehavior attribute saves in member variables the supplied callback type and the thread name, if any. The attribute uses the ThreadAffinityHelper class presented earlier to attach the AffinitySynchronizer to the dispatcher. Unlike the service, there is no host involved, so there is no closing event you can subscribe to as a signal to shut down the worker thread of AffinitySynchronizer. Instead, the constructor uses an anonymous method to subscribe to the process exit event of the current app domain. When the client application shuts down, the anonymous method will use ThreadAffinityHelper to close the worker thread.

While the attribute supports IEndpointBehavior, the only method of interest here is ApplyClientBehavior( ) where you can affect the callback endpoint dispatcher:

```
public interface IEndpointBehavior
{
   void ApplyClientBehavior(ServiceEndpoint serviceEndpoint,
                     ClientRuntime clientRuntime);
   //More members
}
```

In ApplyClientBehavior( ) the attribute extracts from the ClientRuntime parameter its dispatcher in the CallbackDispatchRuntime parameter:

```
public sealed class ClientRuntime
{
   public DispatchRuntime CallbackDispatchRuntime
   {get;}
```

```
    //More members
}
```

and passes it to `ThreadAffinityHelper` to attach the `AffinitySynchronizer`.

While the client-side worker thread used by `AffinitySynchronizer` will automatically be closed once the client application shuts down, the client may want to expedite that and close it sooner. To that end, the client can explicitly call the `CloseThread( )` method of `ThreadAffinityHelper`:

```
MyClient client = new MyClient( );
InstanceContext callbackContext = new InstanceContext(client);
MyContractClient proxy = new MyContractClient(callbackContext);
proxy.DoSomething( );
/* Some blocking operations till after the callback
proxy.Close( );
ThreadAffinityHelper.CloseThread(typeof(MyClient));
```

Asynchronous Calls

When a client calls a service, usually the client is blocked while the service executes the call, and control returns to the client only when the operation completes its execution and returns. However, there are quite a few cases in which you want to call operations asynchronously; that is, you want control to return immediately to the client while the service executes the operation in the background, and then somehow let the client know that the method has completed execution and provides the client with the results of the invocation. Such an execution mode is called *asynchronous operation invocation*, and the action is known as an *asynchronous call*. Asynchronous calls allow you to improve client responsiveness and availability.

 One-way operations are inadequate for asynchronous calls. First, one-way calls are not guaranteed to be asynchronous at all. If the service's incoming calls queue is filled to capacity, WCF will block the caller of a one-way call until it can place the call in the queue. In addition, there is no easy way to notify the client regarding the results or errors of the call when a one-way operation completes. While you could hand-craft a custom mechanism that passes method IDs to every one-way call and then uses a callback to report completion, results, and errors back to the client, such a solution would be cumbersome and proprietary. It would require the service to always catch all exceptions, while communication errors may not reach the client at all. It also mandates the use of a duplex binding, and you will not be able to call the service operation both synchronously and asynchronously.

Requirements for an Asynchronous Mechanism

To make the most of the various options available with WCF asynchronous calls, it is best to first list generic requirements set for any service-oriented asynchronous calls support. These include the following:

- The same service code should be used for both synchronous and asynchronous invocation. This allows service developers to focus on business logic and cater to both synchronous and asynchronous clients.

- A corollary of the first requirement is that the client should be the one to decide whether to call a service synchronously or asynchronously. That in turn implies that the client will have different code for each case (whether to invoke the call synchronously or asynchronously).

- The client should be able to issue multiple asynchronous calls and have multiple asynchronous calls in progress. The client should be able to distinguish between multiple methods completions.

- When a service operation has output parameters or return values, these parameters are not available when control returns to the client. The client should have a way to harvest these results when the operation completes.

- Similarly, communication errors or the service's error should be communicated back to the client side. An exception thrown during the operation execution should be played back to the client later on.

- The implementation of the mechanism should be independent of the binding and transfer technology used. Any binding should support asynchronous calls.

- The mechanism should not use technology-specific constructs such as .NET exceptions or delegates.

- The last item is less of a requirement and more of a design guideline: the asynchronous calls mechanism should be straightforward and simple to use. For example, the mechanism should as much as possible hide its implementation details, such as the worker threads used to dispatch the call.

The client has a variety of options for handling operation completion. The client issues an asynchronous call and then can choose to:

- Perform some work while the call is in progress and then block until completion.

- Perform some work while the call is in progress and then poll for completion.

- Receive notification when the method has completed. The notification will be in the form of a callback on a client-provided method. The callback should contain information identifying which operation has just completed and its return values.

- Perform some work while the call is in progress, then wait for only a predetermined amount of time, and stop waiting, even if the operation execution has not completed yet.

- Wait simultaneously for completion of multiple operations. The client can also choose to wait for all or any of the pending calls to complete.

WCF offers all of these options to clients. The WCF support is strictly a client-side facility, and in fact the service is unaware it is being invoked asynchronously. This means that intrinsically any service supports asynchronous calls, and that you can call the same service both synchronously and asynchronously. In addition, because all of the asynchronous invocation support happens on the client side regardless of the service, you can use any binding for the asynchronous invocation.

 The WCF asynchronous calls support presented in this section is similar but not identical to the delegate-based asynchronous calls support offered by .NET for regular CLR types.

Proxy-Based Asynchronous Calls

Because the client decides if the call should be synchronous or asynchronous, you need to create a different proxy for the asynchronous case. Using the /async switch of SvcUtil, you can generate a proxy that contains asynchronous methods in addition to the synchronous ones. For each operation in the original contract, the asynchronous proxy and contract will contain two additional methods of this form:

```
[OperationContract(AsyncPattern = true,
                   Action = "<original action name>",
                   ReplyAction = "<original response name">)]
IAsyncResult Begin<Operation>(<in arguments>,
                              AsyncCallback callback,object asyncState);
<returned type> End<Operation>(<out arguments>,IAsyncResult result);
```

The OperationContract attribute offers the AsyncPattern Boolean property defined as:

```
[AttributeUsage(AttributeTargets.Method)]
public sealed class OperationContractAttribute : Attribute
{
   public bool AsyncPattern
   {get;set;}
   //More members
}
```

The AsyncPattern property defaults to false. AsyncPattern has meaning only on the client-side copy of the contract. You can only set AsyncPattern to true on a method with a Begin<Operation>( )-compatible signature, and the defining contract must also have a matching method with an End<Operation>( )-compatible signature. These requirements are verified at the proxy load time. What AsyncPattern does is bind the underlying synchronous method with the Begin/End pair, and correlates the synchronous execution with the asynchronous one. Briefly, when the client invokes a method of the form Begin<Operation>( ) with AsyncPattern set to true, it tells WCF not to try to directly invoke a method by that name on the service. Instead, it will use a thread from the thread pool to synchronously call the underlying method (identified by the Action name). The synchronous call will block the thread from the thread pool, not the calling client. The client will only be blocked for the slightest moment it takes to dispatch the call request to the thread pool. The reply method of the synchronous invocation is correlated with the End<Operation>( ) method.

Example 8-26 shows a calculator contract and implementing service, and the generated proxy class when the /async switch is used.

Example 8-26. Asynchronous contract and proxy

```
/////////////////////////// Service Side ///////////////////////////
[ServiceContract]
interface ICalculator
{
   [OperationContract]
   int Add(int number1,int number2);
   //More operations
}
class Calculator : ICalculator
{
   public int Add(int number1,int number2)
   {
      return number1 + number2;
   }
   //Rest of the implementation
}
/////////////////////////// Client Side ///////////////////////////
[ServiceContract]
public interface ICalculator
{
   [OperationContract]
   int Add(int number1,int number2);

   [OperationContract(AsyncPattern = true,
                      Action = ".../ICalculator/Add",
                      ReplyAction = ".../ICalculator/AddResponse")]
   IAsyncResult BeginAdd(int number1,int number2,AsyncCallback callback,
                                                    object asyncState);

   int EndAdd(IAsyncResult result);

   //Rest of the methods
}
public partial class CalculatorClient : ClientBase<ICalculator>,ICalculator
{
   public int Add(int number1,int number2)
   {
      return Channel.Add(number1,number2);
   }
   public IAsyncResult BeginAdd(int number1,int number2,
                                AsyncCallback callback,object asyncState)
   {
      return Channel.BeginAdd(number1,number2,callback,asyncState);
   }
```

Example 8-26. Asynchronous contract and proxy (continued)

```
   public int EndAdd(IAsyncResult result)
   {
      return Channel.EndAdd(result);
   }
   //Rest of the methods and constructors
}
```

Note that the BeginAdd( ) operation on the contract still has the original action and reply names, and in fact, you can just omit them:

```
[OperationContract(AsyncPattern = true)]
IAsyncResult BeginAdd(int number1,int number2,AsyncCallback callback,
                                                   object asyncState);
```

Asynchronous Invocation

Begin<Operation>( ) accepts the input parameters of the original synchronous operation. Input parameters include data contracts passed by value or by reference (using the ref modifier). The original method's return values and any explicit output parameters (using the out and ref modifiers) are part of the End<Operation>( ) method. For example, for this operation definition:

```
[ServiceOperation]
string MyMethod(int number1,out int number2,ref int number3);
```

the corresponding Begin<Operation>( ) and End<Operation>( ) methods look like this:

```
[ServiceOperation(...)]
IAsyncResult BeginMyMethod(int number1,ref int number3,
                     AsyncCallback callback,object asyncState);
string EndMyMethod(out int number2,ref int number3,IAsyncResult asyncResult);
```

Begin<Operation>( ) accepts two additional input parameters, not present in the original operation signature: callback and asyncState. The callback parameter is a delegate targeting a client-side method completed notification event. asyncState is an object that conveys whatever state information is needed by the party handling the method completion. These two parameters are optional: the caller can choose to pass in null instead of either one of them. For example, to asynchronously invoke the Add( ) method of the Calculator service from Example 8-26 using the asynchronous proxy, if you have no interest in the results or the errors:

```
CalculatorClient proxy = new CalculatorClient( );
proxy.BeginAdd(2,3,null,null);//Dispatched asynchronously
proxy.Close( );
```

As long as the client has the definition of the asynchronous contract, you can also invoke the operation asynchronously using a channel factory:

```
ChannelFactory<ICalculator> factory = new ChannelFactory<ICalculator>( );
ICalculator proxy = factory.CreateChannel( );
proxy.BeginAdd(2,3,null,null);
ICommunicationObject channel = proxy as ICommunicationObject;
channel.Close( );
```

The problem with such invocation is that the client has no way of getting its results.

The IAsyncResult interface

Every `Begin<Operation>()` method returns an object implementing the `IAsyncResult` interface, defined in the `System.Runtime.Remoting.Messaging` namespace as:

```
public interface IAsyncResult
{
   object AsyncState
   {get;}
   WaitHandle AsyncWaitHandle
   {get;}
   bool CompletedSynchronously
   {get;}
   bool IsCompleted
   {get;}
}
```

The returned `IAsyncResult` object uniquely identifies the method that was invoked using `Begin<Operation>()`. You can pass the `IAsyncResult` object to `End<Operation>()` to identify the specific asynchronous method execution from which you wish to retrieve the results. `End<Operation>()` will block its caller until the operation it waits for (identified by the `IAsyncResult` object passed in) completes and it can rerun the results or the errors. If the method is already complete by the time `End<Operation>()` is called, `End<Operation>()` will not block the caller and will just return the results. Example 8-27 shows the entire sequence.

Example 8-27. Simple asynchronous execution sequence

```
CalculatorClient proxy = new CalculatorClient();
IAsyncResult asyncResult1 = proxy.BeginAdd(2,3,null,null);
IAsyncResult asyncResult2 = proxy.BeginAdd(4,5,null,null);
proxy.Close();

/* Do some work */

int sum;

sum = proxy.EndAdd(asyncResult1);//This may block
Debug.Assert(sum == 5);

sum = proxy.EndAdd(asyncResult2);//This may block
Debug.Assert(sum == 9);
```

As simple as Example 8-27 is, it does demonstrate a few key points. The first point is that the same proxy instance can invoke multiple asynchronous calls. The caller can distinguish among the different pending calls using each unique `IAsyncResult` object returned from `Begin<Operation>()`. In fact, when the caller makes asynchronous calls, as in Example 8-27, the caller must save the `IAsyncResult` objects. In addition, the caller should make no assumptions about the order in which the pending calls complete. It is quite possible the second call will complete before the first one.

Finally, if you have no more use for the proxy, you can close it immediately after dispatching the asynchronous calls, and still be able to call End<Operation>( ).

Although it isn't evident in Example 8-27, there are two important programming points regarding asynchronous calls:

- End<Operation>( ) can be called only once for each asynchronous operation. Trying to call it more than once results in an InvalidOperationException.

- You can pass the IAsyncResult object to End<Operation>( ) only on the same proxy object used to dispatch the call. Passing the IAsyncResult object to a different proxy instance results in an AsyncCallbackException.

Polling or Waiting for Completion

When a client calls End<Operation>( ), the client is blocked until the asynchronous method returns. This may be fine if the client has a finite amount of work to do while the call is in progress, and if, once that work is done, the client cannot continue its execution without the returned value or the output parameters of the operation, or even just the knowledge that the operation has completed. However, what if the client only wants to check if the operation execution has completed? What if the client wants to wait for completion for a fixed timeout, do some additional finite processing, and then wait again? WCF supports these alternative programming models to calling End<Operation>( ).

The IAsyncResult interface object returned from Begin<Operation>( ) has the AsyncWaitHandle property, of type WaitHandle:

```
public abstract class WaitHandle : ...
{
    public static bool WaitAll(WaitHandle[] waitHandles);
    public static int WaitAny(WaitHandle[] waitHandles);
    public virtual void Close( );
    public virtual bool WaitOne( );
    //More memebrs
}
```

The WaitOne( ) method of WaitHandle returns only when the handle is signaled. Example 8-28 demonstrates using WaitOne( ).

Example 8-28. UsingIasyncResult.AsyncWaitHandle to block until completion

```
CalculatorClient proxy = new CalculatorClient( );
IAsyncResult asyncResult = proxy.BeginAdd(2,3,null,null);
proxy.Close( );

/* Do some work */

asyncResult.AsyncWaitHandle.WaitOne( ); //This may block
int sum = proxy.EndAdd(asyncResult); //This will not block
Debug.Assert(sum == 5);
```

Logically, Example 8-28 is identical to Example 8-27, which called only End<Operation>( ). If the operation is still executing, WaitOne( ) will block. If by the time WaitOne( ) is called, the method execution is complete, WaitOne( ) will not block, and the client proceeds to call End<Operation>( ) for the returned value. The important difference between Examples 8-28 and 8-27 is that the call to End<Operation>( ) in Example 8-28 is guaranteed not to block its caller.

Example 8-29 demonstrates a more practical way of using WaitOne( ), by specifying the timeout (10 milliseconds in this example). When you specify a timeout, WaitOne( ) returns when the method execution is completed or when the timeout has elapsed, whichever condition is met first.

Example 8-29. Using WaitOne() to specify wait timeout

```
CalculatorClient proxy = new CalculatorClient( );
IAsyncResult asyncResult = proxy.BeginAdd(2,3,null,null);

while(asyncResult.IsCompleted == false)
{
   asyncResult.AsyncWaitHandle.WaitOne(10,false); //This may block
   /* Do some work */
}
int sum = proxy.EndAdd(asyncResult); //This will not block
```

Example 8-29 uses another handy property of IAsyncResult, called IsCompleted. IsCompleted lets you find the status of the call without waiting or blocking. You can even use IsCompleted in a strict polling mode:

```
CalculatorClient proxy = new CalculatorClient( );
IAsyncResult asyncResult = proxy.BeginAdd(2,3,null,null);
proxy.Close( );

//Sometime later:
if(asyncResult.IsCompleted)
{
    int sum = proxy.EndAdd(asyncResult); //This will not block
    Debug.Assert(sum == 5);
}
else
{
   //Do something meanwhile
}
```

The AsyncWaitHandle property really shines when you use it to manage multiple concurrent asynchronous methods in progress. You can use WaitHandle's static WaitAll( ) method to wait for completion of multiple asynchronous methods, as shown in Example 8-30.

Example 8-30. Waiting for completion of multiple methods

```
CalculatorClient proxy = new CalculatorClient( );
IAsyncResult asyncResult1 = proxy.BeginAdd(2,3,null,null);
IAsyncResult asyncResult2 = proxy.BeginAdd(4,5,null,null);
```

Example 8-30. Waiting for completion of multiple methods (continued)

```
proxy.Close( );

WaitHandle[] handleArray = {asyncResult1.AsyncWaitHandle,
                            asyncResult2.AsyncWaitHandle};

WaitHandle.WaitAll(handleArray);

int sum;
//These calls to EndAdd( ) will not block

sum = proxy.EndAdd(asyncResult1);
Debug.Assert(sum == 5);

sum = proxy.EndAdd(asyncResult2);
Debug.Assert(sum == 9);
```

To use WaitAll( ), you need to construct an array of handles. Note that you still need to call End<Operation>( ) to access returned values. Instead of waiting for all of the methods to return, you can choose to wait for any of them to return, using the WaitAny( ) static method of the WaitHandle class. Much like WaitOne( ), both WaitAll( ) and WaitAny( ) have a few overloaded versions, which let you specify a timeout to wait instead of waiting indefinitely.

Completion Callbacks

Instead of blocking, waiting, or polling for an asynchronous call to complete, WCF offers another programming model altogether—completion callbacks. The client provides WCF with a method and requests that WCF will call that method back when the asynchronous method completes. The client can provide a callback instance method or static method and have the same callback method handle completion of multiple asynchronous calls. When the asynchronous method execution is complete, instead of quietly returning to the pool, the worker thread calls the completion callback. To designate a completion callback method, the client needs to provide Begin<Operation>( ) with a delegate of the type AsyncCallback defined as:

```
public delegate void AsyncCallback(IAsyncResult asyncResult);
```

That delegate is provided as the penultimate parameter to Begin<Operation>( ).

Example 8-31 demonstrates asynchronous call management by using a completion callback.

Example 8-31. Managing asynchronous call with a completion callback

```
class MyClient : IDisposable
{
   CalculatorClient m_Proxy = new CalculatorClient( );

   public void CallAsync( )
```

Example 8-31. Managing asynchronous call with a completion callback (continued)

```
   {
      m_Proxy.BeginAdd(2,3,OnCompletion,null);
   }
   void OnCompletion(IAsyncResult result)
   {
      int sum = m_Proxy.EndAdd(result);
      Debug.Assert(sum == 5);
   }
   void Dispose()
   {
      m_Proxy.Close();
   }
}
```

Unlike the programming models described so far, when you use a completion callback method, there's no need to save the IAsyncResult object returned from Begin<Operation>() because when WCF calls the completion callback, WCF provides the IAsyncResult object as a parameter. Because WCF provides a unique IAsyncResult object for each asynchronous method, you can channel multiple asynchronous method completions to the same callback method:

```
   m_Proxy.BeginAdd(2,3,OnCompletion,null);
   m_Proxy.BeginAdd(4,5,OnCompletion,null);
```

Instead of using a class method as a completion callback, you can just as easily use a local anonymous method:

```
   CalculatorClient proxy = new CalculatorClient();
   int sum;
   AsyncCallback completion = delegate(IAsyncResult result)
                              {
                                  sum = proxy.EndAdd(result);
                                  Debug.Assert(sum == 5);
                              };
   proxy.BeginAdd(2,3,completion,null);
   proxy.Close();
```

Note that the anonymous method sets an outer variable (sum) to provide the result of the Add() operation.

Callback completion methods are by far the preferred model in any event-driven application. An *event-driven* application has methods that trigger events (or requests) and methods that handle these events and fire their own events as a result. Writing an application as event-driven makes it easier to manage multiple threads, events, and callbacks, and allows for scalability, responsiveness, and performance. WCF asynchronous calls management using callback completion methods fits into such an architecture like a hand in a glove. The other options (waiting, blocking, and polling) are available for applications that are strict, predictable, and deterministic in their execution flow. I recommend that you use completion callback methods whenever possible.

Completion callback and thread safety

Because the callback method is executed on a thread from the thread pool, you must provide for thread safety in the callback method and in the object that provides it. This means that you must use synchronization objects and locks to access the member variables of the client. You need to worry about synchronizing between client-side threads and the worker thread from the pool, and, potentially, synchronization between multiple worker threads all calling concurrently into the completion callback method to handle their respective asynchronous call completion. You need to make sure the completion callback method is reentrant and thread-safe.

Passing state information

The last parameter to `Begin<Operation>()` is `asyncState`. The `asyncState` object, known as a *state object*, is provided as an optional container for whatever need you deem fit. The party handling the method completion can access such a container object via the object `AsyncState` property of `IAsyncResult`. Although you can certainly use state objects with any of the other asynchronous call programming models (blocking, waiting, or polling), they are most useful in conjunction with completion callbacks. The reason is simple: in all the other programming models, it is up to you to manage the `IAsyncResult` object, and managing an additional container is not that much of an added liability. When you are using a completion callback, the container object offers the only way to pass in additional parameters to the callback method, whose signature is predetermined.

Example 8-32 demonstrates how you might use a state object to pass an integer value as an additional parameter to the completion callback. Note that the callback must downcast the `AsyncState` property to the actual type.

Example 8-32. Passing an additional parameter using a state object

```
class MyClient : IDisposable
{
   CalculatorClient m_Proxy = new CalculatorClient();

   public void CallAsync()
   {
      int asyncState = 4; //int, for example
      m_Proxy.BeginAdd(2,3,OnCompletion,asyncState);
   }
   void OnCompletion(IAsyncResult result)
   {
      int asyncState = (int)asyncResult.AsyncState;
      Debug.Assert(asyncState == 4);

      int sum = m_Proxy.EndAdd(result);
   }
   void Dispose()
   {
```

Example 8-32. Passing an additional parameter using a state object (continued)

```
      m_Proxy.Close( );
   }
}
```

A common use for the state object is to pass the proxy used for Begin<Operation>( ) instead of saving it as a member variable:

```
class MyClient
{
   public void CallAsync( )
   {
      CalculatorClient proxy = new CalculatorClient( );
      proxy.BeginAdd(2,3,OnCompletion,proxy);
      proxy.Close( );
   }
   void OnCompletion(IAsyncResult result)
   {
      CalculatorClient proxy = asyncResult.AsyncState as CalculatorClient;
      Debug.Assert(proxy != null);

      int sum = proxy.EndAdd(result);
      Debug.Assert(sum == 5);
   }
}
```

Completion callback synchronization context

The completion callback may require some thread(s) affinity, to run in a particular synchronization context. This is especially the case if the completion callback needs to update some UI about the result of the asynchronous invocation. Unfortunately, you must manually marshal the call from the completion callback to the correct synchronization context, using any of the techniques described previously. Example 8-33 demonstrates such a completion callback that interacts directly with its containing form, assuring that the UI update will be on the UI synchronization context.

Example 8-33. Relying on completion callback synchronization context

```
partial class CalculatorForm : Form
{
   CalculatorClient m_Proxy;
   SynchronizationContext m_SynchronizationContext;

   public MyClient()
   {
      InitializeComponent();
      m_Proxy = new CalculatorClient();
      m_SynchronizationContext = SynchronizationContext.Current;
   }
   public void CallAsync(object sender,EventArgs args)
   {
```

Example 8-33. Relying on completion callback synchronization context (continued)

```
      m_Proxy.BeginAdd(2,3,OnCompletion,null);
   }
   void OnCompletion(IAsyncResult result)
   {
      SendOrPostCallback callback = delegate
                                    {
                                       Text = "Sum = " + m_Proxy.EndAdd(result);
                                    };
      m_SynchronizationContext.Send(callback,null);
   }
   public void OnClose(object sender,EventArgs args)
   {
      m_Proxy.Close( );
   }
}
```

One-Way Asynchronous Operations

There is little sense in trying to invoke a one-way operation asynchronously, because one of the main features of asynchronous calls is retrieving and correlating a reply message, and yet no such message is available with a one-way call. If you do invoke a one-way operation asynchronously, End<Operation>( ) will never block, and no exceptions will ever be thrown. If a completion callback is provided for an asynchronous invocation of a one-way operation, the callback is called immediately after returning from Begin<Operation>( ). The only justification for invoking a one way operation asynchronously is to avoid the potential blocking of the one-way call, in which case, you should pass a null for the state object and the completion callback.

Asynchronous Error Handling

Output parameters and return values are not the only elements unavailable at the time an asynchronous call is dispatched: exceptions are missing as well. After calling Begin<Operation>( ), control returns to the client, but it may be some time before the asynchronous method encounters an error and throws an exception, and it may be some time after that before the client actually calls End<Operation>( ). WCF must therefore provide some way for the client to know that an exception was thrown and allow the client to handle it. When the asynchronous method throws an exception, the proxy catches it, and when the client calls End<Operation>( ), the proxy rethrows that exception object, letting the client handle the exception. If a completion callback is provided, WCF calls the callback method immediately after the exception is received. The exact exception thrown is compliant with the fault contract and the exception type, as explained in Chapter 6.

If fault contracts are defined on the service operation contract, the FaultContract attribute should be applied only on the synchronous operations.

Cleaning Up After End<Operation>

Whenever calling Begin<Operation>( ), the returned IAsyncResult has a reference to a single WaitHandle object, accessible via the AsyncWaitHandle property. Calling End<Operation>( ) on that object does not close the handle. Instead, that handle will be closed when the implementing object is garbage-collected. As with any other case of using an unmanaged resource, you have to be mindful about your application-deterministic finalization needs. It is possible (in theory at least), for the application to dispatch asynchronous calls faster than .NET's ability to collect those handles, resulting with a resource leak. To compensate, you can explicitly close that handle after calling End<Operation>( ). For example, using the same definitions as those in Example 8-31:

```
void OnCompletion(IAsyncResult result)
{
    int sum = m_Proxy.EndAdd(result);
    Debug.Assert(sum == 5);
    result.AsyncWaitHandle.Close( );
}
```

Asynchronous Calls and Transactions

Transactions do not mix well with asynchronous calls. First, well-designed transactions are of short duration, yet the main motivation for using asynchronous calls is the latency of the operations. Second, the client's ambient transaction will not flow by default to the service, because the asynchronous operation is invoked on a worker thread, not the client's thread. While it is possible to develop a proprietary mechanism that uses cloned transactions, this is esoteric at best and should be avoided. Finally, when a transaction completes, it should have no leftover activities done in the background that could commit or abort independently of the transaction, and yet this will be the result of spawning an asynchronous operation call from within a transaction. Do not mix transactions with asynchronous calls.

Synchronous Versus Asynchronous Calls

Although it is technically possible to call the same service synchronously and asynchronously, the likelihood that a service will be accessed both ways is low.

The reason is that using a service asynchronously necessitates drastic changes to the workflow of the client, and consequently the client cannot simply use the same execution sequence logic as with the synchronous access. Consider, for example, an online store application. Suppose the client (a server-side object executing a customer request) accesses a Store service, where it places the customer's order details. The Store service uses three well-factored helper services to process the order: Order, Shipment, and Billing. In a synchronous scenario, the Store service calls the Order service to place the order. Only if the Order service succeeds in processing the order (i.e., if the item is available in the inventory) does the Store service call the Shipment service, and only if the Shipment service succeeds does the Store service access the Billing service to bill the customer. This sequence is shown in Figure 8-4.

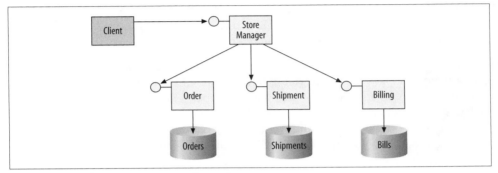

Figure 8-4. Synchronous processing of an order

The downside to the workflow shown in Figure 8-4 is that the store must process orders synchronously and serially. On the surface, it might seem that if the Store service invoked its helper objects asynchronously, it would increase throughput because it could process incoming orders as fast as the client submitted them. The problem in doing so is that it is possible for the calls to the Order, Shipment, and Billing services to fail independently, and if they do then all hell will break loose. For example, the Order service might discover there were no items in the inventory matching the customer request while Shipment service tried to ship the nonexistent item and the Billing service had already billed the customer for it.

Using asynchronous calls on a set of interacting services requires that you change your code and your workflow. To call the helper services asynchronously, the Store service should call only the Order service, which in turn should call the Shipment service only if the order processing was successful (see Figure 8-5), to avoid the potential inconsistencies just mentioned. Similarly, only in the case of successful shipment should the Shipment service asynchronously call the Billing service.

In general, if you have more than one service in your asynchronous workflow, you should have each service invoke the next one in the logical execution sequence. Needless to say, such a programming model introduces tight coupling between services (they have to know about each other) and changes to their interfaces (you have to pass in additional parameters, which are required for the desired invocation of services downstream).

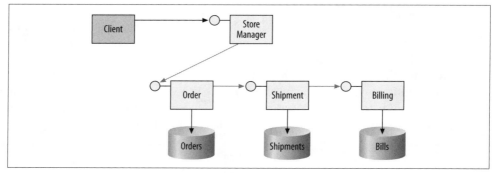

Figure 8-5. Revised workflow for asynchronous processing of an order

The conclusion is that using asynchronous instead of synchronous invocation introduces major changes to the service interfaces and the client workflow. Asynchronous invocation on a service that was built for synchronous execution works only in isolated cases. When dealing with a set of interacting services, it is better to simply spin off a worker thread to call them and use the worker thread to provide asynchronous execution. This will preserve the service interfaces and the original client execution sequence.

CHAPTER 9

Queued Services

WCF enables disconnected work between clients and services. The client posts messages to a queue, and the service processes them. Such interaction enables different possibilities, and in turn a different programming model, from those presented so far. This chapter starts by showing you how to set up and configure simple queued services, and then focuses on aspects such as transactions, instance management, and failures, and their impact on both the business model of the service and its implementation. The chapter ends with my framework for a response service and the HTTP bridge for queued calls over the Internet.

Disconnected Services and Clients

The previous chapters were all predicated on a connected interaction between the client and the service where both sides must to be up and running to be able to interact with each other. However, there are quite a few cases (as well as overall business model justification) for wanting to have disconnected interaction in a service-oriented application.

Availability

The client may need to work against the service even when the client is disconnected; for example, when using a mobile device. The solution is to queue up requests against a local queue, and send them to the service when the client is connected. Much the same way, the service may be offline, perhaps because of network problems. You want to enable clients to continue working against the service even in such a case. When the service is connected again, it can retrieve the pending calls from a queue. Even when both the client and the service are alive and running, the network connectivity may be unavailable, and yet both the client and the service may want to continue with their work. Using queues at both ends will facilitate that.

Disjoint work

Whenever it is possible to decompose a business workflow into several operations (potentially even transactional) that are separated in time, that—is, where each operation must take place, but not necessarily immediately or in a particular order—it is usually a good idea to use queuing because it will improve availability and throughput. You can queue up the operations and have them execute independently of each other.

Compensating work

When your business transaction may take hours or days to complete, you typically split it into at least two transactions. The first queues up the work to be completed immediately, and the second verifies the success of the first and compensates for its failure if necessary.

Load leveling

Load is usually defined as the number of outstanding clients, while *stress* is the number of concurrent calls. If you have a large load, unfettered, it will translate into direct stress on your system. Most systems do not have a constant level of load or stress, as shown in Figure 9-1. If you design the system for the peak load, you will be wasting system resources through most of the load cycle. If you design a system to handle the average load, you will not be able to handle the peak. In a similar manner, you need to examine not just the absolute load level, but also the rate of increase of the load (its first derivative). A sudden spike in load, even if it does not max out your system ability in absolute terms, may still be more than what your system is capable of handling in a timely manner, so responsiveness will be inadequate. With queued calls, the service can simply queue up the excess load and process it at leisure. This enables you to design a system for a nominal average of the desired throughput, as opposed to the maximum load.

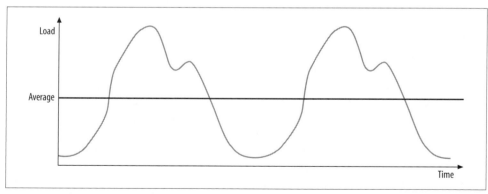

Figure 9-1. Fluctuating load

Queued Calls

WCF provides support for queued calls using the NetMsmqBinding. Instead of transporting the message over TCP, HTTP, or IPC, WCF transports the message over MSMQ. WCF packages the WCF SOAP message into an MSMQ message and posts it to a designated queue. Note that there is no direct mapping of WCF messages to MSMQ messages, just like there is no direct mapping of WCF messages to TCP packets. A single MSMQ message can contain multiple WCF messages, or just a single one, according to the contract session mode, as discussed at length later on. Instead of sending the WCF message to a live service, the client posts the message to an MSMQ queue. All that the client sees and interacts with is the queue, not a service endpoint. As a result, the calls are inherently asynchronous and discounted. The calls will execute later on when the service processes the messages (which makes it asynchronous) and the service or client may interact with local queues (which enables disconnected calls).

Queued Calls Architecture

As with every WCF service, the client interacts with a proxy, as shown in Figure 9-2.

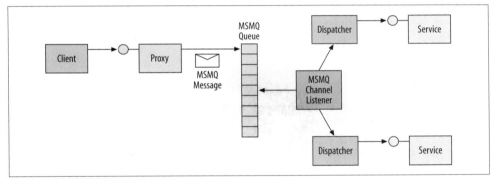

Figure 9-2. Queued calls architecture

However, since the proxy is configured to use the MSMQ binding, it does not send the WCF message to any particular service. Instead, it converts the call (or calls) to an MSMQ message (or messages) and posts it to the queue specified in the endpoint's address. On the service side, when a service host with a queued endpoint is launched, the host installs a queue listener, similar conceptually to the listener associated with a port when using TCP or HTTP. The queue's listener detects there is a message in the queue; it de-queues the message; then it creates the host side's chain of interceptors, ending with a dispatcher. The dispatcher calls the service instance as usual. If multiple messages are posted to the queue, the listener can create new instances as fast as the messages come off the queue, thus ending with asynchronous, disconnected, and concurrent calls.

If the host is offline, messages will simply be pending in the queue. The next time the host is connected, the messages will be played to the service. Obviously, if both the client and the host are alive and running and are connected, then the host will process the calls immediately.

Queued Contracts

A potentially disconnected call made against a queue cannot possibly return any values because no service logic is invoked at the time the message is dispatched to the queue. Not only that, but the call may be dispatched to the service and processed after the client application has shut down, when there is no client available to process the returned values. In much the same way, the call cannot return to the client any service-side exceptions, and there may not be a client around to catch and handle the exception anyway. In fact, WCF disallows using fault contracts on queued operations. Since the client cannot be blocked by invoking the operation, or rather, the client is only blocked for the briefest moment it takes to queue up the message, the queued calls are inherently asynchronous from the client's perspective. All of these are the classic characteristics of one-way calls. Consequently, any contract exposed by an endpoint that uses the NetMsmqBinding can only have one-way operations, and WCF verifies this at the service (and proxy) load time:

```
//Only one-way calls on queued contracts
[ServiceContract]
interface IMyContract
{
   [OperationContract(IsOneWay = true)]
   void MyMethod( );
}
```

Because the interaction with MSMQ is encapsulated in the binding, there is nothing in the service or client invocation code pertaining to the fact that the call is queued. The service and client code look like any other WCF client and service code, as shown in Example 9-1.

Example 9-1. Implementing and consuming a queued service

```
//////////////////////// Service Side ////////////////////////////
[ServiceContract]
interface IMyContract
{
   [OperationContract(IsOneWay = true)]
   void MyMethod( );
}
class MyService : IMyContract
{
   public void MyMethod( )
   {...}
}
```

Example 9-1. Implementing and consuming a queued service (continued)

```
//////////////////////// Client Side ////////////////////////////
MyContractClient proxy = new MyContractClient( );
proxy.MyMethod( );
proxy.Close( );
```

Configuration and Setup

When you define an endpoint for a queued service, the endpoint address must contain the queue's name and designation; that is, the type of the queue. MSMQ defines two types of queues: public and private. *Public queues* require an MSMQ domain controller installation and can be accessed across machine boundaries. Applications in production often require public queues due to the secure and disconnected nature of public queues. *Private queues* are local to the machine they reside on, and do not require a domain controller. Such a deployment of MSMQ is called a *workgroup installation*. During development, and for private queues they set up and administer, developers usually resort to workgroup installation. You designate the queue type (private or public) as part of the queued endpoint address:

```
<endpoint
    address  = "net.msmq://localhost/private/MyServiceQueue"
    binding  = "netMsmqBinding"
    ...
/>
```

In the case of a public queue, you can omit the public designator and have WCF infer the queue type. With private queues, you must include the designator. Also note that there is no $ sign in the queue's type.

Workgroup installation and security

When you're using private queues in a workgroup installation, you must disable MSMQ security on the client and service sides. Chapter 10 discusses how to secure WCF calls, including queued calls. Briefly, the default MSMQ security configuration expects users to present certificates for authentication, and MSMQ certificate-based security requires an MSMQ domain controller. Alternatively, selecting Windows security for transport security over MSMQ requires Active Directory integration, which is not possible with MSMQ workgroup installation. For now, Example 9-2 shows how to disable MSMQ security.

Example 9-2. Disabling MSMQ security

```
<system.serviceModel>
...
    <endpoint name = ...
        address  = "net.msmq://localhost/private/MyServiceQueue"
        binding  = "netMsmqBinding"
        bindingConfiguration = "NoMSMQSecurity"
        contract = "IMyContract"
    />
```

Example 9-2. Disabling MSMQ security (continued)

```
...
   <bindings>
      <netMsmqBinding>
         <binding name = "NoMSMQSecurity">
            <security mode = "None">
            </security>
         </binding>
      </netMsmqBinding>
   </bindings>
</system.serviceModel>
```

Creating the queue

On both the service and the client side, the queue must exist before client calls are
queued up against it. There are several options for creating the queue. The administrator (or the developer, during development) can use the MSMQ control panel
applet to create the queue, but that is a manual step that should be automated. The
host process can use the API of System.Messaging to verify that the queue exists
before opening the host. The class MessageQueue offers the Exists( ) method for verifying that a queue is created, and the Create( ) methods for creating a queue:

```
public class MessageQueue : ...
{
   public static MessageQueue Create(string path);//Nontransactional
   public static MessageQueue Create(string path,bool transactional);
   public static bool Exists(string path);
   public void Purge( );
   //More members
}
```

If the queue is not present, the host process can first create it and then proceed to
open the host. Example 9-3 demonstrates this sequence.

Example 9-3. Verifying a queue on the host

```
ServiceHost host = new ServiceHost(typeof(MyService));

if(MessageQueue.Exists(@".\private$\MyServiceQueue") == false)
{
   MessageQueue.Create(@".\private$\MyServiceQueue",true);
}
host.Open( );
```

In the example, the host verifies against the MSMQ installation on its own machine
that the queue is present before opening the host. If it needs to, the hosting code creates a queue. Not the use of the true value for the transactional queue, as discussed
later on. Note also the use of the $ sign in the queue designation. The obvious prob-
lem with Example 9-3 is that it hardcodes the queue name. It is preferable to read
the queue name from the application config file by storing it in an application setting. But there are additional problems even with that approach. First, you have to

constantly synchronize the queue name in the application settings and in the endpoint's address. Second, you have to repeat this code in every case of a queued service. Fortunately, it is possible to encapsulate and automate the code in Example 9-3 in my ServiceHost<T>, as shown in Example 9-4.

Example 9-4. Creating the queues in ServiceHost<T>

```
public class ServiceHost<T> : ServiceHost
{
   protected override void OnOpening()
   {
      foreach(ServiceEndpoint endpoint in Description.Endpoints)
      {
         QueuedServiceHelper.VerifyQueue(endpoint);
      }
      base.OnOpening();
   }
   //More members
}
public static class QueuedServiceHelper
{
   public static void VerifyQueue(ServiceEndpoint endpoint)
   {
      if(endpoint.Binding is NetMsmqBinding)
      {
         string queue = GetQueueFromUri(endpoint.Address.Uri);
         if(MessageQueue.Exists(queue) == false)
         {
            MessageQueue.Create(queue,true);
         }
      }
   }
   //Parses the queue name out of the address
   static string GetQueueFromUri(Uri uri)
   {...}
}
```

In Example 9-4, ServiceHost<T> overrides the OnOpening( ) method of its base class. This method is being called before opening the host, but after calling the Open( ) method. ServiceHost<T> iterates over the collection of configured endpoints. For each endpoint, if the binding used is NetMsmqBinding—that is, queued calls are expected—ServiceHost<T> calls the static helper class QueuedServiceHelper, passing in the endpoint and asking it to verify the queue. The VerifyQueue( ) method of QueuedServiceHelper parses out of the endpoint's address the queue's name and uses code similar to Example 9-3 to create the queue if needed.

Using ServiceHost<T>, Example 9-3 is reduced to:

```
ServiceHost<MyService> host = new ServiceHost<MyService>();
host.Open();
```

The client too must verify that the queue exists before dispatching calls to it. Example 9-5 shows the required steps on the client side.

Example 9-5. Verifying the queue by the client

```
if(MessageQueue.Exists(@".\private$\MyServiceQueue") == false)
{
   MessageQueue.Create(@".\private$\MyServiceQueue",true);
}
MyContractClient proxy = new MyContractClient();
proxy.MyMethod();
proxy.Close();
```

Yet again, you should not hardcode the queue name and instead read the queue name from the application config file by storing it in an application setting. Yet again, you will face the challenge of constantly keeping the queue name synchronized in the application settings and in the endpoint's address. You can use QueuedServiceHelper directly on the endpoint behind the proxy, but that forces you to create the proxy (or a ServiceEndpoint instance) just to verify the queue. You can extend my QueuedServiceHelper to streamline and support client-side queue verification, as shown in Example 9-6.

Example 9-6. Extending QueuedServiceHelper to verify the queue on the client side

```
public static class QueuedServiceHelper
{
   public static void VerifyQueue<T>(string endpointName) where T : class
   {
      ChannelFactory<T> factory = new ChannelFactory<T>(endpointName);
      VerifyQueue(factory.Endpoint);
   }
   public static void VerifyQueue<T>() where T : class
   {
      VerifyQueue<T>("");
   }
   //Same as Example 9-4
   public static void VerifyQueue(ServiceEndpoint endpoint)
   {...}

   //More members
}
```

Example 9-6 adds two methods to QueuedServiceHelper. The version of the VerifyQueue<T>() method that takes an endpoint name uses the channel factory to read that endpoint from the config file, and then calls the VerifyQueue() method of Example 9-4. The version of VerifyQueue<T>() that takes no arguments uses the default endpoint of the specified contract type from the config file. Using QueuedServiceHelper, Example 9-5 is reduced to:

```
QueuedServiceHelper.VerifyQueue<IMyContract>();

MyContractClient proxy = new MyContractClient();
```

```
proxy.MyMethod( );
proxy.Close( );
```

Note that the client needs to verify the queue for each queued contract.

Queue purging

When the host is launched, it may already have messages in queues, received by MSMQ while the host was offline, and the host will then start processing these messages. Dealing with this very scenario is one of the core features of queued services, enabling you to have disconnected services. While this is exactly the sort of behavior you would like when deploying a queued service, it is typically a hindrance in debugging. Imagine a debug session of a queued service. The client issues a few calls, the service begins processing the first call, and while stepping through the code you notice a defect. You stop debugging, change the service code, and relaunch the host, only to have it process the remaining messages in the queue from the previous debug session, even if those messages break the new service code. Usually, messages from one debug session should not seed the next one. The solution is to programmatically purge the queues when the host shuts down, in debug mode only. You can streamline this with my ServiceHost<T>, as shown in Example 9-7.

Example 9-7. Purging the queues on host shutdown during debugging

```
public static class QueuedServiceHelper
{
   public static void PurgeQueue(ServiceEndpoint endpoint)
   {
      if(endpoint.Binding is NetMsmqBinding)
      {
         string queueName = GetQueueFromUri(endpoint.Address.Uri);
         if(MessageQueue.Exists(queueName) == true)
         {
            MessageQueue queue = new MessageQueue(queueName);
            queue.Purge( );
         }
      }
   }
   //More members
}
public class ServiceHost<T> : ServiceHost
{
   protected override void OnClosing( )
   {
      PurgeQueues( );
      //More cleanup if necessary
      base.OnClosing( );
   }
   [Conditional("DEBUG")]
   void PurgeQueues( )
   {
      foreach(ServiceEndpoint endpoint in Description.Endpoints)
```

Example 9-7. Purging the queues on host shutdown during debugging (continued)

```
      {
          QueuedServiceHelper.PurgeQueue(endpoint);
      }
   }
}
   //More members
}
```

In the example, the `QueuedServiceHelper` class offers the static method `PurgeQueue()`. As its name implies, `PurgeQueue()` accepts a service endpoint. If the binding used by that endpoint is `NetMsmqBinding`, `PurgeQueue()` extracts the queue name out of the endpoint's address, creates a new `MessageQueue` object, and purges it. `ServiceHost<T>` overrides the `OnClosing()` method, which is called when the host shuts down gracefully. It then calls the private `PurgeQueues()` method. `PurgeQueues()` is marked with the `Conditional` attribute, using `DEBUG` as a condition. This means that while the body of `PurgeQueues()` always compiles, its call sites are conditioned on the `DEBUG` symbol. In debug mode only, `OnClosing()` will actually call `PurgeQueues()`. `PurgeQueues()` iterates over all endpoints of the host, calling `QueuedServiceHelper.PurgeQueue()` for each.

 The `Conditional` attribute is the preferred way in .NET for using conditional compilation and avoiding the pitfalls of explicit conditional compilation with `#if`.

Queues, services, and endpoints

WCF requires you to always dedicate a queue per endpoint for each service, meaning, a service with two contracts needs two queues for the two corresponding endpoints:

```
<service name  = "MyService">
   <endpoint
      address  = "net.msmq://localhost/private/MyServiceQueue1"
      binding  = "netMsmqBinding"
      contract = "IMyContract"
   />
   <endpoint
      address  = "net.msmq://localhost/private/MyServiceQueue2"
      binding  = "netMsmqBinding"
      contract = "IMyOtherContract"
   />
</service>
```

The reason is that the client actually interacts with a queue, not a service endpoint, and in fact, there may not even be a service at all, only a queue. Two distinct endpoints cannot share queues because they will get each other's messages. Since the WCF messages in the MSMQ messages will not match, WCF will silently discard those messages it deems invalid, and you will lose the calls. Much the same way, two polymorphic endpoints on two services cannot share a queue, because they will get each other's messages.

Exposing metadata

WCF cannot exchange metadata over MSMQ. Consequently, it is customary even for a service that will always have only queued calls to also expose a MEX endpoint or to enable metadata exchange over HTTP-GET, because the service's clients still need a way to retrieve the service description and bind against it.

Transactions

MSMQ is a WCF transactional resource manager. When you create a queue (either programmatically or administratively), you can create the queue as a transactional queue. If the queue is transactional, then the queue is durable and messages persist to disk. More importantly, posting and removing messages from the queue will always be done under a transaction. If the code that tries to interact with the queue has an ambient transaction, the queue will silently join that transaction. If no ambient transaction is present, MSMQ will start a new transaction for that interaction. It is as if the queue is encased in a `TransactionScope` with `TransactionScopeOption.Required`. Once in a transaction, the queue will commit or roll back along with the accessing transaction. For example, if the accessing transaction posts a message to the queue and then aborts, the queue will reject the message.

Delivery and Playback

When a nontransactional client calls a queued service, client-side failures after the calls will not roll back posting the message to the queue, and the queued call will be dispatched to the service. However, a client calling a queued service may do so under a transaction, as shown in Figure 9-3.

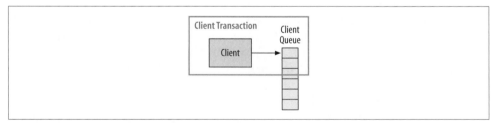

Figure 9-3. Posting to a client-side queue

The client calls are converted to a WCF message (or messages) and then packaged in an MSMQ message (or messages). If the client's transaction commits, these MSMQ messages are posted to the queue and persist there. If the client transaction aborts, the queue discards these MSMQ messages. In effect, WCF provides clients of a queued service with an auto-cancellation mechanism for their asynchronous, potentially disconnected calls. Normal connected asynchronous calls cannot be combined easily, or at all, with transactions, because once the call is dispatched there is no way to recall it in case the original transaction aborts. Unlike connected asynchronous calls, queued services calls are designed for this very transactional scenario. In addition, the client may interact with multiple queued services in the same transaction. Aborting the client transaction due to whatever reason will automatically cancel all calls to those queued services.

Delivery transaction

Since the client may not be on same machine as the service, and since the client, the service, or both could be disconnected, MSMQ maintains a client-side queue as well. The client-side queue serves as a "proxy" to the service-side queue. In the case of a remote queued call, the client first posts the message to the client-side queue. When (or if) the client is connected, MSMQ will deliver the queued messages from the client-side queue to the service-side queue, as shown in Figure 9-4.

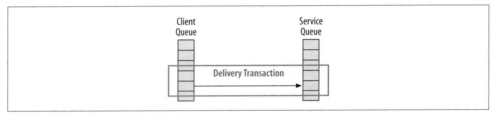

Figure 9-4. The delivery transaction

Since MSMQ is a resource manager, removing the message from the client-side queue will create a transaction (if indeed the queue is transactional). In case MSMQ fails to deliver the message to the service-side queue, for whatever reason (such as a network fault or service machine crash), the message removal from the client-side queue is rolled back, and the message posting to the service-side queue is canceled, resulting in the message being back at the client-side queue, at which point MSMQ tries again to deliver the message. While you could configure and control the failure handling (as you will see later on), excluding fatal errors that can never be resolved, queued services actually enjoy a guaranteed delivery mechanism—if it is technically possible to deliver the message (within the confines of the failure-handling modes), the message will get from the client to the service. In effect, this is WCF's way of providing reliable messaging for queued services. Of course, there is no direct support for the reliable messaging protocol as with connected calls; this is just the analogous mechanism.

Playback transaction

Removing the message by WCF from the queue for playback to the service kick-starts a new transaction (assuming the queue is transactional), as shown in Figure 9-5.

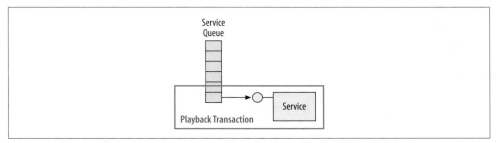

Figure 9-5. Playback transaction

The service is usually configured to participate in the playback transaction. If the playback transaction aborts (usually due to service-side exceptions), the message rolls back to the queue, where WCF detects it and dispatches it again to the service. This in effect yields an auto-retry mechanism. Consequently, you should keep the service processing of the queued call relatively short, or risk aborting the playback transaction.

An important observation here is that it is wrong to equate queued calls with lengthy asynchronous calls. With calls dispatched asynchronously, the service is allowed to take its time processing the call, and usually no client-side transaction is involved. In the case of a queued call, the service processing should not time-out the playback transaction, since that will cause WCF to retry the call, because the service has an incoming transaction.

Service Transaction Configuration

As just demonstrated, in every queued call, assuming transactional queues, there are actually three transactions involved: client, delivery, and playback, as shown in Figure 9-6.

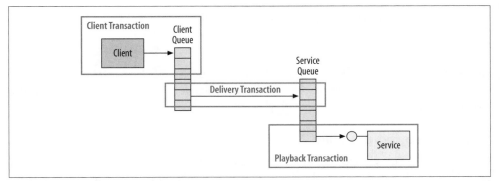

Figure 9-6. Queued calls and transactions

From a design perspective, you rarely, if ever, depict the delivery transaction in your design diagrams and you simply take it for granted. In addition, the service will never participate in the client's transaction, so in effect my four logical transactional modes (Client, Client/Service, Service, None) from Chapter 7 do not apply. If the service contract operation is configured with `TransactionFlowOption.Allowed` and `TransactionFlowOption.NotAllowed`, both of these settings amount to the same result—the client transaction is never provided to the service. Not only that, but `TransactionFlowOption.Mandatory` is disallowed for configuration on a queued contract and it is verified at the service load time. The real question is the relation between the playback transaction and the service transactional configuration.

Participating in playback transaction

From a WCF perspective, the playback transaction is treated as the incoming transaction to the service. To participate in the playback transaction, the service needs to have the operation behavior configured with `TransactionScopeRequired` set to true, as shown in Example 9-8 and graphically in Figure 9-5.

Example 9-8. Participating in the playback transaction

```
[ServiceContract]
interface IMyContract
{
   [OperationContract(IsOneWay = true)]
   void MyMethod( );
}
[ServiceBehavior(InstanceContextMode = InstanceContextMode.PerCall)]
class MyService : IMyContract
{
   [OperationBehavior(TransactionScopeRequired = true)]
   public void MyMethod( )
   {
      Transaction transaction = Transaction.Current;
      Debug.Assert(transaction.TransactionInformation.
               DistributedIdentifier != Guid.Empty);
   }
}
```

An interesting point made in Example 9-8 is that both with MSMQ 3.0 and MSMQ 4.0, every transaction always uses the DTC for transaction management, even in the case of a single service and a single playback.

Ignoring the playback transaction

If the service is configured for not having any transactions (as in Example 9-9 and graphically in Figure 9-7), WCF will still use a transaction to read the message from the queue, except that transaction is always going to succeed (barring an unforeseen failure in MSMQ itself). Exceptions and failures at the service itself will not abort the playback transaction.

Example 9-9. Ignoring the playback transaction

```
[ServiceContract]
interface IMyContract
{
   [OperationContract(IsOneWay = true)]
   void MyMethod( );
}
[ServiceBehavior(InstanceContextMode = InstanceContextMode.PerCall)]
class MyService : IMyContract
{
   public void MyMethod( )
   {
      Transaction transaction = Transaction.Current;
      Debug.Assert(transaction == null);
   }
}
```

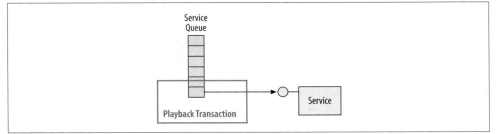

Figure 9-7. Ignoring the playback transaction

Services that do not participate in the playback transaction will not have an auto-mated retry by WCF in the case of a playback failure, and the played-back call could fail while the de-queued transaction commits. The main motivation for configuring services to let go of the benefit of auto-retry is lengthy processing, because by not participating in the playback transaction, the call could take any amount of time to complete.

Using a separate transaction

You can also write the service so that it manually uses a new transaction, as shown in Example 9-10 and graphically in Figure 9-8.

Example 9-10. Using a new transaction

```
[ServiceBehavior(InstanceContextMode = InstanceContextMode.PerCall)]
class MyService : IMyContract
{
   public void MyMethod( )
   {
      using(TransactionScope scope =
                        new TransactionScope(TransactionScopeOption.RequiresNew))
      {
```

Example 9-10. Using a new transaction (continued)

```
        ...
        scope.Complete( );
      }
   }
}
```

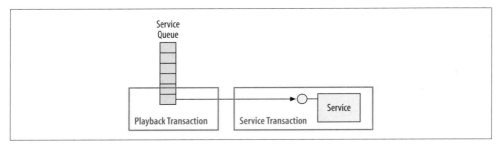

Figure 9-8. Using a new transaction

When the service uses its own new transaction, it should also prevent using the play-back transaction (by defaulting to the `TransactionScopeRequired` value of `false`) so as not to affect the playback transaction in any way. This of course negates the benefit of the auto-retry mechanism. By having a new transaction separate from the play-back transaction, the service is given the opportunity to perform its own transactional work. You would typically configure a service to use its own transaction when the queued operation being called is nice to have and should be performed under the protection of a transaction, yet not retried in case of a failure.

Nondurable Queues

The MSMQ queues described so far were both durable and transactional. The messages persisted to the disk, and posting and reading a message out of the queue was transactional. MSMQ also supports nontransactional volatile queues. Such queues are stored in memory and do not use transactions at all. Because messages are stored in memory, if the machine shuts down or crashes, all messages in the queue are lost. When you create a queue (either using the MSMQ administration tool or programmatically), you can configure it to be transactional or not, and that selection is fixed for the life of the queue. Nondurable queues do not offer any of the benefits of transactional messaging systems such as auto cancellation, guaranteed delivery, and auto-retries. As unadvisable as it is, WCF can work with nondurable queues. `MsmqBindingBase` (the base class of `NetMsmqBinding`) offers the Boolean `Durable` property, which defaults to true.

```
      public abstract class MsmqBindingBase : Binding,...
      {
         public bool Durable
         {get;set;}
         public bool ExactlyOnce
```

```
        {get;set;}
        //More members
    }
    public class NetMsmqBinding : MsmqBindingBase
    {...}
```

When set to `false`, WCF will not use transactions for accessing the queue. Both the client and the service must use the same value for the `Durable` property. The queue itself should be configured to be volatile. When using a volatile queue, if the client transaction aborts, the message or messages will stay in the queue and be delivered to the service. If the playback transaction aborts, the message is lost.

Because of the lack of guaranteed delivery, when using a volatile queue WCF also requires that you set the `ExactlyOnce` property of the binding to `false` (the default is `true`); otherwise, WCF will throw an `InvalidOperationException` at the service load time. Consequently, here is a consistent configuration for a nondurable queue:

```
<netMsmqBinding>
    <binding name ="VolatileQueue" durable = "false" exactlyOnce = "false">
    </binding>
</netMsmqBinding>
```

Instance Management

The contract session mode and the service instance mode have a paramount effect on the behavior of the queued calls, the way the calls are played back to the service, and implications on the overall program workflow and allowed assumptions.

Per-Call Queued Services

In the case of a per-call service, the client has no way of knowing that the calls will eventually end up played to a queued per-call service. All that the client sees is the session mode on the contract. If the `SessionMode` on the contract is either `SessionMode.Allowed` or `SessionMode.NotAllowed`, the queued call (over the `NetMsmqBinding`) is considered to be sessionless. All calls to such sessionless endpoints are placed in separate MSMQ messages, where each call on the proxy yields a single separate MSMQ message.

Nontransactional clients

When a client without an ambient transaction calls a sessionless queued endpoint (as in Example 9-11), the MSMQ messages generated for each call are posted to the queue immediately after each call. If the client has an exception, the messages posted up to that point are not rejected and are delivered to the service.

Example 9-11. Nontransactional client of a sessionless queued endpoint

```
using(TransactionScope scope =
                    new TransactionScope(TransactionScopeOption.Suppress))
```

Example 9-11. Nontransactional client of a sessionless queued endpoint (continued)

```
{
   MyContractClient proxy = new MyContractClient( );

   proxy.MyMethod( );//Message posts to queue here
   proxy.MyMethod( );//Message posts to queue here

   proxy.Close( );
}
```

Transactional clients

With a transactional client (that is, a client code with an ambient transaction) of a sessionless queued endpoint (as in Example 9-12), all messages (corresponding to each call) are posted to the queue when the client's transaction commits. If the client transaction aborts, all messages are rejected from the queue and all calls are canceled.

Example 9-12. Transactional client of a queued sessionless endpoint

```
using(TransactionScope scope = new TransactionScope( ))
{
   MyContractClient proxy = new MyContractClient( );

   proxy.MyMethod( );//Message written to queue
   proxy.MyMethod( );//Message written to queue

   proxy.Close( );
   scope.Complete( );
}//Messages committed to queue here
```

There is no relationship between the proxy and the ambient transaction. If the client uses a transaction scope (as in Example 9-12), the client can close the proxy inside or outside the scope, and may continue to use the proxy even after the transaction or in a new transaction. The client may also close the proxy before or after the call to Complete( ).

Per-call processing

On the host side, the queued calls are dispatched separately to the service, and each call is played to a separate service instance. This is the case even if the service instance mode is per-session. I therefore recommend in the interest of readability that when using a sessionless queued contract, you should always explicitly configure the service as per-call and the contract for disallowing sessions:

```
[ServiceContract(SessionMode = SessionMode.NotAllowed)]
interface IMyContract
{...}

[ServiceBehavior(InstanceContextMode = InstanceContextMode.PerCall)]
class MyService : IMyContract
{...}
```

After each call the service instance is disposed of, just as with a connected per-call service. The per-call service may or may not be transactional, and if it is transactional and the playback transaction is aborted, only that particular call is rolled back to the queue for a retry. As you will see later on, due to the concurrent playback and due to WCF failure-handling behavior, calls to a per-call queued service can execute and complete in whichever order, and the client cannot make any assumptions about call ordering. Note that even calls dispatched by a transactional client may fail or succeed independently. Never assume order of calls with a per-call queued service.

Sessionful Queued Services

To develop and configure a sessionful queued service, the service contract must be configured with SessionMode.Required:

```
[ServiceContract(SessionMode = SessionMode.Required)]
interface IMyContract
{...}

class MyService : IMyContract
{...}
```

When the client queues up calls against a sessionful queued endpoint, all calls made throughout the session are grouped into a single MSMQ message. Once that single message is dispatched and played to the service, WCF creates a new dedicated service instance to handle all the calls in the message. All calls in the message are played back in the original order to that instance. After the last call, the instance is disposed of automatically, since there is no meaning for the client's call to close the proxy. On both the client and the service side, WCF will provide the client and the service with a unique session ID. However, the client session ID will be uncorrelated to that of the service. To approximate the session semantic, all calls on the same instance on the host side will share the same session ID.

Clients and transactions

In the case of a sessionful queued endpoint, the client must have an ambient transaction in order to call the proxy, and a nontransactional client is disallowed, resulting in an InvalidOperationException:

```
[ServiceContract(SessionMode = SessionMode.Required)]
interface IMyContract
{
   [OperationContract(IsOneWay = true)]
   void MyMethod( );
}

using(TransactionScope scope =
                     new TransactionScope(TransactionScopeOption.Suppress))
{
   MyContractClient proxy = new MyContractClient( );
```

```
    proxy.MyMethod( );//Throws InvalidOperationException
    proxy.MyMethod( );

    proxy.Close( );
}
```

In the case of a transactional client of a sessionful queued endpoint, WCF posts a single message to the queue when the transaction commits, and that single message is rejected from the queue if the transaction aborts:

```
using(TransactionScope scope = new TransactionScope( ))
{
    MyContractClient proxy = new MyContractClient( );

    proxy.MyMethod( );
    proxy.MyMethod( );

    proxy.Close( );//Finish composing message, writes to queue

    scope.Complete( );
}//Single message committed to queue here
```

It is important to note that the single message prepared by the proxy must be posted to the queue within the same client transaction—the client must end the session inside the transaction. If the client does not close the proxy before the transaction is complete, the transaction will always abort:

```
MyContractClient proxy = new MyContractClient( );
using(TransactionScope scope = new TransactionScope( ))
{
    proxy.MyMethod( );
    proxy.MyMethod( );

    scope.Complete( );
}//Transaction aborts
proxy.Close( );
```

An interesting side effect of this behavior is that there is no point in storing a proxy to a queued sessionful endpoint in a member variable, because that proxy can only be used once in a single transaction, and cannot be reused across client transactions. The client can only use the proxy inside a single transaction and then close it.

Not only does the client have to close the proxy before the transaction ends, but when using a transaction scope, the client must close the proxy before completing the transaction. The reason is that closing the proxy to a queue's sessionful endpoint requires accessing the current ambient transaction, which is not possible after calling Complete( ). Trying to do so results with InvalidOperationException:

```
MyContractClient proxy = new MyContractClient( );
using(TransactionScope scope = new TransactionScope( ))
{
    proxy.MyMethod( );
    proxy.MyMethod( );
```

```
        scope.Complete();
        proxy.Close(); //Transaction aborts
    }
```

A corollary of this requirement is that you cannot easily stack using statements, because those may result in calling Dispose() in the wrong order, first on the scope, and then on the proxy:

```
    using(MyContractClient proxy = new MyContractClient())
    using(TransactionScope scope = new TransactionScope())
    {
        proxy.MyMethod();
        proxy.MyMethod();

        scope.Complete();

    }//Transaction aborts
```

Services and transactions

A sessionful queued service must be configured to use transactions in all operations by setting TransactionScopeRequired to true. Failing to do so will abort all playback transactions. In addition, the service must provide for transactional affinity to the instance by setting TransactionAutoComplete to false in all but the last operation in the session. Due to a design flaw of WCF, the service cannot rely on setting TransactionAutoCompleteOnSessionClose to true, and must have the last method call in the session complete the transaction, either automatically or manually. Example 9-13 is a template for implementing a queued sessionful service, assuming MyMethod3() is the last operation call in the session.

Example 9-13. Implementing a sessionful queued service

```
[ServiceContract(SessionMode = SessionMode.Required)]
interface IMyContract
{
    [OperationContract(IsOneWay = true)]
    void MyMethod1();

    [OperationContract(IsOneWay = true)]
    void MyMethod2();

    [OperationContract(IsOneWay = true)]
    void MyMethod3();
}

class MyService : IMyContract
{
    [OperationBehavior(TransactionScopeRequired = true,
                       TransactionAutoComplete = false)]
    public void MyMethod1()
    {...}

    [OperationBehavior(TransactionScopeRequired = true,
```

Example 9-13. Implementing a sessionful queued service (continued)

```
                        TransactionAutoComplete = false)]
    public void MyMethod2( )
    {...}
    [OperationBehavior(TransactionScopeRequired = true)]
    public void MyMethod3( )
    {...}
}
```

Obviously, baking into your service code the assumption that a particular method will be the last in the session is often impractical. You can somewhat alleviate this using demarcating operations, and designate the method that terminates the session. Using the same definition as in Example 9-13, you could write:

```
[ServiceContract(SessionMode = SessionMode.Required)]
interface IMyContract
{
    [OperationContract(IsOneWay = true,IsTerminating = false)]
    void MyMethod1( );

    [OperationContract(IsOneWay = true,IsInitiating = false,IsTerminating = false)]
    void MyMethod2( );

    [OperationContract(IsOneWay = true,IsInitiating = false,IsTerminating = true)]
    void MyMethod3( );
}
```

But even that is not a sure cure if the client never calls the terminating operation, in which case the session will abort its transaction. Yet another option is to add an explicit CompleteTransaction( ) operation to the contract whose sole purpose is to complete the transaction and end the session. You need to explicitly document the need to call this method at the end of the session:

```
[ServiceContract(SessionMode = SessionMode.Required)]
interface IMyContract
{
    [OperationContract(IsOneWay = true)]
    void MyMethod1( );

    [OperationContract(IsOneWay = true)]
    void MyMethod2( );

    [OperationContract(IsOneWay = true)]
    void CompleteTransaction( );
}

class MyService : IMyContract
{
    [OperationBehavior(TransactionScopeRequired = true,
                       TransactionAutoComplete = false)]
    public void MyMethod1( )
    {...}
```

```
    [OperationBehavior(TransactionScopeRequired = true,
                       TransactionAutoComplete = false)]
    public void MyMethod2( )
    {...}

    [OperationBehavior(TransactionScopeRequired = true)]
    public void CompleteTransaction( )
    {...}
}
```

That said, avoid a queued sessionful service—it is brittle and introduces coupling.

Singleton Service

A queued transactional singleton service can never have a session and can only implement sessionless contracts. Configuring the SessionMode to either SessionMode.Allowed or SessionMode.NotAllowed has the same result: a sessionless interaction. As a result, I recommend always explicitly configuring the contracts of a queued singleton as sessionless:

```
[ServiceContract(SessionMode = SessionMode.NotAllowed)]
interface IMyContract
{...}

[ServiceBehavior(InstanceContextMode=InstanceContextMode.Single)]
class MyService : IMyContract
{...}
```

A nontransactional queued singleton service behaves like a regular WCF singleton as far as instancing. Regardless of client and proxies, individual calls on the proxies are packaged into separate MSMQ messages and dispatched separately to the singleton, similar to a per-call service. However, unlike the per-call service, all these calls will be played back to the same single instance.

When it comes to a transactional queued singleton, by default it behaves like a per-call service because after every call that completes the transaction, WCF will release the singleton instance. The only difference between a true per-call service and a singleton is that WCF will only allow at most a single instance of the singleton regardless of the number of queued messages. While you could apply the techniques described in Chapter 7 for a state-aware transactional singleton, you can also restore the singleton semantic by setting the ReleaseServiceInstanceOnTransactionComplete property to false. Recall from Chapter 7 that this also constrains the singleton to have at least one operation with TransactionScopeRequired set to true. Example 9-14 shows a template for implementing a transactional queued singleton.

Example 9-14. Transactional queued singleton

```
[ServiceContract(SessionMode = SessionMode.NotAllowed)]
interface IMyContract
{
```

Example 9-14. Transactional queued singleton (continued)

```
    [OperationContract(IsOneWay = true)]
    void MyMethod( );
}

[ServiceBehavior(InstanceContextMode=InstanceContextMode.Single,
                 ReleaseServiceInstanceOnTransactionComplete = false)]
class MySingleton : IMyContract,IDisposable
{
    [OperationBehavior(TransactionScopeRequired = true)]
    public void MyMethod( )
    {...}
    //More members
}
```

 A transactional singleton cannot implement a sessionful contract unless all clients only make a single call in each session, which of course renders the whole idea of a session pointless. The reason for this is that only a per-session service can turn off auto-completion on multiple methods in the same session. Avoid a sessionful transactional queued singleton.

Calls and order

Because the calls are packaged into individual MSMQ messages, the calls may be played in any order to the singleton due to retries and transactions. In addition, calls could also complete in any order, and even calls dispatched by a transactional client may fail or succeed independently. Never assume order of calls with a singleton.

Concurrency Management

As with a connected service, the ConcurrencyMode property governs concurrent play-back of queued messages. With a per-call service, all queued messages are played at once to different instances as fast as they come off the queue, up to the limit of the configured throttle. There is no need to configure for reentrancy to support call-backs, because the operation contexts can never have a callback reference. There is also no need to configure for multiple concurrent access because no two messages will ever share an instance. In short, with a queued per-call service, the concurrency mode is ignored.

When it comes to a sessionful queued service, you are required to configure the ser-vice with ConcurrencyMode.Single. The reason is that it is the only concurrency mode that allows you to turn off auto-complete, which is essential to maintain the session semantic. The calls in the message are always played one at a time to the service instance.

A queued singleton is really the only instancing mode that has any leeway with its concurrency mode. If the singleton is configured with ConcurrencyMode.Single, WCF will retrieve the messages all at once from the queue (up to the thread pool and throttling limits) and then queue up the calls in the internal queue the instance lock maintains. Calls will be dispatched to the singleton one at a time. If the singleton is configured with ConcurrencyMode.Multiple, WCF will retrieve the messages all at once from the queue (up to the thread pool and throttling limits) and play them concurrently to the singleton. Obviously, the singleton must provide for synchronized access to its state. If the singleton is also transactional, it is prone to transactional deadlock over prolonged isolation maintained throughout each transaction. Not only that, but a transactional singleton with ConcurrencyMode.Multiple must have ReleaseServiceInstanceOnTransactionComplete set to false and at least one operation must have TransactionScopeRequired set to true:

```
[ServiceBehavior(InstanceContextMode = InstanceContextMode.Single,
                 ConcurrencyMode = ConcurrencyMode.Multiple,
                 ReleaseServiceInstanceOnTransactionComplete = false)]
class MySingleton : IMyContract
{
    [OperationBehavior(TransactionScopeRequired = true)]
    public void MyMethod( )
    {...}
}
```

Throttling

The throttling of a queued service is your way of controlling the stress of the service and avoiding turning load into stress. The important value to throttle is the number of concurrent playbacks. This is an effective way of throttling the number of played messages because if the number of concurrent calls is exceeded (overall stress) then the maxed-out messages will stay in the queue. For example, if a service has 50 messages in the queue, it may not want to have 50 concurrent instances and worker threads. With a per-call service, the throttle controls the overall number of allowed concurrent instances (and their implied resource consumption). With a per-session service, the throttle controls the number of allowed sessions. In the case of a queued singleton, you can combine a throttled value with ConcurrencyMode.Multiple to control just how many concurrent players are allowed (stress) and how many messages to keep in the queue (buffered load).

Delivery Failures

As discussed in Chapter 6, a connected call may fail both due to communication failures and to service-side errors. Similarly, a queued call can fail due to delivery failure or to service-side playback errors. WCF provides dedicated error-handling mechanisms for both types of errors, and understanding them as well as integrating your error-handling logic with them is an intrinsic part of using queued services.

While MSMQ can guarantee delivery of the message if it is technically possible to do so, there are multiple examples of when it is not possible to deliver the message. These include but are not limited to:

Time out and expiration
> As you will see shortly, each message has a timestamp, and the message has to be delivered and processed within that timeout. Failing to do so will cause the delivery to fail.

Security mismatch
> If the security credentials in the message (or the chosen authentication mechanism itself) do not match up with what the service expects, the service will reject the message.

Transactional mismatch
> The client cannot use a local nontransactional queue while posting a message to a transactional service-side queue.

Network problems
> If the underlying network fails or is simply unreliable, the message may never reach the service.

Machine crashes
> The service machine may crash due to software or hardware failures and will not be able to accept the message to its queue.

Purges
> Even if the message is delivered successfully, the administrator (or any application, programmatically) can purge the messages out of the queue and avoid having the service process them.

Quota breach
> Each queue has a quota controlling the maximum size of data it can hold. If the quota is exceeded, future messages are rejected.

After every delivery failure, the message goes back to the client's queue where MSMQ will continuously retry to deliver it. While in some cases, such as intermediate network failures or quota issues, the retries may eventually succeed, there are many cases where MSMQ will never succeed in delivering the message. In fact, in practical terms, even a large enough number of attempts may be unacceptable and may create a dangerous amount of thrashing. Delivery-failure handling deals with how MSMQ would know it should not retry forever, after how many attempts it should give up, after how long it should give up, and what it should do with the failed messages.

MsmqBindingBase offers a number of properties governing handling of delivery failures:

```
public abstract class MsmqBindingBase : Binding,...
{
   public TimeSpan TimeToLive
   {get;set;}
```

```
//DLQ settings
public Uri CustomDeadLetterQueue
{get;set;}
public DeadLetterQueue DeadLetterQueue
{get;set;}

//More members
}
```

The Dead-Letter Queue

In messaging systems, after an evident failure to deliver, the message goes to a special queue called the dead-letter queue (DLQ). The DLQ is somewhat analogous to a classic dead-letter mailbox at the main post office. In the context of this discussion, failure to deliver constitutes not only failure to reach the service-side queue, but also failure to commit the playback transaction. Note that the service may still fail processing the playback and still commit the playback transaction. MSMQ on the client and on the service side constantly acknowledge to each other receiving and processing messages. If the service-side MSMQ successfully received and retrieved the message from the service-side queue (that is, the playback transaction committed), it sends a positive acknowledgement (ACK) to the client-side MSMQ. The service-side MSMQ can also send a negative acknowledgement (NACK) to the client. When the client-side MSMQ receives a NACK, it posts the message to the DLQ. If the client-side MSMQ receives neither ACK nor NACK, the message is considered in-doubt.

With MSMQ 3.0 (that is, on Windows XP and Windows Server 2003), the dead-letter queue is a system-wide queue. All failed messages from any application go to this single repository. With MSMQ 4.0 (that is, on Windows Vista), you can configure an application-specific DLQ where only messages destined to that specific service go. Application-specific dead-letter queues grossly simplify both the administrator's and the developer's work.

 When dealing with a nondurable queue, failed nontransactional messages go to a special system-wide durable DLQ.

Time to Live

With MSMQ, each message carries a timestamp initialized when the message is first posted to the client-side queue. In addition, every queued WCF message has a timeout, controlled by the TimeToLive property of MsmqBindingBase. After posting a message to the client-side queue, WCF mandates that the message must be delivered and processed in the configured timeout. Note that successful delivery to the service-side queue is not good enough—the call must be processed as well. The TimeToLive property is therefore somewhat analogous to the SendTimeout property of the connected bindings. The TimeToLive property is only relevant to the posting client, and has no affect on the service side, nor can the service change it. `TimeToLive` defaults to one day. After continuously trying and failing to deliver (and process) for as long as `TimeToLive` allows, MSMQ stops trying and moves the message to the configured DLQ.

You can configure the time-to-live value either programmatically or administratively. For example, using a config file, here is how to configure a time to live of five minutes:

```
<bindings>
   <netMsmqBinding>
      <binding name = "ShortTimeout" timeToLive = "00:05:00">
      </binding>
   </netMsmqBinding>
</bindings>
```

The main motivation for configuring a short timeout is dealing with time-sensitive calls that must be processed in a timely manner. However, time-sensitive queued calls go against the grain of disconnected queued calls in general, because the more time-sensitive the calls are, the more questionable the use of queued services is in the first place. The correct way of viewing time to live is as a last-resort heuristic used to eventually bring to the attention of the administrator the fact that the message was not delivered, not as a way to enforce business-level interpretation of the message sensitivity.

Configuring the Dead-Letter Queue

`MsmqBindingBase` offers the `DeadLetterQueue` property of the enum type `DeadLetterQueue`:

```
public enum DeadLetterQueue
{
   None,
   System,
   Custom
}
```

When set to `DeadLetterQueue.None`, WCF makes no use of a dead-letter queue. After a failure to deliver, WCF silently discards the message as if the call never happened. `DeadLetterQueue.System` is the default value of the property. As its name implies, it uses the system-wide DLQ, and after a delivery failure WCF moves the message from the client-side queue to the system-wide DLQ.

When set to `DeadLetterQueue.Custom`, the application can take advantage of a dedicated DLQ. `DeadLetterQueue.Custom` requires the use of MSMQ 4.0, and WCF verifies that at the call time. In addition, WCF requires that the application specify the name of the custom DLQ address in the `CustomDeadLetterQueue` property of the binding. The default value of `CustomDeadLetterQueue` is null, but when `DeadLetterQueue.Custom` is employed, `CustomDeadLetterQueue` cannot be null:

```
<netMsmqBinding>
   <binding name = "CustomDLQ"
      deadLetterQueue = "Custom"
      customDeadLetterQueue = "net.msmq://localhost/private/MyCustomDLQ">
   </binding>
</netMsmqBinding>
```

Conversely, when the `DeadLetterQueue` is set to any other value besides `DeadLetterQueue.Custom`, then `CustomDeadLetterQueue` must be `null`.

It is important to realize that the custom DLQ is just another MSMQ queue. It is up to the client-side developer to also deploy a DLQ service that processes its messages. All WCF does on MSMQ 4.0 is automate the act of moving the message to the DLQ once a failure is detected.

Custom DLQ verification

If a custom DLQ is required, then, like any other queue, it is up to the client to verify at runtime, before issuing queued calls, that the custom DLQ exists and, if necessary, to create it. Following the pattern presented previously, you can automate and encapsulate this with my `QueuedServiceHelper.VerifyQueue()` method, shown in Example 9-15.

Example 9-15. Verifying a custom DLQ

```
public static class QueuedServiceHelper
{
   public static void VerifyQueue(ServiceEndpoint endpoint)
   {
      if(endpoint.Binding is NetMsmqBinding)
      {
         string queue = GetQueueFromUri(endpoint.Address.Uri);
         if(MessageQueue.Exists(queue) == false)
         {
            MessageQueue.Create(queue,true);
         }
         NetMsmqBinding binding = endpoint.Binding as NetMsmqBinding;
         if(binding.DeadLetterQueue == DeadLetterQueue.Custom)
         {
            Debug.Assert(binding.CustomDeadLetterQueue != null);
            string DLQ = GetQueueFromUri(binding.CustomDeadLetterQueue);
            if(MessageQueue.Exists(DLQ) == false)
            {
               MessageQueue.Create(DLQ,true);
            }
         }
      }
   }
   //More members
}
```

Processing the Dead-Letter Queue

The client needs to somehow process the accumulated messages in the DLQ. In the case of the system-wide DLQ, the client can provide a mega-service that supports all contracts of all queued endpoints on the system to enable it to process all failed messages. This is clearly an impractical idea, because that service could not possibly know about all queued contracts, let alone have meaningful processing for all applications. The only feasible way to make this work is to restrict the client side to at most a single queued service per system. Alternatively, you can write a custom application for direct administration and manipulation of the system DLQ using System. Messaging. That application will parse and extract the relevant messages and process them. The problem with that approach (besides the inordinate amount of work involved) is that if the messages are protected and encrypted (as they should be), the application will have a hard time dealing with and distinguishing between them. In practical terms, the only possible solution for a general client-side environment is the one offered by MSMQ 4.0; that is, a custom DLQ. When using a custom DLQ, you also provide a client-side service whose queue is the application's custom DLQ. That service will process the failed messages according to the application-specific requirements.

Defining the DLQ service

Implementing the DLQ service is done like any other queued service. The only requirement is that the DLQ service be polymorphic with the original service's contract. If multiple queued endpoints are involved, you will need a DLQ per contract per endpoint. Example 9-16 shows a possible setup.

Example 9-16. DLQ service config file

```
/////////////////// Client side ///////////////////////
<system.serviceModel>
   <client>
      <endpoint
         address  = "net.msmq://localhost/private/MyServiceQueue"
         binding  = "netMsmqBinding"
         bindingConfiguration = "MyCustomDLQ"
         contract = "IMyContract"
      />
   </client>
   <bindings>
      <netMsmqBinding>
         <binding name = "MyCustomDLQ" deadLetterQueue = "Custom"
            customDeadLetterQueue = "net.msmq://localhost/private/MyCustomDLQ">
         </binding>
      </netMsmqBinding>
   </bindings>
</system.serviceModel>
/////////////////// DLQ service side ///////////////////////
<system.serviceModel>
   <services>
```

Example 9-16. DLQ service config file (continued)

```
      <service name  = "MyDLQService">
        <endpoint
            address  = "net.msmq://localhost/private/MyCustomDLQ"
            binding  = "netMsmqBinding"
            contract = "IMyContract"
        />
      </service>
   </services>
</system.serviceModel>
```

The client config file defines a queued endpoint with the IMyContract contract. The
client uses a custom binding section to define the address of the custom DLQ. A separate queued service (potentially on a separate machine) also supports the
IMyContract contract. The DLQ service uses as its address the DLQ defined by the
client.

Failure properties

The DLQ service typically needs to know why the queued call delivery failed. For
that, WCF offers the MsmqMessageProperty class, used to find out the cause of the failure and the current status of the message. MsmqMessageProperty is defined in the
System.ServiceModel.Channels namespace:

```
public sealed class MsmqMessageProperty
{
   public const string Name = "MsmqMessageProperty";

   public int AbortCount
   {get;internal set;}
   public DeliveryFailure? DeliveryFailure
   {get;}
   public DeliveryStatus? DeliveryStatus
   {get;}
   public int MoveCount
   {get;internal set;}
   //More members
}
```

The DLQ service needs to obtain the MsmqMessageProperty from the operation context's incoming message properties:

```
public sealed class OperationContext : ...
{
   public MessageProperties IncomingMessageProperties
   {get;}
   //More members
}
public sealed class MessageProperties : IDictionary<string,object>,...
{
   public object this[string name]
```

```
      {get;set;}
      //More members
   }
```

When a message is passed to the DLQ, WCF will add to its properties an instance of
`MsmqMessageProperty` detailing the failure. `MessageProperties` is merely a collection of
message properties that you can access using a string as a key. To obtain the
`MsmqMessageProperty`, use the constant `MsmqMessageProperty.Name`, as shown in
Example 9-17.

Example 9-17. Obtaining the MsmqMessageProperty

```
[ServiceContract(SessionMode = SessionMode.NotAllowed)]
interface IMyContract
{
   [OperationContract(IsOneWay = true)]
   void MyMethod( );
}
[ServiceBehavior(InstanceContextMode = InstanceContextMode.PerCall)]
class MyDLQService : IMyContract
{
   [OperationBehavior(TransactionScopeRequired = true)]
   public void MyMethod( )
   {
      MsmqMessageProperty msmqProperty = OperationContext.Current.
   IncomingMessageProperties[MsmqMessageProperty.Name] as MsmqMessageProperty;

      Debug.Assert(msmqProperty != null);
      //Process msmqProperty
   }
}
```

Note in Example 9-17 the practices discussed so far of session mode, instance management, and transactions—the DLQ service is, after all, just another queued service.

The properties of `MsmqMessageProperty` detail the reasons for failure and offer some
contextual information. `MoveCount` is the number of attempts made to play the message to the service. `AbortCount` is the number of attempts made to read the message
from the queue. `AbortCount` is less relevant to recovery attempts, because it falls
under the responsibility of MSMQ and usually is of no concern. `DeliveryStatus` is a
nullable enum of the type `DeliveryStatus` defined as:

```
   public enum DeliveryStatus
   {
      InDoubt,
      NotDelivered
   }
```

`DeliveryStatus` will be set to `DeliveryStatus.InDoubt` unless the message was posi-
tively not delivered (a NACK was received). For example, expired messages are considered in-doubt because their time to live elapsed before the service could
acknowledge them one way or the other.

The DeliveryFailure property is a nullable enum of the type DeliveryFailure defined as follows (without the specific numerical values):

```
public enum DeliveryFailure
{
   AccessDenied,
   NotTransactionalMessage,
   Purged,
   QueueExceedMaximumSize,
   ReachQueueTimeout,
   ReceiveTimeout,
   Unknown
   //More members
}
```

Implementing a DLQ service

The DLQ service cannot affect the message properties, such as extending its time to live. Handling of delivery failures typically involves some kind of compensating transaction: notifying the administrator; trying to resend a new message, or resending a new request with extended timeout; logging the error; or perhaps doing nothing, merely processing the failed call and returning, thus discarding the message.

Example 9-18 demonstrates one such implementation.

Example 9-18. Implementing a DLQ service

```
[ServiceBehavior(InstanceContextMode = InstanceContextMode.PerCall)]
class MyDLQService : IMyContract
{
   [OperationBehavior(TransactionScopeRequired = true)]
   public void MyMethod(string someValue)
   {
      MsmqMessageProperty msmqProperty = OperationContext.Current.
         IncomingMessageProperties[MsmqMessageProperty.Name] as MsmqMessageProperty;
      //If tried more than 25 times: discard message
      if(msmqProperty.MoveCount >= 25)
      {
         return;
      }
      //If timed out: try again
      if(msmqProperty.DeliveryStatus == DeliveryStatus.InDoubt)
      {
         if(msmqProperty.DeliveryFailure == DeliveryFailure.ReceiveTimeout)
         {
            MyContractClient proxy = new MyContractClient();
            proxy.MyMethod(someValue);
            proxy.Close();
         }
         return;
      }
      if(msmqProperty.DeliveryStatus == DeliveryStatus.InDoubt ||
         msmqProperty.DeliveryFailure == DeliveryFailure.Unknown)
```

Example 9-18. Implementing a DLQ service (continued)

```
      {
         NotifyAdmin();
      }
   }
   void NotifyAdmin()
   {...}
}
```

The DLQ service in Example 9-18 examines the cause of the failure. If WCF tries more than 25 times to deliver the message, the DLQ service simply drops the message and gives up. If the cause for the failure was a timeout, the DLQ service tries again by creating a proxy to the queued service and calling it, passing the same arguments from the original call (the in parameters to the DLQ service operation). If the message is in-doubt or unknown failure took place, the service notifies the application administrator.

Playback Failures

Even after successful delivery, the message may still fail during playback to the service. Such failures typically abort the playback transaction, which would cause the message to go back to the service queue. WCF will detect the message in the queue and retry. If the next call fails too, the message will go back again to the queue, and so on. Continuously retrying this way is often unacceptable. If the motivation for the queued service in the first place was load leveling, the auto-retry behavior will generate considerable stress on the service. You need a smart failure-handling schema that deals with the case when the call never succeeds (and of course, defines "never" in practical terms). The failure handling will determine after how many attempts to give up, after how long to give up, and even how often to try. Different systems need different retry strategies, and have different sensitivity to the additional thrashing and probability of success. For example, retrying 10 times, a single retry once every hour, is not the same strategy as retrying 10 times 1 minute apart, or the same as retrying 5 times, each with a batch of 2 successive attempts separated by a day. In addition, once you have given up on retries, what should you do with the failed message and what should you acknowledge to its sender?

Poison Messages

Transactional messaging systems are inherently susceptible to repeated failure because they can bring the system to its knees. Messages that continuously fail playbacks are referred to as *poison messages*, because they literally poison the system with futile retries. Transactional messaging systems must actively detect and eliminate poison messages. Since there is no telling if just one more retry will actually succeed, you can use the following simple heuristic: The more the message fails, the higher the likelihood of failing again. For example, if the message has failed just once, then retrying seems reasonable. If they message has already failed 1,000 times, it is very likely it will fail the 1,001st time, and so it is pointless to try again. What exactly constitutes pointless (or just wasteful) is obviously application-specific, but it is a configurable decision. `MsmqBindingBase` offers a number of properties governing the handling of playback failures:

```
public abstract class MsmqBindingBase : Binding,...
{
    //Poison message handling
    public int ReceiveRetryCount
    {get;set;}

    public int MaxRetryCycles
    {get;set;}

    public TimeSpan RetryCycleDelay
    {get;set;}

    public ReceiveErrorHandling ReceiveErrorHandling
    {get;set;}
    //More members
}
```

Poison Messages Handling in MSMQ 4.0

With MSMQ 4.0 (available on Windows Vista only), WCF retries playing back a failed message in series of batches. WCF provides each queued endpoint with a retry queue and a poison messages queue. After all the calls in the batch have failed, the message does not return to the endpoint queue. Instead, it will go to the retry queue. Once the message is deemed as poisonous, you may have WCF move that message to the poison queue.

Retry batches

In each batch, WCF will immediately retry for `ReceiveRetryCount` times after the first call failure. `ReceiveRetryCount` defaults to five retries, or a total of six attempts, including the first attempt. After a batch has failed, the message goes to the retry queue. After a delay of `RetryCycleDelay` minutes, the message is moved from the retry queue to the endpoint queue for another retry batch. The retry delay defaults to 30 minutes. Once that batch fails, the message goes back to the retry queue, where it will be tried again after the delay has expired. Obviously this cannot go on indefinitely. The `MaxRetryCycles` property controls how many cycles at the most to try. The default of `MaxRetryCycles` is two cycles only. After `MaxRetryCycles` number of retry batches, the message is considered a poison message. When configuring nondefault values for `MaxRetryCycles`, I recommend setting its value in direct proportion to `RetryCycleDelay`. The reason is that the longer the delay is, the more tolerant your system will be for additional retry batches, because the overall stress will be somewhat mitigated, having been spread over a longer period of time. With a short `RetryCycleDelay` you should minimize the number of allowed batches, because you are trying to avoid approximating continuous thrashing.

Finally, the `ReceiveErrorHandling` property governs what to do after the last retry fails and the message is deemed as poisonous. The property is of the enum type `ReceiveErrorHandling`, defined as:

```
public enum ReceiveErrorHandling
{
    Fault,
    Drop,
    Reject,
    Move
}
```

ReceiveErrorHandling.Fault

The `Fault` value considers the poison message as a catastrophic failure. It actively faults the MSMQ channel and the service host. By doing so, the service will not be able to process any other messages, be they from a queued client or a regular connected client. The poison message will remain in the endpoint queue and must be removed from it explicitly by the administrator or by some compensating logic. In order to continue processing client calls of any sort, you must either recycle the hosting process, or open a new host (after you have removed the poison message from the queue). While you could install an error-handling extension (as discussed in Chapter 6) and do some of that work, in practice there is no avoiding involving the application administrator. `ReceiveErrorHandling.Fault` is the default value of the `ReceiveErrorHandling` property. No acknowledgement of any sort is sent to the sender.

ReceiveErrorHandling.Drop

The `Drop` value, as its name implies, silently ignores the poison message by dropping it and having the service keep processing messages. You should configure for `ReceiveErrorHandling.Drop` if you have high tolerance for both errors and retries. If the message is not crucial or it is a nice-to-have service, then dropping and continuing is acceptable. In addition, dropping the message does allow for retries, but conceptually, you should not have too many reties because if you care too much about the message, you should not just drop it after the last failure. Configuring for `ReceiveErrorHandling.Drop` also sends an ACK to the sender, so from the sender's perspective, the message was delivered and processed successfully.

ReceiveErrorHandling.Reject

The `Reject` value actively rejects the poison message and refuses to have anything to do with it. Similar to `ReceiveErrorHandling.Drop`, it drops the message, but it also sends a NACK to the sender, thus signaling ultimate delivery and processing failure. The sender responds by moving the message to the sender's dead-letter queue.

ReceiveErrorHandling.Move

The Move value is probably the best and most practical value of them all. It moves the message to the dedicated poison messages queue, and it does not send back an ACK or a NACK. Acknowledging processing the message will be done after the processing from the poison messages queue.

Configuration sample

Example 9-19 shows a configuration section from the host config file, setting poison message handling on MSMQ 4, and Figure 9-9 illustrates graphically the resulting behavior in the case of a poison message.

Example 9-19. Poison message handling on MSMQ 4

```
<bindings>
   <netMsmqBinding>
      <binding name = "PoisonMessageHandling"
         receiveRetryCount   = "2"
         retryCycleDelay      = "00:05:00"
         maxRetryCycles       = "3"
         receiveErrorHandling = "Move"
      />
   </netMsmqBinding>
</bindings>
```

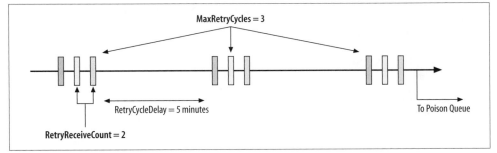

Figure 9-9. Poison message handling of Example 9-19

Poison message service

Your service can provide a dedicated poison message–handling service to handle messages posted to its poison messages queue when the binding is configured with ReceiveErrorHandling.Move. The poison message service must be polymorphic with the service's queued endpoint contract. WCF will retrieve the poison message from the poison queue and play it to the poison service. It is therefore important that the poison service does not throw unhandled exceptions or abort the playback transaction (configuring it to ignore the playback transaction as in Example 9-9 or to use a new transaction as in Example 9-10 is a good idea). Such a poison message service typically engages in some kind of a compensating work associated with the failed message, such as refunding a customer for a missing item in the inventory. Alternatively, a poison service could do any number of things, including notifying the administrator, logging the error, or just ignoring the message altogether by simply returning. The poison message service is developed and configured like any other queued service. The only difference is that the endpoint address must be same as the original endpoint address suffixed by ;poison. Example 9-20 demonstrates the required configuration of a service and its poison message service. In Example 9-20 the service and its poison message service share the same host process, but that is certainly optional.

Example 9-20. Configuring a poison message service

```
<system.serviceModel>
   <services>
      <service name  = "MyService">
         <endpoint
            address = "net.msmq://localhost/private/MyServiceQueue"
            binding = "netMsmqBinding"
            bindingConfiguration = "PoisonMesssageSettings"
            contract = "IMyContract"
         />
      </service>
      <service name = "MyPoisonServiceMessageHandler">
         <endpoint
            address = "net.msmq://localhost/private/MyServiceQueue;poison"
            binding = "netMsmqBinding"
            contract = "IMyContract"
         />
      </service>
   </services>
   <bindings>
      <netMsmqBinding>
         <binding name = "PoisonMesssageSettings"
            receiveRetryCount   = "2"
            retryCycleDelay     = "00:05:00"
            maxRetryCycles      = "3"
            receiveErrorHandling = "Move"
         />
      </netMsmqBinding>
   </bindings>
</system.serviceModel>
```

Poison Message Handling on MSMQ 3.0

With MSQM 3.0 (available on Windows XP and Windows Server 2003), there is no retry queue or a dedicated automatic poison queue. As a result, WCF only supports at most a single retry batch out of the original endpoint queue. After the last failure of the first batch, the message is considered poisonous. WCF therefore behaves as if `MaxRetryCycles` is always set to 1 and the value of `RetryCycleDelay` is ignored. The only values available for the `ReceiveErrorHandling` property are `ReceiveErrorHandling.Fault` and `ReceiveErrorHandling.Drop`. Configuring other values throws an `InvalidOperationException` at the service load time.

Neither `ReceiveErrorHandling.Fault` or `ReceiveErrorHandling.Drop` are attractive options. On MSMQ 3.0, the best way of dealing with a playback failure on the service side (that is, a failure that stems directly from the service business logic as opposed to some communication issue) is to use a response service, as discussed later on.

Queued Versus Connected Calls

Although it is technically possible (with simple changes such as configuring operations as one way, or adding another contract with the one way operations) to use the same service code both connected and queued, in reality it is unlikely that you will actually use the same service both ways. The reasons are similar to the arguments made in the context of asynchronous calls discussed in Chapter 8. Synchronous calls and asynchronous calls addressing the same business scenario often have to use different workflows, and these differences will necessitate changes to the service code to adapt it for each case. The use of queued calls adds yet another barrier for using the same service code (both connected and disconnected): changes to the transactional semantics of the service.

Consider, for example, the application in Figure 9-10, which depicts an online store application that uses connected calls only.

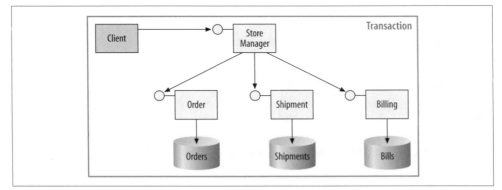

Figure 9-10. A connected application relies on a single transaction

The `Store` service uses three well-factored helper services to process the order: `Order`, `Shipment`, and `Billing`. In the connected scenario, the `Store` service calls the `Order` service to place the order. Only if the Order service succeeds in processing the order (that is, if the item is available in the inventory) does the Store service call the Shipment service, and only if the Shipment service succeeds does the Store service access the Billing service to bill the customer. The connected case involves exactly one transaction created by the client. All operations commit or abort as one atomic operation. Now, suppose the Billing service exposes also a queued endpoint for the use of the Store service, as shown in Figure 9-11.

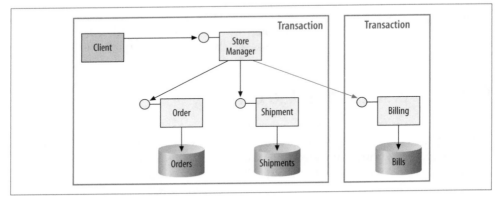

Figure 9-11. A disconnected application relies on multiple transactions

The queued call to the Billing service will be played to the service in a separate transaction from that of the rest of the store, and could also commit or abort separately from the transaction that groups Order and Shipment. This could in turn jeopardize the system consistency, so you must include some logic in the Billing service to detect the failure of the other service and to initiate some compensating logic in case it fails to do its work. As a result, the Billing service will no longer be the same service used in the connected case.

Requiring Queuing

Since not every service can be connected and queued, and since some services may be designed for a particular option and only that option, WCF lets you constrain the communication pattern with such services. The DeliveryRequirements attribute presented in Chapter 1 lets you also insist on a queued or connected delivery of messages to the service:

```
public enum QueuedDeliveryRequirementsMode
{
    Allowed,
    Required,
    NotAllowed
}
[AttributeUsage(AttributeTargets.Interface|AttributeTargets.Class,
                AllowMultiple = true)]
public sealed class DeliveryRequirementsAttribute : Attribute,...
```

```
{
    public QueuedDeliveryRequirementsMode QueuedDeliveryRequirements
    {get;set;}
    public bool RequireOrderedDelivery
    {get;set;}
    public Type TargetContract
    {get;set;}
}
```

The attribute can be used to constrain a contract (and all its supporting endpoints) or
a particular service type. The default value of the QueuedDeliveryRequirements property is QueuedDeliveryRequirementsMode.Allowed, so these definitions are equivalent:

```
[ServiceContract]
interface IMyContract
{...}

[ServiceContract]
[DeliveryRequirements]
interface IMyContract
{...}

[ServiceContract]
[DeliveryRequirements(QueuedDeliveryRequirements =
                     QueuedDeliveryRequirementsMode.Allowed)]
interface IMyContract
{...}
```

QueuedDeliveryRequirementsMode.Allowed grants permission for using the contract or
the service with either connected or queued calls. QueuedDeliveryRequirementsMode.
NotAllowed explicitly disallows the use of the MSMQ binding, and all calls on the
endpoint must therefore be connected calls. Use this value when the contract or the
service is explicitly designed to be used in a connected fashion only. The
QueuedDeliveryRequirementsMode.Required is the opposite—it mandates the use of
the MSMQ binding on the endpoint, and it should be used when the contract or the
service is designed from the group up to be queued.

Note that even though the DeliveryRequirements attribute offers the
RequireOrderedDelivery property (Chapter 1), if QueuedDeliveryRequirementsMode.
Required is used, then RequireOrderedDelivery must be false, because queued calls
inherently are unordered and messages may be played back in any order.

When the DeliveryRequirements attribute is applied on an interface, it affects all services that expose endpoints with that contract:

```
[ServiceContract]
[DeliveryRequirements(QueuedDeliveryRequirements =
                     QueuedDeliveryRequirementsMode.Required)]
interface IMyQueuedContract
{...}
```

The client as well can apply the `DeliveryRequirements` attribute on its copy of the service contract.

When the `DeliveryRequirements` attribute is applied on the service class, it affects all endpoints of that service:

```
[DeliveryRequirements(QueuedDeliveryRequirements =
                      QueuedDeliveryRequirementsMode.Required)]
class MyQueuedService : IMyQueuedContract,IMyOtherContract
{...}
```

When applied on the service class while using the `TargetContract` property, the attribute affects all endpoints of the service that expose the specified contract:

```
[DeliveryRequirements(TargetContract = typeof(IMyQueuedContract),
                      QueuedDeliveryRequirements =
                      QueuedDeliveryRequirementsMode.Required)]
class MyService : IMyQueuedContract,IMyOtherContract
{...}
```

Response Service

The programming model of queued calls described so far was one-sided: the client posted a one-way message to a queue, and the service processed that message. This model is sufficient when the queued operations are one-way calls by design. However, the queued service may need to report back to its client on the result of the invocation, returned results, and even errors. By default, however, this is not possible. WCF equates queued calls with one-way calls, which inherently forbids any such response. In addition, queued services (and their clients) are potentially disconnected. If the client posts a queued call to a disconnected service, when the service finally gets the messages and processes them, there may not be a client to return the values to because the client may be long gone. The solution is to have the service report back to a client-provided queued service. I call such a service a *response service*.* Figure 9-12 shows the architecture of such a solution.

The response service is just another queued service in the system. The response service may be disconnected toward the client as well and may be hosted in a separate process or a separate machine, or it can share the client's process. If the response service shares the client's process, then when the client is launched the response service will start processing the queued responses. Having the response service in a separate process (or even machine) from the client's helps to further decouple lifeline-wise the response service from the client or clients that use it.

---

* I first published my techniques for a response service in *MSDN Magazine*, February 2007.

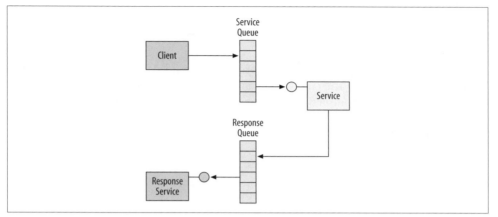

Figure 9-12. A response service

 Not all queued services require a response service, and as you will see, responses add complexity to the system. Be pragmatic, and use a response service only where appropriate; that is, where it adds the most value.

Designing a Response Service Contract

Similar to the use of any WCF service, the client and the service need to agree beforehand on the response contract and what it will be used for, such as for returned values and error information or just returned values. Note that you can also split the response service into two services, and have one response service for results and another for faults and errors. For example, consider the ICalculator contract implemented by the queued MyCalculator service:

```
[ServiceContract]
interface ICalculator
{
   [OperationContract(IsOneWay = true)]
   void Add(int number1,int number2);
   //More operations
}
[ServiceBehavior(InstanceContextMode = InstanceContextMode.PerCall)]
class MyCalculator : ICalculator
{...}
```

The MyCalculator service is required to respond back to its client with the result of the calculation and report on any errors. The result of the calculation is an integer, and the error is in the form of the ExceptionDetail data contract presented in Chapter 6. For the response service, you the ICalculatorResponse contract could be defined as:

```
[ServiceContract]
interface ICalculatorResponse
```

```
    {
        [OperationContract(IsOneWay = true)]
        void OnAddCompleted(int result,ExceptionDetail error);
    }
```

The response service supporting ICalculatorResponse needs to examine the returned error information, notify the client application, the user, or the application administrator on the method completion, and make the results available to the interested parties. Example 9-21 shows a simple response service that supports ICalculatorResponse.

Example 9-21. A simple response service

```
[ServiceBehavior(InstanceContextMode = InstanceContextMode.PerCall)]
class MyCalculatorResponse : ICalculatorResponse
{
    public void OnAddCompleted(int result,ExceptionDetail error)
    {
        MessageBox.Show("result =  " + result,"MyCalculatorResponse");

        if(error != null)
        {
            //Handle error
        }
    }
}
```

Response address and method ID

There are two immediate problems with the implementation of both MyCalculator and MyCalculatorResponse. The first is that the same response service could be used to handle the response (or completion) of multiple calls on multiple queued services, and yet, as listed in Example 9-21, MyCalculatorResponse (and more importantly the clients it serves) has no way of distinguishing between responses. The solution for that is to have the client that issued the original queued call tag the call by associating it with some unique ID, or at least an ID that is unique across that client's application. The queued service MyCalculator needs to pass that ID to the response service MyCalculatorResponse, so that it can apply its custom logic regarding that ID. The second problem is discovering the address of the response service by the queued service. Unlike duplex callbacks, there is no built-in support in WCF for passing the response service reference to the service, so the queued service needs to construct a proxy to the response service and invoke the operations of the response contract. While the response contract is decided upon at design time, and the binding is always NetMsmqBinding (or variations of it as configured), the queued service lacks the address of the response service to be able to respond. While you could place that address in the service host config file (in a client section) such a course of action is to be avoided. The main reason is that the same queued service could be called by multiple clients, each with its own dedicated response service and address. One possible solution is to explicitly pass both the client-managed ID and the desired response service address as parameters to every operation on the queued service contract:

```
[ServiceContract]
interface ICalculator
{
    [OperationContract(IsOneWay = true)]
    void Add(int number1,int number2,string responseAddress,string methodId);
}
```

Much the same way, the queued service could explicitly pass the method ID to the response service as a parameter to every operation on the queued response contract:

```
[ServiceContract]
interface ICalculatorResponse
{
    [OperationContract(IsOneWay = true)]
    void OnAddCompleted(int result,ExceptionDetail error,string methodId);
}
```

Using message headers

While passing the address and the ID as explicit parameters would work, it does distort the original contract, and introduces plumbing-level parameters along business-level parameters in the same operation. A better solution is to have the client store the response address and operation ID in the outgoing message headers of the call. Using the message headers this way is a general-purpose technique for passing out-of-band information to the service, information that is otherwise not present in the service contract.

The operation context offers collections of incoming and outgoing headers, available with the IncomingMessageHeaders and OutgoingMessageHeaders properties:

```
public sealed class OperationContext : ...
{
    public MessageHeaders IncomingMessageHeaders
    {get;}
    public MessageHeaders OutgoingMessageHeaders
    {get;}
    //More members
}
```

Each collection is of the type MessageHeaders—a collection of MessageHeader objects:

```
public sealed class MessageHeaders : IEnumerable<...>,...
{
    public void Add(MessageHeader header);
    public T GetHeader<T>(int index);
    public T GetHeader<T>(string name,string ns);
    //More members
}
```

The class `MessageHeader` is not intended for application developers to interact with directly. Instead, use the `MessageHeader<T>` class, which provides type-safe and easy conversion from a CLR type to a message header:

```
public abstract class MessageHeader : ...
{...}

public class MessageHeader<T>
{
   public MessageHeader();
   public MessageHeader(T content);
   public T Content
   {get;set;}
   public MessageHeader GetUntypedHeader(string name,string ns);
   //More members
}
```

As the type parameter for `MessageHeader<T>` you can use any serializable or data contract type. You can construct a `MessageHeader<T>` around a CLR type, and then use the `GetUntypedHeader()` method to convert it to a `MessageHeader` and store it in the outgoing headers. `GetUntypedHeader()` requires you to provide it with the generic type parameter name and namespace. The name and namespace will be used later on to look up the header from the header collection. You perform the lookup via the `GetHeader<T>()` method of `MessageHeaders`. Calling `GetHeader<T>()` obtains the value of the type parameter of the `MessageHeader<T>` used.

The ResponseContext class

Since the client needs to pass in the message headers both the address and the method ID, a single primitive type parameter will not do. Instead, use my `ResponseContext` class, defined in Example 9-22.

Example 9-22. The ResponseContext class

```
namespace ServiceModelEx
{
   [DataContract]
   public class ResponseContext
   {
      [DataMember]
      public readonly string ResponseAddress;

      [DataMember]
      public readonly string FaultAddress;

      [DataMember]
      public readonly string MethodId;

      public ResponseContext(string responseAddress,string methodId) :
                                      this(responseAddress,methodId,null)
      {}
      public ResponseContext(ResponseContext responseContext) :
```

Example 9-22. The ResponseContext class (continued)

```
                   this(responseContext.ResponseAddress,responseContext.MethodId,
                                            responseContext.FaultAddress)
    {}
    public ResponseContext(string responseAddress) : this(responseAddress,
                                            Guid.NewGuid().ToString())
    {}
    public ResponseContext(string responseAddress,string methodId,
                     string faultAddress)
    {
       ResponseAddress = responseAddress;
       MethodId = methodId;
       FaultAddress = faultAddress;
    }
    //More members
  }
}
```

ResponseContext provides a place to store both the response address and the ID, and, in addition, if the client would like to use a separate response service for faults, ResponseContext also provides a field for the fault response service address. This chapter makes no use of that feature. The client is responsible for constructing an instance of ResponseContext with a unique ID. While the client can supply that ID as a construction parameter, the client could also use the constructor of ResponseContext, which takes just the response address, and have that constructor generate a GUID for the ID.

Client-Side Programming

The client can provide an ID for each method call, even when dealing with a sessionful queued service, by using a different instance of ResponseContext for each call. The client needs to store an instance of ResponseContext in the outgoing message headers. In addition, the client must do so in new operation context, and the client cannot use its existing operation context. This requirement is true for services and non-service clients alike. WCF enables a client to adopt a new operation context for the current thread with the OperationContextScope class, defined as:

```
public sealed class OperationContextScope : IDisposable
{
   public OperationContextScope(IContextChannel channel);
   public OperationContextScope(OperationContext context);
   public void Dispose();
}
```

OperationContextScope is a general technique for spinning a new context when the one you have is inadequate. The constructor of OperationContextScope replaces the current thread's operation context with the new context. Calling Dispose() on the OperationContextScope instance restores the old context (even if it was null). If you do not call Dispose(), that may damage other objects on the same thread that expect the previous context. As a result, `OperationContextScope` is designed to be used inside a `using` statement and provide only a scope of code with a new operation context, even in the face of exceptions; hence its name:

```
using(OperationContextScope scope = new OperationContextScope(...))
{
   //Do work with new context
   ...
}//Restore previous context here
```

When constructing a new `OperationContextScope` instance, you provide its constructor with the inner channel of the proxy used for the call. The client needs to instantiate a new `ResponseContext` object with the response address and ID, add that `ResponseContext` to a message header, create a new `OperationContextScope`, add that header to the outgoing message headers of the new context, and call the proxy. Example 9-23 shows these steps.

Example 9-23. Client-side programming with a response service

```
string methodId = GenerateMethodId();
string responseQueue = "net.msmq://localhost/private/MyCalculatorResponseQueue";
ResponseContext responseContext = new ResponseContext(responseQueue,methodId);

MessageHeader<ResponseContext> responseHeader =
                        new MessageHeader<ResponseContext>(responseContext);

CalculatorClient proxy = new CalculatorClient();
using(OperationContextScope contextScope =
                        new OperationContextScope(proxy.InnerChannel))
{
   OperationContext.Current.OutgoingMessageHeaders.Add(
         responseHeader.GetUntypedHeader("ResponseContext","ServiceModelEx"));

   proxy.Add(2,3);
}
proxy.Close();


//Helper method
string GenerateMethodId()
{...}
```

In Example 9-23, the client uses the helper method `GenerateMethodId()` to generate a unique ID. It then creates a new instance of `ResponseContext` using the response address and the ID for construction parameters. The client uses `MessageHeader<ResponseContext>` to wrap the `ResponseContext` instance with a message header. The client constructs a new proxy to the queued service and uses its inner channel as a construction parameter for a new `OperationContextScope`. The scope is encased in a `using` statement to automatically restore the previous operation context. Inside the new context scope, the client accesses its new operation context, and obtains from it the `OutgoingMessageHeaders` collection. The client calls the

GetUntypedHeader( ) method of the typed header to convert it to a raw `MessageHeader` while providing the name and namespace of the response context, and adds that header to the outgoing headers collection. The client calls the proxy, disposes of the operation context scope, and closes the proxy. The queued message now contains the out-of-band response address and ID. In Example 9-23 you can easily use a channel factory instead of a proxy class, by querying the returned proxy for the context channel to seed the operation context scope:

```
ChannelFactory<ICalculator> factory = new ChannelFactory<ICalculator>("");
ICalculator proxy = factory.CreateChannel( );
using(OperationContextScope contextScope =
                        new OperationContextScope(proxy as IContextChannel))
{...}
```

Service-Side Programming

The queued service accesses its incoming message headers collection and reads from it the response address as well as the method ID. The service needs the address so that it can construct the proxy to the response service, and the ID so that it can provide that ID to the response service. The service usually has no direct use for the ID. The service can use the same technique as the client to pass the method ID to the response service; namely, instead of explicit parameters, use the outgoing message headers to pass the ID out-of-band to the response service. Much like the client, the service too must use a new operation context via `OperationContextScope` in order to be able to modify the outgoing headers collection. The service can programmatically construct a proxy to the response service and provide the proxy with the response address and an instance of `NetMsmqBinding`. The service can even read the binding settings from the config file. Example 9-24 shows these steps.

Example 9-24. Service-side programming with a response service

```
[ServiceBehavior(InstanceContextMode = InstanceContextMode.PerCall)]
class MyCalculator : ICalculator
{
   [OperationBehavior(TransactionScopeRequired = true)]
   public void Add(int number1,int number2)
   {
      int result = 0;
      ExceptionDetail error = null;
      try
      {
         result = number1 + number2;
      }
      //Don't re-throw
      catch(Exception exception)
      {
         error = new ExceptionDetail(exception);
      }
      finally
      {
```

Example 9-24. Service-side programming with a response service (continued)

```
        ResponseContext responseContext =
                        OperationContext.Current.IncomingMessageHeaders.
                GetHeader<ResponseContext>("ResponseContext","ServiceModelEx");

        EndpointAddress responseAddress =
                        new EndpointAddress(responseContext.ResponseAddress);

        MessageHeader<ResponseContext> responseHeader =
                        new MessageHeader<ResponseContext>(responseContext);

        NetMsmqBinding binding = new NetMsmqBinding();
        CalculatorResponseClient proxy =
                        new CalculatorResponseClient(binding,responseAddress);

        using(OperationContextScope scope =
                            new OperationContextScope(proxy.InnerChannel))
        {
            OperationContext.Current.OutgoingMessageHeaders.Add(
              responseHeader.GetUntypedHeader("ResponseContext","ServiceModelEx"));

            proxy.OnAddCompleted(result,error);
        }
        proxy.Close();
    }
  }
}
```

In Example 9-24, the service catches all exceptions thrown by the business logic operation, and wraps that exception with an ExceptionDetail object. The service does not rethrow the exception. As you will see later on in the context of transactions and response services, rethrowing would also cancel the response. Moreover, when using a response service, being able to respond in case of an error is a much better strategy than relying on the WCF playback error-handling.

In the finally statement, regardless of exceptions, the service responds. It accesses its own operation context collection of incoming headers and using the GetHeader<T>() method, it extracts the client-provided response context. Note the use of the name and namespace to look up the response context from the incoming headers collection. The service then constructs a proxy to the response service using the address from the response context and a new instance of NetMsmqBinding. The service uses the proxy's inner channel to seed a new OperationContextScope. Inside the new scope, the service adds to the new context's outgoing headers the same response context it got in (although admittedly it could have just added the ID), and calls the response service proxy, in effect queuing the response. The service then disposes of the context scope and closes the proxy. Sending the entire response context (not just the ID) to the response service is beneficial if the response service has any use for the fault response address.

Response Service–Side Programming

The response service accesses its incoming message headers collection, reads from it the method ID, and responds accordingly. Example 9-25 demonstrates a possible implementation of such a response service.

Example 9-25. Implementing a response service

```
[ServiceBehavior(InstanceContextMode = InstanceContextMode.PerCall)]
class MyCalculatorResponse : ICalculatorResponse
{
   public static event GenericEventHandler<string,int> AddCompleted = delegate{};
   public static event GenericEventHandler<string> AddError = delegate{};

   [OperationBehavior(TransactionScopeRequired = true)]
   public void OnAddCompleted(int result,ExceptionDetail error)
   {
      ResponseContext responseContext =
                            OperationContext.Current.IncomingMessageHeaders.
               GetHeader<ResponseContext>("ResponseContext","ServiceModelEx");

      string methodId = responseContext.MethodId;

      if(error == null)
      {
         AddCompleted(methodId,result);
      }
      else
      {
         AddError(methodId);
      }
   }
}
```

The response service in Example 9-25 provides two public static events, one for completion notification and the other for error notification. The response service invokes these delegates to notify subscribers about completion and errors, respectively. The response service accesses its operation-context incoming headers, and just like the queued service, it extracts out of them the response context and from that the method ID. The response service then invokes the completion delegate, providing the result of the operation and its ID. In the case of an exception, the response service invokes the fault delegate, passing only the method ID.

 A queued response service is not limited to use only with a queued service. You can use the same technique to pass the address and method ID to a connected service and have that service respond to a client-provided queued response service.

Streamlining the Response Service

While the technique shown so far for implementing and consuming a response service certainly works, it is problematic. The problem with the techniques shown in Examples 9-23, 9-24, and 9-25 is that what was supposed to be business-logic service or client code is inundated with low-level WCF programming. Fortunately, it is possible to streamline and encapsulate this technique in helper classes to the point that each participating party can just interact with the other without the plumbing in the open.

The first act is to encapsulate the interaction with the raw message headers by adding the static Current property to ResponseContext:

```
[DataContract]
public class ResponseContext
{
    public static ResponseContext Current
    {get;set;}
    //Rest of the members
}
```

The Current property is listed in Example 9-26.

Example 9-26. The ResponseContext.Current property

```
[DataContract]
public class ResponseContext
{
    public static ResponseContext Current
    {
        get
        {
            OperationContext context = OperationContext.Current;
            if(context == null)
            {
                return null;
            }
            try
            {
                return context.IncomingMessageHeaders.
                       GetHeader<ResponseContext>("ResponseContext","ServiceModelEx");
            }
            catch
            {
                return null;
            }
        }
        set
        {
            OperationContext context = OperationContext.Current;
            Debug.Assert(context != null);
            //Having multiple ResponseContext headers is an error
            bool headerExists = false;
```

Example 9-26. The ResponseContext.Current property (continued)

```
      try
      {

          context.OutgoingMessageHeaders.GetHeader<ResponseContext>
                                      ("ResponseContext","ServiceModelEx");
          headerExists = true;
      }
      catch(MessageHeaderException exception)
      {
       Debug.Assert(exception.Message == "There is not a header with name
                                    ResponseContext and namespace
                                    ServiceModelEx in the message.");
      }
      if(headerExists)
      {
          throw new InvalidOperationException("A header with name ResponseContext
                                      and namespace ServiceModelEx
                                      already exists in the message.");
      }
      MessageHeader<ResponseContext> responseHeader
                                  = new MessageHeader<ResponseContext>(value);
      context.OutgoingMessageHeaders.Add
          (responseHeader.GetUntypedHeader("ResponseContext","ServiceModelEx"));
   }
  }
  //Rest same as Example 9-22.
}
```

The get accessor of Current returns null if the incoming headers do not contain the response context. This enables the queued service to verify if there is anyone to respond to:

```
if(ResponseContext.Current != null)
{
   //Respond here
}
```

Note that the set accessor of Current verifies that no other ResponseContext exists in the outgoing headers collection of the current operation context.

Streamlining the client

To streamline and automate the client's work, you need a proxy base class that encapsulates the response service setup steps of Example 9-23. Unlike with duplex callback, WCF does not provide such a proxy class, so you have to handcraft one. To ease that task I provide the ResponseClientBase<T>, defined as:

```
public abstract class ResponseClientBase<T> : ClientBase<T> where T : class
{
   public readonly string ResponseAddress;

   public ResponseClientBase(string responseAddress);
```

```
      public ResponseClientBase(string responseAddress,string endpointName);
      public ResponseClientBase(string responseAddress,
                            NetMsmqBinding binding,EndpointAddress remoteAddress);
      /* More constructors */
      protected string Enqueue(string operation,params object[] args);
      protected virtual string GenerateMethodId();
   }
```

To use ResponseClientBase<T>, derive a concrete class out of it, and provide for the type parameter the queued contract type. Unlike a normal proxy, do not have the subclass also derive from the contract. Instead, provide a similar set of methods that all return a string for the method ID, not void (this is why you cannot derive from the contract, because the operations on the contract do not return anything—they are all one-way). For example, using this queued service contract:

```
   [ServiceContract]
   interface ICalculator
   {
      [OperationContract(IsOneWay = true)]
      void Add(int number1,int number2);
      //More operations
   }
```

Example 9-27 shows the matching response service aware proxy.

Example 9-27. Deriving from ResponseClientBase<T>

```
class CalculatorClient : ResponseClientBase<ICalculator>
{
   public CalculatorClient(string responseAddress) : base(responseAddress)
   {}
   public CalculatorClient(string responseAddress,string endpointName) :
                                          base(responseAddress,endpointName)
   {}
   public CalculatorClient(string responseAddress,
                        NetMsmqBinding binding,EndpointAddress remoteAddress)
                                   : base(responseAddress,binding,remoteAddress)
   {}
   /* More constructors */

   public string Add(int number1,int number2)
   {
      return Enqueue("Add",number1,number2);
   }
}
```

Using ResponseClientBase<T>, Example 9-23 is reduced to:

```
   string responseAddress = "net.msmq://localhost/private/MyCalculatorResponseQueue";

   CalculatorClient proxy = new CalculatorClient(responseAddress);
   string methodId = proxy.Add(2,3);
   proxy.Close();
```

The virtual method GenerateMethodId( ) of ResponseClientBase<T> uses a GUID for a method ID. Your subclass of ResponseClientBase<T> can override it and provide any other unique string, such as a static incremented integer:

```
class CalculatorClient : ResponseClientBase<ICalculator>
{
    static int m_MethodId = 123;
    protected override string GenerateMethodId( )
    {
        lock(typeof(CalculatorClient))
        {
            int id = ++m_MethodId;
            return id.ToString( );
        }
    }
    //Rest of the implementation
}
```

Example 9-28 shows the implementation of ResponseClientBase<T>.

Example 9-28. Implementing ResponseClientBase<T>

```
public class ResponseClientBase<T> : ClientBase<T> where T : class
{
    public readonly string ResponseAddress;

    public ResponseClientBase(string responseAddress)
    {
        ResponseAddress = responseAddress;
        QueuedServiceHelper.VerifyQueue(Endpoint);
        Debug.Assert(Endpoint.Binding is NetMsmqBinding);
    }
    public ResponseClientBase(string responseAddress,string endpointName)
                                                        : base(endpointName)
    {
        ResponseAddress = responseAddress;
        QueuedServiceHelper.VerifyQueue(Endpoint);
        Debug.Assert(Endpoint.Binding is NetMsmqBinding);
    }
    public ResponseClientBase(string responseAddress,
                        NetMsmqBinding binding,EndpointAddress remoteAddress)
                                                : base(binding,remoteAddress)
    {
        ResponseAddress = responseAddress;
        QueuedServiceHelper.VerifyQueue(Endpoint);
    }
    protected string Enqueue(string operation,params object[] args)
    {
        using(OperationContextScope contextScope =
                                    new OperationContextScope(InnerChannel))
        {
            string methodId = GenerateMethodId( );
            ResponseContext responseContext =
                            new ResponseContext(ResponseAddress,methodId);
```

Example 9-28. Implementing ResponseClientBase<T> (continued)

```
        ResponseContext.Current = responseContext;

        Type contract = typeof(T);
        //Does not support contract hierarchy or overloading
        MethodInfo methodInfo = contract.GetMethod(operation);
        methodInfo.Invoke(Channel,args);

        return responseContext.MethodId;
      }
   }
   protected virtual string GenerateMethodId( )
   {
      return Guid.NewGuid().ToString( );
   }
}
```

The constructors of ResponseClientBase<T> accept the response address and the regular proxy parameters such as endpoint name, address, and binding. The constructors store the response address in a read-only public field. ResponseClientBase<T> derived from a regular ClientBase<T>, and so all constructors delegate to their respective base constructors. In addition, the constructors use my QueuedServiceHelper. VerifyQueue( ) method to verify that the queue (and the DLQ) exists and create it if necessary. The constructors also verify that the binding used for the service endpoint is NetMsmqBinding, because this proxy can only be used with queued calls. The heart of ResponseClientBase<T> is the Enqueue( ) method. Enqueue( ) accepts the name of the operation to invoke (actually queue a message to) and the operation parameters. Enqueue( ) creates a new operation context scope, generates a new method ID, and stores the ID and the response address in a ResponseContext. Then, it assigns the ResponseContext to the outgoing message headers by setting ResponseContext. Current. Enqueue( ) then uses reflection to invoke the provided operation name. Due to the use of reflection and late binding, ResponseClientBase<T> does not support contract hierarchy or overloaded operations. For those, you need manual coding such as in Example 9-23.

If you want to use a queued response service with a connected service (that does not use NetMsmqBinding), rework ResponseClientBase<T> so that it only uses Binding, rename Enqueue( ) to Invoke( ), and avoid asserting the use of a queued call.

Streamlining the queued service

To streamline and automate the work required by the service to extract the response parameters from the headers and respond, I created the ResponseScope<T> class:

```
public class ResponseScope<T> : IDisposable where T : class
{
   public readonly T Response;
```

```
        public ResponseScope( );
        public ResponseScope(string bindingConfiguration);
        public ResponseScope(NetMsmqBinding binding);

        public void Dispose( );
    }
```

ResponseScope<T> is a disposable object—it installs a new operation context, and when it is disposed of, the scope restores the old operation context. To automate that even in the face of exceptions, ResponseScope<T> should be used in a using statement. ResponseScope<T> takes a type parameter representing the response contract, and it offers the Response public, read-only field of the same type. Response is a proxy to the response service, and the clients of ResponseScope<T> use Response to call operations on the response service. There is no need to dispose of Response because ResponseScope<T> does that in Dispose( ). ResponseScope<T> will instantiate Response based on the default endpoint in the config file or using the binding information (the config section name or an actual binding instance) provided to the constructor. Using ResponseScope<T>, the finally statement of Example 9-24 is reduced to:

```
    finally
    {
        using(ResponseScope<ICalculatorResponse> scope
                                = new ResponseScope<ICalculatorResponse>( ))
        {
            scope.Response.OnAddCompleted(result,error);
        }
    }
```

Example 9-29 shows the implementation of ResponseScope<T>.

Example 9-29. Implementing ResponseScope<T>

```
public class ResponseScope<T> : IDisposable where T : class
{
    OperationContextScope m_Scope;

    public readonly T Response;

    public ResponseScope() : this(new NetMsmqBinding( ))
    {}
    public ResponseScope(string bindingConfiguration) :
                                this(new NetMsmqBinding(bindingConfiguration))
    {}
    public ResponseScope(NetMsmqBinding binding)
    {
        ResponseContext responseContext = ResponseContext.Current;

        EndpointAddress address
                        = new EndpointAddress(responseContext.ResponseAddress);

        ChannelFactory<T> factory = new ChannelFactory<T>(binding,address);
        QueuedServiceHelper.VerifyQueue(factory.Endpoint);
```

Example 9-29. Implementing ResponseScope<T> (continued)

```
      Response = factory.CreateChannel( );

      //Switching context now
      m_Scope = new OperationContextScope(Response as IContextChannel);

      ResponseContext.Current = responseContext;
   }
   public void Dispose( )
   {
      IDisposable disposable = Response as IDisposable;
      disposable.Dispose( );
      m_Scope.Dispose( );
   }
}
```

The constructor of ResponseScope<T> uses ResponseContext.Current to extract the incoming response context. It then uses a channel factory to both verify that the response queue exists and to initialize Response with a proxy to the response service. The trick in implementing ResponseScope<T> is using OperationContextScope not inside a using statement. By constructing a new OperationContextScope, ResponseScope<T> establishes a new operation context. ResponseScope<T> encapsulates an OperationContextScope and it saves the newly created OperationContextScope. The old context will be restored once ResponseScope<T> is disposed of in a using statement. ResponseScope<T> then uses ResponseContext. Current to add to the new operation context's outgoing headers the response context and returns.

Streamlining the response service-side

The response service needs to extract the method ID from the incoming message headers. To automate that, simply use ResponseContext.Current. Once you have done so, the OnAddCompleted( ) method of Example 9-25 is reduced to:

```
   public void OnAddCompleted(int result,ExceptionDetail error)
   {
      string methodId = ResponseContext.Current.MethodId;

      if(error == null)
      {
         AddCompleted(methodId,result);
      }
      else
      {
         AddError(methodId);
      }
   }
```

Transactions

A queued service typically queues up the response as part of the incoming playback transaction. Given the queued service definition of Example 9-30, Figure 9-13 depicts the resulting transaction and the participating actions.

Example 9-30. Queuing up a response as part of the playback transaction

```
[ServiceBehavior(InstanceContextMode = InstanceContextMode.PerCall)]
class MyCalculator : ICalculator
{
   [OperationBehavior(TransactionScopeRequired = true)]
   public void Add(int number1,int number2)
   {
      ...
      try
      {
         ...
      }
      catch//Do not re-throw
      {
         ...
      }
      finally
      {
         using(ResponseScope<ICalculatorResponse> scope
                              = new ResponseScope<ICalculatorResponse>())
         {
            scope.Response.OnAddCompleted(...);
         }
      }
   }
}
```

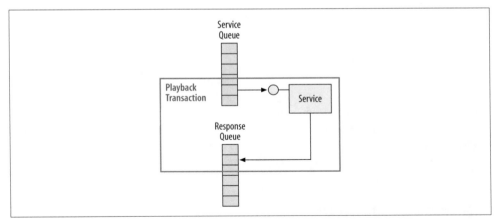

Figure 9-13. Queuing up in the playback transaction

The nice thing design-wise about having the queued call playback and the queued response in the same transaction is that if the playback transaction is aborted for whatever reason (including due to other services in the transaction) the response is canceled automatically. This is by far the common choice for most applications. Note in Example 9-30 that the service catches all exceptions and does not rethrow them. This is important, because any unhandled exception (or rethrown exception) will abort the response, and the service therefore has no point in ever bothering to respond. Using a response service intrinsically means the service does not rely on the automatic retry mechanism of WCF, and it handles its own business logic failures because the clients expect it to respond in a prescribed manner.

Using a new transaction

Alternatively to always having the response be part of the playback transaction, the service can also respond in a new transaction by encasing the response in a new transaction scope, as shown in Example 9-31 and graphically in Figure 9-14.

Example 9-31. Responding in a new transaction

```
[ServiceBehavior(InstanceContextMode = InstanceContextMode.PerCall)]
class MyCalculator : ICalculator
{
   [OperationBehavior(TransactionScopeRequired = true)]
   public void Add(int number1,int number2)
   {
      ...
      finally
      {
         using(TransactionScope transactionScope =
                     new TransactionScope(TransactionScopeOption.RequiresNew))
         using(ResponseScope<ICalculatorResponse> responseScope
                           = new ResponseScope<ICalculatorResponse>())
         {
            scope.Response.OnAddCompleted(...);
         }
      }
   }
}
```

Responding in a new transaction is required in two cases. The first is when the service wants to respond regardless of the outcome of the playback transaction, which could be aborted by other downstream services. The second case is when the response is nice to have, and the service does not mind if the playback transaction commits but the response aborts.

Response service and transactions

Since the response service is just another queued service, the mechanics of managing and participating in a transaction are just like those of any other queued service.

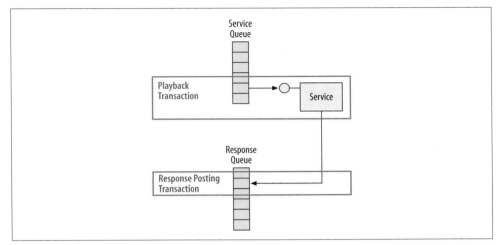

Figure 9-14. Responding in a new transaction

However, there are a few points worth mentioning in this particular context. The response service can process the response as part of the incoming response playback transaction:

```
[ServiceBehavior(InstanceContextMode = InstanceContextMode.PerCall)]
class MyCalculatorResponse : ICalculatorResponse
{
   [OperationBehavior(TransactionScopeRequired = true)]
   public void OnAddCompleted(...)
   {...}
}
```

This is by far the most common option because it allows for retries. That said, the response service should avoid lengthy processing of the queued response because it may risk aborting the playback transaction. The response service can process the response in a separate transaction if the response is nice to have (as far as the provider of the response service in concerned):

```
[ServiceBehavior(InstanceContextMode = InstanceContextMode.PerCall)]
class MyCalculatorResponse : ICalculatorResponse
{
   public void OnAddCompleted(int result,ExceptionDetail error)
   {
      using(TransactionScope scope =
                     new TransactionScope(TransactionScopeOption.RequiresNew))
      {...}
   }
}
```

By processing the response in a new transaction, if that transaction aborts, WCF will not retry the response out of the response service queue. Finally, for response processing of long duration, you could configure the response service not to use a transaction at all (including the playback transaction):

```
[ServiceBehavior(InstanceContextMode = InstanceContextMode.PerCall)]
class MyCalculatorResponse : ICalculatorResponse
{
   public void OnAddCompleted(...)
   {...}
}
```

HTTP Bridge

The MSMQ binding is designed to be employed on the intranet. It cannot go through firewalls by default, and more importantly, it uses a Microsoft-specific encoding and message format. Even if you could tunnel though the firewall, you would need the other party to use WCF. While requiring WCF at both ends is a reasonable assumption on the intranet, it is unrealistic to demand that from Internet-facing clients and services, and it violates a core service-oriented principle that service boundaries are explicit and that the implementation technology used by the service is immaterial to its clients. That said, Internet services may benefit from queued calls just like intranet clients and services, and yet the lack of an industry standard for such queued interoperability (and the lack of support in WCF) prevents such interaction. The solution to that is a technique I call the HTTP bridge. Unlike most of my other techniques shown in this book, the HTTP bridge is a configuration pattern rather than a set of helper classes in a small framework. The *HTTP bridge*, as its name implies, is designed to provide queued calls support when going over the Internet to a service or a client. The bridge requires the use of WSHttpBinding because it is a transactional binding. The bridge has two parts to it. The bridge enables WCF clients to queue up calls to an Internet service that uses the WS binding. The bridge also enables a WCF service that exposes an HTTP endpoint over WS binding to queue up calls from its Internet clients. You can use each part of the bridge separately, or you can use them in conjunction. The bridge can only be used if the remote service contract can be queued (that is, the contract has only one-way operations), but that is usually the case; otherwise the client would not have been interested in the bridge in the first place.

Designing the Bridge

Since you cannot really queue up calls with the WS binding, you would facilitate that instead using an intermediary bridging client and service. When the client wishes to queue up a call against an Internet-based service, the client would queue up a call against a local (that is, intranet-based) queued service called MyClientHttpBridge. The client-side queued bridge service in its processing of the queued call will use the WS binding to call the remote Internet-based service. When an Internet-based service wishes to receive queued calls, it will use a queue. Because that queue cannot be accessed by non-WCF clients over the Internet, the service will use a façade—a dedicated connected service called MyServiceHttpBridge that exposes a WS-binding endpoint. In its processing of the Internet call, MyServiceHttpBridge simply makes a queued call against the local service. Figure 9-15 shows the HTTP bridge architecture.

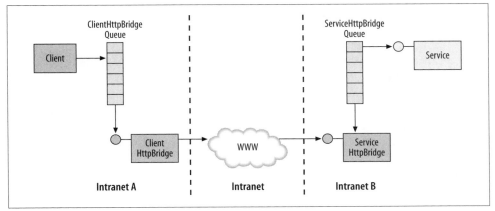

Figure 9-15. The HTTP bridge

Transaction Configuration

It is important to use transactions between MyClientHttpBridge, the client side of the bridge, and the remote service, and it is important to configure the service-side bridge (MyServiceHttpBridge) to use the Client transaction mode of Chapter 7. The rationale is that by using a single transaction from the playback of the client call to the MyClientHttpBridge to the MyServiceHttpBridge (if present) you will approximate the transactional delivery semantic of a normal queued call, as shown in Figure 9-16.

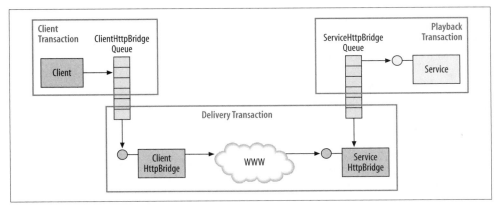

Figure 9-16. The HTTP bridge and transactions

Compare Figure 9-16 with Figure 9-6. If the delivery transaction in the bridge aborts for whatever reason, the message will roll back to the `MyClientHttpBridge` queue for another retry. To maximize the chances for successful delivery, you should also turn on reliability for the call between the `MyClientHttpBridge` and the remote service.

Service-Side Configuration

`MyServiceHttpBridge` converts a regular connected call over the WS binding into a queued call and posts it to the service queue. `MyServiceHttpBridge` implements a similar, but not identical, contract to the queued service. The reason is that the service-side bridge should be able to participate in the incoming transaction, but transactions cannot flow over one-way operations. The solution is to modify the contract to support and even mandate transactions. For example, if this is the original service contract:

```
[ServiceContract]
public interface IMyContract
{
    [OperationContract(IsOneWay = true)]
    void MyMethod( );
}
```

then `MyServiceHttpBridge` should expose this contract instead:

```
[ServiceContract]
public interface IMyContractHttpBridge
{
    [OperationContract]
    [TransactionFlow(TransactionFlowOption.Mandatory)]
    void MyMethod( );
}
```

In essence, you need to set `IsOneWay` to `false` and use `TransactionFlowOption. Mandatory`. For readability's sake, I recommend you also rename the interface by suffixing `HttpBridge` to it. The `MyServiceHttpBridge` can be hosted anywhere in the service's intranet, including the service's own process. Example 9-32 shows the required configuration of the service and its HTTP bridge.

Example 9-32. Service-side configuration of the HTTP bridge

```
//////////////////// MyService Config File ////////////////////////
<services>
   <service name = "MyService">
      <endpoint
         address  = "net.msmq://localhost/private/MyServiceQueue"
         binding  = "netMsmqBinding"
         contract = "IMyContract"
      />
   </service>
</services>
//////////////////// MyServiceHttpBridge Config File ////////////////
```

Example 9-32. Service-side configuration of the HTTP bridge (continued)

```
<services>
   <service name = "MyServiceHttpBridge">
      <endpoint
         address = "http://localhost:8001/MyServiceHttpBridge"
         binding = "wsHttpBinding"
         bindingConfiguration = "ReliableTransactedHTTP"
         contract = "IMyContractHttpBridge"
      />
   </service>
</services>

<client>
   <endpoint
      address = "net.msmq://localhost/private/MyServiceQueue"
      binding = "netMsmqBinding"
      contract = "IMyContract"
   />
</client>

<bindings>
   <wsHttpBinding>
      <binding name = "ReliableTransactedHTTP" transactionFlow = "true">
         <reliableSession enabled = "true"/>
      </binding>
   </wsHttpBinding>
</bindings>
```

The service MyService exposes a simple queued endpoint with IMyContract. The service MyServiceHttpBridge exposes an endpoint with WSHttpBinding and the IMyContractHttpBridge contract. MyServiceHttpBridge is also a client of the queued endpoint defined by the service. Example 9-33 shows the corresponding implementation. Note that MyServiceHttpBridge is configured for Client transaction mode.

Example 9-33. Service-side implementation of the HTTP bridge

```
[ServiceBehavior(InstanceContextMode = InstanceContextMode.PerCall)]
class MyService : IMyContract
{
   //This call comes in over MSMQ
   [OperationBehavior(TransactionScopeRequired = true)]
   public void MyMethod()
   {...}
}

[ServiceBehavior(InstanceContextMode = InstanceContextMode.PerCall)]
class MyServiceHttpBridge : IMyContractHttpBridge
{
   //This call comes in over HTTP
   [OperationBehavior(TransactionScopeRequired = true)]
   public void MyMethod()
   {
```

Example 9-33. Service-side implementation of the HTTP bridge (continued)

```
      MyContractClient proxy = new MyContractClient( );

      //This call goes out over MSMQ
      proxy.MyMethod( );

      proxy.Close( );
   }
}
```

Client-Side Configuration

The client uses queued calls against the local `MyClientHttpBridge` service. The `MyClientHttpBridge` can even be hosted in the same process as the client, or it can be on a separate machine on the client's intranet. `MyClientHttpBridge` uses `WSHttpBinding` to call the remote service. The client needs to retrieve the metadata of the remote Internet service (such as the definition of `IMyContractHttpBridge`) and convert it to a queued contract (such as `IMyContract`). Example 9-34 shows the required configuration of the client and its HTTP bridge.

Example 9-34. Client-side configuration of the HTTP bridge

```
//////////////////////// Client Config File ///////////////////////////
<client>
   <endpoint
      address = "net.msmq://localhost/private/MyClientHttpBridgeQueue"
      binding = "netMsmqBinding"
      contract = "IMyContract"
   />
</client>
//////////////////////// MyClientHttpBridge Config File ////////////////
<services>
   <service name = "MyClientHttpBridge">
      <endpoint
         address = "net.msmq://localhost/private/MyClientHttpBridgeQueue"
         binding = "netMsmqBinding"
         contract = "IMyContract"
      />
   </service>
</services>
<client>
   <endpoint
      address = "http://localhost:8001/MyServiceHttpBridge"
      binding = "wsHttpBinding"
      bindingConfiguration = "ReliableTransactedHTTP"
      contract = "IMyContractHttpBridge"
   />
</client>
<bindings>
   <wsHttpBinding>
      <binding name = "ReliableTransactedHTTP" transactionFlow = "true">
```

Example 9-34. Client-side configuration of the HTTP bridge (continued)

```
          <reliableSession enabled = "true"/>
      </binding>
   </wsHttpBinding>
</bindings>
```

MyClientHttpBridge exposes a simple queued endpoint with IMyContract. MyClientHttpBridge is also a client of the connected WS-binding endpoint defined by the service. Example 9-35 shows the corresponding implementation.

Example 9-35. Client-side implementation of the HTTP bridge

```
MyContractClient proxy = new MyContractClient( );

//This call goes out over MSMQ
proxy.MyMethod( );

proxy.Close( );

////////////////  Client-side bridge implementation ////////////
[ServiceBehavior(InstanceContextMode = InstanceContextMode.PerCall)]
class MyClientHttpBridge : IMyContract
{
   //This call comes in over MSQM
   [OperationBehavior(TransactionScopeRequired = true)]
   public void MyMethod( )
   {
      MyContractHttpBridgeClient proxy = new MyContractHttpBridgeClient( );

      //This call goes out over HTTP
      proxy.MyMethod( );

      proxy.Close( );
   }
}
```

CHAPTER 10

Security

There are several aspects pertaining to secure interaction between a client and a service. Similar to traditional client-server and component-oriented applications, the service needs to authenticate its callers and often also authorize the callers before executing sensitive operations. In addition, regardless of the technology, when securing a service (and its clients) as in any distributed system, you need to secure the messages while en route from the client to the service. Once the messages arrive securely and are authenticated and authorized, the service has a number of options regarding the identity it uses to execute the operation. To these classic security aspects of authentication, authorization, transfer security, and identity management, I add something more abstract, which I call *overall security policy*: that is, your own personal and your company's (or customer's) approach and mindset when it comes to security. This chapter starts by defining the security aspects in the context of WCF and the options available for developers when it comes to utilizing WCF and .NET security. Then, you will see how to secure the canonical and prevailing types of applications. Finally, I will present my declarative security framework that grossly simplifies the need to understand and tweak the many details of WCF security.

Authentication

Authentication is the act of verifying that the caller of a service is indeed who the caller claims to be. While authentication is typically referred to in the context of verification of the caller, from the client perspective there is also a need for service authentication; that is assuring the client that the service it calls really is the service it intends to call. This is especially important with clients who call over the Internet, because if a malicious party subverts the client's DNS service, it could hijack the client's calls. WCF offers various authentication mechanisms:

No authentication
    The service does not authenticate its callers, and virtually all callers are allowed.

Windows authentication

> The service typically uses Kerberos when a Windows Domain Server is available or NTLM when deployed in a workgroup configuration. The caller provides the service with its Windows credentials (such as a ticket or a token) and the service authenticates that against Windows.

Username and password

> The caller provides the service with a username and a password. The service then uses these credentials against some kind of a credentials store, such as Windows accounts or a custom credentials store such as a dedicated table in a database.

X509 certificate

> The client identifies itself using a certificate. Typically, that certificate is known in advance to the service. The service looks up the certificate on the host side and validates it, thus authenticating the client. Alternatively, the service may implicitly trust the issuer of the certificate and hence the client presenting it.

Custom mechanism

> WCF allows developers to replace the authentication mechanism with any protocol and credential type, such as using biometrics. Such custom solutions are beyond the scope of this book.

Issued token

> The caller and the service can both rely on a secure token service to issue the client a token that the service recognizes and trusts. Such a service is typically federated, and encapsulates the act of authenticating and securing the call. Windows CardSpace is an example of such a secure token service. However, federated security and CardSpace are beyond the scope of this book.

Authorization

Authorization deals with what the caller is allowed to do, typically which operations the client is allowed to invoke on the service. Authorizing of the caller is done under the assumption that the caller is indeed who the caller claims to be—in other words, authorization is meaningless without authentication. The service typically relies on some kind of a credentials store where callers are mapped to logical roles. When authorizing an operation, the operation declares or explicitly demands that only certain roles access it. The service needs to look up the caller's role or roles from the store and verify that the caller is a member of the requested roles. Out of the box WCF supports two credentials stores: the service can use Windows groups (and accounts) for authorization, or the service can use an ASP.NET provider (such as the SQL Server provider) to store user accounts and roles. WCF also supports custom role repositories, but I have found that the easiest option by far for implementing a custom store is to implement a custom ASP.NET provider. This chapter will address the ASP.NET providers at length later on.

WCF offers an elaborate and extensible infrastructure for authenticating and authorizing the caller based on a set of claims contained in the message. However, the discussion of this mechanism is beyond the scope of this book.

Transfer Security

Both authentication and authorization deal with two local aspects of security—how (and to what extent) to grant access to the caller once the message was received by the service. In this respect WCF services are not much different from traditional client-server classes. But both authentication and authorization are predicated on secure delivery of the message itself. The *transfer* of the message from the client to the service has to be secure, and without it, both authentication and authorization are moot. Transfer security has three essential aspects to it, and all three aspects must be enforced to provide for secure services. Message *integrity* deals with how to ensure the message itself was not tampered with en route from the client to the service. A malicious party or intermediary could in practice intercept the message and modify its content; for example, providing wrong account numbers in case of a transfer operation in a banking service. Message *privacy* deals with ensuring the confidentiality of message, so that no third party can even read the content of the message. Privacy complements integrity. Without it, even if the malicious party does not tamper with the message, it can still cause harm by gleaning sensitive information such as account numbers from the message. Finally, transfer security must provide for *mutual authentication*; that is, ensuring the client that only the proper service is able to read the context of the message—in other words, that the client connects to the correct service. Once the credentials in the message are received, the service must authenticate the credentials locally. Mutual authentication also needs to detect and eliminate replay attacks and denial of service attacks (DOS). In both cases a malicious party could replay a valid message to the service or even just bogus invalid messages but in such a frequency as to degrade the service's availability.

Transfer Security Modes

WCF supports five different ways of accomplishing the three aspects of transfer security. Choosing the correct transfer security mode is perhaps the prime decision made in the context of securing a service. The five transfer security modes are None, Transport security, Message security, Mixed, and Both.

None transfer security mode

As its name implies, the *None* transfer security mode has transfer security completely turned off. No client credentials are provided to the service, and the message itself is wide open to any malicious party to do with it as it pleases. Obviously, setting transfer security to None is highly unadvisable.

Transport security

When configured for *Transport* security, WCF uses a secure transport. The available secure transports are HTTPS, TCP, IPC, and MSMQ. Transport security encrypts all communication on the channel, and thus provides for integrity, privacy, and mutual authentication. Integrity is provided because without knowing the encryption key, any attempt to modify the message will corrupt it so that it will become useless. Privacy is provided because no party other than the recipient can see the content of the message. Mutual authentication is partly supported because the client's credentials are encrypted along with the rest of the message, and only the intended recipient of the message can read it, so the client need not be concerned with message rerouting to malicious endpoints, as those will not be able to use the message. Once the message is decrypted, the service can read the credentials and authenticate the client.

Transfer security requires the client and the service to negotiate the details of the encryption, but that is done automatically as part of the communication protocol in the respective binding. Transfer security can benefit from hardware acceleration done on the network card so as to avoid burdening the host machine CPU with the encryption and decryption of the messages. Hardware acceleration obviously caters to high throughput and it may even make the security overhead unnoticeable. Transport security is the simplest way of achieving message security and the most performant one. Its main downside it that it can only guarantee transfer security point-to-point, meaning when the client connects directly to the service. Having multiple intermediaries between the client and the service renders transport security questionable, as those intermediaries may not be secure. Consequently, transport security is often used by intranet applications only, where you can ensure a single hop between the client and the service in a controlled environment.

 When configuring any of the HTTP bindings for transport security, WCF verifies at the service load time that the corresponding address on the endpoint uses HTTPS rather than mere HTTP.

Message security

The *Message* transfer security mode simply encrypts the message itself. By encrypting the message, you gain integrity, privacy, and enable mutual authentication for the same reason that transport security provides them when the communication channel is encrypted. However, encrypting the message rather than the transport enables the service to communicate securely over nonsecure transports, such as HTTP. Because of that, message security provides for end-to-end security, regardless of the number of intermediaries involved in transferring the message and regardless of whether or not the transport is secure. In addition, message security is based on a set of industry standards designed for both interoperability and thwarting of common attacks such as replays and DOS, and the support WCF offers is both rich and extensible. The downside of message security is that it may introduce call latency due to its inherit overhead. Message security is typically used by Internet applications, where the call patterns are less chatty and the transport is not necessarily secure.

Mixed transfer security

The *Mixed* transfer security mode uses Transport security for message integrity and privacy as well as service authentication, and it uses Message security for securing the client credentials. The Mixed mode tries to combine the advantages of both Transport and Message security by benefiting from secure transport and even hardware acceleration offered by Transport security to cater to high throughput, and from the extensibility and richer type of client credential types offered by the Message security. The downside of the Mixed mode is that it is only secure point-to-point as a result of the use of Transport security. Application developers rarely need to use the Mixed mode, but it is available for advanced cases.

Both transfer security

As its name implies, the *Both* transfer security mode uses both Transport security and Message security. The message itself is secured using Message security, and then it is transferred to the service over a secure transport. The Both mode maximizes security, yet it may be overkill for most applications, with the exception perhaps of disconnected applications where its additional latency will go unnoticed.

Transfer Security Mode Configuration

Configuring the transfer security mode is done in the binding, and both the client and the service must use the same transfer security mode, and of course comply with its requirements. Like any other binding configuration, you can configure transfer security either programmatically or administratively in a config file. All bindings (with the exception of the peer network binding) offer a construction parameter indicting the transfer security mode, and all bindings offer a Security property with a Mode property identifying the configured mode using a dedicated enumeration. As shown in Table 10-1, not all bindings support all transfer security modes, and the supported modes are driven by the target scenario for the binding.

Table 10-1. Bindings and transfer security modes

Name	None	Transport	Message	Mixed	Both
BasicHttpBinding	Yes (Default)	Yes	Yes	Yes	No
NetTcpBinding	Yes	Yes (Default)	Yes	Yes	No
NetPeerTcpBinding	Yes	Yes (Default)	Yes	Yes	No
NetNamedPipeBinding	Yes	Yes (Default)	No	No	No
WSHttpBinding	Yes	Yes	Yes (Default)	Yes	No

Table 10-1. Bindings and transfer security modes (continued)

Name	None	Transport	Message	Mixed	Both
WSFederationHttpBinding	Yes	No	Yes (Default)	Yes	No
WSDualHttpBinding	Yes	No	Yes (Default)	No	No
NetMsmqBinding	Yes	Yes (Default)	Yes	No	Yes

The intranet bindings (NetTcpBinding, NetNamedPipeBinding, and NetMsmqBinding) all default to Transport security. The reason for that is that the intranet is a relatively secure environment compared with the Internet, and Transport security yields the better performance. Note that the three transport protocols (TCP, IPC, and MSMQ) are also inherently secure transports, and no special programming is required on behalf of the service or client developer. However, the intranet bindings can also be configured for the None transfer mode; that is, they can be used on the same transports, only without security. Note that the NetNamedPipeBinding only supports None and Transport security—there is no sense in using Message security over IPC, since with IPC you have exactly one hop from the client to the service. Also note that only the NetMsmqBinding supports the Both mode.

The Internet bindings all default to Message security, to enable them to be used over nonsecure transports; that is, HTTP. Note that while the WSHttpBinding can be configured for Transport security, the WSDualHttpBinding cannot. The reason is that this binding uses a separate HTTP channel to connect the service to the callback client, and that channel to the client-hosted callback object cannot be easily made to use HTTPS, unlike a service that is likely to be hosted in a real web server.

With one noticeable exception, all of the WCF bindings are configured with some kind of transfer security and are therefore secure by default. Only BasicHttpBinding defaults to having no security. The reason is that the basic binding is designed to make a WCF service look like a legacy ASMX service, and ASMX is unsecured by default. That said, you can and should configure the BasicHttpBinding to use transfer security such as Message security.

Specific bindings configuration

The BasicHttpBinding uses the BasicHttpSecurityMode enum for transfer mode configuration. The enum is available via the Mode property of the Security property of the binding:

```
public enum BasicHttpSecurityMode
{
   None,
   Transport,
   Message,
   TransportWithMessageCredential,
   TransportCredentialOnly
}
```

```
    public sealed class BasicHttpSecurity
    {
        public BasicHttpSecurityMode Mode
        {get;set;}
        //More members
    }
    public class BasicHttpBinding : Binding,...
    {
        public BasicHttpBinding();
        public BasicHttpBinding(BasicHttpSecurityMode securityMode);
        public BasicHttpSecurity Security
        {get;}
        //More members
    }
```

Security is of the type BasicHttpSecurity. One of the constructors of BasicHttpBinding takes the BasicHttpSecurityMode enum as a parameter. To secure the basic binding for Message security, you can either construct it secured or set the security mode post-construction. Consequently, in Example 10-1 binding1 and binding2 are equivalent.

Example 10-1. Programmatically securing the basic binding

```
BasicHttpBinding binding1 = new BasicHttpBinding(BasicHttpSecurityMode.Message);

BasicHttpBinding binding2 = new BasicHttpBinding();
binding2.Security.Mode = BasicHttpSecurityMode.Message;
```

Instead of programmatic settings, you can use a config file as in Example 10-2.

Example 10-2. Administratively securing the basic binding

```
<bindings>
   <basicHttpBinding>
      <binding name = "SecuredBasic">
         <security mode = "Message">
         </security>
      </binding>
   </basicHttpBinding>
</bindings>
```

The rest of the bindings all use their own enumerations and dedicated security classes, yet they are configured just as in Examples 10-1 or 10-2. For example, the NetTcpBinding, NetPeerTcpBinding, and WSHttpBinding all use the SecurityMode enum, defined as:

```
    public enum SecurityMode
    {
        None,
        Transport,
        Message,
        TransportWithMessageCredential//Mixed
    }
```

Not all of these bindings offer a matching constructor parameter, but they all offer a Security property. The `NetNamedPipeBinding` uses the `NetNamedPipeSecurityMode` enum that supports only None and Transport:

```
public enum NetNamedPipeSecurityMode
{
   None,
   Transport
}
```

The `WSDualHttpBinding` uses the enum `WSDualHttpSecurityMode` that supports only None and Message:

```
public enum WSDualHttpSecurityMode
{
   None,
   Message
}
```

The `NetMsmqBinding` uses the `NetMsmqSecurityMode` enum:

```
public enum NetMsmqSecurityMode
{
   None,
   Transport,
   Message,
   Both
}
```

`NetMsmqSecurityMode` is the only enum that offers the Both transfer mode.

The reason that almost every binding has its dedicated enum for security mode is that the designers of WCF security opted for increased safety at the expense of overall complexity. They could have defined just a single all-inclusive enum with values corresponding to all possible transfer security modes, but then it would have been possible at compile time to assign invalid values such as Message security for the `NetNamedPipeBinding` or Transport for the `WSDualHttpBinding`. By opting for specialized enums, configuring security becomes less error-prone, yet there are more moving parts to come to terms with.

Transport Security and Credentials

WCF lets you select from a number of possible client credentials types. The client can identify itself using a classic username and password, or the client can use a Windows security token. Windows credentials can then be authenticated using NTLM or Kerberos when available. The client can use an X509 certificate, or the client can choose to provide no credentials at all and be anonymous. When configuring transfer security as Transport security, not all bindings support all client credential types, as shown in Table 10-2.

Table 10-2. Bindings and transfer security client credentials

Name	None	Windows	Username	Certificate
BasicHttpBinding	Yes (Default)	Yes	Yes	Yes
NetTcpBinding	Yes	Yes (Default)	No	Yes
NetPeerTcpBinding	No	No	Yes (Default)	Yes
NetNamedPipeBinding	No	Yes (Default)	No	No
WSHttpBinding	Yes	Yes (Default)	Yes	Yes
WSFederationHttpBinding	N/A	N/A	N/A	N/A
WSDualHttpBinding	N/A	N/A	N/A	N/A
NetMsmqBinding	Yes	Yes (Default)	No	Yes

Which binding supports which credentials type is largely a product of the target scenario the binding is designed for. For example, all of the intranet bindings default to Windows credentials since they are used in a Windows environment, and the BasicHttpBinding defaults to no credentials, just as with a classic ASMX web service. The WSFederationHttpBinding and WSDualHttpBinding cannot use Transport security at all.

Message Security and Credentials

When it comes to using Message transfer security, WCF lets applications use the same type of credentials as with Transport security, with the addition of the issued token credential type. When configured for Message security, not all bindings support all client credentials types, as shown in Table 10-3.

Table 10-3. Bindings and message security client credentials

Name	None	Windows	Username	Certificate	Issued token
BasicHttpBinding	No	No	No	Yes	No
NetTcpBinding	Yes	Yes (Default)	Yes	Yes	Yes
NetPeerTcpBinding	N/A	N/A	N/A	N/A	N/A
NetNamedPipeBinding	N/A	N/A	N/A	N/A	N/A
WSHttpBinding	Yes	Yes (Default)	Yes	Yes	Yes
WSFederationHttpBinding	N/A	N/A	N/A	N/A	N/A
WSDualHttpBinding	Yes	Yes (Default)	Yes	Yes	Yes
NetMsmqBinding	Yes	Yes (Default)	Yes	Yes	Yes

While it makes sense that all intranet bindings that support Message security will default to Windows credentials, it is interesting to note that the Internet bindings (WSHttpBinding and WSDualHttpBinding) also default to Windows credentials, even though (as discussed later on), Internet applications rarely use Windows credentials over HTTP. The reason for this is to enable developers to securely use these bindings out of the box, without resorting first to custom credentials stores.

 The `BasicHttpBinding` supports username client credentials for message security only with Mixed mode. This might be a source of runtime validation errors since the `BasicHttpMessageCredentialType` enum contains the `BasicHttpMessageCredentialType.UserName` value.

Identity Management

Identity management is the security aspect that deals with which security identity the client sends to service and, in turn, what the service can do with the client's identity. Not only that, but when designing a service, you need to decide in advance which identity the service executes under. The service can execute under its own identity; it can use the client identity (when applicable); or the service can use a mixture, where it will alternate in a single operation between its own identity, the client identity, or even a third identity altogether. Selecting the correct identity has drastic implications on the application scalability and administration cost. In WCF, when enabled, the security identity flows down the call chain, and the service can find out who its caller is, regardless of the identity of the service.

Overall Policy

To the traditional commonplace security aspects of authentication, authorization, transfer security, and identity management, I would like to add one that is less technical and conventional, but to me just as important: what is your business's approach and even your personal approach to security; that is, what is your *security policy*? I believe that in the vast majority of cases, your application simply cannot afford not to be secured. And while security carries with it performance and throughput penalties, these should be of no concern. Simply put, it costs to live. Paying the security penalty is an unavoidable part of designing and administering modern connected applications. Gone are the days when developers could afford not to care about security and deploy applications that relied on the ambient security of the target environment, such as physical security with employees' access cards or firewalls.

Since most developers cannot afford to become full-time security experts (nor should they), the approach I advocate for overall security policy is simple: crank security all the way up until someone complains. If the resulting application performance and throughput is still adequate with the maximum security level, so be it. If the resulting performance is inadequate, only then should you engage in detailed threat analysis to find out what can you trade in security in exchange for performance. My experience is that rarely do you need to actually go this route, and that mostly developers never need to compromise security this way. The security strategies described in this chapter follow my overall security policy. WCF's overall approach to security is very much aligned with my own, and I will explicitly point out the few places it is not, and how to rectify it. With the noticeable exception of the BasicHttpBinding, WCF is secured by default, and even the BasicHttpBinding can easily be secured. All other WCF bindings by default authenticate all callers to the service and rely on transfer security.

Scenario-Driven Approach

Security is by far the most intricate area of WCF. For example, the following list shows the elements that govern security in every WCF operation call:

- Service contract
- Operation contract
- Fault contract
- Service behavior
- Operation behavior
- Host configuration
- Method configuration and code
- Client-side behavior
- Proxy configuration
- Binding configuration

Each of the items on the list may have a dozen or more security-related properties. Obviously, there is an overwhelming number of possible combinations and permutations. In addition, not all combinations are allowed or supported, and not all allowed combinations make sense or are consistent. For example, while technically possible, it does not make sense to use a certificate for client credentials in a homogenous Windows intranet, much like it makes little sense to use Windows accounts in an Internet application. The solution I chose for this book is to focus on a few key scenarios (and slight variations of them) that address the security needs of the majority of applications today.

The scenarios are:

- Intranet application
- Internet application
- Business-to-business application
- Anonymous application
- No security

I will demonstrate how to make the scenarios consistent and secure. In each scenario I will discuss how to support the security aspects of transfer security, authentication, authorization, and identity management. If you need an additional scenario, you can follow my analysis approach to derive the required security aspects and settings.

Intranet Application

The characteristics of the intranet application are that both clients and service use WCF, and that the client and the service are deployed in the same intranet. The clients reside behind the firewall, and you can use Windows-based security for transfer security, authentication, and authorization. You can rely on Windows accounts and groups to store the client's credentials. The intranet scenario addresses a wide range of business applications, from finance to manufacturing to in-house IT applications. The intranet scenario is also the richest scenario of all in the options it offers developers for configuring security. The following section on the intranet scenario will also define the terminology, techniques, and types used in the other scenarios.

Securing the Intranet Bindings

For the intranet scenario, you should use the intranet bindings; namely, `NetTcpBinding`, `NetNamedPipeBinding`, and `NetMsmqBinding`. You can rely on Transport mode for transfer security because the calls are invariably point-to-point. Conveniently, Transport security is the default transfer mode of the intranet bindings (see Table 10-1). For client credentials type, you set the transport client credentials type to Windows, which again is the default (see Table 10-2). You need to configure this on both the client and the service.

Transport security protection level

The three intranet bindings need to be configured for transport security. Each of the three intranet bindings has a configurable protection level, which is the master switch for transport protection. The three protection levels are:

None
> WCF does not protect the message on transfer from the client to the service. Any malicious party can read the content of the message or even alter it.

Signed
> When configured for this protection level, WCF ensures that the message could have come only from an authenticated sender by appending an encrypted checksum to the message. Upon receiving the message, the service calculates the checksum and compares it to the original. If the two do not match, the message is rejected. As a result, the message is impervious to tampering. However, the message content is still visible during the transfer.

Encrypted and Signed
> When configured for this protection level, WCF both signs the message and encrypts its content. Encrypted and Signed provides integrity, privacy, and authenticity.

The Signed protection level is a clear trade-off between a measured degree of security and performance. However, I consider this to be a trade-off to avoid, so you should always opt for the Encrypted and Signed protection level. WCF represents the protection level with the ProtectionLevel enum, defined as:

```
public enum ProtectionLevel
{
   None,
   Sign,
   EncryptAndSign
}
```

Not all Internet bindings default to the same protection level. Both NetTcpBinding and NetNamedPipeBinding default to Encrypted and Signed, yet the NetMsmqBinding defaults to Signed only.

NetTcpBinding configuration

NetTcpBinding takes a construction parameter indicating the desired transfer security mode:

```
public class NetTcpBinding : ...
{
   public NetTcpBinding(SecurityMode securityMode);
   public NetTcpSecurity Security
   {get;}
   //More members
}
```

The Security property of the type NetTcpSecurity contains the transfer mode—Transport or Message—and two respective properties for the specific settings:

```
public sealed class NetTcpSecurity
{
   public SecurityMode Mode
   {get;set;}
   public MessageSecurityOverTcp Message
   {get;}
   public TcpTransportSecurity Transport
   {get;}
}
```

In the intranet security scenario, select Transport security for transfer security and set the values of the Transport property of the type TcpTransportSecurity:

```
public sealed class TcpTransportSecurity
{
   public TcpClientCredentialType ClientCredentialType
   {get;set;}

   public ProtectionLevel ProtectionLevel
   {get;set;}
}
```

The `Transfer` property should be initialized with the client credential type set to Windows using the `TcpClientCredentialType` enum, defined as:

```
public enum TcpClientCredentialType
{
   None,
   Windows,
   Certificate
}
```

The `Transfer` property should have the protection level set to `ProtectionLevel.EncryptAndSign`. Since both settings are the default for this binding, these two declarations are equivalent:

```
NetTcpBinding binding1 = new NetTcpBinding( );

NetTcpBinding binding2 = new NetTcpBinding(SecurityMode.Transport);
binding2.Security.Transport.ClientCredentialType = TcpClientCredentialType.Windows;
binding2.Security.Transport.ProtectionLevel = ProtectionLevel.EncryptAndSign;
```

Or alternatively, using a config file:

```
<bindings>
   <netTcpBinding>
      <binding name = "TCPWindowsSecurity">
         <security mode = "Transport">
            <transport
               clientCredentialType = "Windows"
               protectionLevel = "EncryptAndSign"
            />
         </security>
      </binding>
   </netTcpBinding>
</bindings>
```

For completeness' sake, although not required by the Internet scenario, here is how to configure `NetTcpBinding` for Message security with username client credentials:

```
public enum MessageCredentialType
{
   None,
   Windows,
   UserName,
   Certificate,
   IssuedToken
}
public sealed class MessageSecurityOverTcp
{
   public MessageCredentialType ClientCredentialType
   {get;set;}
   //More members
}
NetTcpBinding binding = new NetTcpBinding(SecurityMode.Message);
binding.Security.Message.ClientCredentialType = MessageCredentialType.UserName;
```

NetTcpSecurity offers the Message property of the type MessageSecurityOverTcp. You need to set the credentials type using the MessageCredentialType enum. Most bindings use the MessageCredentialType enum for representing Message security client credentials.

Figure 10-1 shows the security-related elements of the NetTcpBinding.

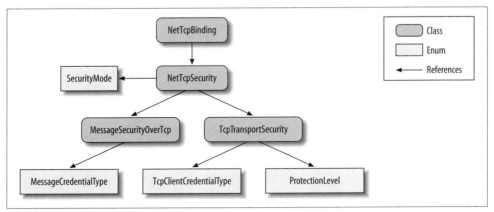

Figure 10-1. NetTcpBinding and security

NetTcpBinding has a reference to NetTcpSecurity, which uses the SecurityMode enum to indicate the transfer security mode. When Transport security is used, NetTcpSecurity will use an instance of TcpTransportSecurity containing the client credential type via the TcpClientCredentialType enum, and the configured protection level via the ProtectionLevel enum. When Message security is used, NetTcpSecurity will use an instance of MessageSecurityOverTcp containing the client credential type via the MessageCredentialType enum.

NetNamedPipeBinding configuration

NetNamedPipeBinding takes a construction parameter indicating the desired transfer security mode:

```
public class NetNamedPipeBinding : Binding,...
{
   public NetNamedPipeBinding(NetNamedPipeSecurityMode securityMode);

   public NetNamedPipeSecurity Security
   {get;}
   //More members
}
```

The Security property of the type NetNamedPipeSecurity contains the transfer mode, Transport or None, and a single property with the specific Transport settings:

```
public sealed class NetNamedPipeSecurity
{
   public NetNamedPipeSecurityMode Mode
```

```
      {get;set;}
      public NamedPipeTransportSecurity Transport
      {get;}
   }
```

For the intranet security scenario, select Transport security for transfer security, and set the values of the Transport property of the type NamedPipeTransportSecurity:

```
   public sealed class NamedPipeTransportSecurity
   {
      public ProtectionLevel ProtectionLevel
      {get;set;}
   }
```

The Transfer property should be initialized with the protection level set to ProtectionLevel.EncryptAndSign. Because this is the default for the binding, these two declarations are equivalent:

```
   NetNamedPipeBinding binding1 = new NetNamedPipeBinding();

   NetNamedPipeBinding binding2 = new NetNamedPipeBinding(
                                           NetNamedPipeSecurityMode.Transport);
   binding2.Security.Transport.ProtectionLevel = ProtectionLevel.EncryptAndSign;
```

Or alternatively, using a config file:

```
   <bindings>
      <netNamedPipeBinding>
         <binding name = "IPCWindowsSecurity">
            <security mode = "Transport">
               <transport protectionLevel = "EncryptAndSign"/>
            </security>
         </binding>
      </netNamedPipeBinding>
   </bindings>
```

There is no need (or option) to set the client credentials type since only Windows credentials are supported (see Table 10-2). Figure 10-2 shows the security-related elements of the NetNamedPipeBinding.

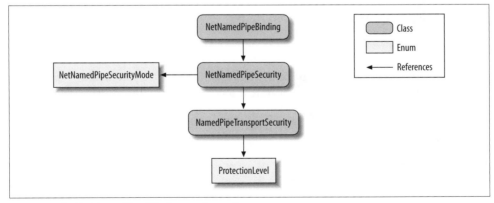

Figure 10-2. NetNamedPipeBinding and security

NetNamedPipeBinding has a reference to NetNamedPipeSecurity, which uses the NetNamedPipeSecurityMode enum to indicate the transfer security mode. When Transport security is used, NetTcpSecurity will use an instance of NamedPipeTransportSecurity containing the configured protection level via the ProtectionLevel enum.

NetMsmqBinding configuration

NetMsmqBinding offers a construction parameter for the transfer security mode and a Security property:

```
public class NetMsmqBinding : MsmqBindingBase,...
{
   public NetMsmqBinding(NetMsmqSecurityMode securityMode);
   public NetMsmqSecurity Security
   {get;}
   //More members
}
```

The Security property of the type NetMsmqSecurity contains the transfer mode, Transport or Message, and two respective properties with the specific settings:

```
public sealed class NetMsmqSecurity
{
   public NetMsmqSecurityMode Mode
   {get;set;}
   public MsmqTransportSecurity Transport
   {get;}
   public MessageSecurityOverMsmq Message
   {get;}
}
```

For the intranet security scenario, select transfer security for Transport security and set the values of the Transport property of the type MsmqTransportSecurity:

```
public sealed class MsmqTransportSecurity
{
   public MsmqAuthenticationMode MsmqAuthenticationMode
   {get;set;}
   public ProtectionLevel MsmqProtectionLevel
   {get;set;}
   //More members
}
```

The Transfer property should be initialized with the client credential type set to Windows domain using the MsmqAuthenticationMode enum:

```
public enum MsmqAuthenticationMode
{
   None,
   WindowsDomain,
   Certificate
}
```

Windows domain is the default credentials type. In addition, you need to set the protection level to `ProtectionLevel.EncryptAndSign` because the MSMQ binding defaults to the `ProtectionLevel.Signed` protection level. The following two definitions are equivalent:

```
NetMsmqBinding binding1 = new NetMsmqBinding( );
binding1.Security.Transport.MsmqProtectionLevel = ProtectionLevel.EncryptAndSign;

NetMsmqBinding binding2 = new NetMsmqBinding( );
binding2.Security.Mode = NetMsmqSecurityMode.Transport;
binding2.Security.Transport.MsmqAuthenticationMode =
                                       MsmqAuthenticationMode.WindowsDomain;
binding2.Security.Transport.MsmqProtectionLevel = ProtectionLevel.EncryptAndSign;
```

Or, alternatively, using a config file:

```
<bindings>
   <netMsmqBinding>
      <binding name = "MSMQWindowsSecurity">
         <security mode = "Transport">
            <transport
               msmqAuthenticationMode = "WindowsDomain"
               msmqProtectionLevel = "EncryptAndSign"
            />
         </security>
      </binding>
   </netMsmqBinding>
</bindings>
```

Figure 10-3 shows the security-related elements of the `NetMsmqBinding`.

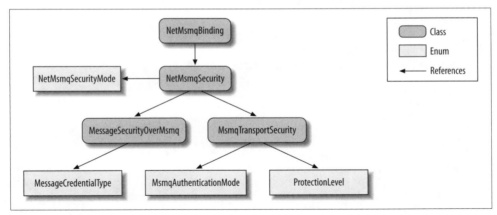

Figure 10-3. NetMsmqBinding and security

`NetMsmqBinding` has a reference to `NetMsmqSecurity`, which uses the `NetMsmqSecurityMode` enum to indicate the transfer security mode. When transport security is used, `NetMsmqSecurity` will use an instance of `MsmqTransportSecurity` containing the client credential type via the `MsmqAuthenticationMode` enum, and the configured protection level via the `ProtectionLevel` enum. In a similar manner, there are references to types controlling Message security.

Message Protection

While a service should use the highest level of security, it is actually at the mercy of its host because the host is the one configuring the binding. This is especially problematic if the service is to be deployed in an unknown environment with an arbitrary host. To compensate, WCF lets service developers insist on a protection level, or rather, constrain the minimum protection level their service is willing to work with. Both the service and the client can constrain the protection level independently of the other. You can constrain the protection level at three places. When applied at the service contract, all operations on the contract are considered sensitive and protected. When applied at the operation contract, then only that operation is protected; other operations on the same contract are not. Finally, you can also constrain the fault contract, because sometimes the error information returned to the client is sensitive, containing parameter values, exception messages, and the call stack. The respective contract attributes offer the `ProtectionLevel` property of the enum type `ProtectionLevel`:

```
[AttributeUsage(AttributeTargets.Interface|AttributeTargets.Class,
                Inherited = false)]
public sealed class ServiceContractAttribute : Attribute
{
   public ProtectionLevel ProtectionLevel
   {get;set;}
   //More members
}
[AttributeUsage(AttributeTargets.Method)]
public sealed class OperationContractAttribute : Attribute
{
   public ProtectionLevel ProtectionLevel
   {get;set;}
   //More members
}
[AttributeUsage(AttributeTargets.Method,AllowMultiple = true,
                Inherited = false)]
public sealed class FaultContractAttribute : Attribute
{
   public ProtectionLevel ProtectionLevel
   {get;set;}
   //More members
}
```

Here is how to set the protection level on a service contract:

```
[ServiceContract(ProtectionLevel = ProtectionLevel.EncryptAndSign)]
interface IMyContract
{...}
```

Setting the `ProtectionLevel` property on the contract attributes merely indicates the low-water mark; that is, the minimum accepted protected level by this contract. If the binding is configured for a lower protection level, it will result in an `InvalidOperationException` at the service load time or the time the proxy is opened. If the binding is configured for a higher level, then that is acceptable by the contract. The default of the `ProtectionLevel` property on the contract attributes defaults to `ProtectionLevel.None`, meaning it has no effect.

The desired protection constraint is considered a local implementation detail of the service and so the required protection level is not exported with the service metadata. Consequently, the client may require a different level, and enforce it separately from the service.

 Even though the nonintranet bindings do not offer a protection level property, the protection level constraint at the service, operation, or fault contract is satisfied when using Transport or Message security. The constraint is not satisfied when turning off security in the None scenario.

Authentication

By default, when a client calls a proxy that targets an endpoint whose binding is configured for using Windows credentials with Transport security, there is nothing explicit the client needs to do to pass its credentials. WCF will automatically pass the Windows identity of the client's process to the service:

```
class MyContractClient : ClientBase<IMyContract>,IMyContract
{...}

MyContractClient proxy = new MyContractClient();
proxy.MyMethod(); //Client identity passed here
proxy.Close();
```

When the call is received by the service, if the client credentials represent a valid Windows account, WCF on the service side will authenticate the caller, and the caller will be allowed to access the operation on the service.

Providing alternative Windows credentials

Instead of using the identity of the process the client happens to be running in, the client can pass alternative Windows credentials. The `ClientBase<T>` base class offers the `ClientCredentials` property of the type `ClientCredentials`:

```
public abstract class ClientBase<T> : ...
{
   public ClientCredentials ClientCredentials
   {get;}
}
public class ClientCredentials : ...,IEndpointBehavior
```

```
{
    public WindowsClientCredential Windows
    {get;}
    //More members
}
```

`ClientCredentials` contains the property `Windows` of the type `WindowsClientCredential`, defined as:

```
public sealed class WindowsClientCredential
{
    public NetworkCredential ClientCredential
    {get;set;}
    //More members
}
```

`WindowsClientCredential` has the property `ClientCredential` of the type `NetworkCredential`, which is where the client needs to set the alternative credentials:

```
public class NetworkCredential : ...
{
    public NetworkCredential();
    public NetworkCredential(string userName,string password);
    public NetworkCredential(string userName,string password,string domain);

    public string Domain
    {get;set;}
    public string UserName
    {get;set;}
    public string Password
    {get;set;}
}
```

Example 10-3 demonstrates how to use these classes and properties in providing alternative Windows credentials to the process identity.

Example 10-3. Providing alternative Windows credentials

```
NetworkCredential credentials = new NetworkCredential();
credentials.Domain   = "MyDomain";
credentials.UserName = "MyUsername";
credentials.Password = "MyPassword";

MyContractClient proxy = new MyContractClient();
proxy.ClientCredentials.Windows.ClientCredential = credentials;

proxy.MyMethod();
proxy.Close();
```

Note in Example 10-3 that the client must instantiate a new object of the type `NetworkCredential`, and that it cannot simply assign the credentials in the existing `ClientCredential` property of `WindowsClientCredential`. Once using an assigned identity, the proxy cannot use any other identity later on. Clients use the technique of Example 10-3 when the credentials provided are collected dynamically at runtime,

---

perhaps using a login dialog box. If, on the other hand, the alternative credentials are static, the client developer can encapsulate them in the proxy constructors:

```
public partial class MyContractClient: ClientBase<IMyContract>,IMyContract
{
   public MyContractClient()
   {
      SetCredentials();
   }
   /* More constructors */
   void SetCredentials()
   {
      ClientCredentials.Windows.ClientCredential =
                  new NetworkCredential("MyClient","MyPassword","MyDomain");
   }
   public void MyMethod()
   {
      Channel.MyMethod();
   }
}
```

When working with a channel factory instead of a proxy class, the `ChannelFactory` base class offers the `Credentials` property of the type `ClientCredentials`:

```
public abstract class ChannelFactory : ...
{
   public ClientCredentials Credentials
   {get;}
   //More members
}
public class ChannelFactory<T> : ChannelFactory,...
{
   public T CreateChannel();
   //More members
}
```

Simply set alternative credentials in the `Credentials` property just as in Example 10-3:

```
ChannelFactory<IMyContract> factory = new ChannelFactory<IMyContract>("");

factory.Credentials.Windows.ClientCredential = new NetworkCredential(...);

IMyContract proxy = factory.CreateChannel();
using(proxy as IDisposable)
{
   proxy.MyMethod();
}
```

Note that you cannot use the static `CreateChannel()` methods of `ChannelFactory<T>` since you first have to instantiate a factory in order to access the `Credentials` property.

Identities

All Windows processes run with an authenticated security identity, and the process hosting a WCF service is no different. The identity is actually a Windows account whose security token is attached to the process and, by default, to all threads in that process. However, it is up to the application administrator to decide which identity to use. You can have the host run with an interactive user identity; that is, the identity of the user who launched the host process. Simply launching the process by a user will use that user account as the identity of the host process. *Interactive identity* is typically used when self-hosting, and is ideal for debugging because the debugger will automatically attach itself to the host process when launched from within Visual Studio. However, relying on an interactive identity is impractical for deployment on a server machine where there is not necessarily a logged-on user, and besides, the logged-on user may not have the necessary credentials to perform the service work. For production deployment, you typically rely on a *designated account*—a pre-set Windows account used primarily by your service or services. To launch the service under a designated account you can use the Run as... shell option to launch the service. However, Run as... is only useful for simple testing. You can also have an NT service as your host, and use the Control Panel Services applet to assign a designated identity to the host. If hosting in IIS6 or in the WAS, you can use those environments' configuration tools to assign a designated identity.

The IIdentity interface

In .NET, the IIdentity interface from the System.Security.Principal namespace represents a security identity:

```
public interface IIdentity
{
   string AuthenticationType
   {get;}
   bool IsAuthenticated
   {get;}
   string Name
   {get;}
}
```

The interface lets you know if the identity behind the interface is authenticated (and which authentication mechanism was used) as well as allows you to obtain the name of the identity. Out of the box, WCF takes advantage of three implementations of IIdentity offered by .NET. The WindowsIdentity class represents a Windows account. The GenericIdentity class is a general-purpose class whose main use is to wrap an identity name with an IIdentity. With both GenericIdentity and WindowsIdentity, if the identity name is an empty string, that identity is considered unauthenticated, and any other nonzero-length name is considered authenticated. Finally, X509Identity is an internal class that represents an identity that was authenticated using an X509 certificate. The identity behind X509Identity is always authenticated.

Working with WindowsIdentity

The `WindowsIdentity` class offers a few useful methods above and beyond the mere implementation of `IIdentity`:

```
public class WindowsIdentity : IIdentity,...
{
   public WindowsIdentity(string sUserPrincipalName);
   public static WindowsIdentity GetAnonymous();
   public static WindowsIdentity GetCurrent();
   public virtual bool IsAnonymous
   {get;}
   public virtual bool IsAuthenticated
   {get;}
   public virtual string Name
   {get;}
   //More members
}
```

The IsAnonymous Boolean property indicates if the underlying identity is anonymous and the GetAnonymous() method returns an anonymous Windows identity, typically used for impersonation to mask out the real identity:

```
WindowsIdentity identity = WindowsIdentity.GetAnonymous();
Debug.Assert(identity.Name == "");
Debug.Assert(identity.IsAuthenticated == false);
Debug.Assert(identity.IsAnonymous == true);
```

The GetCurrent() static method returns the identity of the process where it is called. That identity is by default nonanonymous and authenticated:

```
WindowsIdentity currentIdentity = WindowsIdentity.GetCurrent();
Debug.Assert(currentIdentity.Name != "");
Debug.Assert(currentIdentity.IsAuthenticated == true);
Debug.Assert(currentIdentity.IsAnonymous == false);
```

The Security Call Context

Every operation on a secured WCF service has a security call context. The security call context is represented by the class ServiceSecurityContext, defined as:

```
public class ServiceSecurityContext
{
   public static ServiceSecurityContext Current
   {get;}
   public bool IsAnonymous
   {get;}
   public IIdentity PrimaryIdentity
   {get;}
   public WindowsIdentity WindowsIdentity
   {get;}
   //More members
}
```

The main use for the security call context is the custom security mechanism, as well as analysis and auditing. While presented here in the context of the intranet scenario, all other scenarios have use for the security call context.

Note that in spite of the name, this is a per-call security context, not per-service. The security call context is stored in the TLS, so every method on every object down the call chain from the service can access the security call context, including your service constructor. To obtain your current security call context, simply access the `Current` static property. Another way of accessing the security call context is via the `ServiceSecurityContext` property of the `OperationContext`:

```
public sealed class OperationContext : ...
{
   public ServiceSecurityContext ServiceSecurityContext
   {get;}
   //More members
}
```

Regardless of which mechanism you use, you will get the same object:

```
ServiceSecurityContext context1 = ServiceSecurityContext.Current;
ServiceSecurityContext context2 = OperationContext.Current.ServiceSecurityContext;
Debug.Assert(context1 == context2);
```

 Your service has a security call context only if security is enabled. When security is disabled, `ServiceSecurityContext.Current` returns null.

The `PrimaryIdentity` property of `ServiceSecurityContext` contains the identity of the immediate client up the call chain. If the client is unauthenticated, `PrimaryIdentity` will reference an implementation of `IIdentity` with a blank identity. When Windows authentication is used, the `PrimaryIdentity` property will be set to an instance of `WindowsIdentity`.

The `WindowsIdentity` property is meaningful only when using Windows authentication, and it will always be of the type `WindowsIdentity`. When valid Windows credentials are provided, the `WindowsIdentity` property will contain the corresponding client identity, and will match the value of the `PrimaryIdentity`.

 The constructor of a singleton service does not have a security call context, since it is called when the host is launched, not as a result of a client call.

Impersonation

Some resources, such as the filesystem, SQL Server, sockets, and even DCOM objects, grant access to themselves based on the security token of their caller. Typically, the host process is assigned an identity with elevated credentials that are required to access such resources in order to function properly. Clients, however, typically have restricted credentials compared with those of the service. Traditionally, developers used *impersonation* to address this credentials gap. Impersonation lets the service assume the client's identity primarily in order to verify if the client can perform the work it asks the service to do. Impersonation has a number of key detrimental effects on your application discussed at the end of this section. Instead of impersonation, you should apply role-based security to authorize the callers. That said, many developers are used to design systems using impersonation, so both .NET and WCF have supporting this need in mind.

Manual impersonation

The service can impersonate its calling client by calling the Impersonate( ) method of the WindowsIdentity class:

```
public class WindowsIdentity : IIdentity,...
{
   public virtual WindowsImpersonationContext Impersonate( );
   //More members
}
public class WindowsImpersonationContext : IDisposable
{
   public void Dispose( );
   public void Undo( );
}
```

Impersonate( ) returns an instance of WindowsImpersonationContext containing the service's previous identity. To revert back to that identity, the service needs to call the Undo( ) method. To impersonate, the service needs to call Impersonate( ) on the identity of the caller available with the WindowsIdentity property of its security call context, as shown in Example 10-4.

Example 10-4. Explicit impersonation and reversion

```
class MyService : IMyContract
{
   public void MyMethod( )
   {
      WindowsImpersonationContext impersonationContext =
                     ServiceSecurityContext.Current.WindowsIdentity.Impersonate( );
      try
      {
         /*  Do work as client */
      }
      finally
      {
         impersonationContext.Undo( );
      }
   }
}
```

Note in Example 10-4 that the service reverts to its old identity even in the face of exceptions by placing the call to Undo() in the finally statement. To somewhat simplify reverting, the implementation of Dispose() of WindowsImpersonationContext also reverts, which enables you to use it in conjunction with a using statement:

```
public void MyMethod()
{
   using(ServiceSecurityContext.Current.WindowsIdentity.Impersonate())
   {
      /* Do work as client */
   }
}
```

Declarative impersonation

Instead of manual impersonation, you can instruct WCF to automatically impersonate the caller of the method. The OperationBehavior attribute offers the Impersonation property of the enum type ImpersonationOption:

```
public enum ImpersonationOption
{
   NotAllowed,
   Allowed,
   Required
}
[AttributeUsage(AttributeTargets.Method)]
public sealed class OperationBehaviorAttribute : Attribute,IOperationBehavior
{
   public ImpersonationOption Impersonation
   {get;set;}
   //More members
}
```

The ImpersonationOption.NotAllowed value is the default value. It indicates that WCF should not auto-impersonate, but you can write code (as in Example 10-4) that explicitly impersonates.

ImpersonationOption.Allowed instructs WCF to automatically impersonate the caller whenever Windows authentication is used. ImpersonationOption.Allowed has no effect with other authentication mechanisms. When WCF auto-impersonates, it will also auto-revert to the previous service identity once the method returns.

The ImpersonationOption.Required value mandates the use of Windows authentication and will throw an exception otherwise. As its name implies, WCF will always auto-impersonate (and revert) in every call to the operation:

```
class MyService : IMyContract
{
   [OperationBehavior(Impersonation = ImpersonationOption.Required)]
   public void MyMethod()
   {
      /* Do work as client */
   }
}
```

Note that there is no way to use declarative impersonation with the service constructor because you cannot apply the `OperationBehavior` attribute on a constructor. Constructors can only use manual impersonation. If you do impersonate in the constructor, always revert as well in the constructor, to avoid side effects on the operations of the service and even other services in the same host.

Impersonating all operations

If you need to enable impersonation in all the operations of the service, the `ServiceHostBase` class has the `Authorization` property of the type `ServiceAuthorizationBehavior`:

```
public abstract class ServiceHostBase : ...
{
   public ServiceAuthorizationBehavior Authorization
   {get;}
   //More members
}
public sealed class ServiceAuthorizationBehavior : IServiceBehavior
{
   public bool ImpersonateCallerForAllOperations
   {get;set;}
   //More members
}
```

`ServiceAuthorizationBehavior` provides the Boolean property `ImpersonateCallerForAllOperations`, which is `false` by default. Contrary to what its name implies, when set to true, this property merely verifies that there is no operation on the service configured with `ImpersonationOption.NotAllowed`. This constraint is verified at service load time, yielding an `InvalidOperationException` when violated.

In effect, when Windows authentication is used, this will amount to automatically impersonating in all operations, but you must explicitly have all operations decorated with `ImpersonationOption.Allowed` or `ImpersonationOption.Required`. `ImpersonateCallerForAllOperations` has no effect on constructors.

You can set the `ImpersonateCallerForAllOperations` property programmatically or in the config file. If you set it programmatically, you can only do so before opening the host:

```
ServiceHost host = new ServiceHost(typeof(MyService));
host.Authorization.ImpersonateCallerForAllOperations = true;
host.Open();
```

When set using a config file, you need to reference the matching service behavior at the service declaration:

```
<services>
   <service name = "MyService" behaviorConfiguration= "ImpersonateAll">
      ...
   </service>
</services>
```

```
<behaviors>
   <serviceBehaviors>
      <behavior name = "ImpersonateAll">
         <serviceAuthorization impersonateCallerForAllOperations = "true"/>
      </behavior>
   </serviceBehaviors>
</behaviors>
```

To automate impersonating in all operations without the need to apply the
OperationBehavior attribute on every method, I wrote the SecurityHelper static class
with the ImpersonateAll( ) methods:

```
public static class SecurityHelper
{
   public static void ImpersonateAll(ServiceHostBase host);
   public static void ImpersonateAll(ServiceDescription description);
   //More members
}
```

You can only call ImpersonateAll( ) before opening the host:

```
//Will impersonate in all operations
class MyService : IMyContract
{
   public void MyMethod( )
   {...}
}
ServiceHost host = new ServiceHost(typeof(MyService));
SecurityHelper.ImpersonateAll(host);
host.Open( );
```

Example 10-5 shows the implementation of ImpersonateAll( ).

Example 10-5. Implementing SecurityHelper.ImpersonateAll()

```
public static class SecurityHelper
{
   public static void ImpersonateAll(ServiceHostBase host)
   {
      host.Authorization.ImpersonateCallerForAllOperations = true;
      ServiceDescription description = host.Description;
      ImpersonateAll(description);
   }
   public static void ImpersonateAll(ServiceDescription description)
   {
      foreach(ServiceEndpoint endpoint in description.Endpoints)
      {
         foreach(OperationDescription operation in endpoint.Contract.Operations)
         {
            foreach(IOperationBehavior behavior in operation.Behaviors)
            {
               if(behavior is OperationBehaviorAttribute)
               {
                  OperationBehaviorAttribute attribute =
                                          behavior as OperationBehaviorAttribute;
```

Example 10-5. Implementing SecurityHelper.ImpersonateAll( ) (continued)

```
                    attribute.Impersonation = ImpersonationOption.Required;
                    break;
                }
            }
        }
    }
}
    //More members
}
```

In Example 10-5, ImpersonateAll( ) sets the ImpersonateCallerForAllOperations property of the provided host to true, and then it obtains from the host the service description that contains all the endpoints. That description is passed to an overloaded ImpersonateAll( ) that explicitly configures all operations with ImpersonationOption.Required. This is done by iterating over the endpoints collection of the description. For each endpoint, ImpersonateAll( ) accesses the operations collection of the contract. For each operation, there could be one or more operation behaviors in the form of IOperationBehavior (there is always at least one provided by WCF in the form of OperationBehaviorAttribute, even if you did not provide one explicitly). Each operation behavior is examined until the OperationBehaviorAttribute is found, at which point the Impersonation property is set to ImpersonationOption.Required.

You can further encapsulate and streamline the use of SecurityHelper. ImpersonateAll( ) in ServiceHost<T>:

```
    public class ServiceHost<T> : ServiceHost
    {
        public void ImpersonateAll( )
        {
            if(State == CommunicationState.Opened)
            {
                throw new InvalidOperationException("Host is already opened");
            }

            SecurityHelper.ImpersonateAll(this);
        }
        //More members
    }
```

Using ServiceHost<T> to automatically impersonate all callers is straightforward:

```
    ServiceHost<MyService> host = new ServiceHost<MyService>( );
    host.ImpersonateAll( );
    host.Open( );
```

Restricting impersonation

Authorization and authentication protect the service from being accessed by unauthorized and unauthenticated, potentially malicious clients. However, how should the client be protected from malicious services? One of the ways an adversary service could abuse the client is by assuming the client's identity and credentials and causing harm as the client.

In some cases, the client may not even want to allow the service to obtain its identity at all. WCF lets the client indicate the degree to which the service can obtain the client's identity and use it. Impersonation is actually a range of options indicating the level of trust between the client and the service. The WindowsClientCredential class provides the AllowedImpersonationLevel enum of the type TokenImpersonationLevel found in the System.Security.Principal namespace:

```
public enum TokenImpersonationLevel
{
   None,
   Anonymous,
   Identification,
   Impersonation,
   Delegation
}
public sealed class WindowsClientCredential
{
   public TokenImpersonationLevel AllowedImpersonationLevel
   {get;set;}
   //More members
}
```

The client can restrict the allowed impersonation level both programmatically and administratively. For example, to programmatically restrict the impersonation level to TokenImpersonationLevel.Identification, before opening the proxy the client would write:

```
MyContractClient proxy = new MyContractClient();
proxy.ClientCredentials.Windows.AllowedImpersonationLevel =
                                    TokenImpersonationLevel.Identification;
proxy.MyMethod();
proxy.Close();
```

When using a config file, the administrator should define the allowed impersonation level as a custom endpoint behavior and reference it from the relevant endpoint section:

```
<client>
   <endpoint behaviorConfiguration = "ImpersonationBehavior"
      ...
   />
</client>
<behaviors>
   <endpointBehaviors>
      <behavior name = "ImpersonationBehavior">
         <clientCredentials>
            <windows allowedImpersonationLevel = "Identification"/>
         </clientCredentials>
      </behavior>
   </endpointBehaviors>
</behaviors>
```

TokenImpersonationLevel.None simply means that no impersonation level is assigned, and it amounts to no credentials. When the impersonation level is set to TokenImpersonationLevel.Anonymous, the client provides no credentials at all. In practical terms, TokenImpersonationLevel.None and TokenImpersonationLevel.Anonymous amount to the same behavior—the client provides no identity information. These two values are of course the safest from the client's perspective, but are the least useful options from the application perspective, since no authentication or authorization is possible by the service. Avoiding any credentials is only possible if the service is configured for anonymous access or for having no security, which is not the case with the intranet scenario. If the service is configured for Windows security, these two values yield ArgumentOutOfRangeException on the client side.

With TokenImpersonationLevel.Identification, the service can identify the client; that is, obtain the security identity of the calling client. The service, however, is not allowed to impersonate the client—everything the service does must be done under the service's own identity. Trying to impersonate will throw an ArgumentOutOfRangeException on the service side. TokenImpersonationLevel.Identification is the default value used with Windows security and is the recommended value for the intranet scenario. Note that if the service and the client are on the same machine, then the service will still be able to impersonate the client, even when TokenImpersonationLevel.Identification is used.

TokenImpersonationLevel.Impersonation grants the service permission to both obtain the client's identity and also to impersonate the client. Impersonation indicates a great deal of trust between the client and the service, since the service can do anything the client can do, even if the service host is configured to use a less privileged identity. The only difference between the real client and the impersonating service is that if the service is on a separate machine from the client, it cannot access resources or objects on other machines as the client, because the service machine does not really have the client's password. In the case where the service and the client are on the same machine, the service impersonating the client can make one network hop to another machine, since the machine it resides on can still authenticate the impersonated client identity.

Finally, TokenImpersonationLevel.Delegation provides the service with the client's Kerberos ticket. The service can freely access resources on any machine as the client. If service is also configured for delegation, then when it calls other downstream services, the client identity could be propagated further and further down the call chain. Delegation-required Kerberos authentication is not possible on Windows workgroup installations. Both the client and server user accounts must be properly configured in Active Directory to support delegation due to the enormous trust (and hence security risk) involved. Delegation uses, by default, another security service called *cloaking*, which propagates the caller identity along the call chain.

Delegation is extremely dangerous from the client perspective since the client has no control over who is using its identity or where. When the impersonation level is set to `TokenImpersonationLevel.Impersonation`, the client takes a calculated risk, since it knows which services it is accessing and if those services are on a difference machine, the client identity cannot propagate across the network. I consider delegation as something that enables the service to act as an imposter for the client, not just to impersonate it.

Using impersonation

You should design services so that they do not rely on impersonation, and the client should use `TokenImpersonationLevel.Identification`.

As a general design guideline, the further from the client, the less relevant its identity is. If you use some kind of a layered approach in your system design, each layer should run under its own identity, authenticate its immediate callers, and implicitly trust its calling layer to authenticate its original callers to maintain a chain of trusted, authenticated callers. Impersonation, on the other hand, requires you to keep propagating the identity further and further down the call chain all the way to the underlying resources. Doing so impedes scalability because many resources (such as SQL Server connections) are allocated per identity. With impersonation, you will need as many resources as clients, and you will not be able to benefit from resource pooling (such as connection pooling). Impersonation also complicates resources administration, because you need to grant access to the resources to the original client identities, and there could be numerous such identities to manage. A service that always runs under its own identity poses no such issues, regardless of how many diverse identities access that service. For access control to the resources, you should use authorization, as discussed next. Finally, relying on impersonation precludes non-Windows authentication mechanisms. If you do decide to use impersonation, use it judiciously and only as a sporadic last resort when there is no other and better design approach.

 Impersonation is not possible with queued services.

Authorization

While authentication deals with verifying that the client is indeed who the client claims to be, most applications also need to verify that the client (more precisely, the identity it presents) has permission to perform the operation. Since it is impractical to program access permission for each individual identity, is it better to grant permissions to the roles clients play in the application domain. A *role* is a symbolic category of identities who share the same security privileges. When you assign a role to an application resource, you are granting access to that resource to whomever is a member of that role. Discovering the roles clients play in your business domain is part of your application-requirement analysis and design, just as factoring services and interfaces is. By interacting with roles instead of particular identities, you isolate your application from changes made in real life, such as adding new users, moving existing users between positions, promoting users, or users leaving their jobs. .NET allows you to apply role-based security both declaratively and programmatically, if the need to verify role membership is based on a dynamic decision.

Security principal

For security purposes, it is convenient to lump together the identity and the information about its role membership. This representation is called the *security principal*.

The principal in .NET is any object that implements the IPrincipal interface, defined in the System.Security.Principal namespace:

```
public interface IPrincipal
{
    IIdentity Identity
    {get;}
    bool IsInRole(string role);
}
```

The IsInRole( ) method simply returns true if the identity associated with this principal is a member of the specified role, and false otherwise. The Identity read-only property provides access to read-only information about the identity, in the form of an object implementing the IIdentity interface. Out of the box, .NET offers several implementations of IPrincipal. GenericPrincipal is a general-purpose principal that has to be preconfigured with the roles information. It is typically used when no authorization is required, in which case GenericPrincipal wraps a blank identity. The WindowsPrincipal class looks up role membership information inside the Windows NT groups.

Every .NET thread has a principal object associated with it, obtained via the CurrentPrincipal static property of the Thread class:

```
public sealed class Thread
{
    public static IPrincipal CurrentPrincipal
    {get;set;}
    //More members
}
```

For example, here is how to discover the user name as well as whether or not the caller was authenticated:

```
IPrincipal principal = Thread.CurrentPrincipal;
string userName = principal.Identity.Name;
bool isAuthenticated = principal.Identity.IsAuthenticated;
```

Selecting authorization mode

As presented earlier, the ServiceHostBase class provides the Authorization property of the type ServiceAuthorizationBehavior. ServiceAuthorizationBehavior has the PrincipalPermissionMode property of the enum type PrincipalPermissionMode, defined as:

```
public enum PrincipalPermissionMode
{
    None,
    UseWindowsGroups,
    UseAspNetRoles,
    Custom
}
public sealed class ServiceAuthorizationBehavior : IServiceBehavior
{
    public PrincipalPermissionMode PrincipalPermissionMode
    {get;set;}
    //More members
}
```

Before opening the host, you can use the PrincipalPermissionMode property to select the principal mode; that is, which type of principal to install to authorize the caller.

If PrincipalPermissionMode is set to PrincipalPermissionMode.None, then principal-based authorization is possible. After authenticating the caller (if authentication is required at all), WCF installs GenericPrincipal with a blank identity and attaches it to the thread that invokes the service operation. That principal will be available via Thread.CurrentPrincipal.

When PrincipalPermissionMode is set to PrincipalPermissionMode.UseWindowsGroups, WCF will install a WindowsPrincipal with an identity matching the provided credentials. If no Windows authentication took place (because the service did not require it), then WCF will install a WindowsPrincipal with a blank identity.

PrincipalPermissionMode.UseWindowsGroups is the default value of the PrincipalPermissionMode property, so these two definitions are equivalent:

```
ServiceHost host1 = new ServiceHost(typeof(MyService));

ServiceHost host2 = new ServiceHost(typeof(MyService));
host2.Authorization.PrincipalPermissionMode =
                                PrincipalPermissionMode.UseWindowsGroups;
```

When using a config file, you need to reference a custom behavior section assigning the principal mode:

```
<services>
   <service name = "MyService" behaviorConfiguration = "WindowsGroups">
      ...
   </service>
</services>
<behaviors>
   <serviceBehaviors>
      <behavior name = "WindowsGroups">
```

```
           <serviceAuthorization principalPermissionMode = "UseWindowsGroups"/>
        </behavior>
     </serviceBehaviors>
  </behaviors>
```

Declarative role-based security

You apply service-side declarative role-based security using the attribute
`PrincipalPermissionAttribute`, defined in the `System.Security.Permissions`
namespace:

```
public enum SecurityAction
{
   Demand,
   //More members
}

[AttributeUsage(AttributeTargets.Class | AttributeTargets.Method)]
public sealed class PrincipalPermissionAttribute : CodeAccessSecurityAttribute
{
   public PrincipalPermissionAttribute(SecurityAction action);

   public bool Authenticated
   {get;set; }
   public string Name
   {get;set;}
   public string Role
   {get;set;}
   //More members
}
```

The `PrincipalPermission` attribute lets you declare the required roles membership.
For the intranet scenario, when you specify a Windows NT group as a role, you must
prefix it with the domain name or the local machine name (if the role is defined
locally only). In Example 10-6, the declaration of the `PrincipalPermission` attribute
grants access to `MyMethod( )` only for callers whose identity belongs to the Managers
user group.

Example 10-6. Declarative role-based security on the intranet

```
[ServiceContract]
interface IMyContract
{
   [OperationContract]
   void MyMethod( );
}
class MyService : IMyContract
{
   [PrincipalPermission(SecurityAction.Demand,Role = @"<domain>\Managers")]
   public void MyMethod( )
   {...}
}
```

If the user is not a member of that role, .NET throws an exception of type
SecurityException.

 When experimenting with Windows role-based security, you often
add users to or remove users from user groups. Because user-group
information is cached by Windows at login time, the changes you
make are not reflected until the next login.

If multiple roles are allowed to access the method, you can apply the attribute multiple times:

```
[PrincipalPermission(SecurityAction.Demand,Role=@"<domain>\Managers")]
[PrincipalPermission(SecurityAction.Demand,Role=@"<domain>\Customers")]
public void MyMethod( )
{...}
```

When multiple PrincipalPermission attributes are used, .NET verifies that the caller
is a member of at least one of the demanded roles. If you want to verify that the user
is a member of both roles, you need to use programmatic role membership checks,
discussed later.

While the attribute by its very definition can be applied on methods and classes, in a
WCF service class you can only apply it on methods. The reason is that in WCF
(unlike normal classes) the service class constructor always executes under a
GenericPrincipal with a blank identity, regardless of the authentication mechanisms
used. As a result, the identity that the constructor is running under is unauthenticated, and will always fail any kind of authorization attempt (even when not using
Windows NT groups):

```
//Will always fail
[PrincipalPermission(SecurityAction.Demand,Role = "...")]
class MyService : IMyContract
{...}
```

 Avoid sensitive work that requires authorization at the service constructor. With a per-session service, perform such work in the operations themselves, and with a sessionful service provide a dedicated
Initialize( ) operation where you can initialize the instance and
authorize the callers.

By setting the Name property of the PrincipalPermission attribute, you can even insist
on granting access to a particular user. This practice is unadvisable, however,
because it is wrong to hardcode usernames:

```
[PrincipalPermission(SecurityAction.Demand,Name = "John")]
```

You can also insist on a particular user and that the user is a member of a role:

```
[PrincipalPermission(SecurityAction.Demand,Name = "John",
                     Role = @"<domain>\Managers")]
```

Declarative role-based security hardcodes the role name. If your application looks up role names dynamically, you have to use programmatic role verification as presented next.

Programmatic role-based security

Sometimes you need to programmatically verify role membership. Usually, you need to do that when the decision as to whether to grant access depends both on role membership and on some other values known only during call time, such as parameter values, time of day, and location. Another case in which programmatic role membership verification is needed is when you're dealing with localized user groups. To demonstrate the first category, imagine a banking service that lets clients transfer sums of money between two specified accounts. Only customers and tellers are allowed to call the TransferMoney( ) operation, with the following business rule: if the amount transferred is greater than 5,000, only tellers are allowed to do the transfer. Declarative role-based security can verify that the caller is a teller or a customer, but it cannot enforce the additional business rule. For that, you need to use the IsInRole( ) method of IPrincipal, as shown in Example 10-7.

Example 10-7. Programmatic role-based security

```
[ServiceContract]
interface IBankAccounts
{
   [OperationContract]
   void TransferMoney(double sum,long sourceAccount,long destinationAccount);
}
static class AppRoles
{
   public const string Customers = @"<domain>\Customers";
   public const string Tellers   = @"<domain>\Tellers";
}
class BankService : IBankAccounts
{

   [PrincipalPermission(SecurityAction.Demand,Role = AppRoles.Customers)]
   [PrincipalPermission(SecurityAction.Demand,Role = AppRoles.Tellers)]
   public void TransferMoney(double sum,long sourceAccount,long destinationAccount)
   {
      IPrincipal  principal = Thread.CurrentPrincipal;
      Debug.Assert(principal.Identity.IsAuthenticated);

      bool isCustomer = principal.IsInRole(AppRoles.Customers);
      bool isTeller   = principal.IsInRole(AppRoles.Tellers);

      if(isCustomer && ! isTeller)
      {
         if(sum > 5000)
         {
```

Example 10-7. Programmatic role-based security (continued)

```
            string message = "Caller does not have sufficient authority to" +
                             "transfer this sum";
            throw(new UnauthorizedAccessException(message));
         }
      }
   DoTransfer(sum,sourceAccount,destinationAccount);
   }
   //Helper method
   void DoTransfer(double sum,long sourceAccount,long destinationAccount)
   {...}
}
```

Example 10-7 demonstrates a number of other points. First, even though it uses programmatic role membership verification with the value of the sum argument, it still uses declarative role-based security as the first line of defense, allowing access only to clients who are members of the Customers or Tellers roles. Second, you can programmatically assert that the caller is authenticated using the IsAuthenticated property of IIdentity. Finally, note the use of the AppRoles static class to encapsulate the actual string used for the role to avoid hardcoding the roles in multiple places. In a similar manner, you need to employ programmatic role-based security to enforce additional rules such as that the transfer is allowed only during normal business hours.

 There is a complete disconnect between role-based security and the actual principal type. When the PrincipalPermission attribute is asked to verify role membership, it simply gets hold of its thread's current principal in the form of IPrincipal, and calls its IsInRole( ) method. This is also true of programmatic role membership verification that uses only IPrincipal, as shown in Example 10-7. The separation of the IPrincipal interface from its implementation is the key to providing other role-based security mechanisms besides Windows NT groups, as you will see in the other scenarios.

Identity Management

In the intranet scenario, after successful authentication, WCF will attach to the operation thread a principal identity of the type WindowsIdentity, which will have the value of its Name property set to the username (or Windows account) provided by the client. Since valid credentials are provided, the security call context's two identities, the primary identity and the Windows identity, will be the set to the same identity as the principal identity. All three identities will be considered authenticated. The identities and their values are shown in Table 10-4.

Windows Roles Localization

Declarative role-based security hardcodes the role name. If your application is deployed in international markets and you use Windows groups as roles, it's likely the role names will not match. In the intranet scenario, the principal object attached to the thread accessing the service is of the type `WindowsPrincipal`:

```
public class WindowsPrincipal : IPrincipal
{
   public WindowsPrincipal(WindowsIdentity ntIdentity);

   //IPrincipal implementation
   public virtual IIdentity Identity
   {get;}
   public virtual bool IsInRole(string role);

   //Additional methods:
   public virtual bool IsInRole(int rid);
   public virtual bool IsInRole(WindowsBuiltInRole role);
}
```

`WindowsPrincipal` provides two additional `IsInRole()` methods that are intended to ease the task of localizing Windows NT groups. You can provide `IsInRole()` with an enum of type `WindowsBuiltInRole`, matching the built-in NT roles, such as `WindowsBuiltInRole.Administrator` or `WindowsBuiltInRole.User`. The other version of `IsInRole()` accepts an integer indexing specific roles. For example, a role index of 512 maps to the `Administrators` group. The MSDN Library contains a list of both the predefined indexes and ways to provide your own aliases and indexes to user groups.

Table 10-4. Identity management in the intranet scenario

Identity	Type	Value	Authenticated
Thread principal	WindowsIdentity	Username	Yes
Security context primary	WindowsIdentity	Username	Yes
Security context Windows	WindowsIdentity	Username	Yes

Note that while the host process (and the thread token) retain their designated identity, the principal identity will be that of the caller. I call this behavior *soft impersonation*, and when used in conjunction with role-based security it largely negates the need to ever perform real impersonation and replace the security token with that of the client.

Callbacks

When it comes to security on the intranet, there are several key differences between normal service operations and callbacks. First, with a callback contract you can only ascribe protection level at the operation level, not the callback contract level. For example, this protection-level constraint will be ignored:

```
[ServiceContract(CallbackContract = typeof(IMyContractCallback))]
interface IMyContract
{...}
//Demand for protection level will be ignored
[ServiceContract(ProtectionLevel = ProtectionLevel.EncryptAndSign)]
interface IMyContractCallback
{...}
```

You can only take advantage of operation-level demand for protection level:

```
[ServiceContract(CallbackContract = typeof(IMyContractCallback))]
interface IMyContract
{...}

interface IMyContractCallback
{
   [OperationContract(ProtectionLevel = ProtectionLevel.EncryptAndSign)]
   void OnCallback();
}
```

All calls into the callback object come in with an unauthenticated principal, even if Windows security was used across the board to invoke the service. As a result, the principal identity will be set to a Windows identity with a blank identity, which will preclude authorization and role-based security.

While the callback does have a security call context, the Windows identity will be set to a WindowsIdentity instance with a blank identity that will preclude impersonation. The only meaningful information will be in the primary identity that will be set to service host process identity and machine name:

```
class MyClient : IMyContractCallback
{
   public void OnCallback()
   {
      IPrincipal principal = Thread.CurrentPrincipal;
      Debug.Assert(principal.Identity.IsAuthenticated == false);

      ServiceSecurityContext context = ServiceSecurityContext.Current;
      Debug.Assert(context.PrimaryIdentity.Name == "MyHost/localhost");

      Debug.Assert(context.IsAnonymous == false);
   }
}
```

I recommend avoiding any sensitive work in the callback since you cannot easily use role-based security.

Internet Application

In the Internet scenario, the clients or services may not use WCF or even Windows. If you are writing a service or a client, you cannot assume the use of WCF on the other end. In addition, an Internet application typically has a relatively large number of clients calling the service. These client calls originate from outside the firewall. You need to rely on HTTP for transport, and multiple intermediaries are possible. In an Internet application, you typically do not want to use Windows accounts and groups for credentials and instead the application needs to access some custom credentials store. That said, you could still be using Windows security, as demonstrated later on.

Securing the Internet Bindings

In the Internet application, you must use message security for transfer security to provide for end-to-end security across all intermediaries. The client should provide credentials in the form of username and password. For the Internet scenario you should use the WSHttpBinding and WSDualHttpBinding. In addition, if you have an intranet application that uses the NetTcpBinding but you do not wish to use Windows security for user accounts and groups, you should follow the same configuration as with the WS-based bindings. This is done uniformly across these bindings by selecting MessageCredentialType.Username for the client credentials type used with the message security. You need to configure the bindings this way both at the client and at the service.

WSHttpBinding configuration

WSHttpBinding offers the Security property of the type WSHttpSecurity:

```
public class WSHttpBinding : WSHttpBindingBase
{
   public WSHttpBinding( );
   public WSHttpBinding(SecurityMode securityMode);
   public WSHttpSecurity Security
   {get;}
   //More members
}
```

With WSHttpSecurity, you need to set the Mode property of the type SecurityMode to SecurityMode.Message. The Message property of WSHttpSecurity will then take effect:

```
public sealed class WSHttpSecurity
{
   public SecurityMode Mode
   {get;set;}
   public NonDualMessageSecurityOverHttp Message
   {get;}
   public HttpTransportSecurity Transport
   {get;}
}
```

Message is of the type NonDualMessageSecurityOverHttp, which derives from MessageSecurityOverHttp:

```
public class MessageSecurityOverHttp
{
   public MessageCredentialType ClientCredentialType
   {get;set;}
   //More members
}
public sealed class NonDualMessageSecurityOverHttp :
                                        MessageSecurityOverHttp
{...}
```

You need to set the ClientCredentialType property of MessageSecurityOverHttp to MessageCredentialType.Username. Recall that the default Message credentials type of WSHttpBinding is Windows (see Table 10-3).

Because Message security is the default security mode of WSHttpBinding (see Table 10-1), these three definitions are equivalent:

```
WSHttpBinding binding1 = new WSHttpBinding();
binding1.Security.Message.ClientCredentialType = MessageCredentialType.UserName;

WSHttpBinding binding2 = new WSHttpBinding(SecurityMode.Message);
binding2.Security.Message.ClientCredentialType = MessageCredentialType.UserName;

WSHttpBinding binding3 = new WSHttpBinding();
binding3.Security.Mode = SecurityMode.Message;
binding3.Security.Message.ClientCredentialType = MessageCredentialType.UserName;
```

Or when using a config file:

```
<bindings>
   <wsHttpBinding>
      <binding name = "UserNameWS">
         <security mode = "Message">
            <message clientCredentialType = "UserName"/>
         </security>
      </binding>
   </wsHttpBinding>
</bindings>
```

And since Message security is the default, you can omit explicitly setting the mode in the config file:

```
<bindings>
   <wsHttpBinding>
      <binding name = "UserNameWS">
         <security>
            <message clientCredentialType = "UserName"/>
         </security>
      </binding>
   </wsHttpBinding>
</bindings>
```

Figure 10-4 shows the security-related elements of the `WSHttpBinding`.

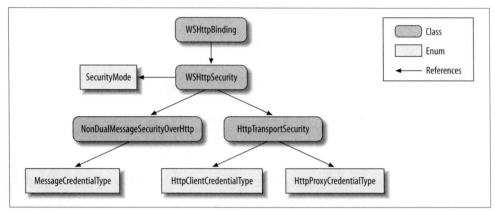

Figure 10-4. WSHttpBinding and security

`WSHttpBinding` has a reference to `WSHttpSecurity`, which uses the `SecurityMode` enum to indicate the transfer security mode. When transport security is used, `WSHttpSecurity` will use an instance of `HttpTransportSecurity`. When Message security is used, `WSHttpSecurity` will use an instance of `NonDualMessageSecurityOverHttp` containing the client credential type via the `MessageCredentialType` enum.

WSDualHttpBinding configuration

`WSDualHttpBinding` offers the Security property of the type `WSDualHttpSecurity`:

```
public class WSDualHttpBinding : Binding,...
{
    public WSDualHttpBinding( );
    public WSDualHttpBinding(WSDualHttpSecurityMode securityMode);
    public WSDualHttpSecurity Security
    {get;}
    //More members
}
```

With `WSDualHttpSecurity`, you need to set the `Mode` property of the type `WSDualHttpSecurityMode` to `WSDualHttpSecurityMode.Message`. The `Message` property of `WSDualHttpSecurity` will then take effect:

```
public sealed class WSDualHttpSecurity
{
    public MessageSecurityOverHttp Message
    {get;}
    public WSDualHttpSecurityMode Mode
    {set;set;}
}
```

`Message` is of the type `MessageSecurityOverHttp` presented earlier.

You need to set the `ClientCredentialType` property of `MessageSecurityOverHttp` to `MessageCredentialType.Username`. Recall that the default Message credentials type of `WSDualHttpBinding` is Windows (see Table 10-3).

Because Message security is the default transfer security mode of `WSDualHttpBinding` (see Table 10-1), these definitions are equivalent:

```
WSDualHttpBinding binding1 = new WSDualHttpBinding( );
binding1.Security.Message.ClientCredentialType = MessageCredentialType.UserName;

WSDualHttpBinding binding2 = new WSDualHttpBinding(WSDualHttpSecurityMode.Message);
binding2.Security.Message.ClientCredentialType = MessageCredentialType.UserName;

WSDualHttpBinding binding3 = new WSDualHttpBinding( );
binding3.Security.Mode = WSDualHttpSecurityMode.Message;
binding3.Security.Message.ClientCredentialType = MessageCredentialType.UserName;
```

Or when using a config file:

```
<bindings>
   <wsDualHttpBinding>
      <binding name = "WSDualWindowsSecurity">
         <security mode = "Message">
            <message  clientCredentialType = "UserName"/>
         </security>
      </binding>
   </wsDualHttpBinding>
</bindings>
```

And since Message security is the default, you can omit explicitly setting the mode in the config file:

```
<bindings>
   <wsDualHttpBinding>
      <binding name = "WSDualWindowsSecurity">
         <security>
            <message  clientCredentialType = "UserName"/>
         </security>
      </binding>
   </wsDualHttpBinding>
</bindings>
```

Figure 10-5 shows the security-related elements of `WSDualHttpBinding`.

`WSDualHttpBinding` has a reference to `WSDualHttpSecurity`, which uses the `WSDualHttpSecurityMode` enum to indicate the transfer security mode: Message or None. When Message security is used, `WSDualHttpSecurity` will use an instance of `MessageSecurityOverHttp` containing the client credential type via the `MessageCredentialType` enum.

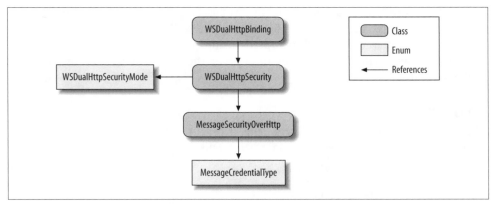

Figure 10-5. WSDualHttpBinding and security

Message Protection

Since in the Internet scenario the client's message sent to the service is transferred over plain HTTP, it is vital to protect its content (both the client's credentials and the body of the message) by encrypting it. Encryption will provide for message integrity and privacy. One technical option for encryption is to use the client's password. However, WCF never uses the client's password for encrypting the message, for a number of reasons. First, there are no guarantees that the password is strong enough, so that anyone monitoring the communication could not break the encryption. Second, it will force the service (more precisely, its host) to have access to the password, and thus couple the host to the credential store. Finally, while the password may protect the message, it will not provide for service authenticity toward the client.

To protect the message, WCF uses an X509 certificate. The certificate provides strong protection, and it uniquely authenticates the service toward the client. The way a certificate works is by using two keys, called the public and private keys, as well as a *common name* (CN) such as MyServiceCert. What is important about those keys is that anything encrypted with the public key can only be decrypted with the private one. The certificate contains the public key and the common name, and the private key is kept in some secure storage on the host machine that the host has access to. The host makes the certificate (and its public key) publicly available; that is, any client can access the host's endpoints and obtain the public key.

In a nutshell, what happens during a call is that WCF on the client's side will use the public key to encrypt all messages to the service. Upon receiving the encrypted message, WCF on the host side will decrypt the message using the private key. Once the message is decrypted, WCF will read the client's credentials from the message, authenticate the client, and allow it to access the service. The real picture is a bit more complex, because WCF also needs to secure the reply messages and callbacks from the service to the client. One of the standards WCF supports deals with setting up such a secure conversation. There are, in fact, several calls done before the first request message from the client to the service, where WCF on the client's side generates a shared secret it passes encrypted (using the service certificate) to the service. The service will then use that to encrypt the reply messages as well as the callbacks if any.

Configuring host certificate

The ServiceHostBase class offers the Credentials property of the type ServiceCredentials. ServiceCredentials is a service behavior:

```
public abstract class ServiceHostBase : ...
{
   public ServiceCredentials Credentials
   {get;}
   //More members
}
public class ServiceCredentials : ...,IServiceBehavior
{
   public X509CertificateRecipientServiceCredential ServiceCertificate
   {get;}
   //More members
}
```

ServiceCredentials provides the ServiceCertificate property of the type X509CertificateRecipientServiceCredential:

```
public sealed class X509CertificateRecipientServiceCredential
{
   public void SetCertificate(StoreLocation storeLocation,
                              StoreName storeName,
                              X509FindType findType,
                              object findValue);
   //More members
}
```

You can use the SetCertificate( ) method to instruct WCF where and how to load the service certificate. You typically provide this information in the host config file as a custom behavior under the serviceCredentials section, as shown in Example 10-8.

Example 10-8. Configuring the service certificate

```
<services>
   <service name = "MyService" behaviorConfiguration = "Internet">
      ...
   </service>
</services>
<behaviors>
   <serviceBehaviors>
      <behavior name = "Internet">
         <serviceCredentials>
            <serviceCertificate
               findValue    = "MyServiceCert"
```

Example 10-8. Configuring the service certificate (continued)

```
            storeLocation = "LocalMachine"
            storeName     = "My"
            x509FindType  = "FindBySubjectName"
        />
      </serviceCredentials>
    </behavior>
  </serviceBehaviors>
</behaviors>
```

Using the host certificate

The client developer can obtain the service certificate using any out-of-band mechanism (such as an email or via a public web page). The client can then include in its config file in the endpoint behavior section detailed information about the service certificate, such as where it is stored on the client side and how to find it. This is by far the most secure option from the client's perspective, because any attempt to subvert the client's address resolving and redirect the call to a malicious service will fail since the other service will not have the correct certificate. This is the least flexible option as well, however, because every time the client needs to interact with a different service, the client administrator will need to rework the client's config file.

A reasonable alternative to explicitly referencing the certificates of all services the client may interact with is to store those certificates in the client's Trusted People certificate folder. The administrator can then instruct WCF to allow calls only to a service whose certificate is in that folder. The client in that case will need to obtain the service certificate at runtime as part of the initial pre-call negotiation, check to see if it is in the Trusted People store and if so, proceed to use it to protect the message. In fact, certificate negotiation this way is the default behavior of WCF, but you can disable it (and use a hard-configured certificate) with both `WSHttpBinding` and `WSDualHttpBinding`. For the Internet scenario, I recommend the use of certificate negotiation coupled with storing the certificates in the Trusted People store.

Service certificate validation

To instruct WCF as to what degree to validate and trust the service certificate, add a custom endpoint behavior to the client's config file. The behavior should use the `ClientCredentials` section. `ClientCredentials` is an endpoint behavior that offers the `ServiceCertificate` property of the type `X509CertificateRecipientClientCredential`:

```
public class ClientCredentials : ...,IEndpointBehavior
{
   public X509CertificateRecipientClientCredential ServiceCertificate
   {get;}
   //More members
}
```

X509CertificateRecipientClientCredential offers the Authentication property of the type X509CertificateRecipientClientCredential:

```
public sealed class X509CertificateRecipientClientCredential
{
   public X509ServiceCertificateAuthentication Authentication
   {get;}
   //More members
}
```

X509CertificateRecipientClientCredential provides the CertificateValidationMode property of the enum type X509CertificateValidationMode:

```
public enum X509CertificateValidationMode
{
   None,
   PeerTrust,
   ChainTrust,
   PeerOrChainTrust,
   Custom
}

public class X509ServiceCertificateAuthentication
{
   public X509CertificateValidationMode CertificateValidationMode
   {get;set;}
   //More members
}
```

Example 10-9 demonstrates setting the service certificate validation mode in the client's config file.

Example 10-9. Validating the service certificate

```
<client>
   <endpoint behaviorConfiguration = "ServiceCertificate"
      ...
   </endpoint>
</client>
<behaviors>
   <endpointBehaviors>
      <behavior name = "ServiceCertificate">
         <clientCredentials>
            <serviceCertificate>
               <authentication certificateValidationMode = "PeerTrust"/>
            </serviceCertificate>
         </clientCredentials>
      </behavior>
   </endpointBehaviors>
</behaviors>
```

X509CertificateValidationMode.PeerTrust instructs WCF to trust the negotiated service certificate if it is also present in the Trusted People store of the client. X509CertificateValidationMode.ChainTrust instructs WCF to trust the certificate if it was issued by a trusted root authority (such as VeriSign or Thwart) whose certificate is found in the Trusted Root Authority folder. X509CertificateValidationMode.ChainTrust is the default value used by WCF. X509CertificateValidationMode.PeerOrChainTrust allows either of these options.

Working with a test certificate

Developers often do not have access to their organization's certificate, and therefore resort to using test certificates such as the ones generated by the *MakeCert.exe* command-line utility. There are two problems with test certificates. The first is that they will fail the default certificate validation on the client side since the client uses X509CertificateValidationMode.ChainTrust by default. That can easily be overcome by installing the test certificate in the client's Trusted People store and using X509CertificateValidationMode.PeerTrust or X509CertificateValidationMode.PeerOrChainTrust. The second problem is that WCF by default expects the service certificate name to match the service host's domain (or machine name). To compensate, the client must explicitly specify the test certificate name in the endpoint identity's DNS section:

```
<client>
   <endpoint
      address  = "http://localhost:8001/MyService"
      binding  = "wsHttpBinding"
      contract = "IMyContract">
      <identity>
         <dns value = "MyServiceCert"/>
      </identity>
   </endpoint>
</client>
```

Authentication

The client needs to provide its credentials to the proxy. The ClientCredentials property (presented earlier) of the ClientBase<T> base class has the UserName property of the type UserNamePasswordClientCredential:

```
public class ClientCredentials : ...,IEndpointBehavior
{
   public UserNamePasswordClientCredential UserName
   {get;}
   //More members
}

public sealed class UserNamePasswordClientCredential
{
   public string UserName
   {get;set;}
   public string Password
   {get;set;}
}
```

The client uses UserNamePasswordClientCredential to pass to the service its username and password as demonstrated in Example 10-10.

 The client need not provide a domain name (if Widows security is used) or application name (if ASP.NET providers are used). The host will use its service domain or a configured application name as appropriate.

Example 10-10. Providing username and passwords credentials

```
MyContractClient proxy = new MyContractClient();

proxy.ClientCredentials.UserName.UserName = "MyUsername";
proxy.ClientCredentials.UserName.Password = "MyPassword";

proxy.MyMethod();
proxy.Close();
```

Unlike the intranet scenario (see Example 10-3) where the client has to instantiate a new NetworkCredential object, with the Internet scenario there is no need (or way) to assign a new UserNamePasswordClientCredential object.

When working with a channel factory instead of a proxy class, set the Credentials property of the factory with the credentials:

```
ChannelFactory<IMyContract> factory = new ChannelFactory<IMyContract>("");

factory.Credentials.UserName.UserName = "MyUsername";
factory.Credentials.UserName.Password = "MyPassword";

IMyContract proxy = factory.CreateChannel();
using(proxy as IDisposable)
{
    proxy.MyMethod();
}
```

Note that you cannot use the static CreateChannel() methods of ChannelFactory<T> since you have to instantiate a factory in order to access the Credentials property.

Once the username and password credentials are received by the WCF on the service side, the host can choose to authenticate them as either Windows credentials, ASP.NET membership provider's credentials, or even custom credentials. Whichever option you choose, make sure it matches your role-based policy configuration.

The ServiceCredentials class (the Credentials property of ServiceHostBase) provides the UserNameAuthentication property of the type UserNamePasswordServiceCredential:

```
public class ServiceCredentials : ...,IServiceBehavior
{
    public UserNamePasswordServiceCredential UserNameAuthentication
    {get;}
    //More members
}
```

`UserNamePasswordServiceCredential` has the `UserNamePasswordValidationMode` property of a matching enum type:

```
public enum UserNamePasswordValidationMode
{
   Windows,
   MembershipProvider,
   Custom
}
public sealed class UserNamePasswordServiceCredential
{
   public MembershipProvider MembershipProvider
   {get;set;}
   public UserNamePasswordValidationMode UserNamePasswordValidationMode
   {get; set;}
   //More members
}
```

By setting the `UserNamePasswordValidationMode` property, the host chooses how to authenticate the incoming username and password credentials.

Using Windows Credentials

While not necessarily common, WCF lets the Internet-facing service authenticate the incoming credentials as Windows credentials. To authenticate the client's username and password as Windows credentials, you need to set `UserNamePasswordValidationMode` to `UserNamePasswordValidationMode.Windows`. Because `UserNamePasswordValidationMode.Windows` is the default value of the `UserNamePasswordValidationMode` property, these two definitions are equivalent:

```
ServiceHost host1 = new ServiceHost(typeof(MyService));

ServiceHost host2 = new ServiceHost(typeof(MyService));
host2.Credentials.UserNameAuthentication.UserNamePasswordValidationMode =
                              UserNamePasswordValidationMode.Windows;
```

When using a config file, add a custom behavior that assigns the username and password authentication mode along with the service certificate information, as shown in Example 10-11.

Example 10-11. Internet security with Windows credentials

```
<services>
   <service name = "MyService" behaviorConfiguration = "UsernameWindows">
      ...
   </service>
</services>
<behaviors>
   <serviceBehaviors>
      <behavior name = "UsernameWindows">
         <serviceCredentials>
            <userNameAuthentication userNamePasswordValidationMode = "Windows"/>
            <serviceCertificate
```

Example 10-11. Internet security with Windows credentials (continued)

```
                ...
            />
        </serviceCredentials>
      </behavior>
   </serviceBehaviors>
</behaviors>
```

As with the programmatic case, adding this line to the config file:

```
<userNameAuthentication userNamePasswordValidationMode = "Windows"/>
```

is optional because it is the default setting.

Authorization

If the `PrincipalPermissionMode` property of `ServiceAuthorizationBehavior` is set to its default value of `PrincipalPermissionMode.UseWindowsGroups`, once the username and password are authenticated against Windows, WCF installs a Windows principal object and attaches it to the thread. This enables the service to freely use Windows NT groups for authorization, just as with the intranet case, both declaratively and programmatically.

Identity management

As long as the principal permission mode is set to `PrincipalPermissionMode. UseWindowsGroups`, the identity management aspect is just as with the intranet scenario, including the identities of the security call context, as shown in Table 10-4. The main difference between an intranet application and an Internet application that uses Windows credentials is that the client cannot dictate the allowed impersonation level, and the host can impersonate at will. This is because WCF will assign `TokenImpersonationLevel.Impersonation` to the Windows identity of the security call context.

Using the ASP.NET Providers

By default, WCF role-based security uses Windows user groups for roles and Windows accounts for security identities. There are several drawbacks to this default policy. First, you may not want to assign a Windows account for every client of your Internet application. Second, the security policy is only as granular as the user groups in the hosting domain. Often you do not have control over your end customer's IT department. If you deploy your application in an environment in which the user groups are coarse or in which the user groups don't map well to actual roles users play in your application, or if the group names are slightly different, Windows role-based security is of little use to you. Roles localization presents yet another set of challenges because role names will differ between customer sites in different locales. Consequently, Internet applications hardly ever use Windows accounts and groups.

.NET 2.0 provides out-of-the-box custom credential management called the ASP. NET Provider Model, though non-ASP.NET applications (like WCF applications) can easily use it to authenticate users and authorize them, without ever resorting to Windows accounts.

One of the concrete implementations of the architecture includes a SQL Server store. SQL Server is often the repository of choice for Internet applications and so I will use it in this scenario. To use the SQL Server provider, run the setup file *aspnet_regsql.exe* found under *%Windir%\Microsoft.NET\Framework\<Version>*. The setup program will create a new database called *aspnetdb*, containing the tables and stored procedures required to manage the credentials.

The SQL Server credential store is well designed, using the latest best practices for credentials management, such as password salting, stored procedures, and so on. This infrastructure helps productivity, saving developers valuable time and effort, not to mention providing a high quality, secure solution. That said, the credential management architecture is that of a provider model, and you can easily add other storage options such as an Access database.

The credentials providers

Figure 10-6 shows the architecture of the ASP.NET 2.0 credentials providers.

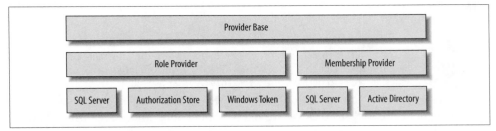

Figure 10-6. The ASP.NET provider model

Membership providers are responsible for managing users (usernames and passwords), and role providers are responsible for managing roles. Out of the box, ASP. NET offers support for membership stores in SQL Server or Active Directory, and roles can be stored in SQL Server, a file (authorization store), or NT groups (Windows token).

Username and password authentication is done using a class called `MembershipProvider` from the `System.Web.Security` namespace, defined as:

```
public abstract class MembershipProvider : ProviderBase
{
    public abstract string ApplicationName
    {get;set;}
    public abstract bool ValidateUser(string name,string password);
    //Additional members
}
```

`MembershipProvider`'s goal is to encapsulate the actual provider used and the details of the actual data access, as well as to enable changing the membership provider without affecting the application itself. Depending on the configured security provider in the host config file, WCF will use a concrete data access class such as `SqlMembershipProvider` targeting SQL Server or SQL Server Express:

```
public class SqlMembershipProvider : MembershipProvider
{...}
```

However, WCF interacts only with the `MembershipProvider` base functionality. WCF obtains the required membership provider by accessing the `Provider` static property of the `Membership` class, defined as:

```
public sealed class Membership
{
    public static string ApplicationName
    {get;set;}
    public static MembershipProvider Provider
    {get;}
    public static bool ValidateUser(string username,string password);
    //Additional members
}
```

`Membership` offers many members, which support the many aspects of user management. `Membership.Provider` retrieves the type of the configured provider from the `System.Web` section in the host config file. Unspecified, the role provider defaults to `SqlMembershipProvider`.

 Because all membership providers derive from the abstract class `MembershipProvider`, if you write your own custom credential provider, it needs to derive from `MembershipProvider` as well.

Since a single credential store can serve many applications, those applications could define the same usernames. To allow for that, every record in the credentials store is scoped by an application name (similar to the way usernames in Windows are scoped by a domain or machine name).

The `ApplicationName` property of `Membership` is used to set and retrieve the application name, and the `ValidateUser( )` method, which authenticates the specified credentials against the store, and returns `true` if they match and `false` otherwise. `Membership. ValidateUser` is shorthand for retrieving and using the configured provider.

If you configure your application to use the ASP.NET credentials store for authorization and if you enabled roles support, after authentication WCF installs an instance of the internal class `RoleProviderPrincipal` and attaches it to the thread invoking the operation:

```
sealed class RoleProviderPrincipal : IPrincipal
{...}
```

`RoleProviderPrincipal` uses the abstract class `RoleProvider` for authorization:

```
public abstract class RoleProvider : ProviderBase
{
    public abstract string ApplicationName
    {get;set;}
    public abstract bool IsUserInRole(string username,string roleName);
    //Additional members
}
```

The `ApplicationName` property of `RoleProvider` binds the role provider to the particular application. The `IsUserInRole( )` method verifies the user's role membership. Like the membership providers, all role providers (including custom role providers) must derive from `RoleProvider`.

`RoleProvider` encapsulates the actual provider used, and the role provider to use is specified in the host config file. Depending on the configured role provider, `RoleProviderPrincipal` uses a corresponding data access class such as `SqlRoleProvider` to authorize the caller:

```
public class SqlRoleProvider : RoleProvider
{...}
```

You can obtain the required role provider by accessing the `Provider` static property of the `Roles` class, defined as:

```
public sealed class Roles
{
    public static string ApplicationName
    {get;set;}
    public static bool IsUserInRole(string username,string roleName);
    public static RoleProvider Provider
    {get;}
    //Additional members
}
```

`Roles.IsUserInRole( )` is shorthand for accessing `Roles.Provider` first and then calling `IsUserInRole( )` on it. `Roles.Provider` retrieves the type of the configured provider from the host config file. Unspecified, the role provider defaults to `SqlRoleProvider`.

Credentials administration

If you choose either Windows or Active Directory to store your application's users and roles, then you need to administer the user credentials using the dedicated tools for those stores, such as the Computer Management control panel applet or the Active Directory tools.

If you use SQL Server, .NET 2.0 installs web site administration pages under *Inetpub*\ *wwwroot\aspnet_webadmin\<version number>*. Developers can configure the application directly from within Visual Studio 2005. When selecting ASP.NET Configuration from the Web Site menu, Visual Studio 2005 will browse to the ASP.NET administration pages and allow you to configure various parameters, including security configuration. You can configure the following aspects for your application:

- Create new users and delete existing ones
- Create new roles and delete existing ones
- Allocate users to roles
- Retrieve a user's details
- Set a user's status
- Use additional features not relevant to this chapter

Shortcomings of Visual Studio 2005

There are a number of significant shortcomings to the Visual Studio 2005-driven administration pages. First, you need Visual Studio 2005. It is unlikely that application or system administrators will have Visual Studio 2005, let alone know how to use it. The administration pages use "/" by default for the application name, and do not offer any visual way to modify that. You must create a web application to activate the administration pages and there is no remote access: the application and Visual Studio 2005 must be co-located so that Visual Studio 2005 can access the application's configuration file. The browser-based user interface is somewhat annoying (you need to frequently click the Back button) and rather dull. Many features that administrators are likely to want to use are not available via the administration pages. This is in spite of the fact that the features are supported by the underlying provider classes. Some of the things missing from the Visual Studio 2005-driven administration pages include the ability to:

- Update most if not all of the details in a user account
- Retrieve a user's password
- Change a user's password
- Reset a user's password
- Retrieve information about the number of current online users
- Remove all users from a role in one operation
- Retrieve information about the password management policy (such as length, reset policy, type of passwords, etc.)
- Test user credentials
- Verify user role membership

Moreover, there are additional features that administrators are likely to want, and yet they are not supported, not even by the provider classes. These features include the ability to retrieve a list of all of the applications in the database, the ability to remove all users from an application, the ability to remove all roles from an application, the ability to delete an application (and all its associated users and roles), and the ability to delete all applications.

Credentials Manager

This tools disparity motivated me to develop the Credentials Manager application—a smart client application that compensates for all of the shortcomings just listed. Figure 10-7 shows a screenshot of Credentials Manager.[*]

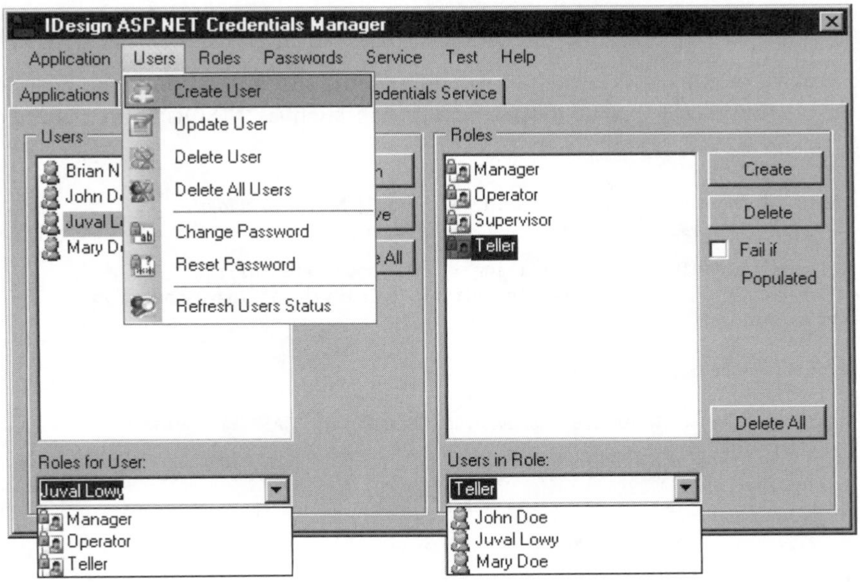

Figure 10-7. The Credentials Manager utility

Credentials Manager is available with the source code of this book at *http://www.oreilly.com/catalog/9780596526993*

I wrapped the ASP.NET providers with a WCF service (that can be self-hosted or be IIS-hosted), and added the missing features, such as deleting an application.

Credentials Manager uses these endpoints to administer the credential store. In addition, it lets administrators to select at runtime the address of the credentials service, and using the MetadataHelper class presented in Chapter 2 it verifies that the address provided does indeed support the required contracts.

---

[*] I first published an earlier version of Credentials Manager in my article "Manage Custom Security Credentials the Smart (Client) Way," *CoDe Magazine,* November 2005. Credentials Manager has since become the de facto standard way of administering the ASP.NET SQL Server credentials store.

Authentication

To authenticate the client's username and password using an ASP.NET provider, set the UserNamePasswordValidationMode property to UserNamePasswordValidationMode. MembershipProvider:

```
ServiceHost host = new ServiceHost(typeof(MyService));
host.Credentials.UserNameAuthentication.UserNamePasswordValidationMode =
                            UserNamePasswordValidationMode.MembershipProvider;
```

Which provider is used depends on the host config file. In addition, the host config file must contain any provider-specific settings such as a SQL Server connection string, as shown in Example 10-12.

Example 10-12. Internet security using an ASP.NET SQL Server provider

```
<connectionStrings>
   <add name= "AspNetDb" connectionString = "data source=(local);
                         Integrated Security=SSPI;Initial Catalog=aspnetdb"/>
</connectionStrings>

<system.serviceModel>
   <services>
      <service name = "MyService" behaviorConfiguration = "ASPNETProviders">
         <endpoint
            ...
         />
      </service>
   </services>
   <behaviors>
      <serviceBehaviors>
         <behavior name = "ASPNETProviders">
            <serviceCredentials>
               <userNameAuthentication
               userNamePasswordValidationMode = "MembershipProvider"/>
               <serviceCertificate
                  ...
               />
            </serviceCredentials>
         </behavior>
      </serviceBehaviors>
   </behaviors>
</system.serviceModel>
```

The default application name will be a useless /, so you must set your specific application name. Once ASP.NET providers are configured, WCF initializes the MembershipProvider property of UserNamePasswordServiceCredential with an instance of the configured membership provider. You can programmatically access that membership provider and set its application name:

```
ServiceHost host = new ServiceHost(typeof(MyService));
Debug.Assert(host.Credentials.UserNameAuthentication.MembershipProvider != null);
Membership.ApplicationName = "MyApplication";
```

You can also configure the application name in the config file, but for that you need to define a custom ASP.NET membership provider, as shown in Example 10-13.

Example 10-13. Configuring the application name for the membership provider

```
<system.web>
   <membership defaultProvider = "MySqlMembershipProvider">
      <providers>
         <add name = "MySqlMembershipProvider"
            type = "System.Web.Security.SqlMembershipProvider"
            connectionStringName = "AspNetDb"
            applicationName = "MyApplication"
         />
      </providers>
   </membership>
</system.web>
<connectionStrings>
   <add name = "AspNetDb"
      ...
   />
</connectionStrings>
```

In Example 10-13, you add a system.Web section with a providers section, where you add a custom membership provider and you set that to be the new default membership provider. Next you need to list the fully qualified type name of the new provider. Nothing prevents you referencing any existing implementation of a membership provider, such as SqlMembershipProvider, as in Example 10-13. When using the SQL provider, you must also list the connection string to use, and you cannot rely on the default connection string from *machine.config*. Most importantly, set the ApplicationName tag to the desired application name.

Authorization

To support authorizing the users, the host must enable role-based security by adding this to the config file:

```
<system.web>
   <roleManager enabled = "true"/>
</system.web>
```

 To enable the role manager programmatically, you have to use reflection.

Enabling roles this way will initialize the Roles class and have its Provider property set to the configured provider. To use the ASP.NET role provider, set the PrincipalPermissionMode property to PrincipalPermissionMode.UseAspNetRoles:

```
ServiceHost host = new ServiceHost(typeof(MyService));
host.Authorization.PrincipalPermissionMode=PrincipalPermissionMode.UseAspNetRoles;
```

Or when using a config file, add a custom behavior to that effect:

```
<services>
   <service name = "MyService" behaviorConfiguration = "ASPNETProviders">
      ...
   </service>
</services>
<behaviors>
   <serviceBehaviors>
      <behavior name = "ASPNETProviders">
         <serviceAuthorization principalPermissionMode = "UseAspNetRoles"
         ...
      </behavior>
   </serviceBehaviors>
</behaviors>
```

After authenticating the client, the RoleProvider property of ServiceAuthorizationBehavior will be set to the configured role provider:

```
public sealed class ServiceAuthorizationBehavior : IServiceBehavior
{
   public RoleProvider RoleProvider
   {get;set;}
   //More members
}
```

The default application name will be a useless /, so you must set your specific application name. Unlike the membership provider, you cannot access the RoleProvider property of ServiceAuthorizationBehavior to set the application name, because its value will be null until after authentication. Instead, use the static helper class Roles:

```
ServiceHost host = new ServiceHost(typeof(MyService));
Debug.Assert(host.Credentials.UserNameAuthentication.MembershipProvider != null);
Roles.ApplicationName = "MyApplication";
```

You can also configure the application name in the config file, but for that you need to define a custom ASP.NET role provider, as shown in Example 10-14.

Example 10-14. Configuring the application name for the role provider

```
<system.web>
   <roleManager enabled = "true" defaultProvider = "MySqlRoleManager">
      <providers>
         <add name = "MySqlRoleManager"
            type = "System.Web.Security.SqlRoleProvider"
            connectionStringName = "AspNetDb"
            applicationName = "MyApplication"
         />
      </providers>
   </roleManager>
</system.web>
<connectionStrings>
   <add name = "AspNetDb"
      ...
   />
</connectionStrings>
```

As with the membership provider, you add a system.Web section with a providers section, where you add a custom roles provider and you set that to be the new default role provider. Next you need to list the fully qualified type name of the new provider. As with the membership provider, you can reference any existing implementation of a role provider, such as SqlRoleProvider, in which case you must also list the connection string to use. Finally, set the ApplicationName tag to the desired application name.

Declarative role-based security

You can use the PrincipalPermission attribute to verify role membership just as with the intranet scenario because all the attribute does is access the principal object attached to the thread, which has already been set by WCF to RoleProviderPrincipal. Example 10-15 demonstrates declarative role-based security using the ASP.NET providers.

Example 10-15. ASP.NET role provider declarative role-based security

```
class MyService : IMyContract
{
   [PrincipalPermission(SecurityAction.Demand,Role = "Manager")]
   public void MyMethod( )
   {...}
}
```

The only noticeable difference between the intranet and Internet scenarios is that in the Internet scenario, when specifying role name, you do not prefix it with the application or domain name.

Identity Management

In the Internet scenario, when using ASP.NET providers, the identity associated with the principal object is a GenericIdentity wrapping the username provided by the client. That identity is considered authenticated. The security call context's primary identity will match the principal identity. The Windows identity, on the other hand, will be set to a Windows identity with a blank username; that is, unauthenticated. Table 10-5 shows the identities in this scenario.

Table 10-5. Identity management in the Internet scenario with ASP.NET providers

Identity	Type	Value	Authenticated
Thread Principal	GenericIdentity	Username	Yes
Security Context Primary	GenericIdentity	Username	Yes
Security Context Windows	WindowsIdentity	-	No

Impersonation

Since no valid Windows credentials were provided, the service cannot impersonate any of its clients.

Callbacks

When you use the ASP.NET providers, while the callback message is protected, all calls into the callback object come in with an unauthenticated principal. As a result, the principal identity will be set to a Windows identity with a blank username, which will preclude authorization and role-based security, as it is considered anonymous. While the callback does have a security call context, the Windows identity will be set to a `WindowsIdentity` instance with a blank identity, which will preclude impersonation. The only meaningful information will be in the primary identity that will be set to an instance of the `X509Identity` class, with a name set to the common name of the service host certificate suffixed by a thumbprint (a hash) of the certificate:

```
class MyClient : IMyContractCallback
{
   public void OnCallback( )
   {
      IPrincipal principal = Thread.CurrentPrincipal;
      Debug.Assert(principal.Identity.IsAuthenticated == false);

      ServiceSecurityContext context = ServiceSecurityContext.Current;
      Debug.Assert(context.PrimaryIdentity.Name ==
                "CN=MyServiceCert; D6E33B50BCF6D9609E68762F2C6A14F65679268B");
      Debug.Assert(context.IsAnonymous == false);
   }
}
```

I recommend avoiding any sensitive work in the callback, since you cannot easily use role-based security.

Business-to-Business Application

In the business-to-business scenario, the service and its clients are disparate business entities. They do not share credentials or accounts, and the communication between them is typically closed to the public. There are relatively few clients interacting with the service, and the client can only interact with the service after an elaborate business agreement and other conditions have been met. Instead of Windows accounts or usernames, the clients identify themselves to the service using X509 certificates. These certificates are usually known a priori to the service. The client or service may not use WCF or even Windows. If you are writing a service or a client, you cannot assume the use of WCF at the other end. The client calls originate from outside the firewall, and you need to rely on HTTP for transport, and multiple intermediaries are possible.

Securing the Business-to-Business Bindings

For the business-to-business scenario, you should use the Internet bindings; namely, `BasicHttpBinding`, `WSHttpBinding`, and `WSDualHttpBinding`. You must use Message security for transfer security to provide for end-to-end security across all intermediaries. The message will be protected using a service-side certificate, just as with the Internet scenario. However, unlike the Internet scenario, the clients provide credentials in the form of a certificate. This is done uniformly across these bindings by selecting `MessageCredentialType.Certificate` for the client credentials type used with the Message security. You need to configure this on both the client and the service. For example, to configure the `WSHttpBinding` programmatically you would write:

```
WSHttpBinding binding = new WSHttpBinding( );
binding.Security.Message.ClientCredentialType = MessageCredentialType.Certificate;
```

Or with a config file:

```
<bindings>
   <wsHttpBinding>
      <binding name = "WSCertificateSecurity">
         <security mode = "Message">
            <message clientCredentialType = "Certificate"/>
         </security>
      </binding>
   </wsHttpBinding>
</bindings>
```

Authentication

The service administrator has a number of options as to how to authenticate the certificates sent by the client. If the certificate is validated, the client is considered authenticated. If no validation is done, then merely sending a certificate will do. If the validation is set to use a chain of trust—that is, a trusted root authority issued the certificate—then the client will be considered authenticated. However, the common way of validating the client's certificate is to use a peer trust. The service administrator should install all the certificates of the clients allowed to interact with the service in the Trusted People store on the service's local machine. When the client's certificate is received by the service, if the certificate is found in the trusted store, the client is authenticated. I will therefore use peer trust in the business-to-business scenario.

The `ServiceCredentials` class offers the `ClientCertificate` property of the type `X509CertificateInitiatorServiceCredential`:

```
public class ServiceCredentials : ...,IServiceBehavior
{
   public X509CertificateInitiatorServiceCredential ClientCertificate
   {get;}
   //More members
}
```

X509CertificateInitiatorServiceCredential provides the Authentication property of the type X509ClientCertificateAuthentication that lets you configure the certificate validation mode:

```
public sealed class X509CertificateInitiatorServiceCredential
{
   public X509ClientCertificateAuthentication Authentication
   {get;}
   //More members
}
public class X509ClientCertificateAuthentication
{
   public X509CertificateValidationMode CertificateValidationMode
   {get;set;} //More members
}
```

Example 10-16 demonstrates the settings required in the host config file for the business-to-business scenario. Note in Example 10-16 that the host still needs to provide its own certificate for message security.

Example 10-16. Configuring the host for business-to-business security

```
<services>
   <service name = "MyService" behaviorConfiguration = "BusinessToBusiness">
      ...
   </service>
</services>
<behaviors>
   <serviceBehaviors>
      <behavior name = "BusinessToBusiness">
         <serviceCredentials>
            <serviceCertificate
               ...
            />
            <clientCertificate>
               <authentication certificateValidationMode = "PeerTrust"/>
            </clientCertificate>
         </serviceCredentials>
      </behavior>
   </serviceBehaviors>
</behaviors>
```

The client needs to reference the certificate to use, by including its location, name, and lookup method. This is done by accessing the ClientCredentials property of the proxy, which offers the ClientCertificate property of the type X509CertificateInitiatorClientCredential:

```
public class ClientCredentials : ...,IEndpointBehavior
{
   public X509CertificateInitiatorClientCredential ClientCertificate
   {get;}
   //More members
```

```
    }
    public sealed class X509CertificateInitiatorClientCredential
    {
        public void SetCertificate(StoreLocation storeLocation,
                                   StoreName storeName,
                                   X509FindType findType,
                                   object findValue);

        //More members
    }
```

However, the client will typically set these values in its config file, as shown in Example 10-17.

Example 10-17. Setting the client's certificate

```
<client>
   <endpoint behaviorConfiguration = "BusinessToBusiness"
      ...
   />
</client>
   ...
<behaviors>
   <endpointBehaviors>
      <behavior name = "BusinessToBusiness">
         <clientCredentials>
            <clientCertificate
               findValue     = "MyClientCert"
               storeLocation = "LocalMachine"
               storeName     = "My"
               x509FindType  = "FindBySubjectName"
            />
            ...
         </clientCredentials>
      </behavior>
   </endpointBehaviors>
</behaviors>
```

The config file needs to also indicate the service certificate validation mode. When using the BasicHttpBinding, since that binding cannot negotiate the service certificate, the client's config file needs to contain in the service certificate section of the endpoint behavior the location of the service certificate to use. Note that when using a service test certificate, as with the Internet scenario, the client's config file must still include the information regarding the endpoint identity.

Once the client certificate is configured, there is no need to do anything special with the proxy class:

```
MyContractClient proxy = new MyContractClient( );
proxy.MyMethod( );
proxy.Close( );
```

Authorization

By default, the service cannot employ principal-based, role-based security. The reason is that the credentials provided, namely the client's certificate, does not map to either Windows or ASP.NET user accounts. Because business-to-business endpoints and services are often dedicated to a small set of clients or even a particular client, this lack of authorization support may not pose a problem. If that is indeed your case, you should set the `PrincipalPermissionMode` property to `PrincipalPermissionMode.None`, so that WCF will attach a generic principal with a blank identity as opposed to a Windows identity with a blank identity.

If, on the other hand, you still would like to authorize the clients, you can actually achieve just that. In essence, all you need to do is deploy some credentials claim store and add the client's certificate name—that is, its common name and its thumbprint—to that repository, and then perform access checks against that store as needed.

In fact, nothing prevents you from taking advantage of the ASP.NET role provider for authorization, even though the membership provider was not used in the authentication. This ability to use the providers separately was a core design goal for the ASP.NET provider model.

First, you need to enable the role provider in the host config file and configure the application name as in Example 10-14, or you can provide the application name programmatically.

Next, add the client certificate and thumbprint to the membership store as a user, and assign roles to it. For example, when using a certificate whose common name is MyClientCert, you need to add a user by the name of "CN=MyClientCert; 12A06153D25E94902F50971F68D86DCDE2A00756" to the membership store, and provide some password. The password, of course, is irrelevant and will not be used. Once you have created the user, assign it to the appropriate roles in the application.

Most importantly, set the `PrincipalPermissionMode` property to `PrincipalPermissionMode.UseAspNetRoles`. Example 10-18 lists the required settings in the host config file.

Example 10-18. ASP.NET role-based security for the business-to-business scenario

```
<system.web>
   <roleManager enabled = "true" defaultProvider = "MySqlRoleManager">
      <providers>
         <add name = "MySqlRoleManager"
            ...
            applicationName = "MyApplication"
         />
      </providers>
   </roleManager>
</system.web>
```

```
<system.serviceModel>
    <services>
        <service name = "MyService" behaviorConfiguration = "BusinessToBusiness">
            ...
        </service>
    </services>
    <behaviors>
        <serviceBehaviors>
            <behavior name = "BusinessToBusiness">
                <serviceCredentials>
                    <serviceCertificate
                        ...
                    />
                    <clientCertificate>
                        <authentication certificateValidationMode = "PeerTrust"/>
                    </clientCertificate>
                </serviceCredentials>
                <serviceAuthorization principalPermissionMode = "UseAspNetRoles"/>
            </behavior>
        </serviceBehaviors>
    </behaviors>
    <bindings>
        ...
    </bindings>
</system.serviceModel>
```

Now you can use role-based security just as in Example 10-15.

Identity Management

If the `PrincipalPermissionMode` property is set to `PrincipalPermissionMode.None`, then the principal identity will be a `GenericIdentity` with a blank username. The security call context primary identity will be of the type `X509Identity` containing the client certificate's common name and its thumbprint. The security call context Windows identity will have a blank username, since no valid Windows credentials were provided. If `PrincipalPermissionMode` property is set to `PrincipalPermissionMode.UseAspNetRoles`, then both the principal identity and the security call context primary identity will be set to an instance of `X509Identity` containing the client certificate and thumbprint. The security call context Windows identity will have a blank username, same as before. Table 10-6 lists this setup.

Table 10-6. Identity management in the business-to-business scenario with ASP.NET role providers

Identity	Type	Value	Authenticated
Thread Principal	X509Identity	Client cert name	Yes
Security Context Primary	X509Identity	Client cert name	Yes
Security Context Windows	WindowsIdentity	-	No

Impersonation

Since no valid Windows credentials were provided, the service cannot impersonate any of its clients.

Callbacks

In the business-to-business scenario, callbacks behave just as in the Internet scenario, since in both cases the same transfer security mechanism is used and the service identifies itself using a certificate. As with the Internet callback scenario, avoid sensitive work in the callback, since you cannot use role-based security and the callers are unauthenticated as far as the principal is concerned.

Host Security Configuration

While Figure 10-8 is not specific to the business-to-business scenario, having covered this scenario, this is the first point in this chapter where I can show all the pieces of the service host pertaining to security.

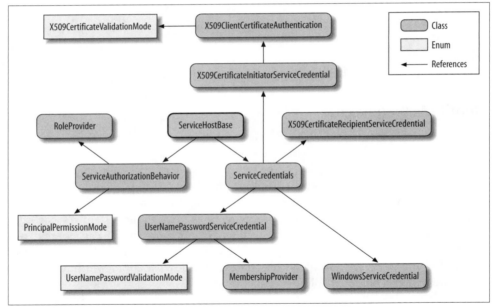

Figure 10-8. The security elements of ServiceHostBase

Anonymous Application

In the Anonymous scenario, the clients access the service without presenting any credentials—they are anonymous. On the other hand, the clients and the service do require secure message transfer, impervious to tampering and sniffing. Both an Internet-facing and intranet-based application may need to provide for anonymous yet end-to-end secure access. The anonymous scenario can have any number of clients, small or large. The clients may connect over HTTP or over TCP.

Securing the Anonymous Bindings

The need to secure the message, and the fact that the clients may be calling over the Internet with multiple intermediaries means that in the Anonymous scenario, you should use Message security, since it can easily accomplish both requirements, by setting the Message credentials to no credentials. The service needs to be configured with a certificate to secure the message itself. For the Anonymous scenario, you can use only the `NetTcpBinding`, `WSHttpBinding`, `WSDualHttpBinding`, and `NetMsmqBinding`— a mixture of both Internet and intranet bindings, as is required in this scenario. Note that you cannot use the `BasicHttpBinding`, `NetNamedPipeBinding`, `NetPeerTcpBinding`, or `WSFederationHttpBinding`, as those bindings either do not support Message security or do not support having no credentials in the message (see Tables 10-1 and 10-3). Configuring the allowed bindings is similar to the previous scenarios. The noticeable difference is in configuring for no client credentials, for example by using `MessageCredentialType.None` in the case of `WSHttpBinding`:

```
WSHttpBinding binding = new WSHttpBinding();
binding.Security.Message.ClientCredentialType = MessageCredentialType.None;
```

Or when using a config file:

```
<bindings>
   <wsHttpBinding>
      <binding name = "WSAnonymous">
         <security mode = "Message">
            <message clientCredentialType = "None"/>
         </security>
      </binding>
   </wsHttpBinding>
</bindings>
```

Authentication

No client authentication is done in the Anonymous scenario of course, and the client need not provide any to the proxy. For service authentication toward the client and for message protection, the service needs to provide its certificate, as in Example 10-8.

Authorization

Since the clients are anonymous (and unauthenticated), authorization and role-based security are precluded. The service host should set the `PrincipalPermissionMode` property to `PrincipalPermissionMode.None` to have WCF install a generic principal with a blank identity, instead of a Windows principal with a blank identity.

Identity Management

Assuming the use of `PrincipalPermissionMode.None`, the identity associated with the principal object is a `GenericIdentity` with a blank username. That identity is considered unauthenticated. The security call context's primary identity will match the principal identity. The Windows identity, on the other hand, will be set to a Windows identity with a blank username; that is, unauthenticated. Table 10-7 shows the identities in this scenario.

Table 10-7. Identity management in the Anonymous scenario

Identity	Type	Value	Authenticated
Thread Principal	GenericIdentity	-	No
Security Context Primary	GenericIdentity	-	No
Security Context Windows	WindowsIdentity	-	No

Impersonation

Since the clients are anonymous, the service cannot impersonate any of its clients.

Callbacks

While the call from the client to the service is anonymous, the service does reveal its identity to the client. The primary identity of the security call context will be set to an instance of the `X509Identity` class, with a name set to the common name of the service host certificate suffixed by the certificate's thumbprint. The rest of the information is masked out. The principal identity will be set to a Windows identity with a blank username, which will preclude authorization and role-based security, as it is considered anonymous. The security call context's Windows identity will be set to a `WindowsIdentity` instance with a blank identity, which will preclude impersonation. Avoid sensitive work in the callback since you cannot use role-based security and the callers are unauthenticated as far as the principal is concerned.

No Security

In this last scenario, your application turns off security completely. The service does not rely on any transfer security, and it does not authenticate or authorize its callers. Obviously, such a service is completely exposed and you generally need a very good business justification for relinquishing security. You can accept any number of clients, and both an Internet and an intranet service can be configured for No Security.

Unsecuring the Bindings

To turn off security, you need to set the transfer security mode to None. This will also avoid storing any client credentials in the message. All bindings support no transfer security (see Table 10-1), but you have no reason to ever use this mode with the WSFederationHttpBinding since the only reason for choosing it in the first place is the need for federated security.

Configuring the allowed bindings is similar to the previous scenarios, except the security mode is set to no transfer security; for example, by using MessageCredentialType.None in the case of NetTcpBinding:

```
NetTcpBinding binding = new NetTcpBinding(SecurityMode.None);
```

Or when using a config file:

```
<bindings>
   <netTcpBinding>
      <binding name = "NoSecurity">
         <security mode = "None"/>
      </binding>
   </netTcpBinding>
</bindings>
```

Authentication

No client authentication, of course, is done in this scenario, and the client needs not provide any credentials to the proxy. Nor does the client ever authenticate the service.

Authorization

Since the clients are anonymous (and unauthenticated), authorization and role-based security are precluded. WCF will automatically set the PrincipalPermissionMode property to PrincipalPermissionMode.None to have WCF install a generic principal with a blank identity.

Identity Management

The identity associated with the principal object is a GenericIdentity with a blank username. That identity is considered unauthenticated. Unlike all the previous scenarios, in the No Security scenario the operation has no security call context, and the ServiceSecurityContext.Current will return null. Table 10-8 shows the identities in this scenario.

Table 10-8. Identity management in the No Security scenario

Identity	Type	Value	Authenticated
Thread Principal	GenericIdentity	-	No
Security Context Primary	-	-	-
Security Context Windows	-	-	-

Impersonation

Because the clients are anonymous, the service cannot impersonate any of its clients.

Callbacks

Unlike all the previous scenarios, in the absence of transfer security, callback comes in under the client's own identity. The principal identity will be set to an instance of WindowsIdentity with the client's username. The callback will be authenticated, but there is no point either in impersonation or using role-based security since the client will only be authorizing itself. In addition, the security call context of the callback will be set to null.

Scenarios Summary

Now that you have seen the making of the five key scenarios, Tables 10-9 and 10-10 serve as a summary of their key elements. Table 10-9 lists the bindings used in each scenario. Note again that while technically you could use other bindings in almost each scenario, my selection of the bindings is aligned with the context in which the scenario is used.

Table 10-9. Bindings and security scenarios

Binding	Intranet	Internet	B2B	Anonymous	None
BasicHttpBinding	No	No	Yes	No	Yes
NetTcpBinding	Yes	Yes	No	Yes	Yes
NetPeerTcpBinding	No	No	No	No	Yes
NetNamedPipeBinding	Yes	No	No	No	Yes
WSHttpBinding	No	Yes	Yes	Yes	Yes
WSFederationHttpBinding	No	No	No	No	No
WSDualHttpBinding	No	Yes	Yes	Yes	Yes
NetMsmqBinding	Yes	No	No	Yes	Yes

Table 10-10 shows how each of the security aspects defined at the beginning of this chapter (transfer security, service and client authentication, authorization, and impersonation) relates to each scenario.

Table 10-10. *The aspects of the security scenarios*

Aspect	Intranet	Internet	B2B	Anonymous	None
Transport	Yes	No	No	No	No
Message	No	Yes	Yes	Yes	No
Service authentication	Windows	Certificate	Certificate	Certificate	No
Client authentication	Windows	ASP.NET	Certificate	No	No
Authorization	Windows	ASP.NET	No/ASP.NET	No	No
Impersonation	Yes	No	No	No	No

Declarative Security Framework

WCF security is truly a vast topic. There is a daunting number of details to master, and intricate relationships exist between the various parts. The programming model is very complex, and at first there is an inescapable feeling of navigating a maze. To make things even worse, there are severe implications both at the application and at the business level for getting it wrong. The solution I came up with is a declarative security framework for WCF. For the service, I provided a security attribute (as well as matching support for the host); and for the client, I provided a few helper classes and secure proxy classes. My declarative framework grossly simplifies applying WCF security, and makes security configuration on par with the other aspects of WCF configuration, such as transactions or synchronization. I wanted a declarative model that would be simple to use and would minimize the need to understand the many details of security. As a developer, all you need to do is select the correct scenario (out of the five common scenarios discussed in this chapter) and my framework will automate the configuration. Not only that, my framework mandates the correct options and enforces my recommendations. At the same time, I wanted a model that maintains granularity and control of the underlying configuration if the need for that ever arises.

The SecurityBehaviorAttribute

Example 10-19 lists the definition of the `SecurityBehaviorAttribute` and the `ServiceSecurity` enum. `ServiceSecurity` defines the five scenarios supported by my framework.

Example 10-19. The SecurityBehaviorAttribute

```
public enum ServiceSecurity
{
   None,
   Anonymous,
   BusinessToBusiness,
   Internet,
   Intranet
}
```

Example 10-19. The SecurityBehaviorAttribute (continued)

```
[AttributeUsage(AttributeTargets.Class)]
public class SecurityBehaviorAttribute : Attribute,IServiceBehavior
{
   public SecurityBehaviorAttribute(ServiceSecurity mode);
   public SecurityBehaviorAttribute(ServiceSecurity mode,
                                    string serviceCertificateName);
   public SecurityBehaviorAttribute(ServiceSecurity mode,
                                    StoreLocation storeLocation,
                                    StoreName storeName,
                                    X509FindType findType,
                                    string serviceCertificateName);
   public bool ImpersonateAll
   {get;set;}
   public string ApplicationName
   {get;set;}
   public bool UseAspNetProviders
   {get;set;}
}
```

When applying the SecurityBehavior attribute you need to provide it with the target scenario in the form of a ServiceSecurity value. You can use just the constructors of the SecurityBehavior attribute, or you can set the properties. Unset, the properties all default to reasonable values in the context of the target scenario. When selecting a scenario, the configured behavior follows to the letter my previous description of the individual scenarios. The SecurityBehavior attribute yields a composable security model, allowing quite a few permutations and subscenarios. When using the attribute, you can even have a security-free host config file, or you can combine settings from the config file with values driven by the attribute. Much the same way, your hosting code can be free of security or you can combine programmatic host security with the attribute.

Configuring intranet service

To configure a service for the intranet security scenario, apply SecurityBehavior with ServiceSecurity.Intranet:

```
[ServiceContract]
interface IMyContract
{
   [OperationContract]
   void MyMethod( );
}
[SecurityBehavior(ServiceSecurity.Intranet)]
class MyService : IMyContract
{
   public void MyMethod( )
   {...}
}
```

Even though the service contract used may not constrain the protection level, the attribute programmatically adds that demand to enforce message protection. You can use Windows NT groups for role-based security:

```
[SecurityBehavior(ServiceSecurity.Intranet)]
class MyService : IMyContract
{
    [PrincipalPermission(SecurityAction.Demand,Role = @"<Domain>\Customer")]
    public void MyMethod( )
    {...}
}
```

The service can programmatically impersonate the callers, or use the operation behavior attribute for individual methods impersonation. You can also configure the service to automatically impersonate all callers in all methods via the ImpersonateAll property. ImpersonateAll defaults to false, but when set to true the attribute will impersonate all callers in all operations without the need to apply any operation behavior attributes or host configuration:

```
[SecurityBehavior(ServiceSecurity.Intranet,ImpersonateAll = true)]
class MyService : IMyContract
{...}
```

Configuring Internet service

With the Internet scenario, you need to both configure for the Internet scenario and to select the service certificate to use. Note in Example 10-19 that the ServiceBehavior attribute constructor may take the service certificate name. Unspecified, the service certificate is loaded from the host config file as with Example 10-8:

```
[SecurityBehavior(ServiceSecurity.Internet)]
class MyService : IMyContract
{...}
```

You can also specify the service certificate name, in which case the specified certificate is loaded from the LocalMachine store from the My folder by name:

```
[SecurityBehavior(ServiceSecurity.Internet,"MyServiceCert")]
class MyService : IMyContract
{...}
```

If the certificate name is set to an empty string, then the attribute will infer the certificate name by using the hosting machine name (or domain) for the certificate name and load such a certificate from the LocalMachine store from the My folder by name:

```
[SecurityBehavior(ServiceSecurity.Internet,"")]
class MyService : IMyContract
{...}
```

Finally, the attribute lets you explicitly specify the store location, the store name, and the lookup method:

```
[SecurityBehavior(ServiceSecurity.Internet,
                StoreLocation.LocalMachine,StoreName.My,
```

```
                    X509FindType.FindBySubjectName,"MyServiceCert")]
class MyService : IMyContract
{...}
```

Note that you can combine explicit location with an inferred certificate name:

```
[SecurityBehavior(ServiceSecurity.Internet,
                  StoreLocation.LocalMachine,StoreName.My,
                  X509FindType.FindBySubjectName,"")]
class MyService : IMyContract
{...}
```

Which credentials store to authenticate the client against is indicated by the `UseAspNetProviders` property. `UseAspNetProviders` defaults to `false`, meaning the default will be to authenticate the client's username and password as Windows credentials, as with Example 10-11. Because of that, when `UseAspNetProviders` is `false` you can by default use Windows NT groups for authorization:

```
[SecurityBehavior(ServiceSecurity.Internet,"MyServiceCert")]
class MyService : IMyContract
{
   [PrincipalPermission(SecurityAction.Demand,Role = @"<Domain>\Customer")]
   public void MyMethod( )
   {...}
}
```

and even impersonate all callers:

```
[SecurityBehavior(ServiceSecurity.Internet,"MyServiceCert",ImpersonateAll = true)]
class MyService : IMyContract
{...}
```

Instead of Windows credentials, if `UseAspNetProviders` is set to true, the attribute will use the ASP.NET membership and role providers as prescribed for the Internet scenario:

```
[SecurityBehavior(ServiceSecurity.Internet,"MyServiceCert",
                  UseAspNetProviders = true)]
class MyService : IMyContract
{
   [PrincipalPermission(SecurityAction.Demand,Role = "Manager")]
   public void MyMethod( )
   {...}
}
```

> The attribute will programmatically enable the role manager section in the config file.

The attribute allows the use of the `NetTcpBinding` with `ServiceSecurity.Internet` along with ASP.NET providers to allow intranet applications to avoid using Windows accounts and groups, as explained previously.

Next is the issue of supplying the application name for the ASP.NET providers. That is governed by the `ApplicationName` property. Unassigned, the attribute will look up the application name from the config file as in Examples 10-13 and 10-14. If no value is found in the host config file, the attribute will not default to using the meaningless / from *machine.config*. Instead, it will default to the host assembly name for the application name. If the `ApplicationName` property is assigned a value, it will override whatever application name is present in the host config file:

```
[SecurityBehavior(ServiceSecurity.Internet,"MyServiceCert",
                 UseAspNetProviders = true,ApplicationName = "MyApplication")]
class MyService : IMyContract
{...}
```

Configuring business-to-business service

Configuring for the business-to-business scenario requires setting `ServiceSecurity` to `ServiceSecurity.BusinessToBusiness`. The attribute will use peer trust for validating the client's certificate. Configuring the service certificate is done just as with the `ServiceSecurity.Internet`; for example:

```
[SecurityBehavior(ServiceSecurity.BusinessToBusiness)]
class MyService : IMyContract
{...}
```

```
[SecurityBehavior(ServiceSecurity.BusinessToBusiness,"")]
class MyService : IMyContract
{...}
```

```
[SecurityBehavior(ServiceSecurity.BusinessToBusiness,"MyServiceCert")]
class MyService : IMyContract
{...}
```

By default, with `ServiceSecurity.BusinessToBusiness`, the attribute will set the `PrincipalPermissionMode` property of the host to `PrincipalPermissionMode.None`, and the service will not be able to authorize its callers. However, setting the `UseAspNetProviders` property to `true` will enable using the ASP.NET role providers, as in Example 10-18:

```
[SecurityBehavior(ServiceSecurity.BusinessToBusiness,UseAspNetProviders = true)]
class MyService : IMyContract
{...}
```

When using the ASP.NET role providers, the application name is looked up and decided upon just as with `ServiceSecurity.Internet`:

```
[SecurityBehavior(ServiceSecurity.BusinessToBusiness,"MyServiceCert",
                 UseAspNetProviders = true,ApplicationName = "MyApplication")]
class MyService : IMyContract
{...}
```

Configuring Anonymous service

To allow callers according to the anonymous scenario, you need to configure the attribute with ServiceSecurity.Anonymous. Configuring the service certificate is done just as with the ServiceSecurity.Internet; for example:

```
[SecurityBehavior(ServiceSecurity.Anonymous)]
class MyService : IMyContract
{...}

[SecurityBehavior(ServiceSecurity.Anonymous,"")]
class MyService : IMyContract
{...}

[SecurityBehavior(ServiceSecurity.Anonymous,"MyServiceCert")]
class MyService : IMyContract
{...}
```

Configuring No-Security service

To turn off security completely, provide the attribute with ServiceSecurity.None:

```
[SecurityBehavior(ServiceSecurity.None)]
class MyService : IMyContract
{...}
```

Implementing SecurityBehaviorAttribute

Example 10-20 is a partial listing of the implementation of SecurityBehaviorAttribute.

Example 10-20. Implementing SecurityBehaviorAttribute

```
[AttributeUsage(AttributeTargets.Class)]
class SecurityBehaviorAttribute : Attribute,IServiceBehavior
{
   SecurityBehavior m_SecurityBehavior;
   string m_ApplicationName = String.Empty;
   bool m_UseAspNetProviders;
   bool m_ImpersonateAll;

   public SecurityBehaviorAttribute(ServiceSecurity mode)
   {
      m_SecurityBehavior = new SecurityBehavior(mode);
   }
   public SecurityBehaviorAttribute(ServiceSecurity mode,
                                    string serviceCertificateName)
   {
      m_SecurityBehavior = new SecurityBehavior(mode,serviceCertificateName);
   }
   public bool ImpersonateAll     //Accesses m_ImpersonateAll
   {get;set;}
   public string ApplicationName  //Accesses m_ApplicationName
   {get;set;}
```

Example 10-20. Implementing SecurityBehaviorAttribute (continued)

```
public bool UseAspNetProviders //Accesses m_UseAspNetProviders
{get;set;}

void IServiceBehavior.ApplyDispatchBehavior(...)
{}

void IServiceBehavior.AddBindingParameters(ServiceDescription description,
                                           ServiceHostBase serviceHostBase,
                                           Collection<ServiceEndpoint> endpoints,
                                           BindingParameterCollection parameters)
{
   m_SecurityBehavior.AddBindingParameters(description,serviceHostBase,
                                                      endpoints,parameters);
}
void IServiceBehavior.Validate(ServiceDescription description,
                              ServiceHostBase serviceHostBase)
{
   m_SecurityBehavior.UseAspNetProviders = UseAspNetProviders;
   m_SecurityBehavior.ApplicationName = ApplicationName;
   m_SecurityBehavior.ImpersonateAll = ImpersonateAll;
   m_SecurityBehavior.Validate(description,serviceHostBase);
}
//Rest of the implementation
}
```

The three public properties of the attribute correspond to three private members where the attribute saves the configured values.

SecurityBehaviorAttribute is a service behavior attribute, so you can apply it directly on the service class. When the AddBindingParameters( ) method of IServiceBehavior is called, SecurityBehaviorAttribute enforces the binding configuration that matches the requested scenario. The Validate( ) method of IServiceBehavior is where SecurityBehaviorAttribute configures the host. Other than that, the attribute does little or no work besides sequencing the overall order of configuration. The actual configuration is accomplished using a helper class called SecurityBehavior. The attribute constructs an instance of SecurityBehavior, providing it with the scenario (the mode parameter) as well as the certificate name in the matching constructor. SecurityBehavior provides systematic meticulous setting of all security scenarios using programmatic calls. SecurityBehavior encapsulates all the explicit steps described previously per scenario. SecurityBehavior is a service behavior in its own right, and it is designed to even be used standalone, independent of the attribute. Example 10-21 contains a partial listing of SecurityBehavior, demonstrating how it operates.

Example 10-21. Implementing SecurityBehavior (partial)

```
class SecurityBehavior : IServiceBehavior
{
   ServiceSecurity m_Mode;
   StoreLocation m_StoreLocation;
```

Example 10-21. Implementing SecurityBehavior (partial) (continued)

```
StoreName m_StoreName;
X509FindType m_FindType;
string m_SubjectName;
bool m_UseAspNetProviders;
string m_ApplicationName = String.Empty;
bool m_ImpersonateAll;

public SecurityBehavior(ServiceSecurity mode) :
                         this(mode,StoreLocation.LocalMachine,StoreName.My,
                                    X509FindType.FindBySubjectName,null)
{}
public SecurityBehavior(ServiceSecurity mode,StoreLocation storeLocation,
                StoreName storeName,X509FindType findType,string subjectName)
{...} //Sets the corresponding members

public bool ImpersonateAll      //Accesses m_ImpersonateAll
{get;set;}
public bool UseAspNetProviders //Accesses UseAspNetProviders
{get;set;}
public string ApplicationName  //Accesses m_ApplicationName
{get;set;}

public void Validate(ServiceDescription description,
                ServiceHostBase serviceHostBase)
{
   if(m_SubjectName != null)
   {
      switch(m_Mode)
      {
         case ServiceSecurity.Anonymous:
         case ServiceSecurity.BusinessToBusiness:
         case ServiceSecurity.Internet:
         {
            string subjectName;
            if(m_SubjectName != String.Empty)
            {
               subjectName = m_SubjectName;
            }
            else
            {
               subjectName = description.Endpoints[0].Address.Uri.Host;
            }
            serviceHostBase.Credentials.ServiceCertificate.
             SetCertificate(m_StoreLocation,m_StoreName,m_FindType,subjectName);
            break;
         }
      }
   }
   .
   .
   .
}
```

Example 10-21. Implementing SecurityBehavior (partial) (continued)

```
public void AddBindingParameters(ServiceDescription description,
                                 ServiceHostBase serviceHostBase,
                                 Collection<ServiceEndpoint> endpoints,
                                 BindingParameterCollection parameters)
{
   .
   .
   .
   switch(m_Mode)
   {
      case ServiceSecurity.Intranet:
      {
         ConfigureIntranet(endpoints);
         break;
      }
      case ServiceSecurity.Internet:
      {
         ConfigureInternet(endpoints,UseAspNetProviders);
         break;
      }
      .
      .
      .
   }
}
internal static void ConfigureInternet(Collection<ServiceEndpoint> endpoints)
{
   foreach(ServiceEndpoint endpoint in endpoints)
   {
      Binding binding = endpoint.Binding;
      if(binding is WSHttpBinding)
      {

         WSHttpBinding wsBinding = (WSHttpBinding)binding;
         wsBinding.Security.Mode = SecurityMode.Message;
         wsBinding.Security.Message.ClientCredentialType =
                                     MessageCredentialType.UserName;
         continue;
      }
      .
      .
      .
      throw new InvalidOperationException(binding.GetType( ) +
                              "is unsupported with ServiceSecurity.Internet");
   }
}
//Rest of the implementation
}
```

The constructors of SecurityBehavior store in member variables the construction parameters, such as the security mode and the details of the certificate. The Validate( ) method is a decision tree that configures the host according to the scenario and the provided information, supporting the behavior of

`SecurityBehaviorAttribute` described earlier. `AddBindingParameters()` calls a dedicated helper method for each scenario to configure the collection of endpoints the host exposes. Each helper method (such as `ConfigureInternet()`) iterates over the collection of endpoints of the service. For each endpoint, it verifies whether the binding used matches the scenario, and then configures the binding according to the scenario.

Host and Declarative Security

While declarative security via the `SecurityBehavior` attribute is easy and handy, often it is up to the host to configure security, and the service just focuses on the business logic. In addition, you may be required to host services you do not develop, and those services do not happen to use my declarative security. The natural next step is to add declarative security to `ServiceHost<T>` with a set of `SetSecurityBehavior()` methods:

```
public class ServiceHost<T> : ServiceHost
{
   public void SetSecurityBehavior(ServiceSecurity mode,
                                   bool useAspNetProviders,
                                   string applicationName,
                                   bool impersonateAll);
   public void SetSecurityBehavior(ServiceSecurity mode,
                                   string serviceCertificateName,
                                   bool useAspNetProviders,
                                   string applicationName,
                                   bool impersonateAll);
   //More members
}
```

Using the declarative security via the host follows the same consistent guidelines as with the `SecurityBehavior` attribute. For example, here is how to configure the host (and the service) for Internet security with ASP.NET providers:

```
ServiceHost<MyService> host = new ServiceHost<MyService>();
host.SetSecurityBehavior(ServiceSecurity.Internet,
                         "MyServiceCert",true,"MyApplication",false);
host.Open();
```

Example 10-22 shows a partial listing of the declarative security support in `ServiceHost<T>`.

Example 10-22. Adding declarative security for ServiceHost<T>

```
public class ServiceHost<T> : ServiceHost
{
   public void SetSecurityBehavior(ServiceSecurity mode,
                                   string serviceCertificateName,
                                   bool useAspNetProviders,
                                   string applicationName,
                                   bool impersonateAll)
   {
```

Example 10-22. Adding declarative security for ServiceHost<T> (continued)

```
    if(State == CommunicationState.Opened)
    {
        throw new InvalidOperationException("Host is already opened");
    }

    SecurityBehavior securityBehavior = new
                                SecurityBehavior(mode,serviceCertificateName);
    securityBehavior.UseAspNetProviders = useAspNetProviders;
    securityBehavior.ApplicationName = applicationName;
    securityBehavior.ImpersonateAll = impersonateAll;

    Description.Behaviors.Add(securityBehavior);
  }
  //More members
}
```

The implementation of SetSecurityBehavior( ) relies on the fact that the
SecurityBehavior class supports IServiceBehavior. SetSecurityBehavior( ) initializes
an instance of SecurityBehavior with the supplied parameters and then adds it to the
collection of behaviors in the service description, as if the service were decorated
with SecurityBehaviorAttribute.

Client-Side Declarative Security

WCF does not allow applying an attribute on the proxy class, and while a contract-
level attribute is possible, the client may need to provide its credentials and other settings at runtime. The first step in supporting declarative security on the client side is
my SecurityHelper static helper class, defined in Example 10-23.

Example 10-23. The SecurityHelper helper class

```
public static class SecurityHelper
{
   public static void UnsecuredProxy<T>(ClientBase<T> proxy)  where T : class;
   public static void AnonymousProxy<T>(ClientBase<T> proxy)  where T : class;
   public static void SecureProxy<T>(ClientBase<T> proxy,
                            string userName,string password) where T : class;
   public static void SecureProxy<T>(ClientBase<T> proxy,
                 string domain,string userName,string password) where T : class;
   public static void SecureProxy<T>(ClientBase<T> proxy,string domain,
        string userName,string password,TokenImpersonationLevel impersonationLevel)
                                                              where T : class;
   public static void SecureProxy<T>(ClientBase<T> proxy,
                            string clientCertificateName) where T : class;
   public static void SecureProxy<T>(ClientBase<T> proxy,
                      StoreLocation storeLocation,StoreName storeName,
            X509FindType findType,string clientCertificateName) where T : class;
   //More members
}
```

You use SecurityHelper to configure a plain proxy according to the desired security scenario and behavior, using the dedicated static methods SecurityHelper offers. You can only configure the proxy before opening the proxy. There is no need for any security settings in the client's config file or elsewhere in the client's code.

SecurityHelper is smart, and it will select the correct security behavior based on provided parameters and the method invoked. There is no need to explicitly use the ServiceSecurity enum.

For example, here is how to secure a proxy for the intranet scenario and provide it with the client's Windows credentials:

```
MyContractClient proxy = new MyContractClient( );
SecurityHelper.SecureProxy(proxy,"MyDomain","MyUsername","MyPassword");
proxy.MyMethod( );
proxy.Close( );
```

For the Internet scenario, the client only needs to provide the username and the password (remember that the decision of whether those are Windows or ASP.NET provider credentials is a service-side decision):

```
MyContractClient proxy = new MyContractClient( );
SecurityHelper.SecureProxy(proxy,"MyUsername","MyPassword");
proxy.MyMethod( );
proxy.Close( );
```

For the business-to-business scenario, the client can specify a null or an empty string for the client certificate name if it wants to use the certificate in its config file, or it can list the certificate name explicitly:

```
MyContractClient proxy = new MyContractClient( );
SecurityHelper.SecureProxy(proxy,"MyClientCert");
proxy.MyMethod( );
proxy.Close( );
```

SecurityHelper will load the certificate from the client's LocalMachine store from the My folder by name. The client can also specify all the information required to find and load the certificate. For simplicity's sake in designing SecurityHelper, when using the BasicHttpBinding in the business-to-business scenario, the client must explicitly specify the service certificate location, either in the config file or programmatically.

For an anonymous client, use the AnonymousProxy( ) method:

```
MyContractClient proxy = new MyContractClient( );
SecurityHelper.AnonymousProxy(proxy);
proxy.MyMethod( );
proxy.Close( );
```

and for no security at all, use the UnsecuredProxy( ) method:

```
MyContractClient proxy = new MyContractClient( );
SecurityHelper.UnsecuredProxy(proxy);
proxy.MyMethod( );
proxy.Close( );
```

Implementing SecurityHelper

Internally, SecurityHelper uses SecurityBehavior to configure the proxy's endpoint as well as set the credentials, as shown in Example 10-24.

Example 10-24. Implementing SecurityHelper (partial)

```
public static class SecurityHelper
{
   public static void SecureProxy<T>(ClientBase<T> proxy,
                                string userName,string password) where T : class
   {
      if(proxy.State == CommunicationState.Opened)
      {
         throw new InvalidOperationException("Proxy channel is already opened");
      }
      Collection<ServiceEndpoint> endpoints = new Collection<ServiceEndpoint>( );
      endpoints.Add(proxy.Endpoint);

      SecurityBehavior.ConfigureInternet(endpoints);

      proxy.ClientCredentials.UserName.UserName = userName;
      proxy.ClientCredentials.UserName.Password = password;
      proxy.ClientCredentials.ServiceCertificate.Authentication.
            CertificateValidationMode = X509CertificateValidationMode.PeerTrust;
   }
   //Rest of the implementation
}
```

The SecureClientBase<T> class

The advantage of using SecurityHelper is that it can operate on any proxy; even a proxy the client developer is not responsible for creating. The disadvantage is that it is a step the client has to take. If you are responsible for generating the proxy, you can take advantage of my SecureClientBase<T> class, defined in Example 10-25.

Example 10-25. The SecureClientBase<T> class

```
public abstract class SecureClientBase<T> : ClientBase<T> where T : class
{
   //These constructors target the default endpoint
   protected SecureClientBase( );
   protected SecureClientBase(ServiceSecurity mode);
   protected SecureClientBase(string userName,string password);
   protected SecureClientBase(string domain,string userName,string password,
                        TokenImpersonationLevel impersonationLevel);
   protected SecureClientBase(string domain,string userName,string password);
   protected SecureClientBase(string clientCertificateName);
   protected SecureClientBase(StoreLocation storeLocation,
                        StoreName storeName,X509FindType findType,
                        string clientCertificateName);
   //More constructors for other types of endpoints
}
```

SecureClientBase<T> derives from the conventional ClientBase<T> and adds the declarative security support. You need to derive your proxy from SecureClientBase<T> instead of ClientBase<T>, provide constructors that match your security scenario, and call the base constructors of SecureClientBase<T> with the supplies credentials and endpoint information:

```
class MyContractClient : SecureClientBase<IMyContract>,IMyContract
{
    public MyContractClient(ServiceSecurity mode) : base(mode)
    {}
    public MyContractClient(string userName,string password) :
                                                base(userName,password)
    {}

    /* More constructors */

    public void MyMethod( )
    {
        Channel.MyMethod( );
    }
}
```

Using the derived proxy is straightforward. For example, for the Internet scenario:

```
MyContractClient proxy = new MyContractClient("MyUsername","MyPassword");
proxy.MyMethod( );
proxy.Close( );
```

or for the Anonymous scenario:

```
MyContractClient proxy = new MyContractClient(ServiceSecurity.Anonymous);
proxy.MyMethod( );
proxy.Close( );
```

The implementation of SecureClientBase<T> simply uses SecurityHelper (as shown in Example 10-26) so SecureClientBase<T> follows the same behaviors, such as regarding the client certificate.

Example 10-26. Implementing SecureClientBase<T> (partial)

```
public class SecureClientBase<T> : ClientBase<T> where T : class
{
    protected SecureClientBase(ServiceSecurity mode)
    {
        switch(mode)
        {
            case ServiceSecurity.None:
            {
                SecurityHelper.UnsecuredProxy(this);
                break;
            }
            case ServiceSecurity.Anonymous:
            {
                SecurityHelper.AnonymousProxy(this);
                break;
            }
```

Example 10-26. Implementing SecureClientBase<T> (partial) (continued)

```
        ...
    }
}
protected SecureClientBase(string userName,string password)
{
    SecurityHelper.SecureProxy(this,userName,password);
}
//More constructors
}
```

Secure channel factory

If you are not using a proxy at all, then both SecurityHelper and SecureClientBase<T> are of little use to you. For that case, I wrote the SecureChannelFactory<T> class, defined in Example 10-27.

Example 10-27. The SecureChannelFactory<T>

```
public class SecureChannelFactory<T> : ChannelFactory<T>
{
    public SecureChannelFactory()
    {}
    public SecureChannelFactory(string endpointName) : base(endpointName)
    {}
    //More constructors
    public void SetSecurityMode(ServiceSecurity mode);
    public void SetCredentials(string userName,string password);
    public void SetCredentials(string domain,string userName,string password,
                              TokenImpersonationLevel impersonationLevel);
    public void SetCredentials(string domain,string userName,string password);
    public void SetCredentials(string clientCertificateName);
    public void SetCredentials(StoreLocation storeLocation,StoreName storeName,
                              X509FindType findType,string clientCertificateName);
}
```

You use SecureChannelFactory<T> just like the WCF-provided channel factory, except you can utilize declarative security. You need to call the SetSecurityMode( ) method or one of the SetCredentials( ) methods that fits your target scenario before opening the channel. For example, with a proxy to an Internet security-based service:

```
SecureChannelFactory<IMyContract> factory =
                                new SecureChannelFactory<IMyContract>("");

factory.SetCredentials("MyUsername","MyPassword");

IMyContract proxy = factory.CreateChannel( );

using(proxy as IDisposable)
{
    proxy.MyMethod( );
}
```

Implementing SecureChannelFactory<T> was very similar to implementing SecurityHelper and so I have omitted detailing that code.

Duplex client and declarative security

I also provided the SecureDuplexClientBase<T,C> class (similar to SecureClientBase<T>), defined in Example 10-28.

Example 10-28. The SecureDuplexClientBase<T,C> class

```
public abstract class SecureDuplexClientBase<T,C> : DuplexClientBase<T,C>
                                                where T : class
{
   protected SecureDuplexClientBase(C callback);
   protected SecureDuplexClientBase(ServiceSecurity mode,C callback);
   protected SecureDuplexClientBase(string userName,string password,C callback);
   protected SecureDuplexClientBase(string domain,string userName,string password,
                       TokenImpersonationLevel impersonationLevel,C callback);
   protected SecureDuplexClientBase(string domain,string userName,string password,
                                                              C callback);
   protected SecureDuplexClientBase(string clientCertificateName,C callback);
   protected SecureDuplexClientBase(StoreLocation storeLocation,
                          StoreName storeName,X509FindType findType,
                          string clientCertificateName,C callback);

   /* More constructors with InstanceContext<C> and constructors that
      target the configured endpoint and a programatic endpoint */
}
```

SecureDuplexClientBase<T,C> derives from my type-safe DuplexClientBase<T,C> class presented in Chapter 5, and it adds the declarative scenario–based security support. As with the DuplexClientBase<T,C> class, you need to derive your proxy class from it, and take advantage of either the callback parameter or the type-safe context InstanceContext<C>. For example, given this service contract and callback contract definition:

```
[ServiceContract(CallbackContract = typeof(IMyContractCallback))]
interface IMyContract
{
   [OperationContract]
   void MyMethod( );
}
interface IMyContractCallback
{
   [OperationContract]
   void OnCallback( );
}
```

your derived proxy class will look like this:

```
class MyContractClient :
             SecureDuplexClientBase<IMyContract,IMyContractCallback>,IMyContract
{
```

```
      public MyContractClient(IMyContractCallback callback) : base(callback)
      {}
      public MyContractClient(ServiceSecurity mode,IMyContractCallback callback)
                                                      : base(mode,callback)
      {}
      /* More constructors */

      public void MyMethod( )
      {
         Channel.MyMethod( );
      }
   }
```

When using it, provide the security scenario or credentials, the callback object, and the endpoint information. For example, when targeting the Anonymous scenario:

```
class MyClient : IMyContractCallback
{...}

IMyContractCallback callback = new MyClient( );

MyContractClient proxy = new MyContractClient(ServiceSecurity.Anonymous,callback);
proxy.MyMethod( );

proxy.Close( );
```

Implementing SecureDuplexClientBase<T,C> was almost identical to SecureClientBase<T>, with the main difference being a different base class.

The SecureDuplexChannelFactory<T,C> class

When you're not using a SecureDuplexClientBase<T,C>-derived proxy to set up the bidirectional communication, you can use my SecureDuplexChannelFactory<T,C> channel factory, defined in Example 10-29.

Example 10-29. The SecureDuplexChannelFactory<T,C>
```
public class SecureDuplexChannelFactory<T,C> : DuplexChannelFactory<T,C>
                                                      where T : class
{
   public SecureDuplexChannelFactory(C callback)
   public SecureDuplexChannelFactory(InstanceContext<C> context,Binding binding) :
                                                      base(context,binding)

   //More constructors

   public void SetSecurityMode(ServiceSecurity mode);
   public void SetCredentials(string userName,string password);
   public void SetCredentials(string domain,string userName,string password,
                        TokenImpersonationLevel impersonationLevel);
   public void SetCredentials(string domain,string userName,string password);
   public void SetCredentials(string clientCertificateName);
   public void SetCredentials(StoreLocation storeLocation,StoreName storeName,
                        X509FindType findType,string clientCertificateName);
}
```

`SecureDuplexChannelFactory<T,C>` derives from the type-safe `DuplexChannelFactory<T,C>` defined in Chapter 5. You construct `SecureDuplexChannelFactory<T,C>` with an instance of the generic type parameter for the callback (or an instance of the type-safe `InstanceContext<C>`). You need to call the `SetSecurityMode()` method or one of the `SetCredentials()` methods that fits your target scenario before opening the channel. For example, when targeting the Internet scenario:

```
class MyClient : IMyContractCallback
{...}

IMyContractCallback callback = new MyClient();

SecureDuplexChannelFactory<IMyContract,IMyContractCallback> factory =
    new SecureDuplexChannelFactory<IMyContract,IMyContractCallback>(callback,"");

factory.SetCredentials("MyUsername","MyPassword");

IMyContract proxy = factory.CreateChannel();
using(proxy as IDisposable)
{
    proxy.MyMethod();
}
```

Implementing `SecureDuplexChannelFactory<T,C>` is very similar to implementing `SecureChannelFactory<T>` with the main difference being the base factory.

Security Auditing

I will end this chapter with presenting a useful feature WCF supports called security audits. As the name implies, a *security audit* is a logbook of the security-related events in your services. WCF can log authentication and authorization attempts, their time and location, and the client's identity. The class `ServiceSecurityAuditBehavior` governs auditing and is listed in Example 10-30 along with its supporting enumerations.

Example 10-30. The ServiceSecurityAuditBehavior class

```
public enum AuditLogLocation
{
   Default,//Decided by the operating system
   Application,
   Security
}
public enum AuditLevel
{
   None,
   Success,
   Failure,
   SuccessOrFailure
}
```

Example 10-30. The ServiceSecurityAuditBehavior class (continued)

```
public sealed class ServiceSecurityAuditBehavior : IServiceBehavior
{
   public AuditLogLocation AuditLogLocation
   {get;set;}
   public AuditLevel MessageAuthenticationAuditLevel
   {get;set;}
   public AuditLevel ServiceAuthorizationAuditLevel
   {get;set;}
   //More members
}
```

`ServiceSecurityAuditBehavior` is a service behavior. The `AuditLogLocation` property specifies where to store the log entries, in the application logfile or in the security log, both in the event log on the host computer. The `MessageAuthenticationAuditLevel` property governs the authentication audit verbosity. For performance's sake, you may want to audit only failures, or both success and failures. For diagnostic purposes you can also audit successful authentication. The default value of `MessageAuthenticationAuditLevel` is `AuditLevel.None`. Similarly, you use the `ServiceAuthorizationAuditLevel` property to control authorization audit verbosity, and it is also disabled by default.

Configuring Security Audits

The typical way of enabling a security audit is in the host config file, by adding a custom behavior section and referencing it at the service declaration, as shown in Example 10-31.

Example 10-31. Configuring a security audit

```
<system.serviceModel>
   <services>
      <service name = "MyService" behaviorConfiguration = "MySecurityAudit" >
         ...
      </service>
   </services>
   <behaviors>
      <serviceBehaviors>
         <behavior name = "MySecurityAudit">
            <serviceSecurityAudit
               auditLogLocation = "Default"
               serviceAuthorizationAuditLevel  = "SuccessOrFailure"
               messageAuthenticationAuditLevel = "SuccessOrFailure"
            />
         </behavior>
      </serviceBehaviors>
   </behaviors>
</system.serviceModel>
```

You can also configure security auditing programmatically by adding the behavior at runtime to the host before opening it. Similar to adding other behaviors programmatically, you can check that the host does not already have an audit behavior, to avoid overriding the config file, as shown in Example 10-32.

Example 10-32. Enabling a security audit programmatically

```
ServiceHost host = new ServiceHost(typeof(MyService));

ServiceSecurityAuditBehavior securityAudit =
                  host.Description.Behaviors.Find<ServiceSecurityAuditBehavior>( );
if(securityAudit == null)
{
   securityAudit = new ServiceSecurityAuditBehavior( );

   securityAudit.MessageAuthenticationAuditLevel = AuditLevel.SuccessOrFailure;
   securityAudit.ServiceAuthorizationAuditLevel = AuditLevel.SuccessOrFailure;
   host.Description.Behaviors.Add(securityAudit);
}
host.Open( );
```

You can streamline the code in Example 10-32 by adding the SecurityAuditEnabled Boolean property to ServiceHost<T>:

```
public class ServiceHost<T> : ServiceHost
{
   public bool SecurityAuditEnabled
   {get;set;}
   //More members
}
```

Using ServiceHost<T>, Example 10-32 is reduced to:

```
ServiceHost<MyService> host = new ServiceHost<MyService>( );
host.SecurityAuditEnabled = true;
host.Open( );
```

Example 10-33 shows the implementation of the SecurityAuditEnabled property.

Example 10-33. Implementing the SecurityAuditEnabled property

```
public class ServiceHost<T> : ServiceHost
{
   public bool SecurityAuditEnabled
   {
      get
      {
         ServiceSecurityAuditBehavior securityAudit =
                     Description.Behaviors.Find<ServiceSecurityAuditBehavior>( );
         if(securityAudit != null)
         {
            return securityAudit.MessageAuthenticationAuditLevel ==
                                                    AuditLevel.SuccessOrFailure
                  &&
                  securityAudit.ServiceAuthorizationAuditLevel ==
                                                    AuditLevel.SuccessOrFailure;
```

Example 10-33. Implementing the SecurityAuditEnabled property (continued)

```
            }
            else
            {
               return false;
            }
         }
         set
         {
            if(State == CommunicationState.Opened)
            {
               throw new InvalidOperationException("Host is already opened");
            }
            ServiceSecurityAuditBehavior securityAudit =
                           Description.Behaviors.Find<ServiceSecurityAuditBehavior>( );
            if(securityAudit == null && value == true)
            {
               securityAudit = new ServiceSecurityAuditBehavior( );
               securityAudit.MessageAuthenticationAuditLevel =
                                             AuditLevel.SuccessOrFailure;
               securityAudit.ServiceAuthorizationAuditLevel =
                                             AuditLevel.SuccessOrFailure;
               Description.Behaviors.Add(securityAudit);
            }
         }
      }
   }
   //More members
}
```

In the get, the SecurityAuditEnabled property accesses the description of the service and looks for an instance of ServiceSecurityAuditBehavior. If one is found, and if both the authentication and the authorization audits are set to AuditLevel. SuccessOrFailure, then SecurityAuditEnabled returns true, and false otherwise. In the set, the property enables the security audit only if the description does not contain a previous value as a result of a config file. If no prior behavior is found, SecurityAuditEnabled sets both the authentication and authorization audits to AuditLevel.SuccessOrFailure.

Declarative Security Audit

You can also write an attribute that surfaces the security audit options at the service level. I chose to add that support in the form of a single Boolean property on the SecurityBehavior attribute called SecurityAuditEnabled:

```
[AttributeUsage(AttributeTargets.Class)]
public class SecurityBehaviorAttribute : Attribute,IServiceBehavior
{
   public bool SecurityAuditEnabled
   {get;set;}
   //More members
}
```

The default of SecurityAuditEnabled is false—no security audit. Using the property complements the rest of the declarative security model; for example:

```
[SecurityBehavior(ServiceSecurity.Internet,UseAspNetProviders = true,
                  SecurityAuditEnabled = true)]
class MyService : IMyContract
{...}
```

Example 10-34 shows how that support was added to the SecurityBehavior attribute.

Example 10-34. Implementing a declarative security audit

```
[AttributeUsage(AttributeTargets.Class)]
public class SecurityBehaviorAttribute : Attribute,IServiceBehavior
{
   bool m_SecurityAuditEnabled;

   public bool SecurityAuditEnabled //Accesses m_SecurityAuditEnabled
   {get;set;}

   void IServiceBehavior.Validate(ServiceDescription description,
                                  ServiceHostBase serviceHostBase)
   {
      if(SecurityAuditEnabled)
      {
         ServiceSecurityAuditBehavior securityAudit = serviceHostBase.Description.
                            Behaviors.Find<ServiceSecurityAuditBehavior>();
         if(securityAudit == null)
         {
            securityAudit = new ServiceSecurityAuditBehavior();
            securityAudit.MessageAuthenticationAuditLevel =
                                                AuditLevel.SuccessOrFailure;
            securityAudit.ServiceAuthorizationAuditLevel =
                                                AuditLevel.SuccessOrFailure;
            serviceHostBase.Description.Behaviors.Add(securityAudit);
         }
         //Rest same as Example 10-20
      }
   }
   //Rest of the implementation
}
```

The Validate() method of IServiceBehavior enables auditing using the same verbosity level as ServiceHost<T>, while avoiding overriding the config file.

Introduction to Service-Orientation

This book is all about designing and developing service-oriented applications using WCF. This appendix presents my understanding of what service-orientation is all about, and what it means to put it in a concrete context. But to understand where the software industry is heading with service orientation, you should first appreciate where it came from, since almost nothing in this new methodology is a leap of thought, but rather, it is based on a gradual evolution that spanned decades. After a brief discussion of the history of software engineering and its overarching trend, the appendix defines service-oriented applications (as opposed to mere architecture), explains what services themselves are, and examines the benefits of the methodology. The appendix then presents the principles of service orientation and augments the abstract tenets with a few more practical and concrete points required by most applications.

A Brief History of Software Engineering

The first modern computer was an electromechanical, typewriter-size device developed in Poland in the late 1920s for enciphering messages. The device was later sold to the German Commerce Ministry, and in the 1930s was adopted by the German military for enciphering all communication. Today we know it as the Enigma. Enigma used mechanical rotors for changing the route of electrical current flow from a key type to a light board with a different letter on it (the ciphered letter). Enigma was not a general-purpose computer: it could only do enciphering and deciphering (today we call it encryption and decryption). If the operator wanted to change the encryption algorithm, he had to change the mechanical structure of the machine by changing the rotors, their order, their initial positions, and the wired plugs that connected the keyboard to the light board. The "program" was therefore coupled in the extreme to the problem it was designed to solve (encryption), and to the mechanical design of the computer.

The late 1940s and the 1950s saw the introduction of the first general-purpose electronic computers for defense purposes. These machines could run code that addressed any problem, not just a single predetermined task. The downside was that the code executed on those computers was in a machine-specific "language" with the program coupled to the hardware itself. Code developed for one machine could not run on another. Initially this was not a cause for concern since there were only a handful of computers in the world anyway. As machines because more prolific, in the early 1960s the emergence of assembly language decoupled the code from specific machines, and enabled code to run on multiple machines. However, the code was now coupled to the machine architecture. Code written for an 8-bit machine could not run on a 16-bit machine, let alone withstand differences in the registers or available memory and memory layout. As a result, the cost of owning and maintaining a program began to escalate. This coincided more or less with the widespread adoption of computers in the civilian and government sectors, where the more limited resources and budgets necessitated a better solution.

In the 1960s, higher-level languages such as COBOL and FORTRAN introduced the notion of a compiler. The developer would write in an abstraction of machine programming (the language), and the compiler would translate that into actual assembly code. Compilers for the first time decoupled the code from the hardware and its architecture. The problem with those first-generation languages was that the code resulted in nonstructured programming, where the code was internally coupled to its own structure, via the use of jump or go-to statements. Minute changes to the code structure had devastating effects in multiple places in the program.

The 1970s saw the eminence of structured programming via languages such as C and Pascal, which decoupled the code from its internal layout and structure, using functions and structures. The 1970s were also the first time that developers and researchers started to examine software as an engineered entity. To drive down the cost of ownership, companies had to start thinking about reuse—what would make a piece of code able to be reused in other contexts. With languages like C, the basic unit of reuse is the function. The problem with function-based reuse is that the function is coupled to the data it manipulates, and if the data is global, a change to benefit one function in one reuse context damages another function used somewhere else.

Object-Orientation

The solution to these problems in the 1980s was object-orientation, with languages such as Smalltalk, and later C++. With object-orientation, the functions and the data they manipulate are packaged together in an object. The functions (now called methods) encapsulate the logic, and the object encapsulates the data. Object-orientation enables domain modeling in the form of a class hierarchy. The mechanism of reuse is class-based, enabling both direct reuse and specialization via inheritance. But object-orientation is not without its own acute problems. First, the generated application (or code artifacts) is a single monolithic application. Languages like C++ have nothing to say about the binary representation of the generated code. Developers had to deploy huge code bases every time, even for minute changes. This had a detrimental effect on the development process, quality, time to market, and cost. While the basic unit of reuse was a class, it was a class in source format. Consequently, the application was coupled to the language used. You could not have a Smalltalk client consuming a C++ class or deriving from it. Moreover, it turned out that inheritance is a poor mechanism for reuse, often harboring more harm than good because the developer of the derived class needs to be intimately aware of the implementation of the base class, which introduces vertical coupling across the class hierarchy. Object-orientation was oblivious of real-life challenges, such as deployment and versioning. Serialization and persistence posed yet another set of problems—most applications did not start by plucking objects out of thin air—they had some persistent state that needed to be hydrated into objects, and yet there was no way of enforcing compatibility between the persisted state and the potentially new object code. If the objects were distributed across multiple processes or machines, there was no way of using raw C++ for the invocation, since C++ required direct memory reference and did not support distribution. Developers had to write host processes and use some remote call technology such as TCP sockets to remote the calls, but such invocations looked nothing like native C++ calls and did not benefit from it.

Component-Orientation

The solution for the problems of object-orientation evolved over time, involving technologies such as a static library (*.lib*) and a dynamic library (*.dll*), culminating in 1994 with the first component-oriented technology called COM (Component Object Model). Component-orientation provided interchangeable interoperable binary components. Instead of sharing source files, the client and the server agree on a binary type system (such as IDL) and a way of representing the metadata inside the opaque binary components. The components are discovered and loaded at runtime, enabling scenarios such as dropping a control on a form and having that control automatically loaded at runtime on the client's machine. The client only programs against an abstraction of the service, a contract called the interface. As long as the interface is immutable, the service is free to evolve at will. A proxy could implement the same interface and thus enable seamless remote calls by encapsulating the low-level mechanics of the remote call. The availability of a common binary type system enables cross-language interoperability, and so a Visual Basic client could consume a C++ COM component. The basic unit of reuse is the interface, not the component, and polymorphic implementations are interchangeable. Versioning was controlled by assigning a unique identifier for every interface, COM object, and type library. While COM was a fundamental breakthrough in modern software engineering, most developers found it unpalatable. COM was unnecessarily ugly because it was bolted on top of an operation system that was unaware of it, and the languages used for writing COM components (such as C++ and Visual Basic) were at best object-oriented but not component-oriented, which greatly complicated the programming model, requiring frameworks such as ATL to bridge the two worlds. Recognizing these issues, Microsoft released .NET 1.0 in 2002. .NET is (in the abstract) nothing more than cleaned-up COM, C++, and Windows, all working seamlessly together under a single, new component-oriented runtime. .NET supports all the advantages of COM, and mandates and standardizes many ingredients such as type metadata sharing, serialization, and versioning. While .NET is at least an order of magnitude easier to work with than COM, both COM and .NET suffer from a similar set of problems:

Technology and platform

> The application and the code are coupled to the technology and the platform. Both COM and .NET are only available on Windows. Both COM and .NET expect the client and the service to be either COM or .NET, and cannot interoperate natively with other technologies, be they on Windows or not. While bridging technologies such as web services make interoperability possible, they force the developers to let go of almost all of the benefits of working with the native framework and introduce their own complexities.

Concurrency management

> When a vendor ships a component, it cannot assume it will not be accessed by multiple threads concurrently by its clients. It fact, the only safe assumption the vendor can make is that the component will be accessed by multiple threads. As a result, the components must be thread-safe and must be equipped with a synchronization lock. If an application developer is building an application by aggregating multiple components from multiple vendors, the introduction of multiple locks renders the application deadlock-prone. Avoiding the deadlock couples the application and the components.

Transactions

> If the application wishes to have the components participate in a single transaction, it requires the application that hosts them to coordinate the transaction and flow the transaction from one component to the next, which is a serious programming fit. It also introduces coupling between the application and the components regarding the nature of the transaction coordination.

Communication protocols

> If components are deployed across process or machine boundaries, they are coupled to the details of the remote calls, the transport protocol used, and its implication on the programming model (such as reliability and security).

Communication patterns

> The components could be invoked synchronously or asynchronously, and could be connected or disconnected. A component may or may not be able to be invoked in either one of these modes, and the application must be aware of the exact preference.

Versioning

> Applications may be written against one version of a component and yet encounter another in production. Dealing robustly with versioning issues couples the application to the components it uses.

Security

> Components may need to authenticate and authorize their callers, and yet how would the component know which security authority it should use or which user is a member of which role? Not only that, but the component may want to ensure that the communication from its clients is secure, and that, of course, imposes certain restrictions on the clients and in turn couples them to the security needs of the component.

Both COM and .NET tried to address some (but not all) of these challenges using technologies such as COM+ and Enterprise Services respectively (similarly, Java had J2EE), but in reality, such applications were inundated with plumbing. In a decent-size application, the bulk of the effort, the development, and the debugging time is spent on addressing such plumbing issues, as opposed to focusing on business logic and features. To make things even worse, since the end customer (or the development manager) rarely cares about plumbing (as opposed to features), the developers are not given adequate time required to develop robust plumbing. Instead, most handcrafted plumbing solutions are proprietary (which hinders reuse, migration, and hiring), and are of low quality, because most developers are not security or synchronization experts and because the developers were not given the time and resources to develop the plumbing properly.

Service-Orientation

If you examine the brief history of software engineering just outlined, you notice a pattern: every new methodology and technology generation incorporates the benefits of its preceding technology and improves on the deficiencies of its preceding technology. However, every new generation also introduces new challenges. I say that *modern software engineering is the ongoing refinement of the ever-increasing degrees of decoupling*.

Put differently, coupling is bad, but coupling is unavoidable. An absolutely decoupled application is useless because it adds no value. Developers can only add value by coupling things together. The very act of writing code is coupling one thing to another. The real question is how to wisely choose what to be coupled to. I believe there are two types of coupling. Good coupling is business-level coupling. Developers add value by implementing a system use case or a feature, by coupling software functionality together. Bad coupling is anything to do with writing plumbing. What was wrong with .NET and COM was not the concept, it was the fact that developers still had to write so much plumbing.

Recognizing the problems of the past, in the late 2000s, the service-oriented methodology has emerged as the answer to the shortcomings of object- and component-orientation. In a service-oriented application, developers focus on writing business logic, and expose that logic via interchangeable interoperable service endpoints. Clients consume those endpoints, not the service code or its packaging. The interaction between the clients and the service endpoint is based on a standard message exchange, and the service publishes some kind of standard metadata, describing what exactly it can do and how clients should invoke operations on it. The metadata is the service equivalent of the C++ header file, the COM type library, or the .NET assembly metadata. The service's endpoint is reusable by any client compatible with its interaction constraints (such as synchronous, transacted, and secure communication) regardless of the client's implementation technology.

In many respects, a service is the natural evolution of the component, just as the component was the natural evolution of the object. Service-orientation is, to the best of our knowledge as an industry, the correct way to build maintainable, robust, and secure applications.

When developing a service-oriented application, you decouple the service code from the technology and platform used by the client; from many of the concurrency management issues; from the transaction propagation and management, and from the communication reliability, protocols, and patterns. By and large, securing the transfer of the message itself from the client to the service is also outside the scope of the service, and so is authenticating the caller. The service may still do its own local authorization as is dictated by the requirements. Much the same way, the client is agnostic of the version of the service: as long as the endpoint supports the contract the client expects, the client does not care about the version of the service. There are also tolerances built into the standards to deal with versioning tolerance of the data passed between the client and the service.

Benefits of Service-Orientation

Because the interaction between the client and the service is based on industry standards that prescribe how to secure the call, how to flow transactions, how to manage reliability, and so on, you could also have off-the-shelf implementation of such plumbing. This in turn yields a maintainable application because the application is decoupled on the correct aspects. As the plumbing evolves, the application remains unaffected. A service-oriented application is robust because the developers can use available, proven, and tested plumbing, and the developers are more productive because they get to spend more of the cycle time on the features rather than the plumbing. This is the true value proposition of service-orientation: enabling developers to extract the plumbing out of their code and invest more in the business logic and the required features.

The many other hailed benefits, such as cross-technology interoperability, are merely a manifestation of the core benefit. You can certainly interoperate without resorting to services, as was the practice until service-orientation. The difference is that with ready-made plumbing you rely on the plumbing to provide the interoperability for you. When you write a service, you usually do not care which platform the client executes on—that is immaterial, which is the whole point of seamless interoperability. But a service-oriented application caters to much more than interoperability. It enables developers to cross boundaries. One type of a boundary is technology and platform, and crossing it is what interoperability is all about. But other boundaries may exist between the client and the service, such as security and trust boundaries, geographical boundaries, organizational boundaries, timeline boundaries, transaction boundaries, and even business model boundaries. Seamlessly crossing each of these boundaries is possible because of the standard message-based interaction. For example, there are standards for how to secure messages and establish a secure interaction between the client and the service, even though both may reside in domains (or sites) that have no direct trust relationship. There is a standard that enables the transaction manager on the client side to flow the transaction to the transaction manager on the service side, and have the service participate in that transaction, even though the two transaction managers never enlist in each other's transactions directly.

Service-Oriented Applications

A service-oriented application is simply the aggregation of services into a single logical, cohesive application (see Figure A-1), much as an object-oriented application is the aggregation of objects.

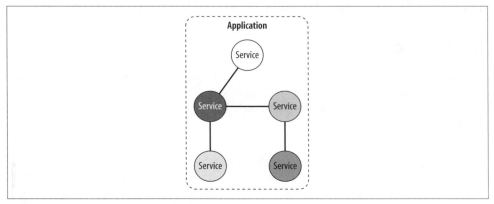

Figure A-1. A service-oriented application

The application itself may expose the aggregate as a new service, much like an object can be composed of smaller objects.

Inside services, developers still use concepts such as specific programming languages, versions, technologies and frameworks, operating systems, APIs, and so on. However, between services you have the standard messages and protocols, contracts, and metadata exchange.

The various services in the application can be all in the same location or be distributed across an intranet or the Internet, or they could come from multiple vendors, developed across a range of platforms and technologies, versioned independently, and even execute on different timelines. All of those plumbing aspects are hidden from the clients in the application interacting with the services. The clients send the standard messages to the services, and the plumbing at both ends marshals away the differences between the clients and the services by converting the messages to and from the neutral wire representation.

Since service-oriented frameworks provide off-the-shelf plumbing for connecting services together, the more granular the services are, the more use the application makes of this infrastructure, and the less plumbing the developers have to write. Taken to the extreme, every class and primitive should be a service to maximize the use of the ready-made connectivity and to avoid handcrafting plumbing. This, in theory, will enable effortlessly transactional integers, secure strings, and reliable classes. In practice, however, there is a granularity limit dictated mostly by the performance of the framework used (such as WCF). I do believe that as time goes by and service-oriented technologies evolve, the industry will see the service boundary pushed further and further inward, making services more and more granular, until the very primitive building blocks will be services. This evidently has been historically the trend of trading performance for productivity via methodology and abstraction.

Tenets and Principles

The service-oriented methodology governs what happens in the space between services (see Figure A-1). There is a small set of principles and best practices for building service-oriented applications referred to as the tenets of service-oriented architecture:

Service boundaries are explicit
> Any service is always confined behind boundaries such as technology and location. The service should not make the nature of these boundaries known to its clients by exposing contracts and data types that betray its technology or location. Adhering to this tenet will make aspects such as location and technology irrelevant. A different way of thinking about this tenet is that the more the client knows about the implementation of the service, the more the client is coupled to the service. To minimize the potential for coupling, the service has to explicitly

expose functionality, and only operations (or data contracts) that are explicitly exposed will be shared with the client. Everything else is encapsulated. Service-oriented technologies should adopt an "opt-out by default" programming model, and expose only those things explicitly opted-in.

Services are autonomous

A service should need nothing from its clients or other services. The service should be operated and versioned independently from the clients. This will enable the service to evolve separately from the client. The service is also secured independently and it protects itself and the messages sent to it regardless of the degree to which the client uses security. Doing so (besides being just common sense) also decouples the client and the service security-wise.

Services share operational contracts and data schema, not type- and technology-specific metadata

What the service does decide to expose across its boundary should be technology-neutral. The service must be able to convert its native data types to and from some neutral representation, and does not share indigenous, technology-specific things such as its assembly version number or its type. In addition, the service should not let its client know about local implementation details such as its instance management mode or its concurrency management mode. The service should only expose logical operations. How the service goes about implementing these operations and how it behaves should not be disclosed to the client.

Services are compatible based on policy

The service should publish a policy indicating what it can do and how clients can interact with it. Any access constraints expressed in the policy (such as reliable communication) should be separate from the service implementation details. Not all clients can interact with all services. It is perfectly valid to have an incompatibility that prevents a particular client from consuming the service. The published policy should be the only way that clients decide if they can interact with the service, and there should not be any out-of-band mechanism by which the clients make such a decision. Put differently, the service must be able to express, in a standard representation of policy, what it does and how clients should communicate with it. Being unable to express such a policy indicates a poor design of the service. Not that the service may not actually publish any such policy due to privacy (if it is not a public service). The tenet implies that the service should be able to publish a policy if it needs to.

Practical Principles

The tenets just listed are very abstract, and supporting them is largely a facet of the technology used to develop and consume the services and the design of the service. Consequently, applications may have various degrees of compliance with the tenets, much the same way as developers can write non-object-oriented code in

C++. However, well-designed applications try to maximize adherence to the tenets. I therefore supplement the tenets with a set of more down-to-earth practical principles:

Services are secure

A service and its clients must use secure communication. At the very least, the transfer of the message from the client to the service must be secured, and the clients must have a way of authenticating the service. The clients may also provide their credentials in the message so that the service can authenticate and authorize them.

Services leave the system in a consistent state

Conditions such as partially succeeding in executing the client's request are forbidden. All resources the service accesses must be consistent after the client's call. A service must not have any leftovers as a result of an error, such as only partially affecting the system state. The service should not require the help of its clients to recover the system back to a consistent state after an error.

Services are thread-safe

The service must be designed so that it can sustain concurrent access from multiple clients. The service should also be able to handle causality or logical thread reentrancy.

Services are reliable

If the client calls a service, the client will always know in a deterministic manner if the message was received by the service. The messages should also be processed in the order they were sent, not in the order they were received.

Services are robust

The service isolates its faults, preventing them from taking down itself or other services. The service should not require the clients to alter their behavior according to the type of error the service encountered. This helps to decouple the clients from the service on the error-handling dimension.

Optional Principles

While I view the practical principles as mandatory, there is also a set of optional principles that may not be required by all applications, although adhering to them as well is usually a good idea:

Services are interoperable

The service should be designed so that it can be called by any client, regardless of its technology.

Services are scale-invariant

They should use the same service code regardless of the number of clients and the load on the service. This will grossly simplify the cost of ownership of the service as the system grows and allow different deployment scenarios.

Services are available

The service should always be able to accept the client's requests, and the service should have no downtime. Otherwise, if the service is unavailable, the client needs to accommodate for that, which in turn introduces coupling.

Services are responsive

The client should not wait long for the service to start processing its request. Having a nonresponsive service means the client needs to accommodate for that, which in turn introduces coupling.

Services are disciplined

The service execution of any operation is relatively short and does not take long to process the client's request. Having long processing means the client needs to accommodate for that, which in turn introduces coupling.

Publish-Subscribe Service

Using raw duplex callbacks for events often introduces too much coupling between the publisher and the subscribers. The subscriber has to know where all the publishing services are in the application and connect to them. Any publisher that the subscriber is unaware of will not be able to notify the subscriber of events. This in turn makes adding new subscribers (or removing existing ones) difficult in an already deployed application. There is no way for the subscriber to ask to be notified whenever anyone in the application raises a particular type of event. In addition, the subscriber must make multiple and potentially expensive calls to each publisher, both to subscribe and to unsubscribe. Different publishers may fire the same event but offer slightly different ways to subscriber and unsubscribe, which of course couples the subscribers to those methods.

Much the same way, the publisher can only notify subscribers it knows about. There is no way for the publisher to deliver an event to whomever wishes to receive it, nor is there an ability to broadcast an event. In addition, all publishers must repeatedly have the necessary code to manage the list of the subscribers and the publishing act itself. This code has almost nothing to do with the business problem the service is designed to solve, and can get fairly complex if you want some advanced features employed, such as concurrent publishing.

Further, the duplex-based callbacks introduce coupling between the lifetime of the publisher and the subscribers. The subscribers have to be up and running in order to subscribe and receive events.

There is no way for a subscriber to ask that if an event is fired, the application should create an instance of the subscriber and let it handle the event.

Security represents yet another coupling dimension: the subscribers need to be able to authenticate themselves against all publishers, across all security modes and credentials used. The publisher too needs to be able to have enough security credentials be allowed to fire the event, and different subscribers may have different role membership mechanisms.

Finally, setting up subscriptions has to be done programmatically. There is no easy administrative way to configure subscriptions in the application or administratively change the subscriber's preferences when the system is running.

These problems actually are not specific to WCF duplex calls, and they also characterize past technologies such as COM connection points or .NET delegates—all are tightly coupled event-management mechanisms.

The Publish-Subscribe Design Pattern

The solution to the problems just listed is to design around them using what is known as the *publish-subscribe* design pattern. The idea behind the pattern is a simple one: decouple the publishers from the subscribers by introducing a dedicated subscription service and a dedicated publishing service in between, as shown in Figure B-1.

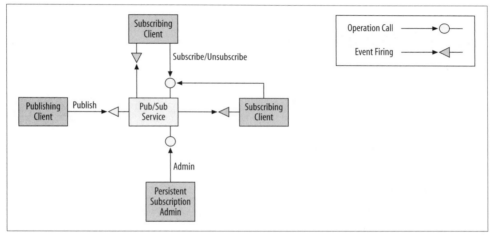

Figure B-1. A publish-subscribe system

Subscribers that want to subscribe to events register with the subscription service, which manages the lists of subscribers, and also provides a similar ability to unsubscribe. Similarly, all publishers use the publisher service to fire their events, and avoid delivering the events directly to the subscribers. The subscription and publishing services provide a layer of indirection that decouples your system. No longer do the subscribers have any knowledge about the identity of the publishers. They can subscribe to a type of an event, and will receive the event from any publisher, and the subscription mechanism is uniform across all publishers. In fact, no publisher has to manage any subscription list, and the publishers have no idea who the subscribers are. They deliver the event to the publishing service to be delivered to any interested subscriber.

Subscriber Types

You can even define two types of subscribers: *transient subscribers* are in-memory running subscribers, and *persistent subscribers* are subscribers that persist on the disk, representing services to invoke when the event takes place. For transient subscribers, you can use the duplex callback mechanism as a handy way of passing the callback reference to the running service. For the persistent subscribers, all you really need to record is the subscriber address as a reference. When the event is raised, the publishing service will call to the persistent subscriber address and deliver the event to it. Another important distinction between the two types of subscriptions is that you can store the persistent subscription on the disk or in a database. Doing so will persist the subscription across application shutdowns or machine crashes and reboots, thus enabling administrative configuration of the subscriptions. Obviously, you cannot save the transient subscription across an application shutdown, and you will need to set up the transient subscription explicitly every time the application starts.

The Publish-Subscribe Framework

The source code available with this book contains a complete publish-subscribe example. I wanted not just to provide sample publish-subscribe services and clients, but also to provide a general-purpose framework that automates implementing such services and adding the support for any application. The first step in building the framework was to factor the publish-subscribe management interfaces, and provide separate contracts for transient and persistent subscriptions and for publishing.*

Managing Transient Subscriptions

For managing transient subscriptions, I defined the ISubscriptionService interface shown in Example B-1.

Example B-1. The ISubscriptionService interface manages transient subscribers

```
[ServiceContract]
public interface ISubscriptionService
{
   [OperationContract]
   void Subscribe(string eventOperation);

   [OperationContract]
   void Unsubscribe(string eventOperation);
}
```

---

* I first published my publish-subscribe framework in my article "WCF Essentials: What You Need to Know About One-Way Calls, Callbacks, and Events," *MSDN Magazine*, October 2006.

Note that ISubscriptionService does not identify the callback contract its implementing endpoint expects. Being a general-purpose interface, it is unaware of particular callback contracts. It is up to the using application to define those callback contracts. The callback interface is provided in the using application by deriving from ISubscriptionService and specifying the desired callback contract:

```
interface IMyEvents
{
   [OperationContract(IsOneWay = true)]
   void OnEvent1();

   [OperationContract(IsOneWay = true)]
   void OnEvent2(int number);

   [OperationContract(IsOneWay = true)]
   void OnEvent3(int number,string text);
}

[ServiceContract(CallbackContract = typeof(IMyEvents))]
interface IMySubscriptionService : ISubscriptionService
{}
```

Typically, every operation on the callback contract corresponds to a specific event. The subinterface of ISubscriptionService (IMySubscriptionService in this example) does not need to add operations. The transient subscription management functionality is provided by ISubscriptionService. In each call to Subscribe() or Unsubscribe(), the subscriber needs to provide the name of the operation (and therefore the event) it wants to subscribe or unsubscribe to. If the caller wishes to subscribe to all events, it can pass an empty or null string.

My framework offers an implementation for the methods of ISubscriptionService in the form of the generic abstract class SubscriptionManager<T>:

```
public abstract class SubscriptionManager<T> where T : class
{
   public void Subscribe(string eventOperation);
   public void Unsubscribe(string eventOperation);
   //More members
}
```

The generic type parameter for SubscriptionManager<T> is the events contract. Note that SubscriptionManager<T> does not implement ISubscriptionService.

The using application needs to expose its own transient subscription service in the form of an endpoint that supports its specific subinterface of ISubscriptionService. To do so, the application needs to provide a service class that derives from SubscriptionManager<T>, specify the callback contract as a type parameter, and derive from the specific subinterface of ISubscriptionService. For example, to implement a transient subscriptions service using the IMyEvents callback interface:

```
[ServiceBehavior(InstanceContextMode = InstanceContextMode.PerCall)]
class MySubscriptionService : SubscriptionManager<IMyEvents>,IMySubscriptionService
{}
```

`MySubscriptionService` doesn't need any code because `IMySubscriptionService` does not add any new operations, and `SubscriptionManager<T>` already implements the methods of `ISubscriptionService`.

Note that just deriving from `SubscriptionManager<IMyEvents>` is insufficient because it does not derive from a contract interface—you must add the derivation from `IMySubscriptionService` to support transient subscriptions.

Finally, the using application needs to define an endpoint for `IMySubscriptionService`:

```
<services>
   <service name = "MySubscriptionService">
      <endpoint
         address  = "..."
         binding  = "..."
         contract = "IMySubscriptionService"
      />
   </service>
</services>
```

Example B-2 shows how `SubscriptionManager<T>` manages transient subscriptions.

Example B-2. The transient subscribers management in SubscriptionManager<T>

```
public abstract class SubscriptionManager<T> where T : class
{
   static Dictionary<string,List<T>> m_TransientStore;

   static SubscriptionManager()
   {
      m_TransientStore = new Dictionary<string,List<T>>();
      string[] methods = GetOperations();
      Action<string> insert = delegate(string methodName)
                              {
                                 m_TransientStore.Add(methodName,new List<T>());
                              };
      Array.ForEach(methods,insert);
   }
   static string[] GetOperations()
   {
      MethodInfo[] methods = typeof(T).GetMethods(BindingFlags.Public|
                                             BindingFlags.FlattenHierarchy|
                                             BindingFlags.Instance);
      List<string> operations = new List<string>(methods.Length);

      Action<MethodInfo> add =  delegate(MethodInfo method)
                                {
                                   Debug.Assert(!operations.Contains(method.Name));
                                   operations.Add(method.Name);
                                };
      Array.ForEach(methods,add);
      return operations.ToArray();
   }
```

```
static void AddTransient(T subscriber,string eventOperation)
{
   lock(typeof(SubscriptionManager<T>))
   {
      List<T> list = m_TransientStore[eventOperation];
      if(list.Contains(subscriber))
      {
         return;
      }
      list.Add(subscriber);
   }
}
static void RemoveTransient(T subscriber,string eventOperation)
{
   lock(typeof(SubscriptionManager<T>))
   {
      List<T> list = m_TransientStore[eventOperation];
      list.Remove(subscriber);
   }
}

public void Subscribe(string eventOperation)
{
   lock(typeof(SubscriptionManager<T>))
   {
      T subscriber = OperationContext.Current.GetCallbackChannel<T>();
      if(String.IsNullOrEmpty(eventOperation) == false)
      {
         AddTransient(subscriber,eventOperation);
      }
      else
      {
         string[] methods = GetOperations();
         Action<string> addTransient = delegate(string methodName)
                                       {
                                          AddTransient(subscriber,methodName);
                                       };
         Array.ForEach(methods,addTransient);
      }
   }
}

public void Unsubscribe(string eventOperation)
{
   lock(typeof(SubscriptionManager<T>))
   {
      T subscriber = OperationContext.Current.GetCallbackChannel<T>();
      if(String.IsNullOrEmpty(eventOperation) == false)
      {
         RemoveTransient(subscriber,eventOperation);
      }
      else
      {
```

Example B-2. The transient subscribers management in SubscriptionManager<T> (continued)

```
            string[] methods = GetOperations();
            Action<string> removeTransient = delegate(string methodName)
                                             {
                                                RemoveTransient(subscriber,methodName);
                                             };
            Array.ForEach(methods,removeTransient);
         }
      }
   }
   //More members
}
```

SubscriptionManager<T> stores the transient subscribers in a generic static dictionary called m_TransientStore:

```
    static Dictionary<string,List<T>> m_TransientStore;
```

Each entry in the dictionary contains the name of the event operation and all its subscribers in the form of a linked list. The static constructor of SubscriptionManager<T> uses reflection to get all the operations of the callback interfaces (the type parameter for SubscriptionManager<T>) and initializes the dictionary to have all the operations with empty lists. The Subscribe() method extracts the callback reference from the operation call context. If the caller specifies an operation name, Subscribe() calls the helper method AddTransient(). AddTransient() retrieves the list of subscribers for the event from the store. If the list does not contain the subscriber, it adds it in.

If the caller specifies an empty string or null for the operation name, Subscribe() calls AddTransient() for each operation in the callback contract.

Unsubscribe() operates in a similar manner. Note that the caller can subscribe to all events and then unsubscribe from a particular one.

Managing Persistent Subscribers

For managing persistent subscribers, I defined the IPersistentSubscriptionService interface shown in Example B-3.

Example B-3. The IPersistentSubscriptionService interface manages persistent subscribers

```
[ServiceContract]
public interface IPersistentSubscriptionService
{
   [OperationContract]
   [TransactionFlow(TransactionFlowOption.Allowed)]
   void Subscribe(string address,string eventsContract,string eventOperation);

   [OperationContract]
   [TransactionFlow(TransactionFlowOption.Allowed)]
   void Unsubscribe(string address,string eventsContract,string eventOperation);
   //More members
}
```

To add a persistent subscriber, the caller needs to call Subscribe( ), providing the address of the subscriber, the event's contract name, and the specific event operation itself. To unsubscribe, the caller uses Unsubscribe( ) with the same information. Note that IPersistentSubscriptionService does not imply in any way where the subscribers persist on the service side—that is an implementation detail.

The class SubscriptionManager<T> presented previously also implements the methods of IPersistentSubscriptionService:

```
[BindingRequirement(TransactionFlowEnabled = true)]
public abstract class SubscriptionManager<T> where T : class
{
   public void Unsubscribe(string address,string eventsContract,
                                              string eventOperation);
   public void Subscribe(string address,string eventsContract,
                                              string eventOperation);
   //More members
}
```

SubscriptionManager<T> stores the persistent subscribers in SQL Server. It is configured to use the Client/Service transaction mode (presented in Chapter 7), and it enforces that mode using my BindingRequirement attribute.

The generic type parameter for SubscriptionManager<T> is the events contract. Note that SubscriptionManager<T> does not derive from IPersistentSubscriptionService. The using application needs to expose its own persistent subscription service, but there is no need to derive a new contract from IPersistentSubscriptionService because no callback references are required. The application simply derives from SubscriptionManager<T>, specifying the events contract as a type parameter and adding a derivation from IPersistentSubscriptionService; for example:

```
[ServiceBehavior(InstanceContextMode = InstanceContextMode.PerCall)]
class MySubscriptionService : SubscriptionManager<IMyEvents>,
                        IPersistentSubscriptionService
{}
```

There is no need for any code in MySubscriptionService because SubscriptionManager<T> already implements the methods of IPersistentSubscriptionService.

Note that just deriving from SubscriptionManager<IMyEvents> is insufficient because it does not derive from a contract interface—you must add the derivation from IPersistentSubscriptionService to support persistent subscriptions.

Finally, the application needs to define an endpoint for IPersistentSubscriptionService:

```
<services>
   <service name = "MySubscriptionService">
      <endpoint
         address = "..."
         binding = "..."
```

```
                contract = "IPersistentSubscriptionService"
            />
        </service>
    </services>
```

The implementation of the methods of IPersistentSubscriptionService by SubscriptionManager<T> is shown in Example B-4. Example B-4 is very similar to Example B-2, except the subscribers are stored in SQL Server, not in memory in a dictionary.

Example B-4. Persistent subscribers management in SubscriptionManager<T>

```
public abstract class SubscriptionManager<T> where T : class
{
   static void AddPersistent(string address,string eventsContract,
                                                string eventOperation)
   {
      //Uses ADO.NET to store the subscription in SQL Server
   }

   static void RemovePersistent(string address,string eventsContract,
                                                string eventOperation)
   {
      //Uses ADO.NET to remove the subscription from SQL Server
   }

   [OperationBehavior(TransactionScopeRequired = true)]
   public void Unsubscribe(string address,string eventsContract,
                                                string eventOperation)
   {
      if(String.IsNullOrEmpty(eventOperation) == false)
      {
         RemovePersistent(address,eventsContract,eventOperation);
      }
      else
      {
         string[] methods = GetOperations();
         Action<string> removePersistent = delegate(string methodName)
                              {
                                 RemovePersistent(address,eventsContract,methodName);
                              };
         Array.ForEach(methods,removePersistent);
      }
   }
   [OperationBehavior(TransactionScopeRequired = true)]
   public void Subscribe(string address,string eventsContract,
                                                string eventOperation)
   {
      if(String.IsNullOrEmpty(eventOperation) == false)
      {
         AddPersistent(address,eventsContract,eventOperation);
      }
      else
```

```
    {
        string[] methods = GetOperations( );
        Action<string> addPersistent = delegate(string methodName)
                                    {
                                    AddPersistent(address,eventsContract,methodName);
                                    };
        Array.ForEach(methods,addPersistent);
    }
    }
    //More members
}
```

If the application wants to support both transient and persistent subscribers for the same events contract, simply derive the subscription service class from both the specialized subinterface of ISubscriptionService and from IPersistentSubscriptionService:

```
[ServiceBehavior(InstanceContextMode = InstanceContextMode.PerCall)]
class MySubscriptionService : SubscriptionManager<IMyEvents>,
                            IMySubscriptionService,IPersistentSubscriptionService
{}
```

and expose the two matching endpoints:

```
<services>
    <service name = "MySubscriptionService">
        <endpoint
            address  = "..."
            binding  = "..."
            contract = "IMySubscriptionService"
        />
        <endpoint
            address  = "..."
            binding  = "..."
            contract = "IPersistentSubscriptionService"
        />
    </service>
</services>
```

Event Publishing

The parts of the publish-subscribe framework shown so far have only dealt with the aspects of subscription management. The framework also enables easy implementation of the publishing service. The publishing service should support the same events contract as the subscribers, and should be the only point of contact known to the publishers in the application. Because the publishing service exposes the events contract in an endpoint, you need to mark the events contract as a service contract, even if you only use it for duplex callbacks with transient subscribers:

```
[ServiceContract]
interface IMyEvents
{
```

```
      [OperationContract(IsOneWay = true)]
      void OnEvent1( );

      [OperationContract(IsOneWay = true)]
      void OnEvent2(int number);

      [OperationContract(IsOneWay = true)]
      void OnEvent3(int number,string text);
   }
```

The publish-subscribe framework contains the helper class `PublishService<T>`, defined as:

```
   public abstract class PublishService<T> where T : class
   {
      protected static void FireEvent(params object[] args);
   }
```

`PublishService<T>` requires as a type parameter the type of the event's contract. To provide your own publishing service, derive from `PublishService<T>` and use the `FireEvent( )` method to deliver the event to all subscribers, be they transient or persistent, as shown in Example B-5.

Example B-5. Implementing an event-publishing service

```
[ServiceBehavior(InstanceContextMode = InstanceContextMode.PerCall)]
class MyPublishService : PublishService<IMyEvents>,IMyEvents
{
   public void OnEvent1( )
   {
      FireEvent( );
   }
   public void OnEvent2(int number)
   {
      FireEvent(number);
   }
   public void OnEvent3(int number,string text)
   {
      FireEvent(number,text);
   }
}
```

Note that you can use `FireEvent( )` to fire any type of event, regardless of the parameters because of the use of the `params` object array.

Finally, the application needs to expose an endpoint for the publishing service with the events contract:

```
   <services>
      <service name = "MyPublishService">
         <endpoint
            address  = "..."
            binding  = "..."
            contract = "IMyEvents"
```

```
        />
      </service>
    </services>
```

Example B-6 shows the implementation of PublishService<T>.

Example B-6. Implementing PublishService<T>

```
public abstract class PublishService<T> where T : class
{
    protected static void FireEvent(params object[] args)
    {
        StackFrame stackFrame = new StackFrame(1);
        string methodName = stackFrame.GetMethod().Name;
        //Parse out explicit interface implementation
        if(methodName.Contains("."))
        {
            string[] parts = methodName.Split('.');
            methodName = parts[parts.Length-1];
        }
        FireEvent(methodName,args);
    }
    static void FireEvent(string methodName,params object[] args)
    {
        PublishPersistent(methodName,args);
        PublishTransient(methodName,args);
    }
    static void PublishPersistent(string methodName,params object[] args)
    {
        T[] subscribers = SubscriptionManager<T>.GetPersistentList(methodName);
        Publish(subscribers,true,methodName,args);
    }
    static void PublishTransient(string methodName,params object[] args)
    {
        T[] subscribers = SubscriptionManager<T>.GetTransientList(methodName);
        Publish(subscribers,false,methodName,args);
    }
    static void Publish(T[] subscribers,bool closeSubscribers,string methodName,
                                                      params object[] args)
    {
        WaitCallback fire = delegate(object subscriber)
                            {
                                Invoke(subscriber as T,methodName,args);
                                if(closeSubscribers)
                                {
                                    using(subscriber as IDisposable)
                                    {}
                                }
                            };
        Action<T> queueUp = delegate(T subscriber)
                            {
                                ThreadPool.QueueUserWorkItem(fire,subscriber);
                            };
        Array.ForEach(subscribers,queueUp);
```

```
    }
    static void Invoke(T subscriber,string methodName,object[] args)
    {
        Debug.Assert(subscriber != null);
        Type type = typeof(T);
        MethodInfo methodInfo = type.GetMethod(methodName);
        try
        {
            methodInfo.Invoke(subscriber,args);
        }
        catch(Exception e)
        {
            Trace.WriteLine(e.Message);
        }
    }
}
```

To simplify firing the event by the publishing service, the FireEvent( ) method accepts the parameters to pass to the subscribers, yet its caller does not provide it with the name of the operation to invoke on the subscribers. To that end, FireEvent( ) accesses its stack frame and extracts the name of its calling method. It then uses an overloaded FireEvent( ) that accepts the method name. That method in turn uses the helper method PublishPersistent( ) to publish to all persistent subscribers, and the PublishTransient( ) helper method to publish to all transient subscribers. Both publishing methods operate in an almost identical way: they access SubscriptionManager<T> to retrieve their respective subscribers list, and then use the Publish( ) method to fire the event. The subscribers are returned in the form of an array of proxies to the subscribers. That array is passed to the Publish( ) method.

Publish( ) could have simply invoked the subscribers at this point. However, I wanted to support concurrent publishing of the events, so that if any subscriber is undisciplined and takes a long time to process the event, this will not preclude the other subscribers from receiving the event in a timely manner. Note that having the event operations marked as one-way is no guarantee for asynchronous invocation, and besides, I wanted to support concurrent publishing even when the event operation is not marked as a one-way operation. Publish( ) defines two anonymous methods. The first calls the Invoke( ) helper method, which will result in firing the event to the individual subscriber provided and then closes the proxy if so specified. Because Invoke( ) was never compiled against the specific subscriber type, it uses reflection and late binding for the invocation. Invoke( ) also suppresses any exceptions raised by the invocation, because those are of no interested to the publishing party. The second anonymous method queues up the first anonymous method to be executed by a thread from the thread pool. Finally, Publish( ) invokes the second anonymous method on every subscriber in the provided array.

Note how uniformly PublishService<T> treats the subscribers—it almost does not matter if they are transient or persistent. The only difference is that after publishing to a persistent subscriber, you need to close the proxy. This uniformity is achieved by the helper methods GetTransientList() and GetPersistentList() of SubscriptionManager<T>. Of these two, GetTransientList() is the simpler one:

```
public abstract class SubscriptionManager<T> where T : class
{
    internal static T[] GetTransientList(string eventOperation)
    {
        lock(typeof(SubscriptionManager<T>))
        {
            if(m_TransientStore.ContainsKey(eventOperation))
            {
                List<T> list = m_TransientStore[eventOperation];
                return list.ToArray();
            }
            return new T[]{};
        }
    }
    //More members
}
```

GetTransientList() looks up in the transient store for all the subscribers to the specified operation and returns them as an array. GetPersistentList() faces a bigger challenge: there is no ready-made list of proxies to persistent subscribers; all that is known about them is their addresses. GetPersistentList() therefore needs to instantiate the persistent subscribers proxies, as shown in Example B-7.

Example B-7. Creating the persistent subscribers proxy list

```
public abstract class SubscriptionManager<T> where T : class
{
    internal static T[] GetPersistentList(string eventOperation)
    {
        string[] addresses = GetSubscribersToContractEventOperation(
                                        typeof(T).ToString(),eventOperation);

        List<T> subscribers = new List<T>(addresses.Length);

        foreach(string address in addresses)
        {
            Binding binding = GetBindingFromAddress(address);
            T proxy = ChannelFactory<T>.CreateChannel(binding,
                                        new EndpointAddress(address));
            subscribers.Add(proxy);
        }
        return subscribers.ToArray();
    }
    static string[] GetSubscribersToContractEventOperation(string eventsContract,
                                                    string eventOperation)
    {
        //Uses ADO.NET to query SQL Server for the subscribers to the event
    }
```

Example B-7. Creating the persistent subscribers proxy list (continued)

```
static Binding GetBindingFromAddress(string address)
{
   if(address.StartsWith("http:") || address.StartsWith("https:"))
   {
      WSHttpBinding binding = new WSHttpBinding(SecurityMode.Message,true);
      binding.ReliableSession.Enabled = true;
      binding.TransactionFlow = true;
      return binding;
   }
   if(address.StartsWith("net.tcp:"))
   {
      NetTcpBinding binding = new NetTcpBinding(SecurityMode.Message,true);
      binding.ReliableSession.Enabled = true;
      binding.TransactionFlow = true;
      return binding;
   }
   /* Similar code for the named pipes and MSMQ bindings */
   Debug.Assert(false,"Unsupported protocol specified");
   return null;
}
//More members
}
```

To create a proxy for each subscriber, GetPersistentList( ) needs the subscriber's address, binding, and contract. The contract is of course the type parameter for SubscriptionManager<T>. To obtain the addresses, GetPersistentList( ) calls GetSubscribersToContractEventOperation( ) to query the database and return an array of all addresses of the persistent subscribers who subscribed to the specified event. All GetPersistentList( ) needs now is the binding used by each subscriber. For that, GetPersistentList( ) calls the helper method GetBindingFromAddress( ), which infers the binding to use from the address schema. GetBindingFromAddress( ) treats all HTTP addresses as WSHttpBinding. In addition, GetBindingFromAddress( ) turns on reliability and transaction propagation for each binding, to enable including the event in the publisher's transaction when one-way operations are not used, such as with this events contract:

```
[ServiceContract]
interface IMyEvents
{
   [OperationContract]
   [TransactionFlow(TransactionFlowOption.Allowed)]
   void OnEvent1( );

   [OperationContract]
   [TransactionFlow(TransactionFlowOption.Allowed)]
   void OnEvent2(int number);

   [OperationContract]
   [TransactionFlow(TransactionFlowOption.Allowed)]
   void OnEvent3(int number,string text);
}
```

Administering Persistent Subscribers

While you can add and remove persistent subscriptions at runtime by using the methods of the IPersistentSubscriptionService interface shown in Example B-3, because of their persistent nature, it is likely that managing the subscriptions will be done via some kind of an administration tool. To that end, IPersistentSubscriptionService defines additional operations that answer various queries of the subscribers store, as shown in Example B-8.

Example B-8. The IPersistentSubscriptionService interface

```
[DataContract]
public struct PersistentSubscription
{
   [DataMember]
   public string Address;

   [DataMember]
   public string EventsContract;

   [DataMember]
   public string EventOperation;
}

[ServiceContract]
public interface IPersistentSubscriptionService
{
   //Administration operations
   [OperationContract]
   [TransactionFlow(TransactionFlowOption.Allowed)]
   PersistentSubscription[] GetAllSubscribers();

   [OperationContract]
   [TransactionFlow(TransactionFlowOption.Allowed)]
   PersistentSubscription[] GetSubscribersToContract(string eventsContract);

   [OperationContract]
   [TransactionFlow(TransactionFlowOption.Allowed)]
   string[] GetSubscribersToContractEventType(string eventsContract,
                                              string eventOperation);
   [OperationContract]
   [TransactionFlow(TransactionFlowOption.Allowed)]
   PersistentSubscription[] GetAllSubscribersFromAddress(string address);
   //More members
}
```

All of these administration operations utilize a simple data structure called PersistentSubscription, which contains the address of the subscriber, the subscribed contract, and the event. GetAllSubscribers() simply returns the list of all subscribers. GetSubscribersToContract() returns all subscribers to a specific contract, and GetSubscribersToContractEventType() returns all subscribers to a particular event operation on a specified contract. Finally, for completeness' sake, GetAllSubscribersFromAddress() returns all subscribers that provided a specified address. My publish-subscribe framework includes a sample persistent subscription administration tool called Persistent Subscription Manager, shown in Figure B-2.

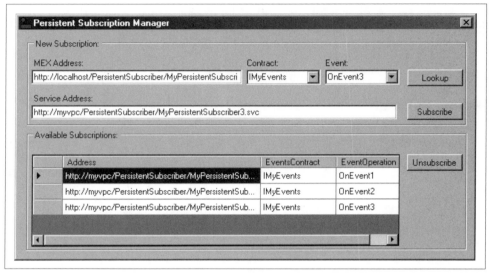

Figure B-2. The Persistent Subscription Manager application

The administration tool uses IPersistentSubscriptionService to add or remove subscriptions. To add a new subscription, you need to provide it with the metadata exchange address of the events contract definition. You can use the metadata exchange address of the persistent subscribers themselves or the metadata exchange address of the publish service (such as the one shown in Example B-5) because they are polymorphic. Enter the metadata exchange base address in the MEX Address text box and click the Lookup button. The tool will programmatically retrieve the metadata of the event service and populate the Contract and Event combo boxes. Retrieving the metadata and parsing its content is done using the MetadataHelper class presented in Chapter 2.

To subscribe, provide the address of the persistent subscriber and click the Subscribe button. Persistent Subscription Manager then adds the subscription by calling to the subscription service (the MySubscriptionService service in the examples so far). The address for the subscription service is maintained in the Persistent Subscription Manager config file.

The publish-subscriber pattern also decouples the system security-wise. All publishers need is to authenticate themselves against a single publishing service, as opposed to multiple subscribers and potentially multiple security mechanisms. The subscribers in turn need only allow the publishing service to deliver them the event, rather than all publishers in the system, trusting the publishing service in turn to properly authenticate and authorize the publishers. Applying role-based security on the publishing service enables you to easily enforce in one place various rules regarding who is allowed to publish an event across the system.

Queued Publishers and Subscribers

Instead of using the synchronous binding for either publishing or subscribing to the events, you can use the NetMsmqBinding. A queued publish-subscribe service combines the benefits of a loosely coupled system and the flexibility of disconnected execution. When using queued events, all events on the contract must of course be marked as one-way operations. As shown in Figure B-3, you can use queuing at either end independently.

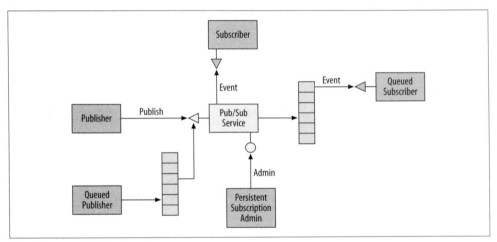

Figure B-3. Queued publish-subscribe

You can have a queued publisher and connected synchronous subscribers. You can have a connected publisher publishing to queued subscribers, or you could have both queued publishers and queued subscribers. Note, however, that you cannot have queued transient subscriptions because there is no support within the MSMQ binding for duplex callbacks, since that would render the disconnected aspect of the communication useless. As before, you can use the administration tool to manage the subscribers, and the administration operations are still connected and synchronous.

Queued publisher

To utilize a queued publisher, the publishing service needs to expose a queued end-point using the MSMQ binding. When firing events at a queued publisher, the publishing service can be offline, or the publishing client itself can be disconnected. Note that when publishing two events to a queued publishing service, there are no guarantees as to the order of delivery and processing of these events by the end subscribers. You can only assume order of publishing when the events contract is configured for a session and only when dealing with a single publishing service.

Queued subscriber

To deploy a queued subscriber, the persistent subscribing service needs to expose a queued endpoint. Doing so will enable it to be offline even when the publisher is on-line. When the subscriber is connected again, it will receive all its queued-up events. In addition, queued subscribers can handle the case when the publishing service itself is disconnected, because no events are lost. When multiple events are fired at a single queued subscriber, there are no guarantees as to the order of delivery of the events. The subscriber can only assume the order of publishing when the event's contract has a session. Of course, having both a queued publisher and subscriber allows both to work offline at the same time.

WCF Coding Standard

A comprehensive coding standard is essential for a successful product delivery. The standard helps in enforcing best practices and avoiding pitfalls, and makes knowledge dissemination across the team easier. Traditionally, coding standards are thick, laborious documents, spanning hundreds of pages and detailing the rationale behind every directive. While these are still better than no standard at all, such efforts are usually indigestible by the average developer. In contrast, the WCF coding standard presented here is very thin on the "why" and very detailed on the "what." I believe that while fully understanding every insight that goes into a particular programming decision may require reading books and even years of experience, applying the standard should not. When absorbing a new developer into your team, you should be able to simply point him or her at the standard and say: "Read this first." Being able to comply with a good standard should come before fully understanding and appreciating it—that should come over time, with experience. The coding standard presented next captures dos and don'ts, pitfalls, guidelines, and recommendations. It uses the best practices and helper classes discussed in this book.

General Design Guidelines

1. All services must adhere to these principles:

   a. Services are secure.

   b. Services leave the system in a consistent state.

   c. Services are thread-safe.

   d. Services can be accessed by concurrent clients.

   e. Services are reliable.

   f. Services are robust.

2. Optional principles services should adhere to:

   a. Services are interoperable.

   b. Services are scale-invariant.

      c. Services are available.

      d. Services are responsive.

      e. Services are disciplined and do not block their clients for long.

3. Avoid message contracts.

Essentials

1. Place service code in a class library and not in any hosting EXE.

2. Do not provide parameterized constructors to a service class unless it is a singleton that is hosted explicitly.

3. Enable reliability in the relevant bindings.

4. Provide a meaningful namespace for contracts. For outward-facing services, use your company's URL or equivalent URN with a year and month to support versioning; for example:

```
[ServiceContract(Namespace = "http://www.idesign.net/2007/08")]
interface IMyContract
{...}
```

For intranet services, use any meaningful unique name, such as `MyApplication`; for example:

```
[ServiceContract(Namespace = "MyApplication")]
interface IMyContract
{...}
```

5. With intranet applications on Windows XP and Windows Server 2003, prefer self-hosting to IIS hosting.

6. On Windows Vista, prefer WAS (IIS7) hosting to self-hosting.

7. Use `ServiceHost<T>`.

8. Enable metadata exchange.

9. Always name all endpoints in the client config file.

10. Do not use SvcUtil or Visual Studio 2005 to generate a config file.

11. Do not duplicate proxy code. If two or more clients use the same contract, factor the proxy to a separate class library.

12. Always close or dispose of the proxy.

Service Contracts

1. Always apply the `ServiceContractAttribute` on an interface, not a class:

```
//Avoid:
[ServiceContract]
class MyService
{
    [OperationContract]
```

```
    public void MyMethod( )
    {...}
}
//Correct:
[ServiceContract]
interface IMyContract
{
    [OperationContract]
    void MyMethod( );
}
class MyService : IMyContract
{
    public void MyMethod( )
    {...}
}
```

2. Prefix the service contract name with I:

```
[ServiceContract]
interface IMyContract
{...}
```

3. Avoid property-like operations:

```
//Avoid:
[ServiceContract]
interface IMyContract
{
    [OperationContract]
    string GetName( );

    [OperationContract]
    void SetName(string name);
}
```

4. Avoid contracts with one member.

5. Strive to have three to five members per service contract.

6. Do not have more than 20 members per service contract. Twelve is probably the practical limit.

Data Contracts

1. Use the `DataMemberAttribute` on properties or read-only public members only.

2. Avoid explicit XML serialization on your own types.

3. When using the `Order` property, assign the same value to all members coming from the same level in the class hierarchy.

4. Support `IExtensibleDataObject` on your data contracts.

5. Avoid setting `IgnoreExtensionDataObject` on the `ServiceBehavior` and `CallbackBehavior` attributes to true. Keep the default of `false`.

6. Do not mark delegates and events as data members.

7. Do not pass .NET-specific types, such as Type, as operation parameters.

8. Do not accept or return ADO.NET DataSet and DataTable (or their type-safe subclasses) from operations. Return a natural representation such as an array.

9. Suppress the generation of a generic type parameter hash code and provide a legible type name instead.

10. Avoid the /ct switch of SvcUtil or any other way of sharing an assembly type across the service boundary.

Instance Management

1. Prefer the per-call instance mode.

2. Avoid a sessionful service.

3. If selecting SessionMode.Required on the contract, always explicitly set service instancing to InstanceContextMode.PerSession.

4. If selecting SessionMode.NotAllowed on the contract, always configure the service instancing to InstanceContextMode.PerCall.

5. Do not mix sessionful contracts and per-call contracts on the same service.

6. Avoid a singleton unless you have a natural singleton.

7. Use ordered delivery with a sessionful service.

8. Avoid instance deactivation with a sessionful service.

9. Avoid demarcating operations.

Operations and Calls

1. Do not treat one-way calls as asynchronous calls.

2. Do not treat one-way calls as concurrent calls.

3. Expect exceptions out of a one-way operation.

4. Enable reliability even on one-way calls. Use of ordered delivery is optional for one-way calls.

5. Avoid one-way operations on a sessionful service. If used, make it the terminating operation:

```
[ServiceContract(SessionMode = SessionMode.Required)]
interface IOrderManager
{
    [OperationContract]
    void SetCustomerId(int customerId);

    [OperationContract(IsInitiating = false)]
    void AddItem(int itemId);

    [OperationContract(IsInitiating = false)]
```

```
    decimal GetTotal( );

    [OperationContract(IsOneWay = true,IsInitiating = false,IsTerminating = true)]
    void ProcessOrders( );
}
```

6. Name the callback contract on the service side after the service contract suffixed by Callback:

```
interface IMyContractCallback
{...}
[ServiceContract(CallbackContract = typeof(IMyContractCallback))]
interface IMyContract
{...}
```

7. Strive to mark callback operations as one-way.

8. Use callback contracts for callbacks only.

9. Avoid mixing regular callbacks and events on the same callback contract.

10. Event operations should be well-designed:

    a. void return type

    b. No out parameters

    c. Marked as one-way operations

11. Avoid using raw callback contracts for event management, and prefer using the publish-subscribe framework.

12. Always provide explicit methods for callback setup and teardown:

```
[ServiceContract(CallbackContract = typeof(IMyContractCallback))]
interface IMyContract
{
    [OperationContract]
    void DoSomething( );

    [OperationContract]
    void Connect( );

    [OperationContract]
    void Disconnect( );
}
interface IMyContractCallback
{...}
```

13. Use the type-safe DuplexClientBase<T,C> instead of DuplexClientBase<T>.

14. Use the type-safe DuplexChannelFactory<T,C> instead of DuplexChannelFactory<T>.

15. When debugging or in intranet deployment of callbacks over WSDualHttpBinding, use the CallbackBaseAddressBehaviorAttribute with CallbackPort set to 0:

```
[CallbackBaseAddressBehavior(CallbackPort = 0)]
class MyClient : IMyContractCallback
{...}
```

Faults

1. Never use a proxy instance after an exception, even if you catch that exception.

2. Do not reuse the callback channel after an exception even if you catch that exception, as the channel may be faulted.

3. Use the FaultContractAttribute with exception classes, as opposed to mere serializable types:

```
//Avoid:
[OperationContract]
[FaultContract(typeof(double))]
double Divide(double number1,double number2);

//Correct:
[OperationContract]
[FaultContract(typeof(DivideByZeroException))]
double Divide(double number1,double number2);
```

4. Avoid lengthy processing such as logging in IErrorHandler.ProvideFault( ).

5. With both service classes and callback classes, set IncludeExceptionDetailInFaults to true in debug sessions, either in the config file or programmatically:

```
public class DebugHelper
{
   public const bool IncludeExceptionDetailInFaults =
#if DEBUG
      true;
#else
      false;
#endif
}
[ServiceBehavior(IncludeExceptionDetailInFaults =
               DebugHelper.IncludeExceptionDetailInFaults)]
class MyService : IMyContract
{...}
```

6. In release builds, do not return unknown exceptions as faults except in diagnostic scenarios.

7. Consider using the ErrorHandlerBehaviorAttribute on the service for both promoting exceptions to fault contracts and automatic error logging:

```
[ErrorHandlerBehavior]
class MyService : IMyContract
{...}
```

8. Consider using the CallbackErrorHandlerBehaviorAttribute on the callback client for both promoting exceptions to fault contracts and automatic error logging:

```
[CallbackErrorHandlerBehavior(typeof(MyClient))]
public partial class MyClient : IMyContractCallback
{
   public void OnCallabck( )
   {...}
}
```

Transactions

1. Never use ADO.NET transactions directly.

2. Apply `TransactionFlowAttribute` on the contract, not the service class.

3. Do not perform transactional work in the service constructor.

4. Using this book's terminology, configure services for either Client or Client/Service transactions. Avoid None or Service transactions.

5. Using this book's terminology, configure callbacks for either Service or Service/Callbacks transactions. Avoid None or Callback transactions.

6. When using the Client/Service or the Service/Callback modes, constrain the binding to flow transaction using the `BindingRequirement` attribute.

7. On the client, always catch all exceptions thrown by a service configured for None or Service transactions.

8. Strive to always configure operations to at least allow transactions:

   ```
   [ServiceContract]
   interface IMyContract
   {
      [OperationContract]
      [TransactionFlow(TransactionFlowOption.Allowed)]
      void MyMethod1(...);
   }
   ```

9. Enable reliability and ordered delivery even when using transactions.

10. In a service operation, never catch an exception and manually abort the transaction:

    ```
    //Avoid:
    [OperationBehavior(TransactionScopeRequired = true)]
    public void MyMethod()
    {
       try
       {
          ...
       }
       catch
       {
          Transaction.Current.Rollback();
       }
    }
    ```

11. If you catch an exception in a transactional operation, always rethrow it or another exception.

12. Always use the default isolation level of `IsolationLevel.Serializable`.

13. Do not call one-way operations from within a transaction.

14. Do not call nontransactional services from within a transaction.

15. Do not access nontransactional resources (such as the filesystem) from within a transaction.

16. Avoid transactional sessionful services.

17. Prefer per-call transactional services.

18. When using a sessionful or transactional singleton, use volatile resource managers to manage state and avoid explicitly state-aware programming or relying on the WCF instance deactivation on completion.

Concurrency Management

1. Always provide thread-safe access to:

    a. Service in-memory state with sessionful or singleton services

    b. Client in-memory state during callbacks

    c. Shared resources

    d. Static variables

2. Prefer ConcurrencyMode.Single (the default). It enables transactional access and it is thread-safe without any effort.

3. Keep operations on single-mode sessionful and singleton services short in order to avoid blocking other clients for long.

4. When using ConcurrencyMode.Multiple, you must use transaction auto-completion.

5. Consider using ConcurrencyMode.Multiple on per-call services to allow concurrent calls.

6. Transactional singleton service with ConcurrencyMode.Multiple must have ReleaseServiceInstanceOnTransactionComplete set to false:

```
[ServiceBehavior(InstanceContextMode = InstanceContextMode.Single,
                 ConcurrencyMode = ConcurrencyMode.Multiple,
                 ReleaseServiceInstanceOnTransactionComplete = false)]
class MySingleton : IMyContract
{...}
```

7. Never self-host on a UI thread and call the service by the UI application.

8. Never allow callbacks to the UI application that called the service unless the callback posts the call using SynchronizationContext.Post( ).

9. Use the asynchronous calls pattern on the client side only.

10. When supplying the proxy with both synchronous and asynchronous methods, apply the FaultContractAttribute only to synchronous methods.

11. Do not mix transactions with asynchronous calls.

Queued Services

1. Always verify that the queue (and a dead-letter queue when applicable) is available before calling the queued service. Use QueuedServiceHelper.VerifyQueue<T>( ) to verify.

2. Always verify that the queue is available when hosting a queued service (done automatically by ServiceHost<T>).

3. Except in isolated scenarios, avoid designing the same service to work both queued and nonqueued.

4. Do enable metadata exchange on a queued service.

5. The service should participate in the playback transaction.

6. When participating in the playback transaction, avoid lengthy processing in the queued service.

7. Avoid sessionful queued services.

8. When using a singleton queued service, use a volatile resource manager to manage the singleton state.

9. When using a per-call queued service, do explicitly configure the contract and the service to be per-call and sessionless:

```
[ServiceContract(SessionMode = SessionMode.NotAllowed)]
interface IMyContract
{...}

[ServiceBehavior(InstanceContextMode = InstanceContextMode.PerCall)]
class MyService : IMyContract
{...}
```

10. Always explicitly set contracts on a queued singleton to disallow sessions:

```
[ServiceContract(SessionMode = SessionMode.NotAllowed)]
interface IMyContract
{...}

[ServiceBehavior(InstanceContextMode = InstanceContextMode.Single)]
class MyService : IMyContract
{...}
```

11. The client should call a queued service inside a transaction.

12. On the client side, do not store a queued service proxy in a member variable.

13. Avoid relatively short values of TimeToLive, as they negate the justification for a queued service.

14. Never use volatile queues.

15. When using a response queue, have the service participate in the playback transaction and queue the response in that transaction.

16. Have the response service participate in the response playback transaction.

17. Avoid lengthy processing in a queued response operation.

18. Prefer a response service to a poison queue service dealing with repeated failures of the service itself.

19. Unless dealing with a sessionful contract and service, never assume the order of queued calls.

Security

1. Always protect the message and provide for message confidentiality and integrity.

2. In an intranet, you can use transport security without message security as long as the protection level is set to `EncryptAndSign`.

3. In an intranet, avoid impersonation. Set the impersonation level to `TokenImpersonationLevel.Identification`.

4. When using impersonation, have the client use `TokenImpersonationLevel.Impersonation`.

5. Use the declarative security framework and avoid manual configuration.

6. Never apply the `PrincipalPermissionAttribute` directly on the service class:

```
//Will always fail:
[PrincipalPermission(SecurityAction.Demand,Role = "...")]
public class MyService : IMyContract
{...}
```

7. Avoid sensitive work that requires authorization at the service constructor.

8. Avoid demanding a particular user, with or without demanding a role:

```
//Avoid:
[PrincipalPermission(SecurityAction.Demand,Name = "John")]
public void MyMethod( )
{...}
```

9. Do not rely on role-based security in the client's callback operations.

10. With Internet clients, always use message security.

11. Allow clients to negotiate the service certification (the default).

12. Use the ASP.NET providers for custom credentials.

13. When developing a custom credentials store, develop it as an ASP.NET provider.

14. Validate certificates using peer trust.

Index

We'd like to hear your suggestions for improving our indexes. Send email to *index@oreilly.com*.

original tools, utilities, and helper classes
(*continued*)
    Transactional<T> class, 297
    TransactionalArray<T> class, 297
    TransactionalDictionary<K,T>, 297
    TransactionalList<T> class, 297
    WsDualProxyHelper class, 194

A

Abort( ) method
    ICommunicationObject interface, 16
    ServiceHost class, 16
aborted transactions, 238
accounts, Windows, 470, 486
ACID (atomic, consistent, isolated, and
    durable) transactions, 239
acknowledgement (ACK), 407
Action and ResponseAction properties,
    OperationContract, 60
activation, instance, 133
    deactivation, 158–163
    per-call activation, 134
    (see also instance management)
Add( ) method, 124, 129
    collection marshaled as an array, 126
AddAllMexEndPoints( ) method,
    ServiceHost<T> class, 32
AddBindingParameters( ) method
    CallbackBaseAddressBehavior
        attribute, 197
    CallbackErrorHandlerBehavior
        attribute, 236
    IEndpointBehavior interface, 197
    IServiceBehavior interface, 227, 527
    SecurityBehavior attribute, 527
    SecurityBehavior class, 530
AddErrorHandler( ) method,
    ServiceHost<T> class, 231–233
addresses, 4–6
    administrative endpoint configuration, 24
    callback
        assigning, 193–195
        assigning declaratively, 195–197
    HTTP, 6
    IPC, 6
    metadata exchange endpoints, 30
    MSMQ, 6
    peer network, 6
    programmatic endpoint configuration, 25

    response service, 424
    self-hosted services, 13, 14
    services using IIS hosting, 12
    TCP, 5
AddServiceEndpoint( ) method, 31
    ServiceHost class, 25
administration pages (Visual Studio
    2005), 503
administrative configuration, programmatic
    versus, 44
ADO.NET, data set and data table
    types, 115
AffinitySynchronizer class, 348, 351, 364
    closing worker thread, 350
    installing, 349
    single concurrency mode, 349
AllowedImpersonationLevel enum, 478
ambient transaction, 255
    setting, 257
anonymous applications, 516
    authentication, 517
    authorization, 517
    callbacks, 518
    identity management, 518
    securing bindings, 517
    SecurityBehavior attribute and
        ServiceSecurity enum, 526
anonymous clients, 479
anonymous Windows identity, 471
App.Config file, 13
Application class
    DoEvents( ) method, 346
    OpenForms collection, 334, 338
    Run( ) method, 332, 337
application name
    configuring for role provider, 508
    default (/), 504
    setting for membership provider, 506
ApplicationName property, 525
    Membership class, 502
    RoleProvider class, 503
applications, event-driven, 374
ApplyClientBehavior( ) method,
    IEndpointBehavior, 234, 364
ApplyDispatchBehavior( ) method, 230, 352
    IEndpointBehavior interface, 234
    IServiceBehavior interface, 228
architecture, WCF, 44–47
    host, 46

arrays, 129
  concrete collections represented as, 124
  marshaling custom collections as, 126
  representing collection interfaces, 123
  using instead of data tables, 117
ASMX web services, 19
ASP.NET providers, 500–510
  authentication, 506–507
  authorization, 507
  callbacks, 510
  credentials administration, 503
    Credentials Manager application, 505
    shortcomings of Visual Studio
      2005, 504
  credentials providers, 501–503
  credentials stores, 449
  identity management, 509
  Internet service configuration, 524
  role-based security for
    business-to-business scenario, 514
  SQL Server, 501
AsyncCallback class, 373
asynchronous calls, 365–380
  asynchronous invocation, 369–371
  cleaning up after End<Operation>( ), 378
  completion callback, 373–377
  error handling, 377
  one-way operations, 377
  polling or waiting for
    completion, 371–373
  proxy-based, 367–369
  requirements for, 366
  synchronous calls versus, 378–380
  transactions and, 378
asynchronous operation invocation, 365
AsyncPattern property,
    OperationContractAttribute, 367
AsyncState property, IAsyncResult
    interface, 375
AsyncWaitHandle property, 371, 378
  managing multiple concurrent
    asynchronous methods, 372
atomic property (transactions), 239
atomic, consistent, isolated, and durable
    (ACID) transactions, 239
AuditLevel.SuccessOrFailure, 541
AuditLogLocation property, 539
authentication, 448
  anonymous applications and, 517
  business-to-business
    application, 511–513

Internet applications, 497–499
  ASP.NET providers, 506–507
  using Windows credentials, 499
intranet applications, 467–469
  providing alternative Windows
    credentials, 467–469
intranet callbacks and, 488
mutual, 450
no security scenario and, 519
security audit verbosity, 539
summary for security scenarios, 521
Authentication property
  X509CertificateInitiatorServiceCredential
    class, 512
  X509CertificateRecipientClientCredential
    class, 496
authorization, 449, 480–487
  anonymous applications and, 517
  business-to-business application, 514
  declarative role-based security, 483–485
  Internet applications
    using ASP.NET provider, 507
    using Windows credentials, 500
  Internet service, using Windows NT
    groups, 524
  intranet callbacks and, 488
  no security scenario and, 519
  programmatic role-based
    security, 485–486
  security audit verbosity, 539
  security principal, 481
  selecting mode, 481
  summary for security scenarios, 521
  using ASP.NET providers, 502
Authorization property, ServiceHostBase
    class, 475
auto-enlistment, transaction resources, 239

B

BasicHttpBinding class, 19, 20
  securing for business-to-business
    application, 511
  security scenarios, use in, 520
  SessionMode.NotAllowed, 145
  setting TransferMode property for
    streaming, 203
  transfer security mode configuration, 453
  transfer security modes, 453
  transport and encoding, 20
  transport-level sessions and, 141

queued publishers, 572
queued services
    coding guidelines, 581
    concurrency management, 404–405
        throttling, 405
    configuration and setup, 385–391
        creating the queue, 386–389
        exposing metadata, 391
        purging the queue, 389
        queues, services, and endpoints, 390
        workgroup installation and
            security, 385
    delivery failures, 405–414
        DLQ (dead-letter queue), 407
        reasons for, 406
        time to live, 407
    HTTP bridge, 442–447
        client-side configuration, 446
        designing, 442
        service-side configuration, 444–446
        transaction configuration, 443
    instance management, 397–404
        per-call, 397–399
        sessionful, 399–403
        singleton service, 403
    nondurable queues, 396
    playback failures, 414–419
        poison messages, 414–419
    queued calls architecture, 383
    queued contracts, 384
    queued versus connected calls, 419–422
        requiring queuing, 420–422
    response service, 422–442
        client-side programming, 427–429
        designing contract, 423–427
        implementing, 431
        service-side programming, 429
        streamlining, 432–438
        transactions, 439–442
    transactions, 391–397
        delivery and playback, 391–393
        service transaction
            configuration, 393–396
queued subscribers, 572
QueuedDeliveryRequirementsMode
        property, DeliveryRequirements
        attribute, 420
QueuedServiceHelper class, 387–390
    PurgeQueue( ) method, 390
    verifying queue on client side, 388
    VerifyQueue( ) method, 436

R

ReadCommitted isolation level, 271
ReadUncommitted isolation level, 271
ReceiveErrorHandling property,
        MsmqBindingBase, 416
    .Drop value, 416
    .Fault value, 416
    .Move value, 417
    .Reject value, 416
    MSMQ 3.0, 419
ReceiveRetryCount property,
        MsmqBindingBase class, 415
recovery, 237
reentrancy, 321–324
    callbacks, 182–184, 323
        configuring for, 357
    designing for, 322
    transactions, 323
rejecting poison messages, 416
ReleaseInstanceMode property
    OperationBehavior attribute, 158
        .None value, 159
    OperationContext
        .AfterCall value, 160
        .BeforeAndAfterCall value, 161
        .BeforeCall value, 160
ReleaseServiceInstance( ) method,
        InstanceContext class, 162
ReleaseServiceInstanceOnTransaction
        Complete property, ServiceBehavior
        attribute, 290–299, 302, 305, 403
reliability, 51–55
    binding and, 51
    configuring, 52
    one-way operations, 172
    queued services, 392
        delivery failures, 405–414
        playback failures, 414–419
    requiring ordered delivery, 53
    sessions and, 146
    transactions, 246
ReliableSession class, 53, 149
RepeatableRead isolation level, 271
replay attack, 450
reply, streaming, 202
request, streaming, 202
request-reply operations, 170
RequireOrderedDelivery property,
        DeliveryRequirements, 421
resource managers per-call service for storing
        state, 288

Resource Managers (RMs), 244
resources
    deadlocked access, 326
        avoiding, 326
    service, synchronizing access to, 325
    sharing by services, reasons to avoid, 328
    synchronization context, 328–336
        UI, 331–336
    transactional, 239
        promotion and, 254
response service, 422–442
    client-side programming, 427–429
    designing contract, 423–427
        message headers, 425
        response address and method ID, 424
        ResponseContext class, 426
    implementing, 431
    service-side programming, 429
    streamlining, 432–438
        client, 433–436
        queued service, 436–438
        ResponseContext.Current, 432
        service side, 438
    transactions, 439–442
        responding in new transaction, 440
        response as part of playback
            transaction, 439
ResponseAction property,
        OperationContract, 60
ResponseClientBase<T> class, 433–436
    Enqueue( ) method, 436
ResponseContext class, 426
    Current property, 432, 436, 438
ResponseScope<T> class, 436–438
retry batches, 415
    MSMQ 3.0, 419
RetryCycleDelay property,
        MsmqBindingBase class, 415, 419
RMs (Resource Managers), 244
Role property, PrincipalPermission
        attribute, 483
role providers, 501
    business-to-business scenario, 525
    Internet scenario, 524
role-based security
    ASP.NET, for business-to-business
        scenario, 514
    declarative, 483–485
        using ASP.NET providers, 509
    enabling for user authorization with
        ASP.NET providers, 507

intranet security scenario, 523
precluded with intranet callbacks, 488
principal type and, 486
programmatic, 485–486
shortcomings of Visual Studio 2005
        configuration, 504
soft impersonation used with, 487
Windows user groups as roles, problems
        with, 487, 500
RoleProvider class, 503
RoleProvider property,
        ServiceAuthorizationBehavior, 508
RoleProviderPrincipal class, 502, 509
Roles class, Provider property, 503, 507
roles localization, 487, 500
Rollback( ) method, 242
root (service) of a transaction, 252
root authority, 497
root scope (transactions), 278
Run as... shell option, 470

S

SafeButton class, 336
SafeLabel class, 334
SafeListBox class, 336
SafeProgressBar class, 336
SafeStatusBar class, 336
SafeTextBox class, 336
scalability
    instance deactivation and, 163
    per-call services and, 135
    singletons and, 154
SecureChannelFactory<T> class, 535
SecureClientBase<T> class, 533
SecureDuplexChannelFactory<T,C>
        class, 537
SecureDuplexClientBase<T,C> class, 536
security, 448–542
    anonymous applications, 516
        authentication, 517
        authorization, 517
        callbacks, 518
        identity management, 518
        securing bindings, 517
    auditing, 538–542
        configuring security audits, 539–541
        declarative security audit, 541
    authentication, 448
    authorization, 449

U

Undo( ) method, WindowsIdentity
class, 473
unknown faults, 212
Unsubscribe( ) and Subscribe( ) methods
ISubscriptionService interface, 557
OperationContract, 200
URIs (Universal Resource Identifiers), 4
UseAspNetProviders property, 524
user groups as security roles, drawbacks
of, 487, 500
username and password authentication, 449
username and password
credentials, 497–499
client authentication with Internet service
using Windows credentials, 499
UserName property, ClientBase<T>
class, 497
UserNameAuthentication property, 498
UserNamePasswordClientCredential
class, 497
UserNamePasswordServiceCredential
class, 498
MembershipProvider property, 506
UserNamePasswordValidationMode
property, 499
.MembershipProvider value, 506
.Windows value, 499
UseSynchronizationContext property, 336
CallbackBehavior attribute, 355
ServiceBehavior attribute, 346
disallowing affinity to UI thread, 347

V

Validate( ) method
IServiceBehavior interface, 263, 527, 542
SecurityBehavior class, 529
ValidateUser( ) method, Membership
class, 502
Value property, EnumMember attribute, 114
VerifyCallback( ) method, 188
VerifyQueue( ) method, 436
QueuedServiceHelper class, 387
VerifyQueue<T>( ) method,
QueuedServiceHelper class, 388
versioning
data contracts, 104–112
missing members, 106–110
new members, 105
versioning round-trip, 110–112
visibility, data members or data contract, 84

Vista
MSMQ 4.0, 415–418
WAS (Windows Activation Service), 17,
36
Visual Studio 2005
adding WCF service an application
project, 14
generating a proxy, 36
IIS-hosted service, 12
shortcomings of credentials
administration pages, 504
volatile queues, 396
voting on transactions, 267–270
callbacks, 311
declarative voting, 268
explicit voting, 269
inside nested scope, 279
TransactionScope, 276

W

WaitHandle class, 371
WaitAll( ) method, 372
WaitAny( ) method, 373
WAS (Windows Activation Service)
hosting, 17
generating a proxy with SvcUtil, 36
WCF (Windows Communication
Foundation), xv
defined, 1
WCF coding standard, 573–582
concurrency management, 580
data contracts, 575
essentials, 574
faults, 578
general design guidelines, 573
instance management, 576
operations and calls, 576
queued services, 581
security, 582
service contracts, 574
transactions, 579
Web Service bindings (see WS bindings)
Web.Config file, 12
Windows Activation Service (see WAS)
Windows authentication, 449
Windows Communication Foundation (see
WCF)
Windows credentials, 456
bindings supporting Message
security, 456
Internet application using, 499

About the Author

Juval Löwy is a software architect and the principal of IDesign (*http://www.idesign.net*), specializing in WCF architecture consulting and advanced WCF training. Juval is Microsoft's Regional Director for Silicon Valley, working with Microsoft on helping the industry adopt WCF. He is author of O'Reilly's bestselling *Programming .NET Components*, widely recognized by many as the best book for developing .NET-based systems. Juval participates in the Microsoft internal design reviews for WCF and related technologies. He publishes numerous articles on nearly every aspect of .NET development and is a frequent presenter at development conferences. Microsoft has recognized Juval as a Software Legend and as one of the world's top .NET experts and industry leaders.

Colophon

The animal on the cover of *Programming WCF Services* is an angelfish. Angelfish are found in tropical and subtropical reefs around the world; there are at least 86 different species. The average size of an angelfish is about 7 to 12 inches (20 to 30 cm), but their size varies greatly, as does their coloring, which changes with maturity. Their diet consists of algae, worms, and various shellfish and small sea creatures. A spine on the gill cover differentiates the angelfish from the also colorful butterfly fish. Depending on the species, angelfish have different mating habits. Some mate for life in territorial pairs, while others create harems of female fish with one dominant male. All angelfish are protogynous hermaphrodites, which means that if the dominant male were to die or leave the group, a female would morph into a male for mating purposes.

In some countries angelfish are used for food, but mostly they are caught for aquariums. Rare species of angelfish can range in price from hundreds to thousands of dollars. In addition to collectors, angelfish are threatened by reef destruction and continual environmental degradation.

The cover image is from Wood's *Reptiles, Fishes, Insects, &c.*. The cover font is Adobe ITC Garamond. The text font is Linotype Birka; the heading font is Adobe Myriad Condensed; and the code font is LucasFont's TheSans Mono Condensed.

Better than e-books

Buy *Programming WCF Services* and access the
digital edition FREE on Safari for 45 days.

Go to www.oreilly.com/go/safarienabled
and type in coupon code VAXGJGA

Search
thousands of
top tech books

Download
whole chapters

Cut and Paste
code examples

Find
answers fast

Search Safari! The premier electronic reference
library for programmers and IT professionals.

Related Titles from O'Reilly

.NET

ADO.NET Cookbook

ASP.NET 2.0 Cookbook

ASP.NET 2.0: A Developer's Notebook

C# Cookbook, *2nd Edition*

C# in a Nutshell, *2nd Edition*

C# Language Pocket Guide

Learning C# 2005, *2nd Edition*

.NET and XML

.NET Gotchas

Programming .NET Components, *2nd Edition*

Programming .NET Security

Programming .NET Web Services

Programming ASP.NET, *3rd Edition*

Programming Atlas

Programming C#, *4th Edition*

Programming MapPoint in .NET

Programming Visual Basic 2005

Programming Windows Presentation Foundation

Visual Basic 2005: A Developer's Notebook

Visual Basic 2005 Cookbook

Visual Basic 2005 in a Nutshell, *3rd Edition*

Visual Basic 2005 Jumpstart

Visual C# 2005: A Developer's Notebook

Visual Studio Hacks

Windows Developer Power Tools

XAML in a Nutshell

Keep in touch with O'Reilly

Download examples from our books

To find example files from a book, go to:
www.oreilly.com/catalog select the book,
and follow the "Examples" link.

Register your O'Reilly books

Register your book at *register.oreilly.com*
Why register your books? Once you've
registered your O'Reilly books you can:

- Win O'Reilly books, T-shirts or discount
  coupons in our monthly drawing.
- Get special offers available only to
  registered O'Reilly customers.
- Get catalogs announcing new books
  (US and UK only).
- Get email notification of new editions
  of the O'Reilly books you own.

Join our email lists

Sign up to get topic-specific email announ-
cements of new books and conferences,
special offers, and O'Reilly Network
technology newsletters at:

elists.oreilly.com

It's easy to customize your free elists subscription so you'll get exactly the O'Reilly news
you want.

Get the latest news, tips, and tools

www.oreilly.com

- "Top 100 Sites on the Web"—PC Magazine
- CIO Magazine's Web Business 50 Awards

Our web site contains a library of comprehensive product information (including book
excerpts and tables of contents), downloadable
software, background articles, interviews with
technology leaders, links to relevant sites, book
cover art, and more.

Work for O'Reilly

Check out our web site for current
employment opportunities:

jobs.oreilly.com

Contact us

O'Reilly Media, Inc.
1005 Gravenstein Hwy North
Sebastopol, CA 95472 USA
Tel: 707-827-7000 or 800-998-9938
      (6am to 5pm PST)
Fax: 707-829-0104

Contact us by email

For answers to problems regarding
your order or our products:
order@oreilly.com

To request a copy of our latest catalog:
catalog@oreilly.com

For book content technical questions
or corrections: **booktech@oreilly.com**

For educational, library, government,
and corporate sales: **corporate@oreilly.com**

To submit new book proposals to our
editors and product managers:
proposals@oreilly.com

For information about our international
distributors or translation queries:
international@oreilly.com

For information about academic
use of O'Reilly books:
adoption@oreilly.com
or visit:
academic.oreilly.com

For a list of our distributors outside
of North America check out:
international.oreilly.com/distributors.html

Order a book online

www.oreilly.com/order_new